Tax by Design for the Netherlands

Tax by Design for the Netherlands

Edited by

SIJBREN CNOSSEN AND BAS JACOBS

OXFORD
UNIVERSITY PRESS

OXFORD
UNIVERSITY PRESS

Great Clarendon Street, Oxford, OX2 6DP,
United Kingdom

Oxford University Press is a department of the University of Oxford.
It furthers the University's objective of excellence in research, scholarship,
and education by publishing worldwide. Oxford is a registered trade mark of
Oxford University Press in the UK and in certain other countries

First Edition published in 2022

Impression: 2

Published in the United States of America by Oxford University Press
198 Madison Avenue, New York, NY 10016, United States of America

British Library Cataloguing in Publication Data
Data available

Library of Congress Control Number: 2021942713

ISBN 978–0–19–285524–4

DOI: 10.1093/oso/9780192855244.001.0001

Printed and bound in the UK by
TJ Books Limited

Acknowledgements

This book is the product of the first *Cnossen Forum—Tax by Design for the Netherlands* that was held on 23–24 May 2019. The forum grew out of the idea that the Netherlands needed a *Mirrlees Review* type of analysis of its tax system. This book attempts to do so by incorporating the peer-reviewed and edited versions of the original papers presented and discussed at the Forum. The Dutch version of the book has been published in 2019 as *Ontwerp voor een beter belastingstelsel* (Amsterdam: ESB). The cut-off date for data on the Dutch tax system is 1 January, 2020.

We would like to thank the Erasmus School of Economics, especially Philip-Hans Franses and Harry Commandeur, for establishing the Sijbren Cnossen Chair in Public Economics. As editors, we are immensely grateful to the authors, commentators, and participants in the Forum, from at home and abroad, without whose enthusiastic and sustained effort this book would not have seen the light of day.

We are most grateful for the financial support of the Dutch Ministry of Finance, represented by Rens Nissen and Erik Kranendonk, and the Erasmus School of Economics. Bas Jacobs thanks the Netherlands Institute for Advanced Study for the Duisenberg Fellowship 2018–19. Indispensable logistical and secretarial support was provided by Ronald de Groot, Annemarie Luchtenberg, Conny Oudshoorn, Thuy Phan, Jany Mes, and Ankimon Vernede. Rachel Lumpkin did a great job in copy-editing and managing the production of this book for which we are truly grateful.

Sijbren Cnossen and Bas Jacobs
The Hague and Amsterdam, September 2021

Acknowledgements

Contents

III. PROFITS: DESIGN

IV. LABOUR INCOME

V. CLIMATE AND MOBILITY

VI. CONSUMPTION

List of Boxes

List of Boxes

List of Figures

List of Tables

List of Contributors

Spencer Bastani (spencer.bastani@ifau.uu.se) is a Researcher at the Institute for Evaluation of Labour Market and Education Policy (IFAU), Uppsala

Lans Bovenberg (a.l.bovenberg@tilburguniversity.edu) is Professor of Relational Economics, Values and Leadership at the Erasmus School of Economics, and Professor of Economics and holder of the F.J.D. Goldschmeding chair on *Innovation in Economics Teaching* at Tilburg University

Koen Caminada (c.l.j.caminada@law.leidenuniv.nl) is Professor of Empirical Analysis of Tax and Social Policy at Leiden University

Sijbren Cnossen (cnossen@ese.eur.nl) is Professor of Economics at the University of Pretoria and Academic Partner at CPB Netherlands Bureau for Economic Policy Analysis. He is also Professor Emeritus of Erasmus University Rottedam and University of Maastricht

Henk-Wim de Boer (h.w.de.boer@cpb.nl) is affiliated with CPB Netherlands Bureau for Economic Policy Analysis

Ruud de Mooij (rdemooij@imf.org) is Advisor in the Fiscal Affairs Department of the International Monetary Fund

Gerben Geilenkirchen (gerben.geilenkirchen@pbl.nl) is a Researcher on Transport and Environment at the Department of Urbanisation and Transport at PBL Netherlands Environmental Assessment Agency

Aart Gerritsen (agerritsen@ese.eur.nl) is Assistant Professor at Erasmus University Rotterdam

Miriam Gielen (mgielen@minszw.nl) is Senior Policy Advisor at the Ministry of Social Affairs and Employment, The Hague

Kees Goudswaard (k.p.goudswaard@law.leidenuniv.nl) is Professor of Applied Economics at Leiden University

Ed Groot (ed.groot230@gmail.com) is editor at Financieele Dagblad

Shafik Hebous (shebous@imf.org) is Deputy Division Chief in the Tax Policy Division, Fiscal Affairs Department of the International Monetary Fund

Patricia Hofmann (patricia.hofmann@pwc.com) is Senior Associate Transfer Pricing at PricewaterhouseCoopers GmbH Wirtschaftsprüfungsgesellschaft, Germany

Bas Jacobs (bjacobs@ese.eur.nl) is Sijbren Cnossen Professor of Public Economics, Erasmus School of Economics, Erasmus University Rotterdam

Egbert Jongen (e.l.w.jongen@cpb.nl) is Program Leader Labour at CPB Netherlands Bureau for Economic Policy Analysis and Associate Professor at Leiden University

Alexander Klemm (aklemm@imf.org) is Division Chief in the Fiscal Affairs Department of the International Monetary Fund

Marko Koethenbuerger (koethenbuerger@ethz.ch) is Professor of Public Economics, ETH Zurich, Department of Management, Technology and Economics

Patrick Koot (p.m.koot@cpb.nl) is researcher at CPB Netherlands Bureau for Economic Policy Analysis, The Hague, Netherlands

Arjan Lejour (a.m.lejour@tilburguniversity.edu) is Professor of Taxation and Public Finance, Tilburg University, and affiliated at CPB Netherlands Bureau for Economic Policy Analysis

Li Liu (lliu@imf.org) is Senior Economist in the Tax Policy Division, Fiscal Affairs Department of the International Monetary Fund

Ben Lockwood (b.lockwood@warwick.ac.uk) is Professor of Economics at the University of Warwick and a Fellow of the CEPR and the Centre for Business Taxation, University of Oxford

Andreas Peichl (peichl@ifo.de) is Director of the Ifo Center for Macroeconomics and Surveys and Professor of Macroeconomics and Public Finance at the University of Munich

Nadine Riedel (nadine.riedel@uni-muenster.de) is Full Professor at the University of Münster

Dirk Schindler (schindler@ese.eur.nl) is Professor of International Taxation at Erasmus University Rotterdam

Peter Birch Sørensen (pbs@econ.ku.dk) is Professor of Economics at the University of Copenhagen

Rick van der Ploeg (rick.vanderploeg@economics.ox.ac.uk) is Professor of Economics at the University of Oxford and Adjunct University Professor of Environmental Economics at the University of Amsterdam

Casper van Ewijk (c.vanewijk@tilburguniversity.edu) is Professor Emeritus of the University of Amsterdam, and researcher at Netspar, Network for Studies in Ageing and Retirement, Tilburg University

Hendrik Vrijburg (h.vrijburg@law.leidenuniv.nl) is Assistant Professor at Leiden University

Daniel Waldenström (daniel.waldenstrom@ifn.se) is Professor of Economics at the Institute of Industrial Economics (IFN), Stockholm

Ludvig Wier (ludvig.wier@econ.ku.dk) is a post-doctoral researcher and lecturer at UC Berkeley

Floris T. Zoutman (floris.zoutman@nhh.no) is Associate Professor at NHH Norwegian School of Economics

1

Tax by Design for the Netherlands

Introduction and Synthesis

*Sijbren Cnossen and Bas Jacobs**

1.1 Introduction

Of every 100 euros earned in the Netherlands, almost 40 euros flow into the treasury in the form of personal income tax (including wage tax), corporate income tax, social security contributions, value added tax (VAT), excise duties, and various other taxes and levies. Consequently, the Dutch tax system influences economic behaviour: whether to work or not and, if so, how many hours; whether to enter business or employment; whether to consume or save; whether to invest in real estate, one's own business or the stock market; how to finance corporations; whether to retain or distribute profits; whether to engage in tax-avoidance activities; whether to ride a bike rather than drive a car; whether to buy low- or high-taxed goods; whether to smoke, drink, or gamble; and many other small and big choices.

Taxation plays a crucial role in raising government revenue, correcting external and internal effects, and redistributing income. This book shows that most taxes in the Netherlands are anything but efficient, neutral, and simple. Taxation generates substantial welfare losses by distorting the economic decisions of individuals and businesses. Jacobs (2015) estimates that the welfare loss of an additional euro of tax revenue is approximately 40–50 eurocents, and the average cost of raising revenue is about 10 cents on the euro.[1] Moreover, the tax system is unnecessarily opaque and complex, which entails high implementation and compliance costs.

The main objective of this book is to design a better tax system for the Netherlands than the current one. In doing so, we take the level of taxation, the

* Sijbren Cnossen (cnossen@ese.eur.nl) is Professor of Economics at the University of Pretoria and Academic Partner at CPB Netherlands Bureau for Economic Policy Analysis. Bas Jacobs (bjacobs@ese.eur.nl) is Sijbren Cnossen Professor of Public Economics, Erasmus School of Economics, Erasmus University Rotterdam.

[1] Taxes can also improve resource allocation if they correct for externalities and internalities in the form of taxes on, for example, CO_2 emissions, traffic congestion, smoking, and drinking—issues that are also dealt with in this book.

Sijbren Cnossen and Bas Jacobs, *Tax by Design for the Netherlands: Introduction and Synthesis* In: *Tax by Design for the Netherlands.* Edited by: Sijbren Cnossen and Bas Jacobs, Oxford University Press.
DOI: 10.1093/oso/9780192855244.003.0001

degree of income redistribution, and the extent of government paternalism as given. Whether to increase the size of the public sector, whether to reduce inequality by redistributing more income, or whether to protect people against harm inflicted on themselves are ethical-normative issues that should be agreed on by the body politic, not prescribed by economists.

Economists can advise policymakers, however, on how the optimality of the tax (and expenditure) system can be enhanced: how the government can raise revenue, redistribute income, and correct for external and internal effects at lower social cost. Therefore, the first main criterion for judging whether tax reforms are desirable is whether the changes raise *economic efficiency*. A more efficient tax system is a better tax system. As the contributions in this book show, the Dutch tax system can be improved.

The second criterion for examining the need for tax reform is *neutrality*, which is closely related to horizontal equity: people whose economic situation is the same should be treated the same for tax purposes. The same amount of labour income should bear the same tax burden, regardless of whether it is earned by an employee, a self-employed person, a proprietor, or a director/dominant shareholder of a closely held company. This also applies to various forms of capital income: the same amount of capital income should be taxed the same, regardless of whether it is earned in the form of a return on equity, debt, know-how, immovable property, pension saving, or in some other form. Departures from tax neutrality introduce costly distortions and tax arbitrage, which, if desired, should be carefully rationalized.

A third criterion is that the tax system should be as *simple and transparent* as possible. Implementation and compliance costs raise the social cost of taxation. Moreover, tax morale is weakened if people have difficulty understanding the tax code or if they perceive taxes to be unfair or arbitrary.

Tax reform is particularly acute at the present time, because the COVID-19 crisis has led to substantial increases in public deficits and debt. Although appropriate at this juncture, it may put government finances under pressure in the near future. The pressure can be alleviated by reforms that allow the government to generate more public revenue with lower efficiency losses, less tax avoidance, and lower compliance costs.

This book lists a large number of evidence-based recommendations for what the authors believe would be a better tax system. Some proposals are incremental, others comprehensive. All proposals have in common that they do not intend to confront people overnight with a major tax overhaul without appropriate transition measures. Trust in government is important. Tax policy reforms require certainty and consistency in the transition to a better tax system.

In the remainder of this introductory chapter, we briefly describe the main features of the Dutch tax system, which should aid readers in understanding the subsequent chapters that focus on specific problem areas. Thereafter, we discuss the issues and options for tax reform that are dealt with in greater detail by the authors of the various chapters.

1.2 The Dutch Tax System

Following a brief overview of the Dutch tax system, we summarize the main features of the various taxes, especially the personal income tax, which is the main focus of the tax debate.

1.2.1 Overview

While the Dutch tax system is largely in line with the systems in other European Union (EU) member states, it has some features that deserve to be noted. We start with a brief overview of the tax bases, rates, and revenue yields of the Dutch tax system over the past thirty years.

Table 1.1 shows that total tax revenue, as a percentage of GDP (i.e. the tax ratio), rose by 2 percentage points since 2000 to 39% in 2017. Particularly significant revenue increases were recorded for the personal income tax and employers' social security contributions. Nonetheless, the total tax ratio in 2017 is 1 percentage point lower than it was in 1990. The shares of the individual taxes in total tax revenue remained approximately the same over the years. Three

Table 1.1 Yield and structure of the Dutch tax system as a percentage of GDP, 1990–2017

	1990	2000	2010	2017
Total tax revenue	**39.7**	**36.9**	**35.7**	**38.7**
Income, profits and capital gains	**12.8**	**9.6**	**9.9**	**11.6**
Of individuals	9.8	5.6	7.7	8.3
Corporate	3.0	4.0	2.3	3.3
Property	**1.5**	**1.9**	**1.4**	**1.6**
Social security	**14.9**	**14.3**	**12.9**	**13.8**
Employees	9.2	7.8	6.5	5.4
Employers	3.0	4.1	4.6	5.1
Self-employed and non-employed	2.7	2.3	1.8	3.3
Goods and services	**10.5**	**10.7**	**11.0**	**11.3**
VAT	6.5	6.4	6.7	6.8
Specific	3.0	3.3	3.1	3.3
Other	1.0	1.0	1.2	1.2
Other	**0.1**	**0.2**	**0.2**	**0.1**

Source: Table 4.47 of OECD (2019). Totals may not add because of rounding.

taxes—the income tax (including the wage tax), social security contributions, and the VAT—still account for more than two-thirds of the total tax revenue.

Currently, the corporate income tax contributes 8% of the total tax revenue, which is more than in 1990. Despite gradual reductions in statutory rates, it has not disappeared from the stage, due to base-broadening measures, a large and increasing amount of foreign profits being routed through the Netherlands, and the rising share of capital income in GDP. The yield of other taxes has not changed much over the period under review. As regards the tax structure and the distribution of the tax burden over consumption, capital, and labour, the Netherlands appears to be broadly in line with other EU member states.

1.2.2 Income Distribution

Compared with other countries, income inequality is rather low in the Netherlands (see Figure 1.1). In an international context, the Netherlands has a

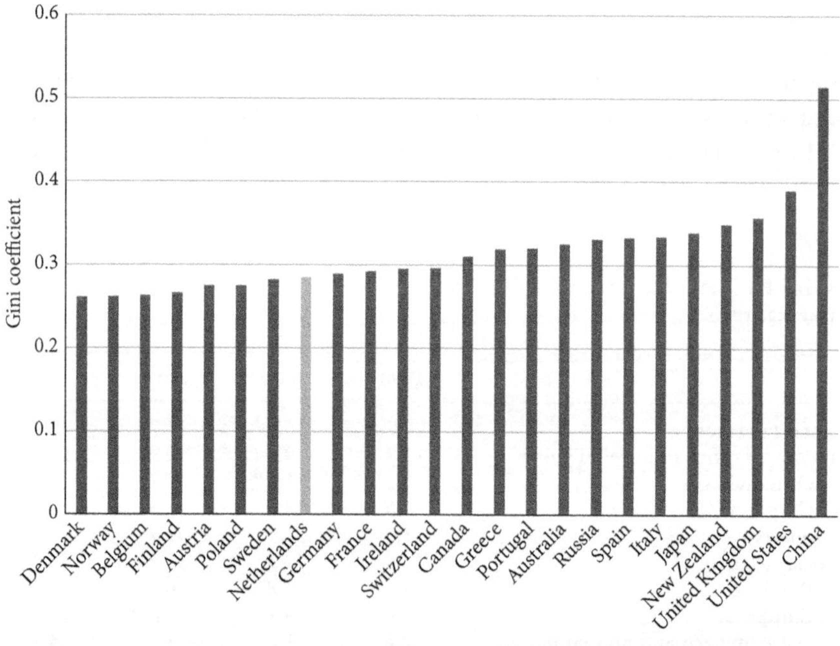

Figure 1.1 International comparison of Gini coefficients of disposable household income

Notes: Gini coefficients refer to the latest estimate available, mostly from 2017/18.
Source: OECD (2020).

relatively low Gini coefficient of disposable household income of around 0.3, which is slightly higher than that of Scandinavian countries, similar to that of France and Germany, and lower than the United Kingdom (OECD, 2020). CBS (2019) shows that the Gini coefficient for disposable income has remained fairly stable since 2001, which is attributable to upward adjustments in income redistribution, despite the increase in primary income inequality in the Netherlands (Caminada and Goudswaard, Chapter 17). Schulenberg and Buitenhuis (2017) show that, to a large extent, the rise in pre-tax inequality is attributable to the greater labour market participation of women, in terms of both entry and duration, the rising level of education, and the ageing of the population. Income is not heavily concentrated in the upper deciles of the income distribution. Indeed, it is lonely at the top in the Netherlands. The income share of the top 1% (10%) of income earners is 6.1% (28.0%) in 2015, which is among the lowest in the world, even lower than in most Scandinavian countries (World Inequality Database, 2020).

1.3 Description and Pressure Points in the Tax System

Most of the attention in the book is devoted to the personal income tax, which is therefore described in somewhat greater detail than the other taxes and duties.

1.3.1 Personal Income Tax

As shown in Table 1.2, the Netherlands has a rudimentary dual income tax with labour and capital income being taxed separately. Income is taxed in three 'boxes'. Employment income, profits of unincorporated firms, the imputed rental value of owner-occupied property, and pension income are subject to a progressive tax rate schedule with two brackets in box 1. The most important tax credits in box 1 are all income-dependent: the general tax credit (*algemene heffingskorting*) for all taxpayers, the earned-income tax credit (EITC) for working taxpayers (*arbeidskorting*), and the EITC for working taxpayers with children (*inkomensafhankelijke combinatiekorting*). The general tax credit is (partly) transferable from the secondary to the primary income earner. The first EITC is phased in with a nonlinear rate up to a taxable income of 34,954 euros, after which it is phased out at a flat rate of 6%. The EITC for people with children increases by 11.45% until it reaches a maximum of 2.881 euros at an income level of 30,233 euros, after which it remains flat.

Table 1.2 Dutch income tax system in 2020

Box 1	**Tax credits box 1**	**Tax rebates**
Employment income	Income-dependent general tax credit	Rental costs
Business income of unincorporated firms	Maximum: €2,711	Formula: quadratic based on household income and rental
Owner-occupied property	Phase-in: none	costs, withdrawal rates vary from 30% to 40% depending
Imputed rent 0.6% of dwelling's value	Phase-out: €20,711 at 6% rate	on household type
Mortgage interest deductible		Maximum per year: €4,416 singles (couples: €3,852)
Pension income	Income-dependent EITC for working taxpayers	Income test: none
Pay-out taxed at reduced rates	Maximum: €3,819	Rental costs: < €737 per month
Contributions tax-deductible	Phase-in 1: €0–9,921 at 2.812%	Wealth test: wealth < €30,846 singles (couples: €61,692)
Tax rates: 37.35%, 49.5%	Phase-in 2: €9,921–21,430 at 28.812%	
	Phase-in 3: €21,430–34,954 at 1.656%	Healthcare costs
Box 2	Phase-out: €34,954 at 6%	Formula: fixed amount, withdrawal rate 13.55%
Substantial share-ownership closely held companies		Maximum per year: €1,248 (couples: €2,388)
>5% shares	Income-dependent EITC for working taxpayers	Income test: < €30,481 (couples: €38,945)
Dividend income	with children	Wealth test: < €116,613 (couples: €147,459)
Capital gains	Maximum: €2,881	
Tax rate: 25%	Phase-in: €5,072–30,233 at 11.45%	Children
	Phase-out: none	Formula: based on household income, withdrawal rate 6.75%
Box 3		Maximum per year: one child €4,375, two children €5,380,
Wealth (savings, portfolio investments, second		each additional child €297 per year
homes, financial products not taxable in box 1)		(couples: one child €1,185, two children €2,190,
Tax rate: 30%		each additional child €297 per year)
Exemption €30,846 (couples: €61.692)		Income test: < €21,431 (couples: €38,181)
Presumptive returns on taxable net wealth		Wealth test: < €116,613 (couples: €147,459)
(Effective wealth tax rates):		
1.789% (0.54%) wealth < €72,798		Childcare
4.185% (1.26%) €72,798 < wealth < €1,005,573		Day-care €8.17 per hour, school-care €7.02 per hour,
5.28% (1.58%) wealth > €1,005,573		childminders €6.27 per hour

Source: Dutch Tax Authorities.

Self-employed people and owners of unincorporated businesses (proprietorships and partnerships) can apply for various tax concessions that ordinary employees are not entitled to, subject to the requirement that they work at least 1,225 hours per annum in their business. Specifically, small and medium-sized enterprises enjoy a 14% exemption of total profits (*mkb vrijstelling*). In addition, these enterprises can claim a tax credit for being self-employed of 7,030 euros (*zelfstandigenaftrek*). For up to three years, they can also claim the start-up credit for the self-employed of 2,123 euros (*startersaftrek*). As a result, the tax burden on the self-employed is substantially lower than that of employees at the same income level.

Important changes have been made in the rate structure of the personal income tax. In particular, the rate structure in box 1 has been made less progressive over time. The Netherlands started with four tax brackets in 1990, but at present only two brackets remain.[2] The top rate of the income tax has been reduced from 62% in 1990 to 52% in 2001, and further to 49.5% in 2020. Another important change is that the household was considered the taxpaying unit in 1990, while the present income tax is levied on an individual basis, although partners can split their deductions to minimize their joint tax liability, transfer (part of) the general tax credit to their partner and average out their taxes on personal wealth holdings. Furthermore, tax rebates are calculated on the basis of household income.

Capital income (interest, dividends, royalties, rental payments, and capital gains) are taxed under a patchwork of different schedules and rates. The imputed rental value of owner-occupied property, deemed to be 0.6% of its estimated value, is taxed at progressive rates in box 1.[3] The top tax rate at which mortgage interest is deductible is gradually being reduced until it reaches the 37% rate of the lowest income tax bracket in 2023. Since 2013, taxpayers can only deduct mortgage interest if they have a linear or annuity type of mortgage. Private pension contributions are deductible, while pension pay-outs are taxed in box 1.[4] Returns on assets in pension funds are not taxed. Benefits from the pay-as-you-go state pension are also taxable in box 1. Income of retirees is taxed at reduced rates in the first income tax bracket.

[2] Because the general tax credit is phased out linearly with income at a 6% rate, the Netherlands effectively still has a three-bracket tax schedule with rates of 37.35%, 43.35%, and 49.5%, respectively.

[3] The imputed rental value of owner-occupied properties with a value larger than 1,090,000 euros is set at 2.35% of the value above 1,090,000 euros and 0.6% on the value below 1,090,000 euros.

[4] The deductibility of pension contributions is capped at a ceiling for employment income of 110,111 euros and above. The tax treatment of pension saving in excess of the ceiling is the same as the tax on personal savings in box 3.

Dividend income and capital gains of shareholders who own 5% or more of the shares in closely held companies are taxed at a flat rate of 26.25% in box 2. Box 3 imposes tax on presumptive returns on savings, portfolio investments, second homes and other real estate, and on pension products, life insurance, and annuities that are not taxed in box 1. The presumptive return is applied to the net value of all assets in excess of a general exemption of 30,846 euros (for couples, 61,692 euros), which is then taxed at a rate of 30%.[5] Presumptive returns are deemed to increase with the size of net wealth holdings, which implies that box 3 is a progressive wealth tax.

The tax treatment of capital income also underwent important changes. Before 2001, the Netherlands had a rudimentary comprehensive income tax, which taxed labour income and capital income at the same progressive rate structure. The main loophole in the system was the exemption of capital gains on individually held assets, which led to a massive conversion of taxable capital income into exempt capital gains. This avenue of tax arbitrage was closed off by the Tax Reform 2001—the last major tax reform in the Netherlands—simply by eliminating the taxation of capital income at the individual level altogether and, instead, taxing the underlying assets. In fact, the income tax on capital income (including rental income) was abolished and the rate of the net wealth tax imposed until 2001 was increased and its basic exemption reduced. The new wealth tax is euphemistically referred to in the tax code as a tax on presumptive capital income. Initially, the new tax was flat: the presumptive return of 4% was taxed at a rate of 30%. In other words, the rate of the net wealth tax was 1.2%. Since 2017, however, the wealth tax has been made progressive, as shown in Table 1.2.

Another notable feature of the personal income tax is the complicated system of tax rebates, introduced in 2005. The rebates are paid out to households with low incomes; they complement the tax credits, which are non-refundable. Tax rebates are provided for the cost of rental housing, health insurance, children, and childcare. IBO (2019) reports that more than 7.5 million rebates totalling 13 billion euros (about 1.6% of GDP) are paid out annually to more than 5 million households (60% of all households). In contrast to the income tax and the tax credits, tax rebates are based on taxable household income rather than taxable individual income. Moreover, all tax rebates (except for the childcare rebate) are means-tested on household wealth. Tax rebates significantly affect the marginal tax burden on labour as they are phased out with household income. For example, the steep phase-out of the rental rebate raises the marginal tax burden on labour income by 30–40% in the phase-out range.

[5] Note that this does not apply to dividends and capital gains from dominant share-ownership in closely held companies that are taxed in box 2 and also not to business income of non-incorporated businesses, which is taxed in box 1.

1.3.2 Other Taxes

The corporate income tax system in the Netherlands can be characterized as a 'classical system'. There is no integration between the corporate income tax and the individual income tax. Moreover, the cost of debt is deductible, whereas the cost of equity is not. The corporate tax regime has made the Netherlands an internationally attractive location for business investment, but also an important conduit country for multinational profits flowing into tax havens. The Netherlands is known worldwide for its extensive network of tax treaties to prevent double taxation, the participation exemption for profits earned abroad, the tax rulings, and the zero withholding tax on royalties. The Netherlands also provides generous tax incentives for research and development (R&D) and permits an innovation box in which wages of R&D workers and profits are taxed at reduced rates. Since the early 1990s, the corporate income tax rate has been gradually reduced from 34% to 25% in 2021.

As regards taxes on goods and services, the Netherlands has a VAT, harmonized with other EU countries under the Common VAT Directive, with a high standard rate and a reduced rate for foodstuffs. Some 60% of total value added is taxed on inputs rather than output (with credit for the tax on inputs) in the form of exemptions for governments, education, healthcare, childcare, media, sports, cultural institutions, finance and insurance, and gambling. The standard VAT rate has been increased gradually from 18.5% in 1990 to 21% in 2012, where it still stands. In 2018, the reduced VAT rate, which for years had been fixed at 6%, was raised to 9%.

The Netherlands levies excises on gas, electricity, motor fuel, alcohol, tobacco, and non-alcoholic beverages. As elsewhere, various measures are in place to internalize the external cost of fossil fuel emissions and other forms of environmentally unfriendly activities, either in the form of special excise duties or restrictive permits. Specifically, the Netherlands imposes a non-linear excise on electricity that declines with the volume of electricity use; the lowest rate applies to business use in excess of 10 million kWh. Similarly, a non-linear excise is levied on natural gas, which gradually declines with the volume of gas use, and reaches the lowest rate for business use in excess of 10 million m^3 a year. Horticulture enjoys a special low rate. Motor fuel is also subject to excise with lower rates on diesel and LPG. The government provides generous tax reductions for electric cars in the form of exemptions from motor vehicle tax, car purchase tax, and a reduced tax rate on imputed income for the private use of company cars. There is no excise on kerosene used for transport by air and sea.

The Netherlands has an inheritance tax with large exemptions for spouses, parents, and children. Tax rates are progressive and increase from 10% to 40%.

Both tax rates and brackets depend on the blood relationship with the deceased. The average tax rate on inheritances received is about 12%.

1.3.3 Peculiar Features of the Dutch Tax System

To complete this overview of the Dutch tax system, it seems useful to summarize its most contentious features.

Capital income taxation is based on presumptive returns. The Netherlands is unique in its tax treatment of capital income. At the personal level, the presumptive capital income tax only taxes normal returns, which converts the tax on capital income into a net wealth tax. No other OECD country exempts dividends, interest and capital gains at the personal level. The rental value of owner-occupied property is also taxed on a presumptive basis, but at lower rates than the presumptive return on other assets. The income of pension funds is not taxed.

Capital income is taxed highly unequally. Equity income is taxed twice, at the corporate level and again on a presumptive basis at the personal level. By contrast, debt income is taxed only once (i.e. presumptively at the personal level), while interest is deductible at the corporate level. The same applies to income from intellectual property (royalties). Generally, capital gains are not taxed when realized, except in a business context or with respect to an individual's dominant shareholding in a closely held company. Owner-ocupied housing and pensions are subsidised on a net basis.

The Netherlands is an important conduit country for shifting profits. Multinational companies can shift their profits to countries with lower tax rates by manipulating transfer prices, shifting debt into high-tax countries (as interest is typically deductible), and by locating intellectual property in countries with low or zero taxes on royalties. The Netherlands enables such profit shifting by exempting the profits of foreign subsidiaries, its wide-ranging tax treaty network, a low withholding tax on royalties, and the practice of advance rulings. Foreign investment is attracted by a comparatively low corporate income tax rate and generous R&D incentives. Revenues of digital platforms are not taxed.

Tax concessions for entrepreneurship are generous. The Netherlands purports to promote entrepreneurship by special concessions for proprietors with tax credits for the self-employed and business start-ups (if applicable), a tax exemption for small and medium-sized businesses equal to 14% of total profits, and by allowing business owners to reduce the tax rate on labour income by conducting their business in the form of a closely held company.

Labour income of workers, self-employed people, and business owners is treated highly unequally depending on the form in which it arises. Wage income from employment tends to be taxed at higher rates than income earned by the self-employed or proprietors. Moreover, the labour income of proprietors of unincorporated firms accruing as profits, tends to be taxed at higher rates than the labour income, also denoted as profits, earned by directors/dominant shareholders of closely held companies.

There are strong tax incentives for the labour supply of secondary earners. In recent decades, the government has implemented an array of policy measures aimed at stimulating labour market participation of secondary earners: the EITC for working taxpayers, the EITC for working taxpayers with children, the gradual phase-out of the transferability of the general tax credit between partners, and the introduction of tax rebates for childcare.

The tax system is highly complex. Income is redistributed through tax credits, tax rebates, and income transfers. There are means-tested tax rebates for healthcare, rent, children, and childcare. These rebates are a perennial headache for taxpayers and the tax administration. Moreover, there is a plethora of tax credits for earned income, old age, education, gifts, work-related travel, life insurance, handicapped people, green investments, and other 'worthy' situations. As a result, the income tax treatment of households in similar economic situations can diverge rather widely.

Pollution and transport externalities are grossly underpriced. The Netherlands has one of the highest CO_2 emissions per capita in the EU and is struggling to meet the requirements of the Paris Agreement. Further, road congestion is not priced, which leads to heavy daily traffic jams and implies a substantial tax on labour. Excise duties are not used as widely as possible to internalize the external costs of alcohol abuse, overconsumption of sugar, and to reduce the amount of plastic waste. No efforts are being made at the EU level to reduce the distortionary effects of the VAT exemptions. The reduced VAT rate on foodstuffs is an ill-targeted instrument to mitigate the tax burden for lower-income groups.

1.4 Issues and Options for Reform

On the basis of the contributions in this book, we draw the following findings and recommendations regarding the tax treatment of capital income, profits (international and design), labour income, climate change and mobility, consumption, and external effects.

1.4.1 Capital Income

Profits, interest, dividends, capital gains, and other forms of capital income should all be taxed once at a uniform, proportional rate, whether related to saving, investment, business, property, or pensions. The taxation of capital income under the current system is a muddle of provisions that distort the efficient allocation of capital and risk, provoke tax arbitrage, involve suboptimal redistribution of income, and promote debt bias that makes the economy financially fragile. Removing these distortions and suboptimalities calls for a uniform and proportional tax rate on all capital income as argued by Bas Jacobs in Chapter 5. Additional revenue from the tax on capital income can be recycled, as much as possible in a distributionally neutral manner, by lowering tax rates on labour income.

Personal capital income should be taxed on an actual rather than a presumptive basis (which is equivalent to a wealth tax). This is maintained by Aart Gerritsen and Floris Zoutman in Chapter 2, Sijbren Cnossen and Peter Birch Sørensen in Chapter 3, and Jacobs in Chapter 5. Because above-normal returns on capital are not included in the tax base, a tax on wealth held in saving deposits, stocks, bonds, and immovable property is more inequitable, more inefficient, and less neutral compared with a tax on actual capital income earned on these assets in combination with full loss offsets. By taxing actual rather than presumptive returns, the government participates in the risk of investments, rents are taxed, taxes on capital income act as automatic stabilizers, and tax progressivity is enhanced.

Capital gains on assets with an evident market value, such as shares and bonds, should be taxed on a mark-to-market basis with loss offsets (Chapters 2, 3, and 5). Capital gains on owner-occupied property can be taxed based on the tri-annually adjusted value estimates under the law on immovable property, which are also used for local property taxes. Capital gains on assets without an evident market value could be taxed on a realization basis at the time of their actual sale. To prevent tax deferral, tax should be levied on the compounded interest on accrued unrealized capital gains at the time of realization, where the interest advantage is calculated based on the holding period of the asset and a comparable market return on the asset. Capital gains should always be taxed in the event of gift, death or migration. An additional policy option, recommended in Chapter 2, is to apply a higher tax rate on above-normal returns on shares, as is done under the Norwegian shareholder tax.

Wealth taxes are a second-best instrument if not all capital income is properly taxed (Jacobs in Chapter 5 and Spencer Bastani and Daniel Waldenström in Chapter 6). This is the case if capital gains are not taxed, housing and pensions are subsidized through the tax system, and actual capital income is left out of the individual income tax base. As Bastani and Waldenström note in Chapter 6, net wealth taxes have largely disappeared from the scene in OECD countries, in part because international capital mobility has limited the feasibility of taxing the very wealthy and because the valuation of illiquid assets, such as unincorporated businesses, is complicated.

The inheritance tax is part of an efficient and equitable tax system. Bastani and Waldenström point out in Chapter 6 that, in contrast to wealth taxes, estate and inheritance taxes are still found in many countries, including the Netherlands and the Scandinavian countries. Taxing inheritances is desirable to complement the income tax system in redistributing income and wealth at the lowest possible social cost and to foster equality of opportunity. Therefore, the preferential regime in the inheritance tax for business succession should be abolished, because it does not serve an economic purpose, causes various non-neutralities and promotes tax avoidance, especially among the very wealthy (see also Jacobs, Chapter 5). At death, unrealized capital gains on bequeathed assets should also be taxed under the personal income tax.

Double taxation of capital income should be avoided. In Chapters 3, 5, 10, and 11, various authors draw attention to the fact that under the current Dutch tax system, equity income is taxed twice, under the corporate income tax and the personal income tax (through the presumptive capital income tax). By contrast, debt income is taxed only once, if at all, under the personal income tax. Double taxation of equity income can be avoided by considering the corporate income tax as a final tax on dividends and on capital gains on shares attributable to profit retention (Chapters 3, 5). Double taxation of dividends can also be prevented by crediting the corporate income tax attributable to dividends against the personal income tax through an imputation tax system, as used to be applied in various EU countries and is still found in Australia (Chapters 3, 5). Double taxation of capital gains on shares can be prevented by increasing the acquisition price with retained corporate profits net of tax.

The director/dominant shareholders of closely held companies who work in their own businesses should no longer be paid a presumptive wage, but instead capital income should be calculated presumptively. Profits net of presumptive capital income should be deemed to be labour income—in line with the Scandinavian dual income tax systems. This conclusion is drawn by Cnossen and Sørensen in Chapter 3. Currently, director/shareholders can transform their higher-taxed labour income into lower-taxed capital income by reducing their salary. The Dutch tax authorities assume that the director/shareholder earns a 'customary' wage of at least 46,000 euros, which is taxed at progressive tax rates in box 1. The authorities have to prove that the customary wage is higher than the reported wage, while the director/shareholder has to prove that it should be lower. This highly contentious issue can be avoided by deeming capital income to be equal to corporate equity or total assets multiplied by a presumptive return set by the government. The profits of the self-employed and proprietorships should also be split into a labour income component, subject to progressive rates, and a capital income component, subject to the proportional rate applicable to other capital income.

Tax arbitrage should be reduced by setting equal tax rates on saving at the personal level and inside closely held companies. Jacobs asserts in Chapter 5 that closely held companies are used as saving banks because taxes on saving inside companies (corporate income tax) are typically lower than on saving outside companies (box 3), which is due to both the lower tax rate under the corporate income tax (15 or 25%) than in box 3 (30%), and the high imputed return in box 3, which lies way above the risk-free interest rate. This tax advantage also provides an incentive to take out company loans for consumption purposes or to buy private assets. Finally, low inheritance taxes on business succession stimulate saving inside closely held companies. All these forms of tax arbitrage are inefficient and disproportionately benefit the well to do. They can be avoided by taxing actual, not presumptive, capital income, and by adopting a uniform tax rate on corporate income and on capital income under the personal income tax, and by eliminating low tax rates on business succession. The call for uniform taxation is especially appropriate if an accrual-based capital gains tax at the time of realization is not introduced.

Owner-occupied property should be taxed symmetrically with other assets. The current tax treatment of owner-occupied property is not efficient, equitable, or neutral, as is made clear by Casper van Ewijk and Arjan Lejour in Chapter 4. Rental values are taxed at lower rates than other forms of capital income and mortgage interest is fully deductible, which generates distortions in the housing market, distorts financing decisions of households, distorts labour markets (due to higher tax rates), and contributes to inequality and financial instability. A symmetric tax treatment of owner-occupied property with other forms of capital can be achieved by gradually reducing the income tax rate at which mortgage interest can be deducted at the rate of the personal income tax on capital income, and by increasing the imputed rental value to 3–4% of the value of the property, which should then be taxed at the rate of the personal income tax on capital income. The property transfer tax should be abolished, as it distorts mobility in the housing and labour market.

Pension holdings should be taxed on an equal footing with other assets. Just like owner-occupied property, pension saving is subsidized through the tax system in two ways. First, income tax rates on pensioners are lower than the tax rates at which pension contributions are deducted from the income tax. Second, returns on assets in pension funds are not subject to tax on capital income. Subsidies on pension savings are inefficient and inequitable, as maintained by Gerritsen and Zoutman in Chapter 2 and Jacobs in Chapter 5. Pension savings in the Netherlands are nearly all compulsory, and they increase income and wealth inequality. These subsidies on pension saving can be reduced by gradually increasing the reduced income tax rates for pensioners and by (partially) taxing the capital income of pension funds.

1.4.2 Profits: International

The corporate income tax is a distortionary tax that harms corporate investment, stimulates excessive debt finance, and enables profit shifting to countries with low corporate income tax rates (Chapter 7, Patricia Hofmann and Nadine Riedel; Chapter 8, Ludvig Wier). The corporate income tax distorts investment as long as not all financing costs (dividend as well as interest) are tax-deductible. The unequal tax treatment of debt and equity creates debt bias (i.e. tax-driven increases in financial leverage of companies), particularly in the financial sector. In addition, multinationals shift their profits to countries with low tax rates by manipulating their internal transfer prices, by shifting debt to countries with high tax rates, and by locating their intellectual property in countries with low taxes. These features induce tax competition. In Chapter 7, Hofmann and Riedel dwell at length on the properties of the Dutch corporation tax, which is explicitly designed to attract foreign investment and to stimulate domestic entrepreneurial activity.

The position of the Netherlands as a conduit country for profits is under increasing international pressure. Lucidly recounted by Ludvig Wier in Chapter 8, the Netherlands is internationally regarded as a country that facilitates profit shifting to tax havens, in part owing to its extensive tax treaty network, no withholding tax on royalties (until recently), the participation exemption for profits earned abroad, advance tax rulings, and tax incentives for corporations. In 2018, multinationals shifted 57 billion US dollars in profits through the Netherlands, an estimated 10% of the global total. If these profits were to remain in the country, an average tax of 8–12% would be charged, which would account for a third of corporate tax revenues. Under international pressure, the Netherlands is implementing the EU's Anti-Tax Avoidance Directive and the OECD's Base Erosion and Profit Shifting (BEPS) guidelines, which could involve a loss of revenue. In the meantime, the Netherlands is trying to maintain its position as an investment location for multinational enterprises by combining a low corporate tax rate with the use of innovation boxes and generous tax incentives for R&D. A further decline in the corporate income tax rate would put this policy under pressure and render tax coordination more urgent.

Sales of advertising revenues of digital platforms, such as Google and Facebook, should be taxed using a digital services tax based on users. This follows from the contribution of Marko Koethenbuerger in Chapter 9. To establish a nexus in the country where users reside, the definition of permanent establishment of companies should be extended with digital establishment. According to Koethenbuerger, the Netherlands should introduce a digital services tax, as discussed in the EU.

1.4.3 Profits: Design

Reduce the debt bias in the corporate income tax. The asymmetric tax treatment of debt and equity of corporations should be partly or fully eliminated, particularly as debt and equity have become largely substitutable. Reducing the debt bias would make the Netherlands financially more robust and less prone to cyclical movements. The debt bias can be removed by treating costs of interest and dividend symmetrically under the corporate income tax (Jacobs, Chapter 5; Shafik Hebous and Alexander Klemm, Chapter 11). This can be achieved by eliminating the deduction of interest in computing taxable profits (comprehensive business income tax, CBIT) or by making interest and dividends both deductible in the form of a deduction for the cost of equity capital or total capital (allowance for corporate equity, ACE, or allowance for corporate capital, ACC). In Chapter 10, Dirk Schindler and Hendrik Vrijburg propose to reduce but not completely remove the debt bias. In doing so, effective tax rates on highly mobile multinationals can be lowered compared to domestic firms. They advocate an earnings-stripping rule, which would partially limit interest deductions to finance a partial deduction of the normal return on investment.

Reforming the corporate income tax in the direction of CBIT or ACE depends crucially on the degree of tax competition and on how effective capital income is taxed at the individual level. If the government wants to remove the investment distortion in the corporate income tax (with an ACE or a form of cash-flow tax), then it should make all financing costs (or all investment costs) deductible from taxable profits. The corporate income tax then only taxes the above-normal return on investment, while exempting normal returns (Hebous and Klemm, Chapter 11). Therefore, the normal returns, in the form of interest and dividends, should be taxed under the personal income tax.[6] If that is not done, then a lower tax on the normal return at the corporate level would involve lower total tax rates on capital income from interest and dividends, less tax revenues, and more income inequality. In addition, higher corporate income tax rates would be required to finance the deduction for financing costs (or investment costs) in a revenue-neutral manner. Higher corporate income tax rates, however, provoke profit shifting and base erosion (Dirk Schindler and Hendrik Vrijburg, Chapter 10). These drawbacks can be prevented only by coordinating tax accounting practices and possibly also corporate income tax rates at the EU level and beyond. However, if tax coordination is not forthcoming, it is not possible to make

[6] As is well known, the residence principle of taxing capital income distorts saving but not investment (capital export neutrality), while the source principle distorts investment but not saving (capital import neutrality). If corporate capital is more mobile than shareholders are, then the residence principle should be favoured over the source principle.

the financing costs for investments (fully) deductible without more profit shifting and base erosion, under an equal-yield assumption.

In a scenario with substantial tax competition, the corporate income tax should move in the direction of a CBIT under which interest and dividends are not deductible for tax purposes. Based on the analyses of Chapters 10, 11, and 12, we conclude that if corporate income tax rates cannot rise due to strong tax competition and lack of tax coordination, then the elimination of the debt bias is possible only if the additional tax revenue due to (further) limiting interest deductions is used to finance a partial ACE. Should tax competition become fiercer, and should the Netherlands, as a result, reduce the corporate income tax rate even further, then the government would be forced to limit the deduction of financing costs even more, which ultimately would result in a CBIT under which neither interest nor dividends are deductible. The economic price of this scenario would be that the normal return on business investment is taxed more heavily so that corporate investment decreases as capital costs rise. At the same time, international profit shifting would be more pronounced due to the lack of tax coordination. This scenario would especially benefit multinationals, as they tend to earn higher above-normal returns. Furthermore, income and wealth inequality would increase if corporate profits are taxed more lightly.

In a scenario with strong tax coordination, the corporate income tax should move in the direction of an ACE/ACC, in which interest and dividends are both tax-deductible. Again based on the analyses of Chapters 10, 11, and 12, we conclude that only greater tax coordination makes it possible to increase corporate income tax rates to finance a tax deduction for financing costs (or investments) in a revenue-neutral manner. Tax coordination is necessary to prevent base erosion and profit shifting to low-tax countries. With an ACE/ACC, the corporate income tax will no longer reduce the normal return on marginal investments. As capital costs are reduced, companies will invest more. However, it is then essential that the entire normal return is taxed effectively under the personal income tax. Tax coordination makes it then possible to increase corporate tax rates to tax above-normal profits at higher effective rates. This is not only optimal, but may also contribute to a reduction of income and wealth inequality.

A harmonized corporate tax base with formulary apportionment terminates profit shifting and base erosion within the EU, but produces new, real distortions to investment and labour demand and may involve a significant loss of revenue for the Netherlands. This is the conclusion of the analysis by Ruud de Mooij, Shafik Hebous, and Li Liu in Chapter 12. The authors suggest that the EU member states could introduce a common consolidated corporate tax base (CCCTB) for all countries with the same tax rules for interest deductions, depreciation, loss offsets, and so on, as proposed by the European Commission. The consolidated profits of multinationals are then apportioned to the EU member states on the basis of a formula incorporating each country's share in the total capital of the multinational, the total payroll and number of employees, and the sales by destination. Subsequently, EU member states would tax the apportioned profits at their own corporate tax rate. Accordingly, multinationals will no longer have incentives to shift profits—through manipulation of transfer prices or by reallocating debt or intellectual property—to lower-taxed countries within the EU. However, they also show that formula apportionment gives rise to other, real economic distortions, as it creates implicit taxes on the factors that are used in the formula. As long as tax rates vary between countries, corporations will try to move their capital, labour, or sales to those countries where tax rates are lowest. Accordingly, larger real economic distortions in production would be the price for halting base erosion and profit shifting. A CCCTB, therefore, is not necessarily welfare improving over the current, separate accounting system. Moreover, the Netherlands would suffer a substantial loss of tax revenue, except if the apportionment formula is confined to sales by destination.

A destination-based cash flow tax (DBCFT) combats profit shifting and base erosion, but can only be meaningfully introduced if all countries in the world adopt it. As discussed by Hebous and Klemm in Chapter 11, the DBCFT is a cash-flow tax on sales minus purchases, payroll and investment expenditures. A border tax adjustment is applied by exempting corporate exports and making imports non-deductible. The DBCFT ensures neutrality of investment and financing decisions, just like the ACE/ACC. Beyond that, a DBCFT only taxes the above-normal return on investment in the country where the corporation's products are actually consumed. Because consumption is less mobile than production, profit shifting to lower-taxed countries is no longer an issue, so that base erosion no longer occurs. Unlike a CCCTB with formula apportionment, there are no real distortions under a DBCFT. However, the benefits of a DBCFT will only materialize if all countries introduce it, which requires extensive international coordination. As long as global implementation is not possible, the consequences are drastic, because effective corporate income tax rates can be reduced to nil by large-scale profit shifting and base erosion.

1.4.4 Labour Income

Lower the income tax burden on the working poor. In Chapter 13, Egbert Jongen points out that an optimal non-linear income tax rate on labour income optimally trades off efficiency and equity at every income level. The current rate structure in the Netherlands has sub-optimally high marginal rates for middle-income groups compared with low-income groups—assuming that society values one euro for low-income groups higher than one euro for middle-income groups. The mirror image of the structure of marginal tax rates is that the average tax burden is too high for the working poor and too low for middle-income groups. This deficiency in the rate structure can be repaired by targeting the EITC more specifically at lower-income groups. Further, Jongen observes that the current top rate maximizes tax revenue in the highest tax bracket and should therefore not be increased.

Tax incentives to boost participation of secondary earners have become too generous. According to Henk-Wim de Boer and Andreas Peichl in Chapter 14, the Netherlands is a world leader with regards to part-time work. In recent years, the government has provided strong tax incentives to encourage secondary earners to work (more) through the EITC for workers, the EITC for workers with children, the childcare tax rebate, and the gradual elimination of the transferability of the general tax credit to the primary earner.[7] As a result, the effective average and marginal tax burden on the second earner has decreased considerably. Further reductions in the already-low marginal tax rates for secondary earners are estimated to have little effect on hours worked. The flip side of strong tax incentives for secondary earners is that income differentials between single-income households and double-income households, and between high-income and low-income households, have substantially widened over time. As de Boer and Peichl demonstrate in Chapter 14, tax incentives for secondary earners have reached the limit of what is socially optimal (based on optimal tax analysis). When the transferability of the general tax credit is completely phased out, the benefits of higher labour participation of secondary earners will be lower than the social cost of larger income inequality. Hence, no further tax incentives to increase the labour supply of secondary workers are recommended.

Simplify the tax rebates. The Dutch tax system has become increasingly complex, partly because of the steady growth of tax rebates for rental payments, health insurance, children and childcare, as shown by Patrick Koot and Miriam Gielen in Chapter 15 and Koen Caminada and Kees Goudswaard in Chapter 17. The tax system has virtually eliminated all income differences in pre-tax incomes that have arisen since 2001. In addition, large differences in tax burdens have emerged between different households with the same household income (Caminada and Goudswaard, Chapter 17). These differences may be the result of deliberate policy choices (e.g. tax incentives for labour market participation of secondary earners). However, they may also be unintended because the revenue from higher taxes is increasingly being recycled in the form of larger tax credits and tax rebates. Koot and Gielen demonstrate in Chapter 15 that it is possible to streamline the tax rebates without major distributional effects. This can be done by bundling all existing tax rebates into one tax rebate, which is based on a limited number of characteristics, such as individual and household income, children, rental payments, and net wealth.

[7] In Dutch policy jargon, the transferability of the general tax credit to the primary earner is referred to as the 'kitchen sink subsidy'.

Reduce the tax benefits for the self-employed. The self-employed (mainly free-lancers) have many tax privileges that ordinary employees do not have, as highlighted by Lans Bovenberg and Ed Groot in Chapter 16. The self-employed benefit from the self-employment credit, the 14% profit exemption and, if applicable, the start-up credit. As a result, the difference in tax burden with regards to ordinary employees has increased considerably. Not surprisingly, the Netherlands has an unprecedented large share of self-employed people compared with other countries. There are no convincing economic arguments that justify the large tax differential. Bovenberg and Groot recommend a more neutral tax treatment between employees and the self-employed in the long run, by converting the EITC and the self-employment credit into an EITC for employees and an EITC for self-employed, and, subsequently, to let these credits gradually converge.

1.4.5 Global Warming and Mobility

Tax all CO_2 emissions in all sectors at a uniform specific rate. Rick van der Ploeg forcefully argues in Chapter 18 that CO_2 emissions need to be priced as the world still has only between five and nine years left to limit global warming to 1.5°C compared with pre-industrial times. With a target of 2°C, the CO_2 budget will run out in 18–33 years. CO_2 emissions need to be priced at an increasing rate, starting from 40–80 euros per tonne of CO_2 for all emissions in all sectors. The CO_2 price can be implemented in the form of carbon taxes or tradable emission permits under the EU's Emissions Trading System (ETS). Higher CO_2 prices should preferably be coordinated internationally to prevent the relocation of business enterprises abroad (carbon leakage). CO_2 taxes are needed for all sectors that are not covered by the ETS in order to implement the correct CO_2 price if the ETS price falls short. An immediate moratorium is required on the burning of coal. All subsidies on the use of fossil fuels should be abolished.

Road pricing is necessary to keep the Dutch mobile. In Chapter 19, Hendrik Vrijburg and Gerben Geilenkirchen focus on road pricing to control externalities from traffic jams, which occur particularly in the western part of the Netherlands. They cause major social costs and are an implicit tax on labour. The authors point out that congestion charges that are differentiated by time and place efficiently prevent traffic jams by confronting people with the external costs they impose on other people when they drive their cars. A cordon levy at rush hours around the big cities can be a good approximation for differentiating congestion charges by place and time. In addition, a relatively low flat user tax of around 3 eurocents per kilometre can be a good proxy for internalizing the damages caused by accidents, wear and tear of the road network, and environmental degradation. Taxes on the purchase and ownership of cars should be differentiated according to anticipated environmental damage and the car's safety.

1.4.6 Consumption

Abolish the VAT exemptions. In Chapter 20, Sijbren Cnossen presents statistics that show that as much as 60% of consumption expenditure in the Netherlands is taxed on inputs (fixed assets and intermediate purchases) rather than on output with credit for the tax on inputs, because governments, healthcare, education, finance and insurance, games of chance, postal services, radio and television broadcasts, and various socio-cultural sectors are exempt from VAT. The exemptions distort both consumer behaviour and producer choices, and involve high administration and compliance costs. The social costs can be as high as one-half of 1% of GDP. If the exemptions were abolished, then part of the additional tax revenue could be used for higher subsidies on healthcare and education to prevent price increases for consumers. Alternatively, as in Canada, healthcare and education, along with governments, might be zero-rated. This would remove the self-supply bias and the input choice distortion, but not the competitive distortion if these sectors supply goods and services that can also be supplied by the private sector. Cnossen recommends that the Netherlands should advocate the removal of the exemptions at the EU level, where agreement on such a reform is required.

Introduce a single VAT rate. Cnossen also argues in Chapter 20 that different VAT rates distort consumer and producer choices and thereby generate welfare losses. The low VAT rate in the Netherlands also redistributes income in the wrong direction. Higher-income groups spend a larger absolute amount of their income on low-taxed goods and services than lower-income groups, and therefore they benefit up to twice as much from the low VAT rate. Cnossen posits that it is more efficient and equitable to levy a single VAT rate and, if necessary, to compensate lower-income groups through the tax-transfer system.

Apply VAT to the financial sector. Ben Lockwood argues in Chapter 21 that it is possible to apply VAT to fee-based financial services, as is done in all countries with a modern VAT. However, VAT cannot be imposed on a transaction-by-transaction basis on margin-based financial services, which is required if the tax on financial services is to be passed on to taxable businesses, which can then take credit for it against their own tax on sales. Alternatively, VAT can be applied to the sum of payroll and business cash flow or profits of financial institutions, as is done in Denmark, Israel, and Iceland, for instance. However, this runs again into the problem that the VAT on financial services cannot be passed on to customers. Lockwood concludes that perhaps the best approach is the solution adopted by New Zealand under which fee-based services are taxed and margin-based services are exempted, while the input tax on business-to-business margin-based services is recoverable by financial institutions. In his view, taxing the financial sector under VAT is preferable to imposing a financial transactions tax that is levied in a number of countries, as this causes cascading effects that distort production.

Taxes and complementary regulations should internalize the external and internal costs of smoking, drinking, gambling, sugar consumption, and the use of plastic. Sijbren Cnossen analyses these issues for the Netherlands in Chapter 22. He points out that various studies indicate that, by and large, smokers pay for the costs they impose on society through the tobacco excise duty. This is probably not the case with drinkers and gamblers, which establishes a case for increasing the excise duties on alcohol and gambling. The drawback, however, is that while excessive drinkers and gamblers are responsible for the majority of external costs, the excise duties affect all consumers, including recreational consumers who do not cause external costs. This implies that information dissemination and regulation should receive more emphasis to control external costs. Individual interventions aimed at addicted consumers may also be called for. Cnossen argues that the minimum duties on alcoholic beverages agreed to in 1992 at the EU level should be increased; their real value has declined by 60%. The duty on non-alcoholic beverages, which also applies to mineral water, should be replaced by an excise duty on sugar sweetened beverages and other sugary products, in order to internalize the external costs of obesity. In addition, excise duties should be levied on plastic items and packaging materials, in combination with a ban on single-use plastics, in order to recover the social cost of plastic pollution from consumers and producers.

1.4.7 Concluding Comment and Summary of Proposals

Obviously, tax reform is not new to the Netherlands. In response to calls for reviews of specific aspects of the tax system, various committees and cabinet members have proposed changes. The reviews include the following reports: Tax System Study Committee (2010), Income Tax and Allowances Committee (2013), Wiebes (2014, 2015), Sustainable Growth Study Group (2016), Snel (2019), and the Ministry of Finance (2020). It is expected that the government will incorporate a tax reform package in its programme for the next cabinet after the general elections in 2021. All these Dutch-language publications are valuable building blocks for tax reform.

The contributions in this book, we believe, add comprehensive theoretical and international insights as well as up-to-date evidence-based analyses to the existing body of knowledge. This is especially relevant in times when the tax-and-expenditure system needs a thorough review to meet the challenges that will arise as a result of the COVID-19 crisis. To aid the reader, Table 1.3 summarizes the recommendations made above by confronting the current system with the reform proposals and providing the economic rationale for the changes. As can be seen, the topic selection spans the full range of tax policy and picks out the most difficult issues for special focus and different perspectives.

Table 1.3 Summary of proposals

Taxable items	Current system	Reform proposal	Rationale
Individual capital income			
1. Dividend, interest, rental payments	Taxation of the value of underlying assets based on presumptive returns	Tax actual returns	Greater neutrality, taxation of above-normal returns, government shares in risk of investment, tax system is more progressive and countercyclical
2. Capital gains	Taxed on presumptive basis at low rates if included in value of underlying asset	Tax capital gains on liquid assets on accrual basis and illiquid assets on realization basis; assume presumptive realization at death or migration	Greater tax neutrality, taxation of above-normal returns, government shares in risk of investment, tax system is more progressive and countercyclical
3. Equity income	Return on equity taxed twice	Tax corporate profits only once, exempt dividends, and gross-up the acquisition cost of shares by corporate profits net of tax	Removal of debt bias, less financial fragility, fewer distortions of investment
4. Rental value of owner-occupied property	Presumptive taxation of rental value at low rates, full deductibility of interest	Increase presumptive rental value to 3%–4% of asset's value and reduce the rate at which mortgage interest is deductible, and imputed rent is taxed, to 30%	Greater tax neutrality, removal of debt bias, less financial fragility
5. Pension fund income	Exempt	Tax capital income of pension funds at low rate	Greater tax neutrality
Business profits			
1.a Self-employed without employees (freelancers)	Allowances as proprietor, small and medium-sized business and start-ups	Merge allowances and reduce their size, approximating employees' earned-income allowance	Less distortion of occupational choice, greater tax neutrality and less tax arbitrage
1.b Self-employed with employees	Same	Split profits into labour and capital income component as proposed for closely held companies	Tax neutrality between self-employed and directors/shareholder of closely held companies, less tax arbitrage

Continued

Table 1.3 *Continued*

Taxable items	Current system	Reform proposal	Rationale
2. Closely held company	Labour–capital income split based on customary labour earnings in similar professions	Capital–labour income split based on presumptive return on business assets or equity; remaining profits taxed as labour income	Tax neutrality between employees and self-employed, less tax arbitrage
Wealth and inheritances			
1. Wealth taxation	Personal assets (excluding pensions, owner-occupied housing and business assets) taxed in box 3	Abolish presumptive income tax if all capital income is taxed on an actual basis	No double taxation of normal returns, capital income taxes more efficient and equitable
2. Inheritance tax	Progressive inheritance tax with large exemptions for family and reduced rates for business succession	Eliminate preferential regime for business succession, raise average inheritance taxes	Closes loopholes for tax avoidance, mitigate lock-in effects by taxing capital gains, remove regressive element of inheritance tax, tax windfalls
Corporation tax: international			
1. Conduit status of country	Participation exemption, zero withholding tax on royalties, tax rulings and tax treaty network cause base erosion and profit shifting	Adopt EU Anti-Tax Avoidance Directive and cooperate in OECD's BEPS project, review participation exemption and impose withholding taxes on interest and royalties	Reduces base erosion and profit shifting
2. Digital platforms	Not taxed	Tax by reference to number of users	Reduces base erosion and profit shifting of tech giants
Corporation tax: design			
1. Debt bias	Interest fully deductible	Symmetric tax treatment of equity and debt finance with ACE, CBIT, or partial deduction for all costs of capital	Removes financing distortions, reduces financial fragility and systemic risks of the financial sector
2. Taxation of normal return	Fully taxed	Exempt normal return through ACE/ACC	Removes investment distortion
3. Formulary apportionment	Not practised; presently separate accounting system	CCCTB	Eliminates incentives for profit shifting, but real distortions could increase

4. DBCFT	Not practised	DBCFT with border tax adjustments	Eliminates incentives for profit shifting, no real distortions, but only desirable if all countries adopt it; if not, large-scale profit shifting and base erosion
Labour income			
1. EITC	Tax rates on low incomes too high	Increase EITC targeted at low incomes	Increases labour market participation, raises tax progressivity or combination of both
2. Work incentives for secondary earners	Strong work incentives via various schemes for secondary earners	Do not increase generosity of tax incentives for secondary workers	Benefits of higher labour participation lower than social cost of greater inequality
3. Tax benefits for freelancers and proprietorships	Allowances for small- and medium-sized businesses and start-ups	Merge allowances and reduce their size	Greater tax neutrality for employees, freelancers, sole proprietors, and directors/substantial shareholders
4. Tax rebates	Tax rebates for healthcare, rent, children and childcare	Merge tax rebates into one rebate based on individual and household income, children and assets	Simplifies current system
Global warming and mobility			
1. CO_2 pricing	Emissions inadequately and unevenly priced	Introduce uniform CO_2 price for all emissions in all sectors of €40–80 per tonne or tighten emissions trading system with equivalent effect	To comply with emission targets in accordance with the Paris Agreement
2. Pricing of road use	Congestion externalities not priced	Introduce road pricing based on time and location and introduce low, flat per km tax on car use	Internalizes congestion costs and externalities of motor vehicles
Consumption			
1. VAT exemptions	Exemptions for governments, healthcare, education, finance, games of chance, postal services, socio-cultural services	Pursue removing exemptions at EU level	Reduces production distortions in input choice and self-supply, and reduces consumption distortions

Continued

Table 1.3 *Continued*

Taxable items	Current system	Reform proposal	Rationale
2. VAT rate structure	Dual rate structure of 9% and 21%	Adopt single uniform rate of around 17%	Reduces distortions in consumption and lowers the cost of income redistribution
3. Tobacco, alcohol, gambling, sugar, plastics	Tobacco adequately taxed, but other items not	Raise EU-wide alcohol duties and introduce excises on sugar and plastics	Promotes internalization of external costs

References

CBS (2019), *Welvaart in Nederland 2019*, CBS, The Hague/Heerlen.

IBO (2019), 'IBO Toeslagen Deelonderzoek 1, Eenvoud of Maatwerk: Uitruilen binnen het Bestaande Toeslagenstelsel', Dutch Ministry of Finance, The Hague.

Income Tax and Allowances Committee (2013), 'Naar een Activerender Belastingstelsel: Eindrapport, Commissie Inkomstenbelasting en Toeslagen', Dutch Ministry of Finance, The Hague.

Jacobs, B. (2015), *De Prijs van Gelijkheid*, Bert Bakker-Prometheus, Amsterdam.

Ministry of Finance (2020), 'Bouwstenen voor een Beter Belastingstelsel', Ministry of Finance, The Hague.

OECD (2019), *Tax Revenue Statistics*, OECD Publishing, Paris.

OECD (2020), 'Income Distribution Data Base' (https://stats.oecd.org/Index.aspx?DataSetCode=IDD).

Schulenberg, R. and Buitenhuis, M. (2017), 'Oorzaken van de Toename in de Primaire Inkomensongelijkheid', *Economisch Statistische Berichten*, 102(4756), 583–6.

Snel, M. (2019), 'Bouwstenen voor een Beter Belastingstelsel', Letter 2019-0000062470, 15 April, Parliament, The Hague.

Sustainable Growth Study Group (2016), 'Kiezen voor Duurzame Groei', Dutch Ministry of Economic Affairs, The Hague.

Tax System Study Committee (2010), 'Continuïteit en Vernieuwing: Een Visie op het Belastingstelsel', Dutch Ministry of Finance, The Hague.

Wiebes, E. (2014), 'Keuzes voor een Beter Belastingstelsel', Letter 32140-5, 16 September, Parliament, The Hague.

Wiebes, E. (2015), 'Belastingherziening 2016, Letter 32140-13', 19 June, Parliament, The Hague.

World Inequality Database (2020), https://wid.world/country/netherlands/.

PART I

CAPITAL INCOME

2
Towards a Tax on Actual Returns

*Aart Gerritsen and Floris T. Zoutman**

2.1 Introduction

Recent years have seen mounting concerns about the distribution of both wealth and the income derived from wealth. These concerns have found popular expression in protests against the so-called top 1%. The publications by Piketty (2014), Piketty and Zucman (2014), and Saez and Zucman (2016), among others, have contributed greatly to a renewed interest in wealth and its distribution. These publications document a spectacular increase in the importance and concentration of capital in today's economy, particularly in the United States. The popular unease about extreme wealth and observed trends in capital concentration emphasize the importance of taxes on capital. A tax on capital can ensure a fairer distribution of resources. However, it may also distort households' saving and investment decisions. The policy challenge is to design a capital tax in such a way that it realizes its distributional gains against the lowest possible distortionary costs.

In the Netherlands, capital is taxed on a personal level with a tax that literally translates to a 'wealth-return levy'. This is a misnomer for two reasons. First and foremost, it does not actually tax the returns on wealth. In the words of the Dutch Tax Authority (our italics): '*We presume* that you obtain a return on your savings and investments. You pay 30% income tax on this return' (Belastingdienst, 2019). Moreover, the *presumptive* rate of return—on the basis of which Dutch households are taxed—does not in any way depend on the *actual* rate of return but only on the household's net wealth.[1] Thus, the Dutch wealth-return levy is really a tax

* Aart Gerritsen (agerritsen@ese.eur.nl) is Assistant Professor at Erasmus University, Rotterdam, and is affilaited with Erasmus School of Economics, Tinbergen Institute, and CESifo. Floris T. Zoutman (floris.zoutman@nhh.no) is Associate Professor, NHH Norwegian School of Economics, and is affilaited with Department of Business and Management Science, Norwegian Center for Taxation (NoCeT), and CESifo. We are grateful to Lans Bovenberg, Sijbren Cnossen, Bas Jacobs and Vinzenz Ziesemer for their elaborate comments on an earlier version. We also thank Mohammed Mardan, Dirk Schindler, Guttorm Schjelderup and Maximilian Todtenhaupt for useful discussions.

[1] In recent years, the Dutch capital tax has been widely criticized. Criticism has focused particularly on the fact that the presumptive rate of return of 4% exceeded the market interest rates of the past decade by a wide margin. In response to the criticism, the government decided that, from 2017 onwards, the presumptive rate of return on wealth below 75,000 euros is considerably lower than the presumptive rate of return on wealth above 75,000 euros. On average, this reform managed to

Aart Gerritsen and Floris T. Zoutman, *Towards a Tax on Actual Returns* In: *Tax by Design for the Netherlands*. Edited by: Sijbren Cnossen and Bas Jacobs, Oxford University Press.
DOI: 10.1093/oso/9780192855244.003.0002

on wealth itself rather than a tax on the returns on wealth. This is something that sets the Netherlands apart from the rest of the industrialized world. No other OECD country taxes the presumptive return on capital while leaving actual returns untaxed (Harding, 2013; Harding and Marten, 2018). The second reason why the wealth-return levy does not do justice to its name is because it only applies to a minor fraction of Dutch household wealth. The two wealth components that account for the vast majority of household wealth (i.e. pensions and owner-occupied houses) are not included in the tax base.

The current capital tax is the result of a major tax reform in 2001. The pre-reform capital tax did tax some actual returns on capital but the tax was relatively easy to avoid because it left capital gains untaxed. Instead of broadening the tax base to include these capital gains, the government decided to not tax any returns at all and to tax presumptive returns instead. Contemporary economic analyses of the reform provide two main takeaways. First, no economist seems to have thought it a good idea to not tax actual returns on wealth; see, for example, the collected volume of Cnossen et al. (1999). Second, the alternative tax reforms that were proposed at the time are still particularly relevant today; see, for example, Cnossen and Bovenberg (2001). Most economists were convinced that the Dutch government would do well (1) to tax the actual returns on wealth, (2) to apply the broadest possible definition of wealth to determine the tax base, and (3) to tax capital gains just like regular capital income, such as dividends and interest income. Twenty years later, the Dutch government is finally willing to seriously consider the first point of advice. The coalition agreement of the current government states that 'a capital tax based on actual returns will be worked out' during the current term of office (VVD et al., 2019, p. 35).

In this chapter, we discuss why it is both equitable and efficient to tax the actual returns instead of the presumptive returns on wealth. Equivalently, it can be read as a plea for taxing capital income rather than wealth itself. We pay particular attention to the most recent insights from the economic literature. What does empirical evidence on the distribution of capital income tell us about the reasons to tax actual returns? What do we know about the possible behavioural effects of such a tax? We also discuss a number of practical aspects of a tax on actual returns. How should such a tax deal with capital gains? To what extent should the tax be differentiated? How should owner-occupied houses and pension wealth be dealt with? On many of these practical points we fully agree with earlier policy proposals, such as those of Cnossen and Bovenberg (2001) and Jacobs (2017). The Dutch Ministry of Finance (2017) has also published a document outlining options for reforming the capital tax. Our policy advice contrasts with that of

somewhat close the gap between actual and presumptive rates of return of the less fortunate. However, the fact remains that the tax depends purely on net wealth alone and therefore is entirely insensitive to variations in capital income.

the Ministry of Finance by emphasizing the importance of also taxing the actual returns on housing and pension wealth.

2.2 Why Government Should Tax the Actual Returns on Capital

In his classic work on public finance, Musgrave (1959) distinguishes between three economic functions of the government: to achieve an equitable distribution of resources, to improve allocative efficiency, and to foster macro-economic stability. A tax on the actual returns to capital is desirable on all three grounds. It improves equity by redistributing income from households that are good at investing their wealth to households that are not so good at investing their wealth. It improves efficiency by making government share in the idiosyncratic risk that households face when investing their wealth. Also, it improves macro-economic stability because actual returns are strongly procyclical, so that a tax on actual returns helps to dampen the business cycle.

2.2.1 Equity: Redistribution from Households with High Returns to Households with Low Returns

Traditionally, the literature on optimal taxation has hardly made any distinction between taxing the returns on capital and taxing capital itself—or, equivalently, presumptive returns on capital. The reason for this is that economists tend to assume that all households have free access to all tradable financial instruments, that they make perfectly rational investment decisions, and that they have identical risk preferences. Under these assumptions, all households will perfectly spread their wealth across the market portfolio, ensuring that they obtain identical rates of return without running unnecessary risks. In that case, there is a one-to-one mapping between capital and capital income, so that a tax on capital has the exact same distributional consequences as a tax on the returns on capital. If everyone obtains the same rate of return, then it simply does not matter whether the government taxes the returns to capital or capital itself. However, recent empirical evidence has documented what must seem trivial to non-economists: there are financial frictions and not everyone is equally good at investing his or her capital. As a result, households do systematically differ in their rates of return, and therefore it does matter whether government taxes the returns on capital or capital itself.

A growing body of literature shows that people differ greatly in their financial literacy. Both survey and experimental evidence show that many people have a weak understanding of simple financial concepts (Hastings, Madrian, and

Skimmyhorn, 2013; Lusardi and Mitchell, 2014; Gerritsen, 2017). For example, van Rooij, Lusardi, and Alessie (2011) find that many Dutch people do not fully understand that shares in a single company are generally riskier than a diversified investment fund. They also show that Dutch people with higher financial literacy invest more in shares and therefore tend to achieve higher returns. People with higher financial literacy are also better able to choose the fund with the lowest fees from a list of otherwise identical investment funds (Choi, Laibson, and Madrian, 2010). Moreover, people with lower financial literacy will be more inclined to take out usury loans or to obtain advice from financial advisers with records of misconduct (Lusardi and Tufano, 2015; Egan, Matvos, and Seru, 2019). Lusardi, Michaud, and Mitchell (2017) estimate that 30–40% of US wealth inequality can be attributed to inequality in returns due to differences in financial literacy.

The most comprehensive and direct empirical evidence of the importance of heterogeneous rates of return comes from Norway. Fagereng et al. (2020) study an administrative data set that covers all Norwegian taxpayers between 2005 and 2015 and contains detailed information on asset holdings and capital income for a broad range of different asset classes. They show that there are large differences in returns across individuals. The standard deviation on rates of return on capital is 8.6 percentage points. The difference in rates of return between the 10th and the 90th wealth percentiles is a full 18 percentage points. Even the returns on risk-free assets differ strongly across households. The most striking part of their analysis is that return heterogeneity appears to be highly persistent within individuals and even across generations. Thus, throughout the ten years under consideration, more or less the same individuals and families keep obtaining either high or low annual rates of return.

From an equity perspective, the policy implications of these empirical findings are clear. While a tax on the presumptive returns on capital redistributes resources from the wealthy to the poor, such a tax does nothing to reduce inequality in actual returns among equally rich or poor households. Under current tax rules, Dutch households with the same amount of wealth pay the same amount of capital taxes, even though they may strongly differ in the actual income that they obtain from their wealth. Virtually any theory of redistributive justice would classify this as unfair. A just tax system requires that, ceteris paribus, people with higher returns on capital carry a larger part of the tax burden. This can be achieved by taxing the actual returns on capital. A tax on actual returns not only redistributes from rich to poor but also, conditional on wealth, from people with high income to people with low income. On equity grounds, a tax on actual returns is therefore preferred to a tax on presumptive returns.[2]

[2] Gerritsen et al. (2020) formally prove that the government ought to tax the actual returns on capital when households face different rates of return.

2.2.2 Efficiency: Redistribution from the Lucky Ones to the Unlucky Ones

A tax on actual returns on capital is not only more equitable than a tax on presumptive returns, it is also more efficient. Rational households with unconstrained access to perfectly working financial markets will diversify their investment portfolio in such a way that they are not exposed to any idiosyncratic risk. In reality, however, many households imperfectly diversify their wealth. The underlying reason for this is most likely a combination of limited financial literacy and financial market frictions. Von Gaudecker (2015) shows that Dutch households with low scores on financial literacy are also more prone to underdiversify their financial portfolios. Moreover, financial frictions may ensure that perfect diversification is simply impossible. For example, there are insufficient financial instruments to insure against the idiosyncratic risk on owner-occupied houses (Giacoletti, 2017). As a result, household wealth is exposed to large idiosyncratic risk (e.g. Benartzi and Thaler, 2001; Choi, Laibson, and Madrian, 2005; Goetzmann and Kumar, 2008). This means that households could in principle reduce their risk for a given expected return, or increase expected returns for a given amount of risk.

The most elaborate empirical evidence on underdiversification of financial portfolios once again comes from Scandinavia. Calvet, Campbell, and Sodini (2007) study the financial portfolios of all Swedish households between 1999 and 2002 to determine the extent to which their wealth is exposed to idiosyncratic risk. They find that households could on average obtain a 0.66% higher return for a given amount of risk by better diversifying their portfolio. This measure is called the return loss and it varies wildly across households. The 25th percentile exhibits a return loss of only 0.09 percentage points but the 95th percentile has a return loss of 2.65 percentage points. Von Gaudecker (2015) determines the return loss for Dutch households on the basis of the DNB Household Survey in the years 2005–6. While these data are much less reliable than the Swedish data, von Gaudecker does find very comparable results. The return loss of Dutch households varies from 0.04 for the 25th percentile to 1.80 for the 95th percentile. Although these numbers are significant in and of themselves—especially in comparison with current interest rates—they are likely underestimating the costs of idiosyncratic risk, because they only focus on financial portfolios and do not take into account households' housing wealth. In this regard, it is important to keep in mind that housing wealth is one of the biggest components of Dutch household wealth (Parlevliet and Kooiman, 2015; CPB Netherlands Bureau for Economic Policy Analysis, 2018) and that the values of houses exhibit a strong degree of idiosyncratic risk (Case and Shiller, 1989; Giacoletti, 2017). In the Netherlands, Dröes and Hassink (2013) show that 89% of the variation in

Dutch housing prices cannot be explained by variation in the housing index, and is therefore idiosyncratic.

If households are unable to (fully) diversify their wealth themselves, the government can provide partial insurance against idiosyncratic risk by taxing the actual returns on capital. When actual returns are taxed, a household carries a higher tax burden when lucky and a lower tax burden when unlucky. This way, the government can absorb part of the idiosyncratic risk on capital returns and thus provide a form of social insurance that is desirable regardless of its redistributive preferences (Varian, 1980; Spiritus and Boadway, 2021). Notice that this is not feasible with the current tax on presumptive returns because it is insensitive to realizations of idiosyncratic risk. Summing up, the government can achieve a more efficient allocation of risk by taxing the actual rather than the presumptive returns on capital.

2.2.3 Macro-Economic Stabilization versus Stable Tax Revenue

The returns on wealth are much more sensitive to the business cycle than wealth itself. As a result of this, the tax revenue from a tax on presumptive returns on capital is much more stable across the business cycle than that of a tax on actual returns. This is often presented by the Dutch government as an important argument in favour of taxing the presumptive returns on capital (e.g. van Goor, 2017; Ministry of Finance, 2017).

However, this argument goes against all macro-economic logic. The fact that returns on capital strongly covary with the business cycle means that a tax on actual returns has an anti-cyclical effect on the economy. This allows the government to absorb part of the macro-economic shocks that would otherwise be borne by households. Thus, a final argument in favour of a tax on actual returns on capital is that it helps to stabilize the economy (see also Jacobs, 2015, 2017).

More generally, even if households do perfectly diversify their wealth and are therefore only exposed to systemic risk, a tax on actual returns is still desirable on efficiency grounds. This is the case because the social benefits of tax revenue are higher in times of economic prosperity than in economic downturns (Christiansen, 1993; Schindler, 2008; Spiritus and Boadway, 2021).

2.2.4 An Efficiency Argument against a Tax on Actual Returns?

To the best of our knowledge, there is only a single study that argues for taxing capital instead of the returns on capital. This is a recent study by Guvenen et al. (2019). They assume that households face borrowing constraints and may therefore be unable to exploit investment opportunities that yield superior rates of return. As households differ in their investment opportunities, they may also differ in their marginal rates of return. In this case, the government can achieve an efficiency gain by redistributing funds from households with low returns on capital to households with high returns on capital—so that these funds are invested at the highest possible return. Guvenen et al. (2019) show that such a redistribution of resources could be achieved with a tax rebate instead of a tax on actual returns.

This finding is at odds with the aforementioned equity argument for taxing actual returns. Ultimately, we believe that this issue comes down to a political question of whether government should rather redistribute from people with high returns on capital to people with low returns on capital, or vice versa. As mentioned before, most theories of redistributive justice would prescribe redistribution from high-return to low-return households. In that case, Gerritsen et al. (2020) show that it is desirable to tax the actual returns on capital. In addition, in their model, Guvenen et al. (2019) assume away risk in the rate of return. As discussed above, if the rate of return is risky, this provides an important efficiency argument for taxing the actual rate of return.

2.3 Behavioural Effects of a Tax on Actual Returns

A tax on actual returns affects economic decision-making. The economic literature has traditionally focused on the effects on savings and risk-taking. Recent studies also estimate the effect on innovation. In this section, we discuss the expected behavioural effects of replacing the tax on presumptive returns with a tax on actual returns. We also discuss how (un)desirable behavioural effects can be encouraged (discouraged).

2.3.1 Behavioural Effects on Savings

Both a tax on actual returns and a tax on presumptive returns reduce the expected rate of return on wealth. This affects the savings decisions of households in two ways. First, a reduction in the after-tax rate of return results in a reduction in future capital income. As a result of this income effect, households will save more. Second, taxation reduces the relative price of current consumption with respect to future consumption. This substitution effect works in the opposite direction and reduces savings.

Empirical studies show that the substitution effect typically dominates the income effect. For instance, Zoutman (2018) studies the Dutch tax reform of 2001. He shows that households that experience a lower (higher) effective tax rate on their wealth after the tax reform save, on average, more (less) than before the reform.

The effect of taxation on savings only plays a role if the total tax burden on wealth changes. As a result, we only expect behavioural effects on aggregate savings if the government decides to change average effective tax rates on wealth.

2.3.2 Behavioural Effects on Risk-Taking

Replacing the current tax on presumptive returns by a tax on actual returns also affects the investment incentives of households. Domar and Musgrave (1944) show that a tax on actual returns reduces both the expected rate of return and the risk. Intuitively, absolute tax payments are largest when returns are high, and vice versa. In contrast to a tax on presumptive returns, a tax on actual returns therefore acts like an insurance against investment risk.

Rational investors will react to this incentive by increasing the risk in their portfolio (Sandmo, 1969). They can do this by investing in risky assets, such as stocks or derivatives, or by increasing the leverage of their portfolio.

This behavioural effect is desirable if the risk on investments is idiosyncratic. The reason is that an increase in risk-taking increases the expected return of households. This, in turn, results in an increase in tax revenue for the government. At the same time, idiosyncratic risk cancels out at the macro-economic level, and therefore tax revenue does not become more volatile (Gordon, 1985).

Although economic theory establishes a clear prediction, there is relatively little empirical research on this relationship. However, the research that exists is in line with theoretical predictions. For instance, using data from the United States, Cullen and Gordon (2007) show that risky investment in private businesses increases when the tax on returns increases. This finding is consistent with the idea that a tax on actual returns increases risk-taking.

The effect of taxation on risk-taking does appear to depend on the opportunities for offsetting losses against future tax payments. If losses cannot be offset, then the insurance value of a tax on actual returns is smaller. Langenmayr and Lester (2018) use data from multinationals to show that a higher corporate tax rate (i.e. a tax on actual returns at the company level) only increases risk-taking if losses can be offset. For companies that cannot offset their losses, they find that a higher corporate tax rate results in less risk-taking. These findings suggest that a tax on actual returns should be combined with a mechanism to offset losses.[3]

[3] However, there are also reasons to limit loss-offset opportunities. In some cases, loss-offset opportunities allow for tax-avoidance opportunities by allowing households to realize losses early on, while postponing gains. We discuss this in more detail below.

Finally, a tax on actual returns can affect risk-taking through the income effect. A tax on actual returns lowers the value of future capital income. This increases (reduces) risk-taking if relative risk aversion increases (decreases) with wealth (Sandmo, 1985). However, the same is true for a tax on presumptive returns. Therefore, this income effect only plays a role if the total tax burden on wealth increases or decreases.

2.3.3 Behavioural Effects on Innovation

The effect of taxation on risk-taking is closely related to the effect of taxation on innovation. Innovation is often seen as a crucial driver of economic growth (e.g. Romer, 1990; Aghion and Howitt, 1992). Akcigit et al. (2018) estimate the empirical relationship between innovation and income taxes in the United States, which taxes income from capital and labour at the same rate. They use variation in the tax rate (1) over time, (2) between states, and (3) between inventors within the same state but within different tax brackets. Their analysis shows that higher tax rates result in a reduction in innovation as measured by the number of patent applications. The reason is that a tax on (capital) income reduces the value of investing in innovation.

Unfortunately, Akcigit et al. (2018) do not answer the question whether a tax on actual returns affects innovation more or less than a tax on presumptive returns. In the theoretical model of Akcigit et al. (2018), both these taxes will result in lower investment in innovation. We tend to believe that a tax on actual returns results in a smaller reduction in innovation than the current tax on presumptive returns. The reason is that investment in innovation is risky and, as discussed in the previous subsection, a tax on actual returns encourages risk-taking.

2.4 Practical Considerations

2.4.1 Tax on an Accrual Basis

In the Netherlands, before the 2001 tax reform, regular returns such as interest and dividends were taxed along with other income, but capital gains (i.e. increases in asset values) remained untaxed even upon realization. As a result, it was relatively easy to avoid the capital-income tax entirely by, for instance, investing in mutual funds that only provided returns in the form of capital gains.

To avoid this type of tax avoidance, it is necessary to tax capital gains similarly to regular returns. Capital gains are often taxed on a realization basis when the asset is sold. In that case, it is important that the government does not simply tax the difference between the sales price and the purchase price of the asset. The reason is that this results in an incentive to postpone the realization of capital gains. This is known as the lock-in effect.

As formally shown by Auerbach (1991), the government can solve this issue by charging interest over capital gains that occurred in previous years. However, a disadvantage of taxing capital income at realization is that records on value changes and deductions have to be retained for a long period of time. For this reason, it is preferable to tax capital income on an accrual basis using mark-to-market valuation. In that case, capital gains are taxed on the basis of their current market valuation even if they are not (yet) realized. Governments can easily verify the market valuation of assets that are traded on financial markets. The most important asset that is not traded on financial market is real estate, such as owner-occupied housing. However, the government already has a valuation system in place for real estate, which it uses to determine imputed rents and property taxes. We believe it is reasonable to apply the same valuation method to determine taxable capital gains on real estate.

2.4.2 Taxing Different Assets at Different Rates

A second practical consideration concerning a tax on actual returns is whether the government should tax different types of assets at different rates. In general, tax-rate differentials between assets are undesirable because they distort the investment decisions of households, resulting in efficiency losses. Additionally, differentiation can generate unfairness when households with the same capital income are nevertheless taxed differently because they have different assets in their portfolio.

In this respect, the current tax system has a number of weaknesses. First, the government taxes owner-occupied housing differently from all other assets. Second, pensions are exempted from the tax on presumptive returns. Third, some assets are taxed multiple times.

Tax treatment of owner-occupied housing. In the Netherlands, owner-occupied housing receives a favourable tax treatment relative to other assets. First, the tax-imputed rent lies well below the market-level rent. At the same time, mortgage interest can be fully deducted from labour income. Second, capital gains on owner-occupied housing remain untaxed. Jacobs (Chapter 5) calculates that the favourable treatment of housing results in a revenue loss of around 12.9 billion euros.

The most important economic justification for this favourable tax treatment is that there are positive externalities related to investment in owner-occupied housing. However, van Ewijk et al. (2006) argue convincingly that these positive externalities are likely to be very small, and that investment in owner-occupied housing is associated with negative externalities. Therefore, we do not believe that a convincing justification exists for a favourable tax treatment of owner-occupied housing. On top of this, as discussed earlier, there are large efficiency and redistributive gains associated with taxing the actual returns on housing. Households strongly differ in the rate of return they receive on housing. Fagereng et al. (2020) show that the rate of return on housing is far more heterogeneous between households than the rate of return on other assets. In addition, Giacoletti (2017) shows that the returns on housing are subject to both systemic and idiosyncratic risk. Hence, a tax on the actual returns on housing will result in gains in both equity and efficiency.

Our proposal for determining the income from owner-occupied housing is based on insights by Jordà et al. (2019), who are one of the first to map the actual returns on owner-occupied housing. They calculate the rate of return on housing as the sum of capital gains and market-based rent, and they subtract maintenance costs. According to their methodology, the annual rate of return on housing in the Netherlands between 1980 and 2015 equals around 6.41%.

We propose to use a similar method to determine the taxable income of owner-occupied housing. Taxable income should consist of imputed rent, where the imputation rate is based on comparable rates in the rental market, and capital gains. As discussed earlier, the tax authorities can calculate capital gains based on the valuation of the house in the Dutch property tax. Interest payments on the mortgage, maintenance costs, and investments in owner-occupied housing should be tax deductible.

Tax treatment of pensions. In the Netherlands, pension wealth is exempted from capital-income taxation. Additionally, pension premiums are deductible against a tax rate that is, on average, much higher than the tax rate at which pension benefits are taxed. Jacobs (Chapter 5) calculates that this costs the Dutch government 22.1 billion euros annually.

There is a large body of economic literature that studies the effects of these tax incentives when people suffer from behavioural biases such as present bias. In that case, households tend to save too little for their pensions so that some form of government intervention is desirable. Governments may therefore use tax incentives to encourage households to accumulate pension wealth. For instance, Poterba and Samwick (2003) show that US households store a larger percentage of their wealth in pension accounts that receive a favourable tax treatment. However, Chetty et al. (2014) use Danish data to show that only a small percentage of households are sensitive to fiscal incentives. Moreover, these are likely to be the households that were making rational saving decisions to begin with. This suggests that other methods, such as nudges, are more effective in stimulating the accumulation of pension wealth.

The issue of behavioural biases in retirement savings is less relevant in the Netherlands. Most of the pension premiums are determined in negotiations between unions and employers, and they are binding for all employees. For most households, therefore, tax incentives have little impact on the accumulation of pension wealth at the household level. Moreover, the tax incentives result in large redistributive losses because the households with the largest pension wealth benefit the most from the favourable tax treatment. Therefore, we propose to tax the actual return on pension wealth, similar to the tax treatment of other assets. The government could use the extra tax revenue to reduce the tax on labour income as proposed in Jacobs (2017).

Double Taxation. Investments in real estate are taxed twice in the Netherlands. First, the central government taxes real estate either under the capital tax on presumptive returns or, in the case of owner-occupied housing, along with labour income. Second, municipalities tax real estate via the property tax. This form of double taxation distorts investment decisions and makes it less attractive to invest in real estate. This effect will become more pronounced if the government taxes the actual returns on owner-occupied housing in the manner we propose.

It is possible to eliminate this distortion by making property taxation deductible from the tax on actual returns. However, economic theory suggests a number of reasons to tax real estate more heavily than other assets. First, the return on real estate partly reflects the benefits citizens receive from local public goods and services. Second, the return on real estate partly reflects the economic rents on land. Rents should be taxed at a higher rate than normal returns. For these reasons, it might not be so harmful to tax real estate twice.

Equity investments are also taxed twice, once at the corporate level via the corporate tax, and again at the personal level via the capital-income tax. This double taxation can give entrepreneurs an incentive to finance their companies through debt instead of equity (Cnossen and Bovenberg, 2001). Jacobs (2017) argues that this 'debt bias' overexposes the Dutch economy to macro-economic shocks.

We believe that this unnecessary distortion should be eliminated by adjusting the corporate tax. This can be done by (partly) exempting equity from corporate taxation via the introduction of an allowance for corporate equity (ACE). This would equalize the tax treatment of debt and equity. Hebous and Klemm (Chapter 11) discuss this option in detail.

Alternatively, it is possible to tax the returns on equity at a lower rate at the personal level. For example, the tax rate could be adjusted in such a way that the sum of the Dutch corporate tax rate and the personal tax on equity investments equals the personal tax rate on other assets. Sørensen (2005) describes the design of such a system in Norway.

2.4.3 Distinguishing between Normal Returns and Excess Returns

The returns on wealth can be divided into 'normal' returns and 'supernormal' or 'excess' returns. Investors typically make investment decisions based on the normal rate of return. As a result, the economic literature shows that a tax on excess returns does not affect investment decisions. Therefore, it is optimal to tax excess returns at a relatively high rate. However, taxing normal returns does affect investment decisions, so these normal returns should therefore be taxed at a lower rate (Diamond and Mirrlees, 1971). Additionally, a tax on excess returns results in redistribution from households with high rates of return to households with low rates of return, whereas a tax on the normal returns does not (Spiritus and Boadway, 2021). Therefore, from an economic perspective, it is desirable to tax excess returns at a higher rate than normal returns.[4]

The government can implement this as follows. The effective rate of return of a household is (net) capital income divided by net wealth, W. Formally, $R = (Net\ capital\ income)/W$, and R_{norm} denotes the normal rate of return. Tax payments of the households can then be determined by the following formula:

$$T = \left(\tau_{norm} R_{norm} + \tau_{excess}(R - R_{norm})\right) W$$

where τ_{norm} denotes the tax rate on normal returns, and τ_{excess} denotes the tax rate on excess returns. Note that the tax on excess returns can turn negative if the tax payer has had a bad investment year. In that case, the government should allow for loss-offset opportunities, as discussed above.

In comparison with a flat tax on actual returns, this system requires that the tax authorities gather more data. For a flat tax, the government only needs to determine capital income. To distinguish between normal and excess returns the government also needs to determine net wealth. In our opinion, this is not a large obstacle, because the government is already gathering information on net wealth for the tax on presumptive returns. In addition, the government needs to determine the normal rate of return. It can do so by considering the rate of return on long-term Dutch treasury bonds as proposed in Sørensen (2005). We believe the economic benefits of a higher tax on excess returns outweigh administrative costs associated with gathering more information.

[4] The *Mirrlees Review* (Mirrlees et al., 2011) concludes that normal returns should not be taxed at all (see also Cnossen, 2014). However, there is a multitude of reasons why the normal return should also be taxed (see, for instance, Jacobs, Chapter 5).

2.5 Conclusion

In this chapter, we have argued that a tax on actual returns on wealth is superior to the current Dutch tax on presumptive returns, on grounds of equity, efficiency, and macro-economic stability. Moreover, the behavioural effects on risk-taking and innovation are likely to be more beneficial under a tax on actual returns. To reap the full benefits of a tax on actual returns, it is important that it applies on both regular returns and capital gains, that owner-occupied housing wealth and pension wealth are taxed at similar rates as other wealth components, that there are generous possibilities for loss offset, and that—if possible—excess returns are taxed at a higher rate than the normal return on wealth.

References

Aghion, P. and Howitt, P. (1992), 'A model of growth through creative destruction', *Econometrica*, 60, 323–51.

Akcigit, U., Grigsby, J., Nicholas, T., and Stantcheva, S. (2018), 'Taxation and innovation in the 20th century'. NBER Working Paper no. 24982.

Auerbach, A. (1991), 'Retrospective capital gains taxation', *American Economic Review*, 81(1), 167–78.

Belastingdienst (2019), 'Belasting betalen over uw vermogen' (https://www.belastingdienst.nl/wps/wcm/connect/bldcontentnl/belastingdienst/prive/vermogen_en_aanmerkelijk_belang/vermogen/belasting_betalen_over_uw_vermogen/).

Benartzi, S. and Thaler, R. H. (2001), 'Naïve diversification strategies in defined contribution savings plans', *American Economic Review*, 91(1), 79–98.

Calvet, L. E., Campbell, J. Y., and Sodini, P. (2007), 'Down or out: assessing the welfare costs of household investment mistakes', *Journal of Political Economy*, 115(5), 707–47.

Case, K. E. and Shiller, R. J. (1989), 'The efficiency of the market for single-family homes', *American Economic Review*, 79(1), 125–37.

Chetty, R., Friedman, J. N., Leth-Petersen, S., Nielsen, T. H., and Olsen, T. (2014), 'Active vs. passive decisions and crowd-out in retirement savings accounts: evidence from Denmark', *Quarterly Journal of Economics*, 129, 1141–1219.

Choi, J. J., Laibson, D. I., and Madrian, B. C. (2005), 'Are empowerment and education enough? Underdiversification in 401 (k) plans', *Brookings Papers on Economic Activity*, 2005(2), 151–213.

Choi, J. J., Laibson, D. I., and Madrian, B. C. (2010), 'Why does the law of one price fail? An experiment on index mutual funds', *Review of Financial Studies*, 23(4), 1405–32.

Christiansen, V. (1993), 'A normative analysis of capital income taxes in the presence of aggregate risk', *The Geneva Papers on Risk and Insurance Theory*, 18, 55–76.

Cnossen, S. (2014), 'Van Dijkhuizen en Mirrlees', *Tijdschrift van Openbare Financiën*, 46, 25–34.

Cnossen, S. and Bovenberg, L. (2001), 'Fundamental tax reform in the Netherlands', *International Tax and Public Finance*, 8, 471–84.

Cnossen, S., Bovenberg, L., Rijkers, A., Kavelaars, P., Caminada, K., Goudswaard, K., Vording, H., and Okker, R. (1999), *Vermogensrendementsheffing: Vondst of Miskleun?*, OCfEB, Rotterdam.

CPB Netherlands Bureau for Economic Policy Analysis (2018), 'De verscheidenheid van vermogens van huishoudens'. CPB Notitie, 29 March 2018.

Cullen, J. B. and Gordon, R. H. (2007), 'Taxes and entrepreneurial risk-taking: theory and evidence for the US', *Journal of Public Economics*, 91, 1479–1505.

Diamond, P. A. and Mirrlees, J. A. (1971), 'Optimal taxation and public production I: production efficiency', *American Economic Review*, 61(1), 8–27.

Domar, E. D. and Musgrave, R. A. (1944), 'Proportional income taxation and risk-taking', *Quarterly Journal of Economics*, 58, 388–422.

Dröes, M. I. and Hassink, W. H. J. (2013), 'Housing price risk and the hedging benefits of home ownership', *Journal of Housing Economics*, 22, 92–9.

Egan, M., Matvos, G., and Seru, A. (2019), 'The market for financial advisor misconduct', *Journal of Political Economy*, 127, 233–95.

Fagereng, A., Guiso, L., Malacrino, D., and Pistaferri, L. (2020), 'Heterogeneity and persistence in returns to wealth', *Econometrica*, 88, 115–70.

Gerritsen, A. (2017), 'Belastingen: optimaal afstemmen op gedrag', in R. Dur (ed.), *Gedragseconomie in beleid, KVS Preadviezen 2017*, Ten Brink, Meppel, pp. 75–85.

Gerritsen, A., Jacobs, B., Rusu, A. V., and Spiritus, K. (2020), 'Optimal taxation of capital income when capital returns are heterogeneous', mimeo.

Giacoletti, M. (2017), 'Idiosyncratic risk in housing markets', available at SSRN (http://dx.doi.org/10.2139/ssrn.2995323).

Goetzmann, W. N. and Kumar, A. (2008), 'Equity portfolio diversification', *Review of Finance*, 12, 433–63.

Gordon, R. H. (1985), 'Taxation of corporate capital income: tax revenues versus tax distortions', *Quarterly Journal of Economics*, 100, 1–27.

Guvenen, F., Kambourov, G., Kuruscu, B., Ocampo, S., and Chen, D. (2019), 'Use it or lose it: efficiency gains from wealth taxation', NBER Working Paper no. 26284.

Harding, M. (2013), 'Taxation of dividend, interest, and capital gain income', OECD Taxation Working Paper no. 19.

Harding, M. and Marten, M. (2018), 'Statutory tax rates on dividends, interest and capital gains: the debt equity bias at the personal level', OECD Taxation Working Paper no. 34.

Hastings, J. S., Madrian, B. C., and Skimmyhorn, W. L. (2013), 'Financial literacy, financial education, and economic outcomes', *Annual Review of Economics*, 5, 347–73.

Jacobs, B. (2015), *De Prijs van Gelijkheid*, Derde, geheel herziene druk, Prometheus—Bert Bakker, Amsterdam.

Jacobs, B. (2017), 'Fundamentele herziening van belastingen op kapitaalinkomen', *Economische en Statistische Berichten*, 102, 416–19.

Jordà, Ò., Knoll, K., Kuvshinov, D., Schularick, M., and Taylor, A. M. (2019), 'The rate of return on everything, 1870–2015', *Quarterly Journal of Economics*, 134, 1225–98.

Langenmayr, D. and Lester, R. (2018), 'Taxation and corporate risk-taking', *The Accounting Review*, 93, 237–66.

Lusardi, A., Michaud, P.-C., and Mitchell, O. S. (2017), 'Optimal financial knowledge and wealth inequality', *Journal of Political Economy*, 125, 431–77.

Lusardi, A. and Mitchell, O. S. (2014), 'The economic importance of financial literacy: theory and evidence', *Journal of Economic Literature*, 52, 5–44.

Lusardi, A. and Tufano, P. (2015), 'Debt literacy, financial experiences, and over-indebtedness', *Journal of Pension Economics and Finance*, 14, 332–68.

Ministry of Finance (2017), 'Keuzedocument box 3, Bijlage bij Kamerstukken II 2016/2017', 34552, no. 83, Dutch Ministry of Finance, The Hague.

Mirrlees, J., Adam, S., Besley, T., Blundell, R., Bond, S., Chote, R., Gammie, M., Johnson, P., Myles, G., and Poterba, J. (2011), *Tax by Design: The Mirrlees Review*, Oxford University Press, Oxford.

Musgrave, R. A. (1959), *The Theory of Public Finance: A Study in Public Economy*, McGraw-Hill, New York.

Parlevliet, J. and Kooiman, T. (2015), 'Wealth formation of Dutch households: a policy assessment', *DNB Occasional Studies*, 13(1) (https://www.dnb.nl/media/5baicukv/201502_nr-_1_-2015-_wealth_formation_of_dutch_households_a_policy_assessment.pdf).

Piketty, T. (2014), *Capital in the 21st Century*, Harvard University Press, Cambridge, MA.

Piketty, T. and Zucman, G. (2014), 'Capital is back: wealth-income ratios in rich countries 1700–2010', *Quarterly Journal of Economics*, 129, 1255–1310.

Poterba, J. M. and Samwick, A. A. (2003), 'Taxation and household portfolio composition: US evidence from the 1980s and 1990s', *Journal of Public Economics*, 87, 5–38.

Romer, P. (1990), 'Endogenous technological change', *Journal of Political Economy*, 98, 71–102.

Saez, E. and Zucman, G. (2016), 'Wealth inequality in the United States since 1913: evidence from capitalized income tax data'. *Quarterly Journal of Economics*, 131, 519–78.

Sandmo, A. (1969), 'Capital risk, consumption, and portfolio choice', *Econometrica*, 37, 586–99.

Sandmo, A. (1985), 'The effects of taxation on savings and risk taking', in A. J. Auerbach and M. Feldstein (eds), *Handbook of Public Economics*, Volume 1, North-Holland, Amsterdam, pp. 265–311.

Schindler, D. (2008), 'Taxing risky capital income—a commodity taxation approach', *FinanzArchiv: Public Finance Analysis*, 64, 311–33.

Sørensen, P. B. (2005), 'Neutral taxation of shareholder income', *International Tax and Public Finance*, 12, 777–801.

Spiritus, K. and Boadway, R. (2021), 'Optimal taxation of normal and excess returns to risky assets', Tinbergen Institute Discussion Paper 2021-025/VI.

van Ewijk, C., Koning, M., Lever, M., and De Mooij, R. A. (2006), 'Economische effecten van aanpassing fiscale behandeling eigen woning', *CPB Bijzondere Publicaties* 62, The Hague.

van Goor, M. (2017), 'Reactie: het belasten van werkelijke rendementen op vermogen kent ook nadelen', in R. Dur (ed.), *Gedragseconomie en beleid, KVS Preadviezen 2017*, Ten Brink, Meppel, pp. 86–87.

van Rooij, M., Lusardi, A., and Alessie, R. (2011), 'Financial literacy and stock market participation', *Journal of Financial Economics*, 101, 449–72.

Varian, H. R. (1980), 'Redistributive taxation as social insurance', *Journal of Public Economics*, 14(1), 49–68.

von Gaudecker, H.-M. (2015), 'How does household portfolio diversification vary with financial literacy and financial advice?', *Journal of Finance*, 70, 489–507.

VVD, CDA, D66, and Christenunie (2019), 'Vertrouwen in de toekomst: Regeerakkoord 2017–2021', Bureau Woordvoering Kabinetsformatie, The Hague.

Zoutman, F. T. (2018), 'The elasticity of taxable wealth: evidence from the Netherlands', Bergen, mimeo.

3
Towards a True Dual Income Tax

*Sijbren Cnossen and Peter Birch Sørensen**

3.1 Introduction

Most OECD countries tax capital income at lower rates than labour income. Corporate profits, capital gains, imputed rental values of owner-occupied properties, pension fund income, and various other items are all taxed at concessionary (and differential) rates (and sometimes not at all). The Nordic countries stand out for their systematic approach to the issue by attempting to tax all capital income at the same rate, separately from labour income, under what is called a dual income tax (DIT).[1]

We explore the rationale, design, and introduction of a Nordic type of DIT in the Netherlands, which taxes all actual (instead of presumptive) capital income at a low uniform rate separate from labour income. At the same time, we investigate the greater uniformity of the taxation of labour income at progressive rates. In doing so, we pose the following questions.

- How are income and profits taxed?
- What is wrong with the Dutch personal income and corporation tax?
- What is the rationale of a DIT?
- How should a DIT be designed?
- What are the main features of the Nordic DITs?
- Why not a DIT for the Netherlands?

* Sijbren Cnossen (cnossen@ese.eur.nl) is Professor of Economics at the University of Pretoria and Academic Partner at CPB Netherlands Bureau for Economic Policy Analysis. Peter Birch Sørensen (pbs@econ.ku.dk) is Professor of Economics at the University of Copenhagen. The authors thank Martijn Badir, Bas Jacobs and other participants in the Cnossen Forum for their helpful comments.

[1] Outside the Nordic area, various countries have introduced DIT elements in their tax systems (see Eggert and Genser, 2005; Genser and Reutter, 2007). Furthermore, the German Council of Economic Experts (2003), Sinn (2004), and Spengel and Wiegard (2004) have proposed variants of the DIT for Germany, as have Keuschnigg and Dietz (2007) for Switzerland. Griffith, Hines, and Sørensen (2010) touch on the issues in Mirrlees et al. (2010); and Kleinbard (2010) provides a very thorough analysis of a hypothetical DIT in the US context. For various economic arguments in favour of a DIT, particularly in small open economies, see Zodrow (2006).

Sijbren Cnossen and Peter Birch Sørensen, *Towards a True Dual Income Tax* In: *Tax by Design for the Netherlands*. Edited by: Sijbren Cnossen and Bas Jacobs, Oxford University Press.
DOI: 10.1093/oso/9780192855244.003.0003

3.2 How Are Income and Profits Taxed?

Updating and drawing on Cnossen and Bovenberg (2001), Table 3.1 shows the main elements of the Dutch income tax.

Taxable personal income is assigned to one of three boxes (boxes 4 and 5 have been added to facilitate the analysis). Box 1 taxes labour income at progressive rates. The labour and capital income (jointly called business profits) of sole proprietorships and the presumptive labour income of managers/dominant shareholders (called dominant shareholders hereafter) of closely held companies are also taxed in box 1. The (capital) income from owner-occupied housing (i.e. the presumptive net rental income minus actual mortgage interest) is also taxed in box 1.

The provisions in box 2 are a (rather unsuccessful) attempt to minimize the tax arbitrage opportunities of dominant shareholders who can decide for themselves whether to distribute the company's earnings as wages or dividends, or to retain the profits in the company, which should then accrue to shareholders as capital gains—all depending on the tax rates that are applied to each form of income. Profits of closely held companies (after deduction of the presumptive wage of the dominant shareholder) are taxed in box 4 (as are the profits of widely held corporations), but dividends distributed to shareholders with a dominant holding (5% or more of the voting stock) in closely held companies are taxed in box 2 at 26.25%, as are capital gains that are realized when a part of, or the whole of, a dominant holding is sold.

Box 3 taxes (the returns on) personally held assets, such as deposits, stocks (including the shares of passive shareholders in closely held companies), bonds and immovable property (except owner-occupied housing). The nominal rate is 30%, which is applied to presumptive returns that increase with total net wealth. In 2017, the graduated returns shown in Table 1 replaced the uniform return of 4%, which had been in force since 2001. This return was found to be too blunt a measure, particularly in light of the low interest rates that prevailed after the 2007/2008 recession. Still, the higher the *actual* return, the lower the tax expressed as a percentage of that return—this is a result that does not agree with equity notions.

Box 4 (not identified separately in the income tax act) taxes the current profits of closely held companies and publicly held corporations at a slightly graduated rate. This rate also applies to the labour income of dominant shareholders in excess of the fictitious wage. Box 5 (not identified separately either) indicates that pension savings can accumulate without attracting capital income taxation. In fact, pension savings are treated on a consumption (expenditure) tax basis.

Table 3.1 Taxes on labour and capital income in the Netherlands, 2019

Boxes/tax rate(s)	Labour income	Capital income
Box 1 (Natural persons) 36.65% (€0–20,711) 38.10% (€20,711–€68,507) 51.75% (>€68,507)[a] General tax credit of €2,711, declining with income after €20,711 and vanishing at €68,507 Earned income tax credit of up to €3,819, declining with income after €34,936 and vanishing at €98,587 Other tax credits for children, single parents, handicapped, elderly, green investments	Wages, salaries Labour income of self-employed[b] Presumptive wage income of dominant shareholders of closely held companies fixed at a minimum of €46,000 (unless proven to be more or less) Pensions, social benefits Other labour income	Return on capital of self-employed[b] Presumptive net capital income of owner-occupied housing (returns of 0.25% to 2.35% depending on value) minus mortgage interest Interest, rental income, and capital gains on assets put at the disposal of closely held companies by dominant shareholders[c]
Box 2 (Dominant shareholders)[d] 26.25%[e]	Labour income—masquerading as profits—of dominant shareholders of closely held companies in excess of presumptive wage income of €45,000 (unless proven to be more or less) is taxed at the rates in box 4	Distributed profits and capital gains on shares in closely held companies that form a dominant holding

Box 3 (Personal wealth)		
30%[f]		Presumptive returns of 1.7991% (€30,846–€72,797), 4.2233% (€72,797–€1,005,572) and 5.33% (>€1,005,572) on the value of deposits, stocks, bonds, and immovable property (excluding owner-occupied housing)
Box 4 (Closely held companies and publicly held corporations)		
16.5% (€0–€200,000) 25% (>€200,000)[g]	Labour income of dominant shareholders of closely held companies in excess of presumptive wage income	Profits
Box 5 (Non-taxable entities)		
Exempt		Capital income of pension funds

Notes: [a] From 2021, the three rates will be reduced to two rates of 37.35% and 49.5%.

[b] The labour and capital income of the self-employed is taxed jointly as business profits subject to the progressive personal income tax rates in box 1.

[c] This anti-avoidance provision, not discussed further, prevents dominant shareholders from shifting their taxable income out of box 1, which features high marginal tax rates, into box 3, which has a lower proportional tax rate, albeit applied to progressively higher presumptive returns.

[d] Shareholders are deemed to be dominant shareholders if they (and associated persons) hold at least 5% of the paid-up shares of a (closely held) company.

[e] The nominal rate is 26.25%, but because of accumulation with the corporation tax rate of 16.5% or 25%, the effective tax rate will be higher depending on the time at which profits are distributed. The effective tax rate on profits distributed out of current profits less than €200,000 is 38.42% [16.5% + 26.25% (100 – 16.5)] or 43.75% [25% + 25% (100 – 25)] on profits higher than €200,000. The nominal rate will be increased to 26.9% in 2021.

[f] Effective tax rates are lower because of the basic wealth exemption of €30,846 (€61,692 for couples).

[g] The plan to reduce the top rate to 21.7% in 2021 was shelved.

Source: Dutch Tax Authorities.

3.3 What Is Wrong with the Dutch Personal Income and Corporation Tax?

As this brief description indicates, labour income is not taxed uniformly in the Netherlands, while capital income is sometimes taxed on a presumptive basis, sometimes on an actual basis and sometimes not at all. In addition, the rates at which presumptive or actual capital income are taxed are sometimes proportional but in other cases progressive rates apply, as listed more specifically here.

- Labour income is taxed at progressive rates, except if accruing to dominant shareholders in excess of the presumptive wage of €45,000 (higher or lower if agreed with the tax administration), when it is taxed at the two-rate corporation tax of 16.5%/25%. This discriminates against ordinary employees whose wages in excess of €46,000 are subject to the progressive income tax rate schedule.[2]
- The return on equity, including capital gains, invested in sole proprietorships and closely held companies is taxed on an actual basis—at progressive rates (in box 1) if earned by proprietorships, but at proportional rates (in boxes 2 and 4) if earned by closely held companies. This is a form of discrimination that is hard to justify. Further, capital gains arising in these entities are taxed on a realization basis without interest charged on the deferred tax.
- The return on equity (shares) in publicly held corporations is taxed twice: on an actual basis at the corporate level and on a presumptive basis at the personal level. At both levels, proportional rates apply. As a result, equity has become a less attractive source of finance than debt. This results in a higher cost of equity finance and so creates a debt bias in corporate financing (Bovenberg and ter Rele, 1998), which aggravates the risk of bankruptcy. Further, capital gains are taxed on a realization basis at the corporate level, but on an accrual basis at low effective rates at the personal level (provided the assets are properly valued each year).
- The return on personally held assets, such as deposits, debt claims, and real estate, is generally taxed on a presumptive basis. This applies also to owner-occupied property—albeit that the presumptive return (i.e. the net rental value of 0.25–2.35% depending on value, which is considerably lower than the presumptive returns in box 3), is taxed at progressive rates (in box 1) instead of at a proportional rate (in box 3). As a result, households subject to

[2] Bettendorf, Lejour, and van 't Riet (2017) report significant bunching around the fictitious wage of dominant shareholders. The marginal tax rate on distributed profits in box 2 is approximately 10 percentage points lower than the tax on labour income in box 1. Further, they find that dominant shareholders use retained earnings (including pension contributions) as the primary channel to reduce their tax burdens.

high marginal tax rates in box 1 are encouraged to finance their own homes and businesses with debt, and to invest their equity in assets assigned to box 3.[3]

- The return on savings held in pension funds is not taxed. Depending on the difference between the tax rate at which pension contributions are deductible and the tax rate at which pension pay-outs are taxable, the return on pension savings is in fact subsidized through the tax system.[4]
- Last but not least, incentives remain to re-label highly taxed income items into items subject to lower rates, an effect that the 2001 reform was supposed to eliminate. Tax arbitrage erodes tax revenue, undermines the effective progressivity of the tax, and distorts the allocation of capital and risk.

Perhaps more fundamentally, the presumptive income tax only taxes the normal risk-free return to capital, while a tax on actual income also includes the reward for investor-specific abilities in its base (e.g. in the form of superior insight and information advantages). This form of income, which can also be viewed as remuneration for the application of a form of human capital, should therefore be taxed as labour income. Moreover, apart from representing a reward for risk-taking, actual capital income above the normal return may also include a pure rent that can be taxed at progressive tax rates without harming savings and investments.

Further, the presumptive income tax excludes the government (which may be better equipped to pool investment risks across generations through public debt policy) as a partner in the good and bad luck of investors by taxing the presumptive rather than the actual return. A tax on actual income includes the return attributable to uncertainty in its base if loss offsets are available. With full loss offset, the tax on the risk premium serves as an insurance premium, which is not a burden on the private sector, but rather a price that the private sector is willing to pay to the government for pooling macro-economic risks.

These considerations justify a closer look at taxing all capital income once and only once on an actual basis at a uniform rate—in other words, a DIT.

[3] In recent years, this possibility has been proscribed for homes by gradually lowering the tax rate at which mortgage interest is deductible from income (49% in 2019 against the top rate of 52% in 2014, and so on until a rate of 37% in 2023).

[4] The return on pension savings is taxed at the time the pension benefit is paid out. This tax is exactly equal to the advantage of tax deferral on the paid-in contributions if the rates at which benefits are taxed coincide with the rates at which the contributions are deductible. Under these circumstances, therefore, income from pension saving is in fact tax-exempt. However, because the rate at which pension benefits are taxed tends to be lower than the rates at which contributions can be deducted, pension savings are typically subsidized through the tax system.

3.4 What Is the Rationale of a DIT?

The literature on the principles of taxation has traditionally focused on two main blueprints for personal taxation: the Schanz–Haig–Simons comprehensive income tax, which subjects the sum of income from all sources to a common tax schedule, and the Fisher–Kaldor expenditure tax, which exempts the normal return to saving from tax by taxing only the part of income that is consumed. By contrast, the DIT is a form of schedular tax, which combines progressive taxation of labour income with a positive but relatively low flat tax on all income from capital. This raises the following three issues.

3.4.1 Why Should the Normal Return to Capital Be Taxed?

It is widely accepted that a zero tax rate on the normal return to capital is optimal only under very restrictive assumptions. The various efficiency and equity motives for taxing capital income have been surveyed at length by Sørensen (2007a), Jacobs (2013), and Bastani and Waldenström (2018); here we list just some of them. For example, if leisure and future consumption are complements, as the evidence suggests, a capital income tax may alleviate distortions to labour supply, since it is essentially a tax on future consumption (Erosa and Gervais, 2002). As another example, the distortion to human capital investment caused by the progressive labour income tax may be alleviated through a capital income tax on the return to investment in financial and physical capital (Jacobs and Bovenberg, 2010). A capital income tax can also offset a tendency towards excessive aggregate saving caused by borrowing constraints by redistributing income from unconstrained savers towards liquidity-constrained borrowers (Aiyagari, 1993). In addition to these efficiency arguments for taxing capital income, there are equity arguments if high-ability agents have a tendency to make greater savings than low-ability agents (Saez, 2002) or if they tend to generate higher returns to capital because they have higher innate skills (Cnossen and Bovenberg, 2001; Banks and Diamond, 2010).

3.4.2 Why Should the Capital Income Tax Rate Be Lower than the Top Marginal Tax Rate on Labour Income?

If the normal return should be taxed, why should the tax rate be lower than the top marginal tax rate on labour income? Here, the (efficiency) argument is that the capital income tax base tends to be more elastic than the labour income tax base (see e.g. the empirical study by Kleven and Schultz, 2014). One reason could be high international capital mobility combined with the difficulty of enforcing domestic tax on foreign-source capital income. Another reason could be that the propensity to realize taxable capital gains is very sensitive to the tax rate, especially among the wealthy (Auerbach and Siegel, 2000). This distortion is hard to avoid if valuation and liquidity problems prevent the taxation of capital gains on an accrual basis. However, if the capital income tax rate is not too high, then it may be easier to include all forms of capital gains in the tax base without creating unacceptable lock-in effects.

An argument against separating the taxation of capital income from the taxation of labour income is that a lower tax rate on capital income could increase the elasticity of the labour income tax base by inviting income-shifting from labour income to capital income; these are options that may be available to the self-employed and to owner-managers of small companies. Below, we discuss how such income-shifting can be prevented under the DIT. In any case, the argument put forward by defenders of the comprehensive income tax—that all income should be taxed at the same marginal rate—applies to *real* income, whereas actual tax systems impose tax on the *nominal* income from capital, including the inflation premium. If the nominal return is, say, 2%, and the inflation rate is 1%, implying a real return to saving of 1%, a 50% tax rate on the nominal return amounts to a 100% tax rate on the real return. If policymakers aim at a 50% tax rate on all labour income and real income from capital, and if the capital income tax has to be levied on the nominal return for practical reasons, then they should only impose a 25% tax rate on capital income combined with a 50% tax rate on labour income. This is a pragmatic argument for a DIT.

3.4.3 Why Should the Capital Income Tax Be Proportional Rather than Progressive?

An efficiency argument for proportional rather than progressive taxation of capital income is that the after-tax return to saving will differ across taxpayers when their marginal tax rates are not identical. Progressivity therefore causes the marginal rate of substitution between present and future consumption to differ from one taxpayer to another, causing an inefficient allocation of the overall volume of saving. Progressive taxation of realized capital gains may also push the taxpayer into a much higher tax bracket in the year of realization, exacerbating the distortionary lock-in effects of realization-based capital gains taxation. Proportional taxation alleviates this effect (although it does not eliminate it). Moreover, proportional taxation eliminates the opportunities for certain forms of tax arbitrage that rely on the exploitation of differences in the marginal tax rates faced by different individual taxpayers. In particular, the scope for tax avoidance through transfers of wealth among family members is significantly reduced when all taxpayers face the same tax rate on income from capital.

Further, under the conventional income tax, many types of tax arbitrage have been based on the accumulation within a corporation of the return to assets acquired with borrowed funds. That is, the owners of the corporation take advantage of interest deductibility against a high marginal personal tax rate, combined with a lower corporate income tax rate on the return to the assets and a deferral of the tax on capital gains on shares until the time of realization. Such arbitrage activity becomes unprofitable in the pure version of the DIT, where the flat personal tax rate on capital income is aligned with the corporate income tax rate. Because taxpayers engaging in large-scale tax arbitrage are usually found in the upper-income brackets, these aspects of the DIT system are attractive from the perspective of vertical taxpayer equity.

These arguments for the DIT notwithstanding, the fact that capital income is distributed more unevenly than income from labour provides an equity argument against a relatively low flat tax rate on capital income. However, the highly skewed distribution of capital income arises in large part from huge stocks of inherited wealth. To maintain the overall progressivity of the tax system, policymakers could therefore supplement the DIT with separate taxes on large stocks of inheritance and/or wealth. Indeed, this equity concern is the reason why Norway—a pioneering DIT country—has maintained a progressive wealth tax.

3.5 How Should a DIT Be Designed?

Box 3.1 summarizes the basic features of a pure DIT (Sørensen, 1994, 2007b; Cnossen, 2000). The building blocks of the tax are largely self-explanatory, but three aspects deserve some discussion: (1) the splitting of capital and labour income that accrue jointly in proprietorships and closely held companies; (2) the treatment of risk premia and above-normal returns to capital; and (3) the treatment of capital gains, accrued or realized. These features, in particular, distinguish a DIT from other income tax systems that tax capital income on an ad hoc basis at lower rates than labour income, and do not split jointly accruing capital and labour income.

3.5.1 Splitting Jointly Accruing Capital and Labour Income

The following issues arise in splitting labour and capital income jointly accruing as 'profits'.

Box 3.1 Basic features of a pure DIT

1. Income split

All income is systematically separated into either capital income or labour income (also called earned income or personal income). Personal capital income includes interest, dividends, capital gains, imputed returns on capital invested in non-incorporated businesses, rents and rental values. Labour income consists of wages and salaries (including the value of the labour services performed by owners in their own business), fringe benefits, pension income and social security benefits. Royalties are taxed as labour income or as capital income (if know-how is acquired or capitalized).

2. Tax rates

Capital income—individual as well as corporate—is taxed at the proportional corporation tax (CT) rate, while labour income is subject to additional, progressive personal income tax (PT) rates. To minimize tax arbitrage, the tax rate on labour income applicable to the first income bracket is set at the same level as the proportional CT rate.

3. Costs of earning income

Costs of earning income are deductible only against income subject to the capital income tax rate (which is the same as the lowest rate on labour income). This implies that mixed expenses, containing an element of personal consumption, have the same tax value for high- and low-income groups (except for partnerships and proprietorships, for which expenses are netted out against gross income before this is split into the capital and labour income components).

4. Basic allowance for capital income

Capital and labour income can be taxed entirely separately, or the two forms of income can be taxed jointly at the CT rate, while gross labour income is subsequently taxed at additional, progressive PT rates. The separate taxation of capital income (which accrues mainly to higher-income groups) without permitting a basic allowance makes it possible to impose flat final source taxes on interest and royalties.

5. Offset of negative capital income against labour income

Joint taxation at the capital income tax rate permits the offset of negative capital income against positive labour income. This may be desirable as the distinction between labour and capital income tends to become blurred at the level of proprietorships and closely held companies. If capital and labour

Continued

Box 3.1 *(Continued)*

income are taxed separately, the same effect can be achieved by permitting a tax credit for negative capital income (calculated at the capital income tax rate) against the tax on labour income.

6. CT–PT integration method

The double taxation of distributed profits at the corporate level and the shareholder level can be avoided through a full imputation system. Alternatively but equivalently, double taxation can be avoided by exempting dividend income at the shareholder level. Under either approach, compensatory taxes should ensure that dividends are not paid out of exempt profits without having borne the CT. Double taxation of retained profits is avoided by writing up the acquisition cost of shares by retained corporate profits net of CT.

7. Closely held companies and unincorporated businesses

The taxable profits of partnerships and proprietorships as well as closely held companies, conventionally computed, are split into a capital income component and a labour income component (if the sum of the two components exceeds the first bracket of the labour income tax), and taxed on a current basis. The capital income component is calculated by applying a presumptive return to the value of the gross assets of the business or to equity. Residual profits are considered as labour income.

8. Withholding taxes

The single taxation of capital income can be ensured through withholding taxes or source taxes at the corporate level or at the level of other entities paying interest, royalties, or other capital income. In principle, the rates of withholding or source taxes should be set at the level of the CT rate. Consequently, these rates could represent the final tax liability if capital income is taxed separately from labour income and no basic allowance applies.

- Profit splitting should apply to the self-employed and to 'active' shareholders involved in running their companies (earning labour income as well as capital income), not to 'passive' shareholders only earning a return on capital invested. This requires a definition of what 'active' is, either by ownership and/or by involvement in the management of the company.
- In splitting profits, either the capital income component is determined first or the labour income component is. The determination of the labour income component is difficult at best, as diligence, effort, and ingenuity can diverge widely, as can the hourly wage rate relating to various types of labour and the

number of hours worked. By contrast, capital income can be determined by applying a presumptive return to the historic cost of either gross assets or net assets (net of liabilities), by deducting the resulting amount from total profits (before or after the deduction of interest, respectively) and by considering the remaining profits as labour income.

- On the one hand, under the 'source model', equal treatment of the labour income component of jointly accruing profits with regards to wage-earners is achieved by taxing it on a current basis at progressive rates. On the other hand, under the 'fence model', equal treatment of the capital income component of jointly accruing profits with regards to retained profits in publicly held corporations is achieved by taxing all earnings retained in the company or the proprietorship at the capital income tax rate and not splitting the profits until they are distributed.[5]
- The application of the presumptive capital income return to gross assets encourages investment in the business, if the government sets the return on assets above the going interest rate. This effect is less likely if the presumptive return is applied to net assets. However, this method offers greater opportunities for tax arbitrage in the form of converting business debt into private debt, and vice versa, depending on the difference between the presumptive rate of return and the going interest rate (Sørensen, 2010).
- The presumptive return can be set at the nominal interest rate of, say, three-month government bonds. Furthermore, a premium can be added in order not to discourage risk-bearing investments if (as is usually the case) indefinite loss offsets with interest are not available.

3.5.2 Taxing Above-Normal Returns on Capital

Generally, taxing capital income at progressive labour income tax rates should not deter saving and investment if the income reflects above-normal returns. For shares, such returns can be taxed under a shareholder income tax (Sørensen, 2005). This imposes a personal capital income tax on dividends and realized capital gains exceeding a rate of return allowance (RRA), which is set equal to the after-tax interest on medium-term government bonds. When the personal capital income tax rate is aligned with the corporate income tax rate, the RRA ensures that a corporate investment generating a pre-tax return equal to the pre-tax market interest rate will only bear corporation tax, but no personal tax. Double

[5] If the marginal tax rate on distributed profits remains constant over time, the deferral of tax until the time of distribution does not involve any tax discrimination in favour of entrepreneurs, as long as the tax rate on the retained profits equals the capital income tax rate imposed on the savings of wage-earners.

taxation of the marginal investment that just generates a normal return is thereby avoided. With an appropriate choice of tax rates, the sum of the corporation tax rate and the shareholder income tax rate on the above-normal return roughly equals the top rate on labour income. Accordingly, the normal rate of return on capital is taxed only once (i.e. at corporate level), while economic rents are taxed twice, in total at the same marginal rate as labour income.[6] The shareholder income tax has been introduced in Norway. As a result, as noted by Kleinbard (2010), Norway does not make a distinction between labour and capital income, but between the normal return on capital and all other income.[7]

As pointed out by Sørensen (2005), the chief architect of the shareholder income tax, an advantage of this approach is that it eliminates the incentive for income shifting between jointly accruing labour and capital income in closely held companies in a manner that limits investment distortions. Furthermore, it obviates the need to make a distinction between the active owners of closely held companies and the passive owners.[8] In addition, the shareholder income tax does not induce shareholders to postpone the realization of capital gains, because the accrued RRA (deductible from the gain before tax is applied) effectively exempts the normal return on the reinvestment.

3.5.3 How Should Capital Gains Be Taxed?

The major obstacle to the adoption of a Nordic-type DIT in the Netherlands is the tax treatment of capital gains. While capital gains arising in business have always been taxable, capital gains on privately held assets outside box 2 (see Table 3.1) have never attracted tax. These gains are taxed in the Nordic countries, although on a realization basis, while Norway alleviates the lock-in effect for shares (but not other assets) by allowing a deduction for accumulated RRAs.

A capital gains tax should be a fair and progressive element in any tax on income, although lock-in and deferral are issues that should be taken into account. A capital gains tax can take one of three forms (Cnossen and Bovenberg, 2001): (1) a conventional realization-based tax, as found in most countries and generally applied to capital gains arising in business; (2) a retrospective capital gains tax,

[6] By contrast, the normal rate of return is not taxed under the Mirrlees et al. (2011) proposal for the RRA. Note that investment incentives would still be distorted under the Norwegian shareholder income tax to the extent that the normal rate of return is taxed.

[7] Note, however, that Norway still taxes income from immovable property at progressive labour income tax rates.

[8] The distinction between labour and capital income remains relevant, however, for unincorporated businesses, but only if the total income exceeds the first bracket of the labour income tax schedule, the rate of which equals or closely reflects the corporation tax rate.

which charges interest on the deferred tax at the time of realization; or (3) a mark-to-market tax, which taxes gains as they accrue (and refunds the 'tax' on losses).

The major drawback of a conventional capital gains tax is that taxpayers are encouraged to defer the realization of capital gains and to accelerate the realization of capital losses. Complicated anti-avoidance provisions are often introduced to forestall this tax-driven behaviour. Deferral and lock-in cause ownership and risk patterns to diverge, and they tend to destabilize the stock market and invite tax arbitrage. The effects can be mitigated, but not eliminated, by deeming realization to occur at death.

Deferral and hence lock-in are prevented under a retrospective capital gains tax by charging interest on the deferred tax. Under the method proposed by Auerbach (1991), the value of an asset is deemed to have accrued at the risk-free interest rate from the date of purchase. Tax is due on this accrual, with additional interest thereon to compensate for the value of deferral. This solves the lock-in issue, but leaves the investor-specific risk premium untaxed. This risk premium is taxed under the method of Bradford (1995).[9] While retrospective capital gains taxation eliminates time-shifting tax planning, it also creates an incentive for entity-shifting tax planning because effective tax rates on excess returns vary across assets. Nevertheless, the general idea of maintaining the realization principle with interest on the deferred tax seems worthy of consideration if taxation at the time of accretion is problematic because of valuation and cash-flow problems for particular assets, such as real estate and small businesses.

The best solution to the issue would be to tax capital gains as they accrue, to the largest extent possible (and to refund tax on losses). This points in the direction of a mark-to-market tax, for which information is already provided in box 3 of Table 3.1 for the returns under the current Dutch income tax. Lack of liquidity to pay the tax can hardly be considered a serious issue for securities, which are as liquid as a deposit in a bank. Similarly, box 3 already values real estate on a mark-to-market basis, including owner-occupied housing (albeit in box 1). Real estate, however, is less liquid than securities. For these assets, therefore, a conventional capital gains tax (preferably with a basic interest charge on deferred taxes) would have to be maintained. This would also be the case with the assets of non-incorporated businesses.

[9] See Bradford (1995) for the intricacies of his approach. Auerbach and Bradford (2004) have generalized their work by showing the unique form that must be taken by a tax system based entirely on realization accounting to implement an accrual-based capital income tax or, equivalently, a uniform wealth tax. This system combines elements of an accrual-based capital income tax and a traditional cash-flow tax, having many of the attributes of the latter while still imposing a tax burden on marginal capital income.

Table 3.2 DITs in Norway, Finland, and Sweden (2019)

	Norway	Finland	Sweden
Year of introduction	**1992**	**1993**	**1991**
Tax rates[a]			
Corporate profits	22%	20%	22%
Other capital income	22%	30% ≤ €30,000 > 34%	30%
Labour income	33.4%–49%[b]	24%–55.25%	29.89%–54.89%
Costs of earning income	Deductible at basic rate	Deductible at basic rate	Deductible at basic rate
Basic allowance for capital income	Yes	No	No
Offset of negative capital income against labour income	Against other capital income and labour income in first tax bracket	Against other capital income and against labour income through tax credit at 30%/34%	Against other capital income and against labour income through tax credit at 30%
CT–PT integration method	RRA—risk-free amount	Basic exemption	Basic exemption
CT on corporations			
Distributed	22% on 144% of dividend after deduction of 0.8% RRA (after-tax return on three-month government paper) calculated on cost base of shares Unused RRAs can be carried forward and set-off against future dividends	*Quoted shares*: 30%/34% on 85% of dividend income *Non-quoted shares*: 25% taxed as income from capital;[c] remaining 75% exempt up to €150,000 and 30%/34% on 85% of excess Dividends deemed employment income if based on value of work	*Shareholder not significantly involved*: one-fifth of dividend exempt *Shareholder significantly involved*: one-third of dividend taxed as employment income
Retained (= capital gains tax rate)	22% on 144% of realized capital gains minus unused risk-free amounts	30%/34% on realized capital gains	30% on realized capital gains (25% on unlisted shares)

PT on non-incorporated businesses	22% on risk-free amount (calculated on gross assets) 33.4%–49% on profits (considered labour income), in excess of risk-free amount	Capital income fixed at 20% of previous year's net assets; remaining profits considered labour income[d]	30% on profits deemed to be return on net assets; 22% on remaining retained profitsLabour income tax upon distribution with credit for 22%
Withholding taxes on residents			
Dividends	–	*Quoted shares*: 25.5% advance tax *Non-quoted shares*: 7.5% advance tax up to €150,000; 28% on excess	30%
Interest	22%	30%	30%
Royalties	–	30%	–
Net wealth tax	0.85% > NOK 1,500,000 (double for spouses)	Abolished in 2006	Abolished in 2007

Notes: [a] Including local income taxes, if levied (local tax in country's capital if different).
[b] Including non-deductible social security contributions.
[c] Subject to the proviso that the dividends do not exceed 8% of the mathematical value of the shares (net assets divided by the number of shares). If the dividend exceeds the 8% ceiling, then 25% of dividends in excess of the ceiling are exempt and the remaining 75% are taxed as labour income.
[d] Profit splitting is optional so as not to disadvantage low-income businesses.

Source: International Bureau for Fiscal Documentation, online country reports (see https://www.ibfd.org/IBFD-Products/Online-Collections-and-Tools-Overview).

3.6 What Are the Main Features of the Nordic DITs?

Table 3.2 shows the basic features of the DITs in the Nordic countries, arranged in the order in which they come closest to satisfying the requirements of the pure DIT outlined above. Finland and Sweden tax capital income other than corporate profits at somewhat higher rates, perhaps because the bases are less mobile. Norway subjects returns on immovable property to progressive labour income tax rates, and also imposes a net wealth tax. Further, it permits a basic allowance for capital income not found in Finland and Sweden, which, as a result, can impose final withholding taxes on residents (withholding taxes on non-residents are generally the subject of tax treaties). All three countries provide for the offset of negative capital income against labour income.

Norway prevents the double taxation of the normal rate of return embodied in dividends and capital gains on shares by a RRA, as discussed in Section 3.5. Finland and Sweden mitigate the double imposition by exempting a basic amount of dividend income paid out by publicly held corporations (identified as 'quoted shares' or 'shareholders not significantly involved'). Finland has a rather complicated formula for taxing profits distributed by closely held companies (identified as 'non-quoted shares'). In Sweden, one-third of dividend income is taxed as labour income if 'shareholders [are] significantly involved' in the business. The significant involvement of Swedish shareholders in closely held companies (called managers/dominant shareholders in the Netherlands) is also reflected in the Finnish anti-tax-avoidance provision, which deems dividends to be treated as employment income if based on the value of work. In all three countries, capital gains are taxed on a realization basi.s at the capital income tax rate. Norway applies its comparatively lower rate but steps up the gain's basis.

The capital–labour income dichotomy extends to non-incorporated businesses. In splitting profits, Norway and Finland follow the source model under which the labour income component is taxed on a current basis on a par with the labour income of employees, regardless of whether or not the income is withdrawn from the business. However, Sweden applies the fence model under which a 'fence' is erected between the 'business sphere' and the 'private sphere' of the proprietor (or shareholder in companies and corporations), and the labour income component (like the capital income component) is taxed at the proportional capital income tax rate as long as the income is retained in the business. Upon withdrawal, however, the profit-splitting rules are applied. In splitting profits of proprietorships, all three countries first determine capital income by applying a presumptive return to the historic cost of gross assets (Norway) or net assets (Finland and Sweden). Remaining profits are considered as labour income, taxable at progressive rates.

3.7 Why Not a DIT for the Netherlands?

In their extensive review of recent research on optimal capital income taxation, Bastani and Waldenström (2018, p. 35) draw the following conclusions.

> While, in principle, progressive capital taxation could be desirable on equity grounds, we deem the administrative problems relating to tax avoidance and tax arbitrage to be too great. The Nordic dual income tax, which taxes labour income according to a non-linear progressive tax schedule and capital income according to a proportional rate, could therefore be a constructive way to strike a balance between an optimal and administratively feasible tax system. Even though the dual income tax employs a proportional tax on capital income, and therefore does not reap the potential equity gains of adopting a progressive capital income tax, it is possible to increase the overall progressivity of the tax system by complementing capital income taxes with taxes on property, wealth and inheritance.

They proceed to argue that '[e]mpirical evidence suggests that capital income is more responsive to taxation than labour income, which suggests that the capital income tax rate should be lower than the tax rate on labour income. However, care must be taken so that the divergence is not too large to prevent cross-base income shifting.'

We concur with these views. Moreover, our review has shown that the following rather persuasive arguments can be made for:

- taxing actual rather than presumptive capital income (in order to include above-normal returns in the tax base and to make sure that the government shares in the uncertainty of investment);
- treating all capital income uniformly (to limit tax arbitrage);
- applying the corporation tax rate to all capital income and the lower bracket of the progressive labour income tax schedule (to promote equal treatment and limit profit-splitting issues);
- adopting the Nordic source model to split profits of sole proprietorships and closely held companies by determining the capital income component as a presumptive percentage of the net assets of the business (to treat labour income more equally regardless of the nature of the employment);
- taxing the above-normal return on capital differentially higher through a shareholder income tax (to impose a higher tax on rents);
- taxing capital gains on shares and other liquid assets on an accrual basis and illiquid assets on a realization basis with interest charged on the deferred tax;

- and, if desired, taxing residents differentially higher than foreign investors through a tax on net wealth above a certain level (to increase the tax burden on capital without deterring foreign investment).

Based on these considerations, we believe that it would be worthwhile to examine the case for a Dutch DIT in greater detail.

References

Aiyagari, S. R. (1993), 'Optimal capital income taxation with incomplete markets, borrowing constraints, and constant discounting', *Journal of Political Economy*, 103, 1158–75.

Auerbach, A. J. (1991), 'Retrospective capital gains taxation', *American Economic Review*, 81(1), 167–78.

Auerbach, A. J. and Bradford, D. F. (2004), 'Generalized cash-flow taxation', *Journal of Public Economics*, 88, 957–80.

Auerbach, A. J. and Siegel, J. M. (2000), 'Capital-gains realizations of the rich and sophisticated', *American Economic Review*, 90(2), 276–82.

Banks, J. and Diamond, P. A. (2010), 'The base for direct taxation', in J. Mirrlees et al. (eds), *Dimensions of Tax Design: The Mirrlees Review*, Oxford University Press for the Institute for Fiscal Studies, Oxford, 548–648.

Bastani, S. and Waldenström, D. (2018), 'How should capital be taxed?' Working Paper, Paris School of Economics (http://www.uueconomics.se/danielw/Research_files/BastaniWaldenstrom_Capitaltax.pdf).

Bettendorf, L., Lejour, A., and van 't Riet, M. (2017), 'Tax bunching by owners of small corporations', *De Economist*, 165, 411–38.

Bovenberg, A. L. and ter Rele, H. T. M. (1998), 'Reforming Dutch capital taxation: an analysis of incentives to save and invest', *CPB Research Memorandum* 142, The Hague.

Bradford, D. F. (1995), 'Fixing realization accounting: symmetry, consistency and correctness in the taxation of financial instruments', *New York University Law Review*, 50, 731–84.

Cnossen, S. (2000), 'Taxing capital income in the Nordic countries: a model for the European Union?', in S. Cnossen (ed.), *Taxing Capital Income in the European Union: Issues and Options for Reform*, Oxford University Press, Oxford, 180–213.

Cnossen, S. and Bovenberg, L. (2001), 'Fundamental tax reform in the Netherlands', *International Tax and Public Finance*, 8, 471–84.

Eggert, W. and Genser, B. (2005), 'Dual income taxation in EU member countries', *CESifo DICE Report*, 3(1), 41–7.

Erosa, A. and Gervais, M. (2002), 'Optimal taxation in life-cycle economies', *Journal of Economic Theory*, 105, 338–69.

Genser, B. and Reutter, A. (2007), 'Moving towards dual income taxation in Europe', *FinanzArchiv*, 63, 436–56.

German Council of Economic Experts (2003), 'Staatsfinanzen konsolidieren—Steuersystem reformieren', Annual Report 2003/04, as amplified in German Council of Economic Experts and Max Planck Institute for Intellectual Property, *Dual Income Tax: A Proposal for Reforming Corporate and Personal Income Tax in Germany*, ZEW Economic Studies.

Griffith, R., Hines. J. R., and Sørensen, P. B. (2010), 'International capital taxation', in J. Mirrlees et al. (eds), *Dimensions of Tax Design: The Mirrlees Review*, Oxford University Press for the Institute for Fiscal Studies, Oxford, 914–96.

Jacobs, B. (2013), 'From optimal tax theory to applied tax policy', *FinanzArchiv/Public Finance Analysis*, 69, 338–89.

Jacobs, B. and Bovenberg, A. L. (2010), 'Human capital and optimal positive taxation of capital income', *International Tax and Public Finance*, 17, 451–78.

Keuschnigg, C. and Dietz, M. D. (2007), 'A growth-oriented dual income tax', *International Tax and Public Finance*, 14, 191–221.

Kleinbard, E. D. (2010), 'An American dual income tax: Nordic precedents', *Northwestern Journal of Law and Social Policy*, 5, 40–86.

Kleven, H. J. and Schultz, E. A. (2014), 'Estimating taxable income responses using Danish tax reforms', *American Economic Journal: Economic Policy*, 6, 271–301.

Mirrlees, J., Adam, S., Besley, T., Blundell, R., Bond, S., Chote, R., Gammie, M., Johnson, P., Myles, G., and Poterba, J. (2011), *Tax by Design: The Mirrlees Review*, Oxford University Press, Oxford.

Mirrlees, J. et al. (eds) (2010), *Dimensions of Tax Design: The Mirrlees Review*, Oxford University Press for the Institute for Fiscal Studies, Oxford.

Saez, E. (2002), 'The desirability of commodity taxation under non-linear income taxation and heterogeneous tastes', *Journal of Public Economics*, 83, 217–30.

Sinn, H-W. (2004), *Ist Deutschland Noch zu Retten?*, 5th edn, Econ Verlag, Munich.

Sørensen, P. B. (1994), 'From the global income tax to the dual income tax: recent tax reforms in the Nordic countries', *International Tax and Public Finance*, 1, 57–79.

Sørensen, P. B. (2005), 'Neutral taxation of shareholder income', *International Tax and Public Finance*, 12, 777–801.

Sørensen, P. B. (2007a), 'Can capital income taxes survive? And should they?' *CESifo Economic Studies*, 53, 172–228.

Sørensen, P. B. (2007b), 'The Nordic dual income tax: principles, practices, and relevance for Canada', *Canadian Tax Journal*, 55, 557–601.

Sørensen, P. B. (2010), 'Dual income taxes: a Nordic system', in I. Claus, N. Gemmell, M. Harding, and D. White (eds), *Tax Reform in Open Economies*, Edward Elgar, London, 78–108.

Spengel, C. and Wiegard, W. (2004), 'Dual income tax: a pragmatic tax reform proposal for Germany', CESifo DICE Report, 2, 15–22.

Zodrow, G. R. (2006), 'Capital mobility and source-based taxation of capital income in small open economies', *International Tax and Public Finance*, 13, 269–94.

4

Low Interest Rates Offer the Opportunity to Reform the Tax Treatment of Owner-Occupied Housing

*Casper van Ewijk and Arjan Lejour**

4.1 Introduction

The favourable tax treatment of owner-occupied housing is a recurring theme in every debate about the Dutch tax system. The deductibility of interest payments on mortgage debt combined with a low value of imputed rent in the income tax generates a substantial subsidy for home ownership in the Netherlands, resulting in pressures on both the housing market and spatial planning. This problem has not been solved in recent decades. To the contrary, spurred by the sharp rise in housing prices the tax advantage of owner-occupied housing has only increased further over time. Since 2000, the deduction for mortgage interest payments has risen from around 16 to 35 billion euros in 2012, after which it slightly decreased to 33 billion euros in 2015 (see Figure 4.1). Imputed rent is generally computed as 0.6% of the property value of the house.[1] The value of imputed rent has risen from around 5 to 7.5 billion euros in the same period.

The mortgage interest deduction and the low value of imputed rent are the most important determinants of the subsidy on owner-occupied housing. In addition, the government also levies a transfer tax on property transactions. However, from an economic point of view, the subsidy on owner-occupied housing is much larger than the tax on mortgage interest minus imputed rent would suggest. Other assets are subject to the wealth tax, whereas owner-occupied housing is not. In particular, the government assumes a common, presumptive return on savings, portfolio investments, and other property, which is then taxed

* Casper van Ewijk (c.vanewijk@tilburguniversity.edu) is Professor Emeritus, University of Amsterdam and Netspar, Tilburg University. Arjan Lejour (a.m.lejour@tilburguniversity.edu) is Professor of Taxation and Public Finance, Tilburg University, and affiliated at CPB Netherlands Bureau for Economic Policy Analysis. We thank the editors Sijbren Cnossen and Bas Jacobs for their comments on an earlier version. We are also grateful for the comments of Jeske de Lint and Floris T. Zoutman following the presentation at the Cnossen forum.

[1] For property with a value above 1,090,000 euros, imputed rent equals 2.35% of the property value in excess of 1,090,000 euros.

Casper van Ewijk and Arjan Lejour, *Low Interest Rates Offer the Opportunity to Reform the Tax Treatment of Owner-Occupied Housing* In: *Tax by Design for the Netherlands.* Edited by: Sijbren Cnossen and Bas Jacobs, Oxford University Press.
 DOI: 10.1093/oso/9780192855244.003.0004

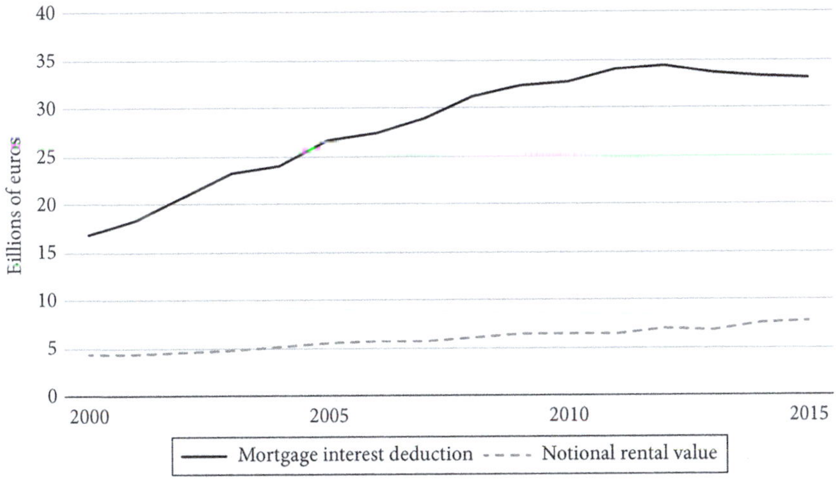

Figure 4.1 Mortgage interest deduction and imputed rent owner-occupied housing
Source: Gidding et al. (2017).

in box 3 of the income tax system at a rate of 30%. This wealth tax is generally much higher than the tax on home equity (via the low tax on imputed rent). The subsidy on owner-occupied housing, and thus its distortionary impact, is therefore also determined by how home equity is treated in comparison with other assets.

In recent years, a major shift has occurred in the distribution of the subsidy for owner-occupied housing. As interest rates have declined, the benefit of the mortgage interest deduction has decreased in importance (relative to the house value), while the benefit of the low tax on imputed rent has remained constant. Put differently, the tax advantage of owning a home that is financed with debt has decreased compared to financing it with equity; the tax advantage now accrues mainly to households that have repaid their mortgage and thus finance their home with equity. For some households, it is even beneficial to pay off the mortgage at current low interest rates by using their savings that are subject to the wealth tax in box 3. This applies mainly to richer households with substantial private wealth that exceeds the general exemption for the wealth tax. However, most households have low wealth and remain below the general tax exemption (see also Jacobs, 2017).

The shift in the distribution of the subsidy on owner-occupied housing has important consequences for the distribution of the subsidy over the life cycle. Younger households mainly finance home ownership with debt, while for older households the property mainly represents equity. Figure 4.2 clearly shows the decreasing importance of mortgage debt relative to the value of the home over the life cycle.

Figure 4.2 Property value of owner-occupied housing and mortgage debt per age cohort (2017)
Source: Statistics Netherlands (2020a).

With the ageing of the population and stricter requirements for mortgages for young people, the importance of home equity will increase in the future. Rising house prices reinforce this further. The net value of the stock of owner-occupied housing (i.e. net of mortgages) in 2017 was approximately 550 billion euros. This amount has increased since the financial crisis of 2008, as shown in Figure 4.3.

From an international perspective, the position of the Netherlands is exceptional. The International Monetary Fund (IMF) concludes that the mortgage interest deduction for owner-occupied housing is the most generous in a sample of twenty highly developed countries, followed by Norway and Denmark (IMF, 2018). Related to this, household debt has also increased. With a size of 92% of GDP in 2018, mortgage debt in the Netherlands is one of the highest in the world (IMF, 2018; OECD, 2018a). Policy measures have been taken in recent years to reduce the generosity of the tax treatment of owner-occupied housing. In particular, the highest tax rate at which mortgage interest can be deducted is gradually lowered from 52% to 37% (the tax rate in the current lowest income tax bracket). Home owners need to obtain a linear or annuity mortgage to be eligible for the mortgage interest deduction. Imputed rent has been increased to 2.35% of property values in excess of about 1 million euro. Despite these policy measures, the mortgage interest deduction is still generous for most households, at least in absolute terms.[2] Relative to the property value, the mortgage interest deduction

[2] See also the analysis by Jacobs (2017) on the tax measures of the previous Dutch government.

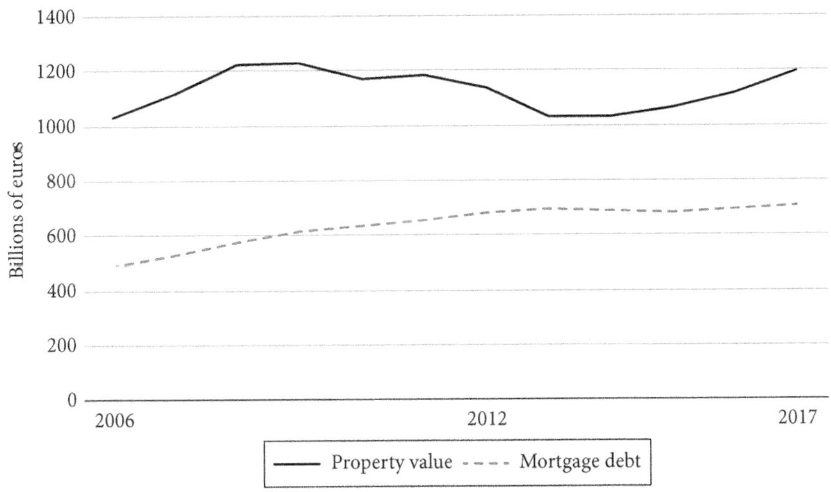

Figure 4.3 Property value of owner-occupied housing and the size of mortgage debt (2006–17)
Source: Gidding et al. (2017).

is declining together with the mortgage interest rates. IMF (2018) and OECD (2018a) give the Dutch government credit for these measures, but emphasize the need to further reduce the subsidy on owner-occupied housing and to bring down debt levels of households. Further reform is necessary because the subsidy on owner-occupied housing causes various distortions in the economy.

Firstly, a substantial subsidy for housing stimulates housing consumption without good reason. Traditional arguments such as better health or a better-maintained neighbourhood, no longer apply, while the negative external effects, such as pressure on spatial planning, come to the fore.[3]

Secondly, households are encouraged—along with buying a home—to incur substantial debt, especially at the start of the life cycle. Because of large, fixed mortgage repayments,[4] they run considerable risks if their income falls, interest rates rise or house prices decline. High household debts also cause systemic risks for the economy as a whole, as proved painfully to be the case during the 2008 financial crisis.

Thirdly, the saving decision is also distorted. The Netherlands has a good pension system with substantial mandatory savings in funded pension schemes. In addition, additional wealth is accumulated through owner-occupied housing,

[3] In addition, little evidence has been found that owning a home leads to better maintenance of the home and the neighbourhood. A correlation has often been found, but this can largely be attributed to selection effects.

[4] Since 2013, mortgage debts have to be repaid via an annuity or linear schedule to be eligible for mortgage deductibility. This further increases the financial pressure at the start of the life cycle.

mainly fuelled by tax incentives; those who do not benefit from the mortgage interest deductibility are considered to be making poor financial decisions. Here, too, the question is whether this additional tax incentive for saving through owner-occupied housing is still appropriate. Knoef et al. (2015) show that a quarter of households have more to spend after retirement than before retirement, while a replacement rate of 70% or 80% is generally regarded as normal. Not only saving too little for old age but also saving too much can lead to considerable welfare losses.[5]

Fourthly, subsidies on owner-occupied housing directly and indirectly distort the labour market. Obstacles to mobility in the housing market (through home ownership and the property transfer tax) exacerbate frictions in the labour market.[6] Subsidies on owner-occupied housing generate inefficiencies in production and consumption. These welfare losses indirectly distort the labour market by reducing the incentives to work.

Fifthly, insofar as housing supply is inelastic, there may be reason to tax housing (or, even better, land) higher than other tax bases. By extracting the rents from home owners, the welfare losses of taxation of, for example in the labour market, can be mitigated.

In this chapter, we focus primarily on economic distortions and on reform options to remedy these distortions. Distributional effects are only dealt with indirectly; these require separate treatment in conjunction with other instruments of income policy. Regarding reform options, we take a 'neutral' treatment of owner-occupied housing as our main reference point, where 'neutral' must be seen as a symmetric tax treatment of owner-occupied housing compared with other assets, such as private saving and portfolio investment, which are subject to the wealth tax in box 3.

4.2 Size of the Subsidy on Owner-Occupied Housing

4.2.1 Macroeconomic Perspective

The size of the subsidy depends on the difference in tax treatment between owner-occupied housing and other assets. As Table 4.1 shows, the tax benefit of the mortgage interest deduction for households amounts to 9.8 billion euros in 2019, which is partially offset by revenues from the tax on imputed rent of 3.4 billion euros. In addition, home owners have the advantage that owner-occupied housing is not subject to the wealth tax in box 3, a benefit that was worth 5.9 billion euros in 2017. From 2014 onwards, the mortgage interest deduction decreases as a result

[5] See van Ewijk et al. (2017). [6] See van Ewijk and van Leuvensteijn (2009).

Table 4.1 Estimates of subsidy on housing (billion euros)

Year	Mortgage interest deduction	Imputed rental value	Exemption capital income tax	Property transfer tax	Net subsidy
2008	12.7	−2.6	7.7	−4.4	13.5
2011	14.3	−2.6	6.3	−1.9	16.1
2014	14.0	−2.9	4.1	−1.6	13.6
2017	11.8	−3.3	5.9	−3.0	11.4
2018	10.9	−3.3	6.9	−3.1	11.4
2019	10.4	−3.4	7.9	−3.2	11.7

Notes: Data are from Statistics Netherlands (2020b), Koelewijn et al. (2019), and Rijksoverheid (2019). The benefit of the mortgage interest deduction includes a special exemption introduced in 2018 to encourage mortgage debt reduction. A rate of 1.2% has been used on the value of owner-occupied housing minus mortgage debt to calculate the benefit for the exemption of the wealth tax in box 3. The one-off exemption for owner-occupied housing with regard to inheritance and gift tax has been ignored. This amounted to about 190 million euros and is not relevant, or is negligible, for years before 2017. The rate of the property transfer tax was 6% until 2010. Values for 2018 and 2019 are estimates.

of declining interest rates, whereas the benefit of the exemption from the wealth tax increases due to rising house prices.

For the subsidy on housing, the mortgage interest deduction and the exemption from the wealth tax are most important. In addition, for purchases of existing property, a property transfer tax of 2% of the property value is due. This generated 3.0 billion euros for the government in 2019 because of the boom in the housing market. Furthermore, municipalities also levy property tax at a rate of 0.11% on average of the estimated value of the property. Similarly, regional water management authorities levy tax on the property value. These local charges can be partly characterized as benefit taxes for locally provided public goods, and are not discussed further. The construction of new houses is also subject to value-added tax (VAT). The VAT on new construction fits in with the neutral treatment of houses, but it is not completely neutral, as discussed later.

4.2.2 The Subsidy on Housing: A Life-Cycle Approach

The size of the implicit subsidy on owner-occupied housing can be calculated in two ways: ex post and ex ante. In the 'macroeconomic' ex post approach (that also has been adopted to make the calculations above), the size of the total tax revenues is related to the total rental value of the stock of owner-occupied housing. This approach is based on measured amounts of tax and thus reflects household decisions about homes and mortgages from the past. Previously, van Ewijk et al. (2007) used this ex post approach. To estimate the distortion of the subsidy, however, it is important to know how households respond to tax incentives now. Therefore, the ex ante or life-cycle approach looks at data (interest, tax provisions, etc.) that are currently relevant to individuals as they buy and finance their own home.

In this chapter, we follow the ex ante approach and calculate the average tax benefit that owning a home provides for an individual over the entire life cycle. In practice, the mortgage interest deduction is lower than in the ex post approach, which reflects higher mortgage interest rates from the past. The ex ante approach also has the advantage that it provides a picture of the tax benefit over the life cycle of households.

The ex ante approach uses the effective marginal tax rate (EMTR), as developed by King and Fullerton (1984). The effective tax burden is calculated for new investment projects by comparing the difference between the return before and after taxes. In essence, this is the present value of the taxes over the entire lifetime of the project. Figure 4.4 provides an overview of EMTRs that are calculated by the OECD for different asset classes for the Netherlands. The EMTR is the total tax rate per euro return on the underlying asset. The figure illustrates the special position of the Netherlands: while ordinary savings and shares are taxed relatively heavily (due to the wealth tax in box 3), the EMTR on owner-occupied housing is low.[7] The Netherlands also treats pension contributions favourably in the tax system.

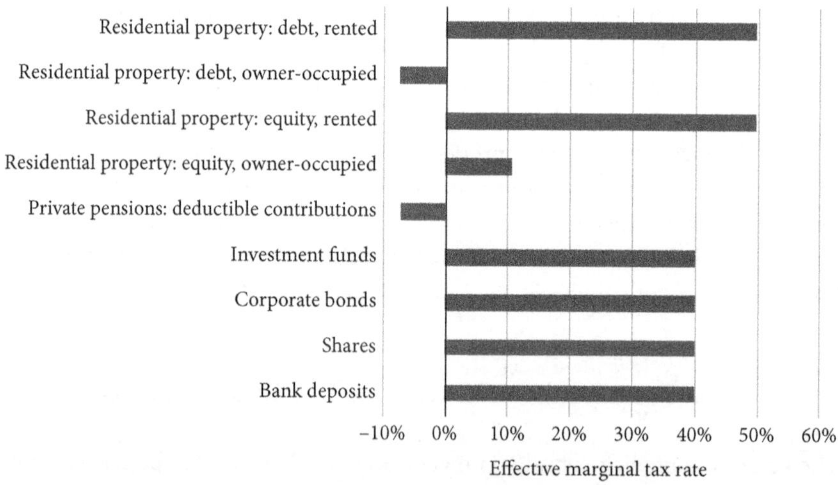

Figure 4.4 Effective marginal tax rates per asset class
Source: OECD (2018b).

[7] This calculation uses a higher interest rate on borrowing.

4.2.3 The Effective Subsidy on Owner-Occupied Housing

We calculate the subsidy on owner-occupied housing as the difference in effective marginal taxes on owner-occupied housing compared with other assets. We thereby focus on the most important items: the interest deduction, imputed rent, and the exemption from the wealth tax in box 3. To illustrate, we consider a household at the start of the life cycle that decides to purchase an owner-occupied home. Suppose, further, that this household owns the home for the whole of its life.[8] The tax benefit of the owner-occupied home can be calculated by determining the present value of the subsidy over the entire life cycle.

Figure 4.5 shows the distribution of the tax benefit per euro invested in an owner-occupied home over the life cycle. The tax benefit is equal to tax savings as a result of the mortgage interest deduction net of imputed rent, and the benefit of the exemption from wealth tax:

$$\text{subsidy} = t_i(rM - r_h H) + t_w r_w (H - M).$$

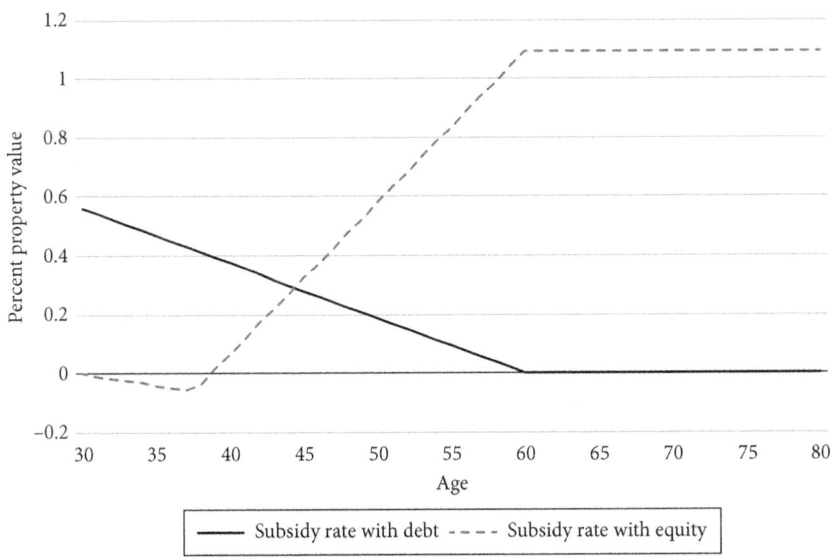

Figure 4.5 Tax benefit broken down by debt and equity (percentage of property value)

Notes: This simulation assumes the purchase of the home at the age of 30, a nominal interest rate of 2%, linear repayment over 30 years, and a threshold for the wealth tax of 25% of the property's value.

Source: Authors' calculations.

[8] This does not necessarily mean that an individual continues to live in the same home for his or her entire life; it is about making a decision to become a home owner, which, in practice, is often a decision for life.

Here, M and H stand for the mortgage and the value of the house, t_i denotes the income tax rate, t_w is the tax rate on presumptive returns in box 3, and r, r_h, and r_w denote the mortgage interest rate, the rate of imputed rent, and the presumptive return used in box 3 for the wealth tax (above the threshold), respectively. If E represents the equity in the owner-occupied home (= $H - M$), we can also break down the tax benefit according to financing with debt (M) and equity (E):

$$\text{subsidy} = t_i(r - r_h)M + (t_w r_w - t_i r_h)E.$$

In the first years after buying a home with a mortgage, the tax benefit mainly consists of the mortgage interest deduction; the net wealth of the household also still falls below the threshold of the wealth tax. The benefit decreases over time with the repayment of the mortgage and becomes zero after 30 years when the household has fully paid off the debt. Over these 30 years, the benefit of the exemption for the wealth tax is growing. In the first few years, equity financing of homes has a negative impact on the subsidy, because imputed rent is taxed but there is still no benefit from avoiding wealth tax as home equity is still below the threshold for the wealth tax. In later years, however, this benefit becomes positive as home equity rises above the threshold for the wealth tax.

The average tax benefit can be calculated by computing the net present value of the annual subsidies. Using a market-based discount rate of 2% (equal to the interest rate) for mortgage debt and 3% (equal to the required return minus the expected increase in the value of the house) for home equity, the effective average subsidy in our example amounts to 25% of the value of the house. If we also take into account the property transfer tax (2% per transaction), the subsidy is slightly lower.

However, the question is whether using a market-based discount rate is relevant for the household in our example. Households—especially at the start of the life cycle—often have limited access to the capital market. As a result, cash flows in the short term should be accorded a larger value than those in the long term, more than is reflected in the market discount rate. For example, if we limit the effective time horizon to 20 years, the effective subsidy falls below 5% (also taking into account the property transfer tax), which is substantially lower than the 25% that we calculated before.[9] This finding also indicates that the subsidy for younger households may be substantially lower than is often assumed. Especially, with the current low interest rates, the incidence of the tax benefit is mainly on to those in the later stages of the life cycle.

It is therefore striking that recent reforms have focused on limiting the mortgage interest deduction together with lowering imputed rent, tilting the balance

[9] An alternative is to calculate net present values with a higher subjective discount rate, which results in a similar result.

even further to the detriment of younger households. The rate of imputed rent will be reduced from 0.65% in 2019 to 0.45% of the house value in 2023.

At the top income tax rate of 49.5%, the net tax equals 0.2% of the property value. This is substantially lower than the wealth tax of 1.3% in 2019 (above a threshold of some 72,000 euros), and this may be raised to 1.4% for risky assets in the near future. The growing importance of the tax-favoured status of home equity in owner-occupied housing has major implications for the life cycle. The tax benefit is shifting from young people without equity to older people with mortgages that have largely been paid off.

4.2.4 Comparison with the Ex Post Approach

The subsidy of 25% (discounted at market interest rates) is roughly in line with the subsidy of 20% that was found by van Ewijk et al. (2007) using an ex post approach. However, these authors use values for 2006, when the interest rate was considerably higher. If we update that ex post approach with recent values, we arrive at a comparable value for the subsidy. Although the lower interest rate has reduced the benefit of the mortgage deductibility, the rental value of houses will also be lowered by lower interest rates. These two factors more or less cancel out.

4.2.5 Distribution of the Tax Benefit by Income Group

With a total amount of 5% of GDP, the mortgage interest payment is one of the largest deductions in the Dutch income tax system, and has, therefore, a significant effect on the income distribution. About half of Dutch households benefit from the tax treatment of housing. The distribution of net benefits is strongly in favour of high incomes, as can be seen in Figure 4.6. The highest two income deciles receive approximately 50% of the tax benefit of 14.2 billion euros in 2014, while the lowest five income deciles receive only 15% of the tax benefit. The redistributive nature of the deductibility of mortgage interest has been one of the reasons that the Dutch government has implemented various reductions in the size of mortgage interest deductibility. It is striking, however, that the benefit of the exemption of the wealth tax in box 3 has received much less attention. Even worse, recent reforms have increased this benefit by reducing the presumptive percentage for imputed rent.

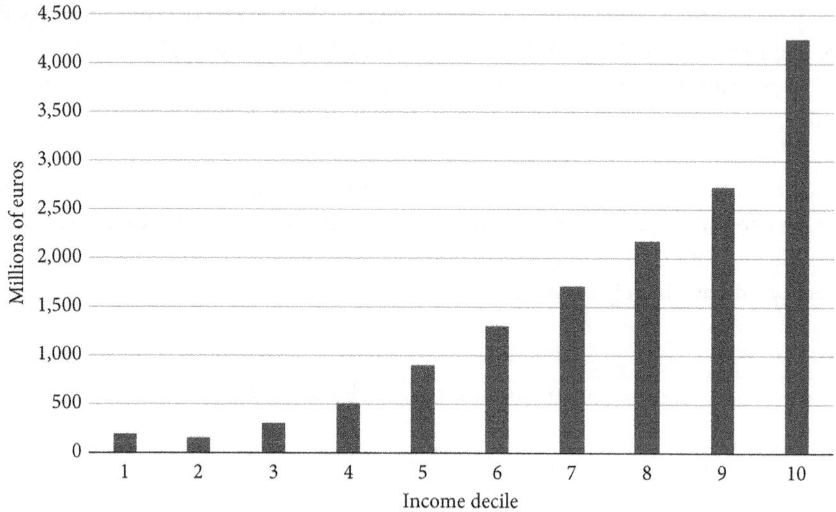

Figure 4.6 Distribution of mortgage interest deduction (in million euros) by income deciles 1–10

Source: Statistics Netherlands (2015). Data apply to 2014.

4.3 Welfare Losses Due to Various Distortions

The implicit subsidy on owner-occupied housing involves various distortions in the economy, causing welfare losses. We distinguish the following distortions:

- Distortions in consumption due to excess housing consumption and pressure on spatial planning;
- Distortions in home ownership patterns, as investing in owning a home is tax-favoured above renting;
- Distortions in financial decisions due to the unequal tax treatment of equity and debt in owner-occupied housing;
- Distortions in saving and portfolio choices, as investing in own property is tax-favoured above other types of saving;
- Distortions in the housing market by restraining mobility (and therefore on the labour market) with the property transfer tax;
- Distortions in production and maintenance of houses due to the incomplete treatment of VAT on owner-occupied housing.

4.3.1 Distortions in Consumption

The subsidy on home ownership distorts household consumption; households spent too much money on owner-occupied housing compared with other goods and services. People decide to buy their first house earlier in life, or to buy larger and better homes instead of other goods and services. There seems little evidence that the housing subsidy can be justified by positive externalities, such as health or better maintenance of the neighbourhood. Accordingly, 'too large' housing consumption involves a welfare loss. This holds even more strongly if we also take possible negative externalities of housing consumption into account (e.g. because there is pressure on spatial planning due to more and larger plots).

The increase in housing consumption depends on the elasticity of housing supply. As the supply of housing is relatively inelastic, because of spatial restrictions and other regulations in the Netherlands, at least in the short run, the subsidy on housing partly results in higher house prices. According to the housing market model of CPB Netherlands Bureau for Economic Policy Analysis, larger demand for housing in the Netherlands translates for about 60% into higher prices.[10] The supply elasticity can vary strongly per region, however. Depending on supply elasticities, van Ewijk et al. (2007) found a welfare loss of 0.2–1.2% of GDP. This welfare loss may now be smaller because the relevant subsidy, as perceived by younger households, has declined (see above). Even then the distortion in housing consumption is still unnecessary and undesirable from an efficiency point of view.

4.3.2 Distortion of Home Ownership Decisions

The home ownership decision is also distorted because the subsidy on home ownership stimulates the purchase of property compared with renting.

Research also points to potential adverse effects of home ownership. Because of the illiquid nature of the home, home owners are less flexible on the labour market (Oswald, 2009). They are therefore less likely to accept a job in another region, which has negative consequences for the labour market and employment.[11] Morescalchi (2016) argues that higher mobility costs lead to higher reservation wages. As a result, home owners may be less inclined to look for a new job outside their own region compared with tenants, as it is easier for people to leave a rental home.

[10] The demand elasticity is 1 above the minimum housing consumption. The supply elasticity is calibrated at 0.65, which involves a price effect of 1/(1 + 0.65).

[11] See also OECD (2018a).

Tax incentives for owner-occupied housing, together with the large social rental sector in the Netherlands, have jeopardized the commercial rental sector. This further hampers mobility in the housing market and in the labour market. The non-transferability of rights and the long waiting lists for social housing, especially in large cities, make residents less mobile and therefore less inclined to accept work in other regions.

4.3.3 Distortion of Financing Decisions

Because younger households have little or no equity (unless parents assist), mortgage interest deductibility of owner-occupied housing is accompanied by large amounts of borrowing. The ensuing leverage in household portfolios entails potential financial vulnerabilities. This became apparent when nominal house prices fell by 20% from 2009–13, leading to negative equity (i.e. the value of mortgage debt exceeded the value of the house) for about one-third of all home-owning households. With the rise in house prices in recent years, this problem has largely disappeared. Free savings of Dutch households are still low, however, due to high mandatory pension obligations and large mortgage debts. As a result, this may involve greater volatility of consumption (Lukkezen and Elbourne, 2015) and stronger business-cycle fluctuations. However, for young people—for whom human capital is the major component of their total wealth—investing in home ownership can actually increase their welfare because it offers an opportunity to take risk early in the life cycle and thus they benefit from the risk premium (Munk, 2016).

4.3.4 Distortions in Saving and Portfolio Choice

Promoting investment in home equity is also seen as a means to stimulate saving for old age. There are good reasons for this, as owner-occupied housing—like pension savings—is relatively illiquid and therefore less easy to use for short-term consumption. In many countries, wealth accumulation in owner-occupied housing is therefore encouraged via the tax system (albeit less so than in the Netherlands; see Figure 4.2). As a rule, an owner-occupied home is held for life. Moreover, because mortgage debt is usually repaid over the course of active life, the rental value of the owner-occupied home can be seen as an annuity for old age. Children often inherit the property.

The question is whether providing tax incentives for home equity is relevant also for the Netherlands. After all, the Netherlands already has a good pension system with mandatory wealth accumulation in fully funded occupational pension schemes. Figure 4.7 shows the composition of retirement income in the

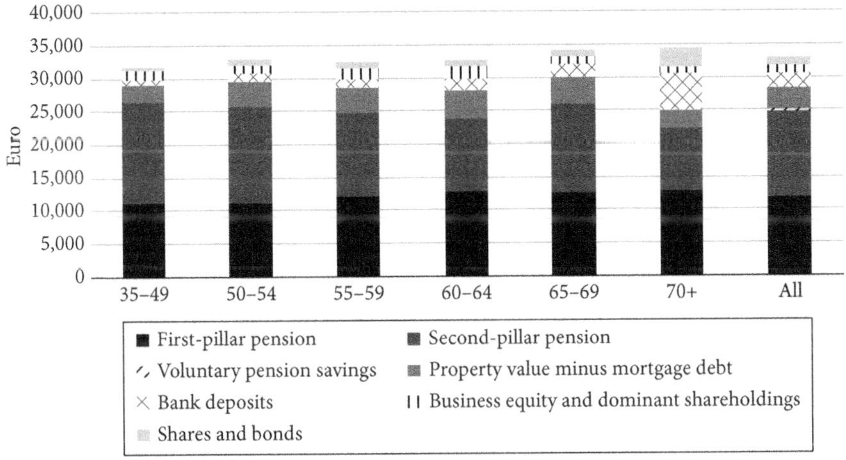

Figure 4.7 Composition of income after retirement
Source: Knoef et al. (2015).

Netherlands. Owner-occupied housing forms around 12% of total retirement income, and here only the rental value of the home is included. This is the average for all households; for higher-income households, the contribution of home ownership is larger, but for the highest incomes it is not. For those households, other wealth components, such as shares, are more important.

Given the solid pension system, stimulating savings through home equity is less relevant for the Netherlands. Actually, it may even lead to over-saving. As can be seen from the figure, about a quarter of all households have a replacement rate (income after retirement relative to income before retirement) of more than 100%. This means that these households have more to spend after retirement than during active life. Saving too little for old age is costly in welfare terms, but saving too much involves welfare losses as well. Tentative calculations show that excess saving through owner-occupied housing may lead to a welfare loss of up to 6% of lifetime consumption (van Ewijk et al. 2017).

It should be noted here that not all households are covered by mandatory pension schemes. A growing group of self-employed and flexible workers does have substantial compulsory pension rights. For them, investing in their own property can be an important provision for old age. However, this may not be optimal; the return on savings then depends entirely on developments in the housing market and their asset portfolio is thus not properly diversified.

Also, in other countries, where pension savings may be less well organized, a subsidy for owner-occupied housing is not always found to be optimal. For example, Nakajima (2010) shows for the United States that tax credits for owner-occupied housing lead to overinvestment in own property. The abolition of these credits increases welfare and improves the labour market in the author's model.

4.3.5 Distortions in the Housing and Labour Market

As indicated above, the virtual lack of a commercial rental market in the Netherlands can also have adverse consequences for the labour market, as it can hinder the mobility of workers. The property transfer tax contributes to this problem, because it is an implicit tax on mobility. De Graaf and van Leuvensteijn (2013) show that an increase in property transfer tax by 1 percentage point leads to a decrease in the number of job changes by approximately 1.5% and to 3–10% fewer relocations. This calls for the abolition of the property transfer tax, as also argued by Mirrlees et al. (2011).

4.3.6 Distortions in Production and Maintenance of Housing

Mirrlees et al. (2011) pay a lot of attention to the VAT on housing services. A neutral treatment of owner-occupied housing requires that the rental value (rent and imputed rent) is also taxed under the VAT, like other goods and services.[12] The owner of the home is, at the same time, an investor who receives the rental value and a consumer who receives the housing service. In the United Kingdom there is no VAT on new construction, while there is in the Netherlands. For residential services, VAT is already included in the price of new buildings. Property owners are able to convert the full purchase price into rent, and therefore tenants implicitly pay VAT. This also applies to residential services through the purchase of an existing house. The VAT is reflected in the purchase price. This makes the VAT on new construction a proxy for a VAT on housing services. This proxy is not a good in the longer term. The problem is that no VAT is levied on capital gains that may occur with improvements in the neighbourhood or with increasing scarcity of housing services now and in the future. We cannot assess the extent of this distortion. Cnossen (2011) proposes to repair this distortion with a VAT on the capital gain of the house upon transfer. A natural moment for this levy is at the time of the sale. To prevent long-term lock-in effects, also a capital gains tax should be levied on gifts and inheritances. When doing this, an adjustment must be made for renovations in owner-occupied housing that are subject to VAT.

[12] See Mirrlees et al. (2011) and Bettendorf and Cnossen (2015).

4.4 Quantifying Some Reform Options

How large are all distortions for the Netherlands, and what are the potential gains of reforms? Little empirical evidence is available. Some guidelines are offered by the housing market model of CPB Netherlands Bureau for Economic Policy Analysis (Möhlmann and Groot, 2019), which is partly based on the model of DiPasquale and Wheaton (1994). For a representative household, housing choices are modelled assuming that households optimize their utility. The model distinguishes between owner-occupied housing, rent-controlled social housing and private, commercial rental housing. Housing market institutions are represented through an (implicit) tax or subsidy on the housing price. It is a long-term model in which the supply of housing is slowly adjusting to demand, based on a low supply elasticity for housing in the Netherlands.[13] The model does not include consumption/savings and labour market decisions, and hence it does not take into account distortions in savings and labour markets. The main distortions concern the consumption choice of housing relative to other goods and services and the choice of home ownership (home ownership or renting). The favourable tax treatment of owner-occupied housing compared with other assets is reflected by a subsidy on owner-occupied housing. According to CPB/PBL (2016), the effective subsidy rate is 27% of the housing price, comparable to the subsidy we calculated above for the subsidy over the life cycle.[14]

The model is used to evaluate potential policy reforms. For example, the limitation of the mortgage deductibility to 30 years in 2001, the tax incentive to redeem mortgage debt[15] and the introduction of a higher top rate for imputed rent (see footnote 1) prove to have had hardly any effect on the efficiency of the housing market. Reducing the deductibility of mortgage interest by bringing it into a lower tax bracket improves efficiency only by 0.1% (in terms of GDP), and the requirement for repayment within 30 years by 0.2%.

Policy reforms that simultaneously abolish tax deductibility of mortgage interest and the taxation of imputed rent have larger effects. Such policies can be accompanied by, in addition, 'neutralizing' the treatment of owner-occupied housing with other assets by levying wealth tax on the net property value (i.e. the value of the house minus the mortgage debt). The results of both reforms are presented in Table 4.2. In each case, the property transfer tax is also abolished and

[13] Caldera and Johansson (2013) find an elasticity of 0.2. Michielsen et al. (2017) find an elasticity of 1.09. This is a lot higher than Caldera and Johansson because the former also include the crisis years 2008–16, when many new housing construction projects were terminated.

[14] If the subjective discount rate is higher, the distortions are smaller and the welfare effects of reform options are smaller. Because it is difficult to gain insight into the actual subjective discount rates, we use the market value of the tax rebate as a benchmark for evaluating the reform options.

[15] According the so-called Hillen Act of 2005, the net tax liability on owner-occupied housing is set to zero if the imputed rent is higher than the mortgage interest payments. This tax incentive mainly benefits older households that have (largely) repaid their mortgage debt.

Table 4.2 Structural ex post long-term effects of policy reforms (percentage change relative to the baseline)

Policy	Price for owner-occupied properties	Efficiency gain (percentage of GDP)	Share of rental properties (percentage point)
Abolish mortgage interest deduction together with taxation of imputed rent	−3.3%	0.3%	1.6
Include the net property value in the wealth tax in box 3 with an exemption of 300,000 euros for owner-occupied housing only	−4.5%	0.4%	2.3
Include the net property value in the wealth tax in box 3 with a general exemption of 300,000 euros	−8.6%	0.7%	5.0

Source: Möhlmann and Groot (2019).

the net proceeds for the government are channelled back to households in the form of lower taxes. Removing tax deductibility of mortgage interest payments, together with taxation of imputed rent, leads to an annual welfare gain of 0.3% of GDP. The drop in the subsidy leads to lower house prices (3.3%), and the share of the commercial rental sector increases by 1.6%. If owner-occupied housing would become subject to the wealth tax in box 3, the efficiency gains in the housing market would be even larger. Depending on the size of the exemption for the wealth tax on owner-occupied housing, the welfare gain ranges from 0.4% to 0.7% of GDP. Donders et al. (2010) found similar results.

If housing wealth is taxed in box 3, it will probably be hard politically to fully abolish specific exemptions for owner-occupied housing. Such exemptions are often seen as a proxy for the consumption character of the home (Donders et al., 2010). This means that the subsidy on owner-occupied housing will partly continue to exist. Exemptions for the wealth tax could be conditioned on owning a house. Alternatively, the general exemption for the wealth tax can be increased. In the latter case, buyers and tenants are treated on an equal footing and the distortion in favour of home ownership is reduced. This involves a larger efficiency gain. A general exemption for the wealth tax is an interesting option if the pension assets are treated in the same way as other private wealth components.

4.5 Now Is the Time to Phase Out the Subsidy on Owner-Occupied Housing

The tax treatment of owner-occupied housing involves a welfare loss due to distortions in saving and portfolio investment decisions. The current, low interest rate offers a good opportunity to phase out the subsidy. Because interest rates are low, the government can implement such a reform without major consequences for younger households; after all, the benefit of the mortgage interest deduction has become much smaller. The main benefit is the exemption from the wealth tax in box 3.

A neutral approach to owner-occupied housing can be achieved by equalizing the tax treatment of investments in owner-occupied housing with that of other assets that are subject to the wealth tax in box 3. The implicit subsidy on housing consumption through owner-occupied housing then expires and there are fewer incentives to save. Just like other debts, mortgage debt is also subject to the wealth tax. Therefore, there is no longer a reason for tax arbitrage between these assets. All these benefits would also materialize if the government were to replace the wealth tax in box 3 with an income tax on actual returns.[16]

There are even arguments to tax owner-occupied housing more heavily than other forms of property. It follows from the well-known Ramsey rule that immobile, and therefore inelastic, tax bases should be taxed more heavily. This is the case for owner-occupied housing (or, even better, land), compared with other, non-compulsory, assets in household portfolios, certainly in the short term. An additional levy can be used to extract rents from home owners. However, this is not possible without intergenerational consequences. With an inelastic housing supply, all taxes now and in the future are effectively borne by the current generation of home owners.

Finally, it is important to have a consistent tax treatment of mandatory private pension savings. There may be arguments for encouraging savings through home equity as part of the provision for retirement income. In many respects, saving through owner-occupied housing is similar to saving through pension products; both are relatively illiquid, and the rental value of owner-occupied housing (when a household has fully paid off the mortgage) can be seen as an annuity for the rest of the life cycle. However, it should be taken into account that the Netherlands already has a solid, funded pension system for most employees, which seems a more natural way to provide for retirement income. Moreover, households should avoid saving too much if they save both via pension funds and through home equity. This requires a comprehensive approach to owner-occupied housing and pensions, for example by creating the possibility of using pension savings partly to

[16] See Jacobs (Chapter 5).

finance owner-occupied housing. In this way, excess saving is avoided. Such a system exists in Switzerland where households can use part of their pension wealth to invest in their own house. When households sell their property, they have to reinvest the proceeds in the pension savings scheme. This possible substitution between owner-occupied housing and pensions gives households more flexibility and reduces the incentive to save. It also prevents tax arbitrage between various assets.

References

Bettendorf, L. and Cnossen, S. (2015), 'The long shadow of the European VAT: exemplified by the Dutch experience', *FinanzArchiv*, 71, 118–36.

Caldera, A. and Johansson, A. (2013), 'The price responsiveness of housing in OECD countries', *Journal of Housing Economics*, 22, 231–49.

Cnossen, S. (2011), 'A proposal to improve the VAT treatment of housing in the European Union', *Fiscal Studies*, 32, 455–81.

CPB/PBL (2016), *Kansrijk Woonbeleid*, CPB, The Hague (in Dutch).

De Graaf, T. and van Leuvensteijn, M. (2013), 'A European cross-country comparison of the impact of homeownership and transaction costs on job tenure', *Regional Studies*, 47, 1443–61.

DiPasquale, D. and Wheaton, W. (1994), 'Housing market dynamics and the future of housing prices', *Journal of Urban Economics*, 35, 1–27.

Donders, J., Romijn, G., and van Dijk, M. (2010), *Hervorming van het Nederlandse woonbeleid*, CPB book no. 84, CPB, The Hague (in Dutch).

Gidding, K., Nieuweboer, J., and Pouwels-Urlings, N. (2017), 'Ontwikkelingen op de koopmarkt', *Economisch Statistisch Berichten*, 102, 13 April 2017 (in Dutch).

IMF (2018), 'The kingdom of the Netherlands—Netherlands', IMF country report.

Jacobs, B. (2017), 'Gaan mensen hun hypotheek aflossen onder Rutte III?', *Economisch Statistische Berichten*, blog 15 October 2017 (Dutch).

King, M. and Fullerton, D. (eds) (1984), *The Taxation of Income from Capital*, University of Chicago Press, Chicago.

Knoef, M., Goudswaard, K., Been, J., and Caminada, K. (2015), 'Veel variatie in de pensioenopbouw van Nederlandse huishoudens', Netspar Brief 2, Netspar, Tilburg (in Dutch).

Koelewijn, C., van de Ven, Y., and Vodegel, D. (2019), 'The subsidy on owner-occupied housing: ripe for reform', Working paper, Erasmus School of Economics, Rotterdam.

Lukkezen, J. and Elbourne, A. (2015), 'De Nederlandse consumptie: goede tijden, slechte tijden', CPB Policy Brief, 2015/03, CPB, The Hague (in Dutch).

Michielsen, T., Groot, S., and van Maarseveen, R. (2017), 'De prijselasticiteit van het woningaanbod', CPB notitie, 17 August 2017, CPB, The Hague (in Dutch).

Mirrlees, J., Stuart, A., Besley, T., Blundell, R. Bond, S., Chote, R., Gammie, M., Johnson, P., Myles, G., and Poterba, J. M. (2011), *Tax by Design: The Mirrlees Review*, Oxford University Press, Oxford.

Möhlmann, J. and Groot, S. (2019), 'Ex post effecten woningmarktmaatregelen', CPB notitie, July 2019, CPB, The Hague (in Dutch).

Morescalchi, A. (2016), 'The puzzle of job search and housing tenure: a reconciliation of theory and empirical evidence', *Journal of Regional Science*, 56, 288–312.

Munk, C. (2016), 'The role of housing in life-cycle portfolio and consumption decisions', presentation, Netspar International Pension Workshop, Netspar, Tilburg.

Nakajima, M. (2010), 'Optimal capital income taxation with housing', Working Paper no. 10–11, Federal Reserve Bank of Philadelphia.

OECD (2018a), *OECD Economic Surveys: Netherlands*, OECD Publishing, Paris.

OECD (2018b), *Taxation of Household Savings*, OECD Tax Policy Studies 25, OECD Publishing, Paris.

Oswald, A. (2009), 'The housing market and Europe's unemployment: a non-technical paper', in C. van Ewijk and M. van Leuvensteijn (eds), *Homeownership and the Labour Market in Europe*, Oxford University Press, Oxford, pp. 43–52.

Rijksoverheid (2019), *Beleidsinformatie kaart*, The Hague (in Dutch).

Statistics Netherlands (2015), 'Belastingvoordeel woningbezit is 280 euro per maand' (https://www.cbs.nl/nl-nl/nieuws/2015/43/belastingvoordeel-woningbezit-is-280-euro-per-maand).

Statistics Netherlands (2020a), 'Vermogen van huishoudens; huishoudenskenmerken, vermogensbestanddelen' (https://opendata.cbs.nl/statline#/CBS/nl/dataset/83834NED/table?ts=1597433251299).

Statistics Netherlands (2020b), 'Overheid; ontvangen belastingen en wettelijke premies' (https://opendata.cbs.nl/statline/#/CBS/nl/dataset/84120ned/table?ts=1598256930456).

van Ewijk, C., Hoet, C., Mehlkopf, R., and van den Bleeken, S. (2017), *De waarde van maatwerk in pensioenen*, Netspar Brief 8, Netspar, Tilburg (in Dutch).

van Ewijk, C., Jacobs, B., and De Mooij, R. (2007), 'Welfare effects of fiscal subsidies on homeownership in the Netherlands', *De Economist*, 155, 323–36.

van Ewijk, C. and van Leuvensteijn, M. (eds) (2009), *Homeownership and the Labour Market in Europe*, Oxford University Press, Oxford.

5
Fundamental Reform of Taxes on Capital Income in the Netherlands

*Bas Jacobs**

5.1 Introduction

Taxation of capital income in the Netherlands exhibits neither economic consistency nor economic logic. Capital income from saving, portfolio investment, owner-occupied housing, business ownership, and pensions is taxed in very different ways: with flat or progressive rates, based on realized returns or on presumptive returns and capital income from the most important assets (owner-occupied housing and pensions) is not taxed but subsidized. Effective tax rates on capital income are low, also in international comparison. As a result, the mix of taxes on labour and capital income is neither efficient nor equitable. Moreover, the tax treatment of capital income distorts the allocation of capital and risk in the Dutch economy. Furthermore, business cycles in the Dutch economy have become volatile due to high financial leverage, which is strongly promoted by the tax system. Against this backdrop, this chapter proposes a fundamental tax reform of the entire tax regime for capital income and wealth in the Netherlands.

A major cause of the inconsistent tax treatment of capital income is the fundamental tax reform of 2001. Then, the so-called 'box system' was introduced by the State Secretary of Finance, Willem Vermeend. The box system moved the Dutch income tax system from a hybrid comprehensive income tax system to a hybrid dual income tax system, where capital income and labour income are taxed separately. Since 2001, labour income—including the earnings (labour and capital income) of the self-employed—is taxed at progressive rates in 'box 1'. Incomes from owner-occupied housing and pensions are also taxed in box 1. Dividends and capital gains on 'substantial share-ownerships' in closely held companies are

* Bas Jacobs (bjacobs@ese.eur.nl) is Sijbren Cnossen Professor of Public Economics, Erasmus School of Economics, Erasmus University Rotterdam. This contribution draws on Jacobs (2017). All references to specific details of the Dutch tax system (bases, rates, brackets, etc.) draw on information from the web site of the Dutch tax authorities (www.belastingdienst.nl). The author acknowledges support from the Netherlands Institute for Advanced Study (Duisenberg Fellowship 2018–2019). The author is grateful for excellent comments and suggestions by Sijbren Cnossen, Arjan Lejour and Peter Sørensen.

Bas Jacobs, *Fundamental Reform of Taxes on Capital Income in the Netherlands* In: *Tax by Design for the Netherlands*. Edited by: Sijbren Cnossen and Bas Jacobs, Oxford University Press.
DOI: 10.1093/oso/9780192855244.003.0005

taxed on a realization basis in 'box 2'. Income from all other assets is imputed and taxed at a rate of 30%, under what is euphemistically referred to as the 'presumptive capital income tax' in 'box 3'.[1] However, the tax in box 3 is simply a wealth tax, because tax liabilities are solely dependent on the wealth of taxpayers and not on the capital income they earn.[2] The Dutch wealth tax in box 3 is an international fiscal oddity.[3] Nowhere in the OECD are interest income, dividends, and capital gains completely exempt from taxation at the personal level (Harding and Marten, 2018).

Moreover, owner-occupied housing and pensions are subsidized at a huge net fiscal cost of about 35 billion euros (4.5% of GDP). These subsidies create inefficiencies in the mix of taxes on labour and capital income, as tax rates on labour income in box 1 need to increase with about 9 percentage points in all brackets to finance these subsidies. The tax treatment of housing and pensions also distorts the asset allocation of the Dutch economy; an inefficiently large amount of wealth is accumulated via largely (housing) or completely (pensions) illiquid forms of wealth.[4]

Another important problem is that the Dutch tax system plays a major role in promoting leverage ('debt bias') by allowing for the deductibility of mortgage interest in the personal income tax (PIT) and the costs of debt in the corporate income tax (CIT); see also IMF (2016). The Great Recession (2008–15) made it abundantly clear that the Dutch economy is financially fragile as a result of the high leverage of households, firms, and banks.

The wholly inconsistent tax treatment of capital income, the ample opportunities for tax arbitrage, and the financial fragility of the Dutch economy have been known for many years. However, many committees and politicians have only recommended partial and marginal adjustments to the existing tax regime for capital income, certainly not fundamental tax reforms.[5] Therefore, this chapter

[1] Originally, the aim of the presumptive capital income tax was to tax the normal return on assets, which was assumed to be 4% until 2017. In its defence in various law suits that have been filed over the years by tax payers earning small or even nil returns on their risk-free assets, the Dutch government has been putting up more and more smoke screens in order to justify the high presumptive return on risk-free assets (FD, 2018).

[2] Since 2017, the wealth tax in box 3 has been made progressive with a three-bracket schedule.

[3] Since its introduction in the Tax Reform 2001, the presumptive capital income tax has been a thorn in the eyes of prominent economists and tax specialists. See, for example, the contributions in Cnossen (1998) and Cnossen and Bovenberg (2001). On the initiative of Sijbren Cnossen, all but two Dutch professors with relevant expertise in the economics of taxation and tax law subscribed to an open letter sent in 1999 to members of parliament opposing the introduction of the new box system.

[4] Pension wealth is illiquid, because Dutch workers or pensioners do not have direct access to their pension entitlements. Pension wealth is stored in collective pension funds that are managed by representatives of employees' and employers' organizations.

[5] The Study Committee Tax System (Studiecommissie Belastingstelsel, 2010), the Committee Income Tax and Allowances (Commissie Inkomstenbelasting en Toeslagen, 2013), State Secretary of Finance (Wiebes, 2014, 2015) and the Sustainable Growth Study Group (Studiegroep Duurzame Groei, 2016). In 2019, the State Secretary of Finance (Snel, 2019) announced that he was gathering 'building blocks' for fundamental tax reform during the period of the current Rutte III government.

proposes a fundamental reform of the tax treatment of capital income in the Netherlands: (1) to reduce the welfare losses of redistributive taxation by raising the share of taxes on capital income in the total tax mix; (2) to reduce distortions and avoid tax arbitrage in portfolio choices; and (3) to eliminate the debt bias to promote financial stability.

To that end, a dual income tax system is proposed with a progressive tax schedule on labour income and a uniform flat rate on all real (not presumptive) capital income from savings, portfolio investment, pensions, owner-occupied housing and business income. Moreover, all capital gains should be taxed either on a realization basis for illiquid assets or on an accrual basis for liquid assets. Double taxation of capital income via the CIT and PIT should be avoided. The tax mix can be made more efficient by abolishing the overly generous tax concessions for owner-occupied housing and pensions, but also by closing down various loopholes in the tax regime for director-shareholders of closely held companies in box 2. In addition, taxes on inheritance and property can be raised. Finally, the entire Dutch tax system should be freed of debt biases. Taxes on labour income can then be cut with approximately 10 percentage points in all brackets.

The rest of this chapter proceeds as follows. Section 5.2 describes how capital income and wealth are taxed in the Netherlands. Section 5.3 argues, based on optimal tax theory, that capital income ought to be taxed in an optimal tax system. Section 5.4 suggests that flat tax rates on capital income should be in the order of 30–35% by confronting theoretical arguments with the available empirical evidence. Section 5.5 recommends replacing the wealth tax in box 3 with a comprehensive, uniform tax on all capital income, including capital gains, from saving, portfolio investment, housing, pensions, and closely held companies. Section 5.6 analyses how owner-occupied housing and pensions should be treated for tax purposes and how current subsidies should be eliminated. Section 5.7 discusses how the taxation of director-shareholders in closely held companies should be improved and integrated with taxes on other capital income. Section 5.8 recommends that all capital income should be taxed only once and discusses policy options to integrate the CIT with the PIT. It also presents options to remove the debt bias in the CIT. Section 5.9 argues that no taxes on wealth are necessary if all capital income is taxed, but that they can be desirable as a second-best instrument if not all capital income is taxed. Moreover, it argues that inheritance taxes can be increased for efficiency reasons. Section 5.10 discusses various transitional issues of the fundamental tax reform proposed in this chapter. Section 5.11 concludes.

5.2 Taxation of Capital Income in the Netherlands

This section provides some background to guide the discussion in this chapter. It aims to answer the following questions. How does the taxation of capital income in the Netherlands compare to other countries? How is capital income taxed, at what rates and how much revenue does this generate? How does the tax treatment of different assets affect the Dutch asset allocation? How does the tax treatment of capital income affect wealth inequality?

Capital income is lightly taxed in the Netherlands, also from an international perspective. The implicit tax rate on capital income (14.4%) is among the lowest of all European Union (EU) countries (including Norway) for which data are available (see Figure 5.1).

The implicit tax rate provides a rough estimate of the total effective tax burden on capital as a fraction of the total capital tax base. The GDP-weighted EU average of the implicit tax rate on capital income of all countries shown is 31.6%. The share of capital taxes in total tax revenue in the Netherlands is 19.3%. This is lower than the EU average of 21.9%. Some Eastern European countries and the Baltic States have a substantially lower share of capital taxes in total revenue. The implicit tax rate on capital income in the Netherlands has fallen sharply in recent years. In 2016, it was 5.3 percentage points lower than it was in 1995 (European Commission, 2018).

How is capital income taxed, at what rates and how much revenue does this generate? Table 5.1 breaks down total tax revenue on capital income by various asset classes.[6] The total revenue from taxes on capital income and wealth in the Netherlands in 2018 amounts to approximately 31 billion euros (4.0% of GDP). Revenue from capital taxes is relatively low mainly as a result of the subsidies on owner-occupied housing and pension savings, which are jointly subsidized by more than 13 billion euros (this estimate does not take into account revenue losses from exempting owner-occupied housing and pensions from the wealth tax in box 3, only the revenue losses in box 1).

Moreover, the total revenue from taxes on capital income and wealth is biased upwards for two reasons. First, in a small open economy, such as the Netherlands, the CIT is, to a large extent, shifted to labour (Jacobs, 2015; Fuest, Peichl, and Siegloch, 2018). Second, the property transactions tax, the local property tax, and the landlord levy are all included in the total revenue from taxing capital. Some of these levies can be considered as benefit taxes for locally provided public goods that raise property values.

The tax treatment of capital income shows neither economic consistency nor economic logic. Private assets—excluding owner-occupied housing, pension wealth and assets from non-listed businesses—are taxed under the progressive wealth tax in box 3, but capital income from interest and dividends are exempted from PIT. Income from owner-occupied housing is treated as labour income under the progressive tax schedule in box 1, where imputed rent is taxed and

[6] The definitions of capital income in Figure 5.1 and Table 5.1 differ because of, among other things, the inclusion of taxes on cars in the EU definition of taxes on capital income.

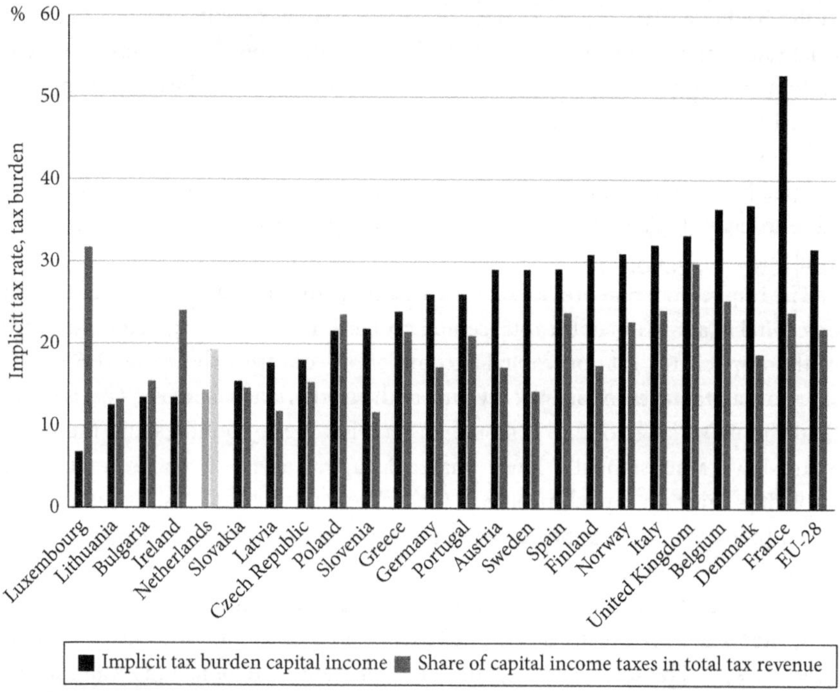

Figure 5.1 Implicit tax rate on capital income (2016) and contribution of taxes on capital to total tax revenue (2017)

Note: The implicit tax on capital is the ratio of tax revenue of all taxes on capital to total capital income. EU averages are GDP-weighted averages of the member states included in the graph.

Source: See the Appendix to this chapter.

mortgage rent is deductible. However, the revenue loss from the deduction for mortgage interest is much larger than the revenue gain of taxing imputed rent. As a result, owner-occupied housing is not progressively taxed but regressively subsidized. Ownership of second houses is taxed under the wealth tax in box 3, where mortgage interest is not deductible and rental income is untaxed. Pensions are considered (deferred) labour income and taxed at reduced rates under the progressive labour tax schedule in box 1. Pension contributions are tax-deductible at a tax rate that is, on average, 17 percentage points higher than the tax rate at which pension benefits are taxed (CPB, 2010).[7] Capital gains on portfolio investments and home ownership at the personal level and capital gains on assets in pension funds are not taxed. Non-incorporated businesses, typically small and medium-sized enterprises (SMEs), file tax under the progressive tax in box 1, where a profit exemption of 14% is applied to business income after the standard

[7] More recent estimates of this tax differential are unavailable.

Table 5.1 Taxes on capital income in the Netherlands (2018)

Base	Revenue (billion euros)	Rate
Box 1: owner-occupied housing (mortgage interest deduction—tax on imputed rent)	-7.0	36.55–51.95%, imputed rent: 0.7%/2.35% property value
Box 1: pensions (taxes on pension benefits—tax deductions of pension contributions)	-6.5	36.55–51.95%
Box 2: substantial ownerships closely held businesses	2.4	25%
Box 3: saving and portfolio investment	4.4	0.6051–1.614%
Inheritance and gift tax	2.3	10–40%
Corporate income tax	23.0	20–25%
Dividend withholding tax	3.4	15%
Transactions tax on property	2.7	2–6%
Local property tax	4.0	variable, av. 0.118% (owner-occupied housing), 0.274% (owner non-housing), 0.2043% (user non-housing)
Landlord levy on public social housing companies	1.7	0.591% property value
Banking tax	0.5	0.044%/0.022% overshort-term/long-term debts
Total (billion euros)	30.9	
Total (percentage of GDP)	4.0	

Sources: See the Appendix to this chapter.

business deduction. Hence, the effective top rate on business income of unincorporated firms in box 1 equals 44.7% in 2018. Incorporated businesses file tax under the CIT. Dividends and realized capital gains on business assets of listed and non-listed firms are taxed under the CIT and the PIT. Dividend distributions are subject to a dividend withholding tax, which shareholders can credit against their PIT liability. Distributed dividends and capital gains on shares (if sold) of dominant shareholders in closely held companies are taxed at a flat rate of 25% in box 2. This implies that the combined rate of the CIT and PIT on dividends and capital gains in non-listed firms equals 43.8%. The transfer of wealth is taxed under the gift and inheritance tax, but family-business succession facilities subsidize the transfer of business assets (not shown in Table 5.1).

How does the tax treatment of different assets affect the asset allocation in the Netherlands? With the patchwork of different tax regimes for different sources of capital (income), the government distorts the efficient allocation of capital and risk in the Dutch economy. See also Table 5.2, which shows the asset allocation of

Table 5.2 Asset composition of the Netherlands (2017)

	Billion euros	Percentage of GDP
Financial assets	427.9	58
Net assets of owner-occupied housing	491.4	67
Gross value of owner-occupied housing	1,199.4	163
Value of mortgage debt	–708.0	–96
Other real estate	161.8	22
Other property	38.2	5
Business assets	65.0	9
Business assets substantial ownerships	190.3	26
Debts (except mortgages)	–115.1	–16
Pension wealth[a]	1,328.0	180
Net government wealth[b]	199.0	27
Gross public assets	728.0	99
Gross public debt	–529.0	–72
Total wealth	2,786.5	378

Source: All data are from Statistics Netherlands (2019b) unless indicated otherwise. [a] Data 2017, fourth quarter, De Nederlandsche Bank (2019). [b] Data 2016, Statistics Netherlands (2019c).

the Netherlands. Households mainly accumulate wealth through owner-occupied housing and pension funds, with a joint value of 343% of GDP in 2017. This is hardly surprising, as both assets are heavily subsidized via the tax system. Dutch mortgage debt is a staggering 96% of GDP. As a result, the Netherlands has the highest household debt in the entire OECD after Denmark: household debt stands at 243% of net disposable household income (OECD, 2019).

The tax system discriminates against financing investment with equity or retained earnings as a result of interest deductibility in the CIT ('debt bias'). Excessive debt financing distorts the optimal allocation of capital and risk as it promotes tax-driven increases in financial leverage of households and firms, especially in financial institutions, and it renders the Dutch economy financially fragile. Moreover, because of the tax facilities for owner-occupied housing, household portfolio decisions are distorted due to excessive exposure of households to housing-market risk. The massive amount of accumulated pension wealth is entirely illiquid, which causes liquidity constraints and amplifies the business cycle; households in financial distress (e.g. as a result of declines in house prices) cannot access their (pension) wealth.

A plethora of capital (income) tax bases and rates opens doors for tax arbitrage. Different types of assets can be transformed into one another to avoid taxation, for example, through various vehicles for pensions or company loans in box 2 where director-shareholders of closely held companies are taxed.[8] Moreover, the

[8] Tax consultants often refer to box 2 as the 'fun box', because of the many possibilities to defer or avoid taxation.

capital–labour income split for director-shareholders in box 2 is difficult to enforce. The tax treatment of closely held companies in box 2 induces shifting of labour income (taxed in box 1) to profits (taxed in box 2), because the combined rate of the corporate tax and box 2 (43.75%) is lower than the top rate on labour income in box 1 (49.5%).[9] Director-shareholders therefore have strong financial incentives to reduce their labour earnings to the minimum presumed labour earnings of 46,000 euros.[10] There are no strong incentives to change the legal form from unincorporated to incorporated businesses, however, as effective top tax rates for both legal forms are roughly aligned at around 44%.

Finally, the transactions tax on property transactions does not have a good economic rationale, but causes considerable welfare losses due to lower mobility in the housing and labour market (van Ewijk et al., 2006; van Ewijk and Lejour, Chapter 4).

Low taxes on capital income and wealth imply that—for given total tax revenue—the tax burden is shifted to labour via taxes on labour income and on consumption. In particular, if owner-occupied housing and pensions were to be taxed as personal savings and portfolio investment (i.e. both housing and pensions are taxed in box 3 rather than in box 1), while tax rates for pensioners and workers were equalized, then the government would raise a large amount of additional revenue equal to about 35.0 billion euros, or 4.5% of GDP (pensions, 22.1 billion euros; owner-occupied housing, 12.9 billion euros; see the chapter Appendix for the calculations). Forgone tax revenue, due to the concessionary tax treatment of housing and pensions, is nearly as large as all expenditure on the entire education system of 38.5 billion euros in 2019 (Ministry of Finance, 2019a). Removing all tax breaks for housing and pensions would permit a cut in tax rates on labour income of about 9 percentage points in all tax brackets ignoring behavioural responses (see the chapter Appendix).

Finally, how does the tax treatment of capital income affect wealth inequality? The tax treatment of capital income affects not only the allocation of assets, but also the distribution of wealth. It is likely that the favourable tax treatment of capital income contributes to a very skewed wealth distribution in the Netherlands. The top 10%, top 1%, and top 0.1% of the wealth distribution owned 64%, 26%, and 11% of total wealth in 2017, respectively (Statistics Netherlands, 2019a).[11] The

[9] Note that these figures apply to 2020, while the discussion on Table 5.1 applied to 2018, when the top rate on labour income was slightly higher.

[10] Presumptive labour income should be a maximum of 75% of the labour income in a similar job, the labour earnings of the highest-paid employee or a minimum of 46,000 euros. If the tax authorities suspect that the presumptive labour earnings of business owners are larger, then they need to prove this. If taxpayers argue that it should be lower than 46,000 euros, then they need to prove that to the tax authorities.

[11] Total wealth includes all personal financial assets (saving deposits, bonds, shares), property, shares in non-listed businesses, minus all debts (including mortgages). However, official statistics do not include pension wealth.

bottom 60% of the wealth distribution has no net wealth. Therefore, wealth inequality in the Netherlands is comparable with other continental European countries, such as France, Germany, and the United Kingdom, but is more unequal than Scandinavian countries (Piketty, 2014). Wealth inequality has been remarkably stable over time, unlike the developments that are documented by Piketty (2014) for other countries.

Although there are currently no statistical signs of rising wealth inequality (Statistics Netherlands, 2019a), some measurement issues prevent definitive conclusions from being drawn. First, reported wealth statistics exclude pension wealth. If all Dutch pension wealth is assigned to individual workers and pensioners—which is a highly complex exercise—the wealth distribution becomes less skewed, as individuals with less wealth own relatively more pension wealth compared with other forms of wealth. By taking pension wealth into account, Caminada, Goudswaard, and Knoef (2014) estimate that the wealth share in 2012 of the top 10% is 50% (61% without pension wealth) and 17% for the top 1% (25% without pension wealth).

Second, there are various measurement issues related to recording capital incomes in the statistics. Because capital gains are generally untaxed, they are not recorded in the income and wealth statistics. Moreover, capital transactions larger than 250,000 euros of director-shareholders of non-listed firms are recorded only as financial transactions, but not as dividend income or capital gains (Frederik, 2014). The income and wealth statistics may therefore understate the true amount of inequality in income and wealth.

5.3 Capital Income Should Be Taxed

Should capital income be taxed? This is one of the oldest questions in public finance. Although some contributions suggest that zero taxation of capital income might be desirable (Atkinson and Stiglitz, 1976; Chamley, 1986; Judd, 1985), these contributions have little relevance for applied tax policy.[12] Taxes on capital income are socially desirable for both efficiency and equity reasons (Banks and Diamond, 2010; Diamond and Saez, 2011; Jacobs, 2013, 2015). Taxes on capital income generate efficiency gains by alleviating the distortions of taxes on labour income and consumption. The latter reduce the incentives to participate in the labour market, to work more hours, to retire later and to invest in human capital (Erosa and Gervais, 2002; Jacobs and Boadway, 2014; Jacobs and Bovenberg,

[12] Moreover, Jacobs and Rusu (2018) show that the contributions of Chamley (1986) and Judd (1985) have been incorrectly interpreted in the literature. They argue that the optimal tax on capital income is zero in the steady state, because the Corlett–Hague argument—leisure complements should be taxed at higher rates—vanishes in the long run.

2010). Taxes on capital income generate wealth effects, which raise both hours worked and participation, and delay retirement. Moreover, investments in human capital are encouraged as investment in financial capital becomes less attractive.

Taxes on capital income are also necessary to prevent tax arbitrage between labour and capital income so as to maintain the integrity of the entire income tax system (Christiansen and Tuomala, 2008). For example, if capital income were not taxed at all, then individuals would try to transform all their labour income into untaxed capital income (e.g. by starting closely held companies that pay out dividends rather than labour income).

Taxes on capital income are also desirable if not all capital income is a pure compensation for postponing consumption or bearing risk, but also contains 'unearned income' that is not a compensation for economic efforts, such as capital gains on (inelastic) housing and land, monopoly profits, and information rents.

These efficiency arguments to tax capital income are dependent on the presence of distortionary labour taxes, and apply irrespective of the redistributional goals of the government.[13] By shifting the tax burden from labour to capital income, the inevitable welfare losses of taxation can be smoothed better over the tax bases for labour and capital income.

However, taxes on capital income are not only desirable for efficiency reasons. Taxes on capital income also contribute to achieving the government's redistributional objectives at lowest social costs. It is generally not sufficient to organize all income redistribution exclusively via the progressive tax on labour income, as not all inequality in income originates from inequality in labour earnings (Diamond and Spinnewijn, 2011; Piketty and Saez, 2013; Piketty, 2014; Gerritsen et al., 2020; Gerritsen and Zoutman, Chapter 2). In particular, individuals with higher ability to earn labour income also tend to save more, to inherit more wealth, and to obtain higher returns on their capital because they invest in riskier portfolios. They also have better access to investment opportunities, and have on average a higher earning ability in the capital market. Therefore, it is optimal to tax capital income for redistributional reasons, because more income redistribution can be achieved than with the progressive tax on labour income alone.

All these efficiency and equity arguments for an optimal positive tax on capital income imply that it is not desirable to exempt the normal return to capital from taxation via a so-called rate-of-return allowance, as Mirrlees et al. (2011) recommended. Moreover, it is desirable—if possible—to differentiate taxes on normal and above-normal returns, by applying a lower tax rate on the normal return than

[13] Naturally, the level of labour tax is determined by the redistributional goals of the government. However, the role of the tax on capital income is to raise efficiency, not to *directly* redistribute income. By lowering the efficiency costs of the labour tax, however, taxes on capital income *indirectly* help to redistribute more income.

the above-normal return, as is done in Norway (Cnossen and Sørensen, Chapter 3; Gerritsen and Zoutman, Chapter 2).

5.4 How High Should the Tax on Capital Income Be?

The optimal tax on capital income trades off the welfare gains of lower distortions in taxing labour income and greater income redistribution against larger distortions in saving and portfolio choices. The welfare losses of taxes on capital income are critically determined by the elasticity of taxable capital income or wealth with respect to its tax rate. There are few empirical studies that credibly estimate the elasticity of taxable capital income or wealth. Recent estimates suggest that the elasticity of taxable capital income or wealth can be substantial. The paper by Kleven and Schultz (2014) appears to be the only study that estimates the elasticity of taxable capital income with respect to the net-of-tax rate on capital income at around 0.1–0.3 for Denmark. Brülhart et al. (2017) estimate an elasticity of wealth with respect to the net-of-tax rate on wealth equal to 1.2 for Switzerland. Seim (2017) reports elasticities of wealth with respect to the net-of-tax rate equal to 0.09–0.27 for Sweden. Jakobsen et al. (2020) estimate the long-run wealth elasticity with respect to the net-of-tax rate for top-wealth taxpayers of 0.77–1.15 for Denmark.

The only available estimates for the Netherlands are those of Zoutman (2018), who estimates the elasticity of wealth with respect to the after-tax return (not the net-of-tax rate) on wealth. He cannot directly identify the elasticity of wealth with respect to the net-of-tax rate, but his estimates imply elasticities that lie in between the estimates of Seim (0.09–0.27) and Brühlhart et al. (1.2). Moreover, Zoutman (2018) suggests that the Dutch wealth taxes mainly trigger saving and portfolio shifts 'on paper', rather than real behavioural changes in saving and portfolio decisions.

Based on this empirical evidence, one can—ceteris paribus—conclude that the optimal tax rate on capital income is likely to be lower than the tax rate on labour income, as taxes on capital income are probably more distortionary and result in relatively more tax avoidance and evasion due to the higher international mobility of capital.

However, capital income is certainly also more unequally distributed than labour income, and capital income is relatively more important for the top-income earners (Saez and Stantcheva, 2016). Hence, taxes on capital income also have redistributional benefits beyond the redistributional benefits of progressive taxes on labour income. How high the optimal tax on capital income should be depends on inequality in capital income *conditional* on labour income. Such information is currently not available for the Netherlands.

The optimal tax on capital income should presumably be of the order of 30–35% for the Netherlands (Jacobs, 2015). On the one hand, the elasticity of taxable capital income is presumably higher than that of labour income, which implies a lower optimal rate on capital income. On the other hand, larger inequality in capital income—conditional on labour income—implies a higher optimal tax rate on capital income. However, a tax of 30–35% is more an educated guess than a precise estimate. Currently, Scandinavian countries levy taxes on capital income of the order of 20–35% (Cnossen and Sørensen, Chapter 3). The possibility that a comprehensive income tax is optimal—where the sum of labour and capital income is taxed under a single progressive tax schedule—cannot be rejected on the basis of available evidence.

5.5 How Should Capital Income Be Taxed?

Given that governments should optimally tax capital income, how should this be done in practice? Should all assets be taxed symmetrically? Should presumptive capital income or actual capital income be taxed? How should lock-in effects be avoided when taxing capital gains?

Optimal tax theory suggests that it is optimal to levy separate non-linear tax schedules on separate tax bases (see, for example, Mirrlees, 1976). By doing so, the government can raise the tax burden on tax bases that either are less elastic or feature larger intrinsic inequality (so that the distributional benefits of taxing such bases are greater). However, in order to tax each tax base with a separate non-linear tax schedule, the government requires information regarding how much capital income is earned on each tax base. This is problematic if various assets can easily be transformed into one another (e.g. by setting up closely held companies or financial vehicles), resulting in income shifting towards tax bases with lower tax rates.

To prevent such tax arbitrage, it is desirable to tax all interest, dividend and capital gains from savings, portfolio investment, home ownership, pensions, and share ownership in closely held businesses as much as possible with a uniform, flat rate.[14] As argued above, differential taxes on capital income may also affect portfolio choices if different types of assets receive a differential tax treatment. However, if taxes on capital income are uniform, and full loss-offsets are

[14] The tax rate on capital income earned by pension funds may be somewhat lower than the standard rate on capital income for other assets, because the equity reasons for taxing capital income are weaker for pension funds. In particular, inequality in pension incomes originates mainly from differences in labour incomes, and much less from differences in capital returns, saving behaviour and portfolio choices—although these, too, may differ across pension funds. It still remains optimal to tax capital income in pension funds for efficiency reasons (i.e. to lower distortions of labour income taxes, to avoid arbitrage, and to tax rents). Lower taxes on capital income from pension funds can only be implemented, however, if tax arbitrage with other capital incomes can be adequately prevented.

permitted, portfolio choices will no longer be distorted by the tax treatment of capital income.

Moreover, actual returns to capital, not presumptive returns, should be taxed. A capital income tax should therefore be introduced, which taxes not only the normal returns to capital, but also the risk premium and rents (Spiritus and Boadway, 2017). By taxing actual capital income, the government shares in the good and bad financial luck of households. Taxes on rents are a non-distortionary source of public finance. By taxing the risk premium and rents, tax revenue increases. Furthermore, a tax on actual capital gains is countercyclical and progressive (Cnossen, 1998; Cnossen and Bovenberg, 2001; Jacobs, 2013, 2015; Cnossen and Sørensen, Chapter 3; Gerritsen and Zoutman, Chapter 2).

The wealth tax in box 3 is the diametrical opposite of what the Mirrlees Review (Mirrlees et al., 2011) recommended: box 3 taxes normal returns to capital and exempts the above-normal returns to capital. The wealth tax in box 3 is also the opposite of what an optimal tax on capital income should be. For the same equivalent tax rate, tax revenues of a wealth tax are lower than of a capital income tax by not taxing excess returns and risk premiums.[15] Moreover, the government does not insure financial risk of households, but exacerbates their exposure to financial risk.

Higher financial risk for households is the mirror image of the 'robust tax revenue yield', which is often referred to by Dutch policymakers in defence of the wealth tax in box 3. This argument is an economic fallacy. Making tax revenue more robust lowers social welfare, as households' exposure to financial risk increases if the government lowers the volatility of the tax base. By the same token, the wealth tax in box 3 is pro-cyclical. Average tax rates on capital income decline in upswings of the business cycle and rise in downswings. Box 3 thereby contributes to the volatility of the Dutch economy. Box 3 is also formidably regressive, because average tax rates decline steeply as capital income rises. As a result, box 3 contributes to wealth inequality. For all these reasons, the wealth tax in box 3 should be replaced by a tax on all realized or accrued capital income; see also Gerritsen and Zoutman (Chapter 2) and Cnossen and Sørensen (Chapter 3).

Liquid assets with a clear market valuation can be taxed with an accrual-based, or market-to-market, capital gains tax. This applies, for example, to all tradable assets, such as stocks and bonds. Moreover, the government also provides yearly estimates of property values to implement a property tax. These data could also be used to estimate capital gains on housing and tax them accordingly (Gerritsen and Zoutman, Chapter 2). However, illiquid assets without an evident market value

[15] Suppose that the wealth tax is t% of all assets a, the capital income tax rate is τ on all asset returns r, the normal return is ρ and the excess return is π ($r = \rho + \pi$). A capital income tax and a wealth tax imply the same tax rate on the safe return if $t = \tau\rho$. In that case, the wealth tax raises revenue of $ta = \tau\rho a$, while the capital income tax raises revenue τra. The difference is the tax revenue from taxing the excess return $\tau\pi a$.

cannot be properly taxed with an accrual-based capital gains tax, such as shares in non-listed firms or works of art. Hence, capital gains on these assets can only be taxed with a capital gains tax upon realization. If capital gains are taxed, then capital losses should also be made deductible against capital gains.

For many decades, Dutch policymakers have consistently rejected a capital gains tax by referring to complications with 'lock-in effects': taxpayers defer realization of capital gains and forward the realization of capital losses (Ministry of Finance, 2016). This argument is, again, largely a fallacy—not because lock-in effects are not empirically relevant, but because these lock-in effects are present precisely because the government provides tax incentives to postpone the realization of capital gains. Lock-in effects are not an intrinsic characteristic of a capital gains tax, but are a symptom of government failure to correctly implement it. To avoid lock-in effects, it is necessary to tax the accrual of interest in unrealized capital gains on illiquid assets (Auerbach, 1991; Bradford, 1995; Auerbach and Bradford, 2004). Then, the most important incentive for deferral of the realization of capital gains has been removed. In the Netherlands, this applies mainly to shares in closely held companies (see below). If lock-in effects nevertheless occur, their impact can be mitigated by only allowing the deduction of capital losses against realized capital gains for a limited number of years.

5.6 Treat Owner-Occupied Housing and Pensions Symmetrically with Other Capital Income

A uniform regime for capital income implies that savings, portfolio investment, housing, pension wealth and business profits are taxed symmetrically. How should the tax treatment for housing and pensions then change compared to the current situation?

The first step towards a comprehensive tax on all capital income is to move the taxation of owner-occupied housing and pensions from the labour base in box 1 to box 3 (which would tax actual rather than presumptive income) by including capital income of owner-occupied housing (imputed rent) and returns on pension wealth in the tax base for capital income. In addition, all capital gains on property should be included as well. Mortgage interest can then be made deductible, while imputed rent is increased to approximately 3–4% of the value of the house. Both mortgage interest and imputed rent are then taxed at the rate of the uniform capital income tax of 30–35%. Doing so eliminates all incentives for excessive debt financing of owner-occupied housing; see also van Ewijk and Lejour (Chapter 4) who recommend removing the debt bias by moving owner-occupied housing to box 3.

Moreover, the government can abolish the requirement of having a linear or annuity mortgage to be eligible for the mortgage interest deduction. This measure has been taken to curb excessive debt financing of houses, but ceases to have a clear rationale if all debt bias has been removed from the tax system. To address short-term liquidity issues, the government could consider introducing a borrowing facility to defer taxation of imputed rent or capital gains until the property is sold or the owner dies (Jacobs, 2013).

The system of deductible pension contributions and taxed pension benefits can remain in place if the reduced tax rates on pensioners are eliminated and aligned with those on workers. Social-security contributions for the pay-as-you-go state pension (*Algemene Ouderdomswet*, AOW) should then also be levied on pensioners' income. Capital income of pension funds (interest, dividends, and capital gains on their portfolios) can be taxed under the new tax regime for capital income, possibly at a reduced rate. Furthermore, all costs of borrowing should be made deductible, such as interest on consumer credit, student loans, and mortgages (for second homes also). The distortionary transfer duty on property transactions should be abolished.

By allowing for a general tax exemption in the tax regime for capital income, the government can provide incentives to accumulate wealth (e.g. for retirement saving). However, it no longer distorts household saving and portfolio choices: via pensions, savings, portfolio investment, housing, or shares in closely held companies. Of course, such a major tax reform requires a careful transition, and the tax treatment of housing and pensions may need to be phased in gradually, along with possible compensation for the biggest losers from the tax reform.

5.7 Stop the Fun in Box 2

How should dividends and capital gains on shares in closely held corporations be taxed under the proposed uniform regime for capital income? The current tax regime in box 2 consists of a capital income tax of 25% on dividend payments and capital gains of dominant shareholders in closely held companies, mostly directors who work in their own firm. Therefore, box 2 already is a tax on actual capital incomes so that it can be merged easily with box 3, while aligning the tax rates at 30–35%. However, the current tax regime in box 2 offers all kinds of possibilities for lowering tax liabilities via deferral of profit distributions and capital gains realizations (lock-in effects), tax arbitrage with box 1 and box 3 (e.g. by allowing dominant shareholders to borrow from their closely held company), and via pension constructions. These loopholes need to be closed.

In particular, if profits are retained, capital income inside the firm is subject to additional CIT. In contrast, if dividends are distributed or capital gains are realized, taxpayers become liable to the tax on wealth in box 3 of the PIT in the current tax system (or to the tax on capital income in the regime proposed in this chapter). In both cases, taxpayers are liable to CIT on profits and the tax on dividend income in box 2. Because the tax rate in box 3 (of 30%) can be twice as high as the CIT rate (the lowest bracket is 15% in 2021), and risk-free interest rates have fallen to near zero, there are strong tax incentives to delay profit distributions and realizing capital gains.[16] In addition, the incentive to delay profit distributions is strengthened, because there is no correction for untaxed interest on unrealized capital gains. Furthermore, firm owners can save tax-free for retirement inside the firm, and they can benefit from reduced rates in the inheritance tax for business succession.

The Dutch Ministry of Finance (2019b) reports that Dutch non-listed companies have issued about 55 billion euros (7% of GDP) of debt to its dominant shareholders. Company loans are attractive because they allow the shareholders to take funds out of their company while avoiding taxation on dividend distributions or on realized capital gains on their shares. Moreover, if director-shareholders default on their company loans, they do not pay any tax on the income taken out of the company as a loan. Furthermore, and as explained above, the tax treatment of closely held companies in box 2 induces shifting of labour income (taxed in box 1) to profits (taxed in box 2), because the combined rate of the CIT and box 2 (43.75%) is lower than the top rate on labour income in box 1 (49.5%). To stop the fun in box 2, it should be integrated into the uniform regime for all capital income, which requires at least four adjustments.

First, to prevent tax arbitrage with the labour tax in box 1, the tax treatment of the presumptive wage income of the director-shareholder should be changed, which is only 46,000 euros in practice. Empirical evidence reveals massive bunching around the minimum presumptive labour income of director-shareholders in non-listed firms (Bettendorf, Lejour, and van 't Riet, 2017). To solve this form of tax arbitrage, director-shareholders should no longer receive a presumptive wage income (which is taxed under the labour tax in box 1), but a presumptive capital income of, say, 10% of all invested equity in the company (Sørensen, 2010; Cnossen and Sørensen, Chapter 3). Presumptive capital income is then taxed under the capital income tax and the remainder is progressively taxed as labour income in box 1. Doing so will close an important tax loophole in box 2.

Second, non-listed companies are used as savings banks because of their possibility to accumulate wealth while benefitting from various tax loopholes. Empirical evidence in Bettendorf et al. (2017) shows that dividend distributions are rare and are extremely sensitive to tax changes. In particular, the bulk of all dividend distributions has taken place in years where the tax rate in box 2 has been temporarily reduced. To prevent endless deferral of profit distributions or realization of capital gains (i.e. lock-in effects) and large-scale issuance of company

[16] The condition for being indifferent between distributing profits and saving in the PIT or retaining them and saving inside the firm is $r\tau^{\text{CIT}} = \tau^{\text{box3}}$ where r is the risk-free interest rate, τ^{CIT} is the CIT rate, and τ^{box3} is the wealth tax in box 3.

loans to pay out undistributed profits, the government should therefore tax financial savings inside non-listed companies in the same way as financial savings are taxed under PIT. This can be accomplished by setting the CIT rate (τ^{CIT}) at the same rate as the PIT rate on capital income (τ^{PIT}) and taxing real, not presumptive, capital income under the PIT.

However, as long as the CIT rate remains lower than the PIT rate, tax neutrality can be achieved only by levying an additional tax (τ^{+}) on capital income generated inside businesses equal to the difference between the PIT and CIT rate on all capital income, i.e. $\tau^{+} = \tau^{PIT} - \tau^{CIT}$. If the PIT remains a wealth tax, as is currently the case in box 3 (τ^{box3}), then tax neutrality can be achieved by levying an additional wealth tax (τ^{wealth}) on business assets equal to $\tau^{wealth} = \tau^{box3} - r\tau^{CIT}$, where r is the risk-free interest rate. If the risk-free rate is near zero, this wealth tax is close to the standard wealth tax in box 3 of the PIT. Under these schemes, the main incentive disappears to exploit closely held companies as savings banks in which returns to saving are taxed at much lower rates, or are even completely tax exempt, compared with saving at the personal level. Moreover, the main incentive to take out company loans will be eliminated.

Third, to completely remove the lock-in effect in realizing capital gains, it would also be necessary to tax the accrual of interest in unrealized capital gains. This can be accomplished by retrospective capital gains taxation, where interest is imputed at the moment of realization, based on the holding period of the business asset and market information on interest rates (Auerbach, 1991; Bradford, 1995; Auerbach and Bradford, 2004). This method has not been applied in the real world, however.

Fourth, generous tax concessions for retirement saving and business succession should also be abolished. Business owners should receive the same tax treatment for retirement saving as normal workers, since this chapter proposes to remove all tax incentives for retirement saving. Moreover, there are no clear indications that business succession arrangements correct a market failure or internalize externalities. These facilities are used mainly by very rich families to avoid paying inheritance tax.

Maintaining tax neutrality between incorporated and unincorporated businesses requires special care under the fundamental tax reform proposed in this chapter, especially if tax rates on labour income will be cut substantially. The effective tax rate on dividend income of closely held businesses equals 44% (45%) in 2019 (2021).[17] At the same time, non-incorporated businesses that file taxes in box 1 can apply for the SME profit exemption of 14%. With a top rate of 49.5%, the effective tax rate on non-incorporated business income thus equals 43%. As income tax rates are basically the same for unincorporated and incorporated

[17] The CIT rate is 25% in 2019 (19% for profits below 200,000 euros). The CIT rate in the lowest bracket will fall to 15% in 2021. The tax rate on dividend distributions in box 2 is 25% (26.9% in 2021).

businesses, there is tax neutrality across incorporated and unincorporated businesses (Commissie Inkomstenbelasting en Toeslagen, 2013). This tax neutrality would be lost if top tax rates on personal income were to be reduced by 9 percentage points, to about 40%. In that case, the effective rates on non-incorporated business income would drop from 43% to about 34%. Raising the tax rate in box 2 to 30–35% would generate even stronger non-neutralities. To restore tax neutrality between incorporated and unincorporated businesses, the SME profit exemption can then be reduced, top rates may need to be reduced by less and the income of unincorporated businesses can be split into a capital and a labour component, similar to director-shareholders in incorporated businesses.

5.8 Integrate the Corporate Income Tax in the Personal Income Tax and Remove the Debt Bias in the Corporate Income Tax

In a good tax system capital income ought to be taxed, and it should be taxed only once. However, due to the interaction with the CIT double taxation of capital income may occur. In particular, the Netherlands has a classical CIT in which interest is deductible, but dividend payments are not. Hence, the normal returns on equity of corporations are taxed twice, first, under the CIT and, second, under the PIT, where the normal return to all wealth is taxed in box 3, while interest is taxed only once in the PIT.

How can double taxation of capital income in the CIT and the PIT be eliminated? Double taxation of dividend income can be prevented via a dividend imputation system by allowing for a tax credit in the PIT for CIT paid as in, for example, Australia and New Zealand. The CIT is then only a withholding tax, much like the dividend withholding tax or the wage tax.

An administratively simpler alternative is a pure dual income tax system, where the rate of the CIT is set at the same rate as the PIT rate on capital income. The CIT is then a final withholding tax on dividend incomes so that no PIT is due on dividend income or capital gains on shares of incorporated businesses attributable to retained profits (Sørensen, 2010; Cnossen and Sørensen, Chapter 3). As a result, it is no longer necessary to introduce a tax credit system for the CIT in the PIT.

However, a pure dual income tax only works well if the CIT rate is equal to the desired rate on capital income in the PIT. In the Netherlands, the CIT rate is 25% in 2021 (15% in the lowest CIT bracket). This CIT rate might generate a too large differential with the proposed tax rate on capital income of 30–35% in the PIT. A dual income tax, such as implemented in the Scandinavian countries, therefore requires removal of the lowest CIT bracket and a somewhat higher CIT rate, around 30–35%.

Furthermore, the CIT is a very distortionary tax that promotes leverage through the deductibility of interest (debt bias). The CIT also reduces incentives to invest and it provokes international movements of firms or their profits. These impacts of the CIT on corporate behaviour are empirically relevant and have been extensively documented in the literature (e.g. De Mooij, 2011; Hofmann and Riedel, Chapter 7).

From an international perspective, Dutch firms have relatively high degrees of leverage (Hebous and Klemm, Chapter 11). Moreover, the Dutch banking sector has a balance-sheet total of about four times GDP, which is among the largest in the EU (European Central Bank, 2018). A weakly capitalized banking system causes financial fragility and generates negative externalities by increasing the probability of financial crashes (Admati and Hellwig, 2013). The Great Recession demonstrated that a financial crisis causes large and long-lasting damage to GDP; the structural loss of GDP in the Netherlands amounted to about 10% (Jacobs, 2016). The CIT promotes financial leverage (European Central Bank, 2018) and the leverage of banks in particular (De Mooij and Keen, 2016).

The debt bias in the CIT should be removed entirely to contain financial leverage and to promote financial stability (IMF, 2016). Elimination of debt bias in the CIT contributes to preventing future financial crises and promotes financial stability. This is even more urgent if it turns out to be impossible to substantially raise capital requirements of banks via the Basel Committee. Hence, as long as banks remain weakly capitalized, and negative externalities of bank leverage remain unaddressed, the tax system should certainly not encourage financial leverage.

Removal of the debt bias can be done in a budget-neutral way by introducing a partial deduction for the costs of both debt and equity; that is, a partial allowance for corporate equity (ACE) together with a partial interest deduction. This would ensure that debt and equity are treated symmetrically for tax purposes.[18] However, part of the revenue of the introduction of a single tax regime for all capital income in the PIT—as recommended in this chapter—could also be used to finance a full ACE. Then, not only financing distortions would be eliminated, but also all investment distortions, as all costs of finance have been made tax-deductible. The CIT then only taxes the above-normal returns of companies.

A far-reaching option would be to introduce a destination-based cash-flow tax (DBCFT); see also Auerbach et al. (2017) and Hebous and Klemm (Chapter 11). In the DBCFT, all investments are made deductible and there is a border tax adjustment to exempt exports, while not allowing deductions for imports for the

[18] It is undesirable to introduce debt bias in the CIT to facilitate debt shifting so as to lower effective corporate tax rates on multinational enterprises (Schindler and Vrijburg, Chapter 10). The first-best solution is to differentiate CIT rates (like the ones that are currently present in the CIT) to reduce the tax burden on multinationals without having to introduce debt bias.

CIT in order to make sure that the above-normal return to investment is taxed in the country of the destination of the firm's product. Like the ACE, the DBCFT removes all investment and finance distortions. Moreover, it removes all location distortions and profit shifting.

However, the DBCFT is, at this moment, a risky policy option for two reasons. First, without international cooperation, international profit shifting will explode and this might lead to the end of the CIT as we know it (Hebous and Klemm, Chapter 11). Second, the prime reason for having a CIT is to tax capital income at source so as to prevent a situation in which capital income is not taxed at all if the tax authorities have difficulties tracing down shareholders and their incomes. Any CIT based on cash flow exempts the normal return to capital at the corporate level. If the normal return cannot be properly taxed in the PIT, then moving to a cash-flow tax on corporate income will be undesirable as it reduces the tax burden on capital income even further and will raise income inequality. Therefore, there are two necessary requirements for introducing cash-flow taxes on corporate income. First, there should be international cooperation in introducing such tax reforms. Second, all capital income should be properly taxed under the PIT.

5.9 Wealth Taxes Can Be Abolished if All Capital Income Is Taxed and the Inheritance Tax Can Be Increased

Should wealth be taxed if all capital income is taxed as well under the PIT? The answer is: no, subject to an important caveat. A wealth tax is superfluous if all capital income is already taxed. The reason is that a wealth tax can be seen as a tax on the normal return on the underlying assets, as has been argued above. The normal returns to all assets are taxed if all capital income from interest, dividends, and capital gains are taxed. A wealth tax on top of the tax on capital income then generates double taxation of capital, which should be avoided.

However, as long as the Dutch government does not tax all capital income (interest, dividends, and capital gains), and it does not tax all sources of capital income under the PIT (housing, pensions), then a wealth tax can be defended as a second-best instrument to tax capital income indirectly. A wealth tax taxes at least the normal return on assets. Taxing wealth should then be preferred over fully exempting capital from any taxation for both efficiency and equity reasons as listed above.

The same logic applies to inheritance; if all income from all assets in the inheritance is taxed, then it is no longer necessary to also tax the inheritance itself. However, two exceptions can be made to this rule of thumb.

First, the value of property may mainly reflect rents from the value of the land on which it is built. This is the case especially when housing supply is inelastic, as is the case in the Netherlands (van Ewijk et al., 2006; van Ewijk and Lejour,

Chapter 4). Therefore, capital gains on property are partly unearned income, because no economic effort is made by sacrificing consumption or bearing risk to earn housing rents. Second, inheritances are also unearned income for the recipients if the testator did not have an explicit bequest motive. As a result, the inheritance yields a windfall gain for the recipient (Jacobs, 2015).

It is highly efficient to levy non-distortionary taxes on rents and unearned income in order to lower taxes on more distortionary tax bases. Therefore, (local) property taxes and inheritance taxes may be raised. A doubling of the inheritance and property tax may yield around 5 billion euros in revenue (0.7% of GDP), which can be rebated in the form of lower taxes on labour income.

5.10 Transition Issues

A fundamental reform of the entire tax treatment of capital income in the Netherlands—as proposed in this chapter—can only be implemented with a carefully designed transition path as some of the proposed tax reforms can have major economic and distributional impacts. In particular, the changes in the tax treatment of owner-occupied housing and pensions can only be done gradually and should include income compensation for the largest losers of the reforms, so as not to breach the trust that citizens should have in the government when it is making important long-term decisions. Nevertheless, a gradual transition path might look as follows.

- **Distribution-neutral recycling of revenue.** As a general rule, rebate all revenue from taxing owner-occupied housing, pensions, and closely held assets, and all other forms of capital income, back to households via cuts in PIT rates in box 1 so as to offset the distributional impacts of these reforms as much as possible. The proposed tax reforms are not intended to make the tax system more (or less) progressive, but to raise the efficiency of the tax system.
- **Owner-occupied housing.** Take twenty years for the entire transition. Gradually phase out the tax rate for the interest deductibility to the desired rate of the capital income tax of 30–35%. Raise imputed rent from 0.6% of the property value (for property under 1,090,000 euros) to 1.8–2.4% in box 1. At a top rate of 49.5%, this is equivalent to a tax of 30% on imputed rent of 3–4% in box 3. When the transition is complete, owner-occupied housing can be moved to the new box where all other capital income is taxed. Gradually raise the property tax. Allow individuals to reduce the share of linear/annuity mortgages to be able to qualify for mortgage interest deductibility as the debt bias in home financing is gradually eliminated. Aim to compensate for the distributional consequences as much as possible by lowering the tax rates in box 1 for those who are hit hardest by the reform.

- **Pensions.** Take twenty years for the entire transition. Gradually eliminate the exemption of retirees for state-pension contributions in the first two brackets of the PIT in box 1. Gradually introduce a tax on the returns of pension funds. Remove tax concessions for tax-free saving retirement of director/shareholders in closely held companies. Compensate for adverse distributional losses for poorer retirees.
- **Director-shareholders of closely held businesses.** Immediately abolish the presumptive labour earnings of the director-shareholder and adopt the Nordic system of taxing presumptive capital income. Moreover, stop tax arbitrage and ensure saving neutrality at the personal and corporate level by equalizing the tax rates in the CIT, box 2 and box 3 to the desired rate on capital income. As long as CIT rates and capital income taxes in box 3 are not aligned, levy additional taxes on capital income or wealth generated inside businesses to ensure neutrality with the tax treatment of saving in the PIT. Apply retrospective capital gains taxation to tax accrual of interest in unrealized capital gains to eliminate lock-in effects.
- **Taxes on personal portfolio-investment.** Immediately introduce a combination of a realization-based and a market-to-market capital gains tax. Introduce a dividend imputation system to avoid double taxation of dividends, as in Australia and New Zealand. Consider taxing excess returns at higher rates than normal returns, as in Norway.
- **Corporate income tax.** Immediately eliminate the debt bias by allowing for a partial deduction for the costs of debt and (newly issued) equity. Use the CIT as a withholding tax for box 3 in the PIT. The CIT can only be used as a final withholding tax if the rate of the CIT is increased to that of the PIT on capital income. Gradually aim to reform the current CIT towards an ACE or DBCFT, under two conditions: first, such a reform is coordinated internationally; second, all normal returns to capital income should be liable to tax in the PIT.
- **Inheritance.** Immediately raise rates and reduce exemptions. Abolish the business succession facilities directly.

5.11 Conclusions

Fundamental reform of the taxation of capital income in the Netherlands is long due. The tax treatment of capital income is wholly inconsistent and defies economic logic. Greatly differing tax treatments of various sources of capital income influence the allocation of capital and risk-taking, trigger deadweight losses, contribute to inequality in income and wealth, cause tax arbitrage and generate financial fragility. Fundamental tax reform can reduce the welfare losses of redistributive taxation by raising the share of taxes on capital income in the tax mix, reduce distortions and tax arbitrage in portfolio choices, and eliminate the debt bias to promote financial stability.

This chapter proposes a uniform tax regime for all capital income for capital income deriving from savings, portfolio-investments, housing, business ownership, and pension funds. A flat tax rate above a general exemption is applied to all interest, dividend, capital gains, rents, and rental values. Possibly, a somewhat lower tax rate on capital income earned by pension funds might be applied. Capital gains on all assets can be taxed with a capital gains tax on market-to-market basis for liquid assets and on realization basis for illiquid assets.

The tax-favoured status of debt financing should be abolished entirely; the tax treatment of debt finance should be identical to that of equity finance by neutralizing the impact of the mortgage interest deduction and by treating debt and equity symmetrically in the CIT. Inheritances and immovable properties can be taxed at higher rates to shift the tax burden to less distortionary tax bases.

All revenue generated by this fundamental tax reform should be rebated by reductions in tax rates on labour income, the elimination of the property transactions tax, and the introduction of tax credits in the PIT for corporate taxes paid on dividends and capital gains.

The tax regime for capital income then no longer unnecessarily distorts the allocation of capital and risk of the Dutch economy, potentially yields large efficiency and equity gains and makes the Dutch economy financially less fragile.

Appendix

This Appendix provides the sources of Table 5.1, the calculation of the revenue cost of the tax treatment of owner-occupied housing and pensions and the data used in Figure 5.1.

Sources of Table 5.1

Unless indicated otherwise, all data are from Statistics Netherlands (2019d). The revenue loss due to deductible pension contributions amounts to 19.78 billion euros (Ministry of Finance, 2019a). Tax revenues in box 2 and box 3 are available only for the year 2016 and are derived from personal communications with the Ministry of Finance. Revenues from the property tax are taken from Statistics Netherlands (2018). The tax rates for box 1, box 2, box 3, the inheritance and gift tax, the CIT, the dividend withholding tax, and the property transactions tax in 2018 all come from the web site of the Tax Authorities.[19] This also applies to the

[19] See www.belastingdienst.nl.

rent imputation for owner-occupied housing. All tax rates in box 3 have been converted into an effective rate of the wealth tax. In box 3, 30% tax is levied on a fictitious return of 2.017% for wealth up to 100,000 euros, 4.326% for assets between 100,000 and 1,000,000 euros, and 5.38% for assets above 1,000,000 euros (Tax Authorities, 2019a). The property tax rates are taken from COELO (2018). The rates of the landlord tax are obtained from the Tax Authorities (2019b) and the bank tax rates are derived from the Tax Authorities (2019c).

Estimated Revenue Loss as a Result of the Tax Treatment of Pensions and Housing

Table 5.A1 provides the total revenue loss due to the tax facilities for pensions and home ownership. This calculation is made by assuming that capital income of pension funds and owner-occupied housing are taxed under the same regime as private saving and portfolio investment. Moreover, the tax rates in the PIT on workers and retirees are equalized by eliminating the reduced rates in the PIT for retirees. This is a rough ex ante estimate of the budgetary impact of the tax treatment of owner-occupied housing and pensions.

The low tax rate on pensioners relative to workers cost 6.5 billion euros in 2017 on a net basis. Not only are pension contributions deductible, future pension benefits are taxed at lower rates. The net benefit is equal to the tax differential between workers and retirees of 17% (CPB, 2010). The revenue loss due to deductible pension contributions is 19.78 billion euros (Ministry of Finance,

Table 5.A1 Net revenue loss of the tax treatment of owner-occupied housing and pensions (in billion euros)

Pensions		
Revenue loss because pension contributions are deductible at higher rates than pension benefits are taxed	17% of 26.873 billion euros pension contributions	6.5
Untaxed capital incomes pension funds	Average of 1.2% over pension wealth of 1,300 billion euros	15.6
Total revenue loss of tax treatment of pensions		22.1
Owner-occupied housing		
Revenue loss due to mortgage-interest deduction minus tax on imputed rent		7.0
Untaxed net wealth of owner-occupied housing	Average of 1.2% over 491 billion euros net property value	5.9
Total revenue loss of tax treatment owner-occupied housing		12.9
Total revenue loss of tax treatment of pensions and owner-occupied housing		35.0

2019a). Using an effective deduction rate of 52% on pension contributions (CPB, 2010), total pension contributions are estimated to be 38.0 billion euros. The net revenue loss amounts to 17% of the pension contributions of 38.0 billion euros.

In addition, the government loses 15.6 billion euros in revenue in box 3, because capital incomes of pension funds are not taxed. This is equivalent to an average of a 1.2% wealth tax over approximately 1,300 billion euros of pension assets in 2018 (De Nederlandsche Bank, 2019). Although the wealth tax in box 3 has been made progressive in the meantime, it was introduced in a budget-neutral way in 2017 (House of Representatives, 2015). This implies that the rate of the wealth tax in box 3 is still approximately 1.2%.

For owner-occupied housing, the revenue loss from the mortgage interest deduction minus the tax on imputed rent is 7.0 billion euros (Ministry of Finance, 2019a). In addition, the government loses 5.9 billion euros in box 3 because the net property value is not liable to wealth taxation in box 3. Once again, it has been assumed that the wealth tax in box 3 is 1.2%. This yields a revenue loss of 1.2% of 491 billion euros in net property wealth. This net value of owner-occupied housing is the gross value (1,199 billion euros; Statistics Netherlands, 2019a) minus total mortgage debts (708 billion euros; Statistics Netherlands, 2019a).

Taken together, the tax facilities for pensions and owner-occupied housing result in a revenue loss of 6.5 + 15.6 + 7.0 + 5.9 = 35.0 billion euros. A reduction in the tax rate of 1 percentage point in all tax brackets costs 3.799 billion euros (Ministry of Finance, 2019c). Hence, tax rates on labour income can, ex ante, be reduced in all brackets by more than 9 percentage points if pensions and owner-occupied housing are taxed in the same way as savings and portfolio investments in box 3.

Data for Figure 5.1

All tax data in Figure 5.1 come from the European Commission (2018). The implicit tax rates on capital income and the revenue shares of taxes on capital income are weighted with GDP for each country in 2017. Data for GDP are taken from the Eurostat database (http://ec.europa.eu/eurostat/data/database).

References

Admati, A. and Hellwig, M. (2013), *The Banker's New Clothes: What's Wrong with Banking and What to Do about It*, Princeton University Press, Princeton, NJ.

Atkinson, A. B. and Stiglitz, J. B. (1976), 'The design of tax structure: direct versus indirect taxation', *Journal of Public Economics*, 6, 55–75.

Auerbach, A. J. (1991), 'Retrospective capital gains taxation', *American Economic Review*, 81(1), 167–78.

Auerbach, A. J. and Bradford, D. F. (2004), 'Generalized cash-flow taxation', *Journal of Public Economics*, 88, 957–80.

Auerbach, A. J., Devereux, M. P., Keen, M., and Vella, J. (2017), 'Destination based cash flow taxation', Oxford University Centre for Business Taxation Working Paper no. 17/01, Oxford University.

Banks, J. and Diamond, P. A. (2010), 'The base for direct taxation', in J. Mirrlees, S. Adam, T. Besley, R. Blundell, S. Bond, R. Chote, M. Gammie, P. Johnson, G. Myles, and J. Poterba (eds), *Dimensions of Tax Design: The Mirrlees Review*, Volume 1, Oxford University Press for the Institute for Fiscal Studies, Oxford, pp. 548–648.

Bettendorf, L., Lejour, A., and van 't Riet, M. (2017), 'Tax bunching by owners of small corporations', *De Economist*, 165, 411–38.

Bradford, D. F. (1995), 'Fixing capital gains: symmetry, consistency and correctness in the taxation of financial instruments', *Tax Law Review*, 50, 731–85.

Brülhart, M., Gruber, J., Krapf, M., and Schmidheiny, K. (2017), 'The elasticity of taxable wealth: evidence from Switzerland', working paper, University of Lausanne.

Caminada, K., Goudswaard, K., and Knoef, M. (2014), 'Vermogen in Nederland gelijker verdeeld sinds eind negentiende eeuw', *Me Judice*, 27 June.

Chamley, C. (1986), 'Optimal taxation of capital income in general equilibrium with infinite lives', *Econometrica*, 54, 607–22.

Christiansen, V. and Tuomala, M. (2008), 'On taxing capital income with income shifting', *International Tax and Public Finance*, 15, 527–45.

Cnossen, S. (1998), *Vermogensrendementsheffing: Vondst of Miskleun?*, OCfEB, Rotterdam.

Cnossen, S. and Bovenberg, A. L. (2001), 'Fundamental tax reform in the Netherlands', *International Tax and Public Finance*, 8, 471–84.

COELO (2018), *Atlas van de Lokale Lasten 2018*, COELO, Groningen.

Commissie Inkomstenbelasting en Toeslagen (2013), *Naar een Activerender Belastingstelsel—Eindrapport*, Ministry of Finance, The Hague.

CPB (2010), 'Vergrijzing verdeeld—Toekomst van de Nederlandse overheidsfinanciën', CPB Speciale Publicatie no. 86, CPB, The Hague.

De Mooij, R. A. (2011), 'The tax elasticity of corporate debt: a synthesis of size and variations', IMF Working Paper no. 11/95, IMF, Washington, DC.

De Mooij, R. A. and Keen, M. (2016), 'Debt, taxes, and banks', *Journal of Money, Credit and Banking*, 48, 5–33.

De Nederlandsche Bank (2019), 'Statistieken: toezichtsgegevens pensioenfondsen' (https://statistiek.dnb.nl/downloads/index.aspx#/?theme=pensioenfondsen).

Diamond, P. A. and Saez, E. (2011), 'The case for a progressive income tax', *Journal of Economic Perspectives*, 25(4), 165–90.

Diamond, P. A. and Spinnewijn, J. (2011), 'Capital income taxes with heterogeneous discount rates', *American Economic Journal: Economic Policy*, 3, 52–76.

Erosa, A. and Gervais, M. (2002), 'Optimal taxation in life-cycle economies', *Journal of Economic Theory*, 105, 338–69.

European Central Bank (2018), 'Statistical data warehouse, ESRB risk dashboard' (sdw.ecb.europa.eu).

European Commission (2018), *Taxation Trends in the European Union*, European Commission, Brussels.

FD (2018), 'Haalt de gehate spaartaks 2020?', *Het Financieele Dagblad*, 21 December 2018 (https://fd.nl/economie-politiek/1282589/haalt-de-gehate-spaartaks-2020).

Frederik, J. (2014), 'De ongelijkheid in Nederland is waarschijnlijk groter dan gedacht', *De Correspondent*, 5 May 2014 (https://decorrespondent.nl/1112/de-ongelijkheid-in-nederland-is-waarschijnlijk-groter-dan-gedacht/66899364488-b3ea020a).

Fuest, C., Peichl, A., and Siegloch, S. (2018), 'Do higher corporate taxes reduce wages? Micro-evidence from Germany', *American Economic Review*, 108(2), 393–418.

Gerritsen, A., Jacobs, B., Rusu, A. V., and Spiritus, K. (2020), 'Optimal taxation of capital income with heterogeneous rates of return', working paper, Erasmus University Rotterdam.

Harding, M. and Marten, M. (2018), 'Statutory tax rates on dividends, interest and capital gains: the debt equity bias at the personal level', OECD Taxation Working Paper no. 34, OECD Publishing, Paris.

House of Representatives (2015), 'Belastingplan 2016', Document no. 34302-3, 15 September, House of Representatives, The Hague.

IMF (2016), 'Tax policy, leverage and macroeconomic stability', IMF Policy Paper no. 16/151, International Monetary Fund, Washington, DC.

Jacobs, B. (2013), 'From optimal tax theory to applied tax policy', *FinanzArchiv*, 69, 338–9.

Jacobs, B. (2015), *De Prijs van Gelijkheid*, Bert Bakker-Prometheus, Amsterdam.

Jacobs, B. (2016), 'Langdurige stagnatie? Je gaat het pas zien als je het door hebt', *Economisch Statistische Berichten*, 101(4741), 616–19.

Jacobs, B. (2017), 'Fundamentele herziening van belastingen op kapitaalinkomen', *Economisch Statistische Berichten*, 102(4753), 416–19.

Jacobs, B. and Boadway, R. (2014), 'Optimal linear commodity taxation under optimal non-linear income taxation', *Journal of Public Economics*, 117, 201–10.

Jacobs, B. and Bovenberg, A. L. (2010), 'Human capital and optimal positive taxation of capital income', *International Tax and Public Finance*, 17(5), 451–78.

Jacobs, B. and Rusu, A. V. (2018), 'Why is the long-run tax on capital income zero? Explaining the Chamley–Judd result', working paper, Erasmus University Rotterdam.

Jakobsen, K., Jakobsen, K., Kleven, H., and Zucman, G. (2020), 'Wealth taxation and wealth accumulation: theory and evidence from Denmark', *Quarterly Journal of Economics*, 135, 329–88.

Judd, K. L. (1985), 'Redistributive taxation in a simple perfect foresight model', *Journal of Public Economics*, 28, 59–83.

Kleven, H. J. and Schultz, E. A. (2014), 'Estimating taxable income responses using Danish tax reforms', *American Economic Journal: Economic Policy*, 6, 271–301.

Ministry of Finance (2016), 'Heffing in box 3 op basis van werkelijk rendement', Dutch Ministry of Finance, The Hague.

Ministry of Finance (2019a), 'Miljoenennota 2019', Dutch Ministry of Finance, The Hague (https://www.rijksoverheid.nl/documenten/begrotingen/2018/09/18/miljoenennota-2019).

Ministry of Finance (2019b), 'Wet excessief lenen bij eigen vennootschap—memorie van toelichting', Dutch Ministry of Finance, The Hague (https://www.internetconsultatie.nl/bovenmatiglenen).

Ministry of Finance (2019c), 'Sleuteltabel 2019', Dutch Ministry of Finance, The Hague (https://www.rijksoverheid.nl/documenten/kamerstukken/2018/09/18/bijlage-1.-sleuteltabel-2019).

Mirrlees, J., Adam, S., Besley, T., Blundell, R., Bond, S., Chote, R., Gammie, M., Johnson, P., Myles, G., and Poterba, J. (2011), *Tax by Design: The Mirrlees Review*, Oxford University Press, Oxford.

Mirrlees, J. A. (1976), 'Optimal tax theory: a synthesis', *Journal of Public Economics*, 6, 327–58.

OECD (2019), 'OECD data: household debt', OECD Publishing, Paris.

Piketty, T. (2014), *Capital in the Twenty-First Century*, Belknap Press, Cambridge, MA.

Piketty, T. and Saez, E. (2013), 'A theory of optimal inheritance taxation', *Econometrica*, 81, 1851–86.

Saez, E. and Stantcheva, S. (2016), 'A simpler theory of optimal capital taxation', *Journal of Public Economics*, 162, 120–42.

Seim, D. (2017), 'Behavioral responses to wealth taxes: evidence from Sweden', *American Economic Journal: Economic Policy*, 9, 395–421.

Snel, M. (2019), 'Bouwstenen voor een beter belastingstelsel,', Kamerbrief 2019-0000062470, 15 April, House of Representatives, The Hague.

Sørensen, P. B. (2010), 'Dual income taxes: a Nordic tax system', in I. Claus, N. Gemmell, M. Harding, and D. White (eds), *Tax Reform in Open Economies*, Edward Elgar, Cheltenham, pp. 78–108.

Spiritus, K. and Boadway, R. (2017), 'Optimal taxation of risky capital income: the rate of return allowance', CESifo Working Paper no. 6297.

Statistics Netherlands (2018), 'Gemeenten heffen 9,7 miljard euro in 2018' (https://www.cbs.nl/nl-nl/nieuws/2018/09/gemeenten-heffen-9-7-miljard-euro-in-2018).

Statistics Netherlands (2019a), 'Ongelijkheid in inkomen en vermogen; huishoudens' (https://www.cbs.nl/nl-nl/achtergrond/2019/19/ongelijkheid-in-inkomen-en-vermogen).

Statistics Netherlands (2019b), 'Vermogen van huishoudens; huishoudenskenmerken, vermogensbestanddelen' (https://www.cbs.nl/nl-nl/cijfers/detail/83834NED).

Statistics Netherlands (2019c), 'Overheidsbalans; activa en passiva' (https://www.cbs.nl/nl-nl/cijfers/detail/84422NED).

Statistics Netherlands (2019d), 'Overheid; ontvangen belastingen en wettelijke premies' (https://www.cbs.nl/nl-nl/cijfers/detail/84120NED).

Studiecommissie Belastingstelsel (2010), *Continuïteit en Vernieuwing: Een Visie op het Belastingstelsel*, Ministry of Finance, The Hague.

Studiegroep Duurzame Groei (2016), *Kiezen voor Duurzame Groei*, Ministry of Economic Affairs and Climate Policy, The Hague.

Tax Authorities (2019a), 'Berekening belasting over inkomen uit vermogen over 2018', Belastingdienst, Heerlen.

Tax Authorities (2019b), 'Berekening verhuurderheffing', Belastingdienst, Heerlen.

Tax Authorities (2019c), 'Tarief bankenbelasting', Belastingdienst, Heerlen.

van Ewijk, C., Koning, M., Lever, M., and De Mooij, R. A. (2006), 'Economische effecten van aanpassing fiscale behandeling eigen woning', CPB Bijzondere Publicatie no. 62, CPB, The Hague.

Wiebes, E. (2014), 'Keuzes voor een Beter Belastingstelsel', Kamerbrief 32140-5, 16 September, House of Representatives, The Hague.

Wiebes, E. (2015), 'Belastingherziening 2016', Kamerbrief 32140-13, 19 June, House of Representatives, The Hague.

Zoutman, F. (2018), 'The elasticity of taxable wealth: evidence from the Netherlands', working paper, Norwegian School of Economics.

6

Wealth and Inheritance Taxation

Theory and Evidence from the Nordic Countries

*Spencer Bastani and Daniel Waldenström**

6.1 Wealth Taxation

A wealth tax commonly refers to as a tax on the stock of net household wealth.[1] The exact definition of the wealth tax base varies across jurisdictions and over time, but in principle it includes all kinds of real estate property (housing, holiday homes, land, etc.), financial assets in bank deposits, fixed-interest securities, and corporate shares, listed and closely held, and sometimes also valuables such as cars, boats, antiquities, art, etc., everything net of debt. Because most countries also tax income from property and capital, the wealth tax tends to become a form of 'surtax' on property and financial assets.

From a technical point of view, a wealth tax can be understood as a tax on the (common) normal return on all assets. When combined with a tax on capital income that also taxes the normal return, the wealth tax effectively becomes a 'double tax' on the normal return to capital and this is not what many believe to be a proper tax system. Instead, one would typically like to have a higher tax on above-normal returns. The main reason is that many scholars view excess returns as reflecting economic rents with weak connection to individual effort. There are, of course, counter-arguments to this view. Guvenen et al. (2019) argue that additional taxation of excess returns (beyond that which is levied on the normal rate of return) is inefficient if this extra taxation disproportionally falls upon high-skill investors (who are more likely to achieve above-average returns). However, this alludes to the existence of a market failure, which could be addressed directly through other instruments (see Gerritsen et al., 2020, for a discussion). Norway taxes above-normal returns through their so-called

* Spencer Bastani (spencer.bastani@ifau.uu.se) is a Researcher at the Institute for Evaluation of Labour Market and Education Policy (IFAU), Uppsala. Daniel Waldenström (daniel.waldenstrom@ifn.se) is Professor of Economics at the Institute of Industrial Economics (IFN), Stockholm.

[1] An exception is Luxembourg that has a net wealth tax on corporations.

Spencer Bastani and Daniel Waldenström, *Wealth and Inheritance Taxation: Theory and Evidence from the Nordic Countries* In: *Tax by Design for the Netherlands*. Edited by: Sijbren Cnossen and Bas Jacobs, Oxford University Press.
 DOI: 10.1093/oso/9780192855244.003.0006

shareholder model where dividends and capital gains corresponding to a normal rate of return are exempt from tax, and any excess returns are fully taxed according to the personal tax rate on capital income (see Södersten, 2020, for a recent discussion).

If the government could tax all sources of income that accrue to individuals, a wealth tax would not be needed. Hence, the main argument in favour of wealth taxation derives from situations where the government (for different reasons) cannot properly tax capital income. This can be because the returns on many assets are deliberately not taxed (e.g. housing wealth) and, when they are taxed, there are problems to do so properly. Especially in the case of capital gains, it can be difficult to levy capital income taxes at desired rates due to lock-in effects. If capital gains cannot be properly taxed, then a wealth tax is perhaps the only way to target the wealth holdings of the wealthiest. In short, the main role of the wealth tax is to serve as an instrument to correct for the incompleteness of the tax code when it comes to taxing capital income.

Some distinct arguments in favour of wealth taxation have been proposed. First, people can derive utility from holding wealth itself, for example, due to the power and influence it can convey (see Saez and Stantcheva, 2016). For this reason, an egalitarian wealth distribution can be desirable, motivating direct redistribution of wealth. Second, the wealth holdings of one individual can impose (negative) positional externalities on others (see e.g. Konrad 1992; Aronsson, Ghosh, and Wendner, 2020), which implies that wealth should be taxed to counter the inefficient accumulation of wealth for positional reasons. Third, a wealth tax with a large basic exemption is a way to tax the wealth holdings of the wealthiest, as argued by Saez and Zucman (2019) in their recent proposal for a wealth tax in the United States.

6.1.1 Defining an Appropriate Wealth Tax Base

One of the main challenges when implementing wealth taxation concerns the definition of an appropriate wealth tax base. Although the wealth tax, in principle, should be a broad-based tax that covers all assets, this has turned out to be difficult to achieve in the real world.

In the case of non-financial assets, some are relatively easily observed, such as dwellings, urban and agricultural land, and forest, and this is also the reason why historically taxes in the pre-industrial era often were defined in terms of asset ownership rather than income streams. However, the valuation of these non-financial assets has not always been simple. Many times, thin markets make it difficult to assess market values, as there is no proper trading and pricing that can inform tax collectors about the proper value. Furthermore, there are also more conceptual valuation problems, as in the case of agricultural land and forests.[2]

In the case of financial assets, some of them are relatively straightforward to include in the wealth tax base, such as bank deposits, fixed-interest securities and listed corporate shares. These assets are also generally denominated in market values, which makes them easy to assess for taxation. However, there are specific forms of financial assets that give rise to considerable problems for tax administrators: business assets and pension wealth. We will deal with these below.

Finally, the wealth tax base sometimes includes valuable consumer durables such as cars, boats, and antiquities, as well as precious metals, jewellery, and fine arts. All these items have sizeable influence on the actual wealth position of individuals, but are difficult to observe and tax appropriately. Thus, for practical reasons, both durables and valuables are usually exempted from wealth taxation.

6.1.2 The Taxation of Business Equity

Arguably, the biggest concern with the wealth tax is the taxation of business assets (corporate equity). Business assets represent a complex mix of non-financial and financial assets, and to determine their correct market values is, many times, extremely difficult as the vast majority of firms are not listed on any stock exchange. A large error margin can have serious real consequences when translated into a tax. For this reason, most countries implemented large discounts, in some cases total tax exemptions, on the value of business assets when determining the wealth tax base. For households, similar problems arise.

A wealth tax on the stock of capital is equivalent, at least in principle, to a tax on an imputed capital income flow. This gives rise to specific problems in the case of businesses. When a firm has no cash flow, or maybe even a negative cash flow (if it is suffering losses), then the tax can cause liquidity problems. This may lead to difficulties in the financing of new investments because retained earnings are the largest single source of firms' funding. In some cases, the owner may even need to sell shares in the company to pay the tax, which could trigger additional capital gains taxes that elevate the effective tax rates. This is the double taxation on normal returns that arises when the wealth tax is imposed on top of capital income taxes (see the discussion above). In Sweden, during the 1950s, 1960s, and 1970s, the combined tax effect led to effective wealth tax rates on large corporations of over 6% (Du Rietz and Henrekson, 2015). In other words, a wealth tax can cause both corporate finance and corporate governance problems for firms. Because

[2] These properties are well defined in terms of size and location, but their value is also a function of how much the soil yields. For example, the value of forest land reflects both the current mass of timber tracts and their future growth.

large closely held companies tend to dominate the portfolios of the wealthy, the wealth tax can generate serious problems for the share of the private business sector that relies on domestic investors for their marginal source of corporate finance.

6.1.3 The Taxation of Pension Wealth

A specific set of challenges are associated with including certain forms of pension wealth into the wealth tax base. Private pension savings in designated accounts, life insurance arrangements, and other similarly funded private income-maintenance arrangements are equivalent to normal savings and therefore not difficult to include in the wealth tax base. However, collective pension savings in defined-contribution plans administered by a third party, often an insurance company, are more problematic to include. While these assets are held in an account with the insured person's name on it, the funds cannot typically be withdrawn until retirement, after which it is paid out either all at once or sequentially. This raises the question of how wealth with such restrictions should be valued for tax purposes and how potential liquidity problems associated with such taxation should be handled.

A specific set of challenges arises in the case of unfunded pensions (defined-benefit or pay-as-you-go), where the wealth is related to a promise of future pension entitlements. Such pension assets are common in the public social security systems of many countries, but are also used extensively in the private sector as part of occupational pension plans. Because of this heterogeneity in pension assets, pension wealth has not systematically been incorporated into the wealth tax base in any country that we know of. Pension income is usually taxed as labour income in most countries.

In sum, the challenges associated with defining and measuring the wealth tax base are substantial. The exemption of large business assets, valuable durables, or pension assets from the tax base has made the wealth tax less legitimate because the principally important broad-based feature of the wealth tax is not respected in practice. Furthermore, exemptions can make wealth taxation less progressive, or even regressive, because exemptions, to a large extent, benefit households in the very top of the wealth distribution.

6.2 Experiences with Wealth Taxation

6.2.1 Prevalence of Wealth Taxes

Wealth taxation, in the sense of a specific tax on the stock of household net worth, is not used by many countries today. In Europe, only four countries (Luxembourg, Norway, Spain, and Switzerland) still have such taxes, while in the mid-1990s more than a dozen countries employed wealth taxation. There is thus a clear downwards trend in the use of wealth taxation among rich countries.

However, some countries are using variants of wealth taxation. One of these variants is to tax imputed capital income, calculated from the stock value of net assets. For example, the Netherlands has a so-called box tax system where one of the boxes (box 3) contains financial assets such as bank deposits, bonds and shares, annuities, and real estate (other than owner-occupied property). A rate of return (a presumptive return) is assumed to be earned on the net value of the assets in the box, with the rates gradually increasing in the net value of the assets in the box. The imputed capital income is then taxed at a flat rate of 30%. In contrast to the broad base in the Netherlands, Sweden levies a presumptive tax on the imputed capital income from certain financial assets (held in special savings accounts), but debt is not deducted and the same rate of return applies independently of the net value of assets.[3]

The fiscal importance of wealth taxation can be assessed in several ways. One way is to look at tax rates, which have usually been around 0.5–1%, many times with some degree of progressiveness and always with a large basic exemption. Another way to assess the fiscal importance of wealth taxes is to examine the total amount of wealth taxes (including real estate and wealth transfer taxes) paid by individuals and to relate it to either GDP or total tax revenues. Figure 6.1 presents revenue statistics for individually paid wealth taxes in 10 OECD countries as a share of GDP since 1980. Wealth tax receipts have ranged from between 0.1% (the OECD average has been stable at just over 0.2%) to 1% of GDP, with Norway and Switzerland standing out as the countries where the wealth tax has had the greatest fiscal importance. Considering that total capital tax revenues usually are around 5% of GDP (see Bastani and Waldenström, 2020), the wealth tax has thus represented about one-twentieth of all capital tax revenues in most countries.

In the Nordic countries, wealth taxes have been used until the late 1990s, but today only Norway has a wealth tax. Denmark abolished its tax in 1997, Finland in 2006, and Sweden in 2007. In Norway, the tax base contains heavily discounted values of property and the basic exemption is 1.5 million Norwegian kroner, equivalent to 150,000 euros. The tax rate is flat at 0.85% of the tax-assessed value.

The reasons for abolishing the wealth tax in the Nordic countries have been widely discussed. One important reason was the increased international mobility of capital in the wake of the capital account liberalizations that swept through the Western world in the 1990s. These liberalizations made it easier for wealthy individuals to avoid the wealth tax. Another reason for abolishing the wealth tax

[3] The Swedish system of taxing imputed capital income has some additional details. For example, it uses different tax rates across asset types (imputed pension wealth returns are taxed at 15% whereas all other imputed capital income is taxed at a rate of 30%, which is the standard flat capital income tax rate). See Bastani and Waldenström (2020) for details.

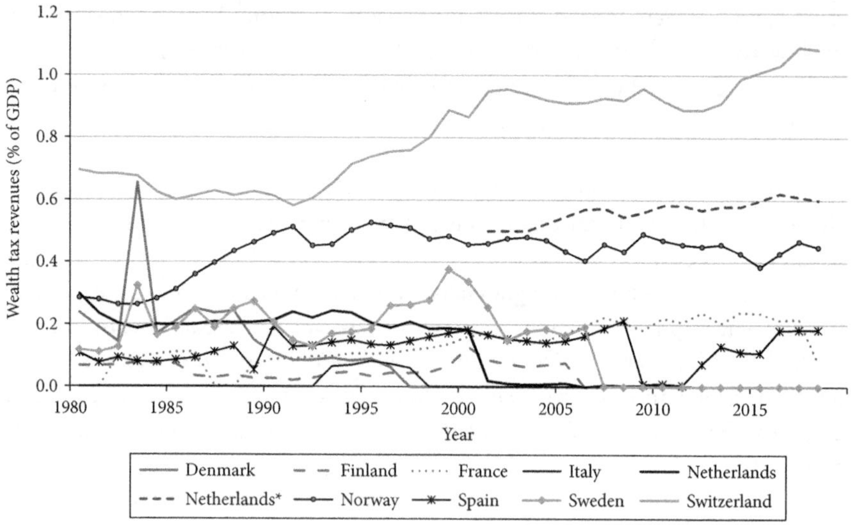

Figure 6.1 Wealth tax revenue as a share of GDP in nine OECD countries (percentage of GDP)

Notes: Series are from OECD Revenue Statistics, item 4210 'Individual recurrent taxes on net wealth', except for 'Netherlands*', which shows revenues from the imputed return to the total of box 3 capital assets (the data were compiled by Bas Jacobs using information from Statistics Netherlands, CPB Netherlands Bureau for Economic Policy Analysis and the Ministry of Finance of the Netherlands).

in the Nordic countries was the increased political tension between different groups of wealthy households that were treated differently by the various wealth tax regimes. The increase in house prices during the 1990s and 2000s had made many home owners liable to the tax but, at the same time, owners of family businesses, who often commanded much larger fortunes, were typically exempt from the tax altogether. With the wealth tax representing a relatively small share (0.2–0.3%) of total tax revenues, well-organized groups lobbying against the tax eventually succeeded in eroding its political support.

6.2.2 Economic Effects of Wealth Taxation

Few studies have analysed the effects of wealth taxation on wealth accumulation and wealth inequality. The main reason for this is a lack of detailed microdata on asset ownership in the population. Two recent studies of Nordic wealth tax data attempt to study the effects of wealth taxation on efficiency and avoidance.

Jakobsen et al. (2020) have perhaps made the most ambitious attempt so far to identify the real effects of wealth taxation by analysing behavioural responses of taxpayers. Using a rich Danish administrative data set and the gradual abolition of the Danish wealth tax between 1989 and 1997, they find clear reduced-form effects of wealth taxes in the short and medium run, with larger effects on the very wealthy than on the moderately wealthy. Connecting these reduced-form estimates to a calibrated model, they obtain an implied long-run elasticity of taxable wealth with respect to the after-tax rate of return of 0.77 for the moderately wealthy and 1.15 for the very wealthy. The order of magnitude of the estimated effects indicates fairly notable efficiency costs of the wealth tax. The estimates should, however, be interpreted with some caution because the estimates capture the effect of wealth taxes on those who are already wealthy, omit migration responses related to wealth tax, and do not capture general equilibrium effects on asset prices and wage rates.[4]

Seim (2017) analyses the elasticity of taxable wealth in Sweden, also using administrative data, but instead employing an empirical approach focusing on measuring the bunching of taxpayers around kink points in the wealth tax schedule. He studies a shorter time period and a more restrictive set of assets, but finds that wealth taxation in Sweden did not spur any large behavioural responses in terms of bunching at kink points. The responses that were observed could mainly be attributed to reporting issues and avoidance behaviour, and not to real accumulation effects.

A recurrent question when it comes to the abolition of the Swedish wealth tax in 2006 is whether the abolishment had any effect on wealth inequality. Unfortunately, answering this question is hindered by two circumstances. The first is that most of wealth data on individuals ceased to be collected after the tax repeal. The second is the almost simultaneous occurrence of the financial crisis of 2008–9. Lundberg and Waldenström (2018) used capital income tax data and property holdings from tax assessments to estimate Swedish wealth inequality before and after the repeal of the Swedish wealth tax. Their main finding is that wealth gaps increased during the end of the 2000s, with one potential explanation being that the tax repeal was capitalized into asset values, benefitting wealthier households.[5] Asset decomposition analyses also show that the poor seemed to empty their bank holdings during the crisis years, which caused widening gaps in financial assets.[6]

Tax-driven capital flight to offshore tax havens has been another, lively debated, aspect of Sweden's wealth taxation. The discussion has concerned both its order of magnitude and the distributional profile of hidden offshore wealth. Recent

[4] See also Ring (2019) for a recent paper analysing wealth tax responses using Norwegian data, finding evidence of a positive effect on savings in response to wealth taxation, financed mostly by increased labour earnings.

[5] For an individual with a taxable wealth of 10 million Swedish kronor (SEK), the wealth tax in 2006 was 127,000 SEK. Assuming a lifetime real return of 3%, the net present value of all future wealth tax payments is 4.25 million SEK (127.000/3%), which thus would imply a mechanical tax-reform effect of an increase by 40% for previously taxed fortunes.

[6] Another aspect is that the value of financial assets tends to decline more rapidly than the value of real estate in downturns, while the opposite holds during upturns.

scholarly efforts have shed some light on both of these questions, but it is fair to say that a lot of uncertainty remains. Roine and Waldenström (2009) used two complementary macro-statistical models, one based on calculating the gap in financial savings between national and financial accounts and the other based on accumulated net errors and omissions in the balance of payments. These sources are uncertain by construction, and they have been shown to be sensitive to adjustments in the computation of the national accounts and the financial accounts. Their estimate suggests that Swedes hold roughly 5% of total domestic financial assets in offshore tax havens. Alstadsæter, Johannesen, and Zucman (2019) present similar estimates for Sweden, but instead use differences in national balance sheets across countries to back out hidden wealth. Their estimate for 2007 is that 3% of households' financial assets were held in tax havens.

As for the distributional effects of offshore wealth, Roine and Waldenström (2008) estimated the effect on the income distribution by adding an assumed return from the offshore wealth to the disclosed domestic incomes of the top decile and percentile in the income distribution. They find that the effect on income shares is moderate for the top decile; their income share increases from 25% to 27% of total income after adding the offshore wealth returns. Looking at the top percentile, adding the same amounts has a relatively larger effect, increasing the top percentile income share from 7% to 9%, which is an increase by roughly one-quarter. Roine and Waldenström (2009) did a similar exercise for the wealth distribution. They found that adding the estimated offshore wealth to the reported wealth of Swedish households belonging to the top percentile in the domestic wealth distribution leads to an increase in their share of total private wealth from around 20%, up to 25–30% of total wealth. This is a relative increase by one-quarter, up to one-half. Alstadsæter et al. (2019) provide another estimate of the effect of hidden wealth in foreign tax havens on the wealth distribution in Denmark, Norway, and Sweden. Using information about named tax evaders linked to administrative wealth registers in Sweden, they found that the majority of tax evaders belong to the top wealth groups in Sweden; about 80% of them were in the top 0.01 percentile. These findings highlight the difficulties in targeting the wealthiest groups in society with a wealth tax.

Altogether, our knowledge about the effect of wealth taxation on wealth accumulation, tax avoidance, and the economic distribution is inconclusive. Studies conducted in different countries are difficult to compare because of the differing implementation of wealth taxation. Moreover, the data are not always comparable. The studies cited above have found indications that wealth taxes prevent the accumulation of business assets, especially in the very top of the wealth distribution, whereas the accumulation of housing wealth or other popularly held assets seems to respond much less. Tax-driven capital flight to offshore havens seems to be related to the relatively high levels of capital taxation in rich countries, and it seems that it is the predominantly richest households who are engaging in these activities. These pieces of evidence suggest that wealth taxation dampens wealth accumulation in the very top of the distribution while inducing the wealthiest to hide wealth in offshore havens.

6.3 Inheritance Taxation

The taxation of intergenerational wealth transfers can practically be designed in different ways. The *inheritance tax* is paid by someone who inherits from a deceased person, the *estate tax* is a tax on the assets of a deceased person, and the *gift tax* is a tax on gifts between people during their lifetime.[7]

Bequests can have substantial behavioural impacts on recipients, mainly due to income effects affecting labour supply and early retirement. These income effects are not distortionary per se, but it is important to take these into account as behavioural responses to the acquisition of inheritances can lower tax revenue from labour income taxes, and increase pension-related government expenses. This provides an efficiency reason to tax bequests (see Kindermann, Mayr, and Sachs, 2020). On the donor side, however, there can be efficiency costs of inheritance taxation if a major motivation to work or accumulate wealth is the desire to transfer wealth across generations. The efficiency costs of taxing bequests are smaller if bequests are unexpected, as substitution effects are avoided.

The main equity argument for inheritance taxation is that those who receive inheritances tend to have higher incomes and are therefore better off. For many people, the central equity argument in favour of inheritance taxation is that receiving an inheritance represents an 'unearned advantage' that should be taxed to equalize opportunities in society. However, the equity role of inheritance taxes is not entirely straightforward to assess. First, an inheritance gives utility both to the donor (through the 'joy of giving') and to the receiver. This 'double-dividend' of giving is considered an argument in favour of subsidizing inheritances (Farhi and Werning, 2010). Second, the power of inheritance taxation to redistribute wealth is in practice greatly undermined by the difficulties to properly tax the succession of (non-listed) family businesses, which represent a major share of aggregate inheritance flows.

As with the wealth tax, the interaction between the bequest tax and the rest of the tax system is important. On the one hand, one may argue that if all bequests are intentional (i.e. like a form of saving), and all capital incomes are taxed, then there would be no reason to tax bequests at all if the entire returns to the assets that constitute the bequests are fully taxed. On the other hand, given that bequests often consist of real estate, and governments lightly tax or even subsidize housing,

[7] See Cremer and Pestieau (2011), Kopczuk (2013), and Bastani and Waldenström (2020) for reviews.

or family-firm succession, which is often subject to reduced rates as well, an inheritance tax might be necessary to counter this distortion.

An important question is whether an optimal inheritance tax (that trades off the costs and benefits of inheritance taxation) is positive. In the standard infinite-horizon model with a representative agent where generations are perfectly linked through altruistic bequests, the taxation of bequests is isomorphic to the taxation of capital income in the Chamley–Judd framework. However, this is not a very realistic framework to analyse optimal inheritance taxation as it misses the fact that individuals are heterogeneous both in terms of their earnings abilities and in terms of their bequest behaviour, which can create substantial inequality in the long run. Farhi and Werning (2013) extend the work of Farhi and Werning (2010) by introducing heterogeneity in parental altruism and find that estate taxes can be positive if preferences for redistribution are sufficiently egalitarian. Piketty and Saez (2013) construct a model where each generation both gives and receives bequests and there is a correlation in earnings abilities across generations. They find that if those who receive large inheritances are more likely to be individuals with a high earnings ability, then the optimal tax rate is positive and quantitatively large if the elasticity of bequests is low, bequests are relatively concentrated, and those who receive small inheritances carry a large weight in the social welfare function.

The administrative definition of the inheritance or estate tax base is similar to the one used for wealth taxation. Thus, inheritance and wealth taxes share many practical problems. In principle, all transferred assets should be part of the tax base and they should be valued at market prices. In practice, however, many assets are assigned values for tax purposes that are far from their true market values because of heavy discounts or, in some cases, full exemptions. Business equity typically enjoys large discounts and the inheritance tax base only includes a fraction of the full value of business equity. Listed shares are relatively easy to handle, whereas shares in closely held corporations, or business assets in unincorporated enterprises, are more problematic to value. Most countries have introduced valuation discounts on business equity in non-listed firms. In Sweden, such discounts were first introduced in the 1970s, and from 1991 they imply that only 15% of business assets should be included in the estate tax base.

The issue of taxing family-firm successions is arguably the most hotly debated aspect of inheritance taxation. For example, in the Netherlands, there is a very friendly regime for family firms, which allows for large tax concessions for family businesses. Mainly the very wealthy benefit from it and the tax advantages can be very large. A popular argument in favour of such concessions and against inheritance taxation, in general, is that inheritance taxation can destroy family firms because of liquidity problems that the heirs face when exposed to the tax. Those who propose to include family firms in the tax base emphasize the equity argument and the need for treating all assets and heirs equally. However, there are also efficiency arguments for the inclusion of family firms in the inheritance tax base. For example, taxing these inheritances reduces lock-in effects in the taxation of capital income at the corporate or personal level. Moreover, some studies show that heirs may actually not be the best suited to run the businesses they inherit, implying that there could be efficiency gains from taxing bequests so that family firms are diverted to professional owners and managers (see Bennedsen et al., 2007).

Another issue is that liabilities and latent tax debt on capital gains are not transferred to heirs in most countries. These exclusions could have important real effects but, despite this, they have not been discussed much by researchers. For example, the fact that heirs do not inherit any net debt the decedent may have upon death contributes to equalizing the distributional effects of inheritances.

6.4 Experiences with Inheritance Taxation

Inheritance and estate taxes have existed in all Western countries for several centuries. Contributing to their popularity was surely the fact that they represented taxes on well-defined tax bases in times when governments typically had much less developed technologies for tax collection relative to modern economies, and also people's debts always needed to be settled at death before any funds could be distributed to heirs. Many rich countries still tax inheritances in one form or another, as indicated by Figure 6.2.

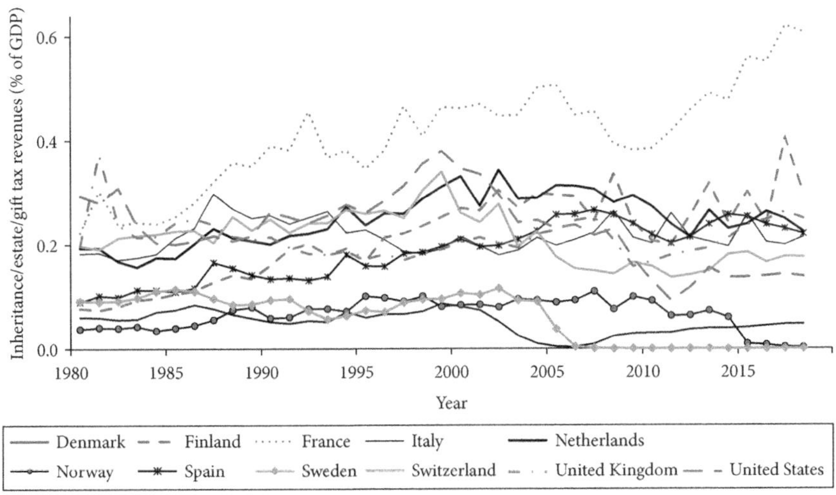

Figure 6.2 Inheritance, gift, and estate tax revenues in eleven OECD countries (percentage of GDP)

Source: OECD Revenue Statistics, item 4310, 'Estate and inheritance taxes'.

Figure 6.2 depicts the share of tax revenue relative to GDP for inheritance, gift, and estate taxes in OECD countries since 1980. It is clear that taxes on intergenerational transfers represent a small fraction of tax revenues, about one-half of 1% of all taxes and about one-twentieth of capital taxes.[8] Looking at the trends over time, the figure shows that the levels vary somewhat between years, but there is not much drift in the overall level, which lies around 0.2–0.3% of GDP over the entire period for these countries (the OECD average has been 0.1–0.2% of GDP). The fact that inheritance tax revenue as a percentage of GDP has been relatively constant over time, combined with the fact that tax rates on inheritances have remained roughly constant over this period in most countries, indicates that the inheritance tax base has not experienced base erosion in any significant way due to the increasing mobility of capital.[9] However, estimates for France and Sweden indicate that aggregate annual inheritance flows in the economy have increased substantially since the 1990s, largely due to the increases in the relative values of private wealth over the same period (Piketty, 2011; Ohlsson, Roine, and Waldenström, 2020), indicating a possibly increasing trend in tax avoidance.

It is instructive to compare how marginal tax rates and basic exemption amounts for inheritance and estate taxes differ across countries. We focus on the case when the beneficiary is a child, which represents the largest group of heirs who generally face the lowest marginal inheritance tax rates and the most generous basic exemptions (EY, 2019). In the Netherlands, child beneficiaries start paying an inheritance tax of 10% on bequests over 20,000 euros and the tax increases to its highest marginal rate, 20%, on bequests over 124,727 euros. Denmark uses a flat inheritance tax of 15%, paid on bequests exceeding roughly 22,000 euros. In Finland, an inheritance tax of 7% is paid on bequests exceeding 20,000 euros, and the marginal tax increases on larger bequests up to a top tax rate of 19%, paid on inheritances above 1,000,000 euros. In Iceland, there is a flat 10% inheritance tax on bequests of 10,000 euros and higher. In an historical perspective, these tax rates are lower than those many countries had during the early post-war era, when marginal tax rates on large bequests and estates often reached levels of 60–90% (Scheve and Stasavage, 2012; Henrekson and Waldenström, 2016). The basic exemptions vary greatly across countries.

Empirical studies of the economic consequences of inheritance taxation are few. The main reasons are that data are scarce and it is extremely difficult to distinguish real capital accumulation effects from tax avoidance responses, where the former are the most interesting from an economic perspective. In a survey of the literature, Kopczuk (2013) concludes that the effects of inheritance taxation on

[8] Taxes over GDP range between 30% and 50% in the post-1980 era and the capital taxes have been roughly one-tenth of total taxes in all countries and years (Bastani and Waldenström, 2020).

[9] The fact that this is the case also for many of the small, open European economies, including the Nordic countries and the Netherlands, is also an important observation.

taxable inheritances appear to be relatively small in magnitude. In an early influential study, the same author examined estate tax planning in the United States, exploiting the timing of receipt of news about terminal illness (Kopczuk, 2007). The results show that the estates of individuals who received the bad news early decreased in value, primarily due to tax planning. Goupille-Lebret and Infante (2018) examine the effects of changes in the French inheritance taxation on private savings in life insurance funds. Using discontinuities in the tax code with respect to time and age, they attempt to disentangle real accumulation effects from avoidance responses and they find modest effects on real capital accumulation.

In the Nordic countries, inheritance taxation has been studied in a few papers. Henrekson and Waldenström (2016) examine the evolution of the Swedish inheritance tax over a century and point to evidence that the historically high tax rates in the 1950s, 1960s, and 1970s were associated with significant avoidance behaviour and cross-border capital flight among the wealthiest. In an unpublished study of Swedish administrative register data on inheritances and firm performance, Escobar (2017) finds that firms whose owners inherit significant amounts tend to last longer than other comparable firms do. However, this phenomenon does not seem to be driven by higher productivity, measured as firm profits or owners' incomes, but instead by enabling small business owners of lower ability to carry on longer.

When assessing the distributional implications of inheritance taxation, it is necessary to take into account the distribution of inheritances as well as the economic position of those who acquire them. The empirical literature has generally found an equalizing effect of inheritances because the distribution of wealth among the decedents tends to be more equal than the distribution of wealth among the heirs (see e.g. Elinder, Erixson, and Waldenström, 2018). Still, sufficiently progressive inheritance taxation combined with appropriate adjustments of taxes and transfers can also serve as an instrument to enhance redistribution.

To properly understand the evolution of inheritance taxation in the Western world, it is necessary to take into account political economy considerations. Scheve and Stasavage (2012) analyse the political determinants of inheritance taxation over the past two hundred years. They argue that historically important increases in inheritance taxation during the first half of the twentieth century can be explained by mass mobilization for warfare, rather than the extension of suffrage. The proposed explanation is that mobilization in times of war implies that people will risk their lives in war. Therefore, people will demand that the rich also make sacrifices by contributing with their wealth.

The dismantling of the inheritance tax in Sweden in 2004 is an interesting story from a political-economy perspective. The exceptionally low basic exemption for bequests in Sweden (see Bastani and Waldenström, 2021) in combination with rising house prices during the 1990s meant that a large fraction of heirs, about one-third in 2000, had to pay the tax. At the same time, the government introduced extended tax reliefs for business equity in the 1990s, which effectively meant that most large bequests were almost tax-exempt. In other words, more and more taxpayers at the lower end of the distribution had to pay the tax while fewer and fewer at the top had to do so. In addition, there was a wide perception that inheritance tax avoidance was common, which further undermined the perceived effectiveness of the tax. When the Social Democratic government eventually proposed abolishing the tax, not even the left-wing party opposed it.

6.5 Concluding Discussion

In this chapter, we have reviewed central themes in the economic analysis of wealth and inheritance taxation as well as practical experiences of wealth and inheritance taxation in the Nordic countries. We have discussed the most important theoretical arguments in favour of and against such taxes and we have surveyed a selection of the empirical research literature.

Wealth taxes have almost disappeared from the fiscal policy toolbox in modern economies, whereas many countries still use inheritance taxes, notably some of the world's largest economies. In the Nordic countries, only Norway employs a proper wealth tax, while Denmark, Finland, and Iceland still employ inheritance taxes.

A wealth tax can be a useful instrument to tax the wealth holdings of the wealthiest, especially if there are restrictions on the optimal use of capital income taxation. However, the possibility for small, open economies to tax internationally mobile wealth and inheritance flows has limitations, especially when it comes to the top of the wealth distribution. The liberalization of capital accounts in the 1990s implied that cross-border flows became more common, and this has had a large impact on the perceived effectiveness of capital taxation in the Nordic countries.

In the Nordic countries, and in the Netherlands, the tax revenue from wealth and inheritance taxes, as a fraction of GDP, has been on an almost constant level for decades. Inheritance flows and aggregate private wealth (as a fraction of GDP) seem to have increased, which can be explained by either an eroding tax base or falling tax rates. The fact that some countries have chosen to abolish wealth and inheritance taxes, and others not, seems to be explained by practical tax design issues and political economy aspects, rather than purely economic reasons.

One important and contentious issue in the context of wealth and inheritance taxation is the potential need for the preferential treatment of wealth pertaining to family firms. In Sweden, the concern for family-firm successions led to extensive tax discounts and even full exemptions. These exemptions shifted the tax burden from the very wealthy to upper middle-class households with expensive residential property. In Sweden, this gradually eroded the political support for wealth and inheritance taxes, ultimately leading to their abolishment. An important lesson for other countries is therefore that it is not only the economic rationale for inheritance and wealth taxes that determine their support in the population, but perhaps, most importantly, their perceived legitimacy.

References

Alstadsæter, A., Johannesen, N., and Zucman, G. (2019), 'Tax evasion and inequality', *American Economic Review*, 109(6), 2073–103.

Aronsson, A., Ghosh, S., and Wendner, R. (2020), 'Positional preferences and efficiency in a dynamic economy', Umeå Economic Studies no. 969, Department of Economics, Umeå University.

Bastani, S. and Waldenström, D. (2021), Perceptions of Inherited Wealth and the Support for Inheritance Taxation. *Economica*, 88: 532–569.

Bastani, S. and Waldenström, D. (2020), 'How should capital be taxed?', *Journal of Economic Surveys*, 34, 812–46.

Bennedsen, M., Meisner Nielsen, K., Perez-Gonzalez, F., and Wolfenzon, D. (2007), 'Inside the family firm: the role of families in succession decisions and performance', *Quarterly Journal of Economics*, 122, 647–91.

Cremer, H. and Pestieau, P. (2011), 'Wealth and wealth transfer taxation: a survey', in E. Albi and J. Martinez-Vasquez (eds), *The Elgar Guide to Tax Systems*, Edward Elgar, Cheltenham, pp. 183–217.

Du Rietz, G. and Henrekson, M. (2015), 'Wealth taxation', in M. Henrekson and M. Stenkula (eds), *Swedish Taxation: Developments since 1862*, Palgrave Macmillan, New York.

Elinder, M., Erixson, O. and Waldenström, D. (2018), 'Inheritance and wealth inequality: evidence from population registers', *Journal of Public Economics*, 165, 17–30.

Escobar (2017), 'Inheritance tax evasion: spousal bequests and under-reporting of inheritances in Sweden', Mimeo, IFN Stockholm.

EY (2019), 'Worldwide estate and inheritance tax guide 2019' (https://www.ey.com/en_gl/tax guides/worldwide-estate-and-inheritance-tax-guide-2019).

Farhi, E. and Werning, I. (2010), 'Progressive estate taxation', *Quarterly Journal of Economics*, 125, 635–73.

Farhi, E. and Werning, I. (2013), 'Estate taxation with altruism heterogeneity', *American Economic Review*, 103(3), 489–95.

Gerritsen, A., Jacobs, B., Rusu, A. W., and Spiritus, K. (2020), 'Optimal taxation of capital income with heterogeneous rates of return', mimeo.

Goupille-Lebret, J. and Infante, J. (2018), 'Behavioral responses to inheritance tax: evidence from notches in France', *Journal of Public Economics*, 168, 21–34.

Guvenen, F., Kambourov, G., Kuruscu, B., Ocampo, S., and Chen, D. (2019), 'Use it or lose it: efficiency gains from wealth taxation', mimeo.

Henrekson, M. and Waldenström, D. (2016), 'Inheritance taxation in Sweden, 1885–2004: the role of ideology, family firms and tax avoidance', *Economic History Review*, 69, 1228–54.

Jakobsen, K., Jakobsen, K., Kleven, H., and Zucman, G. (2020), 'Wealth taxation and wealth accumulation: theory and evidence from Denmark', *Quarterly Journal of Economics*, 135, 329–88.

Kindermann, F., Mayr, L., and Sachs, D. (2020), 'Inheritance taxation and wealth effects on the labor supply of heirs', *Journal of Public Economics*, in press (https://doi.org/10.1016/j.jpubeco.2019.104127).

Konrad, K. A. (1992), 'Wealth seeking reconsidered', *Journal of Economic Behavior & Organization*, 18, 215–27.

Kopczuk, W. (2007), 'Bequest and tax planning: evidence from estate tax returns', *Quarterly Journal of Economics*, 122, 1801–54.

Kopczuk, W. (2013), 'Taxation of intergenerational transfers and wealth', in A. Auerbach, R. Chetty, M. Feldstein, and E. Saez (eds), *Handbook of Public Economics*, Volume 5, Elsevier, Amsterdam, pp. 329–390.

Lundberg, J. and Waldenström, D. (2018), 'Wealth inequality in Sweden: what can we learn from capitalized income data?', *Review of Income and Wealth*, 64, 517–41.

Ohlsson, H., Roine, J., and Waldenström, D. (2020), 'Inherited wealth over the path of development: Sweden, 1810–2016', *Journal of the European Economic Association*, 18, 1123–57.

Piketty, T. (2011), 'On the long-run evolution of inheritance—France 1820–2050', *Quarterly Journal of Economics*, 61, 1071–1131.

Piketty, T. and Saez, E. (2013), 'A theory of optimal inheritance taxation', *Econometrica*, 81, 1851–86.

Ring, M. A. K. (2019), 'Wealth taxation and household saving: evidence from assessment discontinuities in Norway', mimeo.

Roine, J. and Waldenström, D. (2008), 'The evolution of top incomes in an egalitarian society: Sweden, 1903–2004', *Journal of Public Economics*, 92, 366–87.

Roine, J. and Waldenström, D. (2009), 'Wealth concentration over the path of development: Sweden, 1873–2006', *Scandinavian Journal of Economics*, 111, 151–87.

Saez, E. and Stantcheva, S. (2016), 'Generalized social marginal welfare weights for optimal tax theory', *American Economic Review*, 106(1), 24–45.

Saez, E. and Zucman, G. (2019), 'Progressive wealth taxation', working paper prepared for the Fall 2019 issue of *Brookings Papers on Economic Activity*.

Scheve, K. and Stasavge, D. (2012), 'Democracy, war, and wealth: lessons from two centuries of inheritance taxation', *American Political Science Review*, 106, 81–102.

Seim, D. (2017), 'Behavioral responses to wealth taxes: evidence from Sweden', *American Economic Journal: Economic Policy*, 9, 395–421.

Södersten, J. (2020), 'Why the Norwegian shareholder income tax is neutral', *International Tax and Public Finance*, 27, 32–7.

PART II

PROFITS

International

7

Corporate Tax Competition

A Dutch Perspective

*Patricia Hofmann and Nadine Riedel**

7.1 Introduction

We start out by sketching key features of the Dutch corporate tax system. We further draw on insights from the empirical academic literature to derive a notion of what the country has gained from different elements of its corporate tax scheme, with a particular focus on schemes that were designed to attract multinational profits and investment. Implications for tax policy design are discussed. In addition, we sketch how ATAD (Anti-Tax Avoidance Directive), BEPS, and further tax coordination proposals may affect the Netherlands.

7.2 The Dutch Corporate Tax System

We start with a short description of the key elements of the Dutch corporate tax system. Corporate income below (above) 200,000 euros is taxed at a rate of 20% (25%). The tax levy is thus close to the average corporate tax rate in the European Union (EU) and the OECD (and has been so for recent decades; see Figure 7.1). In autumn 2018, the Dutch government announced a reduction of the upper bracket corporate income tax rate to 23.9% in 2020 and 20.5% in 2021, and of the lower bracket rate to 19% in 2019, 17.5% in 2020, and 15% in 2021.

To get an idea of the effective corporate tax burden on investments (which is determined by the tax rate and the tax base definition), Figure 7.2a and 7.2b plot the effective marginal and the effective average corporate tax rates and compare these to the EU and OECD averages. The effective marginal tax rate is constructed as the (forward-looking) corporate tax burden on marginal firm investments at a given location. The effective average tax rate is constructed as the (forward-looking) corporate tax burden on discrete investment projects (e.g. a new factory in the Netherlands). While both effective rates depend on statutory tax provisions

* Patricia Hofmann (patricia.hofmann@pwc.com) is Senior Associate Transfer Pricing at PricewaterhouseCoopers GmbH Wirtschaftsprüfungsgesellschaft, Germany. Nadine Riedel (nadine.riedel@uni-muenster.de) is Full Professor at the University of Münster.

Patricia Hofmann and Nadine Riedel, *Corporate Tax Competition: A Dutch Perspective* In: *Tax by Design for the Netherlands.* Edited by: Sijbren Cnossen and Bas Jacobs, Oxford University Press.
DOI: 10.1093/oso/9780192855244.003.0007

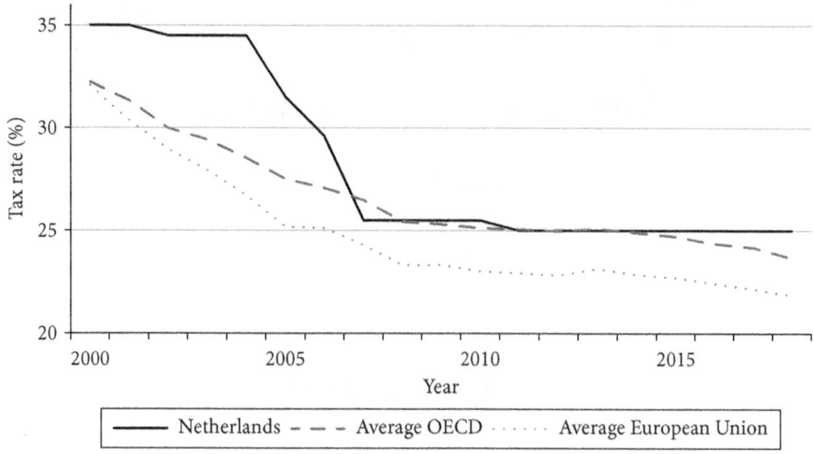

Figure 7.1 Statutory corporate tax rate in the Netherlands relative to the average statutory corporate tax rate in the EU (EU 28) and the OECD
Source: Oxford CBT Corporate Tax Database.

and the tax base definition, the effective average tax rate is mainly determined by the former and converges towards the statutory tax rate if project profitability is high (Devereux and Griffith, 2003). The Dutch average effective tax rate is close to the EU and OECD averages, while the effective marginal tax rate has been lower than these averages since 2008, when the Dutch corporate tax base was broadened.

On top of that, the Netherlands levies withholding tax rates on interests and royalty payments that are effectively zero: qualifying payments to EU member countries are exempt under the EU Interest and Royalty Directive. Because of the extensive Dutch bilateral double taxation network (comprising 102 bilateral double tax treaties), interests and royalty payments to other countries, including tax havens, are also tax-exempt, implying that routing funds through the Netherlands offers a 0% exit from the EU. Investors, moreover, benefit from a fully-fledged participation exemption regime that provides 100% exemption of dividends and capital gains of subsidiary companies abroad from corporate income tax in the Netherlands (if a number of criteria are met). The withholding tax rate on dividend payments of Dutch public limited liability companies (NVs) and Dutch private limited liability companies (BVs) is 15% but these rates are reduced to zero in double taxation treaties. Cooperatives are, in general, exempt from withholding tax obligations except in abusive situations. Effective from January 2018, new provisions imply that holding cooperatives may become subject to dividend withholding tax if they do not engage in active business in the Netherlands.[1]

[1] A cooperative qualifies as a holding cooperative if it is part of an international structure and the actual activities of the cooperative mainly (of more than 70%) consist of holding participations and/or the direct or indirect financing of affiliated persons or entities.

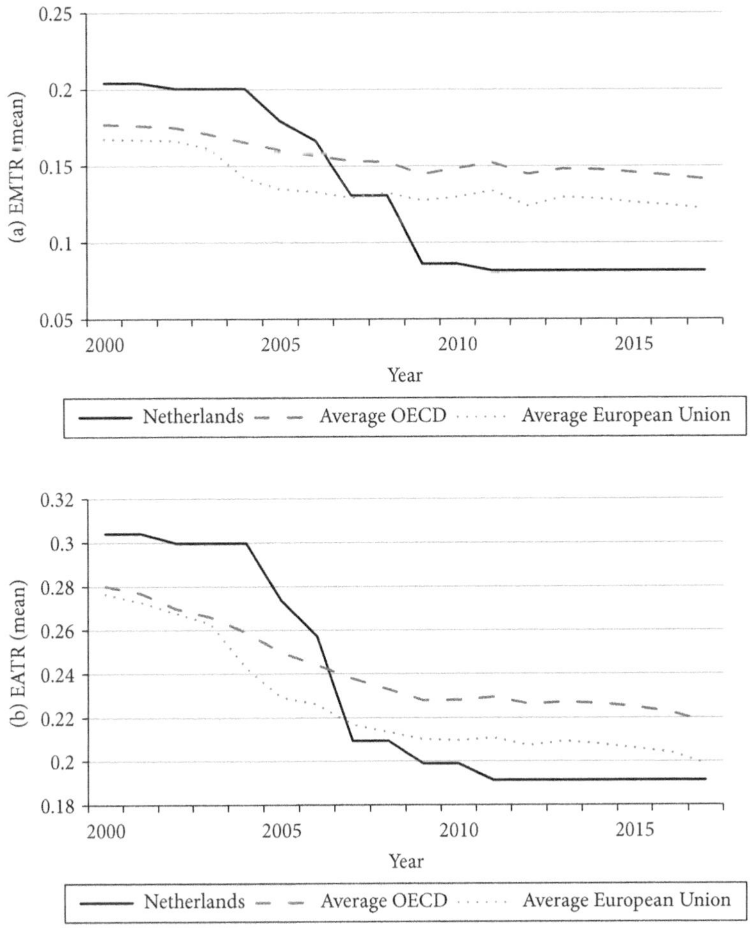

Figure 7.2 Effective marginal (a) and effective average (b) tax rates in the Netherlands compared with the averages in the EU (EU 28) and in the OECD
Source: Oxford CBT Corporate Tax Database.

In addition, the Dutch tax system grants special incentives for R&D activities in the private sector. The granted support is equivalent to about 0.18% of GDP (see OECD, 2021) and the country ranks high in terms of the generosity of the incentives provided in 2018 (see Figure 7.3).

The R&D tax relief in the Netherlands is granted in the form of a payroll withholding tax credit. The headline credit rate is 32%. For eligible R&D costs above 350,000 euros, a reduced credit rate of 16% applies (for details, see OECD, 2021). Also, the Netherlands taxes income from R&D activities at a reduced rate of 7%. Initially, a 'patent box' was introduced in 2007, specifying a patent income tax of 10% at the time of introduction. In 2010, the patent box scheme was extended to an 'innovation box' (also accounting for the proceeds from non- patented R&D

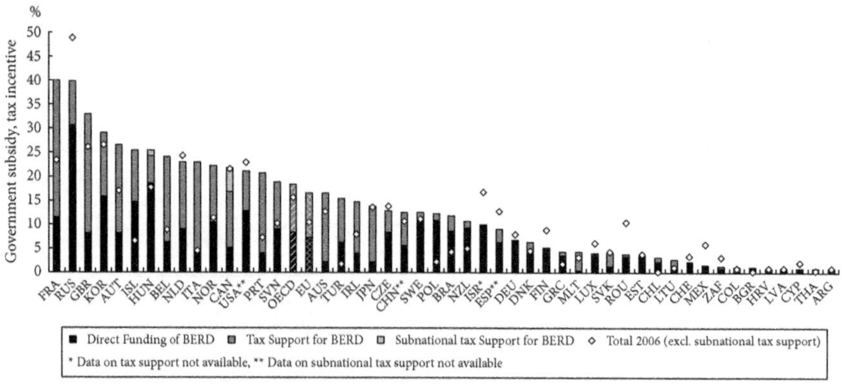

Figure 7.3 Direct government funding for business R&D and tax incentives for business R&D: the Netherlands versus other OECD countries
Source: OECD (2021).

processes) and the tax rate was lowered to 5%—to be increased later to the present rate of 7%. Moreover, from 1 January 2017, the Netherlands applied the nexus requirements specified in Action 5 of the OECD's BEPS process (but had already put R&D requirements in place). Figure 7.4 plots the marginal tax costs related to R&D investments in the Netherlands as captured by the so-called 'B-index' (see McFetridge and Warda, 1983), relative to the EU average of this index.[2] See Gerretsen and Kuipers (2017) and Alstadsæter et al. (2018) for further details.

Last but not least, the Netherlands has a reputation for offering companies easy access to tax authorities and maintaining a flexible and reliable tax administration system, where advance rulings and advance agreements give certainty to multinational enterprises (MNEs) about how the income of their Dutch subsidiaries will be taxed (Gerritsen and Kuipers, 2017).

In recent years, the Netherlands has, moreover, tried to counter the perception that the design of the country's corporate tax system is geared towards supporting tax avoidance activities. The Dutch government has implemented a number of regulations to curb multinational profit shifting, where some provisions resulted from the OECD's BEPS project and the EU's ATAD, while others were implemented unilaterally.

The Netherlands has now enacted all common anti-tax avoidance rules. Transfer price documentation has been required since 2003. In January 2019, moreover, in order to comply with ATAD, the Netherlands introduced an

[2] If investment in R&D can be fully deducted in the fiscal year, the B-index has a value of one. More generous R&D tax credits and tax allowances reduce the B-index below 1. The lower the B-index, the smaller the required pre-tax return for an R&D investment project to break even and the more attractive the tax incentive scheme. The marginal tax costs for R&D in the Netherlands have been below the EU and OECD average in the indicated sample frame, in particular since the reforms around 2008.

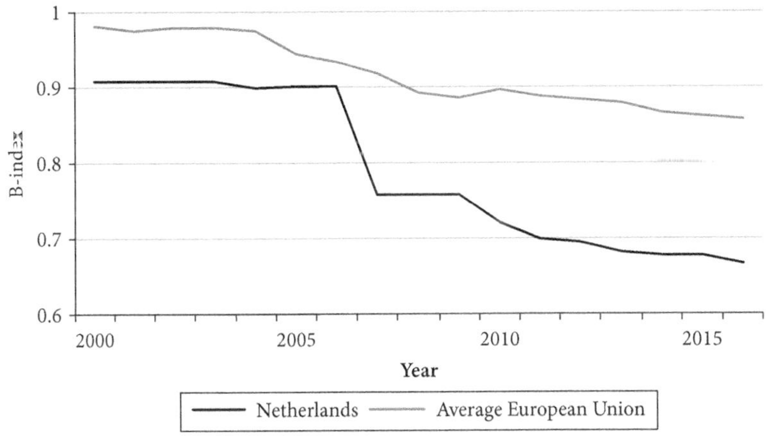

Figure 7.4 The B-index in the Netherlands versus the average B-index in the EU (EU 28)
Source: Schwab and Todtenhaupt (2019).

earnings stripping rule that limited the deductibility of interest payments and enacted controlled foreign company (CFC) regulations.[3] In February and March 2019, the Dutch House of Representatives and the Senate passed the bill for the adoption of the Multilateral Convention to Implement Tax Treaty Related Measures to Prevent Base Erosion and Profit Shifting (MLI). Importantly, the Netherlands will apply a principal purpose test and will hence not grant tax treaty benefits if it is reasonable to assume that obtaining these benefits was one of the principal purposes of the arrangement or the transaction.[4] While the provision is rather vague, it is expected to counter treaty shopping activities.[5] As another tax avoidance provision, the Budget Proposal for 2019 announced limits to tax treaty shopping by introducing a conditional withholding tax on interest and royalties

[3] The earnings stripping rule regulates that excess interest costs are only deductible up to 30% of the adjusted Dutch taxable profit (i.e. earnings before interest, taxes, depreciation, and amortization, EBITDA). The deduction limitation does not apply to excess interest expenses up to 1,000,000 euros. The new CFC provisions regulate that, if a Dutch corporate taxpayer has a direct or indirect interest of more than 50% in a low-taxed foreign subsidiary or has a low-taxed permanent establishment, then passive income earned by the establishment becomes taxable in the Netherlands. An entity is considered low-tax if it is tax-resident in a jurisdiction without corporate income tax, or in a jurisdiction with a statutory corporate income tax rate of lower than 9%, or in a jurisdiction included in the EU's blacklist of non-cooperative jurisdictions. An exception to the CFC rules is available if the passive income derived by the subsidiary makes up less than 30% of the total income or if the subsidiary carries out substantial economic activities.

[4] The Netherlands applies the MLI provision to eighty-two of its current tax treaties, which is the large majority of its treaty networks. Countries where bilateral negotiations are ongoing are excluded from the MLI.

[5] The business sector has criticized that, regarding the principal purpose test, there is little guidance by the OECD or implementing countries as to how to interpret the test. This may give rise to uncertainty and international disputes between tax authorities and firms (see Gottlieb, 2018).

(starting in January 2021 with a rate of 20.5%), which applies to payments made directly to low-tax jurisdictions in abusive situations.

7.3 What Is Gained from a Competitive Corporate Tax System?

To evaluate the current tax system and understand what is gained (and what is lost) from certain provisions, in the following, we briefly review the related academic literature on the topic.

The literature leaves no doubt that corporate taxes influence corporate decision-making. There is comprehensive evidence that tax rates and tax base definitions affect foreign direct investment (FDI) activity in a country. In a meta-analysis study, Feld and Heckemeyer (2011) derived a semi-elasticity estimate for the tax effect on FDI of –2.55. This implies that a reduction in the corporate tax rate by 1 percentage point is associated with an increase in FDI of 2.55%. In line with the notion that internationally mobile investments by large MNEs are highly profitable and yield high returns, the evidence suggests that reductions in the statutory corporate tax rate have a stronger effect on FDI activity than a narrowing of the corporate tax base. Analogously, effective average tax rates have been shown to be a more important determinant of FDI than effective marginal tax rates (see Feld and Heckemeyer, 2011). Moreover, there is response heterogeneity across industries: the tax sensitivity of FDI in the manufacturing sector is, for example, systematically larger than the tax sensitivity of service activities (see Overesch and Wamser, 2009).[6]

In addition to the described link between corporate taxation and real investments, the literature provides comprehensive evidence that corporate taxes affect the profit location of MNEs. Multiple academic papers—complementary to the anecdotal evidence gathered in parliamentary and journalistic inquiries—provide evidence that MNEs transfer profits from high-tax to low-tax countries to reduce their corporate tax burden; see, for example, Huizinga and Laeven (2008), Dharmapala and Riedel (2013), Tørsløv et al. (2018), and Dharmapala (2014) for surveys. Consistent with profit-shifting behaviour, the reported pre-tax profitability of MNEs in high-tax countries falls significantly short of their reported pre-tax profitability in low-tax countries and the pre-tax profitability of their affiliates is observed to decline significantly in response to corporate tax reforms that raise the statutory corporate tax burden. In their meta-study, Heckemeyer and Overesch (2017) review the existing literature and find a consensus semi-elasticity estimate of –0.8. This means that an increase in the corporate tax rate by

[6] Hebous et al. (2011) show that greenfield investments react more sensitively to corporate tax provisions than mergers and acquisitions.

10 percentage points is associated with a reduction of 8% in reported corporate profits, conditional on investment, by multinational affiliates.

In line with these considerations, in the following chapter, Figure 8.2 (taken from Tørsløv et al., 2018) depicts the reported pre-tax corporate profits as a percentage of employee compensation for firms in the Netherlands and other countries in Europe. The figure indicates that foreign firms' in low-tax countries are significantly more profitable than foreign firms in high-tax countries, and significantly more profitable than domestic businesses. While the Netherlands levies a moderate, but not aggressively low, statutory corporate tax rate, foreign entities in the country are also shown to report high levels of pre-tax profits relative to domestic firms. This may, among other things, reflect that special tax provisions, such as the innovation box, coupled with generous tax authority practices allow foreign firms to reduce their corporate tax rate below the statutory corporate tax burden (Gerritsen and Kuipers, 2017). Tørsløv et al. (2018) quantify the corporate tax rate of affiliates of US MNEs in the Netherlands at 12%, on average.[7]

Empirical studies have identified several channels through which the profits of MNEs are located to low-tax countries. Cristea and Nuygen (2016), Liu et al. (2019), and Lassmann and Zoller-Rydzek (2018), among others, provide evidence that MNEs manipulate intra-firm trade prices to reduce their corporate tax burden. Büttner and Wamser (2013) and Møen et al. (2018), among others, show that MNEs adjust their intra-firm financing structure such that profits are relocated from high-tax to low-tax countries.[8] Evidence by Karkinsky and Riedel (2012) and Griffith et al. (2014), and others, suggests that MNEs distort the location of valuable immaterial assets to low-tax countries in order to reduce tax costs. Last but not least, Becker et al. (2020) provide evidence in line with the notion that MNEs transfer risk to low-tax countries in order to shift profits there.[9] The relative importance of profit-shifting channels is still debated. Broadly speaking, the evidence suggests that the mis-pricing of intra-firm trade (especially of trade related to immaterial assets) and the strategic location of immaterial property to low-tax locations tend to be quantitatively important shifting channels (see Heckemeyer and Overesch, 2017).

In conclusion, low corporate tax rates are found to be instrumental in attracting real investments and mobile profits. The Dutch government has, in the past,

[7] The number is constructed from BEA survey information of the operations of US multinationals abroad.

[8] As interest payments are commonly deductible from the corporate tax base, providing debt to high-tax entities from lower-tax affiliates within the same group allows for a transfer of the associated interest payments from the high-tax to the low-tax country (without a change in the aggregate debt-to-equity ratio of the group).

[9] The arm's length principle implies that profits within the MNE must be allocated to affiliates according to their functions, assets, and risk-taking. As a consequence, affiliates within multinational groups that take on risk must be compensated for that risk-taking at arm's length.

ensured that the country's statutory corporate tax rate and tax base definitions are internationally competitive, which—as suggested by the empirical evidence described above—has contributed to attracting mobile investments and profits to the country. However, tax policy in the Netherlands has also been characterized by 'smart' tax competition elements, where the country has opted for tax concessions that target particularly mobile and particularly valuable firm activities. One such element is the introduction of an innovation box that grants special low tax rates on income from innovative activities. The empirical literature suggests that low tax rates on patent and other intellectual property (IP) income trigger significant inflows of mobile IP-related profits, reflecting that R&D activities are important value-drivers in modern MNEs and their proceeds can be disentangled from production activities at low costs (making IP income tax-sensitive and mobile). While the quantitative estimates vary across studies, estimated response rates are high across the board. Studies determining the effect of corporate taxes on patent location within MNEs derive semi-elasticities of –0.5 to –6, where a semi-elasticity of –3 means that a reduction in the corporate tax rate by 10 percentage points increases the patent stock at a given affiliate by 30% (see Karkinsky and Riedel, 2012; Griffith et al., 2014; Alstadsæter et al., 2018). The literature, moreover, suggests that firms sort high-value patents to low-tax countries, making the patent-related income response even larger than elasticities derived based on patent numbers (see Böhm et al., 2015; Bradley et al., 2015; Bösenberg and Egger, 2017; Alstadsæter et al., 2018).

Alstadsæter et al. (2018) assess the effect of patent and intellectual property box regimes on the location of mobile patents, reporting positive and significant patent inflows when IP regimes are introduced or when their scope is expanded (e.g. in terms of lower IP box rates or broader income coverage). Interestingly, they also show that patent (and hence profit) inflows are smaller when IP boxes come with a development condition and require research to be undertaken locally. Development conditions are, in turn, shown to increase local innovative activity (while IP box regimes without a development condition fail to do so). Thus, this suggests that the Dutch innovation box—which has a development condition—expands R&D activity (rather than mobile profits) in the country.

As described above, R&D tax support in the Netherlands comprises a payroll withholding tax credit regime. Recent years have seen the emergence of a flourishing literature that confirms an inverse link between R&D tax costs and the level of corporate R&D activities within countries (e.g. Bloom et al., 2002; Wilson, 2009; Mulkay and Mairesse, 2013; Agrawal et al., 2014; Dechezleprêtre et al., 2016; Guceri and Liu, 2019). The size of the estimates varies across studies, reflecting differences in the studied policy reforms and the applied empirical methodology. Most studies report elasticity estimates larger than –0.5 in absolute terms (see Guceri and Liu, 2019), where an estimate of –0.5 implies that a reduction in R&D user costs by 1% increases R&D spending by 0.5%. Lokshin and Mohnen (2012) assess the (historic) R&D tax incentive scheme in the Netherlands (based on R&D survey data for 1996–2004) and derive a user cost elasticity of around –0.3 in the short run and –0.7 in the long run.

Both output-related R&D tax incentives (e.g. IP boxes with a development condition) as well as input-related R&D tax incentives (e.g. special R&D tax deductions or tax credits) have thus been found to be instrumental in fostering R&D activities in a country. As local R&D is associated with positive knowledge spill-overs to the local economy and with positive growth effects, R&D investments are arguably of particular importance to countries. Output-related incentives in the form of low tax rates may, thereby, be especially effective in attracting the often highly profitable and internationally mobile R&D activities of MNEs. On the downside, output-related incentives only grant tax benefits at the time when innovations materialize and generate income, which may be several years after the initial R&D spending. Therefore, output-related incentives may be less effective in expanding the R&D activities of credit-constrained—often small and medium-sized—firms. Here, input-related incentives tend to be more effective as these tax benefits accrue directly at the time of the R&D spending. See, for example, the discussion in Ernst et al. (2014).

In addition to the generous R&D tax incentive schemes, a second particularity of the Dutch tax system is the fully fledged participation exemption regime and the country's comprehensive tax treaty network. This makes the Netherlands attractive as a location for conduit companies that allow multinational companies to route royalty, dividend and interest flows through the country to save withholding taxes (i.e. treaty shopping).

The country's attractiveness as conduit location is reflected in its FDI positions. Figure 7.5a and 7.5b depict the inward FDI stock of the Netherlands and other countries in levels and as a percentage of GDP. The Netherlands, despite being a comparably small country, has the largest inward FDI stock in Europe (in levels) and also ranks high in terms of inward FDI relative to GDP (a staggering 535%). The high levels of FDI inflows are matched by high levels of FDI outflows (see Figure 7.6). This pattern is widely regarded to be an indicator for the conduit nature of related foreign activities (see EPRS, 2018). In line with that notion, evidence shows that large portions of this FDI position are held by special purpose entities (SPEs) with no or few employees, and little or no physical presence in the host economy, whose assets and liabilities represent investments in or from other countries, and whose core business consists of group financing or holding activities. According to the European Parliamentary Research Service (EPRS), 80% of inward FDI and 73% of outward FDI in the Netherlands are related to such SPEs (EPRS, 2018).[10]

[10] Hebous and Weichenrieder (2014) report that the Netherlands is the most important location of so-called conduit entities for German company structures.

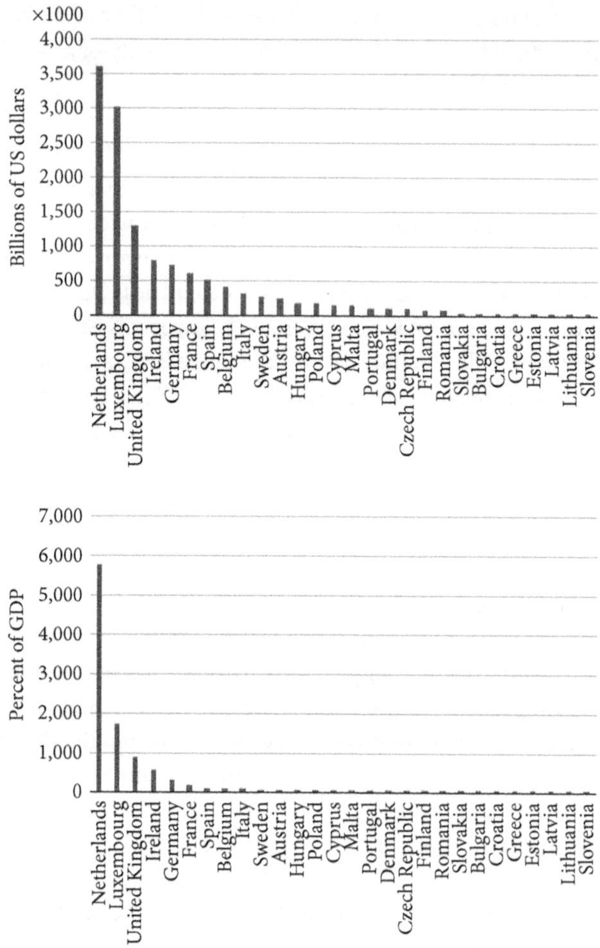

Figure 7.5 Inward FDI stock (top panel) in millions of US dollars (2015) and (bottom panel) as a percentage of GDP
Source: IHS (2017).

The total asset position of these SPEs in the Netherlands amounted to 4,228 billion euros in 2016 (up from 1,524 billion euros in 2004; see Lejour et al., 2019). Related income flows (dividends, interest, and royalties) were about 200 billion euros in 2016, up from about 70 billion euros in 2014 (Lejour et al., 2019). Tax havens are important destination and source countries for these flows. Lejour et al. (2019) show that about 60% of the outgoing royalties flow to haven economies. Channelling royalties through the Netherlands gained attractiveness in 2003 when the EU's Interest and Royalty Directive was adopted and made it attractive for companies to use the Netherlands to reduce their tax burden on royalty flows from the EU (see Figure 7.7, which depicts the Netherlands's aggregate royalty receipts

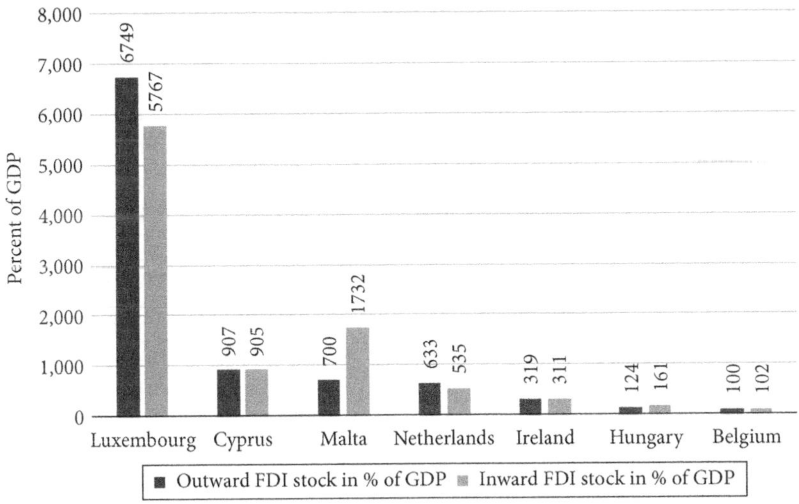

Figure 7.6 FDI positions as a percentage of GDP (2015), for member states with FDI exceeding GDP
Source: IHS (2017).

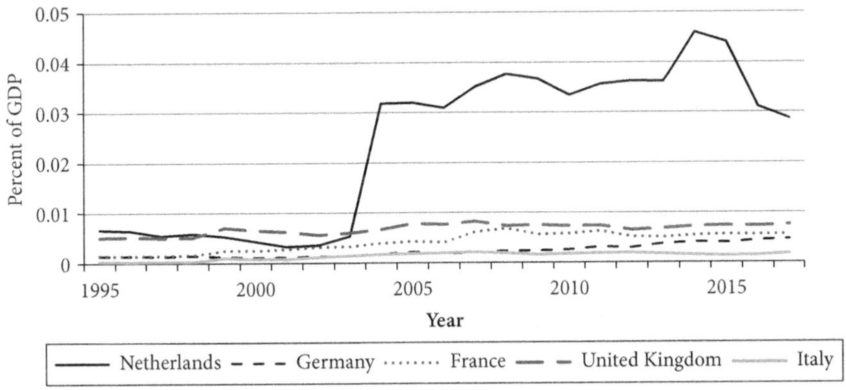

Figure 7.7 Royalty receipts: Netherlands versus Germany, France, Italy, and the United Kingdom
Source: World Development Indicators, Royalty Inflows as a Percentage of GDP.

as a fraction of GDP compared with other countries). Note that a smaller fraction of the Dutch dividend and interest flows goes to low-tax countries, partly reflecting that the direct partners are not the final destination and that tax savings are achieved later in the chain. The evidence in Lejour et al. (2019), in general, implies that income tends to be channelled through several conduit countries in a row and that the Netherlands often just serves as one link in the chain.

Furthermore, note that evidence rejects the notion that the Netherlands gains significant economic activity from treaty shopping activities. As described above, FDI in the country is mainly associated with SPEs. A study of the Danish National Bank (DNB; DNBulletin, 2018) quantifies the number of SPEs at about 15,000, 94% of which have no employees, however. The other SPEs employed a mere 8,100 full-time equivalents.[11] The estimated combined wage costs and social insurance contributions of SPEs is approximated as 0.3% of Dutch total compensation of employees and their tax payments around 0.9% of total tax revenues.

Concluding, the Dutch corporate tax system features several 'smart' tax competition elements. The R&D-related tax incentive schemes have likely contributed to fostering R&D activity in the country. With regard to special tax incentives for conduit entities, the evidence is more mixed. While the schemes plausibly raised corporate income earned within the country (e.g. fees for conduit services), the evidence largely rejects that substantial economic real activity was attracted.

7.4 Should the Netherlands Stop Tax Competition? If Yes, Then How?

The above assessment forms the basis for an evaluation of the Dutch corporate tax regime. Correspondingly, we discuss the potential benefits and costs of international initiatives for tax policy coordination from the perspective of the Netherlands (and a global perspective). Before doing so, two major developments need to be sketched.

7.4.1 Background 1: Refuelled Corporate Tax Competition?

First, several large countries recently cut their corporate tax rates substantially, including France, the United Kingdom, and the United States. Most prominently, the United States decreased its corporate tax rate from 35% to 21% in 2018. Furthermore, among other measures, it implemented new and tighter rules to counter profit shifting from its borders: the Base Erosion and Anti-Abuse Tax (BEAT) and taxes on Global Intangible Low-Taxed Income (GILTI) (see below). It is unlikely that these reforms will leave economic activity and tax revenues in other countries unaffected. However, from a theoretical perspective, the impact of the tax rate cuts on FDI in other countries is ambiguous, and depends on whether investments at different locations are substitutes or complements. If MNEs shift investments from one location to the other, tax decreases in one country (e.g. the

[11] Also, their indirect contribution to job creation is estimated to be small (and quantified with 3,800 jobs).

United States) will lower investment in foreign countries (e.g. the Netherlands). If production chains span several group locations, more investment at one location—in the wake of a tax cut—might also expand investments at other group locations. Positive investment responses in foreign countries may also emerge because of tax-induced increases in global demand for goods and services.

If the investments at different locations are substitutes, firms are expected to invest more in the United States and less in the Netherlands after the US reform. Supporting this notion, Egger et al. (2009) and Bénassy-Quéré et al. (2005) show that corporate taxes in the investor country and corporate taxes in third countries exert a positive and statistically significant effect on bilateral FDI inflows. Figures from the US State Department show that US companies invested 70.7 billion dollars less in the Netherlands in the first quarter of 2018, which may in part reflect responses to the US tax reform; note that the implied drop is quite substantial relative to a total US investment in the Netherlands of 946 billion dollars in 2017 (see Pieters, 2018).[12]

In order to retain an internationally attractive corporate tax system, the Netherlands might be well advised to equally grant more favourable tax conditions to businesses. Given the empirical insights discussed above, corporate tax rate cuts appear particularly attractive as tax rates exert a stronger effect on FDI than adjustments in the tax base definition. Lower tax rates on top of that may attract mobile profits and result in tax revenue gains (or prevent tax revenue losses). The enacted corporate tax rate cuts for the upcoming years do exactly this.

Note, however, that this type of corporate tax competition and mutual undercutting of each other's corporate tax rates—while being welfare-maximizing from a national perspective—may result in inefficiently low corporate tax rates from a global perspective. Specifically, countries disregard the fact that tax cuts attract resources from abroad and hence exert a negative externality on foreign economies. In other words, tax competition erodes the possibility for countries to tax investments and profits. If a particular country lowers its corporate tax rate, other countries will follow and hence diminish or fully erase the potential benefits in the economy that initially cut its tax rate. The international distribution of investments and profits across countries may be unchanged before and after the tax cuts, but the tax revenues may be lower. Devereux et al. (2008) provide empirical evidence for such a 'race-to-the-bottom' in corporate tax rate choices.[13]

[12] There is some evidence that—at least in specific contexts—related effects may emerge (e.g. Desai et al., 2005).

[13] While Devereux et al. (2008) assess corporate tax competition between countries, recent evidence from quasi-experimental settings at the subnational level found little evidence for positive responses of the tax rate choices of neighbouring jurisdictions, hence casting some doubt on the tax competition hypothesis (see Lyttikäinen, 2012; Baskaran, 2014; Garmann, 2018). In part, however, the observed difference in findings may relate to specific features of the local and regional testing ground of recent studies.

Note that similar tax competition behaviour between countries may emerge in other tax instruments. A prominent example is IP boxes and R&D tax incentives. In recent years, there has been a steep increase in the number of countries with IP box regimes or/and special R&D tax incentives (see Alstadsæter et al., 2018; Knoll et al., 2019). Evidence suggests that these regimes are hardly suited to expand global R&D but mainly help to attract mobile R&D activities from neighbouring economies (Bloom and Griffith, 2001; Wilson, 2009; Knoll et al., 2019). In consequence, neighbouring jurisdictions have incentives to counter expansions of R&D tax incentives by equally raising the scope of their R&D tax provisions. From an international perspective, granted provisions are therefore inefficiently generous. This implies that countries might do better by coordinating their corporate tax policies.

7.4.2 Background 2: BEPS AND ATAD—Coordinated Fight against International Tax Avoidance

Recent years have seen such coordination in one particular policy area, which is the fight against international tax avoidance in the context of the OECD's BEPS project and the EU's ATAD (see Section 7.2). Both initiatives put forth a number of provisions to tighten and internationally coordinate anti-tax avoidance measures. The Netherlands endorsed these regulations and implemented tighter anti-avoidance regulations in response (see Section 7.2), including CFC regulations, earnings stripping rules, country-by-country reporting and a principal purpose test for the provision of tax treaty benefits. While the related provisions were implemented very recently and, to the best of our knowledge, no systematic evaluation of these reforms exists, empirical evidence from prior unilateral reforms suggests that anti-tax avoidance measures have some effectiveness in limiting tax-avoidance behaviour; see Beer and Loeprick (2015) and Riedel et al. (2015) for transfer-pricing rules, Büttner et al. (2012) and Blouin et al. (2014) for provisions that limit debt-shifting activities and Ruf and Weichenrieder (2013) for CFC regulations.

As the Netherlands was a recipient of mobile multinational profits in the past (see the evidence Section 7.3), the tightening of anti-profit-shifting legislations in foreign higher-tax economies in the wake of the ATAD and BEPS reforms may reduce these inflows. Expanded anti-profit-shifting provisions in the Netherlands might, in turn, exert the opposite effect and limit outflows to lower-tax countries. Unilateral measures, such as the introduction of a conditional withholding tax on interest and royalty payments (planned for January 2021), may add to this effect. Note that the new Dutch CFC and withholding tax rules blacklist countries that levy a corporate tax rate of less than 9%. While this haven definition may appear lax at first glance, twenty-one low-tax countries are blacklisted, including the

Bermudas, which at present receive more than 60% of outward royalty flows from the Netherlands (Lejour et al., 2019). The latter flows will likely cease with the new rules; however, corporates might not stop tax avoidance altogether but might channel funds through other routes than the Netherlands if such channels remain open after ATAD and BEPS.

We can also ask whether BEPS and ATAD affect real economic activity in the Netherlands. Empirical evidence suggests that anti-tax avoidance provisions do exert investment effects. This relates to the fact that shutting down profit-shifting opportunities raises firms' effective tax costs when operating in high-tax countries and this might, for this reason, trigger investment reductions. Moreover, anti-profit-shifting provisions often come with significant compliance costs, which may amplify negative investment effects. See Büttner et al. (2018), Merlo et al. (2020), De Mooji and Liu (2018) for evidence. The tax sensitivity of the real investment of firms may hence increase in the post-BEPS and post-ATAD world, as high statutory corporate tax burdens would to a lesser extent be avoided by outward profit shifting (see Egger et al., 2014). High-tax countries may lose not only tax revenues through profit shifting (as before) but also jobs and capital investment. Lower-tax countries such as the Netherlands may actually benefit and attract more real investment from abroad. Significant reductions of real activity in the Netherlands—related to these reforms—are hence unlikely. Note that this also holds true with regard to limits put on tax treaty shopping activities in the context of Action 6 of the BEPS process. While these may reduce the number of conduits in the country (see Gerritsen and Kuipers, 2017), the effects are likely to be moderate as economic activity related to these entities is small in the first place (see above); the activity requirements in the new regulations may, in turn, even imply that more real holding company activity will be relocated to the country.

Note, however, that given these corporate incentives, corporate tax competition between countries is likely to prevail. While corporate tax cuts now attract less mobile shifting profits, which dampens tax competition incentives, real investments may become more tax-sensitive. As the latter are plausibly associated with higher welfare gains, tax competition might even intensify. In this case, ironically, the BEPS and ATAD process might—while lowering multinational profit shifting—result in a lower contribution of the corporate sector to government revenues.[14]

In consequence, tax policy coordination may make countries better off. A first-best solution would be to coordinate internationally both corporate tax rates and the tax base definition. Especially, the coordination of corporate tax rates offers

[14] The distribution of the tax burden would plausibly be more equal across firms than in the current system, where it is mainly large international firms that manage to lower their corporate tax burden through profit shifting, while smaller (national) entities do not engage—or to a lesser extent—in these activities (see Dharmapala, 2014).

potential for welfare gains, given that tax rates exert a stronger effect on the location of international investment activities (and mobile shifting profits) than the tax base definition. Along the same lines, the international coordination of tax policy instruments that relate to particularly mobile or/and particularly valuable investments, such as IP boxes and R&D tax incentives, may involve non-negligible welfare gains. Partial coordination of one or a subset of tax policy instruments, in turn, comes with the downside that tax competition in the other instrument may be intensified (see Keen and Konrad, 2013). Moreover, previous attempts to coordinate corporate tax rates at the EU level have been unsuccessful because of the reluctance of countries to give up tax sovereignty.[15]

Recent years have nevertheless seen a number of proposals to internationally coordinate corporate tax policies. In the following, we briefly describe three suggestions that are currently discussed in the policy arena and reflect on their potential effects on the Dutch economy: (1) minimum corporate taxation; (2) destination-based corporate taxation; (3) corporate tax base harmonization and the introduction of a formula apportionment regime.

7.4.3 International Tax Coordination: Minimum Corporate Taxation

In terms of minimum taxation, academic discussions have traditionally focused on 'classic' minimum tax regimes where several jurisdictions agree on a binding minimum statutory corporate tax rate. The current policy debate on minimum taxation is, in turn, inspired by two minimum tax schemes implemented in the US tax reform of 2018 (see OECD, 2019). The first is a regime called GILTI, which establishes a minimum tax on US outbound investment, namely a tax on foreign excess earnings of US companies.[16] The second is a minimum tax on inbound investments, called BEAT, which adds base erosion payments to firms' taxable income to arrive at a 'modified' taxable income base on which a BEAT tax burden is calculated. The taxpayer then pays the maximum of the BEAT tax burden and the regular tax liability.

One appeal of minimum taxation relative to full harmonization of corporate tax rates is that countries retain tax autonomy and the tax setting can respond to structural or macro-economic developments. Moreover, with a GILTI-type

[15] In tax competition models, where countries are symmetric and identical, and can commit over a full range of instruments and time periods, they benefit from a small, common increase in the corporate tax rates. This no longer holds, however, if countries differ in size (capital endowment), as then there is no harmonized tax rate at which both countries are better off (see Keen and Konrad, 2013).

[16] This essentially implies that foreign income is taxed on a worldwide basis in the United States without deferral (but at a rate lower than the US statutory corporate tax rate).

minimum taxation of outbound investment, and conditional on the location of the headquarters, the minimum tax is applied to all foreign operations, irrespective of whether the host country of the foreign entity is part of the minimum-tax agreement or not.[17] Hence, the GILTI-type regime, conditional on tax rates and locations of headquarters, reduces profit-shifting incentives and acts like a second line of defence against tax avoidance. This may allow countries to limit or withdraw anti-profit-shifting rules (which come with significant administration and compliance costs).

On the downside, MNEs may respond to GILTI-type regimes by strategically distorting the location of their headquarters to countries that are not part of the minimum-tax agreement or to countries that offer low foreign minimum tax rates. This issue might potentially be addressed by levying a minimum tax also at the sales destination if the location of the headquarters fails to do so. However, this would further increase the—arguably, in any case, high—administrative and compliance costs of the system. Moreover, corporate tax rates in equilibrium might increase.[18]

From the perspective of the Netherlands, two aspects should be noted. First, minimum-tax regimes for outbound FDI may limit profit-shifting activities. As the Netherlands arguably received some mobile profit inflows in the past, these inflows might be reduced when minimum tax regimes are implemented. However, given the recent tightening of anti-profit-shifting provisions, the change in profit inflows and tax revenues is likely to be limited (and the Dutch corporate tax rate is, moreover, likely above the chosen outbound minimum tax rates—at least, it is above the current US GILTI rate). Secondly, the Netherlands may be in a good position to attract mobile headquarters to the country under such a regime (given that it also provides attractive location characteristics for headquarters in non-tax areas). If equilibrium corporate tax rates rose under such a regime, then this might establish further welfare gains.

The US tax reform complemented GILTI by a so-called BEAT regime. BEAT-type taxes on base eroding payments may be a helpful complementary measure to

[17] One problem of this traditional minimum-tax regime is that countries may not join the club of those that agree on the minimum tax rate. This may weaken the (potentially) positive welfare effects of minimum taxes as MNEs can open up affiliates in low-tax countries that do not participate in the minimum-tax agreement and they can shift profits there.

[18] Implementing such a system may, moreover, alter corporate tax rate choices in equilibrium. Keen and Konrad (2013) review the theoretical literature that assesses the link between the introduction of a 'classic' minimum tax and corporate tax rate choices. They conclude that the introduction of a minimum tax may lead to Pareto-improvement and may increase corporate tax rates in equilibrium, but the results are sensitive to model assumptions (e.g. regarding the nature of the strategic interaction between governments). It is also unclear whether these insights carry over to GILTI-type minimum taxation. If the locations of headquarters are fixed, intuition suggests that low-tax countries may increase their corporate tax rate to the level of the minimum tax charged on foreign profits by the high-tax country and the higher-tax country may adjust its corporate tax rates upwards. If the locations of headquarters are mobile, then the response pattern may look different.

combat outward profit shifting by subsidiaries of multinational groups that are headquartered in foreign countries without minimum-tax regimes for outbound investment, or if profits flow to lower-tax countries that fall outside the scope of existing minimum-tax provisions on outbound FDI (e.g. this applies if the minimum tax is 10% and profits are shifted to lower-tax countries with tax levies above 10%).[19] OECD (2019) suggests the application of such taxes only on income streams to low-tax locations. Given that royalty and interest flows may follow complex routes (see Lejour et al., 2019), international coordination seems important to ensure that the rules are effective in combating income relocation to low-tax countries.

With regard to the Netherlands, the implementation of minimum taxes on inbound investment likely reduces the attractiveness of the country as a conduit location. However, the related effect on economic activity is probably limited, given that current gains from these structures appear to be moderate.

7.4.4 Destination-Based Corporate Taxation

In recent years, there have been discussions about a potential move to destination-based corporate taxation. The proposal was pushed by the Republicans in the US House of Representatives in 2017 but it was discarded later in reaction to strong public opposition. Recent corporate tax policy proposals of the OECD, however, include destination-based elements (see OECD, 2019). The core appeal of destination-based corporate taxation is that levying corporate taxes at the customer location may reduce the efficiency costs of taxation, given that sales destinations can hardly be manipulated by firms for tax reasons.

Hebous et al. (2019) quantify the short-term revenue consequences of moving to destination-based taxation, at unchanged corporate income tax rates. According to this study, corporate income tax revenues in the Netherlands would be largely unchanged by the regime change.

[19] This type of source-country taxation may come in the form of the following: (1) measures that limit the deductibility of 'base erosion payments', such as interest and royalties, from the corporate tax base if these payments exceed pre-defined thresholds; (2) withholding tax rates; (3) alternative minimum taxes such as the BEAT regime introduced with the recent US tax reform. Note that under (1) interest and royalty payments are untaxed up to a pre-defined threshold level (i.e. deductible from the corporate tax base) and beyond the threshold they are taxed at the statutory corporate tax rate of the source country (i.e. not deductible from the corporate tax base). With withholding tax rates, royalties, and interest payments are taxed (from the first euro earned) at the withholding tax rate, which may diverge from the country's corporate tax rate. With an alternative minimum tax such as BEAT, the firm's corporate tax burden is calculated twice: first, based on the standard tax provisions and, second, based on a corporate tax base definition that adds base erosion payments to corporate profits, and taxes the sum at a given rate.

7.4.5 Common Tax Base and Formulary Apportionment

Furthermore, in 2016, the European Commission relaunched its proposal for the introduction of a common consolidated corporate tax base in the EU coupled with a formulary apportionment regime. The European Commission envisaged a two-step process, where, in a first step, a common definition of the corporate tax base is implemented in the EU and, in a second step at a later stage, countries move to a regime of tax base consolidation with formula apportionment.

The main benefit of a common tax base definition is the reduced tax-compliance costs, as firms have to deal with only one tax base definition, not with twenty-eight different sets of rules as is the case now. A common tax base definition, in turn, appears hardly suited in itself to reduce corporate tax competition as countries retain autonomy to choose their corporate tax rate—which is arguably the tax instrument with the stronger effect on mobile profits and investments (see above). Thus, harmonizing the tax base definitions does not eliminate—and may even intensify—international tax competition in rates (Keen and Konrad, 2013).

Things may potentially be different with a formula apportionment regime, where profits are consolidated at the level of the multinational group and allocated to individual affiliates based on specified allocation keys that reflect the affiliate's relative share of assets, wages, and sales.

Fuest et al. (2007) assess how the introduction of profit consolidation and formula apportionment in the EU would change the distribution of corporate tax revenues across countries—in the absence of any behavioural changes of MNEs. Their calculations suggest that the Netherlands would lose tax revenues when countries switch from the current separate accounting system to formula apportionment. The loss in revenue thereby depends on the apportionment formula, with tax revenues in the Netherlands being higher when apportionment is based on property rather than sales or number of employees.

The assumption of no behavioural responses to such a regime change is a strong one, however. Specifically, under formula apportionment, firms have incentives to enhance (reduce) the apportionment factor weights in low-tax (high-tax) countries. If apportionment were, for example, to be based on assets, then firms have an incentive to distort asset investment to lower-tax countries as this increases the profit share to be allocated to these economies. Analogously, if apportionment were to be based on employment, then there are incentives to distort the number of workers towards low-tax locations. For the Netherlands, this means that the country might even—given its moderate corporate tax rate—experience inflows of investments and new jobs (if these factors enter the apportionment formula). These formula manipulations may then also dampen the negative tax revenue consequences calculated in Fuest et al. (2007) for the case of no behavioural adjustments.

Again, given firms' incentives to distort factors that are included in the apportionment formula towards low-tax countries, governments can attract investment, employment, and profits by lowering their corporate tax rates, implying that corporate tax competition will likely prevail. Related effects can, to some extent, be mitigated by using destination-based sales as the (sole) apportionment factor (as the latter can to a lesser extent be manipulated by MNEs).

One potential advantage of formula apportionment is that corporate compliance and public administration costs might be significantly reduced. Specifically, because profit consolidation eliminates shifting incentives, anti-shifting legislations—that often come with high compliance and public costs—could be withdrawn or limited in their application.

7.5 Conclusion

In this chapter, we have reviewed Dutch corporate tax policy, with a particular emphasis on international tax competition and tax coordination. Empirical evidence leaves no doubt that corporate taxation is important and affects the allocation of profits and investments across countries. As corporate tax rates are found to be more important in determining this allocation than corporate tax base definitions, policymakers who want to keep their country attractive for multinational business should ensure that their statutory corporate tax rate is internationally competitive. Given that the United States and other major economies have substantially cut their corporate tax rates in recent years, the enacted decrease in the Dutch corporate tax rate goes in that direction.[20]

Furthermore, we stress the benefits of engaging in 'smart tax competition' (i.e. of levying reduced corporate tax rates on business activities that are either particularly mobile or particularly valuable to the local economy). The prime example is generous R&D tax support—like that provided in the Netherlands—reflecting that R&D comes with positive socio-economic spill-overs. In addition, we discuss the potential consequences of tightened anti-profit-shifting provisions by ATAD and BEPS. While the Netherlands may experience some revenue decline through these measures, the overall economic consequences will likely be moderate. In particular, tax avoidance activities in the Netherlands are largely associated with conduit entities—but the latter hardly contribute any real activity and employment to the country in the first place. Moreover, reduced profit-shifting options may help the Netherlands to attract real business activity to the country (given that real economic activity will likely become more tax-sensitive in the years to come).

[20] Negative revenue consequences are likely to be moderate in a small open economy such as the Netherlands.

Finally, it is important to note that ATAD and BEPS did not eliminate corporate tax competition and the associated detrimental consequences for welfare prevail. We argue that, if appropriately designed, further tax policy coordination will likely be beneficial from a global perspective and from a Dutch perspective.

References

Agrawal, A., Rosell, C., and Simcoe, T. S. (2014), 'Do tax credits affect R&D expenditures by small firms? Evidence from Canada', National Bureau of Economic Research (NBER) Working Paper 20,615.

Alstadsæter, A., Barrios, S., Nicodeme, G., Skonieczna, A. M., and Vezzani, A. (2018), 'Patent boxes design, patents location, and local R&D', *Economic Policy*, 33, 131–77.

Baskaran, T. (2014), 'Identifying local tax mimicking with administrative borders and a policy reform', *Journal of Public Economics*, 118, 41–51.

Becker, J., Johannesen, N., and Riedel, N. (2020), 'Taxation and the allocation of risk inside the multinational firm', *Journal of Public Economics*, 183, 104–38.

Beer, S. and Loeprick, J. (2015), 'Profit shifting: drivers of transfer (mis)pricing and the potential of countermeasures', *International Tax and Public Finance*, 22, 426–51.

Bénassy-Quéré, A., Fontagné, L., and Lahrèche-Révil, A. (2005), 'How does FDI react to corporate taxation?', *International Tax and Public Finance*, 12, 583–603.

Bloom, N. and Griffith, R. (2001), 'The internationalization of UK R&D', *Fiscal Studies*, 22, 337–55.

Bloom, N., Griffith, R., and van Reenen, J. (2002), 'Do R&D tax credits work? Evidence from a panel of countries 1979–1997', *Journal of Public Economics*, 85, 1–31.

Blouin, J., Huizinga, H., Laeven, L., and Nicodeme, G. (2014), 'Thin capitalization rules and multinational firm capital structure', International Monetary Fund (IMF) Working Paper no. 14/12.

Böhm, T., Karkinsky, T., Knoll, B., and Riedel, N. (2015), 'The impact of corporate taxes on R&D and patent holdings', working paper.

Bösenberg, S. and Egger, P. (2017), 'R&D tax incentives and the emergence and trade of ideas', *Economic Policy*, 32, 39–80.

Bradley, S., Dauchy, E., and Robinson, L. (2015), 'Cross-country evidence on the preliminary effects of patent box regimes on patent activity and ownership', *National Tax Journal*, 68, 1047–71.

Büttner, T., Overesch, M., Schreiber, U., and Wamser, G. (2012), 'The impact of thin-capitalization rules on the capital structure of multinational firms', *Journal of Public Economics*, 96, 930–8.

Büttner, T., Overesch, M., and Wamser, G. (2018), 'Anti profit-shifting rules and foreign direct investment', *International Tax and Public Finance*, 25, 553–80.

Büttner, T. and Wamser, G. (2013), 'Internal debt and multinational profit shifting: empirical evidence from firm-level panel data', *National Tax Journal*, 66, 63–95.

Cristea, A. and Nguyen, D. (2016), 'Transfer pricing by multinational firms: new evidence from foreign firm ownerships', *American Economic Journal: Economic Policy*, 8, 170–202.

Dechezleprêtre, A., Einiö, E., Martin, R., Nguyen, K-T., and van Reenen, J. (2016), 'Do tax incentives for research increase firm innovation? An RD Design for R&D', CCCEP Working Paper 260.

De Mooji, R. and Liu, L. (2018), 'At a cost: the real effects of transfer pricing regulations', International Monetary Fund (IMF) Working Paper no. 18/03.

Desai, M., Foley, F., and Hines, J. (2005), 'Foreign direct investment and the domestic capital stock', *American Economic Review*, 95(2), 33–8.

Devereux, M. and Griffith, R. (2003), 'Evaluating tax policy for location decisions', *International Tax and Public Finance*, 10, 107–26.

Devereux, M., Lockwood, B., and Redoano, M. (2008), 'Do countries compete over corporate tax rates?' *Journal of Public Economics*, 92, 1210–35.

Dharmapala, D. (2014), 'What do we know about base erosion and profit shifting? A review of the empirical literature', *Fiscal Studies*, 35, 421–48.

Dharmapala, D. and Riedel, N. (2013), 'Earnings shocks and tax-motivated income-shifting: evidence from European multinationals', *Journal of Public Economics*, 97, 95–107.

DNBulletin (2018), 'DNBulletin: special financial institutions have limited impact on Dutch economy', 25 October.

Egger, P., Loretz, S., Pfaffermayr, M., and Winner, H. (2009), 'Bilateral effective tax rates and foreign direct investment', *International Tax and Public Finance*, 16, 822–49.

Egger, P., Merlo, V., and Wamser, G. (2014), 'Unobserved tax avoidance and the tax elasticity of FDI', *Journal of Economic Behavior and Organization*, 108, 1–18.

Ernst, C., Richter, K., and Riedel, N. (2014), 'Corporate taxation and the quality of research and development', *International Tax and Public Finance*, 21, 694–719.

European Parliamentary Research Service (EPRS) (2018), 'An overview of shell companies in the European Union', European Parliament.

Feld, L. and Heckemeyer, J. (2011), 'FDI and taxation: a meta-study', *Journal of Economic Surveys*, 25, 233–72.

Fuest, C., Hemmelgarn, T., and Ramb, F. (2007), 'How would formula apportionment in the EU affect the distribution and the size of the corporate tax base? An analysis based on German multinationals', *International Tax and Public Finance*, 14, 605–26.

Garmann, S. (2018), 'Staggered electoral cycles and strategic interactions in fiscal policy', working paper.

Gerritsen, R. and Kuipers, I. (2017), 'The post-BEPS advantages of the Netherlands', *Atlas*, 25 January 2017 (https://www.atlas.tax/en/news/item/184-the-post-beps-advantages-of-the-netherlands).

Gottlieb, I. (2018), '2019 outlook: "end of treaty shopping" for multinationals', *Bloomberg Tax*, 28 December 2018.

Griffith, G., Miller, H., and O'Connell, M. (2014), 'Ownership of intellectual property and corporate taxation', *Journal of Public Economics*, 112, 12–23.

Guceri, I. and Liu, L. (2019), 'Effectiveness of fiscal incentives for R&D: quasi-experimental evidence', *American Economic Journal: Economic Policy*, 11, 266–91.

Hebous, S. and Weichenrieder, A. (2014), 'What do we know about the tax planning of German-based multinational firms?', WU International Taxation Research Paper Series no. 2014–15.

Hebous, S., Klemm, A., and Stausholm, S. (2019), 'Revenue-implications of destination-based cash-flow taxation', International Monetary Fund (IMF) Working Paper no. 19/07.

Hebous, S., Ruf, M., and Weichenrieder, A. (2011), 'The effects of taxation on the location decision of multinational firms: M&A versus greenfield investment', *National Tax Journal*, 64, 817–38.

Heckemeyer, J. and Overesch, M. (2017), 'Multinationals' profit response to tax differentials: effect size and shifting channels', *Canadian Journal of Economics*, 50, 965–94.

Huizinga, H. and Laeven, L. (2008), 'International profit shifting within multinationals: a multi-country perspective', *Journal of Public Economics*, 92, 1164–82.

IHS (2017), 'Aggressive tax planning indicators, prepared for the European Commission', DG TAXUD Taxation Papers, Working Paper no. 71–2017.

Karkinsky, T. and Riedel, N. (2012), 'Corporate taxation and the location of patents within multinational firms', *Journal of International Economics*, 88, 176–85.

Keen, M. and Konrad, K. (2013), 'The theory of international tax competition and coordination', in A. Auerbach, R. Chetty, M. Feldstein, and E. Saez (eds), *Handbook of Public Economics*, Elsevier, Oxford, pp. 257–328.

Knoll, B., Riedel, N., Schwab, T., Todtenhaupt, M., and Voget, J. (2019), 'Cross-border effects of R&D tax incentives', working paper.

Lassmann, A. and Zoller-Rydzek, B. (2018), 'Decomposing the margins of transfer pricing', Working Paper no. WP18/11, Oxford University Centre for Business Taxation.

Lejour, A., Möhlmann, J., and van 't Riet, M. (2019), 'Conduit country: the Netherlands in the spotlight', CPB Policy Brief.

Liu, L., Schmidt-Eisenlohr, T., and Guo, D. (2019), 'International transfer pricing and tax avoidance: evidence from the linked tax-trade statistics in the UK', *Review of Economics and Statistics*, 102(4), 1–45 (https://doi.org/10.1162/rest_a_00871).

Lokshin, B. and Mohnen, P. (2012), 'How effective are level-based R&D tax credits? Evidence from the Netherlands', *Applied Economics*, 44, 1527–38.

Lyttikäinen, T. (2012), 'Tax competition among local governments: evidence from a property tax reform in Finland', *Journal of Public Economics*, 96, 584–95.

McFetridge, D. and Warda, J. (1983), 'Canadian R&D incentives: their adequacy and impact', Canadian tax papers no. 70, Canadian Tax Foundation, Toronto.

Merlo, V., Riedel, N., and Wamser, G. (2020), 'The impact of thin-capitalization rules on the location of multinational firms' foreign affiliates', *Review of International Economics*, 28, 35–61.

Møen, J., Schindler, D., Schjelderup, G., and Wamser, G. (2018), 'The tax-efficient use of debt in multinational corporations', CESifo Working Paper no. 7133.

Mulkay, B. and Mairesse, J. (2013), 'The R&D tax credit in France: assessment and ex ante evaluation of the 2008 reform', *Oxford Economic Papers*, 65, 746–66.

OECD (2019), 'Addressing the tax challenges of the digitalisation of the economy', Base Erosion and Profit Shifting Project, Public Consultation Document, 13 February–1 March 2019, pp. 24–9.

OECD (2021), 'OECD R&D Tax Incentives Database', March 2021, OECD, Paris.

Overesch, M. and Wamser, G. (2009), 'Who cares about corporate taxation? Asymmetric tax effects on outbound FDI', *The World Economy*, 32, 1657–84.

Pieters, J. (2018), 'Fewer American investments in Netherlands', *NL Times*, 7 August 2018 (https://nltimes.nl/2018/08/07/fewer-american-investments-netherlands).

Riedel, N., Zinn, T., and Hofmann, P. (2015), 'Do transfer pricing laws limit international income shifting? Evidence from Europe', working paper.

Ruf, M. and Weichenrieder, A. (2013), 'CFC legislation, passive assets and the impact of the ECJ's Cadbury Schweppes decision', CESifo Working Paper no. 4461.

Schwab, T. and Todtenhaupt, M. (2019), 'Thinking outside the box: the cross-border effect of tax cuts on R&D, ZEW', Centre for European Economic Research Discussion Paper no. 16–073.

Tørsløv, T., Wier, L., and Zucman, G. (2018), 'The missing profits of nations', NBER Working Paper no. 24701.

Wilson, D. (2009), 'Beggar thy neighbor? The in-state, out-of-state, and aggregate effects of R&D tax credits', *Review of Economics and Statistics*, 91, 431–6.

8
The Dutch Damage Done
How Tax Haven Activities in the Netherlands Affect the World

*Ludvig Wier**

8.1 Introduction

As a key component of the so-called Double Irish Dutch Sandwich, and by granting profits safe passage to exotic ex-colonies, the Netherlands is well known for its role in innovative tax haven activities. As a result of this behaviour, in March 2019 the European Parliament placed the country on their tax haven list (Bowers, 2019). But is the Netherlands a tax haven? And if so, how much tax revenue is lost because of the Netherlands' stance? Finally, what is the harm to society by multinational firms paying lower taxes?

In this chapter, I seek to answer these questions. Let me stress from the beginning that answering these questions is fraught with difficulty and uncertainty. Moreover, the analysis is based on 2015 data. Since that year, the Netherlands has been heavily involved with the OECD/G20 Inclusive Framework on Base Erosion and Profit Shifting (BEPS) and the European Union (EU) Anti-Tax Avoidance Directive (ATAD), and has taken measures to blunt the most egregious features of its international tax system.

First, I discuss the efficiency and incidence of the corporate tax and (related to this discussion) the welfare consequences of profit shifting. Second, based on the findings by Tørsløv, Wier, and Zucman (2020), I aim to determine and quantify the tax haven activities of the Netherlands.

* Ludvig Wier (ludvig.wier@econ.ku.dk) is a post-doctoral researcher and lecturer at UC Berkeley.
I would like to thank Bas Jacobs and Sijbren Cnossen for inviting me to write this chapter. I also wish to thank Aart Roelofsen, Maarten van 't Riet, and the seminar participants at the 'Tax by Design for the Netherlands' conference, held at Erasmus University, Rotterdam, in May 2019, for useful comments and suggestions.

Ludvig Wier, *The Dutch Damage Done: How Tax Haven Activities in the Netherlands Affect the World* In: *Tax by Design for the Netherlands*. Edited by: Sijbren Cnossen and Bas Jacobs, Oxford University Press. © Oxford University Press 2022.
DOI: 10.1093/oso/9780192855244.003.0008

8.2 Corporate Taxes—What Good Are They?

Before looking at the intricacies of profit shifting in the Dutch context, I briefly look at the source of many problems and ask how efficient the corporate tax is (compared with other taxes) and who pays it.

Let us begin with the efficiency question, which is essentially about whether a substantial part of global profits are believed to be pure economic rents or merely a minimal required return as the result of perfect competition. If profits are, to a large extent, the result of pure economic rents, then these can be taxed without causing any harm to economic activity (no efficiency loss), which would place corporate taxation among the most efficient taxes (along with an imputed rent tax and lump-sum taxes). In contrast, if profits are the result of perfect competition and some (exogenous) required return (determined by outside options or a patience discount factor), then the corporate tax will be enormously distortive and it will fall largely on workers and consumers.

The classical argument against the corporate tax follows a simple logic. An increase in the corporate tax lowers after-tax returns to capital, and hence leads to a reduction in investment until the marginal return to capital equals the required rate of return to capital. Lower capital investment lowers the productivity of workers, which in turn lowers wages—implying that the corporate tax is ultimately paid by workers. The key to determining the validity of this argument is to establish what the required rate of return is, and whether firms are currently earning more than this rate (i.e. earning pure economic rents). The required rate of return is often thought of as the global rate of return to capital—implying that global capital markets will ensure that capital flows to countries where it receives the highest return. If this is the case, then a harmonized increase in the corporate tax rate across all countries will have no effect on investments, as such a tax hike will affect the rate of return equally in all countries. The classical models of capital taxation did not concern themselves with the dynamics of international taxation, but instead perceived the required rate of return as the rate that individuals consider high enough for them to postpone consumption (i.e. the patience discount factor).

Where does that leave us: is the corporate tax the most or the least efficient tax there is? Pure economic rents surely seem to exist, particularly amongst multinationals. Take the example of Apple, with a 40% gross profit margin (net profit margin of 20%), a near monopoly status among its loyalists and earnings safely set above $50 billion. Would Apple sell fewer computers or stop its R&D efforts if it were forced to pay 50% in corporate taxes? This seems unlikely. The textbook example of pure economic rents is, of course, resource extraction; indeed, Norway (with the world's fourth largest oil production per capita) manages to tax the profits from oil extraction by an astounding 78%.

Not all companies earn large economic rents. Multinational companies operating in fierce competition with razor-thin profit margins also exist (e.g. Walmart). The neoclassical economic argument in these cases is that investors would not accept a lower after-tax return on their investment, but would instead consume more of their savings. This would lower the capital stock, which in turn raises after-tax returns (to their required level), raises consumer prices, and lowers wages. In the end, workers and consumers would lose and everyone would be better off if the government had taxed consumption or labour directly instead.

These are the theoretical arguments, but what do the data show? The short answer is that we do not know. We do observe that before-tax profits fall drastically whenever governments increase tax rates, but this is largely because of artificial profit shifting (as shown in Tørsløv et al., 2020). Therefore, it is not very informative about the consequences of a truly well-enforced corporate tax. An important example of the difficulties in making definite conclusions regarding the burden of the corporate tax is seen in Fuest, Peichl, and Siegloch (2018). They find that 51% of the burden of corporate taxation falls on workers, but when focusing on multinationals there is no burden on workers, which they argue is the result of profit shifting.

Adding to the complexity is, of course, the interaction between the enforcement of the corporate tax and other taxes on, for example, labour. In tax enforcement, a general rule is that the broader the base, the less room there is for tax avoidance by relabelling income (Piketty, Saez, and Stantcheva, 2014). Efficiency aside, to the extent that some of the tax incidence lies on shareholders, the corporate tax allows countries to tax foreign shareholders operating in their country, hence lowering the tax burden of domestic residents.[1]

8.3 Profit Shifting—Is This a Problem?

A separate question from whether or not a corporate tax is a good idea is whether profit shifting (i.e. the avoidance of corporate tax by multinational enterprises) is a good idea. In general, from a competition point of view, it is a poor idea to have differing corporate tax rates based on firm ownership. A tax rebate that targets multinationals will, over time, grant an unfair competitive advantage and hence put otherwise efficient domestic businesses out of business. That is, if multinational firms pay lower taxes than domestic firms, then multinational firms can deliver a higher return to investors without being more productive than domestic firms. This allows multinational firms to attract more funds without necessarily having stronger real performance (Johannesen, 2012). Not only is

[1] See Auerbach (1997); Bradford (2003); Avi-Yonah and Clausing (2008); Grubert and Newlon (1997); and Huizinga and Nielsen (1997).

profit shifting a tax rebate confined to multinationals, but recent evidence from Wier and Reynolds (2018) also suggests that it is only the very largest multinationals that benefit. Indeed, it is not for reasons of tax collection but on the basis of competition concerns that the EU Commissioner for Competition, Margrethe Vestager, has attacked the innovative profit shifting of major multinationals such as Apple, Starbucks, Fiat, and IKEA (Boffey, 2017).

Some economists argue that a targeted tax rebate for multinationals might in fact be a good idea, as multinationals respond to taxation more than domestic firms (Hong and Smart, 2010). However, this argument is only pertinent to local tax responses to profit shifting; globally, multinationals are no more mobile than domestic firms (inter-planet shifting is not a thing, yet).

Where does all of this leave us? Should we curb profit shifting or not? Governments across the world, the general public and international organizations all seem to think that we should. The corporate tax currently constitutes roughly 10% of total tax receipts in developed countries and 20% in developing countries (UNCTAD, 2015) so to abandon this tax instrument does seem risky. Meanwhile, global profits constitute an increasing share of global income, and multinational profits are further becoming an increasing share of global profits (Tørsløv et al., 2020).

8.4 The Dutch Case—What the Data Show

Recent advances in the collection of balance of payment statistics—following the sixth edition of the IMF's Balance of Payments and International Investment Position Manual (BPM6)—and in foreign affiliate trade statistics (FATS) allow for a detailed analysis of global profit shifting. I have examined these data in a previous paper, together with my colleagues Gabriel Zucman and Thomas Tørsløv (see Tørsløv et al., 2020). Our approach is five-fold.

1. Using national accounts, we map out global profits on a country basis. This yields the first global map of where profits are booked.[2]
2. Using FATS, we are then able to separate the profits accruing to local and foreign-owned firms. Additionally, by separating the production inputs used by local and foreign-owned firms, we can calculate the profitability gap between foreign-owned and local firms. What we observe is that foreign-owned firms operating in tax havens are enormously more profitable than local firms, while foreign-owned firms operating in high-tax countries are less profitable than local firms.

[2] To be precise, we calculate this as 'corporate value added' minus 'indirect taxes and subsidies' minus 'compensation of employees' minus 'net interest paid' minus 'depreciation'.

3. By using newly published bilateral balance of payment statistics, we are able to identify excessive 'high-risk' payments to tax havens. These high-risk payments are known vehicles of profit shifting, and include royalty payments, management fees, and internal interest payments.
4. We estimate the amount of profits shifted to tax havens (a) by estimating the excess profitability of foreign-owned firms in tax havens, and (b) by estimating the excess high-risk payments going to tax havens. We find, reassuringly, that (a) is approximately equal to (b).
5. We distribute the tax base lost based on the excess high-risk payments made by each country.

To start, Figure 8.1 shows how corporate profitability differs among countries. In general, a business paying 1 euro in wages will see this translate into 36 cents of profit. However, in prominent tax haven Luxembourg, this ratio is eight times as high. The Netherlands also stands out with a ratio of 61%.

Of course, it is interesting to further disentangle the profitability of firms into that of locally owned firms and foreign-owned firms. In this case, we see that the entire profitability premium in tax havens is driven by foreign-owned (and hence multinational) firms. For example, in the Netherlands, domestically owned firms earn 41 cents in profits for each euro spent on salaries, which is very close to the overall profitability in non-havens. By contrast, Dutch foreign-owned firms earn 115 cents per euro spent on wages (i.e. triple the profitability of foreign-owned

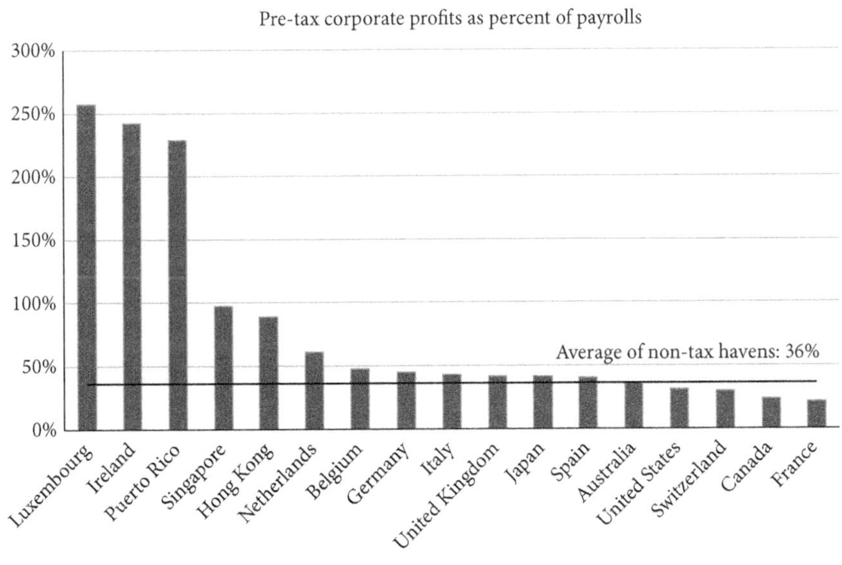

Figure 8.1 Profitability of firms across countries
Source: Tørsløv et al. (2020).

firms in the Netherlands). Standard economic theory would suggest that local businesses in the Netherlands would be put out of business and workers would migrate from the local firms to foreign-owned firms. Additionally, we would anticipate that these enormously productive workers in the foreign-owned firms would be better at wage bargaining. Perhaps, some might argue, the foreign-owned firms just have more machines, yielding large returns to worker salaries. As shown in Tørsløv et al. (2020), this does not seem to be the case. Most likely, workers in foreign-owned firms in the Netherlands are not overly productive, but instead the high profits of these firms are an artefact of artificial profit shifting (i.e. paper profits moving to the Netherlands).

Strikingly, we see the exact opposite pattern in high-tax countries. Systematically, local firms in high-tax countries are more profitable than foreign-owned firms. For example, local firms in Germany earn 51 cents per euro spent on wages, while foreign-owned firms make only 18 cents. Again, the most likely explanation is, of course, that the low profitability of foreign-owned firms in Germany is the result of artificial profit shifting.

It is important to keep in mind that locally owned firms can also be multinational (headquartered firms). For example, Apple, Amazon, Google, and Facebook are local US firms. It seems likely that the pattern in Figure 8.2 would

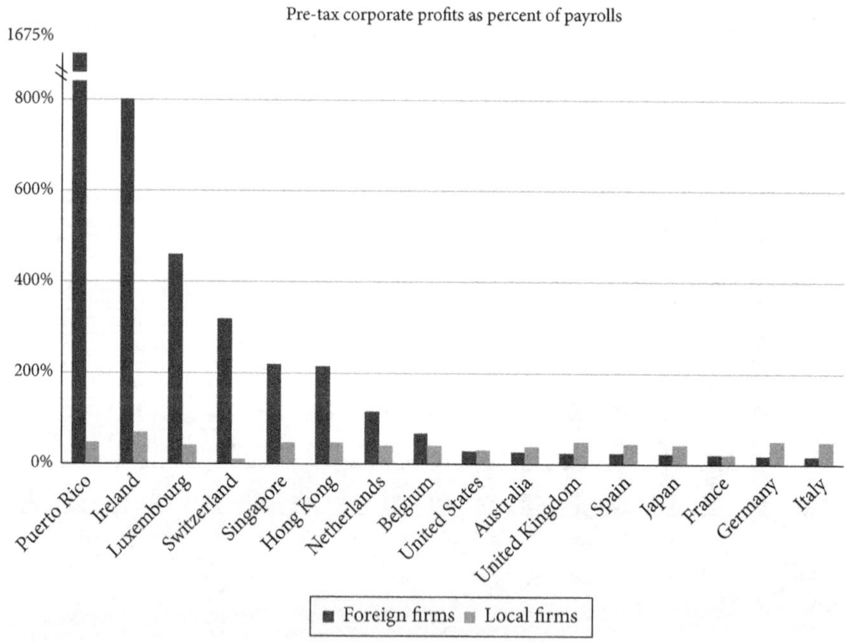

Figure 8.2 Profitability of foreign versus local firms

Source: Tørsløv et al. (2020).

be even more pronounced if we were able to truly separate multinationals from purely domestic firms.

So far, it has been established that foreign-owned firms are excessively profitable in tax havens, but at the same time under-profitable in high-tax countries. The most natural way to estimate the amount of profits shifted to tax havens is simply to assume that profitability in the local and foreign sectors should be identical. In the case of the Netherlands, I assume that the profitability of foreign-owned firms (115%) should equal the profitability of local firms (41%). Making this computation in the case of the Netherlands implies that we estimate that $57 billion are shifted to the Netherlands. This means that the Netherlands is firmly amongst the four largest tax havens in the world and is the second largest tax haven in the EU (see Figure 8.3). Globally, we estimate that more than $600 billion are shifted to tax havens.

With a clear estimate of how much is shifted to tax havens, the question is who pays for this. Here, recent statistical advances in the balance of payment statistics can help answer this. Clearly, we now have data on well-known vehicles of profit shifting: royalty payments, management fees, financial services, insurance services, ICT payments, and internal interest payments. Figure 8.4 shows the flow of these services in the EU. Unsurprisingly, we see the EU tax havens receiving excessive amounts of these high-risk payments. What is astounding is that when we add together the high-risk payments going to tax havens, we find a value of

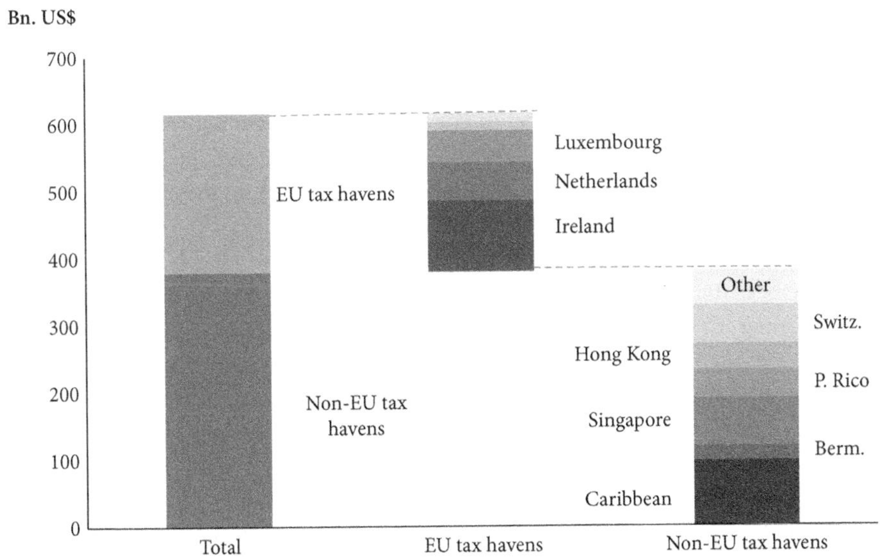

Figure 8.3 The global amount of profits shifted to tax havens

Source: Tørsløv et al. (2020).

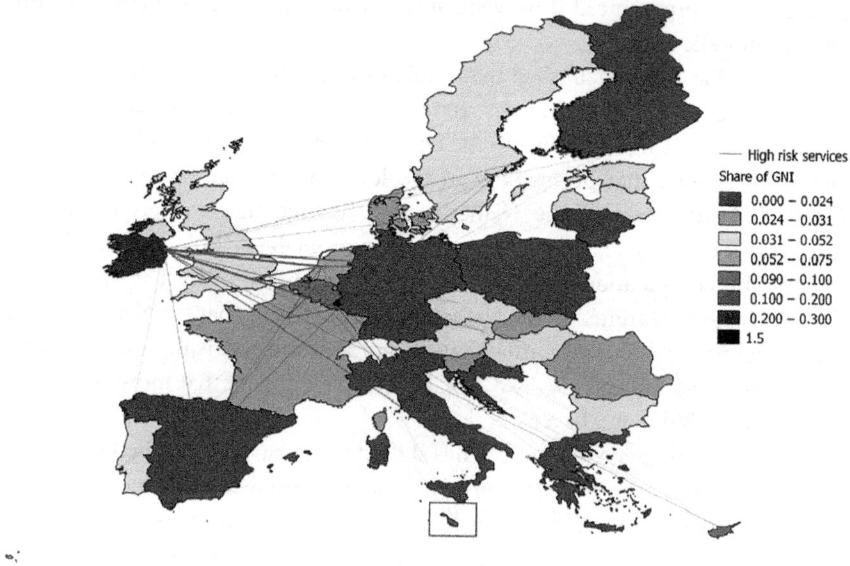

Figure 8.4 High-risk payments in the EU
Source: Tørsløv et al. (2020).

$646 billion, almost exactly the same amount as we estimated for the excess profitability in tax havens. The two methods are hence completely consistent.

We find that the Netherlands receives $81 billion in high-risk payments from countries that are not tax havens plus an additional $31 billion from tax havens—they then transfer back 59 billion euros to other tax havens, leaving the Netherlands with $50 billion net of conduit activities. Remember that the excess profitability of foreign-owned firms in the Netherlands is $57 billion. That is, by using two very different estimation strategies, in fact we find that profits of a very similar magnitude are shifted to the Netherlands.

What does the Netherlands gain by allowing these activities? First, of course these activities lay the ground for an enormous tax planning industry. According to LinkedIn, 34,000 individuals with transfer pricing skills are employed in the Netherlands, which is a remarkable number. Second, and more importantly, the Netherlands earns a great deal of tax revenue. That is, by attracting large artificial amounts of paper profits, and taxing a small fraction of these (while letting most fall outside the tax base), the Netherlands manages to collect a lot of corporate tax. According to our estimates, a third of Dutch corporate tax receipts are the result of artificial profit shifting (Figure 8.5). This tax gain of course comes at great cost—for each euro the Netherlands gains, high-tax countries lose 3 euros.

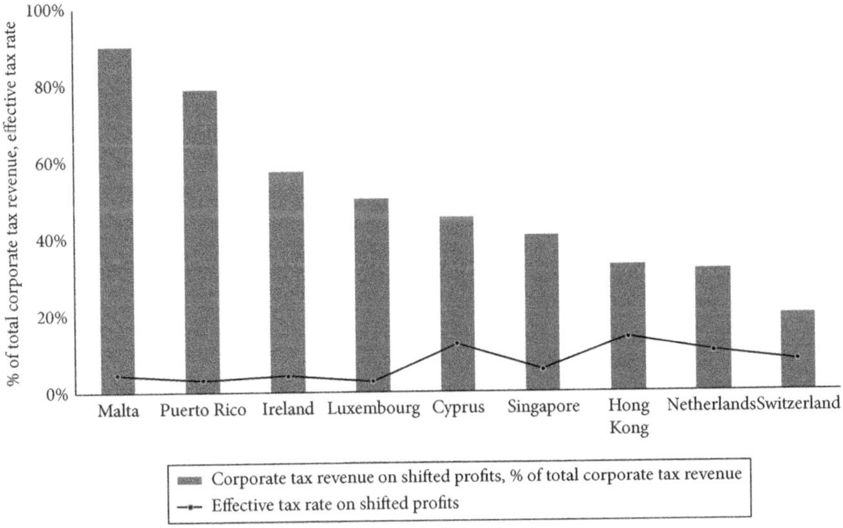

Figure 8.5 Corporate tax revenue collected and tax rate on shifted profits
Source: Tørsløv et al. (2020).

8.5 Conduit or Tax Haven?

The Netherlands is often referred to as a 'conduit' country (see Garcia-Bernardo et al., 2017). A conduit country is defined as a country enabling profit shifting to tax havens or simply put allows safe transfer of profits to tax havens. In our working paper 'The missing profits of nations' (Tørsløv et al., 2020), we simply define tax havens as countries with excessive profitability in multinational firms and low effective corporate tax rates. The Netherlands meets the criteria of being a tax haven according to this definition. That is, profits do not simply seem to pass through the Netherlands to exotic destinations but, according to official FATS, country-by-country reports, and balance-of-payments data, they appear to stay in the Netherlands. While remaining in the Netherlands, these profits are taxed at very low rates (8–12%).

As documented in Tørsløv et al. (2020), it appears that the Netherlands does not recognize all the profits being reported by foreign-owned firms in the Netherlands. For example, US firms report an additional $32 billion in profits in the Netherlands, which the Dutch authorities do not recognize. Of course, this raises the more difficult question of whether the profits are in the Netherlands or just hidden. We take the stance that internationally agreed FATS, country-by-country reports, and balance-of-payments data point towards the profits being in the Netherlands and therefore we allocate these profits to the Netherlands.

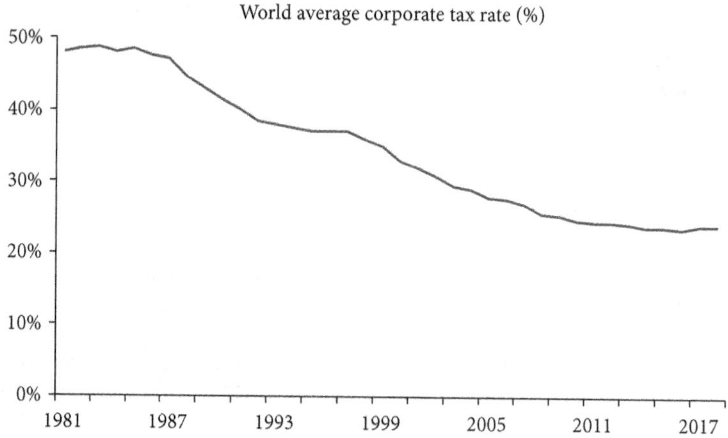

Figure 8.6 The demise of the corporate tax
Source: Tørsløv et al. (2020).

8.6 The End of Corporate Tax?

In the Netherlands, the days of collecting artificial profits may soon end. In the last forty years, the average global corporate tax rate has halved. In the last thirty years alone, it has fallen by 30%. In 2018, the United States finally entered this race by cutting its top statutory tax rate from 40% to 27%. Each year, new tax havens emerge: as the most recent example, Hungary slashed its corporate tax rate to 9% in 2017. As countries try to guard themselves from profit shifting, they cut tax rates and some try to adapt by becoming tax havens. These inclinations are likely to become stronger as multinationals achieve an ever greater position in the world economy. It does not take an economist to make a prognosis based on Figure 8.6: if a fundamental reform is not enacted, then the corporate tax rate is likely to end, and, with it, the Dutch fortune made upon it.

8.7 What Could High-Tax Countries Do?

Why do high-tax countries not intervene? Why do they allow profits to be shifted out of their economies? For example, Germany pays $13 billion in excessive royalty and interest payments to Dutch affiliates. Perhaps high-tax countries could question these payments more aggressively, but they probably will not. The current legal framework of setting 'arm's length' prices is so flawed that the scope for successful enforcement is very small (see Avi-Yonah and Clausing, 2008). Could they impose withholding taxes on the interest and royalty payments? No. The EU Interest and Royalties Directive (I+R Directive) erases the possibility of imposing withholding tax rates on these transactions between EU countries (as long as a minimum of activity is preserved in the Netherlands).[3] This directive makes the Netherlands a supercharged tax haven for high-tax EU countries. The reason why high-tax EU countries do not change the EU legislation is because they need unanimity among all EU member states to do this. So what is left? Germany could abandon the arm's length principle entirely and switch to using, for example, formula apportionment. In this system, Germany would look up the global profits and sales of a multinational company, which are public information. If a firm has 10% of its revenue in Germany, then Germany could apportion 10% of the global profits as the tax base in Germany. This can be done unilaterally or, preferably, in coordination with a group of countries. Unilateral actions are likely to be messy, but the threat of these may in itself drive tax harmonization and coordination. The Netherlands should support these efforts if it wishes to see the corporate tax survive for the next thirty years. There is a straightforward way for the Netherlands to contribute: increase the effective taxation of multinationals operating in the Netherlands.

References

Auerbach, A. J. (1997), 'The future of fundamental tax reform', *American Economic Review*, 87(2), 143–6.

Avi-Yonah, R. and Clausing, K. (2008), 'Reforming corporate taxation in a global economy: a proposal to adopt formulary apportionment', in J. Furman and J. E. Bordoff (eds), *Path to Prosperity: Hamilton Project Ideas on Income Security, Education, and Taxes*, Brookings Institution Press, Washington, DC, pp. 319–44.

Boffey, D. (2017), 'EU investigates Ikea after Dutch deals reduce tax bill by €1bn', *The Guardian* (https://www.theguardian.com/business/2017/dec/18/eu-probes-ikea-after-dutch-deals-reduce-tax-bill-by-1bn).

Bowers, S. (2019), 'Report for the International Consortium of Investigative Journalists' (https://www.icij.org/investigations/luxembourg-leaks/seven-eu-countries-labeled-tax-havens-in-parliament-report/).

Bradford, D. (2003), 'The X tax in the world economy', CEPS Working Paper no. 93.

Fuest, C., Peichl, A., and Siegloch, S. (2018), 'Do higher corporate taxes reduce wages? Micro evidence from Germany', *American Economic Review*, 108(2), 393–418.

Garcia-Bernardo, J., Fichtner, J., Takes, F. W., and Heemskerk, E. M. (2017), 'Uncovering offshore financial centers: conduits and sinks in the global corporate ownership network', *Scientific Reports*, 7, 6246.

[3] Council Directive 2003/49/EC of 3 June 2003 on a common system of taxation applicable to interest and royalty payments made between associated companies of different Member States, Official Journal of the European Union, L157/49.

Grubert, H. and Newlon, T. S. (1997), *Taxing Consumption in a Global Economy*, American Enterprise Institute, Washington, DC.

Hong, Q. and Smart, M. (2010), 'In praise of tax havens: international tax planning and foreign direct investment', *European Economic Review*, 54, 82–95.

Huizinga, H. and Nielsen, S. B. (1997), 'Capital income and profit taxation with foreign ownership of firms', *Journal of International Economics*, 42, 149–65.

Johannesen, N. (2012), 'Optimal fiscal barriers to international economic integration in the presence of tax havens', *Journal of Public Economics*, 96, 400–16.

Piketty, T., Saez, E., and Stantcheva, S. (2014), 'Optimal taxation of top labor incomes: a tale of three elasticities', *American Economic Journal: Economic Policy*, 6, 230–71.

Tørsløv, T. R., Wier, L. S., and Zucman, G. (2020), 'The missing profits of nations', WID.world Working Paper no. 2020/12.

UNCTAD (2015), 'World Investment Report 2015', United Nations Conference on Trade and Development, Geneva.

Wier, L. and Reynolds, H. (2018), 'Big and unprofitable: how 10% of multinational firms do 98% of profit shifting', UNU-WIDER working paper.

9
Taxation of Digital Platforms

*Marko Koethenbuerger**

9.1 Introduction

The increasing importance of services provided by digital platforms, such as Google, Facebook, and YouTube, exemplifies the value that digitalization creates in the economy. Similarly, the sale of digital and non-digital goods via platforms such as Amazon and Apple has experienced tremendous growth over the last decade. The rise in income of digital platforms is related to the use of intellectual property rights and/or the growing demand for advertising via platforms. Although this is a positive reflection of the value added that digital platforms generate, the income is primarily reported in low-tax jurisdictions, which has fuelled the policy discussion of how to re-align the locations of value creation and taxation. Different policy proposals have been developed in recent years, ranging from the OECD proposal for Base Erosion Profit Shifting (BEPS; OECD, 2013), to the recent OECD report on the digital economy (OECD, 2018) and to the more specific proposal of a digital services tax in the EU (European Commission, 2018).

Here, I evaluate the rationale and effects of taxing digital platforms. I focus on two-sided digital platforms that are at the heart of the policy discussion (Google and Facebook, for instance).[1] These are not different to traditional businesses with respect to their preference for tax avoidance, but they are different in important other dimensions. Most notably, they capitalize on user contributions that result from indirect network effects, and this produces significant amounts of advertising income. Indirect network effects have non-conventional implications for the evaluation of taxes and the design of tax policies. I discuss these implications and relate them to tax policies. I start by reviewing the basic characteristics of the business model that two-sided digital platforms use. Then, I turn to the issue of how to modify the concept of nexus for these digital platforms, which traditionally

* Marko Koethenbuerger is Professor of Public Economics, ETH Zurich, Department of Management, Technology and Economics (koethenbuerger@ethz.ch).
I am grateful for helpful comments from Sijbren Cnossen, Bas Jacobs, Nadine Riedel, Jakob Schwab, and Jan van de Streek, as well as from various participants of the Cnossen Forum, Tax by Design for the Netherlands (23–24 May 2019) and the DIE–IMF 8th International Workshop on Domestic Revenue Mobilization: Taxation and Digitalization (1–2 October 2019).

[1] E-commerce is closely related to digital platforms. For example, see Agrawal and Fox (2017) for an analysis of tax policy issues in the context of e-commerce.

Marko Koethenbuerger, *Taxation of Digital Platforms* In: *Tax by Design for the Netherlands.* Edited by: Sijbren Cnossen and Bas Jacobs, Oxford University Press.
DOI: 10.1093/oso/9780192855244.003.0009

requires a physical presence in a country to make it possible for a country to tax them. This is followed by an evaluation of how the two-sidedness of digital platforms leads to unconventional tax responses and efficiency implications. Finally, I discuss the international implications of taxing digital platforms and I review different tax policy proposals for digital platforms. Overall, I recommend that the approach laid down by the EU is followed, that is, to tax digital platforms based on the revenues generated by users of the platform in the respective country.

9.2 Two-Sided Digital Platforms: A Different Business Model

Before discussing the implications of tax policy, first it is important to provide a brief review of the business model of two-sided digital platforms, in order to understand why they are so different from traditional businesses. In a two-sided digital market, two distinct groups of customers or users interact with each other through a digital platform. The decision of each group to join a platform depends on the size of the other group. These across-group interdependences are referred to as indirect network effects.[2] A variety of industries are characterized by such demand spill-overs. Social networks and the media industry are two important examples.[3] Indirect network effects depend not only on the number of users, but also on the 'quality' of users. Advertisers would like to reach the 'right' users and to target their advertising towards users who are most receptive to their advertising efforts. Platforms can generate information about the user side by employing methods of artificial intelligence, and can then use this information to channel advertisements that are more finely tuned to users. In this sense, the key asset for the platforms to be able to generate advertising income is user data. In many cases, most if not all of the income of the platforms is earned on one side of the platform only. For example, Google and Facebook follow a zero-pricing strategy on the user side and charge advertisers for access to their users.

It is important to note that the critical feature that makes two-sided digital platforms different for policy analysis is not the existence of indirect network effects, per se. Rochet and Tirole (2006) offer a refined definition of a two-sided market. Rather than only requiring the existence of cross-group spill-overs, they point to the relevance of the price structure (i.e. the platform charges for both groups) for the market outcome. When the two groups can undo any change in

[2] Indirect network externalities are different to direct network externalities. The latter operate among members of a group (Katz and Shapiro, 1994). They might also operate on two-sided platforms, but are not a defining element of two-sided platforms.

[3] The fact that network industries also share features with two-sided markets (e.g. the software industry and web portals) has implications for the appropriate pricing policy. See Evans, Hagiu, and Schmalensee (2006) for an illuminating discussion of how the economic aspects of two-sidedness were mistakenly ignored during the dot.com boom—a failure that might have contributed to the failure of numerous dot.com firms.

the price structure that the platform implements, the market outcome will not change and the price structure is neutral. In many important examples of digital platforms (e.g. Google and Facebook), this will not be the case, as there are no direct negotiations between users of the digital platforms and firms that place advertisements via these platforms. In contrast, digital platforms such as eBay and Airbnb do not pass this test of two-sidedness. Any change in the prices eBay charges its sellers and buyers on the platform can be neutralized by the two groups, just because sellers and buyers directly interact via the platform and can adjust the price payment between them accordingly.[4] I focus on two-sided platforms that pass this test.

9.3 Implications for Tax Policy

9.3.1 Location of Value Creation: A Dual Role of Users

Traditional methods of corporate taxation rely on the notion that profits are taxed at the location where they have been created. Such source-based tax systems are difficult to sustain in a world in which firms can allocate their profits via profit-shifting strategies to low-tax jurisdictions (Gresik, 2001). A policy to limit profit-shifting is to compare reported profits with the level of economic activity in a given jurisdiction in which the firm has some establishment (the so-called nexus). This comparison primarily tries to see through the 'production function' and to use input measures such as labour and capital to get an idea of value creation in a jurisdiction.[5] In the context of two-sided digital platforms, the comparison becomes somehow meaningless. Labour and capital are not the prime input factors in generating value added. As detailed above, the value creation occurs on both sides of the platform with different inputs. Users enjoy the value created by the service that the platform offers (such as Google search or interaction via Facebook). The service is produced primarily by using intellectual property rights, such as software. At the same time, use of the service creates an audience that advertisers can use for economic or political campaigning. This creates value for advertisers, who capitalize on advertising revenues for the platform.

The allocation of the stream of advertising income to the jurisdiction where it is deemed to be created is a taxing task and it is very much at the core of the policy discussion around digital platforms. In general, many different locations—such as the location of servers, the location where the software is created, and the location

[4] Note that eBay acts 'only' as an e-intermediary between seller and buyers. See e.g. Agrawal and Fox (2017) for an analysis of taxation and e-commerce issues.

[5] Formula apportionment systems are widespread at the subnational level. Such a system of a common consolidated corporate tax base (CCCTB) has been recently proposed at the European level to limit profit-shifting within the EU (European Commission, 2016).

of intellectual property rights, as well as the use of these rights—might be used as the location where the value added is created. These locations typically do not coincide and, in many cases, they can be easily adjusted in order to save on taxes via profit-shifting in a source-based corporate tax system.[6]

An alternative would be to use the second main input factor in value creation: the users. On two-sided digital platforms, users take a dual role. They are consumers of a service provided by the platform, but at the same time they are input factors in the creation of value on the advertiser side of the platform. The value of users for advertisers is magnified by the use of software (artificial intelligence) that uses the characteristics of users to improve the targeting of advertisements. Advertising revenues should reflect the increase in value to advertisers, given the fine-tuned pricing of advertising space that digital platforms use in practice. The location of users is not overly mobile and presumably it is not very responsive to the role of users in allocating profits, given that the pecuniary prices that users pay are zero in many cases and that a shifting of taxes on to users via an adjustment in price payments is not possible.[7]

Multiple concerns are frequently raised in the context of the taxation of digital platforms. First, there are concerns that a user-based tax assignment is a special treatment of two-sided digital platforms, which is inconsistent with the tax treatment of other businesses. With regards to the principles that underlie the current assignment of taxes, a user-based tax system might not be classified as a ring-fenced system. The location of critical input factors is used to assign tax bases in current tax systems. As explained above, for advertising-driven platforms, users become the critical input factor so the location of the users should then be used to assign taxing rights. Secondly, many policy proposals (to be reviewed below) recommend taxes on revenues rather than on corporate profits. In the context of two-sided platforms, the distinction between the two becomes more blurred as the marginal cost of providing services via platforms (such as advertising space) is negligible, if not zero. At least in the short run, the behavioural responses to the two forms of taxation are the same. Digital platforms incur large fixed costs as a result of the development of software and the implementation of the platform. This implies that they incur losses at the beginning of their operations, which are treated differently under revenue-based and profit-based tax systems. In a profit-based tax system, losses can be carried forward, but provisions to carry losses forward are only available for a limited number of years in most tax systems. Another consideration that becomes relevant in this context is that digital

[6] There is a growing body of literature showing that the location of intellectual property rights is tax-sensitive and that intellectual property rights are used for profit-shifting (see Karkinsky and Riedel, 2012; Griffith, Miller, and O'Connell, 2014; Koethenbuerger, Liberini, and Stimmelmayr, 2019).

[7] Becker, Englisch, and Schanz (2018) and Cui (2018) relate this idea to the definition of nexus (i.e. relying on a physical presence) and discuss how this definition needs to be modified from a legal perspective, for instance.

platforms strategically underprice their services in the starting phase in order to create a sufficiently large user base and to drive rival platforms out of business (Evans et al., 2006). From an efficiency perspective, this leaves open the question of whether losses resulting from strategic pricing and the associated creation of market power should be subsidized by providing a loss offset.

The issue of whether to tax revenues or profits is not new, and this has received some prominence in the context of the taxation of natural resources. Therein, a tax on revenues is frequently used, albeit at a low rate in order to minimize the potential disadvantage that arises from not deducting cost (Cui, 2018). A low rate of tax might also be a policy option for digital platforms, an issue that is dealt with in Section 9.4. A final issue is whether current tax treaties accommodate the possibility of taxing revenues at source. Cui (2018) offers an interpretation of a user-based revenue tax on digital platforms that is in line with tax treaties. Current tax treaties allow governments to tax location-specific rents. Advertising revenue might be interpreted as location-specific rents where users are location-specific factors that generate these rents.

9.3.2 Tax Responses by Digital Platforms

Two-sided digital platforms use a business model that has unconventional implications for how two-sided digital platforms respond to public policies, and for the demand for corrective policies.

Turning to the policy responsiveness first, note that two-sided digital platforms frequently receive income streams from the two sides that are subject to different taxes. An example is the media industry where advertising income is subject to the general value added tax (VAT), while the VAT that applies to the sales of media outlets (newspapers or magazines) differs from the general VAT rate. A different example is a multinational platform that earns or reports its income stream in different tax jurisdictions, which have different tax rates. In these environments, indirect network externalities modify the way the platform responds to taxes. For instance, the business model of a digital media platform will generate a higher tax rate on revenues from selling media content, which will result in a lower price for the media content and a higher number of readers. This is contrary to the standard tax response, which entails a higher price and a lower number of users. The different response is rooted in the existence of positive indirect network effects. A higher number of readers makes the platform more attractive for advertisers, and thus generates higher advertising revenues in response. Thus, tax avoidance takes the form of shifting revenues from the more heavily taxed side to the less heavily taxed side of the platform via quantity increases on the more heavily taxed side (Kind et al., 2008, 2010; Kind and Koethenbuerger, 2018).[8]

The welfare effects of these responses might be equally unconventional. While a tax is distortionary in the absence of other sources of inefficiency, two-sided digital platforms are imperfectly competitive markets and thereby are characterized by market power. They exist to capitalize on indirect network effects and this benefit becomes larger when the two sides of the platform are larger. As such, taxes have a corrective role to play in these markets: to counteract both the underprovision of quantities due to market power and the tendencies for underprovision or overprovision due to an imperfect internalization of (inframarginal) indirect network effects.[9] Thus, quantities might be overprovided. Even when the underprovision tendency dominates, the tax policy might be unconventional and might involve a tax just to increase quantities.

The predictions still need to receive empirical support. The tax policies in EU member countries (to be reviewed below) might well serve as a testing ground in future work. At the moment, the theoretical insights should at least be interpreted as a critical assessment of any tax analyses that neglect the basic reason why two-sided digital platforms exist.

9.3.3 International Tax Policy

Digital platforms require a sufficiently large amount of indirect network effects to exist, and hence tend to operate in different countries (e.g. Facebook, Google, and Netflix). The international dimension of firm operation has implications for tax. Multinational platforms have the possibility to avoid paying taxes in one country by shifting profits to another country where taxes are lower (Dharmapala, 2014). In the context of digital platforms, one way of avoiding taxes is to use royalty payments to shift profits to a low-tax country. In the context of, for example, social media, the royalty payment reflects the use of intellectual property such as software (artificial intelligence) or marketing services. As for any other firm, tax differentials across countries incentivize platforms to strategically adjust the payment upwards and to report more income in the low-tax country. Two-sided digital platforms, which earn advertising income on one side of the platform's operation, may organize the profit-shifting differently. Advertising

[8] Two-sided platforms also challenge other well-known and policy-relevant insights in public finance, such as the revenue and welfare dominance of ad valorem taxes (Kind et al., 2009).

[9] More precisely, platforms account for the marginal indirect network effects when setting prices. However, these might differ from inframarginal indirect network effects. In a situation in which users are ad-averse and users with a higher willingness to pay for media content are those that are most averse to advertising, the marginal negative indirect network effect is smaller (in absolute value) than the inframarginal indirect network effects. In isolation, this implies an overprovision of advertising (Kind et al., 2008).

contracts are directly located in low-tax countries and the users in various countries are exposed to the advertising that follows from the contract. The strategic location of contracts, and thereby advertising income, leaves (almost) no reported income in those countries where users are located (apart from the country in which the contract is located).

The issue of profit-shifting is not new and is not restricted to digital platforms. In recent years, multiple policies have been discussed around the globe to combat profit-shifting, including the implementation of so-called arm's-length prices and the apportionment of the profits of an international firm to the different countries in which the firm operates. All these policies have proven to be difficult to implement in practice, and they become even more difficult to implement for two-sided digital platforms. However, digital platforms offer a policy solution that is not available in standard industries, both because of their unique production function for advertising revenue and because of the way taxes work in such industries.

In detail, the concept of arm's-length prices requires that the royalty payment is used for the calculation of tax obligations that unrelated firms use for the pricing of a similar transaction (OECD, 2017). For example, because social media firms are quite large, there are only a few, and there is almost no external market that can be used as a benchmark. This applies to the use of intellectual property, which by construction is unique. It also applies to the 'sale' of the attention of users to advertisers; for example, Facebook users are quite unique in terms of media usage. They cannot easily be compared with magazine readers and the advertising prices that are charged to access their attention. Also, any policy that tries to infer the internal price that should be charged in the absence of tax-saving motives (e.g. by inferring the cost structure of the two-sided digital platform) might yield erroneous outcomes.[10] In the absence of taxes, internal prices of a two-sided platform reflect not only marginal costs (if at all, as marginal costs are close to zero in two-sided digital platforms), but also indirect network effects (Schindler and Schjelderup, 2010). This makes it difficult to apply the OECD guidelines when calculating the 'tax-free' internal price.

A frequently discussed policy to assign tax bases among countries is to implement a formulary apportionment system. If applied universally, royalty payments between divisions of the digital platform would not influence the overall amount of profit and tax-related profit-shifting incentives would be absent. Applied to digital platforms, this system emphasizes the role of users for tax assignment. The general underlying idea is to use critical input factors, which serve as an indicator

[10] There are various ways in which such a concept can be implemented, all of which try to get a good assessment of the cost of producing the good or service that is internally traded (OECD, 2017). The marginal cost of producing the good or service is the metric underlying the arm's-length pricing policy because this is the pricing strategy that firms use in competitive markets.

of real economic activity, for tax assignment. For a digital platform, one of the critical input factors is its users. Another critical input factor is its algorithms, which are public inputs and have no location-specific values that can be used to allocate the income of the digital platform to the different countries. This leaves users as the relevant metric for tax assignment. A limitation of this proposal is that it implies a reallocation of taxable profits across countries, which undermines the incentives for low-tax countries or the home countries of the digital platforms to support such a proposal. A lack of international cooperation to address the issue of profit-shifting might well incentivize countries to focus on user-dependent revenue assignment, which by construction neglects reported costs and thereby royalty payments. This is the essence of many tax proposals that are reviewed next.

9.4 Recent User-Based Tax Reform Proposals

There have been different proposals about how to implement a user-based allocation of tax bases. One proposal would require all advertising contracts that relate to users in a specific country to be located in the platform affiliate in the respective country. Partly going in this direction, the United Kingdom has recently implemented the UK Diverted Profits Tax that requires UK advertisers on digital platforms to sign the contract with the UK platform affiliate (Cuevas et al., 2017). The proposal satisfies the user-based allocation rule only partially. Advertising income earned with UK users is only taxed when UK advertisers target domestic users. A further potential drawback of such a proposal is that profit-shifting incentives are not fully eliminated. The platform still has the possibility to adjust the royalty payments that the UK platform division, for example, has to pay to its parent company in a low-tax country. For instance, in the context of Facebook, it is hard to judge whether a royalty payment is justified based on non-tax reasons, given the lack of an arm's-length relationship that tax authorities can use as a counterfactual. It is only when the tax is not a profit tax but a sales tax that the royalty payment does not lower the tax payment.

The proposed EU digital service tax (DST) goes in this direction, which by and large is a tax on sales that result from active user participation (European Commission, 2018). Some EU member states support the idea, while some states conclude that the challenges that digitalization creates for tax policy are not exclusive to the digital economy and do not require special policies. Given the controversy, the proposal has not been implemented, which has prompted a subset of EU member states to take country-specific actions that reflect the value of users for platforms. For instance, in France, a tax rate of 3% applies to revenues generated from online intermediation services and the sale of targeted digital advertising. It applies to large Internet companies with worldwide taxable revenue exceeding 750 million euros, and French taxable revenue over 25 million euros. The same tax rate will be levied in Austria and is levied in Italy, albeit with a lower domestic revenue threshold. As of 2020, the UK has announced its intention to introduce a 2% tax on the revenues of search engines, social media platforms, and online marketplaces that derive value from UK users. International and domestic revenue thresholds will apply.[11]

The proposed tax policies reflect the importance of users in generating platform revenues, but these policies also tend to include digital platforms that act only as intermediaries between buyers and sellers (e.g. eBay and Airbnb). The policies do not satisfy the aforementioned stringent definition of two-sided markets (where users cannot neutralize changes in the price structure that the platform chooses). These digital platforms earn most of their income via fees rather than advertising income and are not very different in behaviour to other non-platform industries (Grinberg, 2018). It is also advisable to apply a stringent definition of digital platforms that are subject to the DST in order to prevent the inclusion of industries that, for example, use digital marketplaces to sell their products/services, but do not share the basic characteristics of two-sided platforms.

The inclusion of thresholds is compatible with the idea of reducing the administrative costs and compliance costs of tax collection (as is typical for related tax policies such as VAT). In the context of digital platforms, it also addresses the concern that platforms incur large fixed costs and only become profitable with a certain size of operation (i.e. the magnitude of indirect network effects). Thus, a threshold-dependent revenue tax most likely does not apply to loss-making platforms.

Finally, a revenue tax has the disadvantage of creating production inefficiencies as costs are not deductible.[12] As reviewed in Section 9.3.2, the issue is familiar from natural resource taxation, where a low rate of tax is frequently chosen to address the inefficiency. The low tax rates embedded in the different tax reforms are compatible with this line of reasoning.

9.5 Conclusion

The recent rise of tech giants such as Google and Facebook has generated significant amounts of value added, some of which is capitalized in the advertising income these firms earn. The advertising income of these digital platforms has increased tremendously over time, but this income is mainly reported in countries with low tax rates. This has fuelled the discussion about how to tax these firms that operate internationally.

[11] See, for example, OECD (2018) for an overview of policy proposals.

[12] In the context of two-sided markets, production inefficiencies will most likely not occur in the short run, as the marginal cost of putting out advertisements is virtually zero.

The business model that these digital platforms use is different to that of traditional industries. It relies on the existence of indirect network externalities that are the prime reason why they generate advertising income. Any evaluation of tax policies ought to account for this. This includes the fact that an adjusted concept of nexus should be implemented, which should rely on the location of users (i.e. the definition of nexus based on a physical presence should be adjusted to include the notion of a digital presence in a country). The recent EU proposal of a DST builds on this insight. Following this proposal, various EU member countries unilaterally implemented such a tax, which is also a blueprint for the Netherlands.

Finally, a recent proposal for tax policy included the introduction of a destination-based tax system (DBT), possibly supplemented by a cash-flow tax (Auerbach et al., 2017). The DBT implies a shift in taxing rights, away from the norm of taxing profits at source to the idea of taxing profits in the country of final consumption. The issue of where this stream of income has been generated is no longer of relevance for taxation, provided all countries simultaneously adopt a DBT. However, a DBT implies a reallocation of tax revenues and this change in revenues will be higher than the change in revenues that is associated with a DST. To the extent that the DST-related changes are perceived as a political obstacle, the concern might well become even more relevant in the context of a DBT. Thus, the DBT might not become effective in the near future, meaning that the issue of how to tax the income of digital platforms in a source-based tax system policy remains relevant. The DST is one option to address the issue.

References

Agrawal, D. and Fox, W. (2017), 'Taxes in an e-commerce generation', *International Tax and Public Finance*, 24, 903–26.

Auerbach, A., Devereux, M., Keen, M., and Vella, J. (2017), 'International tax planning under the destination-based cash flow tax', *National Tax Journal*, 70, 783–802.

Becker, J., Englisch, J., and Schanz, D. (2018), 'How data should (not) be taxed', working paper, University of Münster and LMU Munich.

Cuevas, A., Cuevas, R., Lassmann A., Liberini, F., and Russo, A. (2017), 'The taxman calls. How does Facebook answer? Global effects of taxation on online advertising', NET Institute, Working Paper 17–09.

Cui, W. (2018), 'The digital service tax: a conceptual defense', working paper, University of British Columbia.

Dharmapala, D. (2014), 'What do we know about base erosion and profit shifting? A review of the empirical literature', *Fiscal Studies*, 35, 421–48.

European Commission (2016), 'Council directive on a Common Corporate Tax Base', Strasbourg.

European Commission (2018), 'Council directive on the common system of a digital services tax on revenues resulting from the provision of certain digital services', Brussels.

Evans, D. S., Hagiu, A., and Schmalensee, R. (2006), *Invisible Engines—How Software Platforms Drive Innovation and Transform Industries*, MIT Press, Cambridge, MA.

Gresik, T. (2001), 'The taxing task of taxing transnationals', *Journal of Economic Literature*, 39, 800–38.

Griffith, R., Miller, H., and O'Connell, M. (2014), 'Ownership of intellectual property and corporate taxation', *Journal of Public Economics*, 112, 12–23.

Grinberg, I. (2018), 'User participation in value creation', *British Tax Review*, 4, 407–21.

Karkinsky, T. and Riedel, N. (2012), 'Corporate taxation and the choice of patent location within multinational firms', *Journal of International Economics*, 88, 176–85.

Katz, M. and Shapiro, C. (1994), 'Systems competition and network effects', *Journal of Economic Perspectives*, 8(2), 93–115.

Kind, H. J. and Koethenbuerger, M. (2018), 'Taxation in digital media markets', *Journal of Public Economic Theory*, 20, 22–39.

Kind, H. J., Koethenbuerger, M., and Schjelderup, G. (2008), 'Efficiency enhancing taxation in two-sided markets', *Journal of Public Economics*, 92, 1531–9.

Kind, H. J., Koethenbuerger, M., and Schjelderup, G. (2009), 'On revenue and welfare dominance of ad valorem taxes in two-sided markets', *Economics Letters*, 104, 86–8.

Kind, H. J., Koethenbuerger, M., and Schjelderup, G. (2010), 'Tax responses in platform industries', *Oxford Economic Papers*, 62, 764–83.

Koethenbuerger, M., Liberini, F., and Stimmelmayr, M. (2019), '(Un)intended effects of preferential tax regimes: The case of European patent boxes', EconPol Working Paper 29.

OECD (2013), *Action Plan on Base Erosion and Profit Shifting*, OECD Publishing, Paris.

OECD (2017), *Transfer Pricing Guidelines for Multinational Enterprises and Tax Administrations*, OECD Publishing, Paris.

OECD (2018), *Tax Challenges Arising from Digitalisation—Interim Report*, OECD Publishing, Paris.

Rochet, J. and Tirole, J. (2006), 'Two-sided markets: a progress report', *Rand Journal of Economics*, 35, 645–67.

Schindler, D. and Schjelderup, G. (2010), 'Profit shifting in two-sided markets', *International Journal of the Economics of Business*, 17, 373–83.

PART III

PROFITS

Design

10
ACE or CBIT for the Netherlands?
Stripping Rules!

*Dirk Schindler and Hendrik Vrijburg**

10.1 Introduction

It is well known that the current corporate income tax (CIT) system is highly imperfect and creates a number of problems, particularly related to excessive debt financing and international profit shifting. In recent years, an old debate on how the CIT should be designed has arisen again, which has provided additional arguments. For fundamental system changes, the main candidates in the discussion are an allowance for corporate equity (ACE), allowing interest deductions and exempting the normal rate of return on firms' equity, and a comprehensive business income tax (CBIT), taxing firms' equity and denying interest deductibility. A less radical alternative is to develop the current system further by adding additional rules and provisions to heal the major problems.[1]

Designing a proper CIT system requires balancing a number of politically delicate issues. In a small open economy, such as the Netherlands, the CIT actually turns into an implicit tax on wages if the standard model of Gordon (1986) applies. Then, at least the part of the CIT that falls on the normal return on capital clearly reduces welfare, and abolishing this part of the tax would exclusively benefit workers, not capital owners. However, there are two important issues to selling a corporate tax reduction as a benefit to workers.[2] First, it will

* Dirk Schindler (schindler@ese.eur.nl) is Professor of International Taxation at Erasmus University Rotterdam. Hendrik Vrijburg (h.vrijburg@law.leidenuniv.nl) is Assistant Professor at Leiden University. We are grateful for helpful comments by Sijbren Cnossen, Bas Jacobs, Alexander Klemm, and participants at the conference on 'Tax by Design for the Netherlands' at Erasmus University Rotterdam in May 2019.

[1] A more radical reform is the destination-based cash-flow tax, proposed by Auerbach and Devereux (2018). Effectively, this is similar to an ACE combined with a VAT-like treatment of taxing intermediate imports and exempting exports from the CIT. We focus on the ACE part and neglect the non-trivial issue of whether destination-based taxation is preferable and superior. See, for example, Bond and Gresik (2020) for a critical discussion.

[2] In principle, the issue is very similar to the pretended 'trickle-down effect' of reducing top marginal tax rates in the US personal income tax. Proponents of this effect have claimed that eventually such tax cuts will benefit all workers by increasing their wages. While the US population has remained sceptical, it now turns out that the income effects hardly appeared. See, for example, the summaries in recent columns by Paul Krugman in the *New York Times* (Krugman, 2017, 2019).

Dirk Schindler and Hendrik Vrijburg, *ACE or CBIT for the Netherlands? Stripping Rules!* In: *Tax by Design for the Netherlands*. Edited by: Sijbren Cnossen and Bas Jacobs, Oxford University Press.
DOI: 10.1093/oso/9780192855244.003.0010

be a long shot to convince the general public (and voters) that the tax relief for the corporate sector indeed raises net wages to the same extent. This mechanism requires a deeper understanding of how general-equilibrium effects determine tax incidence. Second, available empirical evidence shows that a substantial part of the tax incidence still falls on firm owners (Clausing, 2013; Suárez Serrato and Zidar, 2016; Fuest et al., 2018). Indeed, there is no consensus among economists whether the standard model of Gordon applies. Many economists point to issues that suggest limited shifting of tax incidence and speak in favour of a source-based corporate tax also on the normal rate of return.

Hence, in the current political situation with strong populist parties mainly on the right wing, but also on the left, it seems hardly possible to lower the tax burden on the normal return earned by mobile capital. Any reform that apparently gives tax benefits to the corporate sector likely will be a 'gift' for left-wing and populist campaigns that will f7oster the success of the extreme wings in the political arena.[3] Because of this domestic political pressure, a minimum requirement for any CIT reform seems to be budget neutrality where adjustments in the corporate tax regime ensure that corporate tax revenues remain constant. Therefore, in this chapter, we focus on such budget-neutral reforms. Furthermore, it appears unlikely that there will be a coordinated major tax reform in the European Union (EU) in the near future. Even if there is a consensus, it is fully unclear how such a reform would look. Therefore, we derive our proposal based on a unilateral reform in the Netherlands.

By adding further important aspects such as investment shifting, tax avoidance and small firms to the standard model, we take the full picture of decision margins into account and investigate how different tax systems score on the specific margins and in an overall evaluation. We base our policy advice on the criterion that theoretical insights should be robust to changes in the most important modelling assumptions (Diamond and Saez, 2011). Neither the ACE nor the CBIT passes this test. The ACE gives too much tax relief and generates severe distortions on investment shifting and market entry (partly) due to the higher tax rate that follows from the budget-neutrality requirement. The CBIT does not provide sufficient degrees of freedom and implements a high marginal tax burden, which causes severe distortions on the (intensive) investment margin. Therefore, we suggest a reform of the current system that adds stripping rules for interest deductibility and royalty payments. Such a reform pushes the system more towards a CBIT (on the margin for large firms), but provides enough degrees of freedom. The system allows for continuous adjustments, restricts excessive debt financing and profit shifting in those firms that matter most, and leaves other firms unaffected. We believe that the Netherlands has implemented important steps in this direction already.

[3] The discussion on lowering the tax on outgoing dividends in the Netherlands is an informative example of this.

A key underlying claim is that the normal return on investments most likely should be taxed at the corporate level. This claim holds even when it is optimal not to tax the normal return in the personal income tax (i.e. when the Atkinson–Stiglitz theorem applies). Consequently, arguments that capital income should be taxed in case the Atkinson Stiglitz theorem breaks down, come on top of this (Jacobs, Chapter 5).[4]

10.2 Alternative Tax Systems

The traditional corporate tax system treats the return on equity as taxable business income whereas interest expenses on debt are tax deductible. This system is implemented in the overwhelming majority of OECD countries, including the Netherlands, and features a well-known tax preference for debt over equity in case equity and debt are taxed similarly at the personal level. This yields a well-documented tendency by firms to overleverage (see e.g. De Mooij, 2012). In recent years, the use of earnings stripping rules has become popular in order to limit excessive debt financing and to curb international tax avoidance strategies via (internal) debt. The EU Anti-Tax Avoidance Directive (ATAD) will enforce the implementation of these rules in all EU countries in the coming years.

Two systems are usually seen and discussed as alternatives to the traditional system. The US Department of Treasury (1992) proposed the CBIT that continues to treat the return to equity as taxable income, but abolishes tax deductibility of interest expenses. Hence, both returns on debt and equity are treated equally and are fully taxed. Importantly, the original proposal contained the idea that small firms would be exempted from the CBIT and continue to be taxed under the traditional corporate tax system.

The Institute for Fiscal Studies (1991) has already outlined the ACE. Besides eliminating any tax preference for debt, it intends to keep the normal rate of return on capital free of corporate tax. These aims are achieved by maintaining tax deductibility for interest expenses and sheltering equity by an allowance equal to a notional return on equity (e.g. the market interest rate for long-term government bonds). This system is prominently advocated in the Mirrlees Report (Mirrlees et al., 2011). It is based on an earlier proposal for a neutral business tax, called the allowance for corporate capital (ACC), which replaces tax deductibility of effective costs of debt and equity by deductibility of a notional return on total capital in a corporation (Boadway and Bruce, 1984).

[4] We believe, again following Diamond and Saez (2011), that the case where the Atkinson–Stiglitz theorem breaks down is the most policy relevant.

10.3 Important Dimensions for Corporate Income Tax Design

Very often, the tax systems summarized in Section 10.2 are evaluated in partial analyses, mainly focusing on the choice between debt and equity or on the intensive investment margin only. However, in a world with many more decision margins, this cannot be perfectly targeted and controlled by governments, and the presented tax systems need to be evaluated on their impact on all relevant decision margins. As we will see, the systems score differently across all aspects.

10.3.1 Taxing the Normal Rate of Return at the Corporate Level

In a standard model of a small open economy where the government can more or less observe all decision margins, it is well known that a source tax on the normal rate of return on capital is not desirable. By adjusting their capital investment, corporations will ensure that their after-tax return on capital is equal to the world-market interest rate. Reducing investment implies that the tax burden is effectively shifted on to workers, who experience a decrease in their wages. Hence, a source tax on the normal rate of return is equivalent to a wage tax plus additional distortions in capital investment (Gordon, 1986). This view is the foundation for the proposal of an ACE and the recommendation in the Mirrlees Report. The ACE allows approximately all costs of capital to be tax deductible such that the marginal investment (i.e. the intensive margin) remains undistorted. Effectively, an ACE taxes only the above-normal returns in corporations, if any. An ACE is optimal in case all markets and the rest of the tax system function 'perfectly'.

Empirical evidence on the incidence of corporate taxes suggests, however, that the tax burden is shared by labour and capital (and land); see, for example, Suárez Serrato and Zidar (2016), which is not in line with the standard model of the small open economy. The findings in Clausing (2013) even suggest that capital bears the dominant part of the corporate tax. Furthermore, there are good reasons to tax personal capital income (see Jacobs, Chapter 5), showing that only in specific circumstances does the optimal effective tax on the normal return equal zero (see, for instance, the Atkinson–Stiglitz theorem). This implies that optimal non-taxation of the normal return is not sufficiently robust for policy advice (see also Diamond and Saez, 2011, recommendation 3). Indeed, there are several arguments for taxing the normal rate of return at the corporate level if either markets or the tax system as a whole are imperfect.

Importantly, international tax avoidance changes the standard result that the normal return should not be taxed. If firms can shelter their (super)normal return by means of transfer pricing,[5] it is not optimal to fully exempt the normal return in the tax base. This becomes very obvious in the case of supernormal profits ('economic rents'). Governments are constrained in their taxing power of economic rents, for example because of profit shifting. As some firms benefit excessively from their supernormal profits, their investments will not be easily relocated to other countries; that is, a tax on normal returns is an indirect tax on the supernormal profits and partly paid by (foreign) owners of capital.[6]

Furthermore, there is income shifting from labour to capital in closely held firms. With high labour and low capital taxes, self-employed individuals in their closely held corporation have an incentive to declare their labour income as the firm's profits and return on capital. This is known as the 'Achilles heel of the dual income tax' (see Sørensen, 2010). There are possibilities to mitigate and reduce such income shifting, but all available mechanisms are imperfect as soon as one allows for international avoidance schemes (e.g. Alstadsæter et al., 2018). Taxing corporate profits and the normal rate of return reduces the scope for utilizing loopholes in the anti-avoidance regulations.

In a similar vein, the CIT functions partly as a withholding tax on personal earnings. This is desirable when part of personal earnings is undertaxed because the government cannot observe individual personal earnings perfectly, such that there is avoidance of labour income taxes. In particular, enforcement costs might prevent taxing the full compensation for work effort under the labour tax. This holds particularly for income components that are not automatically reported to tax authorities and all benefits-in-kind that do not show up on the personal income tax statement. The latter include the use of a company car, company laptop, employee discounts, etc. In such a world, the corporate tax on the normal rate of return does not constitute an additional tax on the reported wage income, but an implicit tax on the non-reported compensation for work. The implicit tax is much more difficult to avoid for workers. Thus, balancing the distortions in firms' investment against saved enforcement costs for a perfect direct tax on the full compensation for labour yields a positive source tax on the normal rate of return (e.g. Slemrod and Wilson, 2009). Similarly, whenever there is no perfect incidence falling on wages, a corporate tax can be an efficient instrument to amend personal capital income taxes. It is relatively easy to avoid personal capital income taxes. In particular, wealthy investors have various possibilities to structure their portfolio or simply to hide their capital income in tax havens (e.g. Alstadsæter et al., 2018).

[5] Note that we use a broad definition of transfer pricing here. It includes both manipulating internal prices in intra-firm trade of tangible (intermediate) goods and tax-motivated choices of royalty payments and other remuneration for the internal use of intangible goods.

[6] The argument is related to Keen and Piekkola (1997) who show that some source-based taxation of mobile capital is part of the Pareto-optimal policy mix as soon as governments cannot perfectly tax supernormal returns. The tax on the normal rate of return on (international) capital turns into a substitute for the restricted tax on economic rents.

The corporate tax partly taxes domestic evaders (and foreign evaders). Of course, the corporate tax also suffers from international profit shifting, but it should be easier to enforce the corporate tax than the personal capital income tax. This is because there are fewer firms than investors to monitor, businesses are more visible, and last but not least corporations are forced to provide financial reports and are audited on a regular basis.

In addition, following the Diamond–Mirrlees production–efficiency theorem, a distortionary tax on production can be efficient when there are market failures, such as imperfect competition (Diamond and Mirrlees, 1971). For example, imperfect competition with free entry leads to a situation in which, from a social perspective, a single firm produces too little output, but too many firms are active in the market ('business stealing effect'). Such excessive entry is costly, and a corporate tax might reduce this excessive entry. For realistically observed corporate taxes, Brekke et al. (2017) show that the strategic competition effect calls for a CBIT in sectors with increasing returns to scale (e.g. multinationals in the digital economy); under decreasing returns to scale, it allows for some range of corporate tax rates with imperfect deductibility of capital costs.

Similarly, moral hazard in manager behaviour creates another market imperfection that calls for a corporate-level tax on the normal rate of return. If behaviour by firm managers cannot be perfectly monitored by firm owners, the managers have incentives to invest free cash flow into unproductive projects that generate private returns to managers. This well-known agency problem is fostered by an ACE because the ACE reduces capital costs and increases all kinds of investment. In contrast, a CBIT reduces investment and, by this, also the unproductive 'pet projects' of managers. If the CBIT is accompanied by a lower corporate tax rate (due to a larger tax base), it also exerts a substitution effect in favour of productive investment projects, because these projects are relatively less taxed under a CBIT (see Koethenbuerger and Stimmelmayr, 2014).

Although earlier studies focusing on the intensive margin have shown that the welfare losses from a distortion of the intensive investment margin can be significant (e.g. Keuschnigg and Dietz, 2007; Radulescu and Stimmelmayr, 2007), the above arguments together suggest that it is far from obvious that a zero tax burden on the normal rate of return at the corporate level is desirable. All else equal, the conclusion that an ACE system is optimal is not robust to modelling assumptions because both markets and the tax system are imperfect.[7] Rather, in a world with various distortions, the normal return should be taxed, at both the corporate and personal level. However, bearing in mind the gains, and the substantial costs from taxing the normal rate of return at corporate level, full taxation of the normal rate of return likely would be too high. Hence, a CBIT

[7] In other words, one of the main criteria for solid policy advice is violated (see Diamond and Saez, 2011).

system is not optimal either. Balancing marginal gains and costs, some intermediate tax burden on normal capital returns should be desirable, and both the traditional system and an ACC with limited deductibility of capital costs are flexible enough to implement such a tax burden.[8] In any case, the intensive margin will optimally be distorted.

10.3.2 Intensive versus Extensive Investment Margin

Despite the arguments summarized in Section 10.3.1, many economists, including the authors of the Mirrlees Report, still like to focus on an undistorted intensive margin and they advocate an ACE system. Extending the analysis for further aspects and margins, this is critical for at least two reasons.

First, implementing a pure ACE system where the notional deduction meets the normal rate of return on equity perfectly avoids a distortion on the intensive margin only if there are no other deductions related to capital inputs. In reality, however, this condition is violated regularly. As remuneration for the use of sunk research and development (R&D) or marketing investment, the licence fees for the resulting patent are mostly invoiced as sales-dependent royalties (i.e. the size of firm-level sales matters). Higher capital investment increases sales and, by this, tax-deductible licence payments. However, the higher royalties do not constitute real marginal costs in an economic sense. Therefore, the size-dependent royalty payment effectively reduces taxable returns to capital, implying an implicit subsidy on capital investment. Under a normal corporate tax system or a CBIT, the implicit investment subsidy is attractive because it reduces the standard distortion on the intensive margin. Under an ACE, however, all capital costs are tax deductible already and the additional incentive to trigger more tax savings from royalty payments, by increasing capital investment, ends up in a distortive subsidy, creating overinvestment (see Juranek et al., 2018, proposition 3). As the role of intangibles grows in modern economies, the effect of the tax treatment of royalties grows in importance as well.

Second, if there are supernormal profits, it is not only that the Diamond–Mirrlees production–efficiency theorem breaks down. There is also another investment margin that matters: the extensive margin captures non-marginal effects from investment shifting across countries or the discrete location choice about where to open an affiliate or a firm. Then, in a world with various distortions and investment margins, the argument in favour of ACE needs to be

[8] Our conclusion that the normal rate of return on capital should optimally be taxed at source also implies that we do not regard full expensing (or very fast depreciation) of investments for tax purposes desirable. Full expensing would exempt the normal return from taxation and implicitly impose a cash-flow tax.

handled with care. Following standard second-best trade-offs, it is not clear, per se, why one would like to eliminate the distortion on the intensive margin as long as there are other tax distortions left in the economy. The tax burden on the intensive margin under a CBIT system likely remains too high from an optimal tax perspective, but the zero tax burden on the intensive margin under an ACE is no longer optimal either.

In particular, our assumption regarding a budget-neutral reform is important when comparing ACE and CBIT on the investment margin. An ACE has a lower tax base and generates less tax revenue than a CBIT, all else equal. If the compensation is done within the corporate sector, however, this requires a higher corporate tax rate under ACE than under CBIT; see also the simulations in De Mooij and Devereux (2011).[9]

For marginal projects that only earn the normal rate of return, this does not matter. Here, an ACE can actually be beneficial and mute tax competition for such projects (because they effectively remain untaxed). A higher statutory corporate rate, however, leads to a higher effective tax rate on economic profits. This has a negative effect on the extensive investment margin.[10] A lower effective tax rate is more attractive for firms that run high economic profits that are driven by firm-specific knowledge (e.g. returns to intellectual property and R&D).[11] In contrast, location-specific rents (e.g. from exploitation of natural resources) trigger much less tax sensitivity on the extensive margin, because relocating a firm would imply giving up the source of the rents as well. In sum, for a small country that competes with other countries for discrete investments by highly productive companies, a lower effective average tax rate is a clear advantage in attracting (or holding) such knowledge-intensive firms.[12] Consequently, all else equal, a CBIT scores much better than an ACE in countries that host and attract firms with substantial supernormal firm-specific returns, because the extensive margin matters most for their investment decision. Simulations by De Mooij and Devereux (2011) for a unilateral adoption of ACE or CBIT in EU countries confirm the importance of the extensive margin and show that a unilateral CBIT leads to higher welfare than

[9] The Mirrlees Report, for example, alternatively suggests compensating the revenue losses by higher consumption taxes. Besides the issues of political feasibility, discussed in the introduction, we are in doubt whether there is much leeway in the Dutch tax system left to increase the effective tax burden on labour. With a marginal direct labour tax rate around 50%, kicking in at 68,500 euros, and a VAT rate of 21%, the total tax on labour income is very high already.

[10] We discuss the impact on profit shifting separately from the extensive investment margin (i.e. from investment shifting) in the next subsection.

[11] The trade-off between the intensive and extensive investment margin has already been pointed out in Bond (2000) but, except for the careful simulation analysis in De Mooij and Devereux (2011), it is often neglected.

[12] Note that some location-specific rents can still be taxed at high tax rates via special tax regimes. A striking example is the Norwegian petroleum tax code that applies with a 78% tax rate to petroleum business on the Norwegian continental shelf. Similarly, the production of natural gas in the Netherlands yields substantial revenues for the Dutch government.

a unilateral ACE adoption. More precisely, their CORTAX simulations show that a unilateral introduction of a CBIT increased welfare by 0.7% of GDP whereas the adoption of an ACE reduced welfare by 0.2% of GDP, on average. The positive effect of a CBIT matters more for countries with a large multinational sector.

10.3.3 International Profit Shifting

Another important aspect where the statutory and average effective tax rates matter is international profit shifting. Multinational companies structure their internal trade and capital flows (i.e. transfer pricing and debt shifting) such that paper profits are shifted from high-tax countries to countries with a low tax burden. This implies, in particular, that multinationals place intellectual property (e.g. patents, trademarks) and their internal banks in low-tax countries (or tax havens). The affiliates there then invoice royalty payments and interest expenses on internal debt that are deducted at a high rate in high-taxed affiliates, but only trigger low tax burdens in the haven country. The effect is that taxes are saved based on the statutory tax differential between the high-tax and low-tax country.

As a CBIT system comes with a lower corporate tax rate, it suffers less from profit shifting than an ACE system. Similar to economic profits, it becomes more attractive to locate paper profits in the CBIT country, all else equal. Hence, there will be less outward shifting of profits than under an ACE system. A CBIT country with a low corporate tax rate might even turn into a haven for royalty income. De Mooij and Devereux (2011) point out that a substantial part of the welfare effects in their simulations (see the previous subsection) is due to international profit shifting. Once again, the beneficial effect of lowering the statutory tax rate by introducing a CBIT is highest for Western European countries with a large multinational sector and high corporate tax rates.

Two additional points are important. First, it is sometimes argued that an ACE system allows for attracting internal banks of multinationals and benefitting from a tax planning opportunity. As the normal rate of return on equity is tax-exempt, placing equity in an affiliate in an ACE country and using it for internal lending to affiliates in other countries is an attractive strategy. The tax base in the internal bank will only consist of interest receipts that exceed the notional interest deduction. Belgium, for example, managed to benefit from this opportunity when changing from its 'coordination centre regime' to a general ACE system (Hebous and Ruf, 2017). This argument is correct if the counterfactual is the classical corporate tax system. In contrast, under a pure CBIT system, interest income would not be taxable at all (because interest expense is not tax deductible)—financing flows are just not taken into account in determining the tax base. Hence, a unilateral introduction of a CBIT could attract internal banks even more as the effective tax burden on equity-financed interest income would be zero.

Second, a CBIT removes any incentives to debt shifting and interest-rate manipulation on internal debt. In contrast, an ACE eliminates the standard preference of debt over equity, but there can still be an incentive for internal debt financing. As an ACE respects actual interest payments, multinationals still can over-invoice interest payments on internal debt in order to shift profits by transfer pricing.[13] Consequently, an ACE requires additional regulation on limiting interest deductibility. Only under an ACC system does the incentive for transfer price manipulation and internal debt financing vanish for allowance systems.

To summarize, international profit shifting favours lower corporate tax rates or alternative restrictions on corporate tax avoidance. Therefore, it renders a CBIT-like system more attractive than an ACE.

10.3.4 The Debt Bias

Since the financial crisis, the tax preference given to debt has been questioned heavily. This preference leads to excessive debt financing. As debt financing also implies truncated loss distributions, firms and managers can start to take excessive risks and externalize the costs to bondholders and society. Sørensen (2017) points out that the social risk premium on (external) debt is suboptimally high. De Mooij (2012) reviews arguments in favour of a preference of debt over equity and concludes that there are hardly any good arguments to maintain the differential tax treatment. In a rough calibration, Sørensen (2017) suggests that excessive debt financing causes a welfare loss of about 0.14% of GDP. This corresponds to an earlier estimate by Weichenrieder and Klautke (2008) who find a marginal dead weight loss of 0.08–0.23% of GDP. Both estimates indicate rather modest, but still non-negligible welfare effects. Thus, Sørensen (2017) advocates additional limits on interest deductibility (i.e. earnings stripping rules) and argues that a CBIT would be going too far. It would fully eliminate the distortion in the financing decision, but the negative investment effects from banning tax deductibility would be too high. In contrast, De Mooij (2012) favours a complete elimination of the tax preference and points to empirical evidence with ACE systems.

Importantly, these numbers and proposals refer to the economy in general and do not look specifically at the banking sector. In this sector, excessive debt financing is a substantial problem; see, for example, Admati and Hellwig (2013) for a summary. While the tax-induced debt bias surely aggravates the problem, the main driving force should be moral hazard by bank managers ('gambling for

[13] Note that different from debt shifting (i.e. replacing equity by internal debt at the normal rate of return), transfer pricing in interest rates does not trigger beneficial effects and rather should be curbed. See, for example, Schindler and Schjelderup (2016) and Gresik et al. (2017).

resurrection') who perceive their institutes as system-relevant and too big to fail. Indeed, the probability for bailouts is much higher for banks than for other firms.

For external debt, and in a national setting, there is hardly anything to add to these views. In an international setting with both tax competition and profit shifting, however, there is an argument in favour of some tax preference for (internal) debt over equity. Usually, investments of multinational firms are more mobile than investments of purely domestic firms. From an efficiency point of view, CIT systems would therefore apply differentiated corporate tax rates and tax domestic (mainly closely held) firms higher than mobile firms (i.e. multinationals). Typically, however, the schedule of corporate tax rates can hardly be differentiated along this line, either because of legal and political limitations or because of the lack of information. In order to bypass this problem, several studies find that it is optimal for countries under tax competition to give some preference for internal debt and to set weak thin capitalization rules. This targets mobile firms better, relative to immobile firms, as internal debt (i.e. lending among related affiliates) only matters for multinationals. Consequently, weak thin capitalization rules allow for a positive discrimination of multinationals and for a reduction of the tax burden on mobile capital without giving a tax benefit to immobile investors. Such a preference for internal debt is optimal for a government that maximizes national welfare (e.g. Hong and Smart, 2010; Haufler and Runkel, 2012; Haufler et al., 2018).

In sum, there are hardly any arguments for a preference of external debt over equity, but in a setting with profit shifting, the possibility to give some preference for internal debt shifting is welfare-enhancing under unilateral decision-making. Both the ACE (as well as ACC) and the CBIT fully remove this possibility and are rather too strict in their effects. In contrast, earnings stripping rules provide the necessary degrees of freedom. These arguments do not directly apply to the banking sector for which special, sector-specific (non-tax or tax) solutions might be necessary.

10.3.5 The Case of Small Firms

The points raised above are relevant for relatively large, widely held firms that have access to well-functioning capital markets, such that debt and equity are nearly perfect substitutes. The distribution of firms in an economy, however, is heavily skewed, and the CIT also taxes many closely held firms. For closely held firms, policy design is less driven by international tax arbitrage, and more by domestic redistributive considerations. In particular, for closely held firms, the CIT cannot be discussed separately from the personal income tax of the firm's owners. Two stylized facts stand out.

First, the debt-bias aspect is less clear for closely held firms. Though Devereux et al. (2018) report that the asymmetric treatment of debt and equity yields over-leveraging in the United Kingdom, Farre-Mensa and Ljungqvist (2016) do not find a significant effect in the United States. The latter authors suggest that capital market imperfections might prevent some smaller firms from exploiting the preferential treatment of debt. If so, the welfare loss induced by the asymmetric treatment of debt and equity is smaller for closely held firms (and the argument for insisting on neutrality is weaker).

In addition, studies reveal that the observed debt–equity ratios in small firms are also explained by other arguments than taxes. For example, a higher degree of profitability generally tends to reduce debt–equity ratios (Devereux et al., 2018; Mocking and Steegmans, 2017). When the availability of internal funds triggers lower debt–equity ratios, this suggests that some firms perceive debt as a relatively expensive mode of finance. This can partly explain the heterogeneity in observed debt–equity ratios across closely held firms (e.g. Mocking and Steegmans, 2017). A low debt–equity ratio might then (partly) signal the earnings-ability of the owner(s) of the closely held firm. Another argument is provided by Simon (2015) who suggests that in the case of imperfect information, owners might want to use relatively large equity investments to signal a strong commitment to their business. These arguments might lead to some tax differentiation between debt and equity at the corporate level for small and medium-sized enterprises (SMEs).

Second, and related, a budget-neutral CIT reform towards a more neutral treatment of debt and equity ex ante increases the tax burden on firms with relatively high debt–equity ratios. At the same time, it reduces the tax burden on firms with low levels of debt. Depending on general equilibrium effects (i.e. the degree to which market interest rates adjust and firms exit), these changes in tax burden will trigger ex post redistribution and can have structural implications. Given the observed heterogeneity in debt–equity ratios across closely held firms, these redistributive effects can be substantial.

Likely, the best way to tax the owners of closely held firms is by following the structure of a dual-income tax. As explained by, for example, Sørensen (2010), a dual income tax can easily be combined with the current classical CIT. Of course, in theory, an integration with an ACE or CBIT is perfectly possible in a closed economy with well-functioning capital markets. However, in an open economy, where residence-based and source-based taxes are not equivalent, this requires careful design, as neutrality properties might be lost.

Summarizing the above arguments, there seems to be no strong case for either a CBIT or an ACE when it comes to taxing closely held firms, but there are some potential risks related to such major tax reforms.

10.4 The Dutch Situation

The Netherlands is a country with a large multinational sector. It is a major hub for inward and outbound foreign direct investment (FDI); after Luxembourg, the Netherlands is the country with the highest FDI/GDP ratio world-wide. Thereby, there is more outbound than inward FDI. Lejour et al. (2019) report that the Netherlands is in the top three of absolute FDI positions (together with Luxembourg and the United States), holds 15% of the global FDI stock, and features a relative FDI position of five times GDP. 80% of the FDI positions are held by special purpose entities (SPEs), which have their main activities in other countries and are controlled by foreign owners. While a large part of the SPE income is simply routed through the Netherlands, a substantial share of about 24% (or about 37 billion euros per year) still remains in the Netherlands at present. In particular, the growth of royalty payments between 2004 and 2016 was substantial. More generally, it is very likely that the multinational sector in the Netherlands generates substantial economic rents in the industrial areas surrounding the harbour of Rotterdam and the high-tech agglomeration surrounding Eindhoven. Furthermore, the Amsterdam region hosts many financial services. Besides some network effects (and profits from the natural-gas business), these rents appear to be returns on both firm-specific knowledge (Eindhoven, Amsterdam) and location-specific rents (Rotterdam).

These stylized facts suggest that benefits from improving the international competitiveness and the extensive investment margin overcompensate for distortions on the intensive, national investment margin. Consequently, a broader tax base, combined with a lower corporate tax rate, appears to be preferable for the Netherlands. This view is perfectly in line with the simulation outcome for the Netherlands in De Mooij and Devereux (2011, figure 3). For a revenue-neutral reform with an adjustment of the corporate tax rate, an ACE adoption would reduce welfare in the Netherlands by 2.1% of GDP. This tops the list and the loss is 50% higher than the second-largest negative effect (–1.4% for Sweden). The effect is driven by distortions in the location choice of multinationals and the outward shifting of profits. In contrast, the introduction of a CBIT, combined with a reduction in the tax rate, fosters welfare by 1.7% of GDP. Though these simulation results are ten years old, there is no reason to believe that the qualitative implications have changed.

From an optimal-tax perspective, the conditions for some taxation of the normal rate of return on capital are fulfilled in the Netherlands. As pointed out in the paragraphs above, international corporate tax avoidance and transfer pricing are important for the Netherlands. This is no surprise because the Dutch corporate tax rate of 25% is a few percentage points above the EU and OECD averages. Furthermore, as in any country, there is some non-negligible avoidance of personal labour and capital income taxes. Taxes on capital income, for example, are highly fragmented in the Netherlands, with a tax on financial wealth other than pension savings and wealth invested in closely held firms. Therefore, capital income from minority shareholding goes largely untaxed, and in the case of large pension funds, some capital income even is subsidized (Lejour and van 't Riet, 2015; Jacobs, 2015).

In addition, income shifting between labour and capital is important particularly for self-employed managers of closely held firms. The Netherlands does not have a full dual income tax, and the high marginal tax rates on labour of about 50% provide incentives to declare income as business profits and to postpone taxation, if not avoid it completely. Importantly, the tax law only imposes a lower bound for the income that has to be reported as labour income. As a consequence, labour income is typically under-reported and paying tax is postponed by most self-employed managers (see Bettendorf et al., 2017). Moreover, self-employed managers show a preference for borrowing from their own firms instead of paying dividends and paying personal income tax.

10.5 Proposal for Future Development of the Dutch Corporate Tax System

Based on an evaluation of the Dutch situation in light of the aspects discussed in Section 10.3, we do not recommend a major tax reform in the form of either a CBIT or an ACE system. Instead, we recommend introducing a stripping rule that restricts both deductibility of net interest expenses (i.e. the difference between interest expenses and interest income) and royalty payments. This raises the tax burden on multinational firms by broadening the tax base compared with the current system, but it still leaves sufficient room for tax discrimination between domestic and international firms. Such a rule should have two major parameters. First, deductibility is restricted to a certain percentage of EBITDA. Based on the experience with earnings stripping rules to curb excessive debt financing, a deductibility threshold of 25–30% has proven effective, without being too costly. Incorporating royalty payments into an earnings stripping rule, a starting value of 35–40% of EBITDA appears reasonable. Importantly, based on the discussions in Germany and Norway, the rule should restrict expenses on both external and internal debt. Such a general restriction on interest expenses mitigates the debt bias problem. Second, small firms with a total volume of interest expenses and royalty payments below a certain absolute threshold should be exempted from the stripping rule. With respect to royalties, the rule should be designed such that only excessive, tax-motivated royalty payments are targeted. In other words, the deductibility threshold should exempt royalty payments of purely domestic firms to third parties and intra-firm royalty payments that also would have occurred in transactions between unrelated parties.

The reasoning is as follows. We genuinely believe that we live in a world with various distortions in which the normal rate of return on capital should also be taxed at source at the corporate level. For the Netherlands, the extensive investment margin and profit shifting are important. Therefore, it appears more attractive to broaden the corporate tax base and to reduce the corporate tax rate rather than to exempt part of business income from taxation. Such taxation needs to be flexible enough, however, and relying on a full CBIT system appears to be too costly. In particular, it might have a strong negative effect on the intensive investment margin. A CBIT would also potentially cause substantial redistributive income effects for owners of closely held firms.

Thus, we propose to develop the current traditional corporate tax further by implementing additional limitations on interest deductibility. This will push the system more towards a CBIT-like set-up, but at the same time maintains substantial degrees of freedom. For example, the second threshold allows for exempting small firms. By this a reform that mainly targets tax-arbitrage opportunities at multinationals does not affect closely held firms, for which a neutral treatment of debt and equity might have undesirable consequences for income redistribution. The current Dutch earnings stripping rule applies a threshold for the deductibility of (net) interest payments of 1 million euros, which is stricter than the minimum required standard in the EU Anti-Tax-Avoidance Directive (ATAD) 1 (i.e. 3 million euros). This seems sufficient to exempt most closely held firms from the earnings stripping rule.

One potential problem of an EBITDA rule is that it becomes binding in an economic downturn in which firms have low earnings and face liquidity constraints. Denying deductibility of interest expenses would aggravate the latter constraints. This argument was often made in the discussion of the German rules in 2008. To the best of our knowledge, however, there is no consistent evidence that firms suffered from such an effect during the massive economic downturn that followed the financial crisis in 2008/9. The liquidity-constraint argument also was discussed in the Norwegian expert committee on reforming the corporate tax system in Norway (NOU, 2014). There, the conclusion was that while being a problem in principle, it should not matter practically as long as the deductibility threshold does not become too strict.

With respect to profit shifting, CBIT and ACE eliminate debt shifting, but hardly have an effect on abusive transfer pricing. The latter, however, has a much stronger base-eroding effect on tax revenues and it has negative welfare implications. Therefore, a beneficial feature of earnings stripping rules is that they increase the cost of manipulating transfer pricing. Abusive transfer pricing crowds out the available budget for deductible interest expenses, either directly by increasing interest payments on internal debt or indirectly by reducing EBITDA via over-invoicing other production factors. For multinationals, however, maintaining tax deductibility on a broad capital stock is preferable to facing higher tax savings per unit of a limited, low-capital stock.[14] Thus, effectively, earnings stripping rules induce firms to reduce their abusive transfer pricing, whereas debt shifting might even increase. This is welfare-enhancing because debt shifting fosters FDI and ensures a second-best discrimination of mobile and immobile investment (Gresik et al., 2017).[15] In contrast, neither CBIT nor ACE puts additional costs on transfer pricing.

Furthermore, recent research shows that abusive transfer pricing in intangibles (e.g. patents and trademarks) does not trigger any investment effect, it only constitutes revenue losses for high-tax countries. A welfare-improving response is to deny tax deductibility of royalty payments and to compensate negative investment effects by weakening the thin capitalization rules (Juranek et al., 2020). An elegant way of implementing this result should be a 'royalty stripping rule' that exempts the arm's-length component of royalty payments and purely domestic firms in their payments to third parties. Similar to an earnings stripping rule, manipulating royalty payments beyond the deductible threshold does not lead to further tax savings, and incentives to international profit shifting are curbed. Effectively, the rule should apply to internal royalty payments. Because legal constraints might prevent implementing a limitation for multinational companies and internal payments only, a general royalty stripping limitation is also possible. Importantly, then, the threshold should make sure that the average royalty payments by domestic firms to third parties should be tax deductible and the allowance should allow for some normal return on patents in internal transactions. In sum, our proposal for a stripping rule implements two constraints on transfer pricing and simultaneously should mitigate negative investment effects.

Our proposal is largely in line with the idea of strengthening source-based taxation in Cnossen (2018). As a bottom-up strategy, the stripping rule does not require a major change in the system itself, it is easy to implement, and it can benefit from experiences in other countries with earnings stripping rules. Different from withholding taxes, stripping rules that restrict deductibility appear to be viable and sustainable reform options. A political advantage is that the rule can easily be adjusted by updating the two main parameters, based on insights of

[14] Formally, for a multinational that faces a restriction on its level of internal debt (e.g. a safe harbour rule) but no restriction on transfer pricing beyond the arm's-length principle, a marginal reduction of transfer pricing does not have any first-order effect on after-tax profits. The reduced transfer pricing gives slack to the earnings stripping rule and allows for more tax-deductible debt. This generates a first-order gain for investment, after-tax profits and welfare.

[15] This theoretical finding has empirical support. Evidence shows that a direct restriction on the level of internal debt always reduces investment. Büttner et al. (2018) do not find such a negative FDI effect for restrictions on transfer pricing rules.

the real effects on the Dutch economy.[16] The stripping rule would also allow for introducing a full CBIT by reducing the EBITDA threshold and phasing out interest deductibility over time. As Cnossen (2018) shows, the development of CIT systems in the EU is already on the way to a CBIT-like system. While Cnossen seems to be sympathetic to a CBIT under ideal conditions, he clearly advises caution and points to substantial costs related to fully eliminating deductibility of interest and royalty expenses. We fully agree with his advice and want to stress that we view a full CBIT system as too costly a reform option.

In principle, our proposal supports recent Dutch reform steps in corporate tax. The introduction of a general earnings stripping rule to restrict both debt bias and profit shifting is beneficial. However, the absolute threshold for interest deductibility of 1 million euros is stricter than necessary under the EU's ATAD. This implies that the Dutch rule applies to the largest multinational firms in the Netherlands (i.e. the relevant group), but potentially also to some of the larger domestic firms. From our perspective, targeting the second group might not be necessary. In addition, the Dutch government announced introducing a 'conditional' withholding tax on dividends (intended for 2024), interest and royalties (effective from 2021 onwards) in September 2018. We regard the royalty tax as welfare-enhancing. The tax is conditional on royalties being paid to countries with a low (i.e. less than 9%) tax burden on corporations. Instead of limiting the royalty tax to black-listed countries, however, the tax deductibility of royalties should be generalized to a stripping rule that restricts all royalty payments, independent of the target country.

With this development and our proposed rule, the Netherlands would be well embedded in a broad international development, including the OECD Base Erosion and Profit Shifting (BEPS) Action Plan. With the EU ATAD, the use of earnings stripping rules becomes mandatory in the EU from 2024. Norway recently decided to follow the German example of using such rules in a strict sense and to restrict both internal and external debt. Since 2018, the United States has also operated an earnings stripping rule that is very close to the German rule, and it plans to tighten it further by changing the threshold definition from EBITDA to EBIT. Furthermore, in 2018, Germany enacted rules that restrict tax deductibility of royalty payments going to low-tax countries. Also, since 2018, the United States has tried to implement a minimum taxation of royalties via the

[16] This strategy, applied by the Norwegian government in 2014, first introduced an earnings stripping rule falling on internal debt only and guaranteeing deductibility of 30% of EBITDA. In 2016, the threshold was reduced to 25% of EBITDA and, since 2019, deductibility of both internal and external debt is restricted.

'Global Intangible Low-Taxed Income' (GILTI) and the 'Base Erosion and Anti-Abuse Tax' (BEAT) provisions.[17]

Importantly, as discussed in Section 10.3.4, we also believe that debt bias is an important issue for tax reform, but we do not believe that it should be the commanding aspect. The major problem with excessive debt financing lies inside the banking sector and we would suggest finding sector-specific rules, not necessarily tax related, that fix that problem within the banking sector. If we should underestimate the impact of debt bias on the overall economy, or if policymakers have a strong preference with respect to fully eliminating debt bias in the tax system, the alternative to our proposal would be to introduce a partial ACC. Granting some notional deduction of financing costs for total corporate capital fully eliminates the tax preference of debt over equity. Setting the notional deduction significantly below the market interest rate will ensure that the normal rate of return is still taxed. The broader tax base, relative to an ACE, also mitigates problems related to a higher corporate tax rate and distortions on the extensive margin and profit shifting.

10.6 Conclusions

We believe that we live in a world with various distortions where neither the production-efficiency theorem nor the Atkinson–Stiglitz theorem apply. Some distortions on all margins, including the intensive investment margin, are optimal. Consequently, we propose developing the current traditional corporate tax further by introducing a combined stripping rule. This rule restricts tax deductibility of net interest expenses and royalty payments (e.g. to 35–40% of EBITDA). Such a rule limits the debt bias and effectively restricts profit shifting, but still allows for competing for FDI and mitigates the costs of a normal CBIT. Furthermore, an additional size threshold exempting small firms avoids overburdening the SME sector. With its recent decisions on earnings stripping rules and a royalty tax, the Netherlands has taken the first steps on the way to such a system already. Hence, it could be implemented without a major system change and experiment.

As a final cautious remark, our analysis rests on the assumption that there will not be large-scale harmonization of tax reforms on the international level. If the EU, for example, were to introduce a joint tax base and harmonized tax rates for all member countries, this would reduce the distortions on the extensive margin (and, to some extent, also profit shifting) so that the optimal tax systems would move towards an ACE, all else equal. Two important comments apply then. First,

[17] The advantage of a royalty stripping rule, however, is that it is a purely unilateral measure to defend the domestic tax base and it does not require a substantial definition of an 'effectively low tax burden'.

it is not clear whether it is desirable to have the same tax bases and tax rates in a large set of very heterogeneous countries. This would reduce flexibility to adjust to national shocks further and it might lead to similar effects and situations like the adoption of the euro in the European Currency Union. Second, even if all costs on the extensive margin are eliminated, a pure ACE system is not optimal as there always should be some source tax burden falling on the normal rate of return.

References

Admati, A. R. and Hellwig, M. (2013), *The Bankers' New Clothes: What's Wrong With Banking and What to Do About It*, Princeton University Press, Princeton, NJ.

Alstadsæter, A., Johannesen, N., and Zucman, G. (2018), 'Tax evasion and inequality', *American Economic Review*, 109(6), 2073–103.

Auerbach, A. J. and Devereux, M. P. (2018), 'Cash-flow taxes in an international setting', *American Economic Journal: Economic Policy*, 10, 69–94.

Bettendorf, L. J. H., Lejour, A., and van 't Riet, M. (2017), 'Tax bunching by owners of small corporations', *De Economist*, 165, 411–38.

Boadway, R. and Bruce, N. (1984), 'A general proposition on the design of a neutral business tax', *Journal of Public Economics*, 24, 231–9.

Bond, S. R. (2000), 'Levelling up or levelling down? Some reflections on the ACE and CBIT proposals, and the future of the corporate tax base', in S. Cnossen (ed.), *Taxing Capital Income in the European Union*, Oxford University Press, Oxford, pp. 161–79.

Bond, E. W. and Gresik, T. A. (2020), 'Unilateral tax reform: border adjusted taxes, cash flow taxes, and transfer pricing', *Journal of Public Economics*, 184.

Brekke, K. R., Pires, A. J. G., Schindler, D., and Schjelderup, G. (2017), 'Capital taxation and imperfect competition: ACE vs. CBIT', *Journal of Public Economics*, 147, 1–15.

Büttner, T., Overesch, M., and Wamser, G. (2018), 'Anti profit-shifting rules and foreign direct investment', *International Tax and Public Finance*, 25, 553–80.

Clausing, K. A. (2013), 'Who pays the corporate tax in a global economy?', *National Tax Journal*, 66, 151–84.

Cnossen, S. (2018), 'Corporation taxes in the European Union: slowly moving toward comprehensive business income taxation?' *International Tax and Public Finance*, 25, 808–40.

De Mooij, R. A. (2012), 'Tax biases to debt finance: assessing the problem, finding solutions', *Fiscal Studies*, 33, 489–512.

De Mooij, R. A. and Devereux, M. P. (2011), 'An applied analysis of ACE and CBIT reforms in the EU', *International Tax and Public Finance*, 18, 93–120.

Devereux, M. P., Maffini, G., and Xing, J. (2018), 'Corporate tax incentives and capital structure: new evidence from UK firm-level tax returns', *Journal of Banking and Finance*, 88, 250–66.

Diamond, P. A. and Saez, E. (2011), 'The case for a progressive tax: from basic research to policy recommendations', *Journal of Economic Perspectives*, 25(4), 165–90.

Diamond, P. A. and Mirrlees, J. A. (1971), 'Optimal taxation and public production I: production efficiency', *American Economic Review*, 61(1), 8–27.

Farre-Mensa, J. and Ljungqvist, A. (2016), 'Do measures of financial constraints measure financial constraints?' *Review of Financial Studies*, 29, 271–308.

Fuest, C., Peichl, A., and Siegloch, S. (2018), 'Do higher corporate taxes reduce wages? Micro evidence from Germany', *American Economic Review*, 108(2), 393–418.

Gordon, R. (1986), 'Taxation of investment and savings in a world economy', *American Economic Review*, 76(5), 1086–1102.

Gresik, T. A., Schindler, D., and Schjelderup, G. (2017), 'Immobilizing corporate income shifting: should it be safe to strip in the harbor?' *Journal of Public Economics*, 152, 68–78.

Haufler, A. and Runkel, M. (2012), 'Firms' financial choices and thin capitalization rules under corporate tax competition', *European Economic Review*, 56, 1087–1103.

Haufler, A., Mardan, M., and Schindler, D. (2018), 'Double tax discrimination to attract FDI and fight profit shifting: the role of CFC rules', *Journal of International Economics*, 114, 25–43.

Hebous, S. and Ruf, M. (2017), 'Evaluating the effects of ACE systems on multinational debt financing and investment', *Journal of Public Economics*, 156, 131–49.

Hong, Q. and Smart, M. (2010), 'In praise of tax havens: international tax planning and foreign direct investment', *European Economic Review*, 54, 82–95.

Institute for Fiscal Studies (1991), 'Equity for companies: a corporation tax for the 1990s', Institute for Fiscal Studies (IFS), London.

Jacobs B. (2015), 'Belastingen op kapitaalinkomen in Nederland', *Tijdschrift voor Openbare Financiën*, 47(1), 24–48.

Juranek, S., Schindler, D., and Schjelderup, G. (2018), 'Transfer pricing regulation and taxation of royalty payments', *Journal of Public Economic Theory*, 20, 67–84.

Juranek, S., Schindler, D., and Schneider, A. (2020), 'Royalty taxation under tax competition and profit shifting', NHH Discussion Paper FOR 11/2020.

Keen, M. and Piekkola, H. (1997), 'Simple rules for optimal taxation of international capital income', *Scandinavian Journal of Economics*, 99, 447–61.

Keuschnigg, C. and Dietz, M. D. (2007), 'A growth oriented dual income tax', *International Tax and Public Finance*, 14, 191–221.

Koethenbuerger, M. and Stimmelmayr, M. (2014), 'Corporate deductibility provisions and managerial incentives', *Journal of Public Economics*, 111, 120–30.

Krugman, P. (2017), 'Trickle down? Not now, and not for a while at best (wonkish)' (https://www.nytimes.com/2017/12/24/opinion/trickle-down-not-now-and-not-for-a-while-at-best-wonkish.html).

Krugman, P. (2019), 'Bursting the billionaire bubble' (https://www.nytimes.com/2019/11/11/opinion/michael-bloomberg-billionaires.html).

Lejour, A, and M. van 't Riet, 2015. 'Een meer uniforme belasting van kapitaalinkomen', CPB Policy Brief No. 2015/16.

Lejour, A., Möhlmann, J., van 't Riet, M., and Benschop, T. (2019), 'Dutch shell companies and international tax planning', CPB Discussion Paper, June 2019.

Mirrlees, J. A., Adam, S., Besley, T. J., Blundell, R., Bond, S., Chote, R., Gammie, M., Johnson, P., Myles, G. D., and Poterba, J. M. (2011), *Tax by Design: The Mirrlees Review*, Oxford University Press, Oxford.

Mocking, R. and Steegmans, J. (2017), 'Capital structure determinants and adjustment speed: an empirical analysis of Dutch SMEs', CPB Discussion Paper 357.

NOU (2014), 'Kapitalbeskatning i en internasjonal økonomi', Norges offentlige utredninger NOU2014:13, Oslo.

Radulescu, D. M. and Stimmelmayr, M. (2007), 'ACE versus CBIT: which is better for investment and welfare?' *CESifo Economic Studies*, 53, 294–328.

Schindler, D. and Schjelderup, G. (2016), 'Multinationals and income shifting by debt', *International Journal of the Economics of Business*, 23, 263–86.

Simon, J. (2015), 'Optimal debt bias in corporate income taxation', CESifo Working Paper No. 5561.

Slemrod, J. and Wilson, J. D. (2009), 'Tax competition with parasitic tax havens', *Journal of Public Economics*, 93, 1261–70.

Sørensen, P. B. (2010), 'Dual income taxes: a Nordic tax system', in I. Claus, N. Gemmell, M. Harding, and D. White (eds), *Tax Reform in Open Economies*, Edward Elgar, Cheltenham, pp. 78–108.

Sørensen, P. B. (2017), 'Taxation and the optimal constraint on corporate debt finance: why a comprehensive business income tax is suboptimal', *International Tax and Public Finance*, 24, 731–53.

Suárez Serrato, J. C. and Zidar, O. (2016), 'Who benefits from state corporate tax cuts? A local labour markets approach with heterogeneous firms', *American Economic Review*, 106(9), 2582–624.

US Department of Treasury (1992), 'Integration of the individual and corporate tax systems: taxing business income once', US Government Printing Office, Washington, DC.

Weichenrieder, A. J. and Klautke, T. (2008), 'Taxes and the efficiency costs of capital distortions', CESifo Working Paper No. 2341.

11

Options for Origin- and Destination-Based Rent Taxes in the Netherlands

*Shafik Hebous and Alexander Klemm**

11.1 Introduction

Taxes on economic rents are efficient: they are neutral with respect to the level of investment and the source of funding. Nevertheless, most countries, including the Netherlands, continue to use corporate income taxes (CITs) that cover—or at least attempt to cover—broader measures of profit, including normal returns.

When considering the benefits of potential reforms, a starting point is an assessment of the relevance of distortions of the current CIT and the likelihood that alternative systems would address these distortions. Two important problems of the current system are: (1) its distortions with respect to investment and financing decisions (debt bias); and (2) its highly vulnerable international character (i.e. it is prone to tax competition and profit shifting). Traditional rent taxes address the first of these problems but remain vulnerable to tax competition and profit shifting. Destination-based versions of these taxes avoid this problem but have not been tried and are likely to face transitional costs.

We consider different rent taxes and the relative pros and cons for their adoption, as well as their optimal design, from the point of view of a small open economy such as the Netherlands. The chapter is structured as follows. The following section summarizes the problems of the current approach to CITs mentioned above and provides an overview of reform options, covering both rent taxes and the comprehensive business income tax (CBIT) as the main alternative proposal. We then focus entirely on rent taxes. In Sections 11.3 and 11.4, we discuss traditional cash-flow taxes and their destination-based implementation, respectively. In Section 11.5, we deal with allowances for corporate

* Shafik Hebous (shebous@imf.org) is Deputy Division Chief and Alexander Klemm (aklemm@imf.org) is the Division Chief at the Tax Policy Division, Fiscal Affairs Department, International Monetary Fund (IMF). We are grateful for comments from Sijbren Cnossen, Bas Jacobs, Marko Koethenbuerger, Paul Lankhorst, Dirk Schindler, Robin Willemstein, and conference participants. The views expressed in this paper are those of the authors and do not necessarily represent the views of the IMF, its Executive Board or IMF management.

Shafik Hebous and Alexander Klemm, *Options for Origin- and Destination-Based Rent Taxes in the Netherlands* In: *Tax by Design for the Netherlands.* Edited by: Sijbren Cnossen and Bas Jacobs, Oxford University Press.
 DOI: 10.1093/oso/9780192855244.003.0011

equity and related proposals, including their destination-based implementation. We conclude in Section 11.6.

11.2 Problems of the Current Corporate Income Tax System

11.2.1 Debt Bias and Investment Distortions

The tax treatment of interest expenses is one factor that encourages corporate borrowing. The Netherlands provides tax deductions for interest expenses, as do most other countries, whereas returns to equity cannot be deducted. Taxation of dividends and interest at the recipient level typically does not undo this. First, while dividend taxes are usually lower than those on interest, the tax that combines dividends and CIT still exceeds the personal income tax on interest in most countries. Second, many investors are exempt from tax (e.g. pension and investment funds) or are foreign residents benefiting from zero or reduced withholding rates, in which case there is not even a partial mitigation of the debt bias as a result of recipient-level taxation. In the Netherlands, most investors are in this position as there is no tax on actual interest or dividends (instead notional returns, or effectively financial wealth stocks, are taxed). Empirical evidence suggests that the debt bias is not just a theoretical possibility. An international consensus estimate of the elasticity is 0.27, meaning that, ceteris paribus, the debt-to-assets ratio rises by 2.7 percentage points if the marginal tax rate increases by 10 percentage points (Feld, Heckemeyer, and Overesch, 2013).

The debt bias creates direct welfare losses by distorting firms' risk behaviour and investment decisions. For example, agency costs in the form of incentivizing managers to operate efficiently increases the risk premium. Sørensen (2014) studies the deadweight loss associated with debt bias and finds that it is about 0.1% of gross domestic product (GDP) in a calibrated model for Norway. Weichenrieder and Klautke (2008) and Gordon (2010) estimate similar magnitudes for Germany and the United States, respectively.

However, these welfare calculations ignore the negative externalities associated with excessive corporate leverage and other macro-economic implications that are challenging to quantify. Theory and empirics suggest that over-borrowing in the private sector can be a critical component of the financial vulnerability of firms. It is a potential source of systemic credit externality, it propagates macro-economic shocks and it increases not only the probability but also the length of macroeconomic and financial crises (Bernanke and Campbell, 1988; Bianchi, 2011). For example, Giroud and Mueller (2017) find that employment in highly leveraged firms during the global financial crisis declined significantly more than in low-leveraged firms. Sutherland and Hoeller (2012) report that higher leverage ratios in the non-financial corporate sector significantly increase the probability of a recession.

Thus, the empirical literature indicates that the debt bias has real economic costs. This issue is of particular relevance for the Netherlands, where corporate-sector debt is considerably above the average of advanced economies (Figure 11.1).

11.2.2 Tax Competition and Profit Shifting

Under current CIT arrangements, multinational enterprises (MNEs) are able to lower their tax liability by locating profits in low-tax jurisdictions. Estimates of the magnitude of profit shifting vary, but existing results suggest it is sizeable. Tørsløv, Wier, and Zucman (2018) find that the Netherlands is an important location for the profits of foreign affiliates. The attractiveness of the Netherlands for corporate profits is in part driven by its rich tax treaty network, generous rulings, light taxation of dividends and, often, no withholding taxes on interest and royalties.

CIT rates have been on a downward path since the early 1980s. This is often attributed to tax competition (i.e. the efforts of governments to attract tax bases by offering low taxes). Taxes can be lowered in many ways: by lowering the main rates or by narrowing the tax base. However, the dynamics of the competitive process are likely to put stronger pressure on rates than bases. If the issue is profit shifting, then this is intuitive; in most circumstances, any reported profit that is

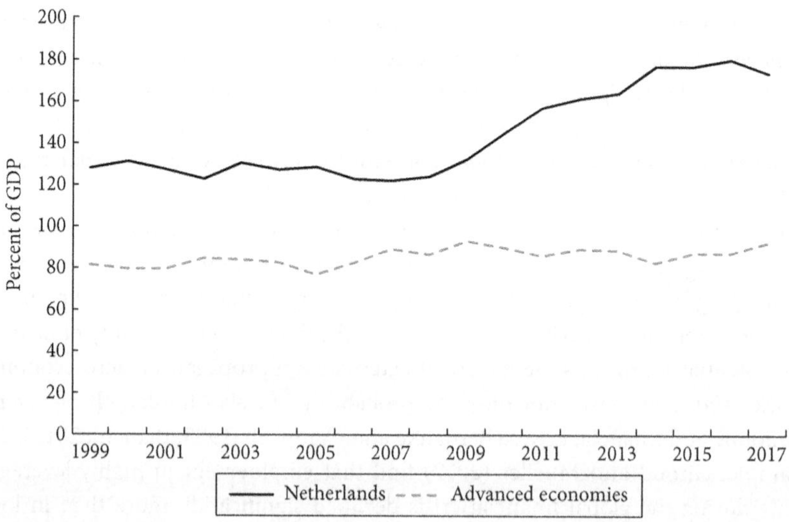

Figure 11.1 Non-financial corporate debt
Source: BIS Statistics.

artificially shifted will benefit from the full tax rate difference.[1] As this is just a reporting exercise, there is normally no effect on investment levels and hence on features of the tax base, such as investment or depreciation allowances. If the issue is competition for real capital, then the most important feature of the tax system is less obvious, as firms could invest in countries offering generous investment allowances or low tax rates. However, as argued, for example, by Devereux, Griffith, and Klemm (2002), the most mobile firms are likely to be large, highly profitable MNEs earning rents, for example as a result of patents, know-how, or economies of scale. They stand to gain more from a cut in the tax rate, which applies to the entire profit, while an investment allowance has a fixed benefit, which is particularly attractive for low-profit operations. Hence, irrespective of whether countries compete for reported profits or real MNE investment, there is likely to be stronger pressure on tax rates than on the definition of tax bases. Indeed, many reforms have combined cuts in tax rates with base broadening.

In line with this trend, the Netherlands announced that it would gradually lower its general CIT rate from 25% to 20.5% by 2021, which is slightly below the current OECD average of 23.5%.[2]

11.2.3 Overview of Reform Options

Rent taxes address the debt bias and other inefficiencies, either fully or partially, depending on their precise design. While the details of the different rent taxes are discussed below, it should be mentioned that rent taxes are not the only possible solution to debt bias. The other main solution is a CBIT system, which achieves debt-equity neutrality by denying all interest deductions. However, this system increases the cost of capital, which potentially negatively affects investment, and it is not efficient insofar as normal returns remain taxed (IMF, 2016). This tax system does not exist in practice.[3]

Between a CBIT and full interest deductibility, there are many systems that limit interest deductibility. Schindler and Vrijburg (Chapter 10) argue that rules limiting interest deductibility to a share of profits are a good compromise solution, reducing the scope for profit shifting, while allowing interest deductibility in many normal business circumstances. Traditionally, the Benelux countries, including the Netherlands, did not have general thin-capitalization rules. However,

[1] Major profit-shifting mechanisms used by firms are the manipulation of transfer pricing, the location of intangible assets and the shifting of debt. Debt shifting (i.e. the overweighting of debt in countries with high taxes) is linked to the interest deductibility, which not only results in the debt bias discussed above, but also allows for profit shifting.

[2] Profits up to 200,000 euros will be taxed at 15%.

[3] For a more in-depth discussion of the CBIT, see Schindler and Vrijburg (Chapter 10). For a discussion that countries may be moving towards the CBIT, see Cnossen (2018). For a general treatment of fundamental CIT reform, see, for example, Auerbach, Devereux, and Simpson (2010).

following the European Union (EU) 2017 Anti-tax Avoidance Directive (ATAD), they are currently in the process of introducing rules that deny interest deductions for net interest payments exceeding 30% of earnings before interest, tax, depreciation, and amortization (EBITDA).[4] Member states should fully comply with ATAD by 2022.

However, it should be emphasized that while such rules may limit debt shifting and the debt bias, they do not eliminate these. Up to the limitation threshold, there is still an incentive to rely on debt rather than other sources of finance.[5] Furthermore, in practice, they are designed as anti-tax avoidance rules, whereby standalone companies and small companies (as defined by some turnover threshold) are not subjected to limitations on interest deductions. Moreover, financial companies, including banks, are also typically excluded.[6]

However, while rent taxes address the debt bias, they do not tackle tax competition and profit shifting (except through debt). Indeed, by moving to a narrower tax base—from normal profits and rents, to rents only—they necessitate a higher tax rate for a given revenue requirement. They thus go in the opposite direction to where tax competition is pushing countries, which may explain the weak uptake of such taxes, despite their well-known efficiency properties. More recently, destination-based versions of rent taxes have been increasingly discussed. With a border adjustment, it is possible to design rent-based taxes that are robust to profit shifting and tax competition.[7]

11.3 Cash-Flow Taxes

11.3.1 Theoretical Background

Meade (1978) systematically classified cash-flow taxes into three types, with different definitions of tax bases, as follows.

- The real (R) base comprises net cash flow from all non-financial transactions and therefore allows immediate expensing of investment. Financial flows are ignored, so that there is no interest deductibility.

[4] This rule has been one topic of the OECD/G20 Base Erosion and Profit Shifting Project (BEPS) initiative (Action 4).

[5] It is only in cases where the desired debt level is above the amount benefitting from preferential treatment that there would be no distortions to the debt stock.

[6] See De Mooij and Hebous (2018) for a detailed discussion about restricting interest deductions and debt bias.

[7] See De Mooij, Hebous, and Liu (Chapter 12) for an assessment of other reform options with a destination-based element (formulary apportionment and residual profits allocation) for the Netherlands.

- The real and financial (R+F) base adds the net financial flows, including interest but also net changes in all types of debt.
- The share transactions (S) base is made up by a firm's net distributions (dividends and share buybacks).

A common feature of all of these taxes is that they restrict the tax base to rents. For the R base tax, this can be seen by noting that an investment leads to an immediate tax deduction. Future returns are taxed, but if the returns match the discount rate, then the present value of future tax payments matches the tax value of the deduction exactly, so the net present value of the tax on an investment earning the normal rate of return is zero. For the R+F base, a similar argument applies. However, to ensure that debt-financed projects are not treated preferentially despite interest deductibility, there is an immediate tax charge on any debt issuance. For the S base, the argument is similar to the R base, but it is capital raised to fund an investment that is deductible rather than the investment itself.

Comparing the three tax bases, the R base is slightly narrower than the other two bases. The difference lies in the rents earned by the financial sector. Under an R+F-base, all rents are included, because all interest receipts are part of the tax base. Similarly, under an S base, all rents are covered because all distributions are taxed equally, whether by financial or non-financial sector firms. Under an R base, however, rents earned by the financial sector from dealing with individuals go untaxed. Rents earned from dealings with businesses are still taxed, but this occurs at the level of non-financial sector businesses through the non-deductibility of interest.

While it is efficient to exempt normal returns at the corporate level and to focus on rents, this does not necessarily mean that normal returns cannot be taxed at all. One way to subject these to taxation, without major negative efficiency costs, is to impose a tax on the normal return (e.g. through a wealth tax), at the individual level on residents only. This avoids much of the tax competition, because people are less mobile than capital. Moreover, provided that all assets are covered, individuals will not reduce their exposure to investment in firms and physical capital, as alternatives are also taxed. One difficulty, in practice, is that some assets tend to be taxed more lightly (most typically owner-occupied housing), and this creates distortions.

11.3.2 Practical Implementation and Challenges

To the best of our knowledge, no country has adopted a pure cash-flow tax of the types described above, but some tax reforms have brought countries close. First, several countries have allowed full expensing of investment, either temporarily (as in the 2017 US reform) or for a subset of firms (small and medium-sized enterprises or the natural resource sector). Because these countries have generally maintained interest deductibility, the system subsidizes debt-financed investment rather than achieving neutrality. In the period 2008–13, Mexico had a tax that approximated an R base (i.e. Impuesto Empresarial a Tasa Única, IETU), but it was implemented as a minimum tax and did not replace the CIT. A few countries (Estonia and Latvia in the EU, and Georgia) have CITs that are levied on distributions only, and therefore resemble an S base, but they typically do not grant a deduction for capital increases.

Given the theoretical advantages of cash-flow taxes, this lack of take up may be puzzling. One explanation is that all of these taxes involve more frequent tax losses, especially regarding new and growing firms, either because investment (R and R+F) or capital increases (S) are deductible. This requires tax refunds either to be paid, which is politically unappealing, or to be carried forward with interest, which creates complications. It is likely that the reasons mentioned in the introduction are more important, such the fact that CIT acts as a backstop to personal income tax, and tax competition, which may have induced countries to prefer lowering tax rates rather than narrowing bases.

11.4 Destination-Based Cash-Flow Taxes

11.4.1 Theory

Bond and Devereux (2002) have proposed a destination-based cash-flow tax (DBCFT), which addresses pressures from tax competition through a border adjustment, under which imports are taxed and exports are exempt from tax. More recent contributions, such as Auerbach et al. (2017a) provide further theoretical analysis and discuss implementation issues. Further, Auerbach et al. (2017b) look more deeply at various profit-shifting channels, such as transfer-pricing manipulation, debt, and the location of intangibles. The upshot of these studies is that global adoption of a DBCFT would eliminate profit-shifting opportunities and tax competition. The basic observation is that consumers are arguably less mobile than capital and there is little room to compete over their location. Furthermore, in theory, the adjustment of the real exchange rate eliminates incentives to relocate capital across countries in order to benefit from differences in the cost of production.[8]

[8] For countries, such as the Netherlands, with a fixed exchange rate within the Euro area, the real adjustment would have to take place through the price level, which would take longer. Even under flexible exchange rates, there is no consensus about instant adjustment. For example, Buiter (2018) argues that, depending on the currency in which prices are set, the initial adjustment could be different. In the long run, however, the real exchange rate should adjust fully, unless there are some hysteresis effects resulting from the transition.

Regarding profit-shifting incentives under the DBCFT, in contrast to current CIT arrangements, affiliates of MNEs in high-tax countries have no incentive to overprice their imports from group members in low-tax countries (i.e. to inflate costs in high-tax countries), because these costs are not deductible. Furthermore, there are no incentives to underprice exports of affiliates in high-tax countries (i.e. to reduce reported income), because revenues from exports are excluded from the tax base. In addition, benefits from debt shifting vanish because the DBCFT denies the deductibility of interest expenses.

However, the outcome of the analysis is dramatically different if the adoption of the DBCFT is not global but unilateral or by a subset of jurisdictions. In that case, there is a very strong incentive to shift profits from other countries into the DBCFT regime through the usual profit-shifting schemes. Note that the country adopting the DBCFT does not benefit from this. Any profit shifted into that country would be untaxed, whether it is reported as exaggerated exports, under-priced imports, or interest inflows; these shifted profits escape taxation entirely. Similarly, it would be attractive to move production into DBCFT countries. It is therefore important to distinguish carefully between global and country-specific adoption of the DBCFT when analysing its effect.

11.4.2 Effect on Revenue When Adopted Globally

Hebous, Klemm, and Stausholm (2020) estimate the effect of a hypothetical DBCFT on revenue in eighty countries. They present various ways of estimating the DBCFT tax base using macro-economic data. One method, which mainly relies on national accounts statistics, is to start with the operating surplus of the corporate sector in the economy and to deduct investment (i.e. a correction term to simulate the cash-flow base) and net exports (i.e. the correction term to simulate the border-adjustment component). The results suggest that, in the case of global adoption of the DBCFT, corporate tax revenues would remain at a similar level, on average, but would be marked by major redistribution across countries.

Hebous et al. (2020) empirically identify three country characteristics that affect the DBCFT revenue especially in the short term. Countries more likely to lose from a shift to a DBCFT, assuming unchanged tax rates, are those with a significant dependency on natural resources, trade surpluses, and high incomes. The short-term effect on revenue might be reversed over time (i.e. as trade balances adjust) and/or offset by changing the tax rate. This is because higher tax rates are feasible in a destination-based tax system, which is robust to profit shifting and tax competition, while the rent base ensures neutrality with respect to investment.

In the case of the Netherlands, two of these factors are particularly relevant (i.e. the trade surplus and the level of development). Additionally, it can be argued that, given the role of the Netherlands as a conduit country for foreign direct investment, a DBCFT system would eliminate any potential benefits from profit shifting into the Netherlands. However, surprisingly, the findings of Hebous et al. (2020) indicate that the Netherlands could achieve a revenue gain (based on 2011 statistics).[9]

To examine the effect on revenues in the Netherlands in greater detail, we expand the analysis in Hebous et al. (2020) to include recent years. A comparison of actual CIT and hypothetical DBCFT revenues in the Netherlands over twenty years reveals that the revenue gain in one particular year is neither an outlier nor typical (Figure 11.2). On average, over this time period, introducing a DBCFT would have reduced revenues by 0.25% of GDP, with the loss approaching 1% of GDP in the two most recent years.

To provide deeper insights into the evolution of the hypothetical DBCFT revenue, Figure 11.3 shows the main determinants of the tax base over time. It reveals that while the investment deduction is similar in size to the deduction for net exports in recent years, the latter is much more volatile and explains the recent decline in the tax base.

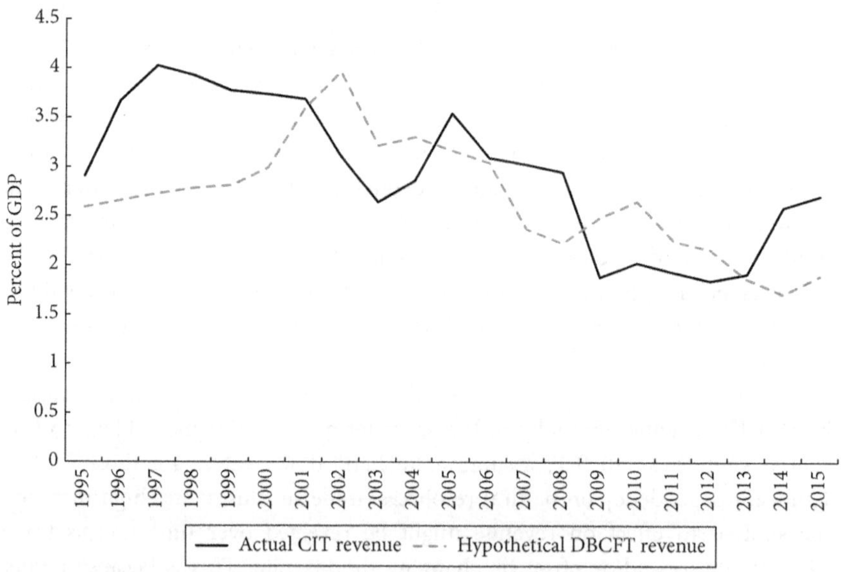

Figure 11.2 DBCFT revenues compared with actual CIT revenues
Source: Authors' calculations.

[9] The study uses the year 2011 because this maximizes the number of observations.

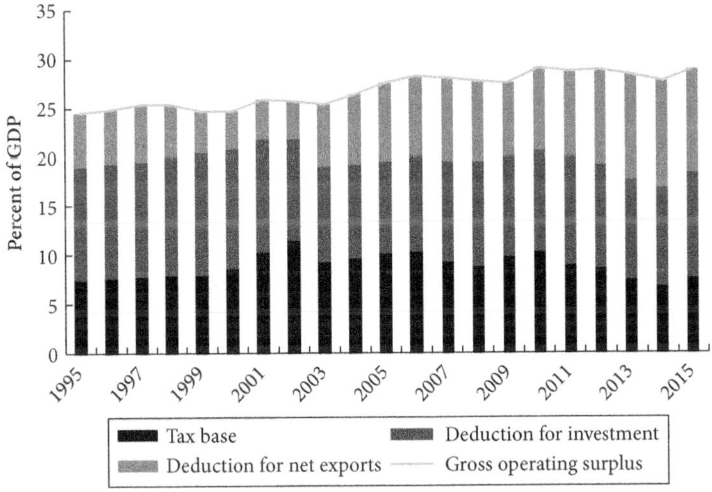

Figure 11.3 The hypothetical DBCFT tax base in the Netherlands
Source: Authors' calculations.

11.4.3 Effect on Revenue When Adopted by Competitors

A different picture emerges when analysing the effect on the Netherlands when the DBCFT is adopted by trading partners.[10] Assuming one country were to adopt a DBCFT, this country would turn into an extreme low-tax jurisdiction for shifted profits and rent-earning investments selling to world markets, with the tax rate effectively dropping to zero (although it would remain unchanged for goods sold in that country). Following Hebous et al. (2020), the negative effect on revenue can be calculated by modelling this as a cut in the foreign tax rate to zero. As it is assumed that all other countries do not change anything, the average foreign tax rate falls by the weight that the foreign country adopting the DBCFT has in international economic relations with the Netherlands. We proxy this using stocks from foreign direct investment. Having calculated the resulting decline in the relative tax rate compared with the rest of the world, the effect on Dutch revenue can then be estimated using elasticities for profit shifting and real-investment responses from the literature.[11]

[10] If, instead, the Netherlands were the only country to adopt a DBCFT, the effect on revenue, abstracting from any retaliation or real adjustments, would be the same as that calculated under global adoption above: there would be negative spill-overs on other countries, but no revenue gain, because profits shifted inward would not be taxed.

[11] We use a profit-shifting elasticity of 1.5 from a meta study by Beer, De Mooij, and Liu (2020). For real investment, we use 2.4 from De Mooij and Ederveen (2008), which we multiply by an assumed capital intensity of 1/3.

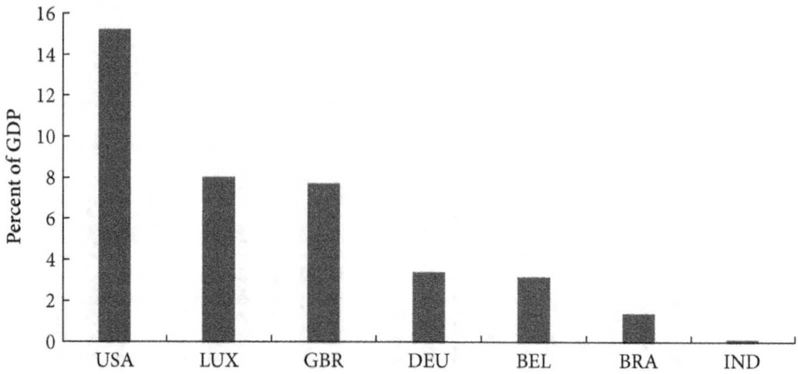

Figure 11.4 Spill-overs on the Netherlands from the adoption of a hypothetical DBCFT by other countries
Source: Authors' calculations.

To illustrate the likely effect, we calculate the expected revenue loss in the Netherlands if one of the neighbouring countries, or the United States as the largest economy, or India or Brazil, as examples of emerging markets, were to adopt a DBCFT. This is purely illustrative and it is not meant to imply that any of these countries are indeed likely to adopt such a tax. As shown in Figure 11.4, the resulting revenue loss could be quite significant for the Netherlands, reaching 14% of its CIT revenue from MNEs if a closely linked country adopted a DBCFT unilaterally. While this is high, the revenue loss could be even higher if the Netherlands also adopted a DBCFT, as shown above, where the loss reached about 1% of GDP in recent years. The loss from the adoption of a DBCFT abroad could, however, be larger than calculated here, for the following reasons. (1) Other countries could follow the first mover, thereby raising the pressure. (2) The elasticities, which were calculated using standard tax systems, might not apply when, all of a sudden, large countries offer effectively zero taxation on shifted profits and rents from international sales. (3) The elasticities are averages across countries but could be larger for the Netherlands where a lot of mobile international activities and holding companies are located.

11.5 Allowance for Corporate Equity

11.5.1 General Design Issues

The allowance for corporate equity (ACE) maintains the deductibility of interest expenses but supplements it with a similar deduction for the normal return on equity, which is calculated as the product of a notional interest rate and a company's equity as determined for tax purposes. The idea of the ACE has been inspired by Boadway and Bruce (1984), who proposed replacing interest deductibility with a notional deduction for all capital, irrespective of whether it is financed by debt or equity; this was later called an allowance for corporate capital (ACC).

The ACE has many desirable features. As a rent tax, it potentially eliminates corporate debt bias and achieves neutrality with respect to investment, which can be intuitively seen from the fact that the normal return, as approximated by the notional interest rate, is deductible. An additional advantage of the ACE system is that it is not dependent on depreciation allowance rates. Accelerated depreciation, for example, reduces the book value of assets in the tax accounts and thereby also reduces the equity, and hence amount, of ACE in later years. This exactly offsets the benefits from earlier depreciation in present-value terms.

However, these neutrality features hinge on choosing the 'right' notional interest rate. Theoretically, the notional rate applied for the ACE should be equal to the rate at which shareholders discount the tax savings from the company's future ACE.[12] In practice, in countries that have implemented an ACE, such as Belgium and Italy, the notional deduction rate is linked to the long-term government bond yield. Other countries that adopted some forms of an ACE include Croatia and Austria. See Hebous and Klemm (2020) for an overview. One concern with the ACE is its revenue cost. This can be reduced by applying the ACE only on new equity compared with a reference year (i.e. an incremental ACE).

Empirical evidence suggests that the Belgian ACE was successful in lowering corporate debt for financial and non-financial corporations (Hebous and Ruf, 2017; De Mooij, Hebous, and Hrdinkova, 2018).[13] Simulations using a computational general equilibrium model for the EU predict a positive welfare effect of the ACE if adopted by all EU countries, and it dominates an EU-wide CBIT. A unilateral revenue-neutral combination of ACE and CBIT is welfare-improving, compared with either an ACE or a CBIT, as it improves efficiency without requiring changes in tax rates (De Mooij and Devereux, 2011). In this origin-based implementation, the increase in rates has the usual disadvantages. The ACE can generate opportunities for domestic and international tax planning if it is not accompanied by appropriate anti-tax avoidance provisions (IMF, 2016; Hebous and Ruf, 2017).

[12] This is equal to the risk-free rate of interest (Bond and Devereux, 1995), provided the future tax saving is certain; that is, it is paid out in case of bankruptcy, which is not likely.

[13] The empirical evidence on the effects of the ACE on investment is mixed (see Hebous and Klemm, 2018). Aus dem Moore (2014) finds that that the expected reduction in leverage is confined to large firms. Petutschnig and Rünger (2017) find evidence that the Austrian ACE lowered corporate debt.

11.5.2 Destination-Based ACE

Hebous and Klemm (2020) have extended the ideas of ACE and ACC to a destination-based variant and have analysed the implications for tax competition and profit shifting. Compared with a DBCFT, the analysis suggests that a destination-based allowance for corporate equity (DBACE) has some advantages in terms of an easier transition from the current system to a destination-based version, and more stable revenues. However, while the DBCFT renders known profit-shifting possibilities entirely useless, the DBACE still permits tax-reducing debt operations to the extent that the ACE rate deviates from the interest rate. The destination-based allowance for corporate capital (DBACC) avoids this, as any interest payment on debt that reduces the tax base is perfectly matched by a loss in notional interest deductibility on equity.

Moreover, under both the DBACE and the DBACC, transfer price manipulation would still be possible, even though to a much more limited extent compared with the existing CIT. For example, if a company imports a capital good and the border adjustment is implemented through a tax collected at the point of entrance, then this firm will want to understate the cost of the investment good, if the notional rate of return is lower than its discount rate. This effect is much smaller than the profit-shifting opportunities under the current system and it does not apply to current goods, because any mispricing at the border would immediately affect current year profits and wash out (i.e. less tax collected at the border, but at the same time an equivalent smaller deduction of costs).

11.6 Conclusions

The case for moving to a rent tax is strong on the grounds of efficiency: it removes distortions to investment and the debt bias. Given these arguments, it is natural to wonder why rent taxes are not more common. The lack of practical proposals or precedence is certainly not the reason. The implementation of these taxes, in particular the ACE, as suggested by the experiences of various countries, generally appears not to encounter significant administrative difficulties (IMF, 2016). For instance, Keen and King (2002) discuss the Croatian experience with the ACE and conclude that concerns about possible bias in favour of capital-intensive enterprises, international complications, and the complexity of the computations of taxable profits were 'less than compelling'.

A more likely explanation is the pressure from tax competition and profit shifting that drives countries toward broad bases and low rates (i.e. the opposite of rent taxes). For a small open economy, such as the Netherlands, this is a particularly important point, as the tax competition literature suggests that small economies are under greater competitive pressure. The decision to move towards a rent tax—whether it is an ACE, ACC, or cash-flow tax—should therefore weigh potential revenue losses against efficiency gains.

Another potential explanation is the use of the CIT as a backstop and enforcement mechanism for the personal income tax. Countries trying to tax personal income comprehensively, also covering income that is saved, will prefer to cover all profits at the corporate level. Otherwise, there is an incentive to save inside corporations. Moreover, this allows revenues to be collected from foreign or tax-exempt investors.

In relative terms among rent taxes (ACE, ACC, and cash-flow tax), the ACE is theoretically the least effective in fully addressing debt bias, but it is also the only tax that has been tested in practice by various countries. A CIT reform in the Netherlands should be in line with the EU Code of Conduct on business taxation and it should comply with the EU state aid rules (the EU competition policy). Versions of the ACE are already in use by three EU member states (i.e. Belgium, Cyprus, and Italy), and have been included in the 2016 European Commission proposal for a common corporate consolidated tax base. As discussed in IMF (2016), the effect of the ACE on revenue can be mitigated by applying it to new equity only. Furthermore, it has transitional benefits compared with the cash-flow tax, as it maintains the tax depreciation rules (i.e. it is closer to the existing system).

While a destination-based implementation would avoid competitive pressures, this faces other major obstacles. First, for economies with large trade surpluses, such as the Netherlands, a destination-based reform is likely to create revenue losses, at least in the short to medium term—although ultimately, as trade rebalances, revenues should recover. (It might even benefit countries with a positive international investment position that adopt a destination-based tax, because it would allow them to run future deficits.) Second, given doubts about the legality of the measure, and the certainty of major negative spill-overs on other economies, there is a strong risk of retaliation.

However, if the international community, or at least a large group of countries, were to agree on a consensual adoption of destination-based rent taxes, the pressure to go along with this would be strong, given the negative spill-overs for any non-participating countries, which will be larger with the greater number of countries that participate. While the DBCFT is likely to be the simpler and more robust form of a destination-based rent tax, the transition to a DBACE is simpler, and revenues are likely to be less volatile. Any destination-based rent tax is extremely unlikely at this point, but it is nevertheless useful to be aware of the consequences and to have a backup plan. Fortunately, increases in the tax rate would be an option under the adoption of destination-based rent taxes.

References

Auerbach, A., Devereux, M. P., and Simpson, H. (2010), 'Taxing corporate income', in J. Mirrlees et al. (eds), *Dimensions of Tax Design: The Mirrlees Review*, Oxford University Press for the Institute for Fiscal Studies, Oxford, pp. 837–93.

Auerbach, A., Devereux, M. P., Keen, M., and Vella, J. (2017a), 'Destination-based cash flow taxation', Oxford University Centre for Business Taxation Working Paper no. 17/01.

Auerbach, A., Devereux, M. P., Keen, M., and Vella, J. (2017b), 'International tax planning under the destination-based cash flow tax', *National Tax Journal*, 70, 783–801.

Aus dem Moore, N. (2014), 'Taxes and corporate financing decisions—evidence from the Belgian ACE Reform', Ruhr Economic Paper no. 533, RWI, Essen.

Bernanke, B. and Campbell, J. Y. (1988), 'Is there a corporate debt crisis?', *Brookings Papers on Economic Activity*, 1.

Beer, S., De Mooij, R., and Liu, L. (2020), 'International corporate tax avoidance: a review of the channels, effect sizes, and blind spots', *Journal of Economic Surveys*, 34, 660–88.

Bianchi, J. (2011), 'Overborrowing and systemic externalities in the business cycle', *American Economic Review*, 101(7), 3400–26.

Boadway, R. and Bruce, N. (1984), 'A general proposition on the design of a neutral business tax', *Journal of Public Economics*, 24, 231–9.

Bond, S. R. and Devereux, M. P. (1995), 'On the design of a neutral business tax under uncertainty', *Journal of Public Economics*, 58, 57–71.

Bond, S. R. and Devereux, M. P. (2002), 'Cash-flow taxes in an open-economy', CEPR Discussion Paper no. 3401.

Buiter, W. (2018), 'Exchange rate implications of Border Tax Adjustment Neutrality', *Economics—The Open Access E-Journal*, 11.

Cnossen, S. (2018), 'Corporation taxes in the European Union: slowly moving toward comprehensive business income taxation?', *International Tax and Public Finance*, 25, 808–40.

De Mooij, R. and Devereux, M. (2011), 'An applied analysis of ACE and CBIT reforms in the EU', *International Tax and Public Finance*, 18, 93–120.

De Mooij, R. and Ederveen, S. (2008), 'Corporate tax elasticities: a reader's guide to empirical findings', *Oxford Review of Economic Policy*, 24, 680–97.

De Mooij, R. and Hebous, S. (2018), 'Curbing corporate debt bias: do limitations to interest deductibility work?', *Journal of Banking and Finance*, 96, 368–78.

De Mooij, R., Hebous, S., and Hrdinkova, M. (2018), 'Growth-enhancing corporate tax reform in Belgium', *Nordic Tax Journal*, 2018(1), 1–17.

Devereux, M. P., Griffith, R., and Klemm, A. (2002), 'Corporate income tax reforms and international tax competition', *Economic Policy*, 17, 451–95.

Feld, L., Heckemeyer, J., and Overesch, M. (2013), 'Capital structure choice and company taxation: a meta-study', *Journal of Banking and Finance*, 37, 2850–66.

Giroud, X. and Mueller, H. (2017), 'Firm leverage and unemployment during the Great Recession', *Quarterly Journal of Economics*, 132, 271–316.

Gordon, R. H. (2010), 'Taxation and corporate use of debt: implications for tax policy', *National Tax Journal*, 63, 151–74.

Hebous, S. and Klemm, A. (2020), 'A destination-based allowance for corporate equity', *International Tax and Public Finance*, 27(3), 753–77.

Hebous, S. and Ruf, M. (2017), 'Evaluating the effects of ACE systems on multinational debt financing and investment', *Journal of Public Economics*, 156, 131–49.

Hebous, S., Klemm, A., and Stausholm, S. (2020), 'Revenue implications of destination-based cash-flow taxation', *IMF Economic Review*, 68(4), 848–74.

IMF (2016), 'Taxes, leverage, and macroeconomic stability', International Monetary Fund Policy Paper, Washington, DC.

Keen, M. and King, J. (2002), 'The Croatian profit tax: an ACE in practice', *Fiscal Studies*, 23, 401–18.

Meade, J. (1978), *The Structure and Reform of Direct Taxation*, George Allen & Unwin, London.

Petutschnig, M. and Rünger, S. (2017), 'The effects of a tax allowance for growth and investment—empirical evidence from a firm-level analysis', WU International Taxation Research Paper Series no. 2017–09.

Sørensen, P. B. (2014), 'Taxation and the optimal constraint on corporate debt finance', CESifo Working Paper no. 5101.

Sutherland, D. and Hoeller, P. (2012), 'Debt and macroeconomic stability: an overview of the literature and some empirics', OECD Economics Department Working Paper no. 1006.

Tørsløv, T., Wier, L., and Zucman, G. (2018), 'The missing profits of nations', NBER Working Paper no. 24701.

Weichenrieder, A. and Klautke, T. (2008), 'Taxes and the efficiency costs of capital distortions', CESifo Working Paper no. 2431.

12

Formulary Methods in International Taxation

Implications for the Netherlands

*Ruud de Mooij, Shafik Hebous, and Li Liu**

12.1 Introduction

Today's century-old international tax framework is under unprecedented stress. Both profit shifting by multinational enterprises (MNEs) and a decline in corporate tax rates over the last three decades have undermined faith in its fairness. This is reinforced by the rise of highly profitable, technology-driven, digital-heavy businesses that pay no or very little tax in many of the countries where they operate. Current rules are also found to be harmful to low-income countries, depriving them of much-needed revenue to help meet the 2030 Sustainable Development Goals.

In recent years, several modifications to the international tax framework have been implemented. For example, the G20/OECD agreed on an action plan in 2015, called the Base Erosion and Profit Shifting (BEPS) project, to addresses the most egregious forms of tax avoidance. However, these actions appear to be insufficient to address the key concerns that countries have. The conceptual and practical difficulties of the current international tax framework have therefore sparked interest in more fundamental reforms, as discussed in, for example, IMF (2014, 2019). Recently, the OECD's Inclusive Framework has launched a new initiative to explore more fundamental changes in the international tax system, with the aim to reach consensus by 2020. Thereby, one of the pillars that is being

* Ruud de Mooij (rdemooij@imf.org), Shafik Hebous (shebous@imf.org) and Li Liu (lliu@imf.org) are staff members of the International Monetary Fund (IMF).

We draw heavily on IMF (2019), with important contributions from other IMF colleagues, including Corry Hillier, Michael Keen, Alex Klemm, Victoria Perry and Christophe Waerzeggers. We are grateful to Victor Mylonas for excellent research support; Dinar Prihardini and Sebastian Beer provided generous support with the quantitative analysis. Excellent comments were received during the conference 'Fundamental Tax Reform in the Netherlands' in Rotterdam on 23–24 May 2019, especially from Bas Jacobs and Sijbren Cnossen. The views expressed in this paper are those of the authors and do not necessarily represent the views of the IMF, its Executive Board or IMF management.

Ruud de Mooij, Shafik Hebous, and Li Liu, *Formulary Methods in International Taxation: Implications for the Netherlands*
In: *Tax by Design for the Netherlands*. Edited by: Sijbren Cnossen and Bas Jacobs, Oxford University Press.
 DOI: 10.1093/oso/9780192855244.003.0012

discussed focuses on reallocation of taxing rights, including through formula apportionment (FA) methods.

In this chapter, we evaluate the implications of using formulary methods to allocate MNE profits across countries. Thereby, we focus on the effects on corporate tax revenue in the Netherlands. We also pay attention to dynamic effects on investment and tax competition. Understanding these implications is important for the Netherlands for two reasons. First, as a member of the OECD's Inclusive Framework, the Dutch government can help to shape the reform agenda and should take a position in this debate. Second, the Netherlands will need to be prepared for its possible future implementation, even if it would not favour the approach, as its influence on the ultimate consensus agreement will likely be modest, given the large number of countries involved in the process.

12.2 The Netherlands as an Investment Hub

The Netherlands is known to host many MNEs. This is clearly reflected in one of the most striking Dutch statistics, namely foreign direct investment (FDI). Table 12.1 illustrates this, showing data for the total stock of inbound and outbound FDI for 10 countries with the largest stock of world FDI. Interestingly, the Netherlands appears to be the world's largest country by this metric, even larger than the United States. The inbound stock exceeds six times its GDP while the outbound stock is more than seven times its GDP. To compare, the shares of China, Germany, and the United States are about 25% of GDP and the global unweighted average is around one-third of it. The most important source and destination of Dutch FDI is the United States (see Table 12.2). Others featuring in the top five are Bermuda, Luxembourg, and Switzerland.

Recently, the OECD has published new FDI data, distinguishing FDI held by special purpose entities (SPEs) and other FDI. Figure 12.1 shows that the Netherlands (together with Luxembourg) stands out in terms of the share of FDI held by SPEs: it is almost four times GDP. This reflects the position of the Netherlands as a so-called 'investment hub'; that is, a country where much financial investment is channelled in and out through these SPEs, but where no tangible capital is actually installed.

Its position as an investment hub does not seem to generate exceptionally high corporate tax revenue in the Netherlands: this ranges between 2% and 3.5% of GDP during the last five years, which is only slightly above averages in the European Union (EU) and the world (see Figure 12.2, top panel). The high investment also does not seem to be caused by an exceptionally low statutory corporate tax rate in the Netherlands which, at 25% (to be reduced to 20.5% in 2021), is slightly above the averages in the EU and the world (see Figure 12.2, bottom panel).

Table 12.1 Top 10 FDI economies (2017)

	Inward FDI			Outward FDI		
	% GDP	%World FDI		% GDP	% World FDI	
1	Netherlands	601	14.5	Netherlands	742	18.0
2	United States	26	14.5	United States	31	17.5
3	Luxembourg	6,387	11.5	Luxembourg	7,707	14.0
4	China	22	7.8	United Kingdom	62	4.7
5	United Kingdom	61	4.7	Germany	43	4.7
6	Hong Kong SAR	463	4.6	Hong Kong SAR	447	4.5
7	Switzerland	170	3.3	Japan	31	4.4
8	Singapore	342	3.3	France	56	4.2
9	Germany	26	2.7	Switzerland	186	3.7
10	Ireland	269	2.6	Canada	54	2.6

Source: IMF Coordinated Direct Investment Survey Database.

Table 12.2 Major FDI partners of the Netherlands (2017)

Top five partner economies			
Inward FDI (% of total)		Outward FDI (% of total)	
United States	19	United States	15
Luxembourg	14	United Kingdom	11
United Kingdom	10	Switzerland	8
Switzerland	6	Luxembourg	8
Bermuda	6	Germany	6

Source: IMF Coordinated Direct Investment Survey Database.

What, then, can explain these large investment flows? SEO (2013, 2018) and Lejour et al. (2019) provide a deeper analysis of the large flows and stocks of FDI held by Dutch SPEs and they point to the role of special Dutch international tax rules. More specifically, the Netherlands has the following features that might help to explain its position as an investment hub.

- *Exemption system.* The Dutch corporate tax system has traditionally been characterized by a generous participation exemption, which makes it attractive for corporate residency. For instance, the ownership share of 5% to qualify for the participation exemption is relatively low. Moreover, whereas many countries only grant an exemption for 95% of the foreign tax payment, the Dutch system grants full exemption. Until recently, the Netherlands also

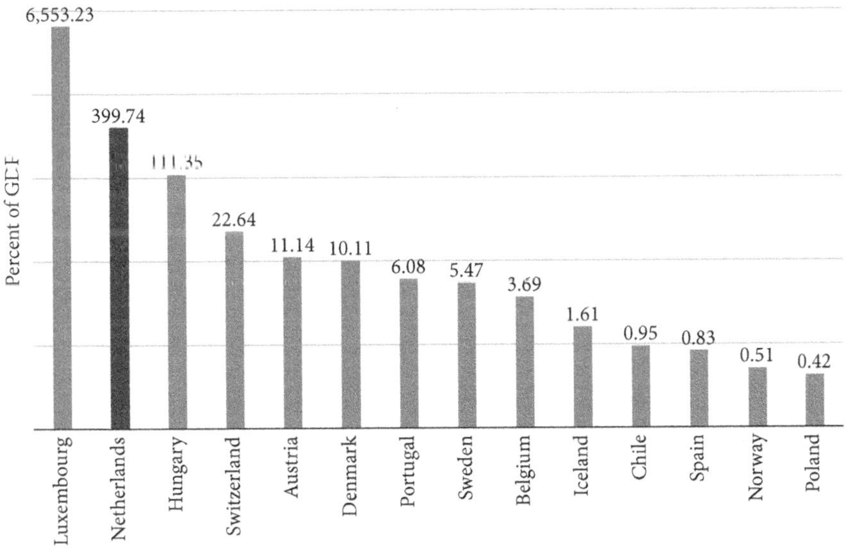

Figure 12.1 Total inbound FDI stock held by SPEs (2017) (% of GDP)
Source: OECD Statistics.

had only a limited controlled foreign corporation regime—through which tax is imposed on foreign-source passive income if that income is taxed less than some minimum. With the implementation of the European Anti-Tax Avoidance Directive, however, the Netherlands will impose such a rule so that Dutch tax will be levied on low-taxed foreign-earned passive income.

- *Ruling practice.* The Dutch government has a tradition to provide extensive tax rulings for international companies. The purpose has always been to offer tax certainty in advance for tax payers about their treatment by tax inspectors on specific interpretations of the tax code. However, the agreements in tax rulings have not always been transparent, while the agreed tax treatment has, in some cases, been suggested to violate European state aid rules (such as for Starbucks and Nike). As per 1 July 2019, the Dutch ruling practice has been reformed to provide more transparency and no longer to provide rulings to companies without sufficient economic nexus in the Netherlands.
- *Tax treaties.* The Netherlands traditionally charges no withholding taxes (WHTs) on interest and royalties paid to foreign entities (this will be modified for interest and royalty payments to low-tax countries and countries on the EU list of non-cooperative jurisdictions in 2021). Moreover, it has built an extensive tax treaty network, with ninety-four bilateral tax agreements (BTAs) in force. This is large compared with an average of seventy-seven BTAs for OECD countries (Figure 12.3). Moreover, the WHT rates agreed in treaties are generally low (Figure 12.4). Because these

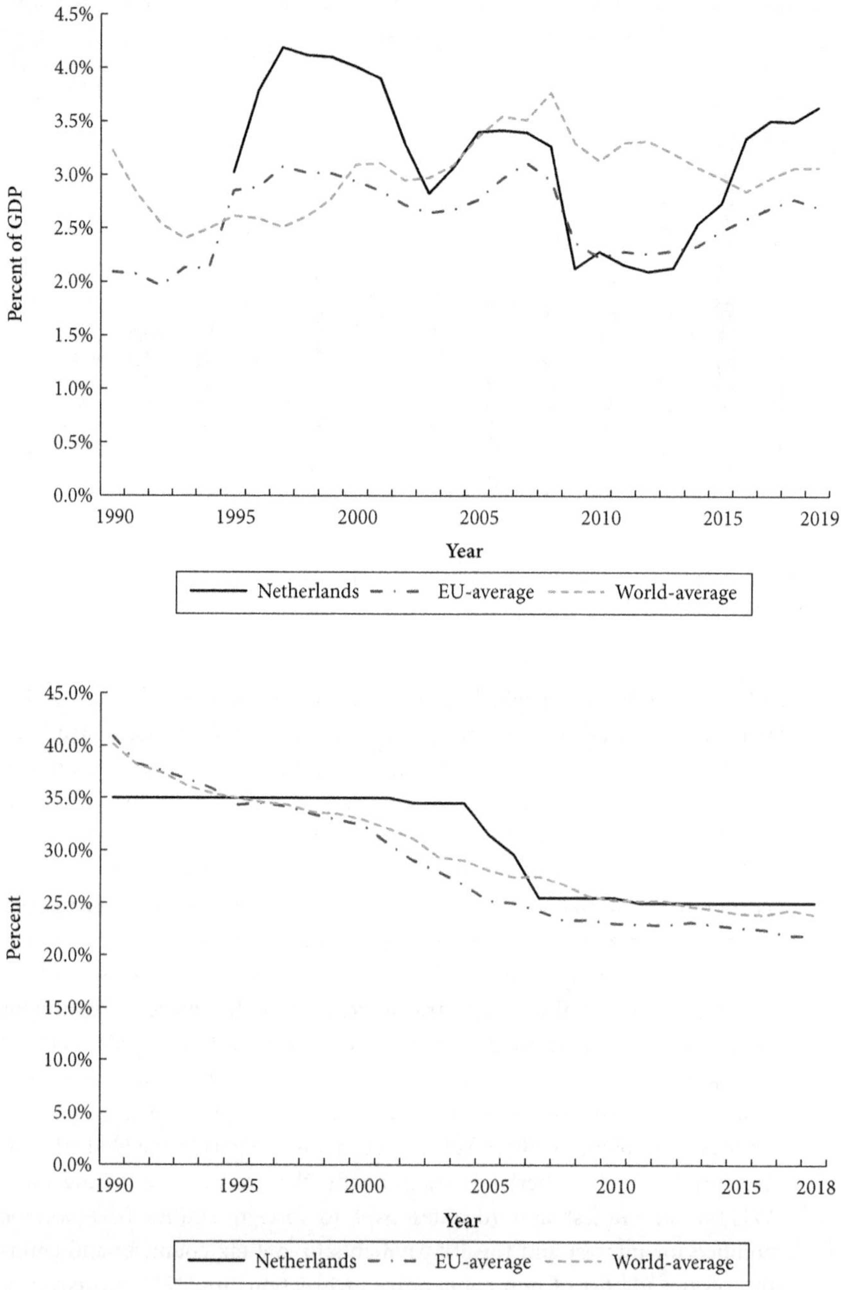

Figure 12.2 Corporate tax revenue to GDP (top) and rate (bottom) (1990–2019)
Source: IMF World Economic Outlook (top panel) and KPMG and OECD data (bottom panel).

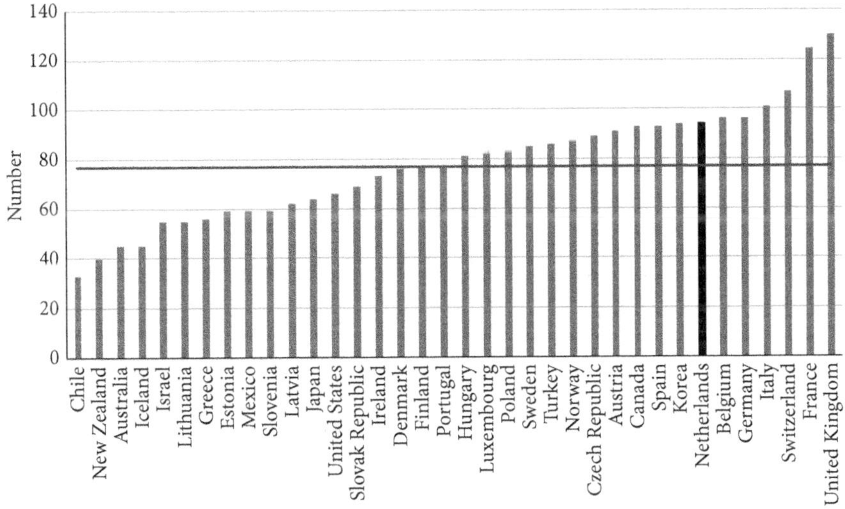

Figure 12.3 Number of BTAs in OECD (2019)
Source: IBFD and IMF staff estimates.

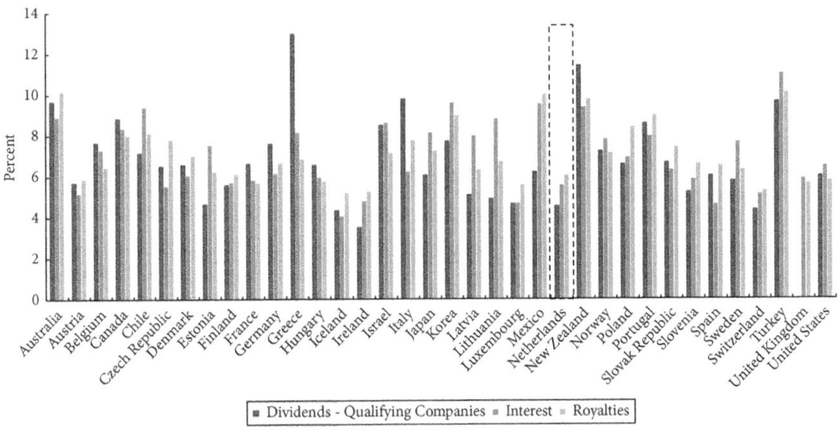

Figure 12.4 Average WHT rates in BTAs (2019)
Source: IBFD and IMF staff estimates.

treaty rates determine the maximum possible rate a country can charge, treaty partners are deprived from using higher WHT rates on payments of dividends, interest, and royalties to Dutch affiliates. Perhaps even more important than the average rates is the fraction of BTAs with zero WHT rates, which deprives other countries entirely from charging WHTs. Figure 12.5 shows that 26% of the Dutch BTAs have a zero WHT rate on dividends (the second highest in the OECD), while 35% impose a zero WHT

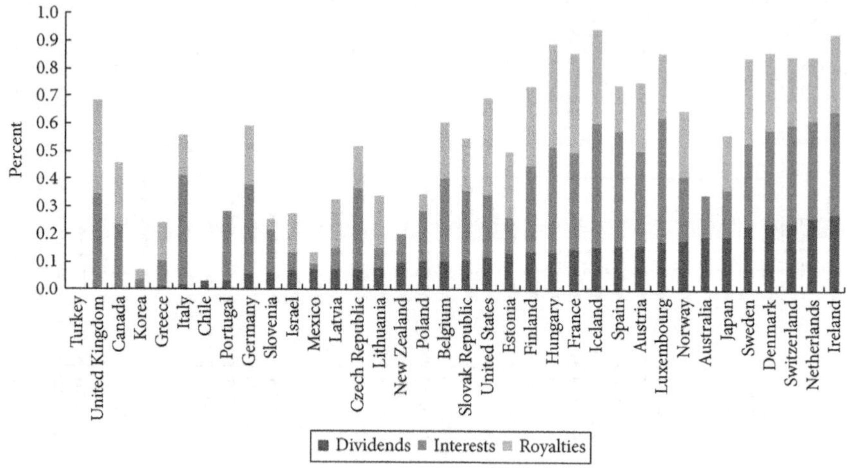

Figure 12.5 Fraction of BTAs with zero WHT rates

Source: IBFD and IMF staff estimates.

rate on interest and 24% on royalties. Importantly, the US–Netherlands treaty imposes a zero WHT rate on dividends, interest, and royalties if certain conditions are met. These features of the Dutch treaty network provide scope for 'treaty shopping' (i.e. channelling international payments between countries indirectly through SPEs located in the Netherlands). Indeed, the Dutch treaty network may explain a good portion of the large FDI stocks reported above and the position of the Netherlands as an investment hub.

There are two reasons why the large stock of FDI might be important for the impact of formulary methods (i.e. FA and residual profit allocation) on corporate tax revenue in the Netherlands. The first is that large FDI flows might be accompanied by an expansion of the Dutch tax base due to profit shifting. This effect will disappear once profit allocation is based on formulary methods (see Section 12.3). The second reason is that the large FDI flows are accompanied by a large financial sector (including SPEs). For that sector, the factors that enter the apportionment formula, such as fixed assets and sales, differ from other businesses—most assets are, for example, in the form of loans or deposits while most revenue might be earned from interest. This can have important implications for the distribution of tax revenues under conventional formula factors.

12.3 Formula Apportionment

Under the current international tax framework, the taxing rights of a country over the business profits of an MNE are based on identifying the source of its profits and its residence. Source refers to where investment is made and where production takes place, and it is largely determined by the physical presence of labour and/or capital. Residence means the place where the MNE receiving the income is deemed to have its primary location, determined by incorporation or its effective place of management. The international convention is that source countries have primary taxing rights over the active business income, while residence countries retain the right to tax passive income. The attribution of income between source countries is based on separate accounting (SA): the accounts of a MNE group are separated between the entities operating in different countries. It depends on the valuation of intra-company transactions within the MNE. To avoid strategic pricing decisions that exploit differences in national tax laws, most countries rely on the arm's-length principle (ALP), which stipulates that internal prices between related parties should resemble prices that would prevail between independent parties.

Under FA, the accounts of all company's affiliates are consolidated to generate a unitary tax base that is apportioned across jurisdictions on a formulaic basis. Jurisdictions then apply their own tax rate to the apportioned base. Subnational business taxes commonly work by FA, notably in Canada, Germany, Japan, and the United States. These subnational experiences indicate that, as economic integration proceeds, FA presents itself as better suited than the ALP for dividing profits of related companies across jurisdictions. In that spirit, the European Commission has proposed a Common Consolidated Corporate Tax Base (CCCTB) for the EU, in which EU-wide taxable profit would be apportioned across member states by three equally weighted factors: assets, sales by destination, and labour (in turn equally weighting payroll and employees). Worldwide FA has also been proposed by, for example, the Independent Commission for the Reform of International Corporate Taxation (2018) and several contributions in Picciotto (2016). As noted before, it is now also being discussed under Pillar 1 of the programme of work by the OECD's Inclusive Framework.

While the principal idea of FA is straightforward, it would be a significant deviation from current norms. FA will need to be implemented through domestic law, supported by tax treaties. Designing such a system requires numerous choices. A unitary group needs to be defined and its consolidated tax base should be calculated on a common set of agreed rules (e.g. building on the International Accounting Standards). The unitary base could also be separated between different types of income or different lines of business undertaken by the MNE. In the United States, for instance, a distinction is made between business income (which is consolidated) and non-business income (which is directly assigned to a jurisdiction). The legal implementation of these policy design choices will be critical to avoiding double taxation (or under taxation) and managing the risk of other adverse spill-overs occurring across jurisdictions. Some flexibility could be achieved by allowing countries to modify their apportioned share of the unitary base, for instance by offering additional R&D deductions. Flexibility is also created if countries can choose their own apportionment formula, as is practised at state level in the United States. However, this can lead to either more or less than 100% of total profits being allocated somewhere. Divergent weights also evidently complicate implementation. Securing agreement on a common apportionment scheme would be difficult though and an equalization scheme might be necessary to achieve that. Ultimately, these issues imply that the precise design of an agreed system of FA would be hard to predict, yet will be critical for its economic and distributional implications.

Specific issues arise for the financial sector. The traditional formula, for example, is based on fixed assets, payroll, and sales. However, fixed assets comprise only a very small fraction of total assets of financial companies, as the majority of their assets are based on loans and deposits. Sales by financial companies are also of a different nature than for other companies (e.g. receipts usually come from margins on interest, money market instruments, or credit cards). Formulary methods might therefore have distinct implications for the allocation of profits of multinational financial firms (Sadiq, 2016). For this reason, Canada uses a specific allocation formula for financial companies, which is based on both payroll (one-third) and loans and deposits (two-thirds, to substitute for the ordinary sales factor). In the United States, the sales factor for financial companies is replaced by a gross receipts factor. In the European CCCTB proposal, 10% of the value of financial assets is added to the asset factor in the formula for financial companies to account for its importance for financial firms. Countries also use sector-specific allocation keys, for example for insurance, transport and extractive industries.

12.4 Attractions and Drawbacks

The primary advantage of FA is that it would simplify the system and greatly reduce the scope for profit shifting through transfer pricing and other devices. By taxing MNEs on a consolidated basis, it cuts a swathe through the problems of the ALP. This would significantly reduce compliance and administrative costs. However, FA would also introduce new forms of shifting through distortions of corporate ownership structures: combining two independent firms, for example, would generally change their combined tax liability (Gordon and Wilson, 1986). Nevertheless, FA is generally thought to be less vulnerable to such manipulation than SA, something that is supported by empirical evidence for Canada (Mintz and Smart, 2004).

FA does not eliminate distortions in factor allocation or tax competition. Under FA, the corporate income tax (CIT) becomes a tax levied on the factors of the formula (McLure, 1981). Hence, tax rate differences between countries may distort the allocation of those factors, especially if those are mobile across borders. Relatedly, the risk of tax competition remains if the factors used for apportionment are mobile. In fact, if production factors are used as weights, tax competition may become more intense, because the revenue gain from attracting such factors comes not from an increase in local activity, but from being allocated a larger share of the MNE's overall profit.

The weighting factors used for FA determine both the efficiency and distributional effects. By allocating the consolidated tax base using proxies for substantial economic activities, FA can align the tax base closely with some obvious fundamentals, where production factors are located, for example, or consumers are based. Ideally, these factors should be easy to verify (to avoid manipulation by companies) and relatively unresponsive to tax differentials (to minimize allocative distortions and tax competition). Commonly used apportionment factors are the following.

- *Production factors.* Payroll, employment, and assets are commonly used. Payroll would be difficult to misrepresent, and much labour is relatively immobile. For tangible assets, valuation can be non-trivial but there are commonly used methods—though these (and some skilled labour) are relatively mobile, so that differences in tax rates across jurisdictions will distort their allocation. Intangible assets are usually excluded because they are hard to value and relatively easy to relocate; to the extent, however, that intangible assets derive from employment (R&D workers) or tangible investments (such as laboratories), they are captured by those other factors. If desired, proxies could also be used in the formula for the value generated by the users of digital services and platforms, although how to best measure this remains unsettled.
- *Third-party sales.* These can be measured on either an origin basis (location of the seller) or on a destination basis. Apportioning by the latter has several advantages of destination-based taxation, which are related to the relative immobility of consumers. However, risks arise because of the channelling of sales through low-margin unrelated firms based in low-tax countries.

Global revenue might increase under FA to the extent that the tax base is reallocated from low-tax countries (to which profits are currently shifted) toward high-tax countries (if a greater share of the apportionment factors is based there). However, it might also decrease, as losses would be immediately offset against the profits of foreign affiliates, while currently they can only be carried forward within each entity. The net effect on global tax revenue is therefore ambiguous.

Irrespective of this global impact, the revenue effect for individual countries can be large. IMF (2019), for instance, evaluates the static revenue changes from FA (i.e. without incorporating behavioural changes). The study finds that advanced economies are likely to gain revenue if FA is by value added, payroll or sales, and likely to lose if it is by employment. Emerging markets and developing countries tend to benefit from FA if FA is by employment or sales, but not by value added or payroll. Significant losses are reported for investment hubs, irrespective of the formula used.

12.5 Revenue Effects for the Netherlands

We look more closely at the effect of FA on tax revenue in the Netherlands, building on the analysis in IMF (2019) and De Mooij, Liu, and Prihardini (2021). We use two data sets for this purpose: ORBIS, which mainly contains European MNEs; and the Bureau of Economic Analysis (BEA), which captures all US-based MNEs. With the ORBIS data, we analyse two apportionment factors: fixed assets and the number of employees. For the BEA, we explore five pure apportionment factors (assets, employment, payroll, sales, and value added) and two composite formulas (the CCCTB formula mentioned before, and a Cobb–Douglas formula that combines payroll and assets).

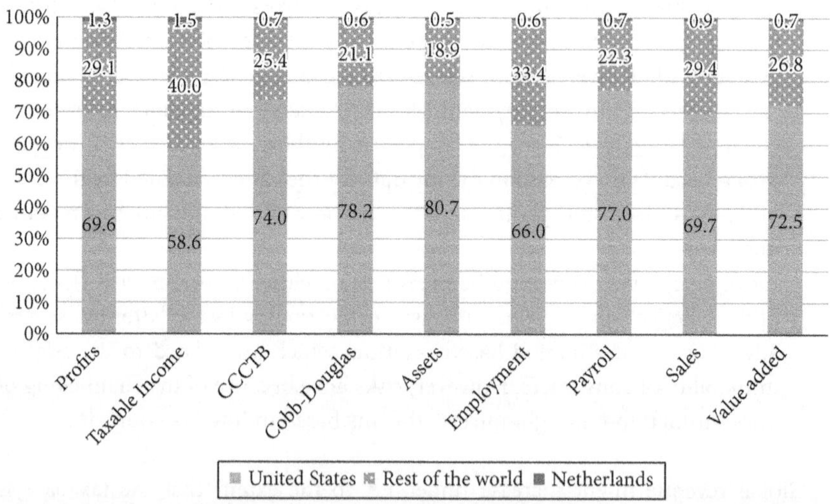

Figure 12.6 Shares of profit and taxable income and apportionment factors in BEA data

Source: BEA and IMF staff estimates.

Using the BEA data, Figure 12.6 shows, for the United States, the Netherlands, and the rest of the world (ROW), the shares of the reported profit (defined as operating profit, excluding foreign equity), taxable income (calculated as tax paid divided by the statutory CIT rate) and the seven apportionment factors. Interestingly, we see that the share of profit reported in the United States is around 65%, while the share of taxable income is 57% of global income. These are much smaller than the shares of assets and payroll, which are close to 80%. Hence, apportionment of consolidated profit based on those factors will likely expand the tax base in the United States. This is in sharp contrast to the Netherlands. Indeed, we see that profit and the taxable base for the Netherlands are, respectively, 1.2% and 1.4% of the consolidated global aggregate. The shares of assets, employment, and payroll, however, are considerably smaller, namely between 0.4% and 0.7%. This discrepancy between the current share of the taxable base and the apportionment factors indicates that the Netherlands will likely experience a significant reduction in tax revenue from the adoption of FA based on production factors. Interestingly, the share of destination-based sales in the United States is more similar to the share of profits (68%), while that in Netherlands is also somewhat closer to the profit share (0.8%). Hence, apportionment by destination-based sales will produce smaller revenue shifts for these countries than apportionment by production factors.

To show the revenue effects for the Netherlands, we compute the difference between, on the one hand, current CIT revenue paid by the MNEs as captured by the data and, on the other hand, the simulated revenue under consolidation of all reported profits and allocation based on the alternative formulas. The effects for ORBIS and BEA are shown in Figures 12.7 and 12.8, respectively. They represent static implications (i.e. without accounting for behavioural effects). The following results are worth noting.

- *The Netherlands will lose revenue under most source-based formulas.* With the firm-level data, the reduction in CIT revenue paid by MNEs exceeds 60% if the employment formula is used. The decline is smaller for the BEA data, but still negative and sizeable for all four source-based factors (assets, payroll, employment, and value added) and the two composite formulas. This reflects the observation from Figure 12.6 that the share of global profit currently reported by MNEs in the Netherlands is much larger than the share of factors of production.
- *Revenue effects for the Netherlands are less negative for the sales apportionment factor.* For US MNEs, revenue in the Netherlands declines by less than 30% if the tax base is apportioned by destination-based sales. This smaller effect is somewhat puzzling in light of the large Dutch trade surplus. Hebous and Klemm (Chapter 11) find that the revenue effect of a hypothetical destination-based cash-flow tax for the Netherlands can be positive in

some years, despite the trade surplus. On average, over the last twenty years, however, they report a loss of 0.25% of GDP. However, this balance may not apply to production and sales by US MNEs. Even more striking is the result for the asset factor: whereas a significant reduction in revenue is reported for the BEA data, the Netherlands would in fact gain revenue from FA according to the ORBIS data (for European MNEs). One explanation might be that the share of fixed assets invested by US-based MNEs in the Netherlands is substantially smaller because they comprise SPEs. European-based MNEs, in contrast, might have invested considerably more in fixed assets.

- *Results for the Netherlands are largely similar to those for other investment hubs*, identified as countries with a high FDI/GDP ratio. This is clear for the ORBIS data, where other investment hubs (Hungary, Ireland, Luxembourg, and Malta) also lose significantly under the employment formula. The same applies to the BEA data (where ten investment hubs are included). Other investment hubs experience a bigger loss in revenue under the sales formula. There are diverging effects for the asset formula between ORBIS and BEA data for other investment hubs. The results for investment hubs might be affected by the significance of the financial sector in these countries, as noted above.
- *Effects for the Netherlands differ markedly from the average OECD country.* With the ORBIS data, the effects for OECD countries are much smaller than

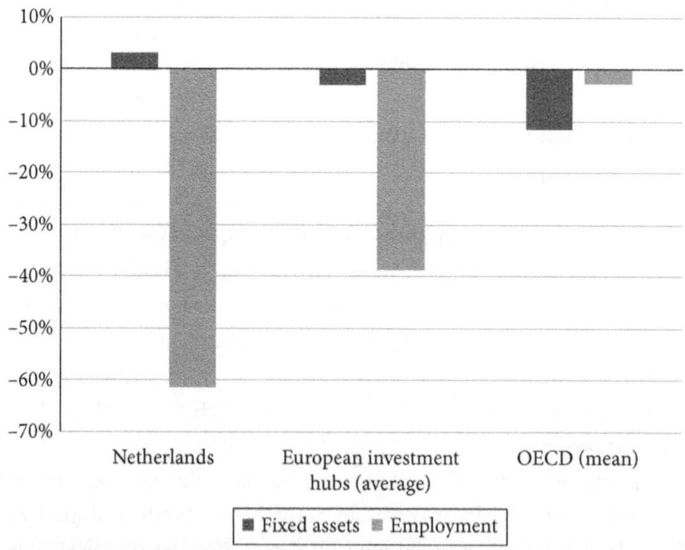

Figure 12.7 Tax revenue effect of FA: firm-level data

Notes: European investment hubs are Hungary, Ireland, Luxembourg, Malta and the Netherlands.
Source: IMF staff analysis based on data from the ORBIS.

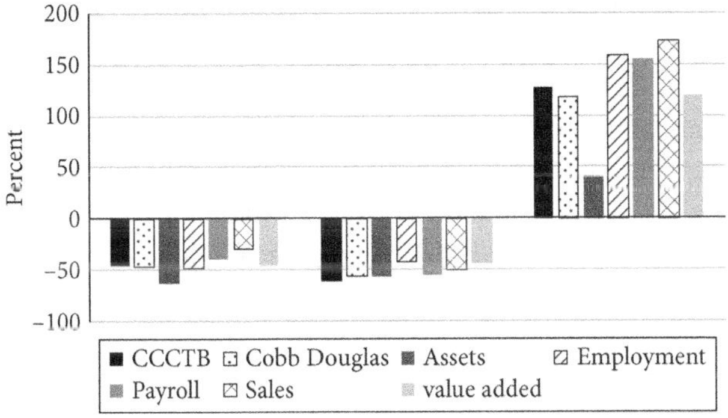

Figure 12.8 Tax revenue effect of FA: US MNEs

Notes: Investment hubs are Cyprus, Hong Kong SAR, Hungary, Ireland, Luxembourg, Malta, Mauritius, the Netherlands, Singapore, and Switzerland.

Source: IMF staff based on data from BEA.

those for the Netherlands, especially for the employment factor. Hence, current profit allocation is more aligned with the number of employees in an average OECD country than it is for the Netherlands. With the BEA data, tax revenue in OECD countries typically increases due to FA, in contrast with the decline found for the Netherlands and other investment hubs.

12.6 Residual Profit Allocation

Recently, policy discussions have focused on a more moderate departure from the ALP, namely proposals for so-called residual profit allocation (RPA). They are essentially hybrid systems, combining elements of the conventional ALP to allocate a portion of profit to source countries and FA to allocate another portion to destination countries. They centre on a distinction between 'routine' and 'residual' profit. The terms are often used loosely, but broadly.

- Routine profit (a term of transfer pricing art) is used to denote an acceptable return to some activity or function—broadly equivalent to a normal return (i.e. the minimum required) on the underlying activity (e.g. assembling a product's subcomponents, or providing warehousing). Most RPA proposals envisage using the conventional ALP for routine profits (see Auerbach et al., 2019). For instance, for activities intense in capital assets, it might be calculated by applying some notional return to those assets based on comparable third-party experiences; in other cases, a mark-up, based on financial statements of comparable independent companies, is applied to purchases from third parties and labour costs. Some RPA schemes simply apply a common mark-up to all cases to calculate routine profit (Avi-Yonah, Clausing, and Durst, 2009).

- Residual profit means the excess of aggregate profit over routine profit. To the extent that routine profit can be identified with a normal return on investment, residual profit is identified with rent. Residual profits tend to include that part of profit that—due to intangibles or risk-bearing, for instance—is hardest to allocate across jurisdictions by standard transfer pricing methods. They would therefore be taxed on a unitary basis and apportioned through FA.

Countries may choose to tax the two elements (i.e. routine profit earned in their jurisdiction, and the residual income they are allocated) at different rates. Variants of RPA are seen in recent proposals discussed in the OECD's Inclusive Framework to tax digital companies or for the separate taxation of the return on marketing intangibles. A common feature of these schemes is that they envisage taxing rights being established in the destination country, even in the absence of a traditional permanent establishment.

The interest in RPA signals the recognition that ALP has proved capable of dealing with relatively straightforward operations, but not of addressing the full complexities of transactions within modern MNEs. Moreover, it facilitates the allocation of taxing rights for some portion of profits to destination countries. While preserving a significant element of source taxation, the RPA approach thus provides a framework within which progress might be made while retaining familiar elements of current arrangements. The taxation of normal returns retains a distortion inherent in most current corporate income taxes and creates incentives for tax competition to attract mobile routine activities. Incentives to compete to attract residual profit depend on the apportionment formula, with an element of FA in RPA schemes meaning that the same forces that potentially encourage tax competition between governments (and game-playing by firms) identified above remain. They are lessened, however, if apportionment is by destination-based sales.

There is little analysis on the possible implications of RPA. Avi-Yonah et al. (2009) and Auerbach et al. (2019) describe how their proposals would work, how they can be implemented, and the benefits of such reforms. However, they offer no analysis. One might think that, as a hybrid system, the effects of RPA would be proportional to the size of the residual profit, as only the allocation of that share of income will be modified; the routine return will be treated the same as under the current system. If so, then the economic implications (e.g. on investment, profit shifting, and tax competition) would also be proportionally adjusted. However, there can be profound non-linearities in the system that can create disproportional effects. For example, profit shifting might currently be disproportionally associated with RPA, rather than with routine profits. RPA would then, like FA, virtually eliminate profit shifting.

The effect of RPA will depend critically on two aspects: (1) how routine profit is determined; and (2) how residual profit is subsequently apportioned across countries. Regarding the first aspect, some initial empirical analysis is reported in Beer et al. (2020), based on data of the consolidated statement of the 10,000 largest global companies. The analysis shows, for instance, that, for a routine return of 7.5% on tangible assets, the average residual profit of an MNE would be around 60% of total income. Between 13% and 20% of the MNEs would report a negative residual. For all MNEs that are headquartered in the Netherlands, their average residual profit is around 59% of total income, with about 12% of them reporting a negative residual. There would also be significant variation across sectors and countries: most of the global residual profits are, for instance, earned by US-based MNEs. One-third of the global residual profit would be earned by the top 1% of MNEs in terms of size. On the second issue, the focus here will be on apportionment to the destination country using a sales factor.

12.7 Revenue Effects for the Netherlands

To understand the revenue implications of RPA proposals for the Netherlands, we follow Beer et al. (2020) in performing two types of analysis. The first is an assessment of the revenue from taxing only the routine return component and comparing that to current tax revenue. The second is an assessment of the full revenue effect, from taxing both the routine return and the residual profit.

The first assessment uses data on the private fixed capital stock of countries, obtained from different sources. The aggregate routine return is then derived by applying alternative rates of return (5%, 7.5%, and 10%) to that capital stock. Beer et al. (2020) discuss how the tax base thus derived compares with the current corporate tax base. The striking outcome is that six countries would see their CIT base expand if they were to fully tax the routine return, even at a rate of return of only 5%. The number of countries that would gain rises if higher rates of return apply: to twenty-six countries for a rate of return of 7.5% and to fifty countries for a rate of return of 10% (out of a total of 113 countries). These countries would thus unambiguously benefit from an RPA system, which would not only tax these routine returns but would add revenue from taxing the residual profits as well. Among them are many developing countries. For the remaining sixty-three countries included in the analysis, however, the tax base for the routine return is always smaller than the current corporate tax base, even for a routine return of 10%. This includes the Netherlands, for which revenue from the routine return is, respectively, 21%, 32%, and 43% of current revenue for a routine return of 5%,

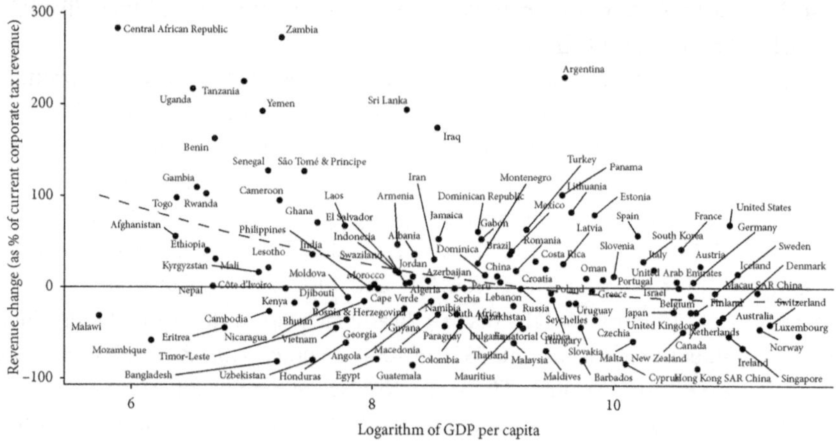

Figure 12.9 Effect of introducing RPA on CIT revenue (in per cent)
Source: IMF staff analysis.

7.5%, and 10%. Of course, this difference might be offset when taxes on the residual returns are added.

The second analysis is a full assessment of the revenue effects from RPA, from both taxing routine returns and residual profits. To that end, we calibrate the share of the routine profit at 40% of total profit, based on the analysis in Beer et al. (2020) (using a fixed routine return of 7.5% on fixed assets). The remaining 60% are residual profits. These residual profits are then apportioned based on sales by destination, which is approximated (admittedly a rough approximation) by the share of GDP minus net exports of countries. Figure 12.9 summarizes the results from this simulation, showing the revenue change in per cent. Interestingly, low-income countries stand out to gain from RPA, as illustrated by the downward slope of the regression line that shows a negative relationship between the revenue effect and GDP per capita. The Netherlands loses approximately 40% of the current corporate tax revenue generated by MNEs.

12.8 Dynamic Effects

An important omission from the analysis above is that it reflects the static effect of reforms, without accounting for changes in the behaviour of MNEs or for changes in corporate tax policies by individual countries. Such dynamic effects could significantly change the impact.

Under formulary methods, CIT rates will induce incentives for MNE investment, employment and production if assets, labour, or value-added factors are included in the formula. For instance, if assets are part of the formula, MNEs will have an incentive to locate more assets in low-tax countries—and less in high-tax countries—because such a location will expand the share of the consolidated profit that is taxed at the low rate. This can induce a significant tax savings for the MNE. A dynamic relocation of assets in response to FA would thus benefit countries with low CIT rates and harm countries with high CIT rates. This effect is opposite from the static effects reported above and will mitigate the revenue effects. Moreover, the relocation of capital will boost labour productivity in low-tax countries and reduce it in high-tax countries, which will be reflected in GDP and welfare.

These effects are illustrated in a study by Bettendorf et al. (2010), who explore the effect of the CCCTB by using a computable general equilibrium model for the EU. From the static analysis in their study, it appears that the Netherlands would lose 0.7% of GDP in corporate tax revenue. However, accounting for dynamic effects on investment, it is found that GDP in the Netherlands would expand by 0.2% and the net welfare loss would be very small.

While behavioural responses might thus significantly alter the results on the revenue and economic effects of formulary methods, they critically depend on the choice of the apportionment formula. For instance, the use of sales by destination is expected to produce much smaller behavioural effects, as consumption is generally less responsive to differences in CIT rates than production. Therefore, sales by destination might provide a more robust formulary system where dynamic effects are less important. As we saw from the analysis, moreover, apportionment based on sales by destination does not produce lower CIT revenue from US-based MNEs for the Netherlands.

Governments can also respond to the changed incentives for tax competition. For instance, if assets receive a significant weight in the formula and MNEs respond to this by relocating assets, governments will have a strong incentive to reduce their CIT rates. Indeed, simulations by Bettendorf et al. (2010) with their general equilibrium model suggest that the welfare gain of a CIT rate cut by an individual country is larger under FA than it is under the current system. These effects would be muted, however, if sales by destination were to be used as an allocation factor.

12.9 Conclusions

In this chapter, we have explored the economic and distributional effects of formulary methods to allocate profits of multinational companies across countries. Existing literature emphasizes the substantial benefits from the elimination of profit shifting and the possible major simplification gains. However, experience from federal states suggests that new distortions will arise in the allocation of formula factors and that opportunities for tax planning will not go away (but will be of a different form). Moreover, tax competition will not disappear under FA and might intensify if the factors in the formula are mobile across borders.

We assess the direct revenue implications of FA and RPA for the Netherlands. These effects are found to be large for certain formulas. The revenue paid by MNEs can decrease by up to 50% or 60% if employment or asset factors are used. Smaller losses are reported if FA is restricted to RPA. Effects are also smaller if US-based MNE profits are allocated using a destination-based sales formula. The results are thus sensitive to the specific design of the formula. If different formulas were to apply to certain sectors, such as the financial sector or extractive industries (an issue not explored in this paper), then the outcomes might also change.

Also, dynamic effects can be important. Formulary methods hold the prospect of generating major simplification benefits, which are ignored in the quantitative analysis here. Moreover, if allocation is geared more towards sales by destination, spill-overs and distortions can be reduced. Analysis suggests, for instance, that the expected negative effect on corporate tax revenue in the Netherlands might be accompanied by positive effects on investment and GDP. While the Dutch might not be expected to be very enthusiastic about the adoption of formulary methods in light of the expected direct revenue losses, its perspective should also focus on the specific aspects of its design as well as a proper understanding of the expected dynamic implications.

References

Auerbach, A., Devereux, M. P., Keen, M., Oosterhuis, P., and Vella, J. (2021), 'Residual profit allocation by income', in Devereux et al (ed.), *Taxing Profit in a Global Economy*, Oxford University Press, UK, pp. 189–266.

Avi-Yonah, R., Clausing, K. A., and Durst, M. C. (2009), 'Allocating business profits for tax purposes: a proposal to adopt a formulary profit split', *Florida Tax Review*, 9, 497–553.

Beer, S., De Mooij, R., Hebous, S., Keen, M., and Liu, L. (2020), 'Exploring Residual Profit Allocation', IMF Working Paper no. 20/49.

Bettendorf, L., Devereux, M., van der Horst, A., Loretz, S., and De Mooij, R. (2010), 'Corporate tax harmonization in the EU', *Economic Policy*, 25, 537–90.

De Mooij, R., Liu, L., and Prihardini, D. (2021), 'An assessment of global formula apportionment', *National Tax Journal*, 74(2).

Gordon, R. H. and Wilson, J. D. (1986), 'An examination of multijurisdictional corporate income taxation under formula apportionment', *Econometrica*, 54, 1357–73.

IMF (2014), 'Spillovers in international corporate taxation', IMF Policy Paper, Washington, DC.

IMF (2019), 'Corporate taxation in the global economy', IMF Policy Paper, Washington, DC.

Independent Commission for the Reform of International Corporate Taxation (2018), 'A roadmap to improve rules for taxing multinationals: a fairer future for global taxation' (https://www.icrict.com/resources/icrict-documents).

Lejour, A., Möhlmann, J., van 't Riet, M., and Benschop, T. (2019), 'Dutch shell companies and international tax planning', CPB Discussion Paper.

McLure, C. E., Jr (1981), 'The elusive incidence of the corporate income tax: the state case', *Public Finance Review*, 9, 395–413.

Mintz, J. and Smart, M. (2004), 'Income shifting, investment, and tax competition: theory and evidence from provincial taxation in Canada', *Journal of Public Economics*, 88, 1149–68.

Piccioto, S. (2016), 'Taxing multinational enterprises as unitary firms', International Centre for Tax and Development, Brighton, UK.

Sadiq, K. (2016), 'Unitary taxation of the finance sector', in S. Piccioto (ed.), *Taxing Multinational Enterprises as Unitary Firms*, Institute of Development Studies, UK, pp. 119–29.

Stichting Economisch Onderzoek (SEO) (2013), 'Uit de Schaduw van het Bankwezen', SEO, Amsterdam (in Dutch).

Stichting Economisch Onderzoek (SEO) (2018), 'Balansen, Inkomsten en Uitgaven van Bijzondere Financiële Instellingen', SEO, Amsterdam (in Dutch).

PART IV

LABOUR INCOME

13
An Exploration of Optimal Income Taxation in the Netherlands

*Egbert Jongen**

13.1 Introduction

There is a lot of discussion about the income tax and transfer system, raising concerns about the complexity, efficiency, and redistribution (van Dijkhuizen Committee, 2013). In 2014, then Treasury Secretary Wiebes proposed a broad overhaul of the tax system, but it proved impossible to achieve a comprehensive reform (Lejour, 2016). As a result, according to various experts, the current system is inefficient, unfair, and can 'be infinitely simpler' (Stevens, 2016). In the policy debate, several proposals for changes to the system are being discussed, such as a flat tax, a basic income, a higher or lower top tax rate, more or less support for single- and/or dual-earners, etc. (CPB, 2017).

What does an efficient but fair income tax look like? This is the domain of optimal-tax theory (Mirrlees, 1971). Optimal-tax theory considers how the optimal tax rate structure depends on the distribution of income, the extent to which taxpayers react to taxes and the social value of an additional euro of income for different income groups. We can compare the optimal tax rate structure that follows from theory with the existing tax rate structure. This gives insight into promising reforms of the tax rate structure, such as the (un)desirability of a flat tax or a higher top tax rate. Thanks in part to the work of Diamond (1998) and Saez (2001, 2002), optimal-tax theory has gained practical relevance for actual policy-making, as they have made the theory more accessible by rewriting the conditions for the optimal structure in terms of sufficient statistics and by using empirical information on these sufficient statistics.

* Egbert Jongen (e.l.w.jongen@cpb.nl) is Program Leader Labour at CPB Netherlands Bureau for Economic Policy Analysis, Associate Professor at Leiden University and also affiliated with IZA.

I am grateful to Sijbren Cnossen, Bas Jacobs, and Rocus van Opstal for comments on an earlier draft. Further, I thank my co-authors of the research on which this chapter is based, in particular Henk-Wim de Boer, Bas Jacobs, Patrick Koot, and Floris Zoutman. The views expressed in this chapter are those of the author and do not necessarily reflect the views of CPB Netherlands Bureau for Economic Policy Analysis, Leiden University or IZA.

Egbert Jongen, *An Exploration of Optimal Income Taxation in the Netherlands* In: *Tax by Design for the Netherlands*. Edited by: Sijbren Cnossen and Bas Jacobs, Oxford University Press. © Oxford University Press 2022.
DOI: 10.1093/oso/9780192855244.003.0013

In this chapter, I apply the methods of optimal-tax theory to the Netherlands. I study the optimal rate structure, seeking to determine the optimal marginal tax rate for different income groups in the Netherlands. Furthermore, I take a closer look at optimal income support for single parents, a group that, relatively, has received much attention in the policy debate.

The results presented here are based on recent models of optimal-tax theory (see Jacobs et al., 2013, 2017; Zoutman et al., 2015; de Boer and Jongen, 2017; de Boer et al., 2018), and on the recent findings of empirical research into the behavioural responses to changes in taxes and income-dependent transfers (see Bettendorf et al., 2014, 2015; Jongen et al., 2015; Mastrogiacomo et al., 2017; Jongen and Stoel, 2019; Bosch et al., 2019), both on the extensive margin (participation) and on the intensive margin (hours per week), in terms of both hours worked and the elasticity of taxable income.

13.2 A Brief Introduction to Optimal-Tax Theory

What is the optimal tax rate structure for given preferences for redistribution? Mirrlees (1971) answered this question, in an article that won him the Nobel Prize in Economics in 1996. His model works as follows. People differ in their earnings capacity. The income of people is determined by a combination of earnings capacity (given) and work effort (choice), where people with a higher earnings capacity ultimately also have a higher income. The government wants to redistribute income from people with a high earnings capacity to people with a low earnings capacity, because an extra euro is worth more for people with a low earnings capacity than for people with a high earnings capacity. However, the government only observes income and not earnings capacity. Redistribution from high to low incomes therefore also increases the marginal tax on effort. This leads to efficiency losses. Therefore, the government is constrained to a second-best solution in which tax rates are set so that, for each income level, the marginal social gains from redistribution equal the marginal losses of efficiency. Mirrlees (1971) solved for the optimal non-linear tax schedule, but his formula was still rather inaccessible and rather general, giving limited direction to policymakers. Based on a number of simplifying assumptions, Diamond (1998) presented the more accessible ABC formula that determines the optimal rate structure; I cover this ABC formula in more detail below. Saez (2001) then described this model in so-called sufficient statistics, which for the most part can be observed empirically (except for the social welfare weights), and applied the model empirically to the United States. Thanks to Diamond (1998) and Saez (2001), optimal-tax theory gives much more direction to policymakers.

Diamond (1998) shows that, using some simplifying assumptions (e.g. the absence of income effects), the optimal marginal tax rate $t(y)$ at income level y follows from the following ABC formula:[1]

$$\frac{t(y)}{1-t(y)} = A(y)\,B(y)\,C(y)$$

A higher value for A, B, or C at any level of income y thus corresponds with higher optimal marginal rates at that income level. The terms A, B, and C consist of the following components.

- $A(y) = 1/\varepsilon$. Here, ε is the elasticity of taxable income with respect to (1 minus) the marginal tax rate. The higher ε is, the greater the distortion caused by higher tax rates, the smaller A is and, hence, the lower the optimal marginal tax rate is at a given income level.
- $B(y) = 1 - G(y)$. Here, $G(y)$ is the average of the social marginal value of an additional euro $g(y)$ for any individual with an income higher than y. $g(y)$ gives the increase in social welfare—in money units—if an individual with income y receives an additional euro. Furthermore, $G(0) = 1$; the average value of an additional euro for all taxpayers is equal to 1. Also, we assume that $G'(y) < 0$; the average social value of a euro decreases higher up in the income distribution, either because the individual marginal utility of an additional euro decreases in income or because the social valuation of the individual marginal utility of an additional euro decreases in income (Saez, 2001). Because $G'(y) < 0$, we have $B'(y) > 0$. Hence, a stronger preference for redistribution corresponds to higher marginal tax rates.
- $C(y) = [1 - F(y)]/[yf(y)]$. In this expression, the numerator $1 - F(y)$ is the proportion of people with an income above y. This term weighs the gains from redistribution $B(y)$. When there are still many people with an income above y, then there are still many people whose income can be redistributed to lower incomes. The denominator $yf(y)$ is the tax base at income y. This term weighs the efficiency loss $A(y)$. The efficiency losses are greater when income y or the proportion of people $f(y)$ at income y is higher. The term $C(y)$ empirically follows a U-shape in income y (with a lower right leg). At low income levels, there are still many people with an income above that income level, $1 - F(y)$ is high, and the tax base that is distorted $yf(y)$ is low. Moving up to the modal income, there are now fewer people with an income

[1] More precisely, Diamond (1998) developed the ABC formula for the (unobserved) underlying skills distribution, as the income distribution is endogenous. In Jacobs et al. (2017), we show that we can also express the ABC formula using income as an argument. In the application, we use a structural model to take into account, among other things, the endogenous income distribution in different tax systems. However, this results in almost identical results as a model where we use sufficient statistics (and ignore the fact that these sufficient statistics are endogenous); see Jacobs et al. (2017).

above that income level, $1 - F(y)$ is lower, but the tax base that is distorted $yf(y)$ is higher, as there are many people $f(y)$ at that income level. At high income levels, both the numerator and denominator fall, and it is an empirical question whether $C(y)$ is increasing or decreasing. Empirically, it turns out that $C(y)$ increases again, and finally becomes a constant as the income distribution converges to a Pareto distribution at the top (Jacobs et al., 2013).

The optimal marginal tax rates largely follow the U-shape of $C(y)$, which is determined by the income distribution. Suppose that the elasticity of taxable income is constant across the income distribution. According to Jongen and Stoel (2019), this is not a bad approximation. Furthermore, $B(y)$ is increasing in income. How fast $B(y)$ increases with income depends on the preferences for redistribution; when there are strong preferences for redistribution, $B(y)$ increases faster. Then, optimal marginal tax rates also follow a U-shape in income (Diamond, 1998): high at the bottom, low for middle incomes, and again slightly higher for the top incomes. This is shown graphically in Figure 13.1. The U-shape is robust to different political preferences for redistribution (as long as the social value of an additional euro decreases in income).

Before moving on to the empirical application to the Netherlands, I briefly consider two variations on the model of Mirrlees (1971). First, the model in Mirrlees (1971) ignores the extensive margin when it comes to labour supply (or, more precisely, it does not consider fixed costs of work). However, taxes distort both the extensive margin (participation) and the intensive margin (hours per week or wage and profit income per employed). The extensive margin can be

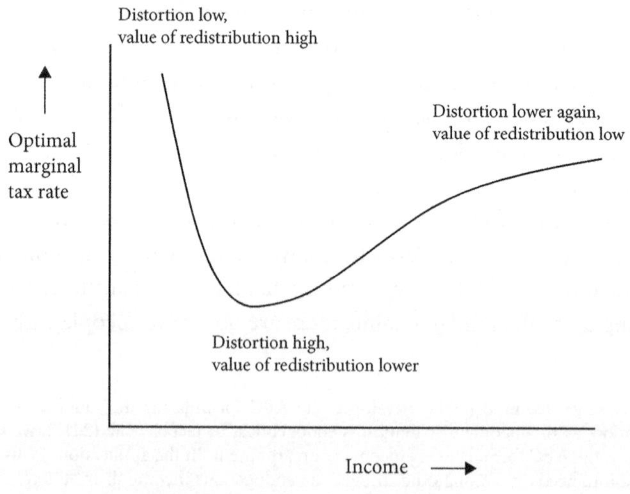

Figure 13.1 Optimal marginal tax rates have a U-shape

modelled by allowing people to make a choice between working and not working, where they have to incur fixed costs of work in order to work. Adding the extensive margin results in an adjusted ABC formula (Jacquet et al., 2013; Jacobs et al., 2017), where the $B(y)$ term is usually slightly lower (higher marginal rates lead to higher average rates higher in the income distribution, which lowers employment rates there, reducing the benefits of redistribution). In the empirical application, I use the adjusted ABC formula with both extensive and intensive margins.

Second, I can also rewrite the ABC formula so that the preference for income redistribution will be on the left-hand side. This is the so-called inverse optimal-tax method, first applied to income taxation by Bourguignon and Spadaro (2012). The question then is the following. For a given distribution of income and knowing how the tax base reacts to taxes, what is the implicit social welfare function (i.e. the set of social welfare weights) that makes the observed tax system the optimal one? It is particularly interesting to see whether all incomes are positively valued in the social welfare function, i.e. $g(y) > 0$ for all y, and whether people with higher incomes have a lower social welfare weight, i.e. $g'(y) < 0$. Note that all the determinants of the social welfare weights in the inverse optimal-tax method can (in principle) be determined empirically.

13.3 Application to the Netherlands

Below, the modified ABC formula, including income and extensive margin effects, is used for an applied optimal-tax analysis for the Netherlands, including an inverse optimal-tax analysis. To begin with, an analysis of the general tax rate structure is made in Section 13.3.1 (model and calibration) and Section 13.3.2 (results) followed by an analysis of optimal income support for single parents in Section 13.3.3.

13.3.1 Optimal Tax Rate Structure: Model and Calibration

First, the general tax rate structure is analysed. What is the optimal rate structure across incomes in the Netherlands for different preferences for redistribution, and how does this compare to the current system?

For the analysis, the optimal-tax model of Jacquet et al. (2013) and Jacobs et al. (2017) is used, where individuals can respond to changes in financial incentives, both on the extensive margin (participation) and on the intensive margin (hours worked or income). Consumption is equal to the net income of the individual. The fact that some of the individuals cohabitate (a discussion of the limitations is given in Section 13.4) and that they can save or borrow is ignored.[2] For an extensive discussion of the model and calibration method, see Jacobs et al. (2017).

For the calibration of the model, the income distribution of 2015 is used (more specifically, the distribution of income in 2012, updated to 2015) of the Income Panel Survey of Statistics Netherlands, a representative sample of about 100,000 people. For the top 10% of the income distribution, a Pareto distribution is used, which gives a good fit for the top of the income distribution (see Jacobs et al., 2013). The utility of individuals is determined by consumption (positive) and effort (negative), and fixed costs or benefits of work (these are incurred only if the individual works). The parameters in the utility function are set in such a way that the uncompensated intensive-margin elasticity is, on average, equal to 0.2. This is more conservative than the estimate of 0.25 for the elasticity of taxable income for employees in Jongen and Stoel (2016) but it is similar to the estimate of 0.20 for the elasticity of taxable income for workers in Bosch and de Boer (2019). The compensated elasticity is, on average, equal to 0.25, implying a low average income elasticity of –0.05, in line with empirical studies (see Saez et al., 2012). The elasticity of taxable income is used as the intensive-margin elasticity in the calibration because the elasticity of taxable income captures more behavioural reactions from changes in marginal rates than just hours worked. The distribution of fixed costs/benefits of employment has been chosen to reach an average extensive-margin elasticity of 0.2, in line with the average extensive-margin elasticity between groups in the MICSIM model,[3] and a participation rate in line with the data. The effective marginal tax rates in the tax and transfer system for 2015 are calculated with the MIMOSI model, taking into account all (national) income-dependent rates, tax deductions, and transfers.[4]

13.3.2 Optimal Tax Rate Structure: Results

When the (modified) ABC formula is applied to the Netherlands, the results in Figure 13.2 are obtained. It can be seen that the optimal marginal rates also have a U-shape in the Netherlands, when taking into account extensive-margin and income effects. The marginal rates should be relatively high for low incomes, much lower for middle incomes and then slightly higher again for top incomes. The exact value of the optimal marginal tax rate for each income level depends on

[2] When calculating the effective marginal tax rate, the partner's income is taken into account.

[3] MICSIM is a behavioural microsimulation model of CPB that focuses on behavioural responses in participation rates and hours worked in response to changes in the tax-benefit system (see Jongen et al., 2015).

[4] MIMOSI is a non-behavioural microsimulation of CPB that, amongst other things, can be used to calculate marginal and average tax rates (see Koot et al., 2016). The marginal rates are also used together with the intensive-margin elasticity to recover the distribution of earnings capacities of workers (see Jacobs et al., 2017).

the preferences for redistribution. This may seem obvious, but the debate is often about the unique optimal system. There is no clear-cut answer to this, but it is possible to get answers on the general shape of the profile of optimal tax rates.

The results for a so-called Rawlsian social welfare function are given,[5] where only the person with the lowest income gets a positive weight, and for a Utilitarian social welfare function, where social welfare equals the sum of individual utilities.[6] In the case of a Rawlsian social welfare function, the optimal marginal tax rates are higher so that there is more redistribution. In the case of a Utilitarian social welfare function, the optimal marginal tax rates are lower so that there is less redistribution. However, note that neither of these social welfare functions generates optimal marginal tax rates that are flat. A flat tax rate is therefore not optimal. In the case of a flat tax rate, there is insufficient redistribution to low incomes and there are unnecessary efficiency losses for the middle-income groups, because the marginal rate has to be the same at the bottom and the top of the income distribution. See Jacobs (2015) for further discussion on the advantages and disadvantages of a flat tax system.

Figure 13.3 gives the actual effective marginal tax rates in the Netherlands in 2015. When the actual rates are compared with the rates of the optimal-tax analysis, a number of things can be observed.

First, the actual marginal tax rates are relatively low for low incomes, as opposed to the optimal marginal tax rates for low incomes. Second, the actual marginal rates close to modal income are relatively high, where the optimal-tax analysis indicates that they should be relatively low there. Third, we see that the top rate is close to the top rate for a Rawlsian social welfare function, generating the maximum tax revenue from the top of the income distribution.

From the perspective of optimal-tax theory, it is remarkable that marginal rates rise at the bottom and spike near the mode of the income distribution. Figure 13.4 shows that this implies that we give a relatively low social weight to low incomes compared with middle incomes, which is an anomaly (see Jacobs et al., 2017, for the method). We should note that there are relatively many secondary earners at the lower end of the individual income distribution, whose personal income is not a good measure of their consumption opportunities (determined by household income). However, when the analysis is carried out just for single people without children, we still find an inverse U-shape for the social welfare weights (see Jacobs et al., 2017). Furthermore, the finding that the marginal tax rate is relatively high for the densest part of the income distribution (i.e. middle incomes) is robust across household types (Jacobs et al., 2017). Hence, the marginal tax rate for

[5] The marginal rates do not go to 100% because this does not generate the maximum amount of tax revenue, as it is beyond the top of the Laffer curve.

[6] The marginal rates do not go to 0% because there is still declining marginal utility in income at the individual level.

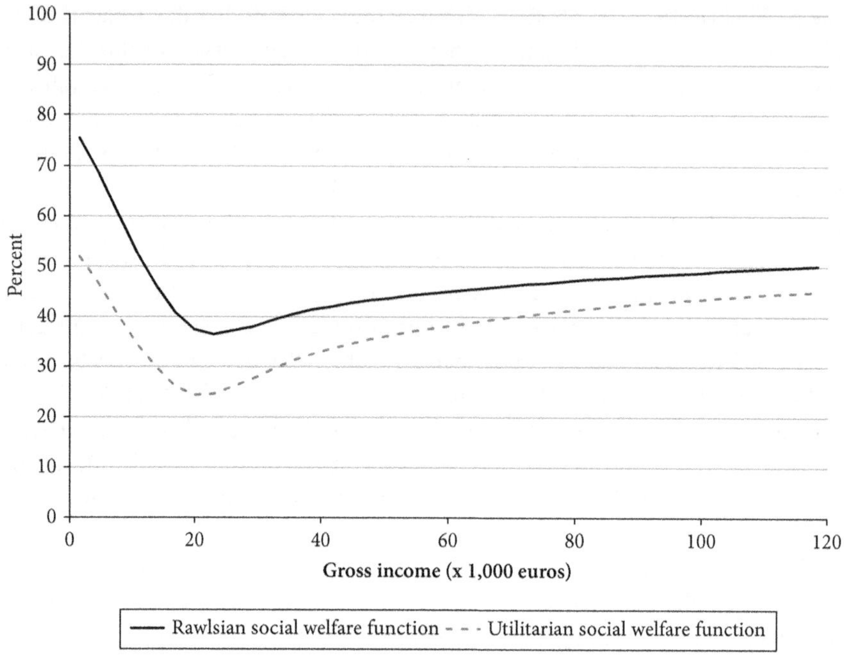

Figure 13.2 Optimal marginal tax rates in the Netherlands (2015)
Source: Zoutman et al. (2015).

middle incomes seems too high according to optimal-tax theory when compared with the marginal tax rate for low incomes (and top incomes). Jacobs et al. (2017) show that this result is also robust to the elasticity of the tax base. The high marginal tax rate for middle incomes is the result of the phase-out of income-dependent transfers between the minimum wage and modal income (such as the tax rebate for rent). The optimal-tax analysis suggests that these income-dependent transfers should be phased out at a lower income level.

Finally, the top tax rate is analysed. Figures 13.2 and 13.3 have shown that the top rate in 2015 was close to the top rate at a Rawlsian social welfare function. In a Rawlsian social welfare function, the term $B(y)$ at the top is equal to 1 (i.e. an additional euro at the top has no social value). This also implies a social welfare weight of about 0 for the top incomes in Figure 13.4. Empirically, the top of the income distribution (at least for the top 10% of the income distribution in the Netherlands) appears to follow a Pareto distribution (see Jacobs et al., 2013). In the case of a Pareto distribution, the term $C(y)$ is constant, equal to $1/a$, where a denotes the so-called Pareto parameter. For the Netherlands, Jacobs et al. (2013) precisely estimate the Pareto parameter to be 3.3. At the top of the income distribution, the ABC formula reduces to:

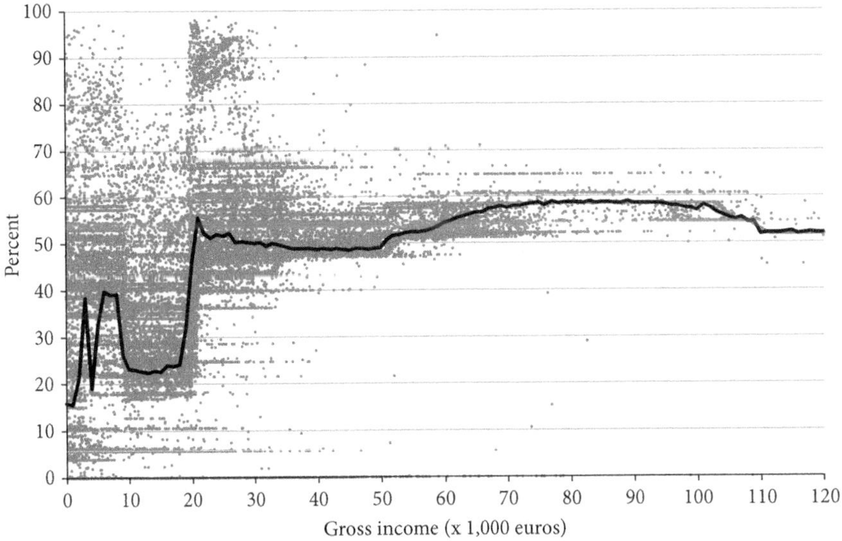

Figure 13.3 Actual marginal tax rates in the Netherlands (2015)
Source: MIMOSI.

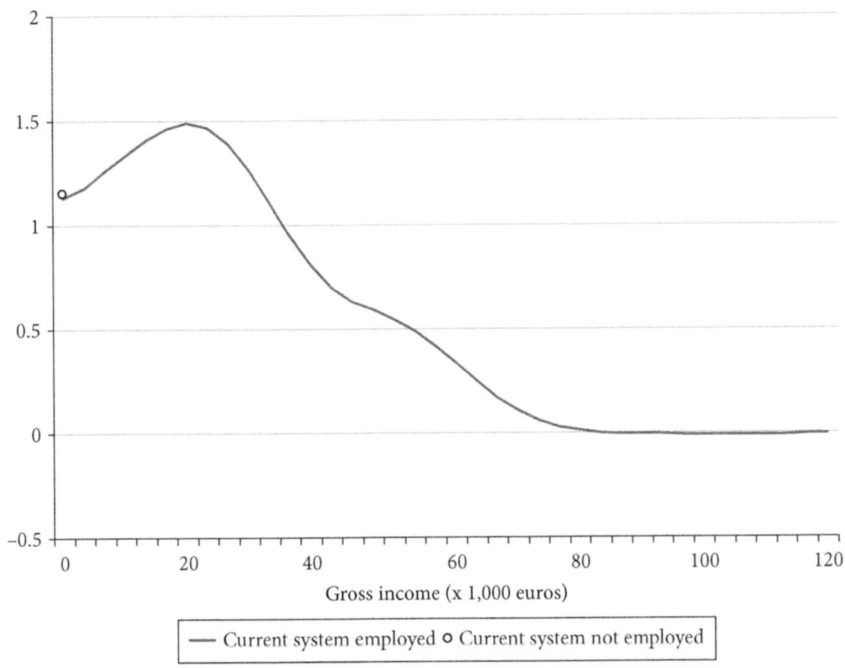

Figure 13.4 Implicit social welfare weights in the Netherlands (2015)
Source: Zoutman et al. (2015).

$$\frac{t(top)}{1-t(top)} = \frac{1}{\varepsilon}\frac{1}{a} <=> t(top) = \frac{1}{1+\varepsilon a}.$$

For an elasticity of taxable income at the top ε of 0.25, the revenue-maximizing top rate is about 55%. This is similar to a top rate of 50%, near the current top rate, and an effective top rate of 55% (taking into account indirect taxes; see Jacobs et al., 2013). This means that the current top rate is near the top of the Laffer curve, and a higher top rate yields little if any additional tax revenue.

13.3.3 Optimal Income Support for Single Parents

A limitation of the previous analysis is that it is assumed that the same tax system applies to everyone. However, in practice this is not the case. Single parents usually receive special treatment, as they are entitled to specific income-dependent transfers and tax deductions. In addition, tax design is particularly challenging for this group. On the one hand, the social benefits of income support are relatively high, as they have a relatively low income and must also provide for children from that income. On the other hand, the social costs of income support are also relatively high, as single parents react relatively strongly to financial incentives; see Jongen et al. (2015) and Mastrogiacomo et al. (2017) for empirical evidence for the Netherlands.

Here, we explore to what extent tax policy has found an optimal balance between providing sufficient income support for different groups of single parents while maintaining sufficient financial incentives for labour supply; see de Boer and Jongen (2017) for a more elaborate analysis. To that end, an inverse optimal-tax analysis is performed for single parents, before and after a major reform of income support for single parents in 2015. The goal of the reform was to improve the financial incentives to supply labour of single parents. It should be noted though that an important limitation of the analysis is that the analysis is partial, in the sense that we do not consider the optimality of the overall income support for single parents relative to other groups. The focus is on the income support for single parents with different income levels, in particular the employed versus the non-employed. Whether income support for single parents as a whole is optimal depends on the social welfare weight of single parents compared with the social welfare weights of other groups.

The reform. Before 2015, there was a complex system of targeted income support for single parents (see Figure 13.5(a)). All single parents were entitled to the general child benefit, which is income-independent. In addition, non-working single parents were entitled to the income-dependent tax rebate for children (this tax rebate was phased out when income passed a certain threshold) and an

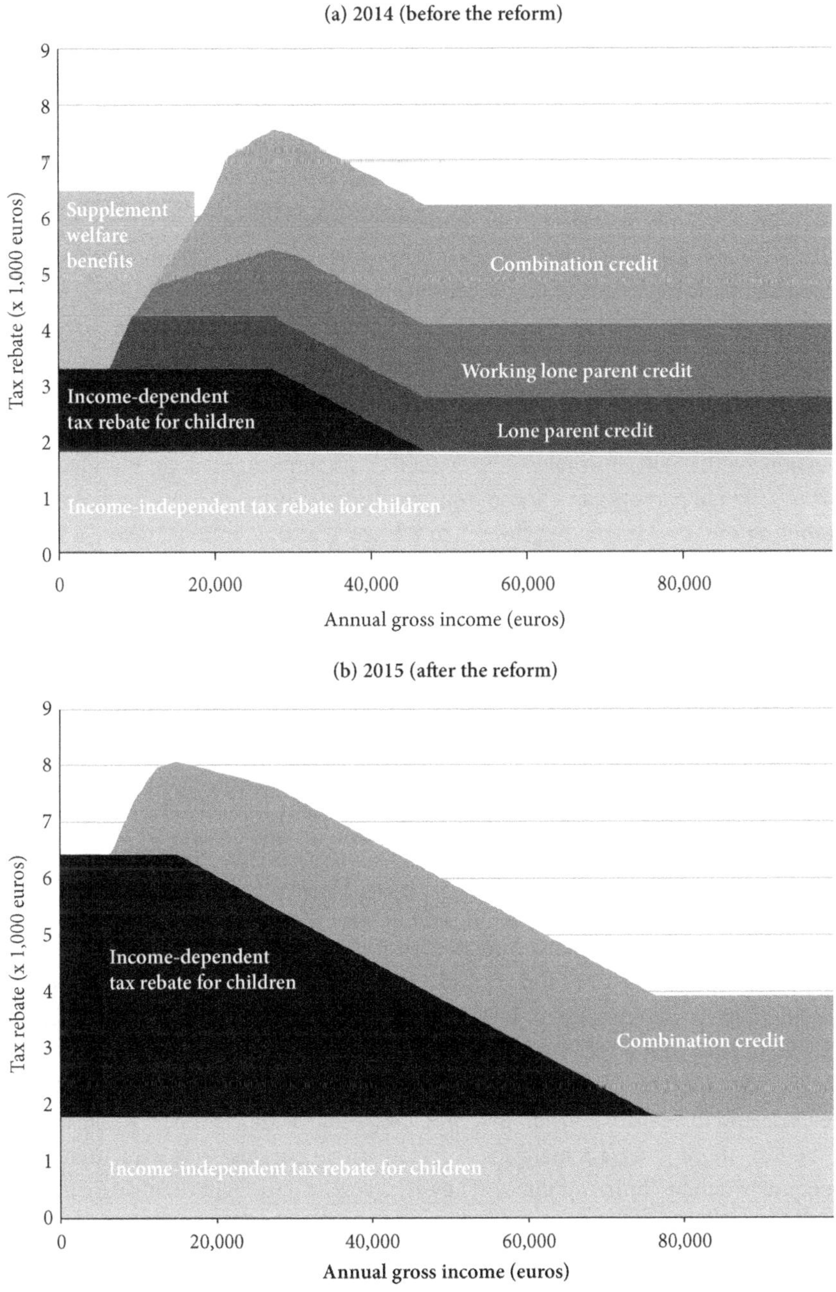

Figure 13.5 Specific income support for single parents (2014–15)
Source: De Boer and Jongen (2017).

additional benefit for single parents on social assistance. In addition to the general child benefit, working single parents were also entitled to the income-dependent tax rebate for children (insofar as their income was not too high), a single parent tax credit, a supplementary single parental tax credit, and the so-called combination credit (for parents who combine work with care for children below the age of 12).

After 2015, the system has become much simpler, and only three specific schemes remain (see Figure 13.5(b)): the general child benefit, the income-dependent tax rebate for children, and the combination credit. Furthermore, the financial incentive to start working was improved for single parents, in particular at relatively low income levels. The incentive to earn a relatively high income (by working many days, for example) was actually reduced in the reform.

Model and calibration. De Boer and Jongen (2017) use the discrete-choice version of the ABC formula of Saez (2002), as implemented by Blundell et al. (2009). Single parents can choose from six discrete income points, with option 0 denoting not working and options 1 to 5 being working options, where a higher number implies a higher income. The choice that single parents make depends on their earnings capacity, which varies across the group of single parents, and their effort/working hours. The distribution of income over the discrete choice points has been calibrated on the income distribution of single parents in the Labour Market Panel of Statistics Netherlands. Net incomes before and after the reform have been calculated with the MIMOSI model of CPB. The extensive- and intensive-margin elasticities of the tax base for single parents are based on the MICSIM model of CPB. See de Boer and Jongen (2017) for further details of the model used and the calibration.

Outcomes for single parents. Figure 13.6 gives the results of the analysis. We present the implicit social welfare weights for the different discrete choice options from which the single parents can choose in the model.[7] Option 0 refers to single parents who do not work (and typically receive social assistance), option 1 refers to single parents with a small job and/or low hourly pay and option 5 refers to single parents with a full-time job and/or a high hourly wage.

We see that, before the reform, although the social welfare weights fall with income and are positive for all incomes, consistent with a 'proper' social welfare function, there is an anomaly for working single parents with a relatively low income (discrete-choice option 1). They receive a lower weight than single parents with higher incomes (discrete-choice options 2–4). After the reform in 2015, this

[7] A complication is that the 'distance' in terms of gross income is not equal between the different points; see de Boer and Jongen (2017) for the gross incomes corresponding to points 0 to 5.

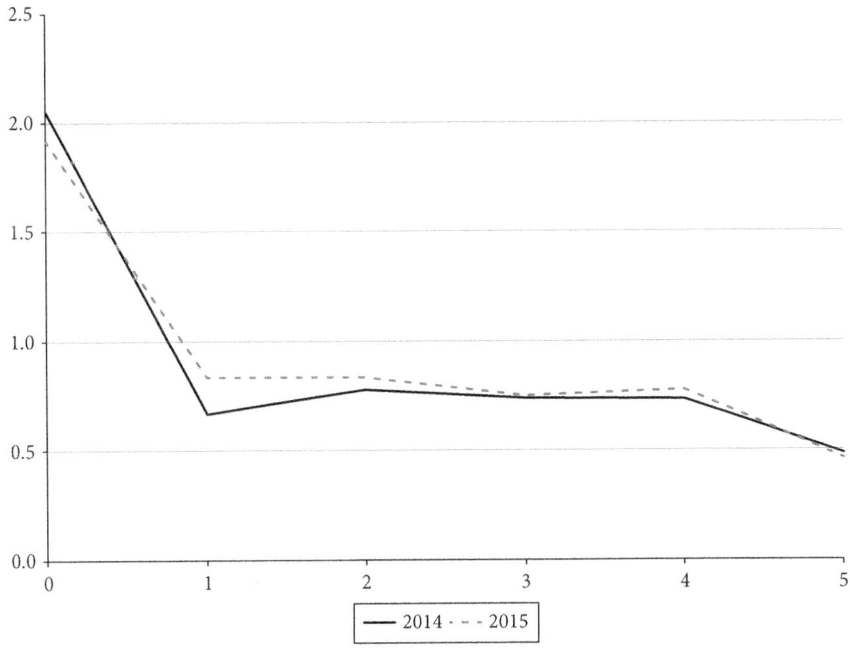

Figure 13.6 Implicit social welfare weights before and after the reform

Notes: Single parents are ordered according to gross income on the x-axis. Single parents at position 0 do not work and receive social assistance. Single parents at position 1 work but have a relatively low income. Single parents at position 5 also work and have a relatively high income.

Source: De Boer and Jongen (2017).

anomaly has largely disappeared, as income support for working single parents with relatively low incomes increased.[8]

Therefore, the reform of 2015 has at least been successful in two dimensions: the system became a lot simpler and an anomaly in the implicit social welfare weights has largely disappeared from the system. So, is income support for single parents now optimal? Unfortunately, there is no clear-cut answer to this, as it depends, among other things, on the preferences for redistribution within the group of single parents and between the group of single parents and other groups in the population.

Considering the level of redistribution within the group of single parents, de Boer and Jongen (2017) analyse optimal income support for single parents for different preferences for redistribution, keeping total income support for single

[8] An analysis for subgroups by age of the youngest child suggests that for single parents with a youngest child 0–3 years old there is still an anomaly in 2015, with the social welfare weights of working single parents with relatively low incomes being lower than for working single parents with higher incomes. Future research should show whether the increase in the earned income tax credit for lower incomes after 2015 also remedied this anomaly.

parents fixed. For both strong and weak preferences for redistribution, they find that income support for single parents with relatively low incomes can be further increased, in line with the increase in the earned income tax credit for low incomes after 2015. Whether income support for non-working single parents or parents with relatively high incomes should go up or down depends on how strong the preference for redistribution is.

Finally, note that the analysis was carried out after the reform took place. An interesting option for future research is to do such an analysis to study potential interesting future reforms, and to see whether a potential reform moves the tax system closer to an optimal tax and transfer system or not, and, more generally, what an optimal design for certain subgroups in the tax system might look like (e.g. income support for single people without children).

13.4 Limitations of the Analysis

The optimal-tax analyses for the Netherlands give interesting insights into promising policies to further optimize the tax and transfer system. At the same time, it is important to note that the analysis, though in some respects already advanced, still has potentially important limitations. Below, a number of important gaps in our knowledge are considered, which at the same time are interesting options for future research.

We still know relatively little about what explains the difference between the elasticity of the number of hours worked and the elasticity of taxable income (Jongen and Stoel, 2019). Part of the explanation is perhaps that contractual hours are used in the empirical analysis, where actual hours worked may respond more strongly to changes in marginal tax rates. Furthermore, tax avoidance and evasion are likely to play a role. To separate real responses from tax avoidance and evasion, it is important to be able to make a decomposition of the changes in the tax base as a result of a change in the marginal tax rates. For example, if tax avoidance leads to an increase in a tax base elsewhere (or in the future—think of pension savings), the elasticity of a certain tax base is not a sufficient statistic for optimal-tax analysis (Chetty, 2009; Saez et al., 2012). In that case, the optimal rates are usually higher than if we do not take these so-called fiscal externalities into account. A further analysis of the elasticity of taxable income, including a decomposition of the underlying behavioural responses that would give a better insight into possible fiscal externalities, is an interesting option for future research.

Another important question is whether people are fully aware of their budget constraint (which is complex due to the large number of income-dependent tax credits and tax rebates), and which rebates and credits they are entitled to. An analysis of the tax rebate for rent shows that there is substantial non-take-up (Bosch et al., 2019). This makes the rent rebate less effective as a tool for redistribution. If people have limited knowledge of the financial incentives relevant to the choice of working (more) or not, this can be an important factor in the extent to which they respond to financial incentives, such as income-dependent tax credits and tax rebates; see, again, Bosch et al. (2019) for an analysis of the behavioural effects of the rent rebate.[9] Informational frictions and other frictions are also important for thinking about the long-term elasticities of the tax base, where low short-term elasticities can be consistent with high long-term elasticities (Chetty, 2012).

A further limitation of the current analysis is that the problem of simultaneously deriving optimal taxes on primary and secondary earners is not solved. Kleven et al. (2009) show that it is possible to solve this problem for a unitary-household model, but so far it has not been possible to implement this for the Netherlands. As indicated in the analysis, an important explanation for the relatively low effective marginal tax rates at the bottom is the high proportion of secondary earners who have a relatively low income. However, the anomaly that rates are relatively high for middle incomes (relative to people with an income below or above), where the distortion is relatively high because many people are located there, is robust across household types. In general, the analysis ignores that individuals live in different household types, for example, where economies of scale and children's costs and benefits may play an important role. The government explicitly distinguishes between the different household types in the tax and transfer system. The question is to what extent these differences can be rationalized with optimal-tax theory. This is an interesting direction for future research (see Jacobs, 2015, for some considerations and references).

Another challenge is an analysis of optimal taxation over the life cycle. For example, income inequality on a lifetime basis is much smaller than on an annual basis (Lever and Waaijers, 2013). Developing an optimal-tax analysis based on a realistic empirical life-cycle model for the Netherlands is also interesting for future research. The same applies to an empirically founded optimal-tax analysis that explicitly takes into account preference heterogeneity, for example in the preference for leisure (Fleurbaey and Maniquet, 2006), when work in itself (in addition to income) has social value (Brett and Jacquet, 2015), or when people do not make privately optimal decisions (Gerritsen, 2016). Furthermore, it is important to realize that existing tax systems are the result not only of an exchange between efficiency and equality, but also of more strategic political considerations (Jacobs et al., 2017). As a result, the implicit social welfare function that I derive for the Netherlands does not necessarily reflect social preferences for redistribution.

[9] The analysis in Jongen et al. (2016) shows that simplifications in the system with limited distributional effects are indeed possible.

13.5 Conclusions

In this chapter, we have analysed the optimality of the current income tax and transfer system, using optimal-tax theory. We have used large representative data sets, an advanced tax-benefit calculator to determine the effective (marginal) tax rates, recent estimates of the elasticity of participation, hours worked and the tax base more generally with respect to financial incentives, and state-of-the-art simulation models.

The analysis suggests the following for the general rate structure: there is not one unique optimal tax system, an optimal rate structure is not flat, the marginal tax rate for middle incomes is (too) high, and a higher top tax rate generates little, if any, additional revenue. This implies that proposals for introducing a flat tax (Beetsma et al., 2012), reducing the average tax rate for middle incomes (and raising the marginal tax rate for middle incomes) and/or increasing the top tax rate (see the election programmes of the left-wing parties in CPB, 2017) are less promising reform options in terms of an efficient and fair tax system.[10] One way to reduce the marginal tax rate for middle incomes is to phase-out income support at lower income levels. This also reduces the number of people who receive income-dependent transfers, reducing the complexity of the tax system, with almost six out of ten households now receiving an income-dependent transfer (Bos, 2017). Furthermore, the analysis of income support for single parents suggests that this part of the tax system is close to an optimal system. Finally, it should be noted that the analysis still has some limitations. Future research can show to what extent these limitations affect the results.

References

Beetsma, R., Bovenberg, L., Caminada, K., Dijkgraaf, E., Eijffinger, S., and Gradus, R. (2012), 'Elke Nederlander gebaat bij sociale vlaktaks', *Me Judice*, January.

Bettendorf, L., Folmer, K., and Jongen, E. (2014), 'The dog that did not bark: the EITC for single mothers in the Netherlands', *Journal of Public Economics*, 119, 49–60.

Bettendorf, L., Jongen, E., and Muller, P. (2015), 'Childcare subsidies and labour supply: evidence from a large Dutch reform', *Labour Economics*, 36, 112–23.

Blundell, R., Brewer, M., Haan, P., and Shephard, A. (2009), 'Optimal income taxation of lone mothers: an empirical comparison of the UK and Germany', *Economic Journal*, 119(535), F101–21.

Bos, W. (2017), 'Toeslag voor bijna 6 op de tien huishoudens', *ESB*, July 11.

[10] To reduce the average tax rate for middle incomes, we need to increase the marginal tax rate for middle income groups, in order to generate more taxes from higher incomes to finance the lower average tax rate for middle incomes.

Bosch, N. and de Boer, H.-W. (2019), 'Income and occupational choice responses of the self-employed to tax rate changes: heterogeneity across reforms and income', *Labour Economics*, 58, 1–20.

Bosch, N., Jongen, E., Leenders, W., and Möhlmann, J. (2019), 'Non-bunching at kinks and notches of income support in the Netherlands', *International Tax and Public Finance*, 26, 1329–52.

Bourguignon, F. and Spadaro, A. (2012), 'Tax-benefit revealed social preferences', *Journal of Economic Inequality*, 10, 75–108.

Brett, C. and Jacquet, L. (2015), 'Workforce or workfare? The optimal use of work requirements when labour is supplied along the extensive margin', *Canadian Journal of Economics*, 48, 1855–82.

Chetty, R. (2009), 'Is the taxable income elasticity sufficient to calculate deadweight loss? The implications of evasion and avoidance', *American Economic Journal: Economic Policy*, 1(2), 31–52.

Chetty, R. (2012), 'Bounds on elasticities with optimization frictions: a synthesis of micro and macro evidence on labor supply', *Econometrica*, 80, 969–1018.

CPB (2017), 'Charting Choices 2018–2021', CPB Netherlands Bureau for Economic Policy Analysis, The Hague.

de Boer, H.-W. and Jongen, E. (2017), 'Optimal income support for lone parents in the Netherlands: are we there yet?' CPB Discussion Paper no. 361, CPB Netherlands Bureau for Economic Policy Analysis, The Hague.

de Boer, H.-W., Jongen, E., and Koot, P. (2018), 'Optimal taxation of secondary earners in the Netherlands: has equity lost ground?' CPB Discussion Paper no. 375, CPB Netherlands Bureau for Economic Policy Analysis, The Hague.

Diamond, P. (1998), 'Optimal income taxation: an example with a U-shaped pattern of optimal marginal tax rates', *American Economic Review*, 88(1), 83–95.

Fleurbaey, M. and Maniquet, F. (2006), 'Fair income tax', *Review of Economic Studies*, 73, 55–83.

Gerritsen, A. (2016), 'Optimal taxation when people do not maximize well-being', *Journal of Public Economics*, 144, 122–39.

Jacobs, B. (2015), *De prijs van gelijkheid*, Bert Bakker, Amsterdam.

Jacobs, B., Jongen, E., and Zoutman, F. (2013), 'Over de top, CPB Policy Brief 2013/04', CPB Netherlands Bureau for Economic Policy Analysis, The Hague.

Jacobs, B., Jongen, E., and Zoutman, F. (2017), 'Revealed social preferences of Dutch political parties', *Journal of Public Economics*, 156, 81–100.

Jacquet, L., Lehmann, E., and van der Linden, B. (2013), 'Optimal redistributive taxation with both intensive and extensive responses', *Journal of Economic Theory*, 148, 1770–1805.

Jongen, E., de Boer, H.-W., and Dekker, P. (2015), 'De effectiviteit van fiscaal participatiebeleid', CPB Policy Brief 2015/02, CPB Netherlands Bureau for Economic Policy Analysis, The Hague.

Jongen, E., Koot, P., and Vlekke, M. (2016), 'Leuker kunnen we het niet maken, wel makkelijker', *ESB*, 4741, 604–7, September 8.

Jongen, E. and Stoel, M. (2019), 'The elasticity of taxable labour income in the Netherlands', *De Economist*, 167, 359–86.

Kleven, H., Thustrup Kreiner, K., and Saez, E. (2009), 'The optimal income taxation of couples', *Econometrica*, 77, 537–60.

Koot, P., Vlekke, M., Berkhout, E., and Euwals, R. (2016), 'MIMOSI: Microsimulatiemodel voor belastingen, sociale zekerheid, loonkosten en koopkracht', CPB Background Document, The Hague.

Lejour, A. (2016), 'De politieke economie van belastinghervormingen', CPB Policy Brief no. 2016/08, CPB Netherlands Bureau for Economic Policy Analysis, The Hague.

Lever, M. and Waaijers, R. (2013), 'Inkomensongelijkheid gedurende de levensloop', *TPEdigitaal*, 7, 140–59.

Mastrogiacomo, M., Bosch, N., Gielen, M., and Jongen, E. (2017), 'Heterogeneity in labour supply responses: evidence from a large tax reform', *Oxford Bulletin of Economics and Statistics*, 79, 769–96.

Mirrlees, J. (1971), 'An exploration of in the theory of optimal income taxation', *Review of Economic Studies*, 38, 175–208.

Saez, E. (2001), 'Using elasticities to derive optimal income tax rates', *Review of Economic Studies*, 68, 205–29.

Saez, E. (2002), 'Optimal income transfer programs: intensive versus extensive labor supply responses', *Quarterly Journal of Economics*, 117, 1039–73.

Saez, E., Slemrod, J., and Giertz, S. (2012), 'The elasticity of taxable income with respect to marginal tax rates: a critical review', *Journal of Economic Literature*, 50, 3–50.

Stevens, L. (2016), 'Belastingstelsel kan oneindig veel simpeler', interview in *De Volkskrant*, September 13, 2016.

van Dijkhuizen Committee (2013), 'Commissie inkomstenbelasting en toeslagen, Naar een activerender belastingstelsel', final report, commissioned by the Ministry of Finance, The Hague (https://www.mejudice.nl/docs/default-source/download/eindrapport.pdf).

Zoutman, F., Jacobs, B., and Jongen, E. (2015), 'Optimal redistributive taxes and redistributive preferences in the Netherlands', mimeo, Erasmus School of Economics/CPB.

14
Taxation and Part-Time Work

*Henk-Wim de Boer and Andreas Peichl**

14.1 Introduction

In this paper, we address the following questions to guide the policy discussion in the Netherlands on this issue. Are the few hours worked on average an economic problem as such? What do we know about the intensive-margin responses of secondary earners? What should Dutch policymakers learn from the evidence? Given that marginal tax rates on secondary earners are not particularly high, should they be reduced even further to promote hours worked? Does such a policy not run into sharp equity–efficiency trade-offs by increasing inequality between single-earner and dual-earner couples?

The chapter proceeds as follows. First, we analyse the labour force participation and part-time employment rates for Dutch men and women with an international comparison. Second, we review the literature on labour supply responses in the Netherlands—especially for women in couples (who are usually secondary earners). Third, we show the distribution of marginal tax rates and participation tax rates for different household types in the Netherlands. Fourth, we discuss policy options for reforming the Dutch tax and transfer system.[1] We believe that our analysis is interesting for policymakers not only in the Netherlands but also in other countries.

14.2 Labour Force Participation

The Netherlands is a world leader with regards to part-time work, as can be seen from Figure 14.1. The figure plots the share of part-time employment (as a percentage of total employment) for men and women, separately and jointly.

* Henk-Wim de Boer (h.w.de.boer@cpb.nl) is affiliated with CPB Netherlands Bureau for Economic Policy Analysis and Andreas Peichl (peichl@ifo.de) is Director of the Ifo Center for Macroeconomics and Surveys and Professor of Macroeconomics and Public Finance at the University of Munich. The views expressed in this paper do not necessarily represent the views of the CPB. We are grateful to Sijbren Cnossen, Albert-Jan Hummel, Bas Jacobs and Alexandra Rusu, as well as conference participants in Rotterdam, for helpful comments on an earlier draft.

[1] We do not discuss the theoretical literature on optimal taxation (see Piketty and Saez, 2013, for a recent survey).

Henk-Wim de Boer and Andreas Peichl, *Taxation and Part-Time Work* In: *Tax by Design for the Netherlands.* Edited by: Sijbren Cnossen and Bas Jacobs, Oxford University Press. © Oxford University Press 2022.
DOI: 10.1093/oso/9780192855244.003.0014

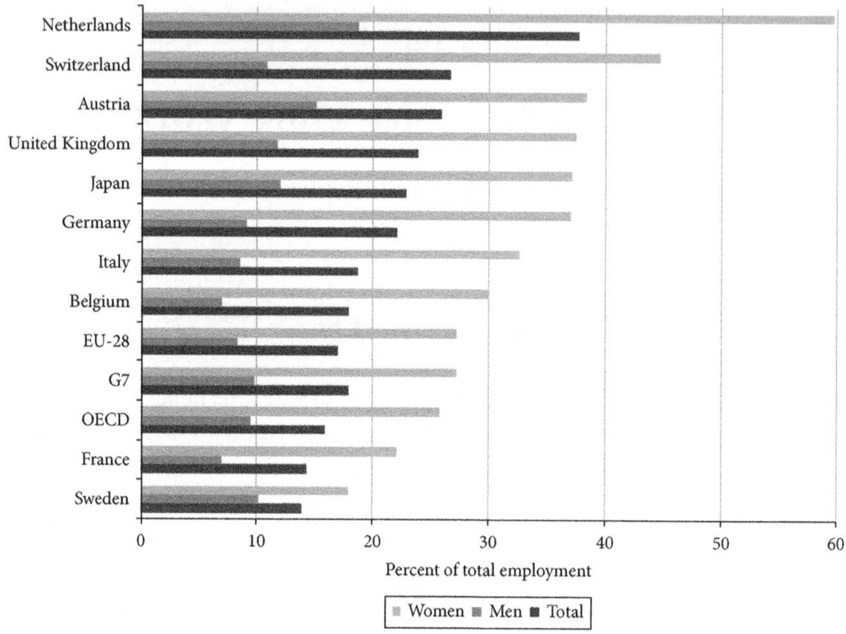

Figure 14.1 Part-time employment rates (as a percentage of total employment)
Source: OECD.

The Netherlands has the highest share in each of the three measures: almost 60% of women and about 20% of men are working part-time. The total share (37.4%) is more than 10 percentage points higher than for the next country (Switzerland) and more than (almost) twice as large as that of neighbouring countries Belgium and Germany.

Over the past decades, the Netherlands, like many other developed countries, has witnessed an increase in the employment rate of women. Figures 14.2 and 14.3 show the employment rates for men and women in the Netherlands over time, along with the development in the employment rate for a number of other countries. Whereas the employment rate of men has increased only slightly over time, the rise in the employment rate of women—mostly secondary earners in the Netherlands—has been spectacular. Indeed, by 2014, the Netherlands had one of the highest employment rates for women of all OECD countries.

However, the average number of working hours for women in the Netherlands has remained relatively stable over the past decade, as indicated by Figure 14.4 (again in comparison with other OECD countries). The changes in hours worked per week by employed men were also limited over the past decades, with a slight downward trend (see Figure 14.5). In both cases, the average hours worked in the Netherland are lowest compared with other OECD countries, reflecting again the high part-time work share.

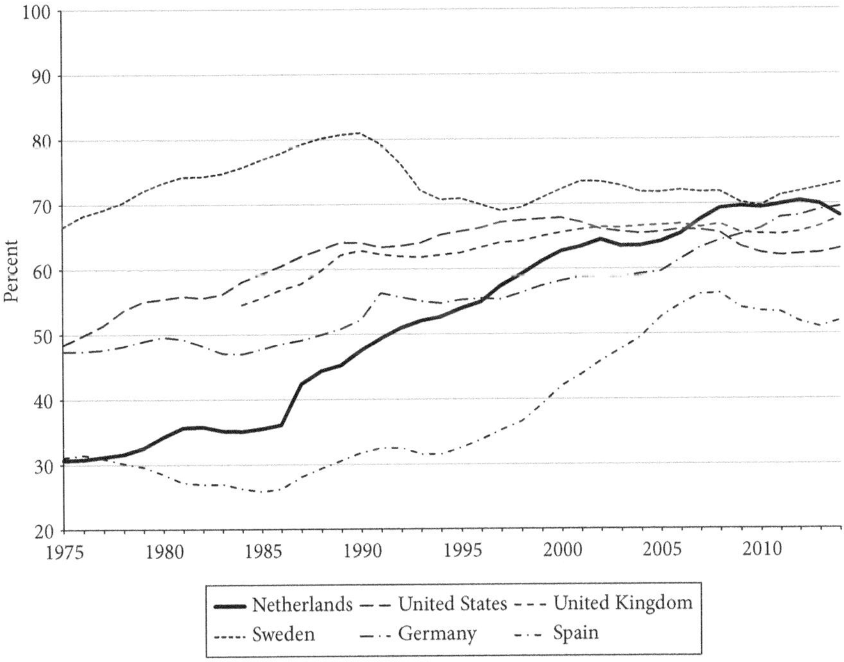

Figure 14.2 Employment rates of women over time for selected OECD countries
Source: OECD (2016).

14.3 Labour Supply Responses of Women in Couples

In terms of labour supply responsiveness to (tax) incentives, both discrete choice models and quasi-experimental studies show us that labour supply elasticities of women in couples, who are mostly secondary earners, are substantially higher than those for men in couples (see Evers, de Mooij, and van Vuuren, 2008; Bargain, Orsini, and Peichl, 2014; Bargain and Peichl, 2016). However, the average female labour supply elasticity has declined substantially over the past decade (see Heim, 2007; Blau and Kahn, 2007; Bargain and Peichl, 2016). A possible explanation for this finding is that a more stable attachment of women to the labour market (due to a rise in female employment rates) is responsible for the modest labour supply responses to financial incentives in the recent period. The Netherlands is no exception in this regard, and we also observe a steep drop in labour supply elasticities of women. With data from the 1980s, Theeuwes and Woittiez (1992) estimated an elasticity of 1.0 for women. A more recent study by Evers et al. (2008), using data from the 1980s and 1990s, gave an elasticity of 0.5.

Bargain and Peichl (2016) report elasticity estimates from several studies for the Netherlands in their survey. Figure 14.6 shows the results in comparison to other

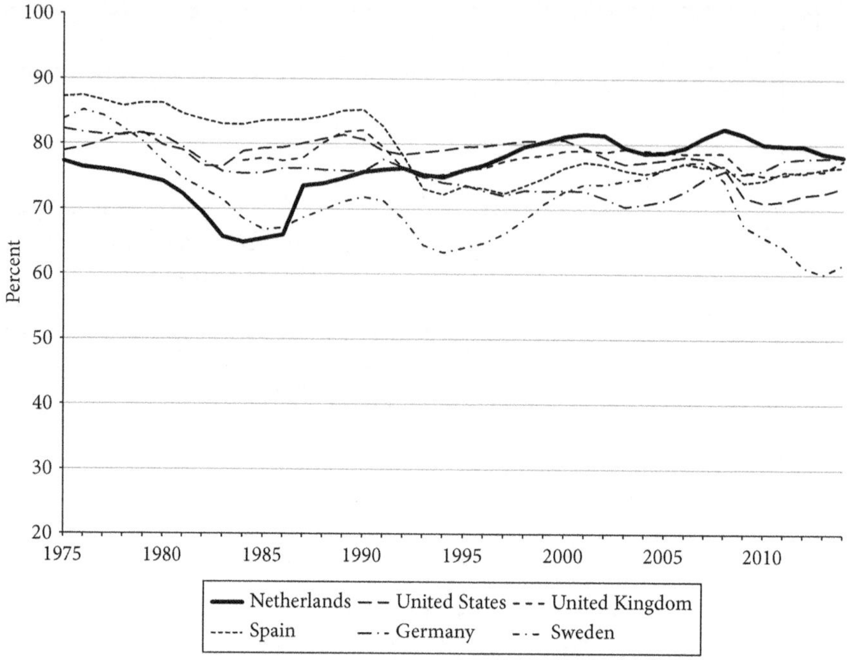

Figure 14.3 Employment rates of men over time for selected OECD countries
Source: OECD (2016).

countries. The Netherlands does not have particularly large elasticities (except perhaps for single women).

One potential problem from such a survey or meta-analysis is that differences in data sources or estimation techniques might drive some of the results. Therefore, Dolls et al. (2019) update the results from Bargain et al. (2014) and estimate labour supply elasticities for several European countries using the same underlying data (EUROMOD based on the European Union Statistics on Income and Living Conditions, EU-SILC) and estimation method (structural discrete choice household labour supply model). Figure 14.7 shows the results. Labour supply elasticities are very small for married men in the Netherlands. They are relatively large for married women in an international comparison but, with a value of 0.27, it is still not large in absolute terms. Moreover, most of the responsiveness comes from the extensive margin. This suggests that tax cuts to incentivize labour supply along the intensive margin will have limited labour supply effects and will be far from self-financing.

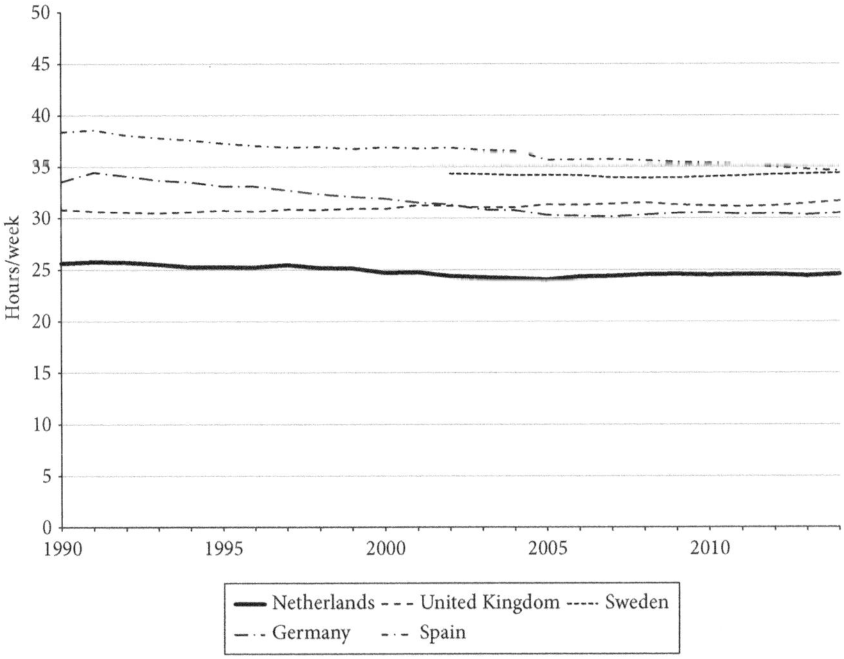

Figure 14.4 Average weekly hours worked by women over time for selected OECD countries
Source: OECD (2016).

The most recent analysis for the Netherlands is by De Boer et al. (2018a) who used panel data for the period 2006–9. Figure 14.8 shows that the total labour supply elasticities for women in couples are between 0.16 and 0.47, depending on the presence and age of children.[2] Intensive margin responses are relatively small (0.05–0.17). The results are in line with those of Dolls et al. (2019) who do not account for differences in the number and age of children.

Obviously, this has important policy implications as we face the law of diminishing returns. First, the labour force participation of women is much higher now than it was in the past. This reduces the remaining potential to stimulate participation by tax-benefit reforms. Second, fiscal incentives in the Dutch tax-benefit system are already targeted at sensitive groups, such as single parents and secondary earners with children, by using childcare subsidies and in-work benefits

[2] We follow Blundell, Bozio, and Laroque (2013) who decompose the total number of hours (H) as $H = p\,h$, where p is the extensive margin (e.g. the fraction of the reference period when the individual is employed) and h represents the intensive margin, which is defined as the total number of hours H divided by the fraction of the reference period in employment.

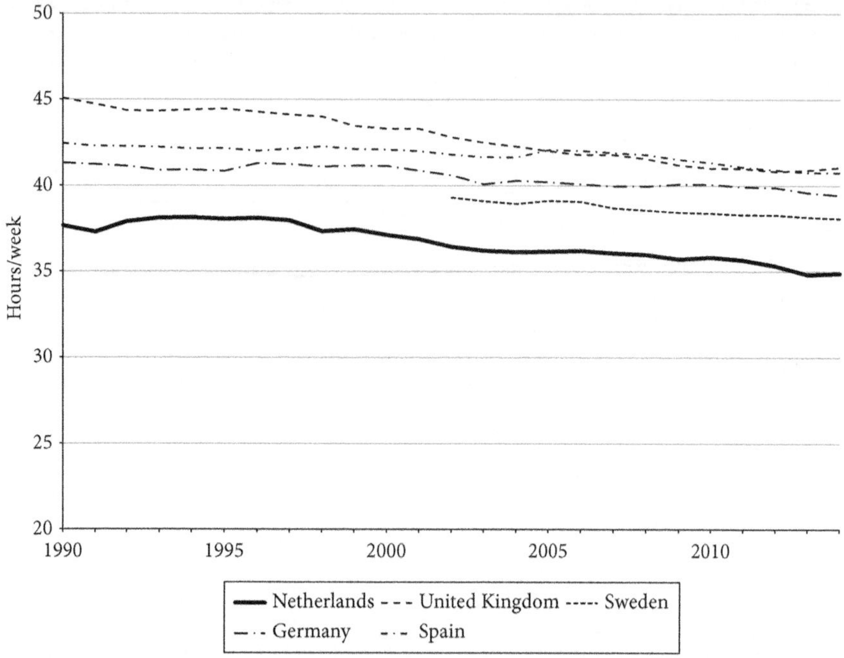

Figure 14.5 Average weekly hours worked by men over time for selected OECD countries
Source: OECD (2016).

for secondary earners and single parents. Hence, further targeting or reducing tax rates along the intensive margin will not have large effects.

14.4 Marginal Tax Rates and Participation Tax Rates

Considering the Dutch tax-benefit system, the Netherlands has an individual tax system, with specific tax credits and subsidies targeted at certain groups. However, income-dependent income support is based on household rather than individual income. The so-called effective marginal tax rates (EMTRs) illustrate how the tax-benefit system plays out for different subgroups. Figure 14.9 shows that the EMTRs for secondary earners, without and with children, were quite low in 2015.

Figure 14.9 shows the average EMTR per income level in 2015, where the right axis shows the EMTR for employees per income category of 1,000 euros. The left axis shows the frequency distribution of the income group in the total population. The three horizontal dashed lines refer to the statutory marginal income tax rates. However, the EMTR is determined not only by marginal income tax rates, but also by tax credits and means-tested benefits. For individuals with an income in the

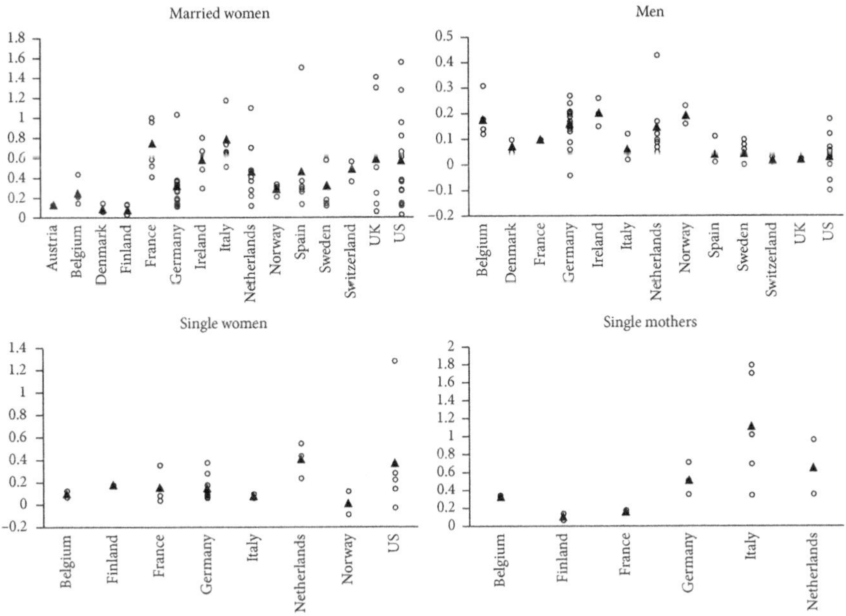

Figure 14.6 Labour supply elasticities across countries

Note: The triangles give the unweighted averages of available estimates per country.

Source: Based on fig. 2 of Bargain and Peichl (2016).

first income tax bracket (in 2015, 0–19,822 euros), the EMTR is lower than the statutory marginal income tax rate of 36.5%. This is due to the general tax credit, the phase-in of the EITC for all workers and those for working parents. However, secondary earners with an income in the second tax bracket (in 2015, 19,822–33,569 euros) face an EMTR that exceeds the marginal income tax rate of 42%. In these cases, the phase-out of the general tax credit, the healthcare benefit, rent subsidy, and the income-dependent child benefit lead to an increase in the EMTR. In addition, pension fund contributions also result in a higher EMTR.

In order to compare EMTRs in the Netherlands with those of other countries, Koot et al. (2018) compare the EMTRs calculated with the OECD tax-benefit model, which provides calculations for eight different hypothetical household types. For most groups in the Netherlands, the marginal tax burden is relatively high compared with the average for the OECD and the Eurozone. The EMTR is relatively low only for single parents, while the marginal tax burden for secondary earners with children is average.

The effective participation tax rates (EPTRs) compare disposable household income when the individual is working with disposable household when the individual does not work, and is calculated as one minus the difference in disposable household income over gross labour income. Figure 14.10 shows that the EPTRs for secondary earners without and with children were quite low in

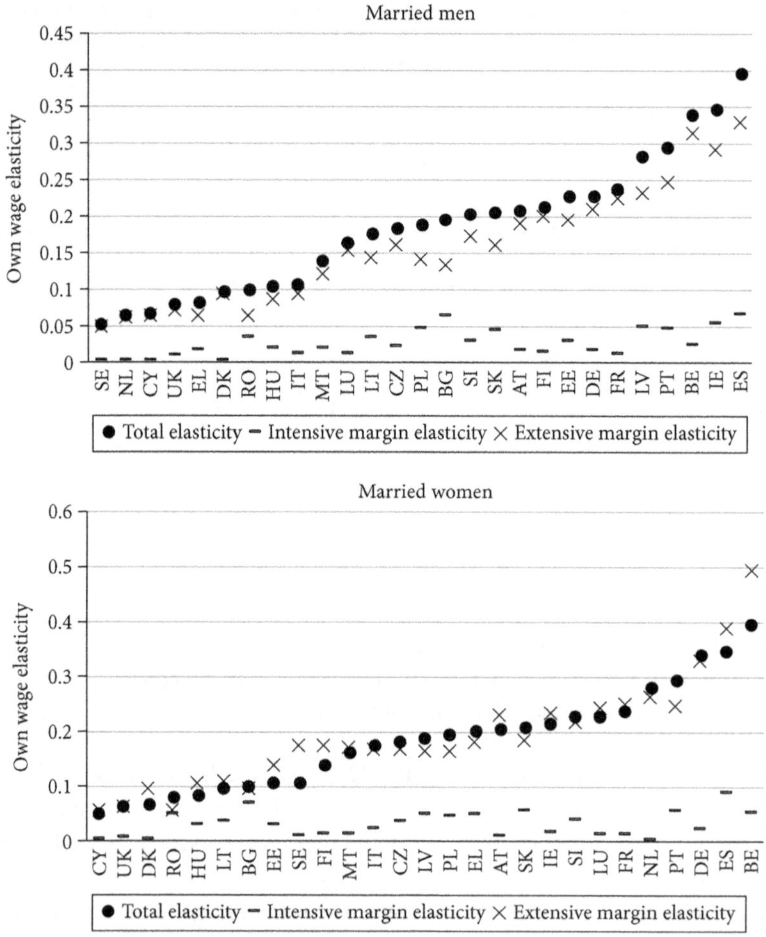

Figure 14.7 Labour supply elasticities across countries for married men and women
Source: Dolls et al. (2019).

2015. EPTRs are relatively low for secondary earners, because these individuals typically do not qualify for income-dependent benefits when they do not work (because of the income of the partner). In addition, EPTRs are particularly low for secondary earners with children, because they qualify for additional in-work benefits.

Next to the EMTRs and EPTRs, the difference in the average tax rates between single-earner and dual-earner households is also important. De Boer et al. (2018b) focus on the different tax treatment of single-earner and dual-earner couples. More specifically, they discuss the tax-benefit system for couples in the Netherlands in 2017, and the changes in this system between 2005 and 2017. After considering the tax-benefit systems in 2005 and 2017, they look at a long-run scenario that

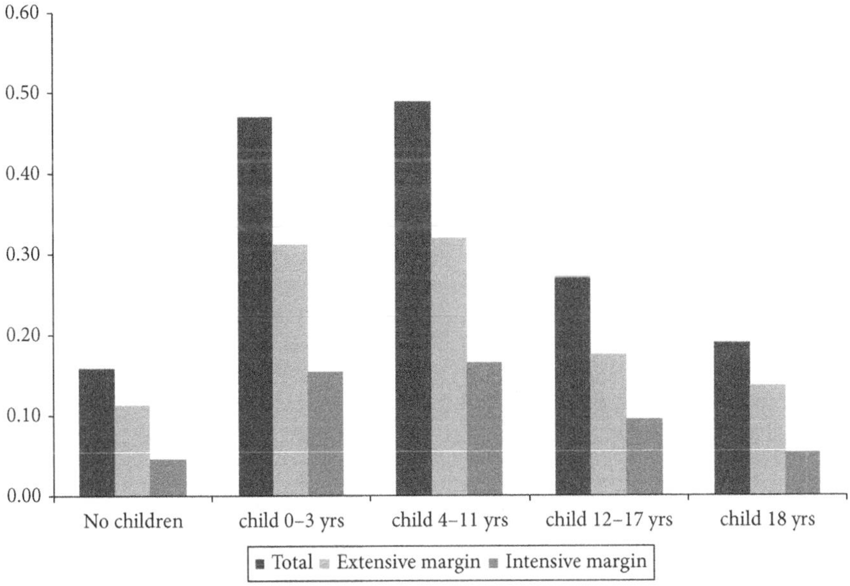

Figure 14.8 Labour supply elasticities of women in couples in the Netherlands
Source: De Boer et al. (2018a).

includes the proposed policy reforms by previous Coalition Agreements and the proposed changes in the tax-benefit system in the recent Coalition Agreement.

Over the past decade, a series of reforms has reduced average effective tax rates on dual-earner couples and increased average effective tax rates on single-earner couples. Furthermore, this policy 'trend' is expected to continue into the future, as proposed policy reforms will further reduce tax rates on dual-earner couples and further increase tax rates on single-earner couples. The Netherlands can be regarded as a front-runner internationally for its preferential tax treatment of dual-earner households. Indeed, the difference in the average tax rates between single- and dual-earner households in the Netherlands is the highest of all OECD countries (OECD, 2014). These reforms have stimulated formal labour participation, but have also increased the inequality in disposable income between single- and dual-earner couples. The question then is how the reforms have affected the trade-off between equity and efficiency, and whether the reforms have moved the system closer to an 'optimal' tax system. We will address this question below.

14.5 Policy Analysis

The analyses by de Boer et al. (2018a) illustrate that there are large differences in labour supply elasticities between demographic groups and decision margins.

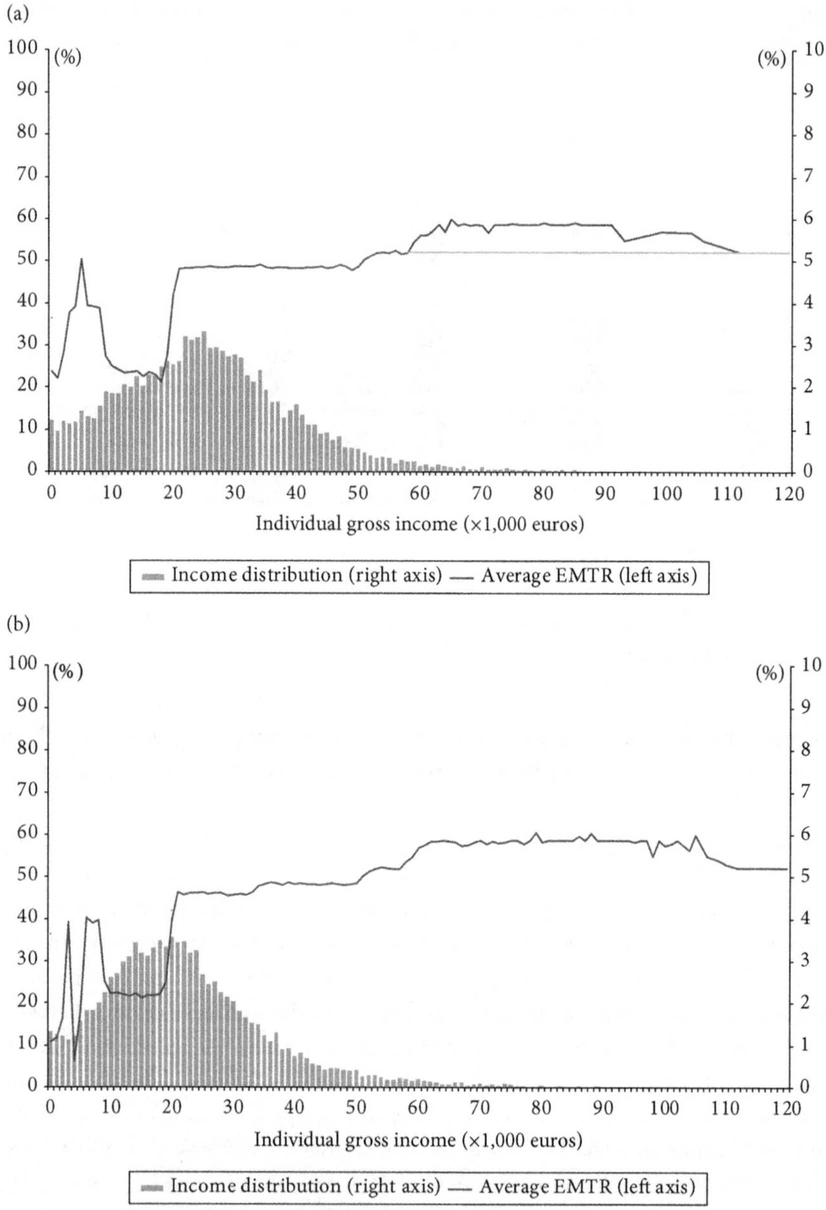

Figure 14.9 EMTRs for secondary earners (a) without and (b) with children

Source: Koot et al. (2018).

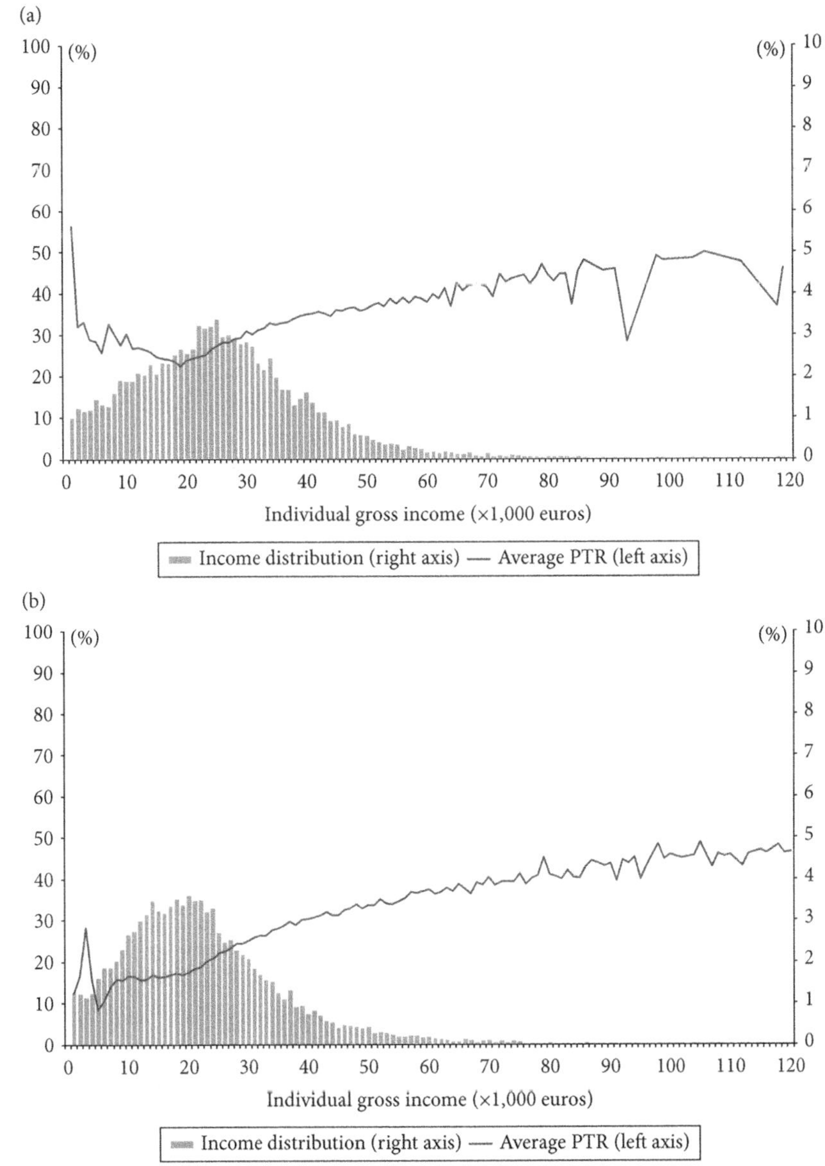

Figure 14.10 EPTRs for secondary earners (a) without and (b) with children
Source: Koot et al. (2018).

Indeed, there are large differences in labour supply elasticities between, for example, singles and couples, primary and secondary earners, and the groups based on the age of their youngest child. They also uncover large differences in the relative importance of the extensive margin (participation) and intensive margin (hours per employed person), with the intensive margin response still substantial for women with young children but small for most other groups. Their main findings are as follows.

- The reduction of marginal income tax rates is not an effective way to promote labour supply. It targets the less sensitive hours-per-week margin (intensive margin), and for couples there is also a cross-effect: a higher net income for men reduces the labour supply of women in couples.
- In-work benefits targeted at low-wage earners appear to be more effective. For instance, an increase in the earned income tax credit targets the more sensitive extensive margin. Similarly, a reduction of income-dependent subsidies is also relatively effective in stimulating labour supply, but then income inequality increases as well.
- Policies targeted at single parents and working mothers with young children (e.g. increases of in-work tax credits for secondary earners and childcare subsidies) generate the largest labour supply response.
- It is, however, important to realize that many policies are already targeted specifically at these groups. Over the past decade, the Dutch government has increased the level of in-work benefits for secondary earners and increased childcare subsidies. Also, the current Coalition has increased these levels even further. Hence, the effectiveness of these reforms has substantially decreased over time.

We focus on four large reforms in order to study the trade-off between inequality and efficiency. The first large reform is the removal of the transferability of the general tax credit (in Dutch: *Beperking overdraagbaarheid algemene heffingskorting*). Individuals received a general tax credit of 2,477 euros in 2019. Non-working individuals, or secondary earners who do not pay enough taxes, can transfer this tax credit to their partners. The transferability of the general tax credit reduces the financial incentive for non-working partners to supply labour. In order to stimulate labour force participation, the Dutch Government restricted this transferability of the general tax credit in 2007 (Ministry of General Affairs, 2007). The transferability of the tax credit is reduced in yearly steps in order to smooth negative income effects, and the transferability will be completely abandoned in 2024. This reform increases income inequality among single-earner couples (who receive the tax credit only once) and dual-earner couples (who receive the tax credit twice). The second large reform is the increase in the EITC for all workers (*Arbeidskorting*) who earn an individual labour income. In 2019, the maximum amount of the EITC for all workers was 3,399 euros. Single-earner households receive this tax credit once, whereas dual-earner households receive this tax credit twice. Consequently, this reform has increased income inequality among single- and dual-earner households. The third tax credit that has increased income inequality among single- and dual-earner couples is the income-dependent combination tax credit (*Inkomensafhankelijke Combinatiekorting*) for working parents with a youngest child up to 12 years of age. Finally, the increase in the childcare subsidy has also increased income inequality among single- and dual-earner couples. Both partners in the household need to work in order to qualify for the childcare subsidy. Hence, dual-earner couples with young children are eligible for this subsidy, whereas single-earner couples are not. Indeed, de Boer et al. (2018b) show that the difference in average tax rates between single- and dual-earner households has increased over the past decade, and they argue that the four above-mentioned reforms have contributed to this increase.

In designing the tax system, policymakers face a trade-off between income equality and economic efficiency. A lower degree of inequality is usually achieved by a decrease in efficiency (Mirrlees, 1971). Income taxes lower the return from work relative to leisure. Consequently, taxes distort individuals' decisions to supply labour when they decide on the number of hours to allocate to leisure and work, and total labour supply is smaller than it would be in the absence of the income tax. What, then, is the optimal tax structure, given a preference for income redistribution? Our analysis is based on Saez (2002), who follows the framework proposed by Mirrlees (1971). A social planner maximizes a social welfare function, which is a weighted total of individual utilities from consumption (net income) and leisure. The income of individuals is determined by a combination of the earning capacity (given) and the effort that they make (hours worked). Individuals differ in earning capacity but the social planner only observes their income. When the social planners redistribute income from individuals with a higher income to individuals with a lower income, they impose a marginal tax on both earning capacity and effort. This leads to efficiency losses. The government will then look for a second-best solution in which the tax rates are chosen in such a way that the marginal burden of the tax is equal to the marginal distributional gain of redistribution.

The reforms described above have stimulated labour force participation but also increased income inequality among single- and dual-earner households. De Boer et al. (2018b) use the inverse-optimal method of optimal taxation, and assume that there are $I + 1$ groups on the labour market, where I groups of individuals work and one group does not work. The resulting optimal tax system is then characterized by a system of equations with expressions for the optimal level of taxes in labour supply option i relative to labour supply option $i - 1$. Then, they invert the optimality conditions to determine the social welfare weights and to show that the implicit social welfare weights of single- and dual-earner couples were relatively well behaved (e.g. monotonically declining in income) before the reforms. However, after the reforms, they are no longer monotonically declining in income, and are sometimes negative. Taken at face value, this suggests an imbalance between equity and efficiency. Furthermore, their optimal tax analysis suggests that, for all the different levels of inequality aversion they consider, optimal net taxes should be lower for single-earner couples, and should be higher for dual-earner couples with a low and average household income.

However, other considerations can rationalize these findings. Stimulating labour force participation itself might be a policy goal of the government. Also, if emancipation is a separate goal of the government, then this could lead to higher social welfare weights for dual earners than for single earners. Indeed, the Dutch Minister of Education, Culture, and Science explicitly states that independence of women, from an economic perspective, is an important policy goal of the government (Ministry of Education, Culture, and Science, 2017). The economic literature on optimal taxation addresses some non-welfarist motives for these anomalies. For instance, Kanbur, Tuomala, and Pirttilä (2006) argue that the government can have non-welfarist motives when maximizing social welfare. Fleurbaey and Maniquet (2006) focus on the fairness concerns in an optimal taxation setting, and show that it can be optimal to give the highest subsidy to the hard-working poor (e.g. individuals who work full-time but have a low earning ability). Finally, non-working women in single-earner couples may have a higher productivity at home, or may have a higher preference for leisure (Apps and Rees, 2009).

14.6 Conclusions

The Netherlands is a world leader with regards to part-time work. Whether this is good or bad news depends on the point of view: is the glass half full or half empty? In other words, what is the counterfactual for evaluating this empirical observation? If the counterfactual is that everybody works full-time, then the resulting equity–efficiency considerations are different, compared with a counterfactual situation where half of the part-time workers worked full-time and the other half were unemployed. The empirical evidence suggests that it is not the tax-benefit system that discourages individuals on part-time contracts to work more hours.

Marginal tax rates on secondary earners are not particularly high in the Netherlands. Further, and in contrast to, for example, Germany (see Peichl et al., 2017), the tax-benefit system in the Netherlands does not provide disincentives for working more hours. Therefore, reducing them further to promote more hours worked is not a very efficient policy reform. Moreover, tax incentives are not the only determinants of (female) labour supply: individual work–leisure preferences, social preferences, the possibility to combine work and the care of children and household production, among others, also play an important role. Further, labour demand responses could play an important role in the general equilibrium effects of policies targeted at the intensive margin (see Peichl and Siegloch, 2012). Given estimates of typically downward-sloping labour demand curves (see Lichter et al., 2015), these labour supply responses are attenuated by labour demand reactions, making increased incentives at the intensive margin less attractive in the Dutch context.

We conclude that reducing marginal tax rates of secondary earners further in order to increase full time work (and reduce part time work) in the Netherlands is relatively ineffective. Rather, in order to increase employment and tax revenues, Blundell (2014) argues that it is more effective to focus on labour market entry and retirement, as these are the two margins that show the greatest labour supply responsiveness. In addition, the broad policy proposals laid out in the Mirrlees Review (Mirrlees et al., 2011) are also potentially important for the Netherlands. These include simplifying and integrating the different benefits and welfare programmes, targeting work incentives where they are most effective (i.e. labour market entry of the young and retirement decisions), and aligning tax rates across similar sources of income to reduce avoidance opportunities and to broaden the tax base. As summarized by Blundell (2014), tax incentives increase lifetime earnings at certain key points in the life cycle, thus suggesting the importance of focusing policy reforms on improving labour market entry for individuals leaving school and for women with young children, keeping older workers in the labour force, and increasing human capital investments in general.

It might be beneficial for the Netherlands to follow these broad recommendations—and for most, if not all, other countries that are in similar situations and that need sustainable fiscal revenues. Such policies also have the potential of reducing inequalities in the long run (especially if human capital investments of disadvantaged types can be encouraged). However, in the short run, an equity–efficiency trade-off might arise (e.g. if those who stay longer in the workforce are those with high incomes). Clever distributional policies should counteract such potential tensions.

References

Apps, P. and Rees, R. (2009), *Public Economics and the Household*, Cambridge University Press, Cambridge.

Bargain, O., Orsini, K., and Peichl, A. (2014), 'Comparing labor supply elasticities in Europe and the US: new results', *Journal of Human Resources*, 49, 723–838.

Bargain, O. and Peichl, A. (2016), 'Own-wage labor supply elasticities: variation across time and estimation methods', *IZA Journal of Labor Economics*, 5, 10.

Blau, F. and Kahn, L. (2007), 'Changes in the labor supply behavior of married women: 1980–2000'. *Journal of Labor Economics*, 25(3), 393–438.

Blundell, R. (2014), 'How responsive is the labor market to tax policy?', *IZA World of Labor*, 2.

Blundell, R., Bozio, A., and Laroque, G. (2013), 'Extensive and intensive margins of labour supply: work and working hours in the US, the UK and France', *Fiscal Studies*, 34, 1–29.

De Boer H.-W., Jongen, E. L. W., and Mastrogiacomo, M. (2018a), 'Tax-benefit reforms and structural models for labour supply', in J. de Haan and J. Parlevliet (eds), *Structural Reforms: Moving the Economy Forward*, Springer, Berlin, 239–64.

De Boer H.-W., Jongen, E. L. W., and Koot, P. (2018b), 'Optimal taxation of secondary earners in the Netherlands: has equity lost ground?', CPB Discussion Paper no. 375.

Dolls, M., Fuest, C., Peichl, A., and Wittneben, C. (2019), 'Automatic stabilization and labor supply' (https://lagv2017.sciencesconf.org/136862/document).

Evers, M., de Mooij, R., and van Vuuren, D. (2008), 'The wage elasticity of labour supply: a synthesis of empirical estimates', *De Economist*, 156, 25–43.

Fleurbaey, M. and Maniquet, F. (2006), 'Fair income tax', *Review of Economic Studies*, 73, 55–83.

Heim, B. T. (2007), 'The incredible shrinking elasticities: married female labor supply, 1978–2002', *Journal of Human Resources*, 42, 881–918.

Kanbur, R., Tuomala, M., and Pirttilä, J. (2006), 'Non-welfarist optimal taxation and behavioral economics', *Journal of Economic Surveys*, 20, 849–68.

Koot, P., de Boer, H.-W., and Jongen, E. L. W. (2018), 'De belastingdruk van een- en tweeverdieners vanaf 2005: een intertemporele en internationale analyse van de belastingdruk voor paren in Nederland', CPB achtergronddocument, The Hague.

Lichter, A., Orsini, K., and Peichl, S. (2015), 'The own-wage elasticity of labor demand: a meta-regression analysis', *European Economic Review*, 80, 94–119.

Ministry of General Affairs (2007), 'Coalition agreement', Ministry of General Affairs (https://www.rijksoverheid.nl/binaries/rijksoverheid/documenten/publicaties/2017/10/10/regeerakkoord-2017-vertrouwen-in-de-toekomst/Regeerakkoord+'Vertrouwen+in+de+toekomst'.pdf).

Ministry of Education, Culture, and Science (2017), 'Opbrengsten Emancipatiebeleid 2013–2017'.

Mirrlees, J. A. (1971), 'An exploration of the theory of optimal income taxation', *Review of Economic Studies*, 38, 175–208.

Mirrlees, J. A., Adam, S., Besley, T. J., Blundell, R., Bond, S., Chote, R., Gammie, M., Johnson, P., Myles, G. D., and Poterba, J. M. (2011), *Tax by Design: The Mirrlees Review*, Oxford University Press, Oxford.

OECD (2014), *Benefits and Wages*, OECD Publishing, Paris.

OECD (2016), *OECD Labour Force Statistics 2016*, OECD Publishing, Paris.

Peichl, A. and Siegloch, S. (2012), 'Accounting for labor demand effects in structural labor supply models', *Labour Economics*, 19, 129–38.

Peichl, A., Buhlmann, F., Löffler, M., and Barišić, M. (eds) (2017), 'Marginal tax rates in the tax-and-transfer system, Bertelsmann Stiftung Policy Brief 2017/4' (https://www.bertelsmann-stiftung.de/de/publikationen/publikation/did/policy-brief-20,174-marginal-tax-rates-in-the-tax-and-transfer-system).

Piketty, T. and Saez, E. (2013), 'Optimal labor income taxation', in A. Auerbach, R. Chetty, M. Feldstein, and E. Saez (eds), *Handbook of Public Economics*, Vol. 5, Elsevier, Amsterdam, pp. 391–474.

Saez, E. (2002), 'Optimal income transfer programs: intensive versus extensive labor supply responses', *Quarterly Journal of Economics*, 117, 1039–73.

Theeuwes, J. J. M. and Woittiez, I. (1992), 'Advising the minister on the elasticity of labour supply', University of Leiden, Research Memorandum 92.06.

15

Towards Simpler Income-Dependent Tax Credits and Tax Rebates

*Patrick Koot and Miriam Gielen**

15.1 Introduction

The Netherlands has a progressive income tax system, which features an extensive system of income-dependent tax credits and tax rebates. Over time, this system has been expanded to meet ambitious policy targets regarding labour participation and income redistribution. At the same time, tax yields had to remain the same.

Policymakers have made tax credits and tax rebates increasingly more dependent on income so as to be able to simultaneously meet different policy objectives. Existing tax rules have often been targeted at specific groups in the population for whom the greatest policy impact could be expected (e.g. in the area of income support or labour participation); at the same time, tax rules have been scaled down for those groups for whom the policy impact was likely to be smaller (e.g. by permitting the tax credit or rebate to be phased out more rapidly with income).

All in all, this has led to a complex income tax system where taxpayers find it difficult to gauge the consequences of income changes on entitlements to tax credits and tax rebates. See Figure 15.1 for an example of the overlap between income-dependent tax credits and tax rebates for various income levels, for couples with children.

Remarkably, income inequality in the Netherlands has remained rather stable over the years, despite the stronger income-dependency of tax policy (Koot, 2019). This observation raises the question of whether the tax system can be made simpler, while retaining its redistributive effects.

* Patrick Koot (p.m.koot@cpb.nl) is a researcher at CPB Netherlands Bureau for Economic Policy Analysis. Miriam Gielen (mgielen@minszw.nl) is a senior policy advisor at the Ministry of Social Affairs and Employment. The authors thank the participants of the Cnossen Forum, discussants Chris Heady and Jesse Hoekstra, and in particular Bas Jacobs for useful comments and suggestions for improvement. This chapter reflects the personal views of the authors.

Patrick Koot and Miriam Gielen, *Towards Simpler Income-Dependent Tax Credits and Tax Rebates* In: *Tax by Design for the Netherlands.* Edited by: Sijbren Cnossen and Bas Jacobs, Oxford University Press.
DOI: 10.1093/oso/9780192855244.003.0015

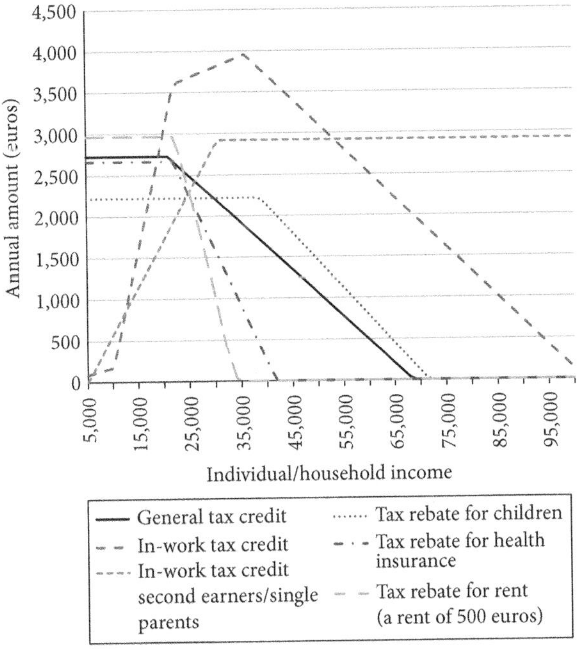

Figure 15.1 Income-dependent tax credit and rebates for couples with children

Notes: Data based on couples with children, below the Dutch state pension entitlement age, in rental housing and excluding the tax rebate for childcare.

Source: CPB calculations based on the MIMOSI micro-simulation model (Koot et al., 2016).

15.2 Income-Dependent Tax Credits and Rebates in the Netherlands

Figures 15.2 and 15.3 present the main income-dependent tax credits and rebates for people below the statutory retirement age.[1] The figures show how these credits and rebates have changed over the 2005–17 period, and how they will change up to 2021.

The Dutch tax system currently features four tax brackets, as it did in 2005. By 2021, the number of brackets will be reduced to two, with a low tax rate of approximately 37% for incomes up to approximately 68,500 euros, and a top rate of 49.5% for higher incomes. Thus, tax rate progressivity will be declining, particularly in future years.

[1] The starting point in Figures 15.2 and 15.3 is the proposed policy laid down in the Coalition Agreement of the Rutte III government. In the meantime, the government announced an increase in the general tax credit and the tax rebate for health insurance for 2020. These additional increases have not been taken into account in this chapter; they do have an effect on the credits, but not on the system's design.

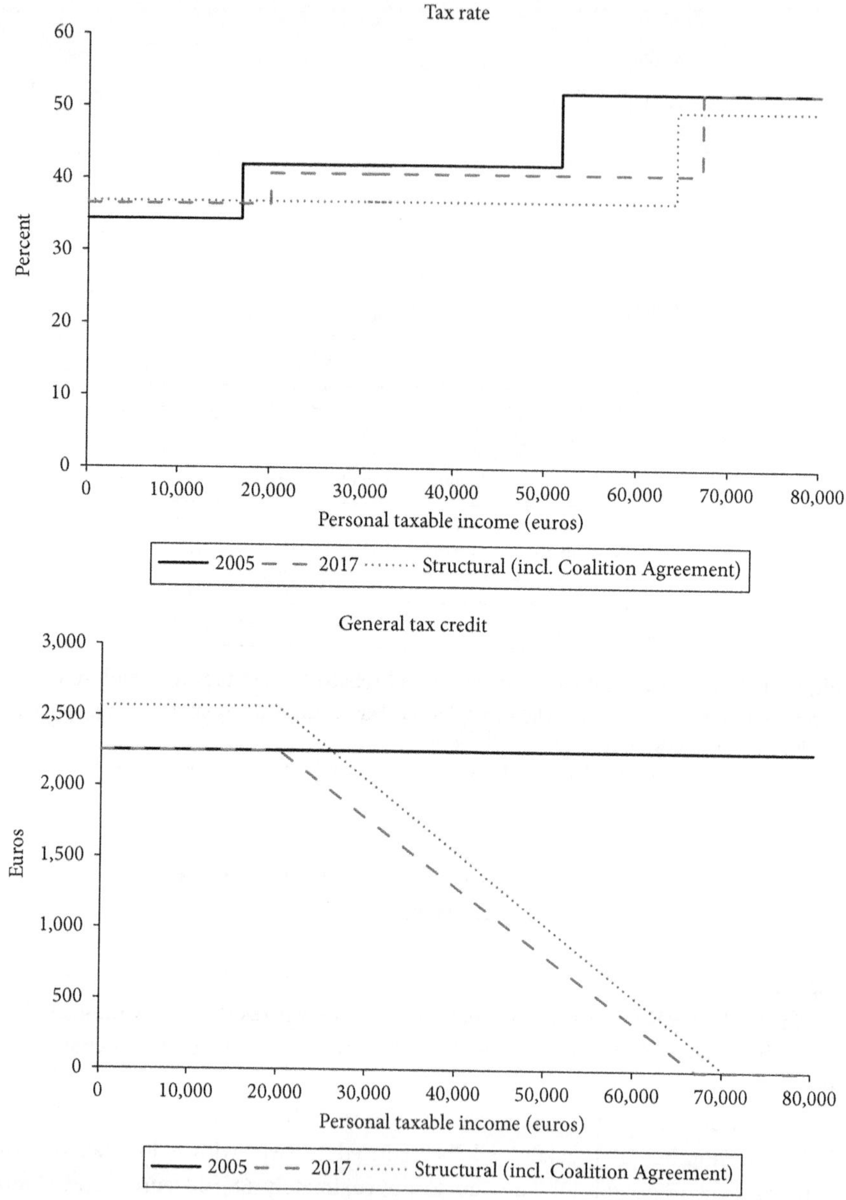

Figure 15.2 Design of income tax schedule and tax credits in 2005, 2017, and 2021 (2017 price level)

Source: Koot et al. (2018).

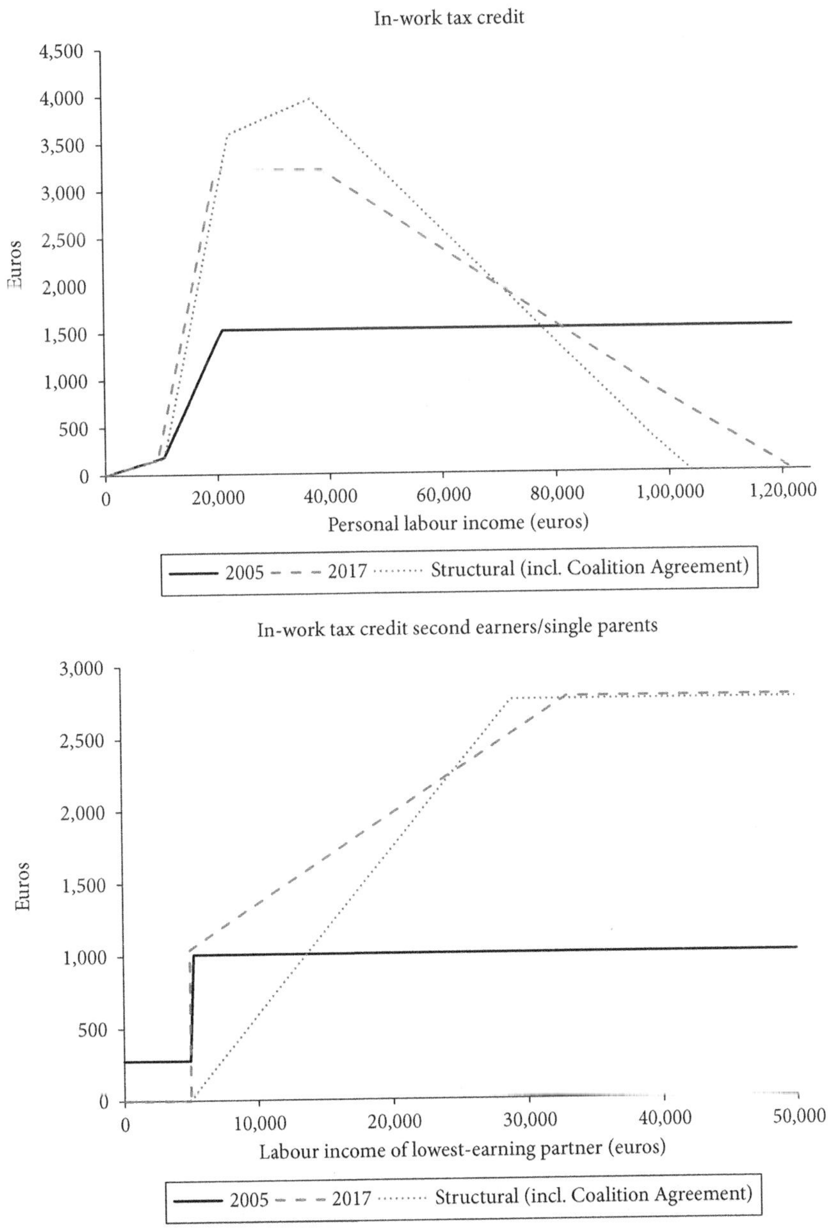

Figure 15.2 Continued

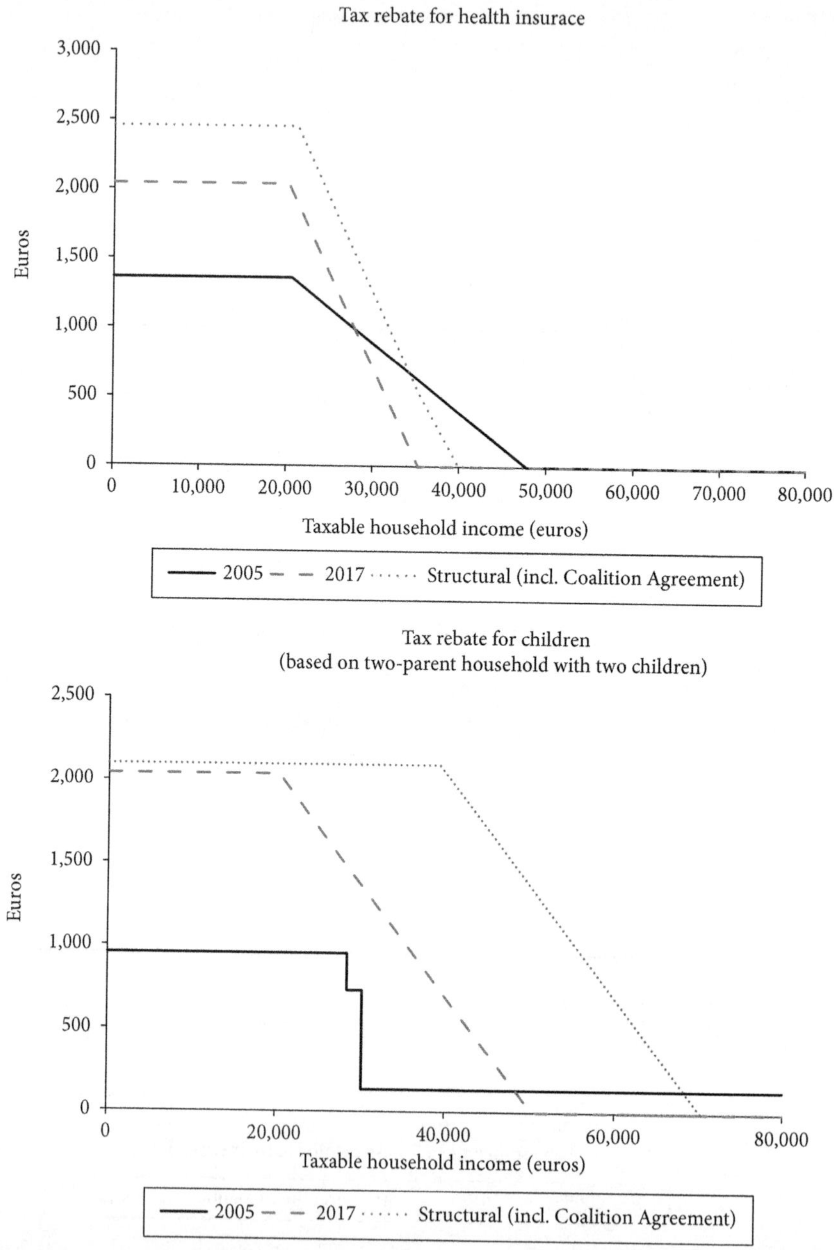

Figure 15.3 Design of tax rebates for a two-person household in 2005, 2017 and 2021 (2017 price level)

Source: Koot et al. (2018).

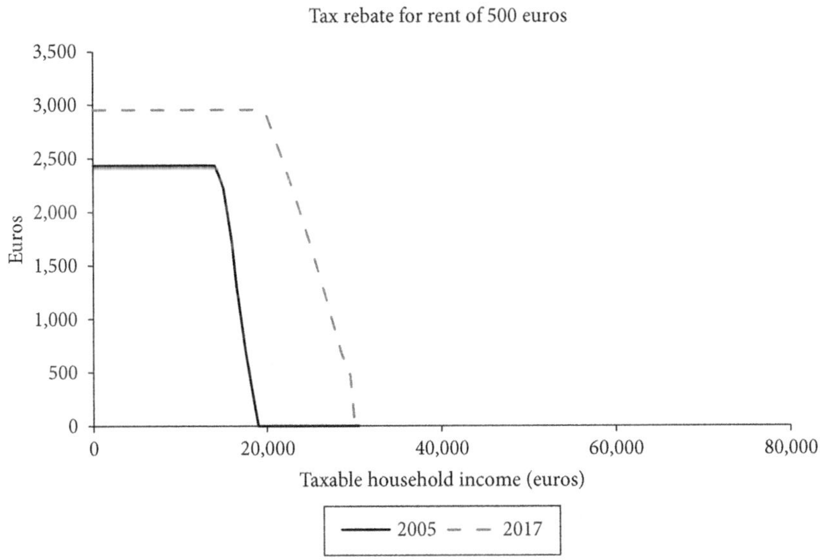

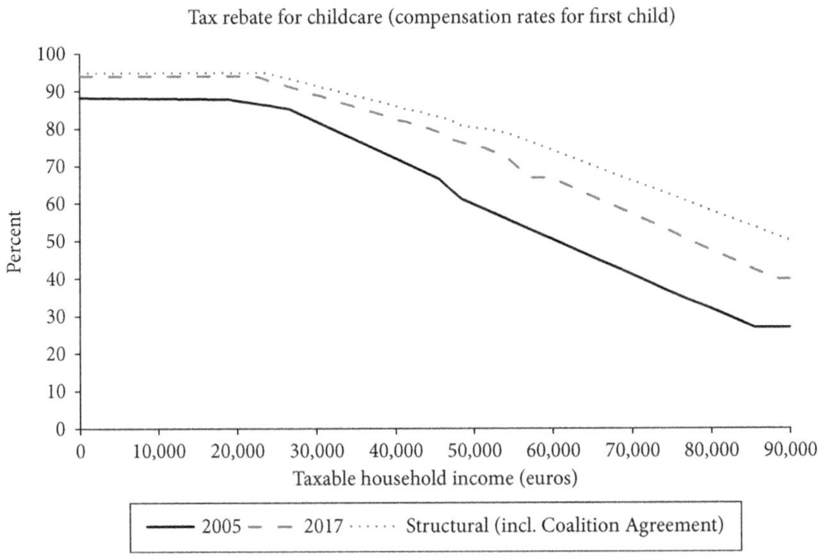

Figure 15.3 Continued

Tax credits are in fact becoming increasingly income-dependent. In 2005, the system had a general tax credit with a fixed amount for nearly all households, whereas, under the current system, tax credits for middle and higher incomes are phased out with income. The general tax credit (*algemene heffingskorting*) is mainly aimed at the lowest incomes and is phased out for incomes starting at around 20,000 euros. The phase-out range coincides with the start of the second and third tax bracket in the current tax system. Over this trajectory, tax credits are phased out to zero, with a phase-out rate of over 6% by 2021.

The in-work tax credit (*arbeidskorting*), up to incomes of 35,000 euros, and the in-work tax credit for second earners/single parents (*inkomensafhankelijke combinatiekorting*) increase with income. These two types of tax credits are intended to promote labour participation and, because they increase with income, they reduce the marginal tax rates in certain income trajectories (see the next section). In-work tax credits are phased out from incomes starting at 35,000 euros (with a phase-out rate of 6%).

Figure 15.3 shows that the tax rebates for rental costs, children, healthcare, and childcare have also changed significantly over time. Currently, the rebates all feature a standard amount for the lowest incomes, which is then phased out with income above a certain income level. The standard amount depends on the type of household, among other things, and is lower—for example, the tax rebate for rent (*huurtoeslag*) and health costs (*zorgtoeslag*)—or higher—for example, the tax rebate for children (*kindgebonden budget*)—for single individuals or single-parent households (not shown in Figure 15.3) than for couples or two-parent households.

The tax rebate for rent has the steepest phase-out range (which is quadratic in income, and, in certain cases, is phased out at a rate of approximately 30%), followed by the tax rebate for health insurance (which, with a phase-out rate of 13.6%, decreases more rapidly than in 2005). The tax rebate for children is phased out over a longer income trajectory (with a rate of 6.75%).

Currently, the tax rebates for children and health insurance are phased out at incomes starting from around 20,000 euros. The phase-out threshold of the tax rebate for children for two-parent households will be increased in 2020 from the current 20,000 euros to over 40,000 euros. With respect to the tax rebate for rental costs, the phase-out threshold depends on the type of household (single individual, couples, single-parent/two-parent households) and age (below or above the statutory retirement age). For single-person households, the phase-out threshold of the rent rebate starts at incomes well below the national minimum wage (NMW).

15.3 Labour Market Incentives versus Redistributive Effects: Income-Dependent Tax Credits and Tax Rebates

Figures 15.4 and 15.5 provide an overview of the redistributive and labour market effects of the various income-dependent tax credits and tax rebates in the

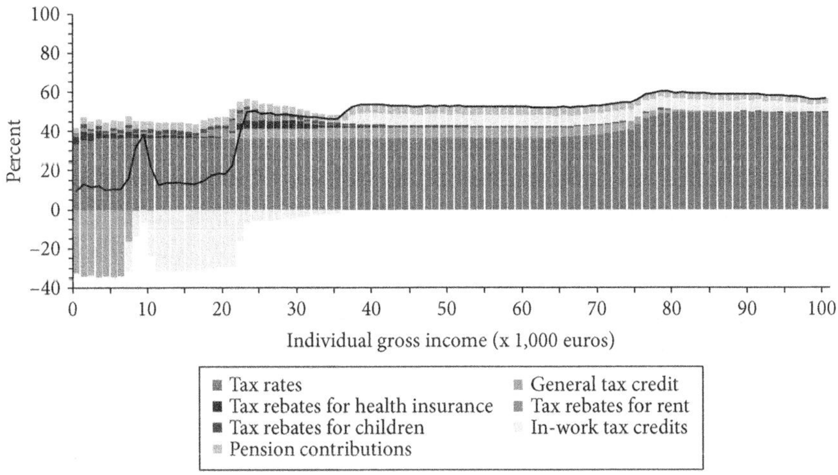

Figure 15.4 Contributions to effective marginal tax rates on labour income of the income-dependent tax credits and tax rebates in the long run
Source: CPB calculations based on the MIMOSI micro-simulation model (Koot et al., 2016).

Netherlands. The labour market effects are measured by the effective marginal tax burden on wage increases in the long-run, with all future policy changes having been fully implemented. For the redistributive effects, we calculated the increase or decrease in inequality (as measured by the Gini coefficient) if the credits and tax rebates were to be abolished. The calculations were carried out using CPB's MIMOSI micro-simulation model (Koot et al., 2016).

The average marginal tax burden in the Netherlands (solid line in Figure 15.4) is largely determined by the tax brackets and tax rates (i.e. the effect of income tax rates; see the tax rates in Figure 15.4). As a result of the two-bracket system that comes into force in 2020, the impact of the statutory tax rate will be flat with income, with an increase of the tax rate at the beginning of the highest tax bracket at around 75,000 euros.

However, the average marginal tax burden differs significantly from the statutory rates in the two-bracket system due to the income-dependent tax credits and tax rebates. The average marginal tax burden for the lowest income groups (up to 20,000 euros) is around 10%. Up to an income of 10,000 euros, the increase in the income tax burden cancels out against the increase in the general tax credit, which is non-refundable at very low incomes. Beyond 10,000 euros, the general tax credit becomes fully refundable. Moreover, the earned income tax credit kicks in (at a rate of 28%) and reaches a maximum at approximately 20,000 euros (i.e. the NMW). As a result, the marginal burden will remain relatively low. Even before the NMW level is reached, the tax rebate for rent for single-person households starts to be phased out, which increases the average marginal burden around the NMW level.

Between incomes of 20,000 and approximately 35,000 euros, all tax rebates are phased out simultaneously. Moreover, at an income of 20,000 euro the general tax credit is also being phased out. This increases the average marginal tax burden. However, in-work tax credits continue to increase slightly, which reduces the marginal tax burden. On balance, the average marginal tax burden along this trajectory will be well over 40%. Starting at an income of around 35,000 euros, the average marginal tax burden increases further, to well over 50%. At this point, the tax rebate for health insurance has been phased out, which reduces the average marginal tax burden. At the same time, the in-work tax credits will be phased out (on top of the higher statutory tax rate and the phase-out of the general tax credit). Furthermore, for households with children, the phasing out of the tax rebate for children will also continue.

At the starting point of the top tax rate, the general tax credit will have been fully phased out, which slightly dampens the impact of the higher tax rate. As a result of phasing out the in-work tax credit, the average marginal burden will exceed 55% at the start of the top bracket. At an income of about 100,000 euros, all in-work tax credits will have been fully phased out, moving the marginal tax burden to the top tax rate in the two-bracket tax system of (ultimately) 49.5%.

To determine the redistributive impact of the income-dependent tax measures, we analysed the redistributive impact of the tax measures on the Gini coefficient of standardized disposable household incomes (Koot, 2019). We calculated how much the Gini coefficient would increase or decrease if the tax measures were to be abolished. The general tax credit gives the largest reduction in income inequality (top panel of Figure 15.5). If the general tax credit were to be abolished, the Gini coefficient would be almost 12% higher than under the current system. The phase-out of the general tax credit starts below the NMW level, which implies that only the lowest incomes would receive the maximum tax credit. However, the large redistributive impact of the general tax credit is also due to its large budgetary size (around 27 billion euros, in 2021). When correcting for differences in budget size (bottom panel of Figure 15.5), the redistributive impact of the general tax credit—as measured by the reduction in the Gini coefficient per euro spent—is smaller than the impact of the tax rebates and also of the top tax rate.

Tax rebates for rent (4 billion euros) and health insurance (6 billion euros) also have major redistributive consequences. Both rebates are aimed at people with the lowest incomes, who would therefore also be affected most if these rebates were to be abolished. The Gini coefficient would then rise by 5% (rent rebate) and 4% (health rebate). Adjusted for differences in budget size (bottom panel of Figure 15.5), these two rebates would have the largest distributional impact.

If the progressivity in tax rates were to be abolished by aligning the top rate with the low rate, under the two-bracket system—which would cost 5 billion euros—then the Gini coefficient would increase by 4%.

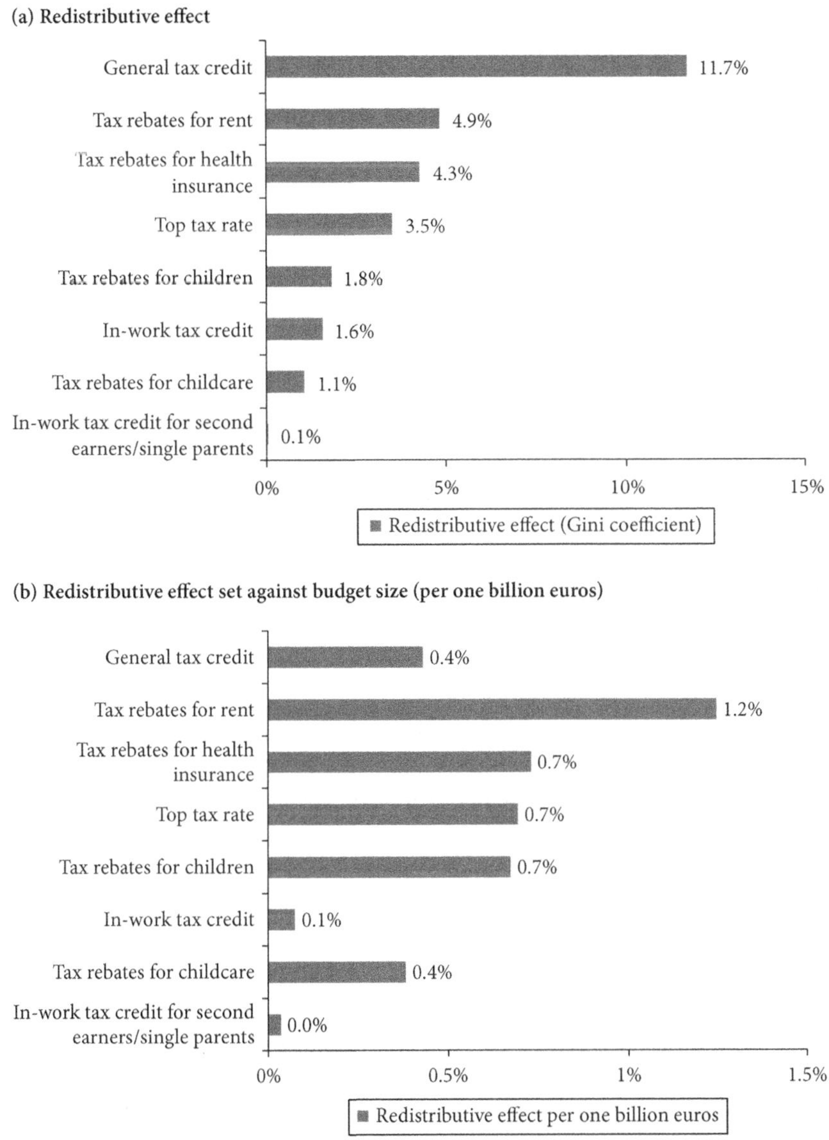

Figure 15.5 Redistributive effect of income-dependent tax credits and tax rebates

Notes: To determine the redistributive effect, we looked at the change of the Gini coefficient if a tax credit or tax rebate were to be abolished. In other words, the redistributive effect = (Gini coefficient without tax credit or tax rebate–Gini coefficient current system)/Gini coefficient current system.

Source: CPB calculations based on the MIMOSI micro-simulation model (Koot et al., 2016).

Smaller rdistributive impacts can be expected from the tax rebates for children and childcare and the in-work tax credits. In the case of the tax rebates for children and childcare, this would partly be due to the limited scope of the rebates. If the differences in budget size are also taken into account (bottom panel of

Figure 15.5), then the redistributive impacts are shown to be more in line with the other tax credits and tax rebates.

The redistributive impact of in-work tax credits is, on balance, limited (certainly in relation to the budget size of 21 billion euros). Whereas social benefit recipients are not entitled to in-work tax credits, they increase with income for lower income earners, but are also phased out with income for higher income earners.

The in-work credit for single parents/secondary earners is a relatively small measure, with hardly any overall redistributive effects, even after correcting for the size of the budget.

15.4 Starting Points for Simplification

In this section, we look at the starting points for simplifying income-dependent tax rebates and tax credits. The starting point is to leave the redistributive impact of the tax-transfer system the same, as much as possible. We analysed two reforms: (1) simplification and standardization of the various tax rebates; (2) elimination of the income-dependent feature of the general tax credit.

15.4.1 Case Study 1: Simplifying Tax Rebates

The first case study takes a close look at the tax rebates for rent, health, children, and childcare. Using regression analyses, we explore whether the design of the rebates can be simplified (with significantly fewer parameters and dependencies than under the current system) and, if so, how this simplification can be brought about and which distributional impacts should be taken into account.

The tax rebates currently feature different income definitions, phase-out thresholds, phase-out rates, and maximum income thresholds (see also Figure 15.1). In addition, entitlements to rebates for rent, health, and children are means-tested on wealth with different wealth thresholds for each tax rebate. Moreover, different household types are treated differently with respect to different tax rebates (e.g. in the treatment of single- and two-person households).

On the basis of the following starting points, we investigated the possibilities for simplifying the tax rebates.

- The simplicity of the tax rebates should be considered of paramount importance. Therefore, the analysis focuses on limiting the number of parameters and cross-dependencies in the tax rebates. Rebates for rent are meant to support people in paying their rent. Rebates for health insurance help people to pay their health insurance premiums and to alleviate the impact of deductibles. And rebates for children are intended to support parents with child-related costs (single-parent households receive additional support under the current system). Rebates for childcare are not included in our analysis, because of its different nature, compared with the other rebates. The rebates for rent, health insurance, and children are mainly aimed at income support, whereas the rebate for childcare is mainly focused on encouraging labour participation.

- All tax rebates feature the same phase-out threshold and the same phase-out rate with income. We have taken the NMW level as the phase-out threshold. The phase-out rate is determined using regression analysis. The main idea is to merge the current tax rebates for rent, health insurance, and children into one, single tax rebate.
- Means testing on wealth for the rebates is harmonized and based on the wealth test that currently applies to the rebates for health and children. Tax rebates are denied to people having over 80,000 euros net wealth above the general exemption for the wealth tax (in box 3 of the income tax system).
- The tax reform should minimize the distributional impacts compared with the current system. After all, the tax rebates are intended to provide income support.
- Total expenditures on tax rebates remains the same.

For households receiving a rebate, regression analyses were carried out in which the current total amount of tax rebates are regressed on the amount of rent,[2] the costs of healthcare,[3] the number of children per household, a dummy variable indicating whether the household is a single-parent household and household income above the NMW (the presumed phase-out threshold). A standard OLS regression minimizes the sum of squared errors in predicting the total level of the tax rebate. Hence, it can be used to derive a tax reform that results in the lowest distributional impacts, and thus complies with the basic principles for a reform. Our analysis also took into account that the total tax rebate predicted from the regression cannot be negative. The estimated regression equation is the following:

$$\begin{aligned} \textit{rebate} = {} & x_1 \times \textit{rent} + x_2 \times \textit{number of children} + x_3 \times \textit{single parent} \\ & + x_4 \times \textit{healthcare costs} - x_5 \times \textit{means-tested income} + \textit{error}_1, \end{aligned}$$

where '*rebate*' is the sum of rebates for rent, health insurance, and children, x_1 up to and including x_5 are estimated parameters, and '*means-tested income*' is max(0, (*household income* − *NMW*)) × (*household income* < *phase-out threshold*) and '$\textit{error}_1$' is the distributional impact in euros.

[2] This particularly concerns the rent between 3,000 and 8,400 euros, annually.

[3] This concerns the premiums paid by households for their basic health insurance and policy excess (deductible) costs.

The advantage of this formula is that we take into account the interactions between the different rebates when determining the phase-out rate x_5. However, the disadvantage is that all rebates are required to have the same maximum income threshold. The estimated phase-out rate is probably underestimated, because minimizing the distributional impact of the reform implies that the highest phase-out threshold of a particular tax rebate will become dominant if the phase-out rate is constrained to be uniform.

An alternative approach is to carry out a regression analysis separately for every tax rebate in order to estimate a phase-out rate for each rebate. The sum of the estimated phase-out rates thus forms the phase-out rate for the reformed, single rebate. This procedure overestimates the estimated phase-out rate, because under the current system, the rent rebate is phased out considerably faster than the other rebates and the sum of phase-out rates would then mainly be determined by the rent rebate. The formula for the alternative method is:

$$\begin{aligned} \textit{rent rebate} &= y_1 \times \textit{rent} - y_2 \times \textit{means-tested income} + \textit{error}_2, \\ \textit{health insurance rebate} &= y_3 \times \textit{healthcare costs} - y_4 \times \textit{means-tested income} + \textit{error}_3, \\ \textit{child rebate} &= y_5 \times \textit{number of children} + y_6 \times \textit{single parent} \\ &\quad - y_7 \times \textit{means-tested income} + \textit{error}_4, \end{aligned}$$

where y_1 up to and including y_7 are the estimated parameters, and $error_2$ up to and including $error_4$ are the distributional impacts measured in euros.

Table 15.1 provides the estimation results from the various methods. In Approach 1, the estimated phase-out rate with income (22.5%) is clearly lower than in Approach 2 (35%). Because the phase-out threshold in both analyses is the same (i.e. the NMW level), Approach 1 benefits, on average,

Table 15.1 Results of a regression analysis of the simplification of the tax rebates

	Approach 1	Approach 2			
	Sum of rebates	Rent rebate	Child rebate	Health insurance rebate	Household rebates (in total)
Rent	0.410	0.830			0.830
Number of children	1,161		1,021		1,021
Single parent	4,002		3,260		3,260
Health insurance premiums and deductibles	1,142			0.760	0.760
Income above the NMW level	22.5%	23.6%	3.3%	12.6%	35%[a]

Notes: [a] Average, based on estimated phase-out rates in separate analyses for the rebates for rent, health insurance, and children.

Source: CPB calculations based on the MIMOSI micro-simulation model (Koot et al., 2016).

better-off households with an income above the phase-out threshold compared with Approach 2. Approach 2 has a higher phase-out rate, and thus is, on average, more favourable for poorer households with an income around the phase-out threshold.

As both methods are not perfect in determining the appropriate phase-out rate, we fixed the phase-out rate at 29% for the uniform rebate, which lies in the middle of both methods. To achieve budget neutrality for this new rebate, we adjusted the other parameters of the regression in Approach 2 (taking into account the interactions between them). We use the parameters of Approach 2, because they are most favourable to the lowest incomes, which is the main focus of income support under the current system. Based on this, we derive a simplified and uniform tax rebate according to the following formula:

$$\begin{aligned} rebate = {} & 80\% \times rent + €980 \times number\ of\ children + €3,130 \times single\ parent \\ & + 73\% \times healthcare\ costs - 29\% \times means\text{-}tested\ income, \end{aligned}$$

where '*rent*' is the rent between 3,000 and 8,400 euros, per year, and '*healthcare costs*' are health insurance premiums plus deductibles, per household.

Table 15.2 shows the distributional impact of the new, uniform tax rebate compared with the current system of tax rebates. This shows that the distributional impact remains limited to a net income increase or decline of 5%. Most of

Table 15.2 Distributional effects of the simplified tax rebate system (compared with the 2018 system)

	< -5%	-5% to -2%	-2% to 0%	No effect	0% to 2%	2% to 5%	≥5%
Income groups							
First 20% (≤ 115% NMW)	3%	43%	23%	4%	8%	7%	13%
Second 20% (115–183% NMW)	0%	15%	20%	19%	8%	13%	25%
Third 20% (183–267% NMW)	2%	6%	12%	68%	5%	4%	3%
Fourth 20% (267–388% NMW)	1%	2%	23%	73%	0%	0%	0%
Fifth 20% (≥ 388% NMW)	0%	0%	25%	74%	0%	0%	0%
Source of income							
Working population	1%	7%	22%	55%	3%	4%	7%
Benefit recipients	5%	39%	17%	17%	6%	6%	10%
Pensioners	0%	19%	19%	38%	6%	7%	11%
All households	1%	13%	21%	47%	4%	5%	8%

Source: CPB calculations based on the MIMOSI micro-simulation model (Koot et al., 2016).

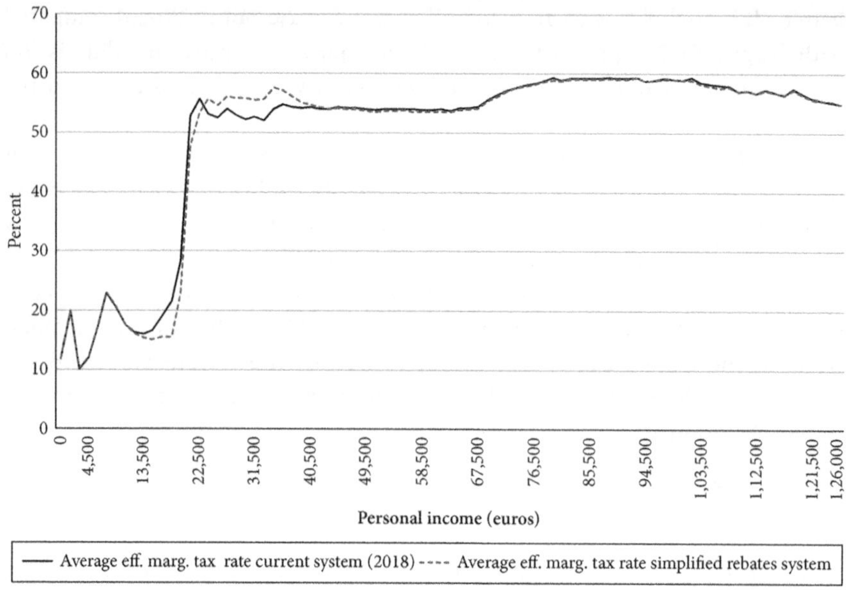

Figure 15.6 Marginal burden of simplified tax rebate system (compared with the system of 2018)

Source: CPB calculations based on the MIMOSI micro-simulation model (Koot et al., 2016).

the adverse distributional effects occur amongst the lowest-income group (< 115% NMW) and among social benefit recipients. These are the groups that, under the current system, often receive the maximum rebates. Since simplifying the rebate comes at the expense of specific targeting, these groups will experience the greatest income declines. However, with supplementary income policy in the tax and transfer system, it should be possible to limit the adverse distributional impacts of a reform.

The redistributive power of the new system of rebates remains virtually the same compared with the existing system. In the new system the Gini coefficient would be 0.1% lower than under the current system.

The average marginal tax burden for incomes below the NMW level will decrease under the uniform rebate system, compared with the current system (Figure 15.6). This is because, under the current system, the rent rebate for single-person households is phased out below the NMW level while under the new system the phase-out does not start until the NMW level. The marginal tax burden, in fact, increases slightly, between the NMW and average income. With a phase-out rate of, on average, 29%, the new tax rebate will be phased out more rapidly than under the current system. A policy option is to lower the phase-out rate for this trajectory.

15.4.2 Case Study 2: Abolition of the Phase-Out of the General Tax Credit

The second case study concerns the abolition of the phase-out range of the income-dependent general tax credit. The phase out of the general tax credit since 2013, has resulted in a very intransparent increase in the marginal tax burden, and has been accompanied by considerable administrative costs (Jongen et al., 2016). The phase-out of the general tax credit (with a rate of 6% for individuals under the statutory retirement age) occurs exactly in the second and third tax bracket, so that the phase-out, in fact, represents a 6% increase in marginal tax rates in these two tax brackets.

For individuals below the statutory retirement age, the phase-out of the income-dependent general tax credit can therefore be abolished with a 6 percentage point increase in statutory rates in the second and third bracket without any distributional consequences. For individuals above the statutory retirement age, the general tax credit is lower, so that the corresponding phase-out rate is also lower. For this group, therefore, marginal tax rates should not be increased to the same extent. However, by simultaneously increasing tax credits for retirees, in addition to the 6 percentage point increase in statutory rates in both tax brackets, it should still be feasible to abolish the phase-out of the income-dependent tax credits with only marginal distributional consequences for pensioners (Jongen

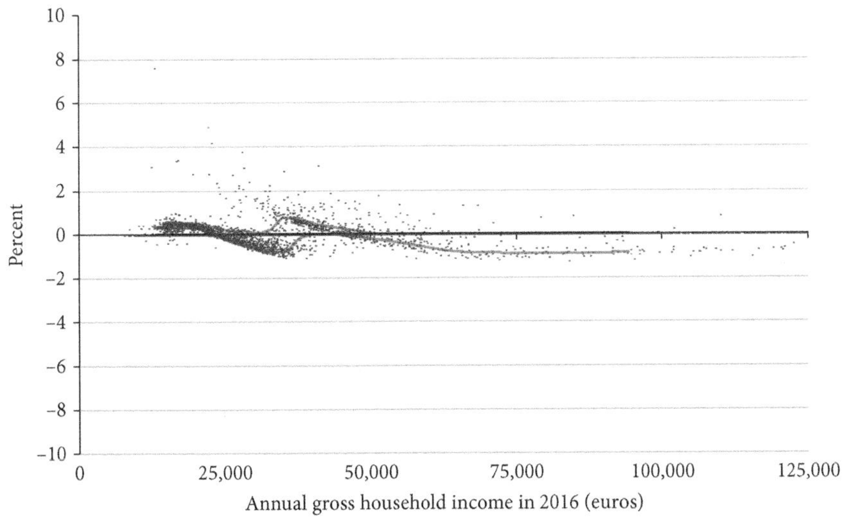

Figure 15.7 Income effects under abolition of the income-dependent general tax credit

Notes: Including compensation via higher tax rates.
Source: Jongen et al. (2016).

et al., 2016). Figure 15.7 shows that such income changes would generally range between −1% and +1%.

The redistributive effects of the tax system would remain the same after the simplification. Abolition of the phase-out of the general tax credit alone would lead to a 2.3% increase in the Gini coefficient, because higher income groups would now receive the full tax credit. However, after raising the tax rates in the second and third tax brackets, this effect is fully neutralized.

15.5 Conclusions

In this chapter, we described the complexity of the income tax, and particularly the increasing income-dependency of the tax credits and tax rebates. The redistributive and labour market effects have played an important role in the current design of the income-dependent tax credits and rebates. We quantify these effects for the current system, and examine the possibility of simplifying the system, while retaining the redistributive effects of the tax-transfer system. The conclusion is that simplification of the tax system is feasible with limited redistributive consequences, which can, moreover, be repaired by additional policy changes in the tax-transfer system. The system of tax rebates for rent, health insurance, and children can be simplified substantially by introducing one tax rebate with a single phase-out threshold, a single phase-out rate and a single means test. Moreover, the phase-out range of the general tax credit can be fully eliminated by offsetting adjustments in tax rates and the tax credit for retirees. However, it should be noted that our analyses are merely exploratory. Follow-up research could, for example, investigate the labour market effects of the proposed reforms.

References

Jongen, E., Koot, P., and Vlekke, M. (2016), 'De politieke economie van inkomensbeleid: makkelijker kunnen we het niet maken?' CPB Background Document, 30 June.

Koot, P. (2019), 'Het ramen van beleidseffecten op de inkomensverdeling via de Gini-coëfficiënt', CPB Background Document, 21 March.

Koot, P., Vlekke, M., Berkhout, E., and Euwals, R. (2016), 'MIMOSI: microsimulatiemodel voor belastingen, sociale zekerheid, loonkosten en koopkracht', CPB Background Document, 30 March.

Koot, P., de Boer, H.-W., and Jongen, E. (2018), 'De belastingdruk van een- en tweeverdieners vanaf 2005: een intertemporele en internationale analyse van de belastingdruk voor paren in Nederland', CPB Background Document, 15 February.

16
Towards a New Tax Balance between Employees and Freelancers

*Lans Bovenberg and Ed Groot**

16.1 Introduction

The Dutch labour market is experiencing rapid growth in the number of self-employed people without staff (i.e. freelancers).[1] This increase is also occurring internationally, but Figure 16.1 shows that this growth is exceptionally large in the Netherlands (Baker and Gielens, 2018). There are now 1.5 million self-employed individuals, of whom 1.1 million are freelancers.

Socio-cultural, technological, and demographic factors are frequently put forward as explanations for these radical changes. However, these factors also play a role in other countries and are therefore not a sufficient explanation for the exceptionally high growth of the self-employed in the Netherlands (Ministry of Finance, 2015; OECD, 2019).

From an employer's point of view, and especially for small- and medium-sized enterprises (SME), the restrictive provisions in collective wage agreements are often suggested as causal factors. These lead to a preference for the recruitment of self-employed individuals and other forms of flexible work, such as temporary contracts, payrolling, and agency work. This is all the more true in a world of open borders, where adjustment speed is becoming increasingly important and wherein businesses are less inclined to contract employees for an indefinite period of time. However, in this case too, these developments also occur in other countries, and therefore cannot explain the exceptional rise of freelancers in the Netherlands.

* Lans Bovenberg (a.l.bovenberg@tilburguniversity.edu) is Professor of Economics at Tilburg School of Economics and Management, Tilburg University. Ed Groot (ed.groot230@gmail.com) is editor at Financieele Dagblad. The authors wish to thank the participants of the Cnossen Forum 2019 'Tax by Design for the Netherlands' in general and Bas Jacobs, Sijbren Cnossen and our discussants Egbert Jongen and Koen van Schie in particular for very useful comments on an earlier version of this chapter.

[1] The following English translations have been made of the concepts used in the Dutch tax law: closely held company = BV (*besloten vennootschap*); director/substantial shareholder = *directeur-grootaandeelhouder*; earned income-tax credit = *arbeidskorting*; employee tax credit = *werknemerskorting*; freelancer = *zelfstandige zonder personeel* (*zzp'er*); unincorporated entrepreneurs = IB-*ondernemers*; small- and medium-sized enterprises (SME) exemption = MKB *vrijstelling*; self-employed (with or without staff) = *zelfstandige* (*met of zonder personeel*); self-employed allowance = *zelfstandigenaftrek* (ZA); self-employed tax credit = *zelfstandigenkorting*.

Lans Bovenberg and Ed Groot, *Towards a New Tax Balance between Employees and Freelancers* In: *Tax by Design for the Netherlands*. Edited by: Sijbren Cnossen and Bas Jacobs, Oxford University Press.
DOI: 10.1093/oso/9780192855244.003.0016

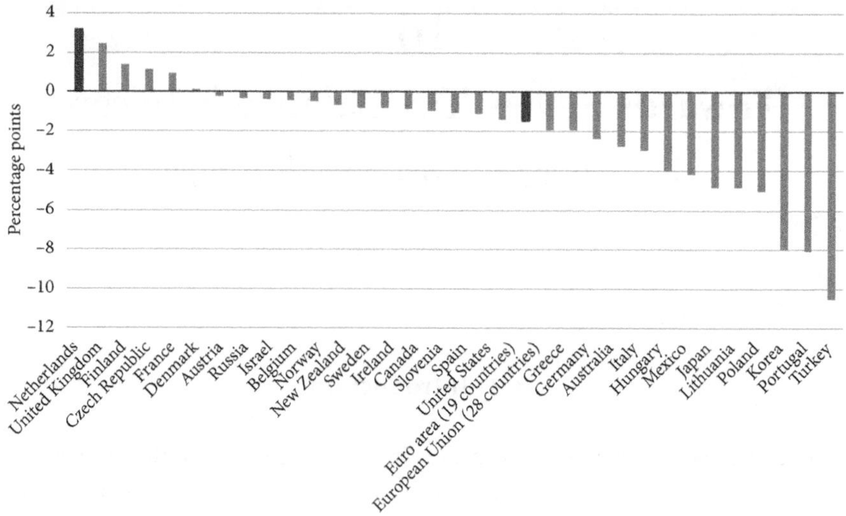

Figure 16.1 Change in the self-employed share of total employment between 2005 and 2016 (in percentage points)
Source: OECD (2019).

In the public debate, reference is often made to the mandatory wage payments for sick employees. But, here too, a direct link with the strong growth in the number of self-employed individuals is difficult to establish. Since 2000, the so-called 'employer's wedge' has remained stable at just under 21% of labour costs. Within the wedge, the share of continued payment of wages in the event of illness has even fallen from 2.9% to 2.5% of the wage costs (CPB, 2018).

16.2 Tax Incentives

A more plausible explanation for the exceptional developments in the Dutch labour market relates to the tax benefits of independent entrepreneurship. The OECD also refers to this factor (Baker et al., 2018; OECD, 2019). In the Netherlands, the self-employed enjoy extensive tax advantages compared with employees: the highest level in the entire OECD area (Milanez and Bratta, 2019). The most important tax advantages are the self-employed allowance and the SME profit exemption.[2] The self-employed allowance was introduced in 1971. Since 2012, a fixed nominal amount applies—currently 7,030 euros—provided that the

[2] In addition, there are a number of other tax concessions, such as the start-up allowance, the employee allowance and various schemes for stimulating investments. These depend on the individual situation of the entrepreneur, and are not discussed in this chapter.

individual works 1,225 hours for his or her own business. The tax expenditure in 2019 was approximately 1.7 billion euros. The SME exemption equals 14% of business profits minus the self-employed allowance. The revenue foregone is 1.9 billion euros. The combination of the self-employed allowance and the SME profit exemption means that the difference in tax burden between employees and the self-employed is considerable. Figure 16.2 compares the (average and marginal) tax burden for employees and the self-employed.

For the self-employed with low earnings, the effect on tax rebates is also important. For the calculation of the right to tax rebates (for healthcare, rent, children, and childcare), self-employed individuals can deduct the self-employed allowance and the SME profit exemption from aggregate income when determining their eligibility for the benefits. As a result, the self-employed are entitled to considerably larger tax rebates than employees with a comparable taxable income. To illustrate, single employees lost the right to the tax rebate for rent in 2019 if they earned more than 22,700 euros, and they received no tax rebate for healthcare at an income above 29,562 euros. A self-employed individual making a profit of 29,562 euros had an eligible income of 19,162 euros, which is

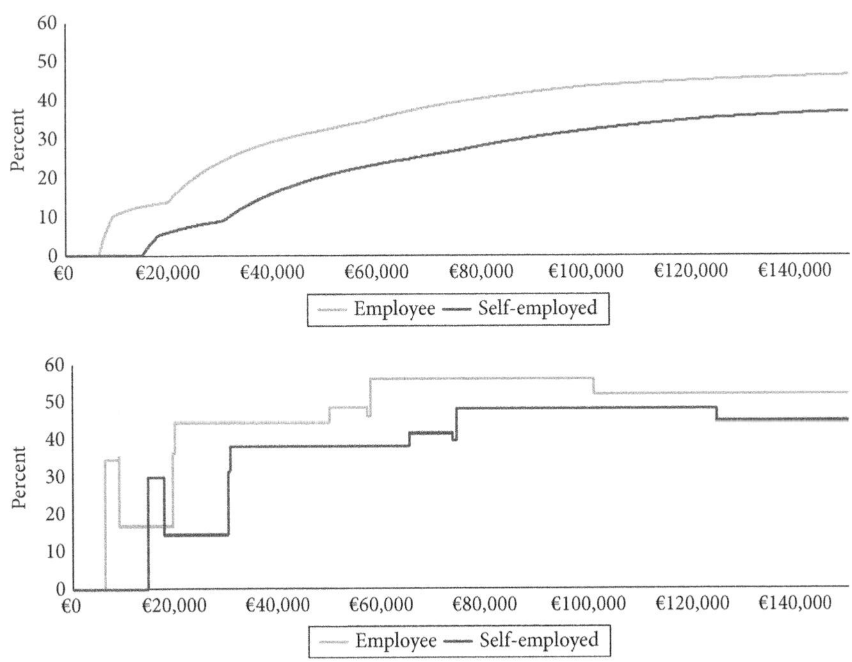

Figure 16.2 Average (top panel) and marginal (bottom panel) tax rates for employees and the self-employed

Source: SEO (2017).

(29,562–7,280) × (1–0.14). This is slightly below the minimum annual wage and therefore entitles the individual to maximum tax rebates.

The self-employed allowance and the SME profit exemption also affect the income-dependent health insurance contribution of 5.7% of taxable profits. Especially with low earnings, this implies a considerably lower tax base than is the case with employees. In addition, there are financial incentives on the client's side. After all, they do not have to pay contributions for pension and employee insurance for the self-employed.

Ministry of Finance (2015) calculates the remuneration at which employees and the self-employed can enter the labour market, assuming equal net incomes. This provides a picture of their relative competitive position. Two alternatives are considered here. In the first alternative, the self-employed do not insure themselves against disability, illness, old age, and closing the income gap between assignments. In the second alternative, they charge a fee to cover the contributions for these insurance policies.

Figure 16.3 shows that the total wage costs of an average employee amount to 184% of their net wage. For comparable unincorporated entrepreneurs who insure themselves, the percentage is 141%. If unincorporated entrepreneurs do not insure themselves, this percentage drops to 106%.

At the minimum income level, employees cost 140% of their net wage, compared with 116% for the comparable self-employed. It is remarkable that if the self-employed do not insure themselves at the minimum level, their total

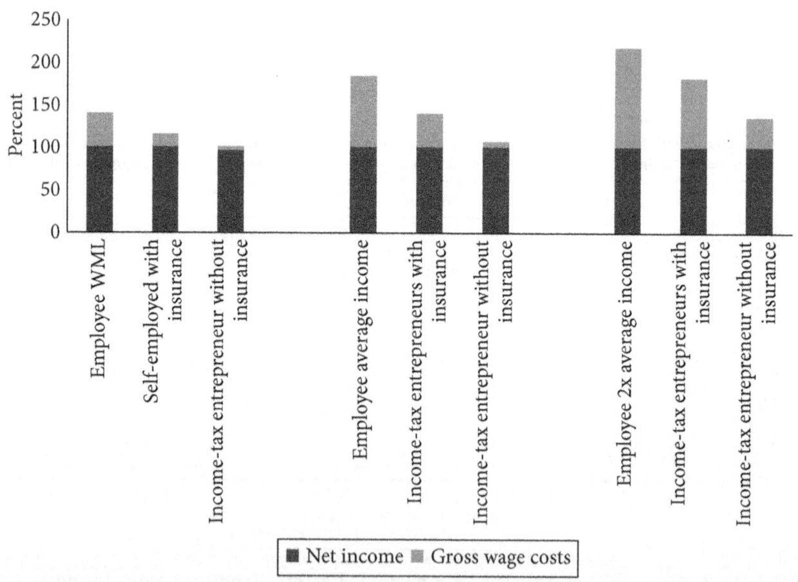

Figure 16.3 Costs of employees versus unincorporated entrepreneurs
Source: Ministry of Finance (2015).

labour costs will be lower than their net income. This is because unincorporated entrepreneurs do not pay tax at the minimum income level, but do receive a health insurance allowance.

Ministry of Finance (2015) compares single employees and/or self-employed individuals who may only be eligible for tax rebates for healthcare. Other tax rebates, such as for rent and children, are not taken into account because they depend strongly on the household situation. If there is a right to other tax rebates in addition to the healthcare rebate, the tax position of the self-employed will improve even further compared with employees. In addition, the self-employed have more options than employees to deduct costs of earning income from taxable profits and to under-declare income for tax purposes.

In all cases, the self-employed can offer their services at a lower price on the labour market than employees can. In practice, many self-employed individuals are not insured. This might be due to short-sightedness (i.e. the self-employed underestimate risks and therefore do not anticipate them). External effects might also play a role for the self-employed with low earnings. After all, social provisions, such as social assistance and the state pension, already protect the self-employed in the event of a fall in income. These income groups therefore have little interest in supplementary insurance.

However, even if the self-employed do want to insure themselves, the question is whether they can pass this on by demanding a higher price for their goods and services. The self-employed are more poorly organized than employees are, and they are not allowed to make pricing agreements. If the self-employed individual is economically weak, then the client can reduce the price so that the self-employed individual must pass on any tax benefits to the client. Ministry of Finance (2015) observed that the tax concessions and the exemption from social and pension contributions function as price subsidies.

It is clear that such price subsidies can be considerable. Figure 16.3 shows that employees at a minimum income level are up to 44% more expensive than the self-employed—as much as 73% at the average income level, and 58% at twice the average income level.

The accelerated growth in the number of self-employed individuals since 2005 is not unrelated to the developments concerning the declaration of labour relations (VAR). Since the introduction of the extensive legal consequences of VAR, clients have been exempted from withholding wage tax and social contributions if the contractor is able to submit a VAR statement. As a result, clients no longer run the risk of additional taxes should it become apparent that they have actually contracted a fictitious employee. This risk came to lie with the contractor but, in practice, it turned out that the tax authorities could barely monitor this. Nevertheless, the VAR eliminated an important institutional brake on companies hiring self-employed people.[3]

[3] Bosch et al. (2012) study the various reasons behind the growth of self-employed people and find only a limited effect of tax factors. They do not take into account the developments around the VAR.

16.3 Optimal Tax Treatment

16.3.1 Positive External Effects

The strong growth in the number of self-employed people was initially generally welcomed. Independent work, where people supervise themselves, was seen in the context of workers' emancipation. Independent entrepreneurship offered workers the freedom to escape regulatory pressure and hierarchical control within companies. Self-employment also gave people who would otherwise end up receiving social security or social assistance an extra option to continue to make a productive contribution to society. Self-employed people without employees (freelancers) would thus generate positive external effects on the government budget.

Moreover, tax concessions can reduce distortions in the labour market (e.g. a lack of downward wage flexibility for older employees). Subsequently, the potentially positive external effects of innovation by self-employed people were noted. Finally, there was the hope that successful self-employed workers would stimulate labour demand by allowing them to expand and take on additional staff in the long run. For example, in a unanimous recommendation in 2010, the Social Economic Council (SER, 2010) spoke of a valuable 'contribution to society and the economy and thus to the socio-economic dynamics'. The SER saw no reason for fundamental system changes.

16.3.2 More Targeted Instruments?

This positive assessment of the social effects of the increase in the self-employed has gradually given way to doubts. For example, a large number of self-employed businesses do not grow and the effects of the business tax concessions on employment and innovation seemed limited (SEO, 2017). The insight that generic tax instruments were unfocused also gained traction. For example, CPB (2015) and SEO (2017) argued for the conversion of the generic self-employed allowance and SME exemption into more targeted instruments, such as a start-up allowance for young innovative companies. With regards to combating distortions on the labour market, CPB (2015) favoured targeted wage-cost subsidies that were not linked to the self-employed status. Many freelancers remain single-person businesses and do not have the ambition to expand and recruit staff (Stam, van der Veen, and Smetsers, 2019). Based on data for the United States, Haltiwanger, Jasmin, and Miranda (2013) show that small companies make little or no contribution to employment growth.

16.3.3 Productivity

According to the OECD, the consensus in academic research leans towards a negative effect of flexible employment and self-employment on the productivity and vigour of the economy.[4] Comparisons between the productivity of employees with that of the self-employed require caution because of possible self-selection: low-productive workers might only be able to participate in the labour process as self-employed individuals. However, empirical studies show that, after correcting for self-selection, independent entrepreneurs are still less productive than employees. The empirical literature that shows a positive relationship between business size and productivity also leads to the conclusion that freelancers are less productive than the average employee in most companies (Bartelsman, Haltiwanger, and Scarpetta, 2009). One reason for the lower productivity of the self-employed is that these workers benefit less from company-specific training. Sustainable employment relationships seem to offer a better basis for clients and contractors to invest in each other (Lisi and Malo, 2017; Borstlap Committee, 2019).

The lower productivity of self-employed entrepreneurs is also consistent with Coase's well-known theorem that companies hire employees if lower transaction costs outweigh the benefits of outsourcing. The tax rebates on self-employed work distort that trade-off between relationship and transaction. The entrepreneurial status is chosen in order to pay less tax, not because the people involved are more productive as entrepreneurs. As a specific example, people in home care are better at offering care than being busy with administering hours worked, writing invoices, and acquisition. Companies are partnerships aimed at saving transaction costs and exploiting economies of scale through specialization. A very rough indication of the differences in productivity is provided by the comparison of the value added of full-time employees with that of the self-employed. According to the OECD, Dutch full-time employees created an average of 80,000 euros in added value in 2015, compared to 40,000 euros for the full-time self-employed (Baker and Gielens, 2018).

It is precisely in a tight labour market that the negative effects on labour productivity count heavily (Stam, van der Veen, and Smetsers, 2019). After all, it is becoming increasingly important to make the best possible use of available labour. In the healthcare sector, it is increasingly common for the self-employed to be hired at times that suit them best. As a result, the permanent employees have to do night shifts or services during the weekends, with the result that they too increasingly opt for independence. There is some risk of a self-reinforcing effect, because the growing number of self-employed individuals makes permanent employment less attractive. Healthcare institutions then encounter the problem

[4] For detailed literature references, see the OECD input for the Discussion Note Committee on Regulation of Work, June 2019.

that the costs of irregular services increase. As a further example, in a letter to the Lower House of Parliament, the Minister of Social Affairs and Employment (Koolmees, 2019) stated that companies in ICT, education, and healthcare in particular want to offer fixed contracts to self-employed people more often nowadays, but that the tax and other benefits of independence are more important for contractors. What mainly started as a tax-driven cost saving now runs the risk of freezing the status quo.

16.3.4 Negative External and Internal Effects of the Self-Employed

There is also increasing attention for possible negative external and internal effects of self-employed people without employees (freelancers). With regards to the labour market, there is a concern that wages in some sectors are not too high, but too low (OECD, 2019). Trade unions are increasingly challenging self-employed workers in court because they cause inappropriate competition in the labour market, undermining the negotiating power of labour. Indications that the tax concessions, in practice, often hardly support the income of self-employed persons, but are skimmed off by the client, can be found in the income statistics (SEO, 2018). According to Ministry of Finance (2015), half of self-employed people earn profits of 24,500 euros or less. This group consists largely of net recipients of public funds because no income tax is due, but there is a right to tax rebates. Hence, a vicious circle may occur in which a shrinking number of employees have to pay for the burdens of the welfare state.

Another issue is that freelancers cause adverse selection in social insurance. The Scientific Council for Government Policy (WRR), for example, points out that the increasing flexibility of work through flex contracts and self-employment is eroding social insurance (Engbersen, Snel, and Kremer, 2017). More generally, fears are rising that a growing group of workers will not have adequate pension provision and other social insurance benefits (Borstlap Committee, 2019; OECD, 2019). This is partly due to the short-sightedness of workers, as long as they are allowed to choose whether or not to insure themselves against risks. The result is more poverty and greater claims on government benefits (such as allowances and social assistance).

These external and internal effects are particularly problematic at the lower end of the labour market. Low-skilled, vulnerable people are the most susceptable to short-sighted decisions and are in a poor negotiating position. It is precisely these people who would benefit from good social protection. Furthermore, embedding them in more sustainable relationships within companies and institutions improves their labour productivity and their human potential. Research indicates that self-employed professionals earn less at the bottom of the income distribution than do employees with the same characteristics (SEO, 2018).

The shift from sustainable employee–employer relationships to loosely established client–contractor relationships may also have negative consequences for the stability of the Dutch economy. Macro-economic risks end up with households facing liquidity constraints rather than shareholders of companies. This distortion increases the exposure of the Dutch economy to macro-economic shocks. The erosion of social security due to the increase in the number of self-employed people lacking adequate social security further reduces the workings of the automatic stabilizers.

16.3.5 Towards Tax Neutrality

Supported by the theoretical arguments and empirical findings provided above, we argue in favour of working towards tax neutrality between self-employed workers and employees.[5] The possible negative internal and external effects of the self-employed can be combated, if necessary, through adequate income protection against major risks for all workers – regardless of the contract form.

16.4 History of the Tax Imbalance

The (distorted) tax balance between unincorporated entrepreneurs and employees is not the result of a conscious policy, let alone of in-depth economic analysis. Rather, the historical development of the business concessions had its own political dynamics that inadvertently led to the tax imbalance with employees.

In a review of the legal history of the self-employed allowance, Vording (2004) distinguishes three main motives for the design of the self-employed allowance: income support for small entrepreneurs, doing justice to the specific (uncertain) characteristics of the entrepreneur's income position, and, finally, contributing to a balanced tax treatment of the self-employed compared with directors/substantial shareholders of closely held companies. The first and last motives dominate in the history of the law. The introduction of the self-employed allowance in 1975 was justified in the Explanatory Memorandum to Parliament with reference to the unfavourable income development of small entrepreneurs and to compensate for high inflation. A year later, the allowance was extended to higher earnings, primarily to prevent entrepreneurs subject to the progressive personal income tax from resorting to the closely held corporate form of doing business and being taxed at the lower corporate tax rate. In the same year, the corporation tax rate was reduced from 48% to 43%. Vording notes that subsequent reductions in the corporation tax

[5] This is consistent with Statement 4 of the Borstlap Committee (2019): 'A more level playing field for workers is promoted by limiting differences in the tax treatment of workers.'

rate were almost always accompanied by an increase in the self-employed allowance. Maintaining 'global balance' between unincorporated entrepreneurs and incorporated entrepreneurs was also the main reason for introducing the SME profit exemption in 2007. The fact that the accumulation of the self-employed allowance and the SME profit exemption in turn led to a tax imbalance between the self-employed and employees was hardly noticed (De Kam, 2009).

Something similar occurred with the conversion of the earned-income deduction into the earned-income tax credit in 2001. Employees lost the tax deduction for professional costs, such as a study and so forth, and received a tax credit in return. Unincorporated entrepreneurs received the same tax credit, but at the same time retained their full cost tax deduction.

Both the employed person's tax credit and the entrepreneurial concessions substantially increased over the years. For unincorporated entrepreneurs, this was a win–win situation: they share in both the concessions for employees and those of entrepreneurs, with the result that tax imbalances between employees and unincorporated entrepreneurs have increased since the turn of the century.

Rather than in politics or ministries, the growing imbalance attracted attention among tax specialists. The committee for reforming the tax system (van Weeghel et al., 2010) suggested that the self-employed allowance should be abolished because it is not aimed at the positive external effects of entrepreneurship and encourages tax-driven self-employment, especially at the bottom of the income distribution. The van Dijkhuizen Committee (2012) offered the same advice in its interim report. The Borstlap Committee (2019) also argued for more tax neutrality.

16.5 Barriers to Balance Restoration

The above discussion shows that there is now a broad consensus in the tax literature and in various committees that the tax balance between employees and the self-employed has been upset. The pressing question is why so little has happened regarding the various recommendations. The simple answer is that successive governments did not dare to address this, or that there was insufficient political support for this.[6] The number of self-employed individuals is now so large that they form a formidable group of very articulate voters. In addition, these are self-employed people with often low earnings, for whom measures such as the abolition of the self-employed allowance are hard to swallow. After the workers disability law (WAO) in the 1980s and 1990s and the mortgage interest deduction

[6] The Rutte II coalition agreement included a cut of 150 million euros of the entrepreneurial income tax concessions. However, this proposal did not get the support of the opposition, which was needed to obtain a majority in the Senate.

in the previous decade, the imbalance in the tax position of employees with regards to the self-employed can therefore be seen as the new taboo in Dutch politics. Reform is difficult if it affects a large group of voters.

Perhaps because of the electoral risks, in the coalition agreement of the Rutte III cabinet only marginal adjustments were foreseen in the tax and institutional arrangements for the self-employed. These include the limitation of the self-employed allowance to the rate of the first income tax bracket and the obligation for clients to offer an employment contract if the hourly rate for self-employed work is below a minimum bandwidth of between 15 and 18 euros.

Remarkably, the minimum rate was already on the table at the IBO working group in 2015, but this was not further pursued because it is difficult to implement. The hourly rate is easy to manipulate by adjusting the working time that is being charged. Apart from that, it is impossible for the tax authorities to check thousands of records of the self-employed for hourly rates. The government proposal also turned out to be incompatible with competition policy in the European Union. The cabinet subsequently decided to set a general minimum rate of 16 euros per hour and to abolish the obligation to offer an employment contract. Other non-tax proposals have also been made to reduce the differences between employees and the self-employed. Consider, for example, the introduction of mandatory pension provision for the self-employed and/or compulsory insurance against disability.

Various proposals have also attempted to combat fictitious employment by better distinguishing employee relationships from independent entrepreneurship. However, the distinction between forms of work is becoming increasingly blurred, partly due to the emergence of all kinds of platforms that, like companies, link supply and demand on the labour market. Making a distinction between an employee relationship and independent entrepreneurship is hardly feasible any longer, and is associated with various costs for the tax authorities, clients, and contractors.

16.6 Restoration of the Tax Balance

In view of political realities, a more efficient labour market with adequate social protection seems feasible only if the tax balance between employment and self-employment is restored gradually. In addition, an abrupt change to the approach, whereby neutrality is quickly restored, would endanger the credibility of a stable tax system. People who make long-term decisions about their labour market status must be able to count on stable tax rules. Therefore, our proposals gradually work towards tax neutrality.

The first step is to split the earned income tax credit into an 'employee tax credit' and a 'self-employed tax credit'. This creates two separate 'switches' with which the tax benefits for employees and unincorporated entrepreneurs can be controlled independently. In this way, the self-employed no longer automatically follow along with future increases in the employee tax credit. This measure can easily be implemented in the automated systems of the tax administration and it does not involve higher implementation costs.

The second step is to gradually merge the self-employed allowance with the self-employed tax credit. The effect of the self-employed allowance on the entitlement to tax rebates and the income-dependent contribution to the care insurance law (Zvw) would thus gradually be phased out. This reform focuses on the tax distortions at the bottom of the income distribution and the associated erosion of social security for vulnerable groups.

In 2015, in the context of the preparation of the 2016 Tax Plan, the distributional effects were calculated if the self-employed allowance were to be merged with the earned income tax credit into a self-employed tax credit in one go. Table 16.1 shows that the income position of 8% of the self-employed deteriorates by 5% or more, that at 9% the loss is between 3% and 5%, and that for more than half of the self-employed the loss of net disposable income is limited to the bandwidth 0–3%. As can be expected, the negative distributional consequences most often occur between the minimum income and 1.5 times the average income. After all, this is the trajectory where the difference in entitlement to benefits between employees and the self-employed is largest.

It is remarkable that a quarter of those who are self-employed benefit from the conversion of a self-employed allowance into a tax credit. This is because tax credits, as opposed to the self-employed allowance, can be credited against the tax in box 2 (director/substantial shareholder) and box 3 (presumptive capital income). There is a substantial group of self-employed individuals who combine low profits with sizable wealth in box 3. This effect appears to be hardly

Table 16.1 Distributional effects of merging the self-employed allowance and earned income tax credit for the self-employed

Income level	< –5%	–5% to 3%	–3% to 1%	–1% to 0%	No effect	0–3%	>3%	Total	Share
Minimum	3%	6%	36%	12%	36%	3%	3%	100%	9%
Minimum–average	12%	6%	43%	15%	4%	10%	9%	100%	18%
1× to 1.5× average	22%	19%	26%	17%	2%	10%	3%	100%	15%
1.5× to 2× average	11%	15%	21%	23%	2%	27%	2%	100%	16%
2× to 3× average	1%	8%	14%	30%	1%	44%	1%	100%	18%
>3× average		1%	6%	67%	2%	23%		100%	24%
Total	8%	9%	22%	32%	5%	22%	3%	100%	100%

Source: 2019 internal memo, Ministry of Social Affairs and Employment, The Hague (not published; can be requested from authors).

objectionable because wealth in box 3 serves as a retirement reserve for many of the self-employed who do not benefit from (tax-deductible) pension contributions.

The negative distributional consequences can be considerably mitigated by gradually phasing out the self-employed allowance and its conversion into the self-employed tax credit. Self-employed people and their clients are then given the time to negotiate new (higher) rates that do justice to the new tax reality. Additional revenue can also be recycled in an income-neutral fashion (e.g. through higher earned-income tax credits).

This brings us to the third step. The tax imbalance between employees and the self-employed can be reduced by increasing the employee tax credit, which unincorporated entrepreneurs would no longer be entitled to. This adjustment process can be speeded up by not adjusting the self-employed tax credit for inflation, or by reducing it by a certain amount each year until tax neutrality is obtained. Limiting the tax concessions for the self-employed in this way can provide budgetary resources for gradually increasing the employee tax credit. To prevent a reduction of unskilled employment, where the low-skilled have to turn to social assistance, higher earned-income tax credits can be targeted primarily at the bottom of the labour market. However, other ways to recycle revenue are also conceivable (e.g. a reduction of income tax rates).

The consequences for the low-paid self-employed of not indexing the self-employed tax credit can be limited by indexing the tax credit for the self-employed who insure themselves against disability and/or old age. It is precisely for the self-employed at the bottom of the income distribution that positive external effects are associated with eliminating these insurance policies. In this way, a future claim on public services (such as tax credits and social assistance) is limited. However, a disadvantage of this option to stimulate insurance through the tax system is the further increasing complexity of the tax system, with negative consequences for feasibility.

It should be noted that the entrepreneurial tax concessions still have an effect on the tax rebates through the SME profit exemption. This exemption, too, could gradually be integrated into the self-employed tax credit, which could ultimately create a single, appropriately designed tax concession for unincorporated entrepreneurs. Apart from that, the level of the SME profit exemption of 14% seems to be generous. It is difficult to justify the fact that unincorporated entrepreneurs pay more than 7 percentage points less tax on an extra euro than employees do, in view of a higher labour supply elasticity of the self-employed than of employees—particularly because the self-employed mainly consist of men who have a lower labour supply elasticity than women do. In order not to distort the overall balance with incorporated entrepreneurs, a gradual reduction of the SME profit exemption could accompany a reduction of the 'efficiency discount' (currently 25%) in the presumptive wage of directors/substantial shareholders, in agreement with the recommendation of the van Dijkhuizen Committee (2013). The proceeds from this operation could be recycled in the form of a general reduction in income tax rates.

16.7 Final Considerations

In recent years, there has been a growing awareness that the rise in the number of self-employed individuals is not so much the result of personal preferences, but is primarily driven by tax incentives. The tax distortions erode social security, undermine the negotiating power of labour, and affect labour productivity. However, tax concessions for the low-paid self-employed contribute to cheap low-paid work.

Various other proposals have been made to reduce the differences between employees and the self-employed. Many of these measures (such as compulsory insurance for the self-employed, prevention of fictitious entrepreneurship by better defining entrepreneurship, or prescribing minimum rates for the self-employed) do not address the cause of the problem: the uneven tax playing field. This is why these proposals call for a restriction of freedom or go hand-in-hand with considerable implementation problems.

Our proposal focuses on the tax cause of the undesired shift from being an employee to being self-employed, and the resulting erosion of social security and the negotiating power of labour, particularly at the lower end of the labour market. Splitting the earned income-tax credit into an employee tax credit and a self-employed tax credit creates two separate switches with which the net disposable incomes of the self-employed and employees can be controlled independently. Tax neutrality can be restored by gradually increasing the employee tax credit and gradually merging the self-employed allowance with the self-employed tax credit.

References

Baker, M. and Gielens, L. (2018), 'Making employment more inclusive in the Netherlands', OECD Economics Department Working Paper no. 1527, OECD Publishing, Paris (https://doi.org/10.1787/da8bc5c4-en).

Baker, M. et al. (2018), 'To what extent do policies contribute to self-employment?' OECD Economics Department Working Paper no. 1512, OECD Publishing, Paris (https://doi.org/10.1787/74c044b1-en).

Bartelsman, E., Haltiwanger, J., and Scarpetta, S. (2009), 'Measuring and analyzing cross-country differences in firm dynamics', in T. Dunne, B. Jensen, and M. Roberts (eds), *Producer Dynamics: New Evidence from Micro Data*, University of Chicago Press, Chicago, pp. 000–000.

Borstlap Committee (2019), 'In wat voor land willen wij werken? Discussienota van de Commissie regulering van werk: over toekomstbestendig arbeidsrecht', sociale zekerheid en fiscaliteit, 20 June (https://www.rijksoverheid.nl/ binaries/rijksoverheid/documenten/rapporten/2019/06/20/discussienota-in-wat-voorland-willen-wij-werken/discussienota-in-wat-voorland-willen-wij-werken.pdf).

Bosch, N., Roelofs, G., van Vuuren, D., and Wilkens, M. (2012), 'De huidige en toekomstige groei van het aandeel zzp'ers in de toekomstige beroepsbevolking', CPB Background document.

CPB (2015), 'Position paper with regard to "IBO, self-employed without staff"', CPB Note, March 12, CPB Netherlands Bureau for Economic Policy Analysis, The Hague.

CPB (2018), 'Central Economic Plan 2018', SDU, The Hague.

De Kam, C. A. (2009), 'Belastingdruk van werknemers en zelfstandigen: globaal evenwicht?', *Weekblad Fiscaal Recht*, 2009/640.

Engbersen, G., Snel, E., and Kremer, M. (2017), *De val van de middenklasse? Het stabiele en kwetsbare midden*, WRR, The Hague.

Haltiwanger, J., Jasmin, R., and Miranda, J. (2013), 'Who creates jobs? Small versus large versus young', *Review of Economics and Statistics*, 95, 347–61.

Koolmees, W. (2019), 'Letter to the Lower House, 0000036153', Ministry of Social Affairs and Employment, The Hague.

Lisi, D. and Malo, M. (2017), 'The impact of temporary employment on productivity: the importance of sectors' skill intensity', *Journal of Labor Market Research*, 50, 91–112.

Milanez, A. and Brata, B. (2019), 'Taxation and the future of work: how tax systems influence choice of employment form', OECD Publishing, Paris.

Ministry of Finance (2015), 'IBO, self-employed without staff', Ministry of Finance, The Hague.

OECD (2019), 'Input to the Netherlands Independent Commission on the Regulation of Work', OECD Publishing, Paris.

SEO (2017), 'Evaluatie ondernemersregelingen', SEO report 2017–17, commissioned by the Ministry of Economic Affairs, Stichting Economisch Onderzoek, The Hague.

SEO (2018), 'Karakteristieken en tarieven van zzp'ers', SEO Report 2018–68, commissioned by Ministry of Social Affairs and Employment, Stichting Economisch Onderzoek, The Hague.

SER (2010), 'Zzp'ers in beeld: een integrale visie op zzp'ers', SER Advice 10/04, Social Economic Council, The Hague.

Stam, E., van der Veen, M., and Smetsers, D. (2019), 'Economische groei vraagt om meer dan zzp'ers', *ESB*, 104, 278–80.

van Dijkhuizen Committee (2012), 'Commissie inkomstenbelasting en toeslagen, Naar een activerender belastingstelsel', interim report, commissioned by the Ministry of Finance, The Hague (https://zoek.officielebekendmakingen.nl/blg-189,757.pdf).

van Dijkhuizen Committee (2013), 'Commissie inkomstenbelasting en toeslagen, Naar een activerender belastingstelsel', final report, commissioned by the Ministry of Finance, The Hague (https://www.mejudice.nl/docs/default-source/download/eindrapport.pdf).

van Weeghel, S. et al. (2010), 'Continuïteit en vernieuwing: een visie op het belastingstelsel', Ministry of Finance, The Hague.

Vording, H. (2004), 'Zelfstandigenaftrek: feiten, trends, en alternatieven', *Weekblad Fiscaal Recht*, 133(6560), 63–71.

17

Dutch Tax Policy Creates Heterogeneity in Tax Burdens

*Koen Caminada and Kees Goudswaard**

17.1 Introduction

Since the Dutch Income Tax Act 2001 (Wet inkomstenbelasting 2001) came into force, successive changes in policy, both small and large, have created a complex tax system. A multiplicity of schemes and exceptions has arisen over the years and so it is important to analyse in detail the system as a whole. In principle, there are two approaches to this. The first approach is to survey the range of tax measures that may have missed their target or have since proved to be ineffective (Caminada and Stevens, 2017a). The other approach, which we have adopted here, is to look at how the volume of schemes and policy changes now affect the distribution of tax and social security burdens across the population (see Caminada, Goudswaard, and Knoef, 2018). Income taxes, social security contributions, and allowances differ between people with different patterns of work, household composition, cohabitation patterns, preferences for raising children, and between rental and owner-occupied housing. The disadvantage of this policy, however, is that in many cases it infringes on the classical assumption that everyone can be asked to contribute to public funds in proportion to their ability to pay (the ability-to-pay principle).

Public discussion of a desirable distribution of the tax burden has a mainly normative nature and so it is important to conduct it on the basis of facts. In the Netherlands, administrative data are provided by the Statistics Netherlands (CBS, 2017) Income Panel Survey (IPO), making it possible to outline a good picture of trends in the distribution of the tax burden since the introduction of the Income Tax Act 2001. The IPO is a huge data set with extensive information on income, covering some 100,000 households (a sample of 280,000 people) in the Dutch

* Koen Caminada (c.l.j.caminada@law.leidenuniv.nl) is Professor of Empirical Analysis of Tax and Social Policy at Leiden University. Kees Goudswaard (k.p.goudswaard@law.leidenuniv.nl) is Professor of Applied Economics at Leiden University. This chapter spins a thread through recent team-based research, and we would like to acknowledge the co-authors (see the references), although they are not responsible for the text of this chapter. We would also like to thank Ed Groot, Monique Fasol, Bas Jacobs and Sijbren Cnossen for their valuable comments.

Koen Caminada and Kees Goudswaard, *Dutch Tax Policy Creates Heterogeneity in Tax Burdens* In: *Tax by Design for the Netherlands*. Edited by: Sijbren Cnossen and Bas Jacobs, Oxford University Press.
DOI: 10.1093/oso/9780192855244.003.0017

population. In this chapter, we use the IPO data to address the distribution of tax burdens over time across households, income levels, and socio-economic groups. This provides significant information for policymakers. We show that there is considerable heterogeneity in the burden of taxes on income between households, even those with the same gross income. These large differences arise from the fact that the government uses characteristics other than income to determine total taxes that are due. There may be good or less good reasons for this; we do not comment further on that. Our analysis is designed merely to provide insights into the differences in tax burden that are not a consequence of income; that is, where the government (deliberately or otherwise) departs from income as the measure for the ability to pay.

The analysis also shows that the fiscal redistribution mechanism has been running at full speed since the introduction of the Income Tax Act 2001 to more or less maintain the existing income distribution. We also show the extent to which the net disposable incomes of many Dutch households have been under pressure as a result of higher taxes and a multitude of tax measures since 2001. The income tax system has become ever more complex, and so calls for reform are growing louder. Following the reports of the van Weeghel Committee (van Weeghel et al., 2010) and the van Dijkhuizen Committee (2012, 2013), the government published its policy paper on options for an improved tax system (Ministry of Finance, 2014) and recently announced a new series of six studies (Ministry of Finance, 2019). The most recent revision was in 2001. It is now also possible to use the insights of the authoritative Mirrlees Review (Mirrlees et al., 2011). This review drew three main conclusions: consider the system as a whole, aim for neutrality and achieve redistribution as efficiently as possible. In this chapter, we make some suggestions for simplification that could contribute to reaching these aims.

17.2 Tax Instrumentalism

17.2.1 Developments since 2001

Table 17.1 shows that the income tax rates in the first two income brackets rose by 4.3 and 0.5 percentage points, respectively, between 2001 and 2019 (observing that the rate in the second bracket was reduced by 2.75 percentage points in 2019). This shift is a result of several small steps. Since the introduction of the Income Tax Act 2001, almost every household has received some concession. The table shows that the maximum rate of the earned income tax credit (*arbeidskorting*) has more than tripled since 2001, the elderly tax credit (*ouderenkorting*) is almost seven times higher and both entrepreneurs' facilities and financial support to families with children have been considerably enhanced. 'Tax instrumentalism'

Table 17.1 Selected income tax rates, credits, and other schemes

	2001	2019	Increase
First bracket rate	32.35%	36.65%	4.3 pp
Second bracket rate	37.60%	38.10%	0.5 pp
General tax credit (maximum)	€1,576	€2,477	57%
Employed person's tax credit (maximum)	€920	€3,399	269%
Elderly person's tax credit	€236	€1,596	576%
Small and medium-sized enterprises profit exemption	0%	14%	14 pp
Child benefit and supplementarytax credit[a]	€2,117		106%
Tax rebate for children[a]		€4,364	
Consumer price index	100.0	133.1	33.1%

Notes: [a] Two children aged between 6 and 11. Percentage point is abbreviated to pp.

Source: Dutch Tax Authorities.

has been on the rise; over time the government has steadily intensified the use of particular tax instruments and financed this by higher tax rates, so that specifically targeted groups of taxpayers have been granted tax advantages without reducing overall revenue for the treasury. Because almost everyone now receives a specific concession or tax advantage, the ultimate result is that tax rates have risen greatly, without major changes in the net income distribution. The most commonly used measure for income inequality, the Gini coefficient, has therefore remained virtually constant in recent years (Caminada, Goudswaard, and Been, 2017). However, the complexity of the system has steadily increased.

17.2.2 Tensions between Ambitions on Distribution and Other Policy Goals

The government reveals a high level of ambition with payroll and income taxes to achieve income redistribution and other policy goals. The principle for income redistribution is based on taxation according to ability to pay. However, policymakers also have the ambition to steer the income distribution with progressive taxes (and tax credits). Consequently, it is not possible to draw a sharp distinction between the part of the progressive rate structure based on the (presumed 'neutral') distribution principle and the instrumental part that serves income redistribution desired for policy purposes. Opinon still differs on this and it continues to be a central theme in the debate on fair taxation. Another problem when aiming for a fair income distribution is that the income definition for this is often not made explicit. Is individual income the main determinant or should policymakers focus on household income? The system is based on the notion of horizontal equity; all taxpayers that are equal in relevant circumstances should be taxed equally. However, the question of what are equal circumstances and what are not is still open to debate. Tax and social security contributions are levied largely on an individual basis (with a few exceptions, if there is a fiscal partner) but many benefits and allowances focus on the household.

Taxation is also made to serve other policy objectives, including labour market, family, housing, environmental and investment policies, and it involves the use of a range of tax instruments. Research by CPB Netherlands Bureau for Economic Policy Analysis (CPB) shows that generic tax stimuli have a limited effect on labour participation (Jongen, de Boer, and Dekker, 2015). To increase labour participation, therefore, it is more effective to focus tax credits and benefits on groups that are relatively responsive to these measures. The following tax instruments are among those introduced in recent years: income-dependent earned income tax credit, income-dependent combination tax credit, age-related employment bonus, income-dependent tax rebate for childcare and a reduction in the transferability of the general tax credit. The promotion of labour participation with tax incentives is reaching its limits. CPB research shows that the difference in burden between, say, single- and dual-earners, whose youngest child is aged between 0 and 3, has become inefficiently large (Jongen, de Boer, and Koot, 2018). The Netherlands Court of Audit (2017) concluded more generally that it is not clear whether a large number of tax facilities achieve their underlying policy objective or at what price. Also the question remains on the extent to which the instrumentalization of taxation has put the central principle of fair distribution of the tax burden under pressure.

17.3 Developments in the Burden of Tax and Social Security Contributions

17.3.1 Developments since 2001

Table 17.2 sets out the income inequality indices and the burden of tax and social security contributions in the period since the introduction of the Income Tax Act 2001. We assume that equivalized household income is the measure for the ability to pay. Equivalization means that household income is corrected for the size and decomposition of the household in order to make all incomes comparable. This is a convention in international empirical distribution research developed by the United Nations Canberra Group.

The system of taxes and social security contributions reduced income inequality by 20% in 2014 (measured by the Gini coefficient), while this had been 15% in 2001. When the Rutte–Asscher government made the general tax credit and the earned income tax credit income-dependent, this was done on purpose to reduce income differences. This involved considerable (disguised) additional tax burdens

Table 17.2 Income inequality: gross and disposable income (Gini coefficient) and redistribution via income taxes, 2001–14

	2001	2005	2010	2014	Change 2001–14
Income inequality					
Gini coefficient: gross standardized income	0.328	0.341	0.345	0.358	0.030
Minus redistribution through income taxes	0.050	0.060	0.066	0.072	0.022
Gini coefficient: standardized disposable income	0.278	0.281	0.279	0.286	0.008
Percentage redistribution	15%	18%	19%	20%	5 pp
Burden of income taxes					
Income taxes as a percentage of gross income	38.8%	41.0%	40.8%	41.3%	2.5 pp
income insurance premiums	20.0%	21.7%	19.1%	18.5%	-1.5 pp
healthcare insurance premiums	9.1%	10.2%	11.0%	11.7%	2.6 pp
taxes on income and capital	9.5%	8.9%	10.5%	11.0%	1.4 pp
Real average disposable household income	€35,000	€34,400	€36,000	€35,000	€0

Notes: Gross income consists of income from labour and income from self-employment and capital, income insurance benefits (related to unemployment, illness and occupational disability, age, and dependants), social assistance provisions and certain related transfers and alimony. Average disposable household income is corrected for inflation (CPI 2001–14 = 1.272).

Source: Authors' calculations using Statistics Netherlands IPO and Statline.

on those with middle and higher incomes: the reduction of the general tax credit raised an extra 5.9 billion euros for the treasury in 2016 (Caminada and Stevens, 2017a).

Policymakers have had to redistribute more income over time to maintain existing income inequality, raising the question of what role income taxation plays in this. Consequently, Table 17.2 shows the level and development in the burden of taxes on income since the introduction of the Income Tax Act 2001. For our research, applying the broad definition of income taxes used by Statistics Netherlands, we took the difference between gross and disposable household income as the tax on income. The starting point is gross income, which consists of income from labour and income from self-employment and capital, income insurance benefits (related to unemployment, illness, occupational disability, age, and dependants), social assistance provisions and certain related transfers, such as housing benefit. Taxes on income comprise taxes on income and capital, employees' social security, and national insurance contributions (including supplementary pensions) and premiums for healthcare insurance—that is, nominal premiums plus the income-related contribution under the Healthcare Insurance

Act (*Zorgverzekeringswet*) less healthcare allowances claimed. Contributions for social security and pensions include both the employer's and employee's portions. Table 17.2 shows the total amount of income taxes as a percentage of gross household income.

The average burden of taxes and social contributions was 41.3% in 2014, which is substantially higher than it was in 2001 (38.8%). Clearly, healthcare financing in particular has left its mark, resulting in a 2.6 percentage point higher burden from premiums. Taxes on income and capital were substantially higher in 2014 than in 2001. There are different trends in income insurance premiums: premiums for disability insurance have fallen, while pension contributions have risen.

Finally, the table shows that it has taken years to get out of the 2008 financial crisis. Real average disposable household income has been calculated (in 2014 euros) using data from Statistics Netherlands. Nominal disposable income at current prices has been corrected for inflation using the consumer price index (CPI) from Statistics Netherlands. Average real disposable household income in 2014 was 35,000 euros, while net disposable income of an average household in the Netherlands in 2001 was also 35,000 euros. In the period 2001–14, average net disposable income fell year-on-year no less than nine times; it rose only in 2004, 2006, and 2007, and not again until 2014. Tax policy has proven to have significant influence on the development of disposable household income.

17.3.2 Tax Burdens by Group

Averages rarely say much about the situation of individual taxpayers and so we present groups that differ in size and level of average gross household income. For clarity, initially we only present group averages. It is relevant to note that these households have different background features and this may significantly influence the measured tax burdens. Composition of the groups may also have changed between 2001 and 2014.

Table 17.3 shows that there is considerable variation in average tax burdens. All identified groups had a substantially higher burden in 2014 than in 2001 but the change differed strongly between groups. Employees, for example, suffered a relatively large increase in their tax burden while entrepreneurs enjoyed a fall. Multi-person households incurred a greater than average increase in burden and single-person households a less than average increase. Notably, single-parent families with children under 18 faced the greatest increase in their total tax burden.

Changes in disposable income arise both from changes in gross income (the red bars in Figure 17.1) and a variety of income taxes deducted from gross income (the grey bars in Figure 17.1). The black bar presents the net effect. Movements in net disposable income could be positive or negative.

Table 17.3 Average household income and burden of income tax and social security contributions (2001 and 2014)

	2014 No. of households (×1,000)	2014 Gross income (×1,000 euros)	2014 Disposable income (%)	2014 Tax burden (%)	2011 Tax burden (%)	2001–14 Change in tax burden (pp)
Total	7,557	59.6	35.0	41.3	38.8	2.5
Single person	2,774	32.0	19.9	37.8	36.0	1.8
Multi-person	4,783	75.6	43.7	42.2	39.3	2.9
Single parent	526	45.2	28.8	36.3	32.3	4.0
Single parent, children aged < 18	283	36.8	24.4	33.7	28.6	5.1
Single parent, children aged > 18	242	55.0	34.0	38.2	35.0	3.2
Couple aged < 65, no children	1,235	80.0	42.9	46.4	42.4	4.0
Couple aged > 65, no children	1,306	89.2	49.0	45.1	42.1	3.0
Couple, children aged < 18	670	101.0	56.9	43.7	40.2	3.5
Couple, at least one child aged >18	913	48.0	35.3	26.5	21.5	4.9
Single man, aged > 65	255	30.7	23.1	24.8	21.5	3.3
Single woman, aged > 65	651	25.5	20.4	20.0	18.8	1.2
Single man, aged < 65	1,056	37.1	20.5	44.7	43.1	1.6
Single woman, aged < 65	813	30.9	17.6	43.0	38.8	4.2
Wage employees	3,153	71.4	37.9	46.9	43.0	4.0
Wage civil servants	500	85.8	42.7	50.2	44.4	5.9
Self-employed	948	81.0	51.3	36.7	37.0	-0.3
Social transfers	2,813	32.7	23.8	27.2	24.3	2.9

Source: Authors' calculations using Statistics Netherlands Statline.

Figure 17.1 shows the full effect of Dutch redistribution efforts via income taxes. Averaged over all individual groups, the increase in gross income in the period from 2001 to 2014 created 7.2 percentage points of additional net disposable income. However, against this, there was a negative effect of much higher

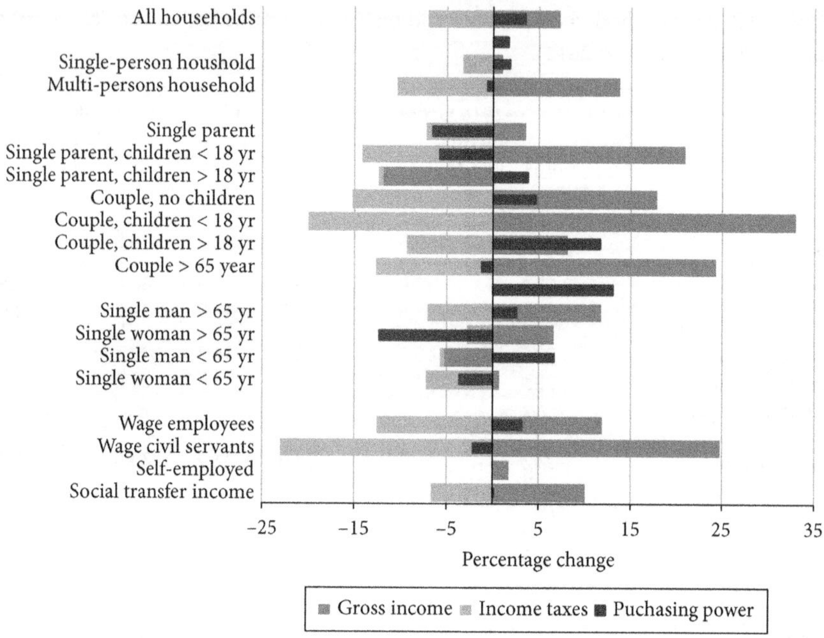

Figure 17.1 Decomposition of movements in net disposable income for groups of households (2001–14)

Source: Authors' calculations using Statistics Netherlands Statline.

income taxes: on average, net disposable incomes were eroded by 7.1 percentage points. As a result, the net disposable income of an average household in the Netherlands in 2014 was, on balance, exactly where it had been in 2001.

A further thing to note is that, on average, taxes on income and capital were substantially higher in 2014 than in 2001 (see Table 17.3) for virtually all groups except entrepreneurs. This is evidently the result of a combination of lower average gross income because of the financial crisis and a tax policy that aimed to spare the self-employed. Single people (aged under 65) saw a fall of about 6% in net disposable income. However, older people and households with young children saw an improvement. This applied to both couples and single-parent families. It should be noted that net disposable income for older people is influenced by cohort effects: on average, new pensioners have a higher pension income. Tax incentives for labour participation have led to a relatively large increase in gross income for households with young children as a result of increased participation and young mothers opting to work more hours part-time.

Since 2001, therefore, the government has had to take extensive measures to redress changes in gross income so that, in the end, policymakers could achieve a distribution of disposable income that they regarded as 'equitable'.

17.4 Large Dispersion of the Tax Burdens by Income

Figure 17.2 presents the distribution of the burden of income taxes, ranking households into one hundred 1% groups (percentiles) based on their standardized gross income. The distribution of tax burdens shows a remarkably varied pattern, including at the top of the income distribution. The average tax burden rises as gross household income rises, in accordance with the ability-to-pay principle. The median burden in the range between 20,000 and 30,000 euros is a little lower as a result of a relatively high concentration of older people, who, in relation their income, are taxed less. The solid black line shows the median. There is considerable dispersion around the median. The dispersion of the tax burden is shown in

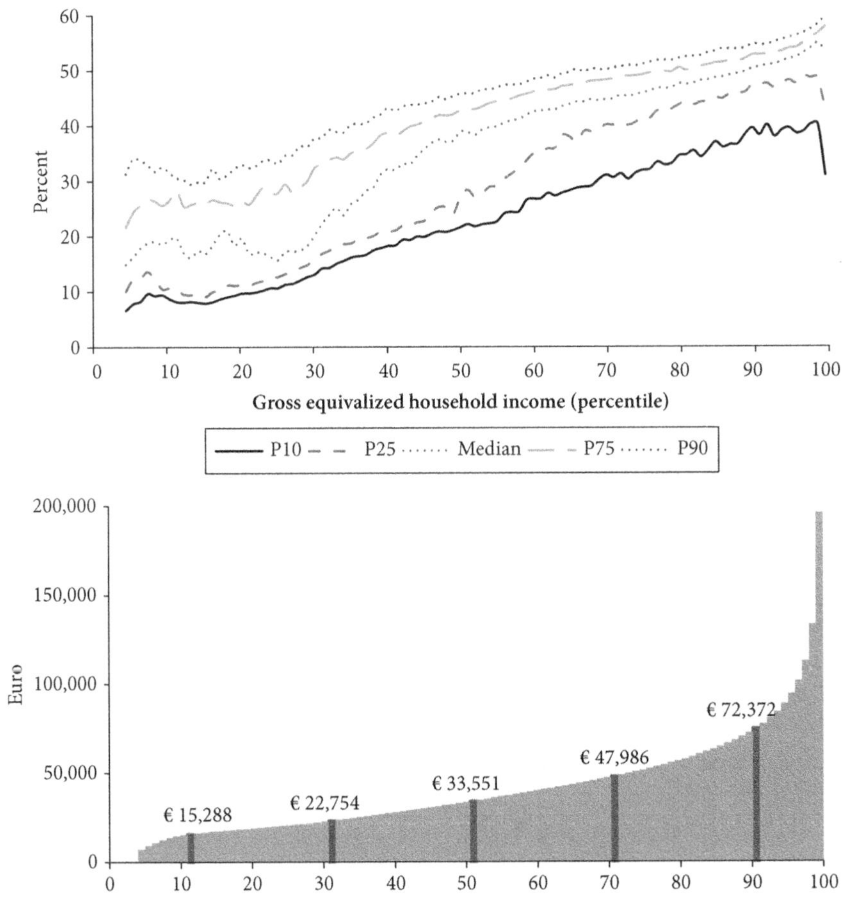

Figure 17.2 Distribution of tax burdens (top panel) and income level per percentile (bottom panel) (2014)

Source: Statistics Netherlands, IPO 2014; authors' calculations.

the five lines in the chart. The vertical axis indicates the extent to which households with a similar income position (approximated by different income percentiles) face similar taxes. Take households in the 50th percentile with a standardized gross income of 33,551 euros and a median tax burden of 39%. In this percentile, 10% of the households face a tax burden of 22% or less (p10) while 10% face a burden of 46% or more (p90). For the same gross income, therefore, there is a dispersion of income taxes to be paid of no less than 8,113 euros (46% minus 22% of 33,551 euros).

Among the 10% of households with the highest income, the median tax burden is 50%, but this ranges between 40% (p10) and 55% (p90). Furthermore, the Statistics Netherlands data show that even among the top 1% of households with the highest income, no less than 10% have a tax burden of less than 31%. However, a considerable proportion of high earners pay more than half of gross household income in income taxes. This major dispersion means that the distribution of the tax burdens is out of line with the ability-to-pay principle for many households.

An identical analysis for 2001 (at the time of the introduction of the Income Tax Act 2001) and an analysis of the differences for the period from 2001 to 2014 show that the heterogeneity of tax burdens has increased, especially at the lower end of the income distribution (see Caminada et al., 2018). Part of the increased dispersion can be explained by the fact that society has become more heterogeneous (e.g. distribution of work between partners, cohabitation patterns, increase in the number of self-employed people) and part by tax policy. Our reading of the data is that there has only been limited greater heterogeneity in the income dimension since 2001, and so the greatest part of the increase in heterogeneity in the tax burden since 2001 can be attributed to tax policy.

17.5 Developments since 2001

Figure 17.3 shows the causes of the increase in the tax burden discussed above, differentiating by percentile of equivalized gross household income. In principle, three channels can change the tax burden for a household: gross income changes so that more euros of income taxes have to be paid (assuming an unchanged average tax burden), the change in income taxes as a result of progressive rates, and the change in the burden as a result of policy. Figure 17.3 clarifies this breakdown (all values have been adjusted for inflation: CPI 2001–14 = 1.272). Finally, the change in gross income per percentile is shown for the period 2001–14.

About two-thirds of all households faced higher taxes. Those with the lowest and higher incomes saw an above-average increase, although successive governments have tried, somewhat, to protect households between the 25th and 50th percentiles. Part of the change in taxes between 2001 and 2014 can be explained by

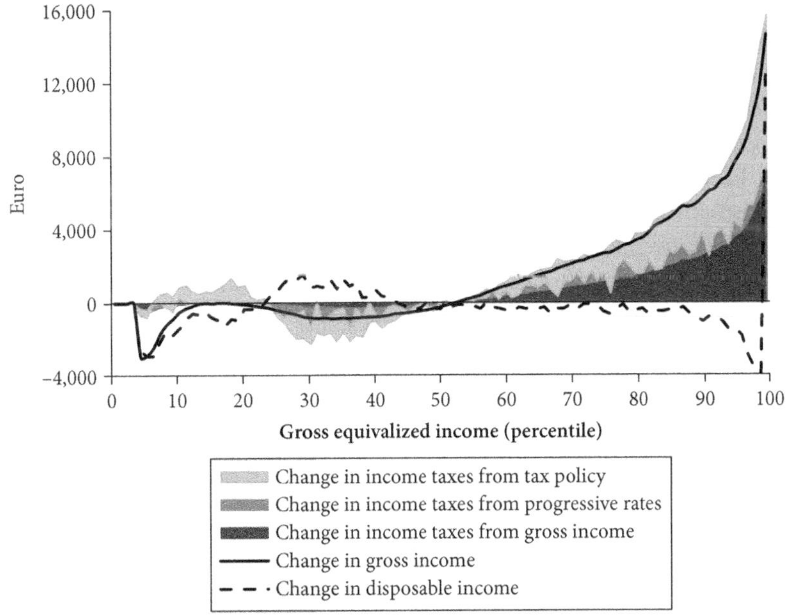

Figure 17.3 Causes of changes in income taxes 2001–14 by percentile, in 2014 euros
Source: Statistics Netherlands, IPO 2001 and IPO 2014; authors' calculations.

movements in relative income. On average, developments in gross income have been relatively favourable for higher income groups, who, partly as a result, experienced a relatively large increase in taxes. Further analysis of the causes of the change in taxes (in euros) in the period 2001–14 shows that about 42% can be attributed to the increases and changes in gross income. Further to this, progressive rates have also contributed to generally higher taxes for households. Policy measures can explain about 54% of the increase in taxes.

Finally, if we compare the percentile distributions, there was very rarely an increase in real net disposable income; in fact, the opposite. On balance, net disposable income was lower for many Dutch households in 2014 than in 2001 (leaving aside the fact that households can move up the income distribution). The vast majority of households have faced higher taxes (lower net disposable income) since 2001.

17.6 Opportunities for Simplification

The Dutch tax system can best be described as an attic that no one wants to tidy up because everyone likes part of the mess. The system has many revenue-reducing regulations (tax deductions, exemptions, and tax credits) alongside a system of tax rebates that is used by 4.5 million households each year. Tax rates are consequently estimated to be 80% higher than they would be without those tax provisions (Caminada and Ros, 2012, p. 164). Fewer tax concessions and base broadening in exchange for lower rates would be appropriate. Consideration could be given to ending 'tax instrumentalism', where all tax provisions that have been introduced since 2001 are phased out again. The reason for this policy recommendation lies in the empirical finding that the distribution of disposable income in 2014 was virtually the same as in 2001, albeit with many more tax instruments in place in 2014 and involving larger amounts. The solution, therefore, is a return to a situation with substantially fewer transfers of money between citizens and government. Naturally, the specific design of the phase out is relevant here. In this context, reference can be made to quantitative analyses and recommendations in that direction, such as the reports of the van Dijkhuizen Committee (2012, 2013), Caminada and Stevens (2017a, 2017b), and Caminada (2015).[1] The van Dijkhuizen Committee saw opportunities to limit deductions and to streamline and simplify tax rebates by introducing a single household tax rebate, thus reducing the number of those entitled to a rebate so that the system (including checks and audits) can focus on fewer households. The Committee also saw opportunities for shifting part of the tax rebates to the healthcare insurer as a way of reducing transfers between the tax authorities, citizens, and insurers.

The phase out of tax provisions and rebates in an exchange for a rate reduction would shorten the fiscal balance sheet for both the government and families. The aim of the reforms should be to arrive at a simpler and more neutral system that puts a priority on lower rates on income from employment. Efforts could then be made on reducing rate-arbitrage and shortening balance sheets, as a result of which the Dutch economy would be less volatile (fewer tax rebates for housing and more restraint in tax credits and rebates) and lower rates could be placed on income from employment. To make this more concrete, Caminada and Stevens (2017b) proposed a tax package in which 34.4 billion euros would be freed up by broadening the tax base and dropping ineffective instruments, the majority of which could be used for reducing rates (see also Caminada, 2015). With this approach, a basic rate (including income-related healthcare insurance premiums) could be set at 33.8%, with a top rate of 43.8% for incomes above 55,000 euros. About 10% of taxpayers with the highest income would face this higher rate and so there would be a flat rate tax of 33.8% for the vast majority of taxpayers. For comparison with the current system, without the measures to free up the 34.4 billion euros for rate reduction, the basic rate (including healthcare insurance premiums) would be 46.3% and the top rate 56.3%. Across the board, the marginal

[1] See also Ministry of Finance (2014).

rate line is 12.5 percentage points lower, making all kinds of arbitrage opportunities less rewarding. This would imply a big step in the direction of restoring a global balance in taxation of various income flows. If other objectives, such as aiming for a fair income distribution, are ignored, employment would substantially be enhanced by the lower rates. Their estimate is that an increase in participation of 120,000 full-time equivalent employees is feasible.

17.7 Conclusion

In this chapter, we have identified the distribution of the burden of income tax and social security contributions and redistribution efforts through tax policy in the Netherlands. We have shown that since 2001 the government has had to take extensive measures to redress changes in gross income so that, in the end, a policy-based disposable income picture regarded as 'equitable' could be achieved. On balance, the net disposable income of many groups was lower in 2014 than in 2001. Much higher income taxes, in particular, have eroded net disposable income.

Tax policy has brought about significant differences in the burden of income taxes between households with different compositions and different income shares of partners, and between socio-economic groups. There are considerable differences in tax burden between households, even those with the same gross income. Among households with the same modal income, 10% of them face a tax burden of 22% or less while 10% face a burden of 46% or more. Differences between high and low income groups are also considerable. The outcome is, for example, that a small proportion of households with the very highest incomes have a similar tax burden as some in the bottom half of the income distribution. Further analysis shows that the dispersion of tax burdens since the last major tax reform in 2001 has increased. This applies to dispersion both between and within income groups. The government applies ample discrimination in income tax and social regulations on differences in working pattern (single- and dual-earners, self-employed), household composition (with or without children), cohabitation patterns (singles, cohabitees), and preferences for raising children (childcare or not), and between rental and owner-occupied housing.

The ability-to-pay principle demands that households with the same ability to pay are taxed the same and that households with greater ability to pay are taxed more heavily. It seems that it is becoming gradually more difficult to align the distribution of tax burdens from taxes on income in the Netherlands with the ability-to-pay principle. This has mainly to do with the use of tax and social security contribution instruments for other policy objectives. The government has regularly explicitly said that achieving socio-economic objectives prevails over theoretical notions on the tax structure. However, the effectiveness of taxation as an instrument to achieve policy goals is in many cases doubtful. There are ever more indications that the income tax system has become deadlocked as a result. Therefore, it would be good if sufficient support arose for an income tax reform that could resolve taboos, simplify complicated (income-related) regulations, and strengthen weak enforcement.

There are good reasons to progressively abandon 'tax instrumentalism'—the ever greater reliance on special tax provisions—since 2001. The main reason is our finding that the distribution of income in 2001 was virtually the same as in 2014, albeit with many more tax instruments in place in 2014 and involving larger amounts. Therefore, the solution is to return to a situation with substantially fewer transfers of money between citizens and government. In exchange for cutting rates, deductions could be limited and tax rebates streamlined and simplified, cutting the number of beneficiaries. With fewer transfers, the system (including checks and audits) can focus better on fewer households.

References

Caminada, K. (2015), 'De tragiek van gefaalde ambities en gemiste kansen rond belastinghervorming', *Me Judice*, 23 September.

Caminada, K. and Ros, A. P. (2012), 'Belastingfaciliteiten', in C. de Kam and J. Donders (eds), *Jaarboek Overheidsfinanciën 2012*, Sdu Uitgevers, The Hague, pp. 157–82.

Caminada, K. and Stevens, L. G. M. (2017a), 'Instrumenteel fiscaal beleid: oorzaak van complexiteit en scheefgroei', *Weekblad Fiscaal Recht*, 7181, 307–26.

Caminada, K. and Stevens, L. G. M. (2017b), 'Blauwdruk voor belastinghervorming', *Weekblad Fiscaal Recht*, 7191, 632–46.

Caminada, K., Goudswaard, K., and Been, J. (2017), 'Neemt de inkomensongelijkheid in Nederland toe?', in K. Chkalova, J. van Genabeek, J. Sanders, and W. Smits (eds), *Dynamiek op de Nederlandse arbeidsmarkt: de focus op ongelijkheid*, CBS/TNO: 85–10, The Hague, pp. 85–100.

Caminada, K., Goudswaard, K. P., and Knoef, M. G. (2018), 'Toenemende spreiding in de drukverdeling van inkomensheffingen', *Weekblad Fiscaal Recht*, 7256, 1245–53.

Jongen, E., de Boer, H.-W., and Dekker, P. (2015), 'De effectiviteit van fiscaal participatiebeleid', CPB Policy Brief 2015-02, The Hague.

Jongen, E., de Boer, H.-W., and Koot, P. (2018), 'Eenverdieners onder druk', CPB Policy Brief 2018/03, The Hague.

Ministry of Finance (2014), 'Keuzes voor een beter belastingstelsel, Tweede Kamer der Staten-Generaal', The Hague (https://www.rijksoverheid.nl/ documenten/kamerstukken/2014/09/16/kamerbrief-keuzes-voor-een-beter-belastingstelsel).

Ministry of Finance (2019), 'Bouwstenen voor een beter belastingstelsel', Tweede Kamer der Staten-Generaal, The Hague (https://www.rijksoverheid.nl/ documenten/

kamerstukken/2019/04/15/kamerbrief-tweede-kamer-bouwstenen-voor-een-beter-belastingstelsel).

Mirrlees, J., Adam, S., Besley, T., Blundell, R., Bond, S., Chote, R., Gammie, M., Johnson, P., Myles, G., and Poterba, J. (2011), *Tax by Design: The Mirrlees Review*, Oxford University Press, Oxford.

Statistics Netherlands (CBS) (2017), 'Inkomensstatistiek: herziene cijfers' (https://www.cbs.nl/nl-nl/nieuws/2017/37/inkomensongelijkheid-en-herverdeling-2001-2015).

The Netherlands Court of Audit (2017), 'Zicht op belastingverlichtende regelingen' (https://www.rekenkamer.nl/publicaties/rapporten/2017/02/01/zicht-op-belasting verlichtende-regelingen).

van Dijkhuizen Committee (2012), 'Commissie inkomstenbelasting en toeslagen, Naar een activerender belastingstelsel', interim report, commissioned by the Ministry of Finance, The Hague (https://zoek.officielebekendmakingen.nl/blg-189,757.pdf).

van Dijkhuizen Committee (2013), 'Commissie inkomstenbelasting en toeslagen, Naar een activerender belastingstelsel', final report, commissioned by the Ministry of Finance, The Hague (https://www.mejudice.nl/docs/default-source/download/eindrapport.pdf).

van Weeghel, S. et al. (2010), 'Continuïteit en vernieuwing: een visie op het belastingstelsel', Ministry of Finance, The Hague.

PART V

CLIMATE AND MOBILITY

18

Climate Policy

Challenges and Obstacles

*Rick van der Ploeg**

18.1 Introduction

At the 2015 United Nations Climate Change Conference (COP 21) in Paris, 194 countries from across the globe committed themselves to the Paris Agreement, a global agreement signed in 2016 to limit global warming to no more than 2°C and to strive for 1.5°C above pre-industrial temperatures. Climate scientists attach great importance to these targets, as these limit the risk of a cascade of tipping points related to the collapse of the Gulf Stream, the melting of the Greenland or Antarctic Ice Caps or the unleashing of nasty positive feedback effects (e.g. the albedo effect or the reduced absorption capacity of the oceans). Thereby, the risk of moving in the direction of a 'Hothouse Earth' is lessened (Steffen et al., 2018). To make sure these targets are met, emissions of carbon have to be cut drastically and, eventually, these need to be cut completely. A two-thirds chance of meeting the 2°C target means that the world as a whole cannot emit more than 600–1100 Giga tonnes of CO_2 ($GtCO_2$) from now on. A cap of 1.5°C requires maximum cumulative emissions of 150–300 $GtCO_2$ (Aengenheyster et al., 2018). This is called the global carbon budget and it is the key factor in determining climate policy. If the world does not cut emissions, then from 2018 onwards the carbon budget will run out in 18–33 years for the 2°C target and in 5–9 years for the 1.5°C target. Hence, there is very little time left before it will no longer be feasible to meet the Paris targets, unless nuclear energy is used to substitute for fossil fuel or unorthodox policies such as geo-engineering are relied on to realize negative carbon emissions. In any case, it is necessary to use bio-based fuel combined with capture and sequestration of at least 90% of the carbon that is emitted, whilst

* Rick van der Ploeg (rick.vanderploeg@economics.ox.ac.uk) is Professor of Economics at the University of Oxford and Adjunct University Professor of Environmental Economics at the University of Amsterdam. This article is an updated and extended version of 'Obstacles to Climate Policy', which was originally published in *The Environmental Scientist*, 9–13 August, 2018. I thank my discussant Herman Vollebergh for constructive comments, and Sijbren Cnossen and Bas Jacobs for their detailed suggestions for improvement.

Rick van der Ploeg, *Climate Policy: Challenges and Obstacles* In: *Tax by Design for the Netherlands.* Edited by: Sijbren Cnossen and Bas Jacobs, Oxford University Press.
DOI: 10.1093/oso/9780192855244.003.0018

the realistic potential of such measures has so far been very modest (Strengers et al., 2018). Running existing coal-powered electricity stations to the end of their normal economic lifetime is enough to overshoot the Paris targets (Pfeiffer et al., 2016). Hence, very ambitious climate policies must be pursued by all countries in order to meet the Paris targets. This will involve painful measures such as scrapping assets that have not been able to fully earn back their investments and last-resort methods to ensure negative emissions such as geo-engineering.

18.2 The Golden Rule: Price the Emissions of Carbon

The best method to achieve such a drastic reduction in emissions is to price carbon. This can be done by committing in advance to a rising path of carbon taxes. Finland, Norway, Sweden, Switzerland, and the United Kingdom have already done this. Alternatively, this can be done via a competitive market for tradable permission permits. The best known is perhaps the European Union (EU) Emissions Trading Scheme (ETS), but in other parts of the world (especially China) these schemes are being introduced more and more. Trading of permits ensures that reduction takes place in those sectors and countries where this can be done in the most cost-effective way (i.e. in a way that minimizes the cost per saved tonne of emitted carbon). The disadvantage of permit markets is that the price can be volatile over time, and thus the signal for industry and households to transition to carbon-free production and consumption is less strong. Since the global financial crisis, the ETS has introduced stability reserves, so that permits are bought up when the price is too low. This has led to an increase in the market price of ETS permits.

The problem with a carbon tax is that policymakers do not know exactly how high the tax should be in order to realize the desired reduction in emissions. It is therefore attractive to combine the best of both by announcing and committing to a rising time path for the CO_2 price, and topping up the ETS price with carbon taxes if the ETS price is below this path. As the budget for cumulative emissions becomes exhausted and permissible emissions are scarcer, the price of emissions has to rise over time. The United Kingdom has done this since 2018, and has said it will continue this after Brexit. This gives clarity and certainty for the longer term, so that businesses can take account of this when they switch from a carbon-intensive to a carbon-extensive production structure.

How high should the carbon price be? Most economists answer this question by equating the price to the Pigouvian tax, namely the expected present discounted value of all current and future marginal damages to production resulting from emitting one tonne of carbon today (also known as the social cost of carbon). Because these damages are highly uncertain and temperature is very difficult to predict, and because they have to be discounted over a very long horizon at a rate that is subject to huge discussions, climate scientists and the Intergovernmental Panel for Climate Change (IPCC), instead of maximizing welfare, choose a time path for the carbon price that ensures that the temperature caps are realized at minimal economic costs. The carbon price at the end of the fossil-fuel era is then determined by the costs of total decarbonization of the economy. The carbon price before the end of this era has to grow at a rate equal to a rate that equals the rate of interest. This reflects the increasing scarcity of permitted emissions as the carbon budget for cumulative emissions becomes exhausted.

The initial price in 2020 could be at least 40–80 euros per tonne of CO_2 and, from then onwards, it could grow steeply at a rate of 3.75% per annum, excluding the inflation correction. This is the interest rate that is corrected for the uncertainties regarding growth of emissions and the reduction of the cost of renewable energy (Gollier, 2019). According to a recent report under the chairmanship of the Nobel Prize winner Joe Stiglitz and Lord Nicholas Stern, such a carbon price path is necessary to meet the Paris targets. This rapidly rising carbon price is necessary for a cap of 2°C. The initial price would need to be much higher for a cap of 1.5°C.

The alternative Pigouvian approach leads to a carbon price that grows slower than the price necessary to implement a temperature cap; that is, a rate of growth that corresponds to the growth rate of the economy (i.e. 2% per year excluding the inflation correction) instead of a rate that equals the interest rate. A combination of the Pigouvian approach and the temperature cap approach leads to a carbon price path that grows at a rate that lies between the growth rate of the economy and the interest rate (van der Ploeg, 2018).

Pricing carbon helps the transition to the carbon-free era in many ways. It curbs demand for fossil-fuel energy, it encourages substitution from carbon-intensive coal to less carbon-intensive oil and gas, it stimulates green innovation and the move towards a circular economy, it makes carbon capture and sequestration economically attractive, and it forces fossil-fuel companies such as BP, Shell, Chevron, and ExxonMobil, as well as oil-, gas-, and oil-rich nations, to lock more fossil fuel in the earth. Also, climate policy has the collateral benefit of improving air quality in cities and saving many early deaths, especially of schoolchildren near busy roads (e.g. Mayrhofer and Gupta, 2016). China shows that such collateral benefits of climate policy are an important catalyst for eliminating diesel-powered modes of transport and for climate policy more generally. The reason for this is that these collateral benefits are locally visible, whilst the direct costs of global warming affect the whole of humanity and concern a global externality. Collateral benefits weaken the free-rider problems in international climate policy.

18.3 Take Climate Sceptics Seriously, but Price Carbon Emissions

One of the biggest obstacles to a successful climate policy is the rise of populism and climate scepticism. The respected Environmental Protection Agency was founded in 1970 by President Nixon, but President Trump has appointed climate denier Scott Pruitt as director. Pruitt denies the scientific consensus that carbon emissions caused by humans are a major contributor to global warming. Furthermore, President Trump has pulled out of the Paris Agreement, and has reversed the emission-reduction measures for coal-fired power stations introduced by President Obama. It is not clear whether populists such as President Trump really believe, despite all the scientific views and evidence, that climate scientists are wrong in believing that the huge rise in carbon emissions since the beginning of the industrial revolution has had no effect on global warming, or whether their scepticism is driven by the coal lobbies.

However, it does not matter much whether climate sceptics are taken seriously or not. Imagine that there is a 10% chance that climate sceptics are right and that climate scientists are wrong. The optimal carbon price is then hardly reduced (Rezai and van der Ploeg, 2017). Also, if policymakers follow the max–min principle of maximizing outcomes under the worst possible scenario for climate change, then they still want to vigorously price carbon. The reason for this is that the welfare costs of unnecessarily pricing carbon if the sceptics are right are modest (especially if the revenues are handed back to households and/or firms in the form of lower income or corporation taxes). However, the welfare costs of not pricing carbon emissions are huge if the climate scientists are right and temperatures rise to 4°C or more above the temperatures recorded at the beginning of the industrial revolution.

18.4 Make Sure That the Costs of Reducing Each Tonne of Carbon Are the Same Everywhere

To make sure that the transition to the carbon-free era is done most efficiently, it is crucial that the price of carbon—and thus the cost per saved tonne of carbon—is the same throughout the world. Businesses and consumers can then compare the costs per abated tonne of carbon with the benefits from doing that (i.e. the emission charge they no longer have to pay). By allowing trade in carbon permits, some countries that can obtain a lot of extra output per unit of carbon emitted (e.g. the cement industry) can buy permits from countries that can reduce emissions more efficiently (e.g. forests in Bohemia or in the Amazon). Thus, from a global perspective, emission reductions are done in a more cost-effective manner. Many poorer countries are not eager to introduce such a carbon price or a fast transition from a coal-based economy to one that relies on solar, wind, and water energy. The success of an international climate agreement thus depends on persuading poorer countries to agree to one global price for carbon emissions, with rich countries transferring funds to poorer countries (and to compensate for past emissions in rich countries). However, despite three decades of summits, such transfers have hardly been forthcoming. The reason for this is the same as the reason why countries are unable to price carbon properly: global collective actions are required to redistribute incomes across countries as well as to internalize external effects due to global warming.

For efficient reductions in emissions, the cost per saved tonne of carbon must also be the same across all sectors for the economy. The price of carbon emissions must thus be the same in the steel industry, transport and construction sectors, in horticulture, agriculture, and in individual households. The EU market for permits ensures this automatically because allowing parties to trade on this market until the price of a permit is the same everywhere leads to the most cost-effective way of abating carbon. Companies that can cut emissions relatively cheaply will sell their permits to companies that can abate less easily but have the highest added value per tonne of emitted carbon. For carbon taxes and for the large variety of subsidies to cut emissions, this does not happen automatically.

In practice, the implied costs per abated tonne of carbon vary hugely, which is inefficient. The reason for this is the piecemeal approach adopted by policymakers. It is also explained, for example, by the fact that a lobby to keep a steel plant open is stronger and more concentrated than the one to eliminate gas from all residential homes. Furthermore, the cost per abated tonne of carbon must be the same for different climate policies, but this is rarely the case.

Abatement is not achieved in a cost-effective manner if there are all kinds of exceptions, which imply that, in practice, mainly households and small enterprises pay for emissions. The reason for this is that the lobby to keep open a steel factory is stronger and more concentrated than, for example, the lobby to encourage people to change from using gas to using heat pumps. It is also desirable that shipping and airlines start to pay as soon as possible for the emissions of carbon and other dangerous substances.

18.5 Dangers with the Proposed Climate Agreement for the Netherlands

Typically, policymakers prefer the carrot to the stick. They do not like taxes or pricing carbon and prefer subsidies to stop using fossil fuel or to encourage the use of renewable energy, even though subsidies are an expensive way to abate carbon—witness the huge solar subsidies in German power generation. We have seen this in the Netherlands with the 'Climate Tables' for negotiating climate reductions. These were introduced by the Dutch Minister of Economic Affairs and Climate Policy, Eric Wiebes. They were divided up into a general table for climate policy and separate tables for the economic sectors: manufacturing, mobility, construction, electricity, and agriculture and land use. Following good Dutch practice, the biggest polluters in each sector were sitting at the same table as other stakeholders such as the trade union movement, the municipalities, the provinces, and the lobby for car manufacturers. To compensate for this, green lobbies such as Greenpeace and Nature and Environment were added to the Climate Tables, although some of them walked away at a later stage. Plans were negotiated to curb emissions with the required amounts, as instructed by the Minister, but the costs of abating one tonne of carbon seemed to be of less importance. As a result, the costs per abated tonne of carbon varied enormously by sector, by table, and by particular policy measure. For example, the cost of cutting the costs of emitting one tonne of CO_2 through subsidies for electrical cars (mostly Tesla cars) was almost 2,000 euros. Van der Meijden and Siegman (2018) calculated that the cost of cutting emissions per table varied from 22 euros for agriculture, to 67 euros for industry, to 70–124 euros for the electricity sector and to 135 euros for construction per abated tonne of CO_2. However, these costs can be much higher for individual policy measures.

CPB Netherlands Bureau for Economic Policy Analysis suggests that government spending will rise by 4.4 billion euros in 2030 including planned additional expenditures on various infrastructure funds. As a result, taxes will rise by 5.3 billion euros in 2030, of which 3 billion euros will have to be paid by households and 2 billion euros by corporations (CPB, 2019). This leads to a reduction in disposable income of 1.3% in 2030 compared with 2018. It is not quite clear yet who will pay for the costs of these plans, but ordinary families will end up paying a substantial share of the bill. Economic sectors, such as the steel industry, do not want to shrink, so they lobby for carbon capture and sequestration, and they demand big subsidies from the government.

The resulting climate plans turn out to be insufficiently ambitious as they imply that the speed of curbing emissions is too slow. Probably, this is the result of the following: expectations being too high during the negotiations; lobbies of existing polluters that try not to change their business practices and do not want to carry the bill for the energy transition; and inefficient policies to cut emissions. It is therefore essential for the government to give clarity by announcing a gradually rising carbon price and committing to it instead of procrastinating on it. It is much better to price carbon vigorously than to hand out all kinds of subsidies that are inefficient and invite all types of rent-seeking. Every effort must be undertaken to ensure that the costs per abated tonne of carbon, after taking into account potential carbon leakage, is the same for each sector and for each type of policy measure. If these costs differ too much, then it will be clear that money is wasted.

This is what happened for the huge subsidies given to solar energy in the electricity sector in Germany, which were many factors higher than the recommended price of carbon emissions. It is much better to price carbon and to leave the hard economic decisions on the basis of the new green reality to business corporations, not to the government.

18.6 Stop Fossil-Fuel Subsidies Immediately

Although pricing carbon is the first-best policy, the decision to immediately abolish all fossil-fuel subsidies should be easy. After all, a uniform carbon price implies that all emissions cost the same price, via either carbon taxes or emission permits, and thus that these negative prices have to be transformed into a uniform positive carbon price. Globally, explicit and implicit subsidies (including those resulting from exemptions) are a colossal \$5.3 trillion (or 6.5% of world GDP) compared to a miserly \$120 billion in subsidies for renewable energies (Coady et al., 2016). Carbon subsidies tend to be largest in countries that are oil or gas producers and that have insufficient state capacity to redistribute incomes towards the poor via the tax system. However, fossil-fuel subsidies are a blunt, costly and CO_2-intensive way of helping the poor.

In Europe, the biggest polluters—such as coal-fired power stations, steel and aluminium producers, and airline companies—have been the most successful in claiming exemptions from the ETS and carbon pricing. Furthermore, the practice of 'grandfathering' ETS permits has meant that the biggest polluters obtained the most permits in the past, especially in the first phase of the ETS. Recent reforms of the ETS have led to a market stability mechanism, which should remove some of these inefficiencies. The government should meticulously go through all unwarranted fossil-fuel subsidies with the aim of stopping them as soon as possible. It can start by abolishing the explicit and implicit subsidies for Schiphol and the airline industry (e.g. not paying tax on kerosene), the shipping industry, the greenhouse industry, and coal-fired power stations.

Sometimes the inefficiencies in climate policy are more subtle. Under the influence of the fossil-fuel lobby in the Netherlands, energy is taxed but CO_2 emissions are not taxed. This implies that coal use is undercharged, even though this is much more damaging than oil or gas. Although fossil-fuel lobbies have been incredibly powerful, we now see a rise in renewable energy lobbies trying to capture the climate policy rents. This is also dangerous and undesirable, because business not government should pick winning technologies as they are much better informed and it is business that should take these risks. Government should promote renewable energies by pricing carbon, but take a neutral stance towards particular technologies.

There are positive external effects that require subsidies for energy-saving technology. For example, every doubling of the number of installed solar panels leads to a reduction in the cost per panel of at least 20%. Similarly, learning-by-doing advantages are observed for wind energy and batteries. To the degree that the development costs that lead to these cost reductions are not internalized by the market, subsidies are justified. However, if there is a learning-by-doing or infant-industry case for such subsidies, one should subsidize regardless of whether there is a carbon tax and additional revenue from such a tax or not (e.g. Acemoglu et al., 2012). In the Paris Agreement, the carbon tax revenues are recycled via subsidies. This is a political compromise that cannot be motivated by economic arguments. If it is worthwhile to subsidize green technology in order to internalize the external effects of learning by doing, then the implementation of these subsidies should not depend on whether or not a carbon tax is implemented. Part of the carbon revenues can be rebated by giving subsidies to the carbon-intensive economic sector that demonstrably suffers most from the leakage of economic activity to neighbouring countries (Fowlie and Reguant, 2018). It is perhaps better to give these companies clarity for the longer term and the necessary investments that have to be made for the green transition by announcing the transition to a carbon-free economy as early as possible, sticking to a well-defined transition by a rising time path of carbon prices and formalizing it in a special climate law.

18.7 Avoid Unintended Adverse Effects Such as the Green Paradox and Carbon Leakage

Politicians procrastinate and commit their successors to more ambitious climate policies. This was also the case when the ministers of 194 countries signed up to the Paris Agreement. Such second-best policies lead coal, oil, and gas barons to deplete their reserves more quickly, as they realize that their reserves will become obsolete more quickly. This depresses energy prices and boosts demand for fossil fuel, thus accelerating global warming in the short run. This so-called Green Paradox (Sinn, 2008; van der Ploeg and Withagen, 2012) can be costly. It is particularly costly if the supply of fossil-fuel reserves does not respond much to price changes, as is the case in the short run. However, such second-best policies do lock up more carbon in the crust of the Earth and thus curb global warming in the long run. To avoid unintended adverse effects, it is better for politicians to price carbon, to commit to a steeply rising price and to start immediately. Incidentally, even without the Green Paradox effect, delaying climate action pushes up the required ultimate carbon price considerably as the marginal damages of global warming rise steeply as global warming becomes worse.

The spatial equivalent of the Green Paradox effect is carbon leakage (World Bank, 2015). This arises if only a subset of countries prices carbon. Some of the burden of the carbon price is shifted to producers, so energy prices abroad fall and thus emissions abroad rise while at home emissions fall. The estimated carbon leakage effect varies from hardly anything to about 20% (e.g. IPCC, 2001). This means that one-fifth of the reduction in emissions resulting from pricing carbon is offset by increases in emissions in countries that do not price carbon. Carbon leakage is much higher in countries such as the Netherlands, which has become a hub for gas trade in Europe. The beneficial effect of carbon pricing, if it were to be introduced in the Netherlands, is partially offset by additional coal and gas imports from Belgium and Luxemburg where carbon is not taxed. This means that the net costs per abated tonne of carbon are much higher if the increase in emissions in neighbouring countries is taken into account. Multilateral carbon pricing is therefore more effective than unilateral carbon pricing. It is best if carbon pricing can be done together with neighbouring countries, if necessary by offering transfers to persuade them to cooperate. For example, it might be efficient to help Germany to close its relatively much more carbon-intensive coal-fired power stations as quickly as possible.

If neighbouring countries do not put a price on carbon emissions, then it makes sense to levy import tariffs on carbon-intensive goods from these countries. This is called a border-tax adjustment. Some argue that this violates international free trade treaties, but it appears possible to have border tax adjustment under the World Trade Organization (Hillman, 2013). However, it may be difficult to introduce these border tax adjustments for the Netherlands as a loyal member of the EU without the cooperation of other member states. If it is not possible to introduce such border tax adjustments in Europe, it might be sensible to mitigate the risk of carbon leakage by fully taxing carbon emissions of polluting sectors such as steel and cement, but to help them by giving a subsidy that rises with the level of their production (Fowlie and Reguant, 2018). In the end, the Dutch government has decided to introduce a very different policy: a carbon charge only for emissions above a certain exemption. This policy has a very weak incentive to cut emissions and is therefore not very efficient (Schoenmaker et al., 2019; van der Ploeg et al., 2019).

18.8 Avoid Adverse Effects on the Poor, Not on Carbon-Intensive Sectors

One of the biggest obstacles to a successful climate policy is the effect of carbon prices on the lowest incomes. Carbon pricing increases electricity prices and this hurts the poor relatively more than the rich, especially if they live in badly insulated houses and cannot afford investments in better insulation. Therefore, a key policy question is to decide what to do with the revenues from the carbon taxes. If the tax system is already efficient, then it does not matter in which way the revenue is rebated as all (small) changes in tariffs, tax credits, and supplements have zero effect on welfare. However, if the revenue from carbon taxes were to be rebated in a lump-sum manner to all households, this would help the lowest earners in society most.

To maximize societal support and to mitigate the effects on those with lower and middle incomes as much as possible, it is important to make this transfer as salient as possible by labelling it as a 'fee' and a 'carbon dividend' (Klenert et al., 2018). It also helps to give subsidies for roof and window insulation for the homes of the poor. If labour income or corporate tax rates are inefficiently high, then the carbon tax revenue can be used to cut these tax rates. This helps to boost employment and labour activity, but in practice it is usually better to recycle the revenue to citizens in order to avoid the type of protests that we have seen in France. This also helps to improve support among companies, especially if such support is combined with taxes on carbon-intensive imports and tax deductibles for carbon-extensive exports. The World Trade Organization should allow such border taxes and deductibles if it can be established that these are 'essential to protect human, animal and plant life and health'.

18.9 Limit the Risk of Stranded Assets

Proven reserves of coal, oil, and gas are worldwide eight to ten times as large as the carbon budget compatible with the target of the Paris Agreement of a maximum temperature of 2°C (McGlade and Ekins, 2015). This means that the big fossil-fuel energy producers cannot sell all of their reserves, because if these are burnt they will lead to excessive warming of the planet. If this is not taken into account by market participants, then the share prices of fossil-fuel energy producers will be overvalued. The alternative is that the market does not take seriously the announced policies resulting from the Paris Agreement, and that fossil-fuel reserves can be sold and burnt. At the same time, private and institutional investors are exposed to the risk that share prices of fossil-fuel energy producers and carbon-intensive companies will drop in value if future climate policy suddenly becomes more ambitious. This risk is not illusionary, as a very large portion of the portfolios of many pension funds consists of shares in Royal Dutch Shell and other carbon-intensive companies. But producers of coal, oil, and gas, just like the coal-fired power stations and the cement and steel industries, lose the most value if policymakers suddenly wake up and finally start implementing a credible and ambitious climate policy. The risk of stranded assets in the case of unanticipated changes in climate policy is highest for those carbon-intensive sectors with high, difficult to reverse, investments (van der Ploeg and Rezai, 2020).

Recently, the biggest pension fund in Sweden, AP7, has dropped all the shares of companies that act against the Paris Agreement (i.e. Exxon Mobil, Gazprom,

TransCanada Corp, Westar WR.N, Entergy, and Southern Corp). Pension funds can also hedge themselves by investing in 'low-carbon' trackers, such as sold by MSCI and other financial providers. Such trackers give a similar return as normal trackers when climate policy is not enacted, but they give a good return by avoiding stranded assets and capital losses when climate policy at some uncertain moment in the future becomes much more vigorous. Financial supervisors in many countries are increasingly concerned not only about the risks of global warming for pension funds, but also for the potential adverse effects on insurance companies and commercial banks. It is therefore important that financial supervisors conduct regular climate stress tests for the financial sector.

18.10 Lessons for an Effective Climate Policy

To keep global temperatures within safe limits, the world needs to end its dependence on fossil fuels in the next few decades. This requires the phasing out of—or, even better, an immediate moratorium on—coal, abolishing all direct and indirect fossil-fuel subsidies and a commitment to a steeply rising path of carbon prices for all regions and sectors of the economy. If the required carbon price is higher than the price of an ETS permit, the government should levy an additional charge that is equal to the difference between the required price and the ETS price of a permit. It is important to act multilaterally, so that carbon emissions are priced uniformly in as many countries as possible and so that permits can be traded internationally and across sectors. If this is not possible, governments can levy an additional border tax to ensure that the emissions associated with carbon-intensive imports are priced the same as at home. This ensures a level playing field. If this not possible either, then governments can help those companies that suffer the most from leakage of business to other countries by giving them a production subsidy that increases in the risk of import leakage.

An effective climate policy also requires that policymakers resist carbon lobbies, and that subsidies for new methods to avoid carbon emissions are avoided unless there are market failures linked to learning by doing and the cost reductions that result. To gain broad support in society, it should be possible to use part of the carbon revenues to visibly and transparently redistribute revenue to the poor by handing out carbon dividends. This can be combined, if necessary, with subsidies for home insulation and carbon-free heating for the poor. Waiting longer before taking actions will drive up the costs of decarbonization and increase the risk of having to implement policies that lead to negative emissions such as geo-engineering. Leaving it to each of the sectors of the economy to come up with top-down plans to cut emissions or to the government to pick particular renewable energies to be subsidized is prone to rent seeking and will be much more expensive than pricing carbon. Delegating climate policy to individual sectors of the economy also leads to an inefficient piecemeal approach to climate policy. Pricing carbon uniformly is much more effective. Finally, the financial sector needs to adjust to survive the energy transition or, better still, to gain from facilitating the energy transition.

The proposed Climate Agreement for the Netherlands takes some important steps. There will be a moratorium on coal in the production of electricity from 2030. The floor for the price of emissions will rise in 2020 from 12.30 to 31.90 euros per tonne of CO_2. The proposed carbon tax for industry contains few incentives to produce in a greener way. The Climate Agreement is still insufficiently ambitious, it will be introduced too slowly, and it offers too little clarity for the longer term. There is a real chance that the Dutch emission targets will not be met. Many of the details of the Climate Agreement still need to be worked out, but for now it looks like it will lead to unnecessarily high costs to meet the agreed upon targets.

References

Acemoglu, D., Aghion, P., Bursztyn, L., and Hemmous, D. (2012), 'The environment and directed technical change', *American Economic Review*, 102(1), 131–66.

Aengenheyster, M., Feng, Q. Y., van der Ploeg, F., and Dijkstra, H. (2018), 'The point of no return for climate action: effects of climate uncertainty and risk tolerance', *Earth System Dynamics*, 9, 1085–95.

Coady, D., Parry, I. W. H., Sears, L., and Shang, B. (2016), 'How large are global energy subsidies?' IMF Working Paper no. 15/105, International Monetary Fund, Washington, DC.

CPB (2019), *CPB Doorrekening Ontwerp Klimaatakkoord*, CPB Netherlands Bureau for Economic Policy Analysis. The Hague (https://www.klimaatakkoord.nl/documenten/publicaties/2019/03/13/cpb-doorrekening-ontwerp-klimaatakkoord).

Fowlie, M. and Reguant, M. (2018), 'Challenges in the measurement of leakage risk', *American Economic Review*, 108(5), 124–9.

Gollier, C. (2019), 'The cost-efficiency carbon pricing puzzle', TSE Working Paper no. 18-952, Toulouse University.

Hillman, J. (2013), 'Changing climate for carbon taxes—who's afraid of the WTO?', Climate and Energy Paper Series, German Marshall Fund, United States.

IPCC (2001), 'Third Assessment Report: Climate Change 2001', ch. 8.7, Working Group 1, The Scientific Basis, Intergovernmental Panel for Climate Change, Geneva.

Klenert, D., Mattauch, L., Combet, E., Edenhofer, O., Hepburn, C., Rafaty, R., and Stern, N. (2018), 'Making carbon pricing work for citizens', *Nature Climate Change*, 8, 669–77.

Mayrhofer, J. and Gupta, J. (2016), 'The science and politics of co-benefits in climate policy', *Environmental Science and Policy*, 57, 22–30.

McGlade, C. and Ekins, P. (2015), 'The geographical distribution of fossil fuels unused when limiting global warming to 2°C', *Nature*, 517, 187–90.

Pfeiffer, A., Millar, R., Hepburn, C., and Beinhocker, E. (2016), 'The "2°C capital stock" for electricity generation: committed cumulative carbon emissions, from the electricity generation sector and the transition to the green economy', *Applied Energy*, 196, 1395–1408.

Rezai, A. and van der Ploeg, F. (2017), 'Climate policies under model uncertainty: max-min and min-max regret', *Energy Economics*, 68 (S1), 4–16.

Schoenmaker, D. et al. (2019), 'Die CO_2-heffing voor de industrie moet er komen', *NRC Handelsblad*, 25 January.

Sinn, H. W. (2008), 'Public policies against global warming', *International Tax and Public Finance*, 15, 360–94.

Steffen, W. et al. (2018), 'Trajectories of the earth system in the Anthropocene'. *Proceedings of the National Academy of Sciences*, 115(33), 8252–9.

Strengers, B., Heerens, H., Smeets, W., van den Born, G. J., and Ros, J. (2018), 'Negatieve emissies—Technisch potentieel, realistisch potentieel en kosten voor Nederland', PLB, The Hague.

van der Meijden, G. and Siegmann, A. (2018), 'Wie betaalt de rekening?' *Christen Democratische Verkenningen*, 4.

van der Ploeg, F. (2018), 'The safe carbon budget', *Climatic Change*, 147, 47–59.

van der Ploeg, F. and Rezai, A. (2020), 'The risk of policy tipping and stranded carbon assets', *Journal of Environmental Economics and Management*, 100, 102258.

van der Ploeg, F. and Withagen, C. (2012), 'Is there really a Green Paradox?' *Journal of Environmental Economics and Management*, 64, 342–63.

van der Ploeg, R. et al. (2019), 'Kabinet: zorg dat iedere ton CO_2-uitstoot dezelfde prijs krijgt', *NRC Handelsblad*, 24 April.

World Bank (2015), 'Carbon leakage—theory, evidence and policy design', PMR Technical Note 11, World Bank, Washington, DC.

19

Road Pricing by Design

The Dutch Case

*Hendrik Vrijburg and Gerben Geilenkirchen**

19.1 Introduction

Cars are not going to disappear from the streets and, apart from the house, they are often a household's largest investment. This makes taxation and regulation of car use and ownership a sensitive political subject. However, the Dutch government sees the car mainly as an attractive source of taxation. For example, the first sentence of a recent position paper by the Dutch government (Autobrief II) states that 'the primary aim of car taxes is to finance government expenditure' (Rijksoverheid, 2015). This perspective on revenue generation yields a focus on inelastic tax bases, which might not be in the public interest. As a result of the energy transition, for example, the Dutch government is looking for ways of encouraging passenger cars[1] with lower CO_2 emissions, and this is putting receipts from fuel duties under pressure. We analyse how current taxation of the purchase and ownership of cars can be replaced by a system of kilometre-based road pricing, which charges for use of the car.

In the Netherlands, motor vehicle taxes are levied on initial registration (*belasting van personenauto's en motorrijwielen*, BPM) of a car and on its ownership (*motorrijtuigenbelasting*, MRB). In addition, car use is taxed mainly by fuel duties, which approximates a 'flat' tax per kilometre. Car use is also regulated by other means than taxation (e.g. by mandatory insurance and traffic enforcement). Since Pigou (1932), economists have analysed whether such regulation internalizes relevant externalities. This is because the pricing of externalities, the unintended side effects of individual choices, leads to greater social welfare. Congestion, for

* Hendrik Vrijburg (h.vrijburg@law.leidenuniv.nl) is Assistant Professor at Leiden University. Gerben Geilenkirchen (gerben.geilenkirchen@pbl.nl) is Economic Policy Adviser at the Department of Urbanisation and Transport, PBL Netherlands Environmental Assessment Agency. This chapter incorporates helpful comments from Sijbren Cnossen, Hans Hilbers, Bas Jacobs, Rick van der Ploeg, Stef Proost and participants at the 'Tax by Design for the Netherlands' conference held at Erasmus University, Rotterdam, in May 2019.

[1] A passenger car is a road motor vehicle, other than a moped or a motor cycle, intended for the carriage of passengers and designed to seat no more than nine persons (including the driver).

Hendrik Vrijburg and Gerben Geilenkirchen, *Road Pricing by Design: The Dutch Case* In: *Tax by Design for the Netherlands.* Edited by: Sijbren Cnossen and Bas Jacobs, Oxford University Press.
DOI: 10.1093/oso/9780192855244.003.0019

example, is an externality caused by car use. Thus, Pigou suggested internalizing this externality with a price to be paid by each additional road-user. The (tax) receipts that follow from such pricing are a side-effect (see Mirrlees et al., 2011; Vollebergh et al., 2016) and should preferably be used to reduce other distorting taxes (see CPB and PBL, 2018). Already since the 1990s, the Dutch government is discussing whether to tax car use. For example, the fuel duty was raised by 25 guilder cents per litre (*kwartje van Kok*) in an attempt to tax car use more compared with use of public transport. A more specific peak-period charge was discussed in the 1990s and a proposal by the Balkenende IV government in 2009, to introduce a kilometre-based levy, came to nothing. Proposals have recently been made to introduce kilometre-based road pricing, including alternatives that specifically address electric cars, by 2026 (see Rijksoverheid, 2019).

In this chapter, we analyse kilometre-based road pricing for passenger cars from the perspective of internalizing external costs of car use for a given road network.[2] Freight traffic is not addressed. We also do not discuss spatial planning aspects, although more efficient use of the road network as a result of road pricing can affect spatial planning (see CPB and PBL, 2016; Proost and Thisse, 2019). As usual with the regulation of utilities, we pay no attention to the redistributional effects of road pricing, despite its political relevance (see Button, 2004; Levinson, 2010; van den Berg and Verhoef, 2011). Finally, we assume that no kilometre-based levy will be introduced in the European Union (EU) in the near future.

19.2 Social Costs of Road Use

In 2010, passenger cars in the Netherlands were driven for 102 billion kilometres (see CBS Statline), leading to a total external cost of some 12 billion euros.[3] Traffic volume increased by 8% between 2010 and 2018 and further growth is expected in the coming decades (CPB and PBL, 2015). Table 19.1 shows an estimate of the monetized value of the various externalities per vehicle-kilometre driven (marginal external cost) for the Netherlands (NL) in 2010 and 2016, the European Union (EU) in 2016 and the United States (US, as a benchmark from the literature). We stress that these estimates have substantial margins of uncertainty for both the physical size of the externality and its social value. We report the marginal external cost because kilometre-based road pricing is aimed at limited (marginal) changes in behaviour. The estimates for the Netherlands for 2016 are

[2] Construction of more roads seems to be hitting limits as a result of rising land prices (see Parry, Walls, and Harrington, 2007), and they simultaneously increase traffic due to additional road space (Duranton and Turner, 2011; CPB and PBL, 2015).

[3] We also include variable infrastructure costs due to passenger cars. CE Delft presents a range of 6–18 billion euros. In the absence of reliable data for the underlying road network, only the costs of the trunk road network are included in the calculations for congestion.

Table 19.1 Marginal external costs of passenger cars (eurocents/km)

	NL10[a] (1)	NL16[b] (2)	EU16[b] (3)	US[c] (4)	Existing instruments that implicitly internalize the externality (5)
Infrastructure	0.3	0.3[b]	0.3[b]	0.1	Fuel duties, energy taxes[d]
Accidents	4.4	(1.0)	(1.0)	2.6	Traffic enforcement, mandatory insurance, fuel duties, energy taxes[d]
Congestion	8.0 [0–41]	– [0–79]	– [0–66]	4.4	Fuel duties, energy taxes, parking charges[d]
Air quality (NOx, SO_2, $PM_{2.5}$, PM_{10})	0.7	1.0	1.0	1.8	Fuel duties, energy taxes, low-emission zones in Rotterdam and Utrecht, parking policy in Amsterdam, taxes on purchase and ownership, EU regulations[d]
Noise	0.4	0.7	0.9	0.1	Fuel duties, energy taxes, noise standards, noise barriers, laying quieter pavement, speed limits[d]
Climate damage (CO_2, CH_4, N_2O, NOx)	1.4	2.1	1.9	0.2	Fuel duties (first-best), energy taxes, taxes on purchase and ownership, taxable company car benefits[d]
Total	15.2	–	–	9.4	

Notes: [a] Based on the mid-value figures for 2010 in CE Delft (2014). CE Delft reported marginal effects per passenger-kilometre in table 104, but we report marginal costs per vehicle-kilometre. Passenger-kilometres are 33% higher than vehicle-kilometres as, on average, there is more than one person in a car. We calculated the kilometre-weighted average of the externalities of petrol (68%), diesel (31%), and LPG cars (1%). [b] Estimate for vehicle-kilometres based on CE Delft (2019) for the Netherlands and the EU in 2016. The same estimate as in CE Delft (2014) has been used for infrastructure (not reported in CE Delft, 2019). CE Delft (2019) reports marginal values for accidents for individual roads; the figures in parentheses reported in the table are based on our estimates. [c] Based on Parry et al. (2007). We used an exchange rate of 1.4 euros to 1 US dollar (applicable for this period). [d] Petrol duties in the Netherlands in 2019 were 79 cents per litre; average consumption of 13 km per litre means 6 cents per km. Diesel duties were 50 cents per litre; 16 km per litre means 3 cents per km. For electricity, 9.8 cents per kWh, in general, and 5.3 cents per kWh specifically for charging. Calculated at 5 km per kWh, this means 1–2 cents per km.

taken from CE Delft (2019) and differ from those for 2010 as a result of both the data used and the method applied. The estimates for 2016 are the preferred benchmark in this study. The issue of how these external costs can best be internalized is discussed in Section 19.3.

Infrastructure and road safety cause by far the largest total social costs from traffic—each about 11 billion euros, according to CE Delft (2014) and KiM (2017).[4] However, some of the total social cost of road safety is borne directly by the individual road user and is therefore not an externality (e.g. part of the damage to the road user's own health following an accident). The total damage to others (e.g. loss of life and lower productivity) is about 5.3 billion euros (CE Delft, 2014, p. 93). It should be noted that the chance of an accident on some roads actually decreases when there is more traffic and, consequently, the marginal cost of accidents is lower than the average cost. It is notable that the more recent study estimated a lower externality for accidents. The estimated marginal cost for infrastructure in Table 19.1 is relatively low since variable costs are only 14% of the total infrastructure costs and are caused mainly by heavier vehicles.[5]

Traffic congestion arises when several road users use the same road. Each road user contributes to the congestion such that other road users reach their destination more slowly: an externality. The total social cost of congestion on the trunk road network in 2016 is estimated at 2.8–3.7 billion euros (KiM, 2017). The cost of congestion includes longer travel time (66.3 million vehicle hours lost in 2018, according to RWS, 2019) and the inconvenience of travelling at another time ('schedule delay costs') or by a different route. On top of this comes the unreliability of journey times (see CE Delft, 2014). The social value of lost time is related to hourly pay (see Small, 1992). In contrast to accidents and infrastructure costs, the average cost for congestion is relatively low (1.4 cents per km) compared with the marginal cost. The high marginal costs follow from the strongly non-linear nature of congestion (CE Delft, 2014). Road users only really cause inconvenience to other users once there are a certain number of cars per kilometre and so congestion varies by time (day and time of day) and place (the Randstad agglomeration dominated the list of the top-50 traffic jams in 2018 according to RWS, 2019). To get a feel for the magnitude of non-linearity in the external cost due to congestion, it should be noted that Table 19.1 reports the mid-value of marginal costs from the study by CE Delft (2014). The full range is from a high of 41 cents per km and a low of zero cents. CE Delft (2019) only reports values for specific road types and not an average value. The ranges in columns 2 and 3 in Table 19.1 report the high value for urban roads in peak periods. The more recent estimates suggest higher external costs from congestion, which is higher in the Netherlands than the EU average.

Car use also damages the environment (climate damage, air quality, and noise). Drissen and Vollebergh (2018) estimated total environmental damages from

[4] Estimates of infrastructure costs are for 2010, and road safety for 2016. Car traffic is estimated at about 75% of total passenger-kilometres travelled.

[5] See CE Delft (2014, p. 40) for further discussion. The total annual infrastructure costs for passenger cars were 5.8 billion euros in 2010. Construction and management of infrastructure are taken as a fixed cost. Maintenance and renewal costs are divided between fixed and variable costs.

atmospheric pollutants and greenhouse gases emitted by traffic in the Netherlands at over 8 billion euros in 2015. The environmental damage estimate depends on the number of people affected by the pollutants and the social valuation of this damage. Damage from particulates in towns is, for example, a factor of 5 higher than average, and noise is ranked a factor of 4 higher at night than during the day (see CE Delft, 2014). The type of car is also important: newer cars are cleaner and quieter as a result of EU regulations. It is expected therefore that damage to air quality by passenger cars will fall in the coming years (see Parry et al., 2007; de Borger and Proost, 2017). Estimates of climate damage vary strongly with the price of CO_2: an implicit 9.50 euros per tonne of CO_2 in column 4, 78 euros per tonne in column 1 and 100 euros per tonne in columns 2 and 3. It is expected that the CO_2 price will increase further in the future. An increase in the price of CO_2 in the range of 100–500 euros per tonne in 2030 fits a path that limits global warming to 2°C (CPB and PBL, 2019). The estimate of climate damage is also corrected for energy-efficiency improvements. Parry et al. (2007) assume 8.8 km per litre of petrol, whereas 13 km per litre of petrol is a better approximation for European cars.

19.3 Road Pricing Policy Design to Internalize the External Costs of Road Use

In this section, we analyse what proportion of the external costs in Table 19.1 could preferably be internalized by kilometre-based road pricing. We take account of existing policy instruments that already implicitly correct the externality (column 5 of Table 19.1).

19.3.1 Theoretical Optimal Regulation of Externalities

Pricing (e.g. by a levy) aims at efficient reduction of externalities (see Kaplow and Shavel, 1996; Hepburn, 2006).[6] If implementation and administration costs are ignored, then the government can best price the action that creates a negative externality directly. This gives individuals the greatest freedom in dealing with the higher price (see Verhoef et al., 2004, for application to kilometre-based road pricing). That is, when all other markets operate efficiently, the optimal Pigovian tax is equal to the marginal external cost. However, such a first-best price is linked to high implementation costs and not all other markets are efficient. Therefore, it

[6] Also, tradable permits potentially reduce externalities efficiently. For example, de Palma et al. (2018) discuss pricing congestion with tradable permits. As the implementation of such a system is unclear (see CPB and PBL, 2016), we have not discussed this option further.

is often more efficient to opt for a combination of pricing an observed action associated with the negative externality and encouraging alternatives (see Sandmo, 1976; Lehman, 2012; Jacobsen et al., 2020). In that case, the rate chosen is different from the marginal cost (see Diamond, 1973; Sandmo, 1976). Application of these arguments to internalizing the externalities in Table 19.1 is set out below.

19.3.2 Congestion Pricing

Congestion arises because the road capacity at a given point (i.e. a 'bottleneck') is inadequate to handle a temporarily high volume of traffic (e.g. during peak periods). As a result, the journey takes longer and not all road users arrive at their intended time. Pigou suggested using a price to make road users aware of the loss of time they cause to others.[7] Vickrey (1963) and Walters (1961) argue that congestion pricing spaces out traffic better and that it will also cause some road users to opt for other means of transport (modal shift) or to travel less (for a discussion, see also Button, 2004; CPB and PBL, 2016). Following Vickrey (1969), Arnott, de Palma, and Lindsey (1990) show that large efficiency gains can be achieved by mainly varying congestion pricing by departure time. Time-variation implies that the traffic flow is distributed differently over time so that the bottleneck is used efficiently (travelling at a different time; see also Verhoef et al., 2004). Congestion pricing initially rises linearly towards the most desired time to pass the bottleneck and then falls linearly. Road users who choose to leave earlier pay a relatively low price but suffer a loss of utility as they arrive early, and vice versa for road users who leave later. Road users who want to arrive at exactly the desired time pay the highest price. Receipts from congestion pricing replace the time lost in traffic jams and, unlike loss of time, can be spent usefully by the government. In the stylized optimum of Arnott et al. (1990), all road users gain from shorter travelling times compared to the unregulated case (even without the receipts from the pricing).

The differences between road users in the value of time, desired arrival times, and inconvenience from arriving late will ensure that congestion pricing leads to changes in road use. Pricing makes the decision to travel more efficient: while it takes less time, it costs more money. The time gain is valuable to road users who put a high value on time but those who have relatively less to spend experience a loss of welfare through the higher price (see also Rouwendal and Verhoef, 2006). Recreational traffic will more likely travel outside priced periods or use alternative transport. A factory worker (specifically, a commuter) gains from the better

[7] French engineers analysed levying tolls between 1840 and 1850 (see Button, 2004).

spacing of traffic (not 'paying to sit in a traffic jam' but 'paying to drive') but the overall price of the journey can be a relatively heavy burden on his or her income. Furthermore, the road network is complex: routes have several bottlenecks (see Arnott et al., 1990; Verhoef, 2002) and 'start–stop traffic' occurs near towns (see Button, 2004). Taking account of these factors makes calculating the first-best charge per trip complex and it will differ from the marginal external cost (Verhoef et al., 2004). Consequently, various authors see a first-best system of congestion pricing mainly as a theoretical construct (see Button, 2004, p. 19; Rouwendal and Verhoef, 2006).

Second-best congestion pricing takes account of limitations in the implementation and administration of taxes and imperfections in related markets (see Rouwendal and Verhoef, 2006). One limitation on implementation is, for example, charging for the use of some roads by location (section) rather than by individual trip. Uniform pricing of a section of road for a given period while the externality varies within this section leads to 'coarse' congestion pricing (i.e. not every driver is priced in accordance with the marginal external damage caused). Arnott et al. (1990) discuss, for example, a regime with two prices for using a bottleneck (during and outside the peak period) and conclude that even such a 'coarse' approach leads to a gain in welfare. The optimum rate for coarse congestion pricing is usually below the marginal cost of congestion during the peak period because account has to be taken of the inherent additional distortion that is created as a result of the price being too high for some road users.[8] If not all roads are priced, then account has to be taken of extra congestion caused by drivers diverting to unpriced roads (see Marchand, 1968). The potential net social benefits from coarse congestion pricing are therefore less than the current external costs of congestion (see Parry et al. 2007). However, the more coarse congestion pricing can vary over time, the higher the welfare gains (see also van den Berg and Verhoef, 2011; CPB and PBL, 2015). Implementation that is too coarse can easily reduce the gains by a factor of 4.

Road use is related to other markets and therefore road use is also affected by demands to regulate these other markets. Therefore, the desired level of congestion pricing may also depend on regulation of those other markets (see also Rouwendal and Verhoef, 2006). Congestion is, for example, reduced by subsidizing public transport (a substitute for road use; see Button, 2004) or other policies that try to ensure 'peak-period avoidance'. Another good example of regulating a complementary market is parking policy: after all, every journey ends by parking at the destination. Higher pricing at popular destinations, such as the flat daily charge in London, indirectly prices the journey (see also Button, 2004). Although

[8] As the base covers individuals who generate externalities of varying sizes, the optimum tariff is a weighted average, where those with the strongest behavioural response carry the greatest weight (Diamond, 1973).

public transport subsidies and parking charges do not lead to an efficient reduction in congestion, in general terms the 'optimum' kilometre price depends on whether public transport and parking are efficiently priced (see Verhoef et al., 2004). The conclusion is that road pricing can be motivated from the perspective of internalizing the congestion externality. However, this demands a road price that varies by location and time.

19.3.3 Pricing Damage from Accidents and Damage to Infrastructure

The external cost of accidents and damage to infrastructure can be priced by a levy proportional to road use. The Dutch car ownership tax (MRB) was originally intended to co-finance infrastructure based on setting user fees, but the tax is unrelated to the extent to which the road is used.

The probability of an accident occurring is not associated only with road use—the probability falls with speed and, therefore, the degree of congestion (Parry et al. 2007; CE Delft, 2014). The probability of an accident also depends strongly on the motorist's specific conduct (e.g. drinking alcohol or tiredness) and the safety systems in the vehicle. Existing legislation and regulations reduce the potential damage from accidents. Car owners must have insurance for injury to others. However, insurance pricing is not an efficient instrument to internalize the damage done by accidents because of inadequate differentiation into risk classes and not pricing 'at the margin' (the premium does not rise with road use; see CE Delft, 2014). In addition, dangerous driving is regulated by traffic enforcement and prosecution of criminal activity. Much of the externality from accidents is therefore already regulated. Besides this, a proportional levy on road use at best indirectly prices accidents.

It seems from column 2 of Table 19.1 that a proportional kilometre-charge of 1 cent per km (rounded) for wear and tear on infrastructure and external costs from accidents could be justified from the literature (0.3 cent for wear and tear on infrastructure and, as a rule of thumb, 0.5 cent per km for accidents, where the rule of thumb corrects for existing regulations). Note that, overall, a policy mix is needed to reduce costs from accidents, as car-design characteristics are also important. See, for example, van Maarseveen, Tijm, and Zwaneveld (2018) for support of varied purchase or ownership taxes based on the traffic-safety argument.

19.3.4 Pricing Environmental Damage

Car use causes pollution from particulates as a result of a combination of wear on tyres, braking, and damage to road surfaces. The weight of the car, driving style, and traffic density (more braking in heavier traffic) determine the degree of air pollution. The use of a car indirectly causes air pollution. This effect is indirectly related to car use as the damage to the air for the same number of kilometres can be reduced by higher fuel efficiency or a cleaner combustion process (e.g. by using soot filters; see Fullerton and West, 2002). Damage to air quality is also strictly regulated by EU directives already (see also de Borger and Proost, 2017) and low-emission zones. Likewise, nuisance from noise can also be solved in other ways than by making less use of cars. Also, for noise there are already regulations and other policies. The climate damage of 2.1 cents per km in column 2 of Table 19.1 comes from the use of fossil fuels. Levying duties on the purchase of fossil fuels is a good example of charging for a transaction that is closely related to the actual emission that causes climate damage, because the location of the greenhouse gas emissions does not influence the resulting climate change (in contrast to emissions of air pollutants). Fossil fuel sales are an almost perfect proxy for the greenhouse gas emissions that arise when fuel is burnt (see Parry et al., 2007),[9] and so kilometre-based road pricing is unnecessary for climate damage.

We conclude that despite environmental damage being strongly location- and time-dependent, the existing policies imply that there is most probably little need for an additional location- and time-dependent kilometre-charge. If a proportional kilometre-based levy were selected, 1 cent per km (rounded) could be justified, based on column 2 of Table 19.1 (assuming half of the air quality damage and noise nuisance as an implicit rule-of-thumb adjustment for existing regulations), to internalize the air quality damage and noise nuisance. Air quality damage is also, to a large extent, car-specific and so a policy mix differentiated by distance and by type of car is needed; see Jacobsen et al. (2020) for further discussion if reported damage differs from actual damage.

19.3.5 Inelastic Base—Tax Revenue Perspective

Besides being related to externalities, kilometres driven are also a relatively inelastic tax base and therefore often seen as an efficient tax base. This follows from the insight that the tax system does not treat use of time neutrally: time spent working is taxed while time that does not deliver taxable income remains untaxed. Therefore, a second-best argument is heavier taxation of goods and services that are complementary to leisure (see Parry and Small, 2005; Parry et al., 2007). A low elasticity may indicate that a good is complementary to leisure (see Mirrlees et al., 2011). West and Williams (2007) suggest that, on average, fuel use is complementary to leisure and so fuel duties should be adjusted upwards. However, Mirrlees et al.

[9] 98% of climate damage is caused by CO_2 emissions. Emissions of other greenhouse gases (N_2O and CH_4) are small and not proportional to fuel consumption but to the type of car.

(2011, p. 289) suggest that fuels are complementary to work and so should bear relatively low taxes. The confusion could come from fuel being used for both work-related and social/recreational traffic. The efficiency argument is not associated with fuel consumption but with recreational kilometre displacement. Parry and Small (2005) talk of 17 cents per gallon and Parry et al. (2007) suggest that this is a lower limit. This implies that a uniform levy of about 1 cent per km can be justified from the perspective that a charge per kilometre raises tax revenues efficiently.[10]

19.3.6 Setting the Rate

It follows from the above that part of the externality in column 2 of Table 19.1 can be internalized by a form of kilometre-based road pricing on top of existing regulations (on accidents, environmental damage, etc.) and fuel duties to internalize climate damage (about 25 cents per litre).[11] However, congestion is by far the largest part and this should preferably be priced by location- and time-dependent congestion pricing. Some 2 cents per km plus 1 cent on revenue-raising efficiency grounds can be justified as a flat tax.

Note that Table 19.1 shows the marginal cost under current regulations. The estimates may therefore change when the above-mentioned policy changes are implemented. In the case of a rising marginal cost curve, pricing, for example, reduces the marginal cost. Nash et al. (2004) suggests that the external cost from congestion after congestion pricing is implemented is only 20% of the initial amount. Finally, effective pricing policies for road users demand some predictability and reliability in the price (see also Parry et al., 2007; Mirrlees et al., 2011; CPB and PBL, 2016). In view of these complications, it seems sensible to increase charges gradually until road use is seen as adequately efficient (applying the insights of Baumol and Oates, 1971).

19.4 Application: Specific Forms of Kilometre-Based Road Pricing

The introduction of kilometre-based road pricing is restricted by implementation costs, but the literature pays relatively little attention to this (see also Button, 2004, p. 15). CPB and PBL (2015) discuss various implementation options and it is

[10] Inelastic demand for mobility as an argument to support kilometre-based road pricing is quantitatively relatively small compared with congestion. Receipts from kilometre-based road pricing are, however, an important argument for the government, and so estimating a justifiable upper limit for a proportional kilometre levy is relevant to policy.

[11] The CO_2 price per litre of petrol follows from a price of 100 euros per tonne for CO_2 (CE Delft, 2019) and an emission factor of 2,371 g per litre for a petrol-driven car giving 24 eurocents per litre (see also Vollebergh et al., 2014, table 4.5). The emissions factor for diesel is 2,657 g per litre, giving 27 eurocents per litre. The admixture with bio-fuels is ignored.

evident that the systems that are capable of implementing a time-varying congestion price involve higher costs. Comprehensive time-variation demands an investment per car, such as a box with GPS functionality or a dedicated short-range communications (DSRC) system, costing approximately 250 and 40 euros, respectively. Measurement by section of road can also be done more coarsely using automatic number-plate recognition (ANPR) camera systems or smart vignettes (stickers in the car and monitoring equipment along the road) at almost no cost per car. The operational costs for a GPS system are estimated to be 25% higher than an ANPR system that can be used for coarser pricing. Implementation with ANPR cameras has the advantages that the government manages the cameras, the access costs for motorists are relatively low and that implementation does not depend on technology with the road user (possibly less fraud and appeals). Technology is still developing, however, and it is conceivable that the cost of GPS-based systems will fall relatively sharply in the next few years.[12]

The introduction of kilometre-based road pricing will also come up against the provisions of the Personal Data Protection Act (*Wet Bescherming Persoonsgegevens*, WBP). It is expected that a higher degree of refinement of kilometre-based road pricing will create greater conflict with the WBP: flat variants of kilometre-based road pricing can meet the requirements of the WBP but implementing varied congestion pricing might not (see CPB and PBL, 2015). It is not clear how far privacy concerns will, in the end, limit implementation and whether this is socially desirable (see Button, 2004; CPB and PBL, 2015; CPB, 2017). There seems to be an inconsistency between how much people say they value privacy (high) and their actual willingness to pay for more privacy (low) (see Athey, Catalini, and Tucker, 2017). This may mean that the actual value put on privacy is low or that consumers need to be protected from frivolously surrendering privacy.

In this section, we evaluate different aspects of a limited number of practical policy options for kilometre-based road pricing (see Table 19.2 for a schematic overview). We discuss different bases. The evaluation is based on the theoretical insights in Section 19.3, cost–benefit analyses by CPB and PBL (2015), analyses in Besseling, Groot, and Lebouille (2005) and documented experience in other countries (in particular on implementation).

19.4.1 First-Best Congestion Pricing (Base Is Departure Time and Specific Route)

An (approximate) first-best congestion charge is a levy that varies strongly by the motorist's departure time and takes account of congestion on the selected route.

[12] From March 2018, EU regulations require all new cars to transmit an emergency signal, including GPS coordinates, in the event of an accident. In 10–15 years, almost all cars will have such GPS technology.

Table 19.2 Assessment of policy options for kilometre-based road pricing

	First-best	Second-best	Cordon fee	Peak-period	Flat
Reduced congestion (+)	+ + + +	+ + +	+ +	+	+ + +
Other benefits (+)	0	0	+	0	+ +
Other costs (–)	0	–	–	–	– – –
Implementation costs (–)	– – – –	– –	–	–	– –
Privacy (–)	– – – –	– – –	– – –	–	0
Net effect on welfare	–	+ +	+	–	0

Notes: The columns represent the policy options discussed below. Benefits are indicated by a plus sign (+). The more plus signs, the better the score, with first-best as the benchmark: first-best (+ + + +), very good (+ + +), good (+ +), poor (+), and almost none (0). Similarly, costs have a number of minuses (–). Other benefits include road safety, noise, and emissions (see CPB and PBL, 2015). Other costs are mainly loss of demand.

Source: Authors' assessment.

This is the best policy option for both maximizing the reduction in external congestion cost and minimizing unnecessary efficiency losses in car use (see also Verhoef et al., 2004). This type of pricing is feasible, in principle: cars can report their real-time location via GPS. However, it has not been put into use anywhere (see Cipriani et al., 2019), as the expected implementation costs are high (see also CPB and PBL, 2016). For the same reason, the implementation costs are also very uncertain (see also Mirrlees et al., 2011). With respect to privacy, this type of pricing requires complete personal journey information to determine the journey-specific price, and so this may conflict with the WBP. First-best congestion pricing generates additional benefits in terms of less environmental damage. These benefits arise jointly with reduced congestion as emissions per kilometre decline with fuel efficiency. However, this benefit is limited as overall car use falls only slightly, and this small decline is often outside towns. Our conclusion is that the potentially large social gains from first-best congestion pricing in terms of reduced congestion still fall short of the currently expected implementation and privacy costs (taking into account the substantial uncertainty of the size of these costs).

19.4.2 Second-Best Congestion Pricing (Base Is the Use of a Section of Road at a Given Time)

Second-best (coarse) congestion pricing is an average price for a number of specific (busy) sections of road and times on the trunk road network (CPB and PBL, 2015, 2016). Coarse congestion pricing reduces congestion strongly (see also Mirrlees et al., 2011) but less efficiently than the first-best levy, and so overall car use falls more than with the first-best levy (see CPB and PBL, 2016).[13] As second-best congestion pricing is largely implemented on trunk roads outside towns, it scores the same as the first-best levy for additional benefits. In privacy terms, second-best congestion pricing requires time and place to be recorded for checks, although for a smaller area.

As the pricing applies to specific sections of road, implementation can require investment in in-car systems (GPS box, DSRC technology) or systems that mainly demand investment along the road (ANPR technology and smart vignettes). DSRC and ANPR systems with smart vignettes are used in various countries (see CPB and PBL, 2015, p. 18).[14] Systems with a limited investment per car make implementation simple.

CPB and PBL (2015, 2016) assess congestion pricing implemented using ANPR or smart vignette technology as socially viable, with both high and low economic growth, but are cautious about implementation. The social benefits come mainly from substantially faster journey times. Furthermore, a little more time-variation delivers greater benefits for a relatively small increase in cost (CPB and PBL, 2015, p. 44). We base our opinion on the net effect of these cost–benefit analyses: second-best congestion pricing yields a net social gain.

19.4.3 Cordon Fees (Base Is Entering a Specific Area during a Given Period)

A cordon fee is a time-varying levy for entering a city such as Amsterdam, Rotterdam, The Hague, or Utrecht, including the ring road, during a given period, irrespective of how long the vehicle remains in the zone; see CPB and PBL (2016) and the pass-through fee in Besseling et al. (2005). A related levy is a flat daily charge where payment is per day or part of a day.

After the introduction of cordon fees, traffic fell in London and Stockholm by 12% (KiM, 2018) and 20% (Richardson and Bae, 2008) respectively. Congestion declined by 30% in London. A cordon fee affects congestion relatively strongly as part of the congestion occurs in cities and their ring roads (for the Netherlands, see figures 3.2, 3.3, and 7.2 in CPB and PBL, 2015). Cipriani et al. (2019) simulate a system of cordon fees for Rome and show that congestion not only falls within the city but the system also indirectly regulates congestion outside the zone. As a

[13] The model that CPB and PBL use to calculate congestion pricing is limited to trunk roads (other roads, including urban roads, have not been modelled). Detailed time-variation is also not possible. 'Optimum' congestion pricing is established iteratively by introducing a price for a given section of road and then looking to see if congestion arises on other sections, such that a price is needed there too.

[14] CPB and PBL (2015) are not in favour of toll roads in the Netherlands. These studies addressed a number of specific new routes where a social cost–benefit analysis was performed, and not tolls specifically focused on reducing congestion.

result of the effect on congestion, Besseling et al. (2005) regard cordon fees around cities, including the ring roads, as positive. However, a daily charge excluding ring roads is evaluated negatively. CPB and PBL (2015) use the same model as Besseling et al. (2005) to evaluate a cordon fee, but are cautious about the robustness of their results as the model primarily covers trunk roads.

Cordon fees are feasible as they have already been implemented in Singapore (since 1975 with an electronic system, and, since 1998, a cordon fee with a flat daily charge), London (since 2003, a flat daily charge between 9.00 a.m. and 5.00 p.m.), Stockholm (since 2007, a time-varied cordon fee), Milan and Gothenburg (since 2013, a cordon fee); see Cipriani et al., 2019, for a discussion. Most systems use ANPR cameras, which many cities have already installed in order to establish low-emission zones. The urban location also correlates strongly with air quality damage and noise nuisance. A cordon fee is therefore expected to have greater additional benefits than second-best congestion pricing (or low implementation costs, if such a low-emission zone already exists). From a national perspective, too few motorists are priced by cordon fees to bring about substantial safety benefits. Based on Besseling et al. (2005), implementation costs are estimated to be lower than for second-best congestion pricing. Time-varying cordon fees will rank the same on privacy as second-best congestion pricing, because the time the motorist enters the zone has to be recorded.

We conclude that this type of pricing has promise (see also de Borger and Proost, 2017) but note that the overall effect of cordon fees depends strongly on their design and a broader policy package (level and variation of rates, size of the zone, quality of and investment in public transport and cycling networks; see PBL and CE Delft, 2010; Mirrlees et al., 2011).

19.4.4 Peak-Period Levy (Base Is Use of Roads in a Given Area and for a Given Period)

The peak-period levy is a levy per kilometre on all main roads in the Randstad and parts of Noord-Brabant and Gelderland during peak periods (see CPB and PBL, 2015). It is coarser than second-best congestion pricing and specific cordon fees around cities: road users are more often priced unnecessarily, while many road users are not priced at all. In the end, this results in lower social benefits from reduced congestion than second-best congestion pricing and cordon fees (see CPB and PBL, 2015). The peak-period levy is less focused on cities and also misses all road users outside the peak period, which means that other benefits are reduced (see CPB and PBL, 2015). As it is not necessary to state where a road user entered the peak-period levy zone, privacy intrusion is smaller.

19.4.5 National Flat Kilometre-Charge (Base Is Kilometres Driven in the Netherlands)

A national flat charge does not distinguish by time or location and is a fixed levy per kilometre. A flat kilometre-charge can be implemented with a relatively simple in-car box (see CPB and PBL, 2015). In view of the crude pricing implementation, the levy is poorly focused on congestion and also yields a strong decline of some 12–15% in kilometres driven (see CPB and PBL, 2015). When, for example, the tax rate of a flat charge is comparable with the tax rate of a second-best congestion price, congestion will be reduced to a similar extent, but on top of that the flat charge will reduce kilometres travelled substantially (an economic cost; see Besseling et al., 2005).

A flat charge can be implemented at relatively low cost (see CPB and PBL, 2015). Several EU countries, including Austria, Belgium, Czech Republic, Germany, Hungary, Poland, Slovakia, and Switzerland, have experience with imposing flat charges for freight vehicles using electronic toll systems with cameras and/or in-vehicle boxes. These levies often cover the entire motorway network and through routes (to prevent diversionary effects). In the Netherlands, a lorry levy is being designed. As no time- or location-specific information has to be collected, privacy intrusion is minimal.

With high congestion, a national flat charge leads to positive welfare gains according to CPB and PBL (2015); there is a welfare loss with low congestion. Apart from the relatively strong fall in car use, there are relatively large additional road safety and environmental benefits.

19.5 Policy Recommendations

Given the above discussion, we reach the following three policy conclusions. Coarse, second-best congestion pricing that is targeted at heavily congested sections of the trunk road network will yield a welfare gain when implemented with, say, ANPR cameras. It is advisable to vary by time as much as possible during the peak period. Time-variation avoids "paying to sit in a traffic jam" and implements user fees.

If (coarse) second-best congestion pricing is not politically feasible, then a cordon fee for the four main cities (Amsterdam, The Hague, Rotterdam, and Utrecht), including ring roads, at busy times is a good alternative as a first step towards implicit congestion pricing (see also Button, 2004, p. 15). Cities are already experimenting with such systems for air pollution, and congestion would seem to be a next step. As local, regional, and national roads will be priced, and as the levy covers both local and through traffic, management of cordon fees will require cooperation between the national government and regional authorities. Cordon fees will probably first appear around cities with high levels of local traffic, partly because there is a risk of reverse tax competition—a race to the top—if local authorities mainly want road users from outside to pay a relatively high levy (Mandell and Proost, 2016). Coordination/regulation at a national level is therefore important (de Borger and Proost, 2017). Maximum fees or receipts could limit such reverse tax competition (see also the Eurovignette Directive).[15]

Alongside (implicit) congestion pricing, a relatively low national flat kilometre-charge of about 3 cents per km is justifiable as implicit pricing for accidents, for wear and tear on the road network and for environmental damage, and as an efficient tax instrument from the revenue perspective.[16] If both a congestion charge and a low national flat kilometre-charge are implemented, then excise duties on fuel of about 25 cents per litre should be part of the policy mix to efficiently internalize climate damage.

Current excise duties on fuel (on average around 6 cents per km for petrol and 3 cents per km for diesel) and the tax on electricity use (2 cents per km) already approximate a national flat kilometre-charge. On the one hand, using fuel duties to approximate a flat kilometre-charge comes at an economic cost because fuel-efficient cars will experience a relative low price per kilometre. On the other hand, the approximation avoids the implementation costs of an actual national flat kilometre-charge. In the short term, therefore, implementing an actual additional national flat kilometre-charge is not likely to yield a welfare gain. When over the long term, as a result of the energy transition, fossil fuels are phased out and electrification increases, a levy on electricity use by cars could take over the role of fuel duties as an approximation of a flat tax on car use. However, for climate reasons, electricity consumption in general should preferably not be taxed as it does not cause climate damage (hence the reduction in energy taxes in the Netherlands; see Rijksoverheid, 2019). Therefore, electricity taxes should be differentiated by type of electricity use. Current Dutch energy taxes are already differentiated for charging electric cars at fuel stations; this will have to be extended to home-charging with all the related implementation costs. Those costs have to be compared with the cost of direct measurement of kilometres driven, which serves as the base for an actual flat kilometre-based levy (e.g. in electric cars, as proposed in Rijksoverheid, 2019).

When energy input instead of kilometres driven is used as the tax base, the optimum rate for pricing external costs other than climate damage should be adjusted downwards. This is because energy as an input is not an exact approximation for kilometres (Parry and Small, 2005). The charge of 3 cents per km

[15] Directive 1999/62/EC of the European Parliament and of the Council of 17 June 1999 on the charging of heavy goods vehicles for the use of certain infrastructures, Official Journal of the European Union (OJ) L187/42.

[16] Note that the charge of 3 cents per km is significantly lower than 7 cents per km for a flat tax on top of the existing duties in the social cost–benefit analysis by CPB and PBL (2015).

translates into about 50 cents per litre for petrol, 60 cents per litre for diesel, and 10 cents per kWh for electricity for the existing car fleet.[17] The duty on diesel could be increased slightly when considering somewhat higher air quality damage, or reduced if diesel is regarded as relatively complementary with work. Cross-border effects could also be a reason for lower optimum rates (see also Parry and Small, 2005). We propose cancelling out these arguments against each other. This implies that when congestion is priced with a targeted congestion charge, in order to approximate an additional flat rate, the current duties on petrol (78 cents) should be reduced while the duties on diesel (currently 50 cents) should be increased (see also Mirrlees et al., 2011; Vollebergh et al., 2014). The combination of a congestion-focused levy plus a relatively low flat tax was not computed in CPB and PBL (2015) and Besseling et al. (2005).

Efficient road pricing, or better pricing of car use, will most probably not generate higher tax revenue. Current receipts from motoring taxes are some 15 billion euros, including 8 billion euros from fuel duties (see Vollebergh et al., 2016). CE Delft (2014) estimates the total external costs from passenger cars at about 12 billion euros. As argued, the size of external cost falls, sometimes substantially, after pricing. The flat daily charge in London, for example, resulted in much lower receipts than expected because of strong changes in behaviour in response to the charge (see Lehe, 2019). CPB and PBL (2015) estimate the receipts from second-best congestion pricing between 200 and 400 million euros; far less than the estimated 3 billion euros in external costs due to congestion. Current petrol duties are higher than the above proposed (approximation of a) low national flat kilometre-charge, which would be efficient alongside targeted congestion pricing.

There are also good arguments for additional taxes on purchase and ownership (see also Mirrlees et al., 2011; Vrijburg, Brink, and Dijk, 2018). Kilometre-pricing would ideally differentiate by type of car if the damage varies by type of car. If such a first-best levy is not feasible, however, corrective taxation of the purchase of a car contributes to guiding the type of car being used (see Fullerton and West, 2000, 2002) and how long it is owned (ownership tax; see Alberini et al., 2018). A purchase and/or ownership tax per car can easily be varied by expected

[17] A significant part of the reduction in energy consumption comes from more fuel-efficient vehicles rather than a reduction in the number of kilometres. Parry et al. (2007) argue that the optimum tariff (t) on fuels is $t = E_c + E_m f\beta$, where E_c denotes climate damage per litre, E_m denotes other external costs per km, β denotes the fraction of the fuel elasticity caused by fuel efficiency and f denotes kilometres driven per unit of energy. We use β equal to 0.5 (see Parry and Small, 2005; Geilenkirchen et al., 2010), and f is 13 for petrol, 16 for diesel, and 5 for electricity. In Section 19.3, we suggested about 2 cents per km for a flat levy for external costs. This results in a levy of 13 cents per litre for petrol, 16 cents per litre for diesel and 5 cents per kWh for electricity (the same β is used for electricity). The Ramsey component is also about 1 cent per km or about 15 cents per litre and 5 cents per kWh. In total, for climate damage, this gives 13 + 24 + 13 = 50 cents per litre for petrol, 16 + 27 + 16 = 59 cents per litre for diesel and 5 + 5 = 10 cents per kWh for electricity. The levy would need to be adjusted when the energy efficiency of the car fleet improves.

environmental damage and safety and so, as part of a policy mix, indirectly reduce a large part of the externality, even if reported emissions differ from actual emissions (Jacobsen et al., 2020). Fullerton and West (2000) estimate that over 70% of the maximum social benefits from pricing cars can be achieved by a policy mix in which both fuel (i.e. car use) and purchase are priced.

References

Alberini, A., Bareit, M., Fillipini, M., and Martinez-Cruz, A. L. (2018), 'The impacts of emissions-based taxes on the retirement of used and inefficient vehicles: the case of Switzerland', *Journal of Environmental Economics and Management*, 88, 234–58.

Arnott, R., de Palma, A., and Lindsey, R. (1990), 'Economics of a bottleneck', *Journal of Urban Economics*, 27, 111–30.

Athey, S., Catalini, C., and Tucker, C. (2017), 'The digital privacy paradox: small money, small costs, small talk', NBER Working Paper no. 23488.

Baumol, W. J. and Oates, W. E. (1971), 'The use of standards and prices for protection of the environment', *Scandinavian Journal of Economics*, 73, 42–54.

Besseling, P., Groot, W., and Lebouille, R. (2005), 'Economische analyse van verschillende vormen van prijsbeleid voor het wegverkeer', CPB Netherlands Bureau for Economic Policy Analysis, The Hague.

Button, K. (2004), 'The rationale for road pricing: standard theory and latest advances', *Research in Transport Economics*, 9, 3–25.

CE Delft (2014), 'Externe en infrastructuurkosten van verkeer, een overzicht voor Nederland in 2010', Rapport CE Delft no. 14.4485.35.

CE Delft (2019), 'Handbook on the External Costs of Transport', Version 2019, European Commission, publication number 18.4K83.131.

Cipriani, E., Mannini, L., Montemarani, B., Nigro, M., and Petrelli, M. (2019), 'Congestion charging policies: design and assessment for the city of Rome', *Transport Policy*, 80, 127–35.

CPB (2017), 'Verkenning maatschappelijke kosten-batenanalyse bij de digitale overheid (Study of cost–benefit analysis for e-government)', CPB Netherlands Bureau for Economic Policy Analysis, The Hague.

CPB and PBL (2015), 'Maatschappelijke Kosten en Baten Prijsbeleid Personenauto's', Planbureau voor de Leefomgeving, PBL Netherlands Environmental Assessment Agency', The Hague.

CPB and PBL (2016), 'Kansrijk mobiliteitsbeleid', CPB Netherlands Bureau for Economic Policy Analysis and PBL Netherlands Environmental Assessment Agency, The Hague.

CPB and PBL (2018), 'De werkgelegenheidseffecten van fiscale vergroening', CPB Netherlands Bureau for Economic Policy Analysis and PBL Netherlands Environmental Assessment Agency, The Hague.

CPB and PBL (2019), 'Economische effecten van CO_2-beprijzing: varianten vergeleken', CPB Netherlands Bureau for Economic Policy Analysis and PBL Netherlands Environmental Assessment Agency, The Hague.

De Borger, B. and Proost, S. (2017), 'What can European experience teach us for Belgian transport policy?', *Reflets et perspectives de la vie economique*, 2017(2), 33–53.

De Palma, A., Proost, S., Seshadri, R., and Ben-Akiva, M. (2018), 'Congestion tolling—dollars versus tokens: a comparative analysis', *Transportation Research Part B*, 108, 261–80.

Diamond, P. A. (1973), 'Consumption externalities and corrective imperfect pricing', *Bell Journal of Economics*, 4, 526–38.

Drissen, E. and Vollebergh, H. (2018), 'Monetaire Milieuschade in Nederland', Planbureau voor de Leefomgeving, The Hague.

Duranton, G. and Turner, M. A. (2011), 'The fundamental law of road congestion: evidence from US cities', *American Economic Review*, 101(6), 2616–52.

Fullerton, D. and West, S. (2000), 'Tax and subsidy combinations for the control of car pollution', NBER Working Paper no. 7774.

Fullerton, D. and West, S. (2002), 'Can taxes on vehicles and on gasoline mimic an unavailable tax on emissions?', *Journal of Environmental Economics and Management*, 43, 135–57.

Geilenkirchen, G. P., Geurs, K. T., van Essen, H. P., Schroten, A., and Boon, B. (2010), 'Effecten van prijsbeleid in verkeer en vervoer', Kennisoverzicht, Planbureau voor de Leefomgeving, The Hague.

Hepburn, C. (2006), 'Regulation by prices, quantities, or both: a review of instrument choice', *Oxford Review of Economic Policy*, 22, 226–47.

Jacobsen, M, R., Knittel, C. R., Sallee, J. M., and van Benthem, A. A. (2020), 'The use of regression statistics to analyze imperfect pricing policies', *Journal of Political Economy*, 128, 1826–76.

Kaplow, L. and Shavel, S. (1996), 'Property rules versus liability rules: an economic analysis', *Harvard Law Review*, 4, 715–90.

KiM (2017), 'Mobiliteitsbeeld 2017', Kennisinstituut voor Mobiliteitsbeleid.

KiM (2018), 'Mobiliteitsbeeld 2018', Kennisinstituut voor Mobiliteitsbeleid.

Lehe, L. (2019), 'Downtown congestion charging in practice', *Transportation Research Part C*, 100, 200–23.

Lehman, P. (2012), 'Justifying a policy mix for pollution control: a review of economic literature', *Journal of Economic Surveys*, 26, 71–97.

Levinson, D. (2010), 'Equity effects of road pricing: a review', *Transport Reviews*, 30, 33–57.

Mandell, S. and Proost, S. (2016), 'Why truck distance taxes are contagious and drive fuel taxes to the bottom', *Journal of Urban Economics*, 93, 1–17.

Marchand, M. (1968), 'A note of optimal tolls in an imperfect environment', *Econometrica*, 36, 575–81.

Mirrlees, J., Adam, S., Besley, T., Blundell, R., Bond, S., Chote, R., Gammie, M., Johnson, P., Myles, G., and Poterba, J. (2011), *Tax by Design: The Mirrlees Review*, Oxford University Press, Oxford.

Nash, C., Mackie, P., Shires, J., and Nellthorp, J. (2004), 'The economic efficiency case for road user charging', Institute for Transport Studies, University of Leeds.

Parry, I. W. H. and Small, K. A. (2005), 'Does Britain or the United States have the right gasoline tax?', *American Economic Review*, 95(4), 1276–89.

Parry, I. W. H., Walls, M., and Harrington, W. (2007), 'Automobile externalities and policies', *Journal of Economic Literature*, 45, 373–99.

PBL and CE Delft (2010), 'Effecten van prijsbeleid in verkeer en vervoer', kennisoverzicht, Planbureau voor de Leefomgeving, The Hague.

Pigou, A. C. (1932), *The Economics of Welfare*, 4th edn, Macmillan, London.

Proost, S. and Thisse, J. F. (2019), 'What can be learned from spatial economics?', *Journal of Economic Literature*, 57, 575–643.

Richardson, H. W. and Bae, C. C. (2008), *Road Congestion Pricing in Europe: Implications for the United States*, Edward Elgar, Cheltenham.

Rijksoverheid (2015), 'Autobrief II', Kamerbrief, 19 June 2015 (https://www.rijksoverheid.nl/documenten/kamerstukken/2015/06/19/autobrief-ii).

Rijksoverheid (2019), 'Voorstel voor een Klimaatakkoord', Kamerbrief, 28 June 2019.

Rouwendal, J. and Verhoef, E. T. (2006), 'Basic economic principles of road pricing: from theory to applications', *Transport Policy*, 13, 106–14.

RWS (2019), 'Rapportage Rijkswegennet', Ministerie van Infrastructuur en Milieu, The Hague.

Sandmo, A. (1976), 'Direct versus indirect Pigovian taxation', *European Economic Review*, 7, 337–49.

Small, K. (1992), *Urban Transportation Economics*, Harwood Academic, Reading, PA.

Van den Berg, V. and Verhoef, E. T. (2011), 'Winning or losing from dynamic bottleneck congestion pricing? The distributional effects of road pricing with heterogeneity in values of time and schedule delay', *Journal of Public Economics*, 95, 983–92.

Van Maarseveen, R., Tijm, J., and Zwaneveld, P. (2018), 'De fiscale behandeling van voertuigveiligheid', CPB Netherlands Bureau for Economic Policy Analysis, The Hague.

Verhoef, E. T. (2002), 'Second-best congestion pricing in general static transportation networks with elastic demands', *Journal of Urban Economics*, 32, 281–310.

Verhoef, E., Koopmans, C., Bliemer, M., Bovy, P., Steg, L., and van Wee, B. (2004), 'Vormgeving en Effecten van Prijsbeleid op de Weg', Report by UVA, SEO, RuG, and TU Delft commissioned by Ministerie van Verkeer en Waterstaat, The Hague.

Vickrey, W. S. (1963), 'Pricing in urban and suburban transport', *American Economic Review*, 53(2), 452–65.

Vickrey, W. S. (1969), 'Congestion theory and transport investment', *American Economic Review*, 59(2), 251–61.

Vollebergh, H., Dijk, J., Drissen, E., Eerens, H., and Geilenkirchen, G. (2014), 'Milieubelastingen en Groene Groei Deel II: Evaluatie van belastingen op energie in Nederland vanuit milieuperspectief', Planbureau voor de Leefomgeving, The Hague.

Vollebergh, H., Dijk, J., Drissen, E., Eerens, H., and Geilenkirchen, G. (2016), 'Belastingverschuiving: meer vergroening en minder complexiteit?', Planbureau voor de Leefomgeving, The Hague.

Vrijburg, H., Brink, C., and Dijk, J. (2018), 'Instrumentkeuze voor efficiënt en effectief klimaatbeleid', in D. van Soest, S. Smulders, and R. Gerlagh (eds), *Klimaatbeleid: Kosten, Kansen en Keuzes*, Koninklijke Vereniging voor de Staathuishoudkunde (https://esb.nu/kvs/20046610/instrumentkeuze-voor-efficient-en-effectief-klimaatbeleid), pp. 79–90.

Walters, A. A. (1961), 'The theory and measurement of private and social costs of highway congestion', *Econometrica*, 29, 676–99.

West, S. E. and Williams, R. C. (2007), 'Optimal taxation and cross-price effects on labor supply: estimates of the optimal gas tax', *Journal of Public Economics*, 91, 593–617.

PART VI

CONSUMPTION

20

Modernizing Value-Added Tax

*Sijbren Cnossen**

20.1 Introduction

The EU's single market is founded on the principles of free trade and free competition between and, consequently, within member states. These principles require that taxes on goods and services should be fully and accurately rebated at export, equivalently imposed at import, and washed out between taxable businesses within member states. To achieve this, the cumulative turnover taxes levied in the1960s and 1970s were replaced by the value-added tax (VAT), whose basic features were harmonized in 1977 and subsequently consolidated in what is now known as the EU VAT Directive.[1] However, while the EU VAT permits the application of border tax adjustments and the set-off of prior-stage tax, multiple exemptions and exclusions still distort trade and complicate administration. The exemptions are not found under the modern VAT—a concept coined by Ebrill et al. (2001)—introduced in other countries, which applies a uniform rate to the broadest possible base. Accordingly, the EU VAT tends to become an anachronism (Cnossen, 2003). Institutionalizing the exemptions and exclusions, as the EU has done, does not lessen the VAT's shortcomings.

In this chapter, I examine the exemptions and exclusions[2] prescribed under the EU VAT Directive and I propose revisions that move the base closer to the base of a modern VAT. This is done on the widely agreed notion that the primary role of the VAT in an overall tax system is to raise revenue, predictably and efficiently. The VAT differs from the excises in that it is not intended to internalize external costs or to change people's behaviour. It differs from import duties in that it

* Sijbren Cnossen (cnossen@ese.eur.nl) is Professor of Economics at the University of Pretoria and Academic Partner at CPB Netherlands Bureau for Economic Policy Analysis.

I am grateful for the comments by Leon Bettendorf, Bas Jacobs, Ben Lockwood, and the participants of the Cnossen Forum held at Erasmus University Rotterdam, 23–24 May 2019.

[1] Council Directive 2006/112/EC of 28 November 2006 on the Common System of Value Added Tax, Official Journal of the European Union (OJ) L347/1, recasting Sixth Council Directive 77/388/EEC of 12 May 1977 on the Harmonisation of the Laws of the Member States relating to Turnover Taxes—Common System of VAT: Uniform Basis of Assessment, (1977) OJ L145/01.

[2] The main difference between exemptions and exclusions is that entities engaging in excluded (i.e. non-taxable) activities, unlike exempt entities, cannot opt for registration and taxation that would enable them to recover their input VAT. Below, exemptions include exclusions, unless the context implies otherwise.

Sijbren Cnossen, *Modernizing Value-Added Tax* In: *Tax by Design for the Netherlands.* Edited by: Sijbren Cnossen and Bas Jacobs, Oxford University Press. © Oxford University Press 2022. DOI: 10.1093/oso/9780192855244.003.0020 should not be used to support trade policy. It also differs from income tax in that it is not the instrument of first choice to influence the tax burden distribution or to stimulate industry through investment incentives. The expenditure system (financed by the VAT, among other sources of revenue) is a much better instrument to mitigate the plight of lower-income groups, while investment incentives, if considered desirable, should be incorporated in taxes on profits, because they purport to raise the net return on investment.

The major design principle that follows from this view is that all goods and services used or consumed in a given country should be taxed equally at a uniform rate. This distorts the efficient allocation of resources brought about by the market as little as possible, as relative prices do not change. With reference to the production-efficiency theorem of Diamond and Mirrlees (1971), Crawford, Keen, and Smith (2010) argue that optimality considerations regarding base and rate differentiation do not fundamentally alter this guiding principle for VAT design.[3] It follows that exemptions should be limited to those strictly necessary on administrative grounds. In this respect, the EU VAT and, by extension, the Dutch version leaves much to be desired. The issue is important because it has been shown that base-broadening and rate unification offset by a reduction in the standard rate foster economic growth (Acosta-Ormaechea and Morozumi, 2019)—more than would an increase in the standard rate in combination with a reduction in the income taxes.

With these considerations in mind, in Section 20.2 I list the exemptions under the EU VAT and note the distortions and complications that these bring about. Next, in Section 20.3, I provide a quantitative analysis of the Dutch VAT base, which, in view of the EU-wide harmonized base, should be fairly representative of the base in other member states. The gap between the actual Dutch VAT (or any other VAT, for that matter) and a modern VAT can be captured by the ratio of actual to potential revenue, found by applying the standard rate to the aggregated consumption expenditures of households, governments, and non-profit organizations. This ratio is called the VAT's collection efficiency (C-efficiency, for short). In Section 20.4, I show that the C-efficiency differs greatly from unity and that the gap involves substantial welfare costs. Subsequently, in Sections 20.5–20.11, I review the most important exemptions in greater detail and suggest how the underlying activities can be integrated into the VAT base. In Section 20.12, I present arguments against rate differentiation—another aspect that distinguishes the Dutch and EU VAT from a modern VAT. In Section 20.13, I summarize and

[3] Further, Keen (2013) points out that "[u]ltimately, the use of uniform taxation as a reference point in evaluating VAT systems reflects the pragmatic judgment that the practical case for a single rate [and a broad base] is so strong as to make this an important benchmark.... The case is especially persuasive in higher-income countries, a central lesson of the literature being that uniform taxation is more likely to be optimal the more sophisticated the range of other instruments by which equity objectives can be pursued."

conclude. Throughout the chapter, I assume that taxes on consumption reduce the disposable income of consumers proportionate to their expenditures on taxable goods and services (Institute for Fiscal Studies, 2011).

20.2 Exemptions and Distortions

Box 20.1 provides a summary of the exemptions under the EU VAT. The exemptions are mandatorily prescribed under the EU's joint VAT Directive, namely in Article 13 (public bodies excluded from VAT), in Article 132 (exemptions for specified activities in the public interest), and in Article 135 (exemptions for other activities). In addition, EU member states can provide a threshold below which small entities, which might have difficulties in complying with the VAT's obligations, are exempted from VAT. For similar reasons, the agricultural sector is often left out of the VAT base.

The exemptions have been introduced not for administrative reasons but because the designers of the EU VAT Directive did not understand the manner in which exempt activities could be included in the VAT base. The need for reconsidering the exemptions is quite evident from the distortions and complications that they cause. As discussed in the literature (e.g. Ebrill et al., 2001), exemptions have the following effects:

- they distort input choices, because exempt entities will buy products that bear a lower VAT, which they would not do if the VAT were creditable;
- they disincentivize investments, which are postponed or acquired second-hand in order to save on non-creditable input VAT;
- they hamper outsourcing (self-supply bias) to avoid the VAT on the labour element in the cost of, say, laundry, cleaning, food, administrative and protection services, which would otherwise be bought from taxable suppliers;
- they distort competition, because taxable entities cannot provide similar goods or services at the same (lower) price as they would have to apply the full VAT;
- they favour imports, which enter the country presumptively free of tax, while similar domestically produced goods and services bear input VAT on purchases from exempt businesses;
- they discriminate against exports, because it is not possible to relieve them of tax on purchases from exempt businesses;
- they cause delineation issues (taxable or exempt?) and complicate input VAT allocation over exempt (non-creditable) and taxable (creditable) supplies if the inputs are used for both forms of supply;
- they induce 'exemption creep' because exempt entities and their suppliers will lobby for an extension of the exemption.

Box 20.1 Exemptions and exclusions under the EU VAT Directive

Mandatory

Public bodies (Article 13)

States, regional, and local government authorities, and other bodies governed by public law in respect of the activities or transactions in which they engage as public authorities.

Activities in the public interest (Article 132)

- Public postal services other than passenger transport and telecommunications services;
- hospital and medical care, ambulance and dental services;
- welfare and social security work, also if supplied by old people's homes;
- protection of children and young persons;
- children's or young people's education, school or university education, vocational training or retraining;
- private tuition by teachers, covering school or university education;
- religious or philosophical institutions with a view to spiritual welfare;
- subscription-based political, trade-union, religious, patriotic, philosophical, philanthropic, or civic organizations;
- sport or physical education by non-profit-making organizations;
- cultural services;
- fund-raising activities by exempt organizations;
- public radio and television bodies.

Other activities (Article 133)

- Insurance and reinsurance, including insurance brokers and agents;
- granting, negotiation, and management of credit and credit guarantees;
- transactions concerning deposit and current accounts, payments, transfers, debts, cheques, and other negotiable instruments, but excluding debt collection;
- currency, bank notes, and coins used as legal tender, with the exception of collectors' items;
- transactions in shares, interests in companies or associations, debentures, and other securities;
- special investment funds;
- postage stamps, fiscal stamps, and similar stamps;
- betting, lotteries, and other forms of gambling;

- buildings or parts thereof, and of the land on which they stand;
- land that has not been built on;
- leasing or letting of immovable property.

Note: not exempt are hotels and similar forms of accommodation, holiday camping sites, parking facilities, permanently installed equipment and machinery, and the hire of safes.

Optional

Small entities (Article 285)

Taxable persons whose annual turnover is no higher than 5,000 euros or the equivalent in national currency.

Agriculture (Article 296)

Farmers in conjunction with a flat-rate scheme designed to offset the VAT charged on purchases of goods and services made by the flat-rate farmers.

Source: EU VAT Directive.

20.3 Analysis of the VAT Base

To get an idea of the quantitative importance of the exemptions (and the lower rate), Table 20.1 shows details of the composition of the Dutch VAT base in 2015, subdivided into predominantly taxable transactions and predominantly exempt or input-taxed transactions subject to VAT on fixed assets and intermediate purchases.

The first and second columns of Table 20.1 identify the component parts of the base of a modern VAT, which consists of the consumption expenditures of households and the value of the services rendered by public bodies and non-profit entities. Government salaries on healthcare, education, cultural services, and government itself are assumed to represent the consumption expenditures on these items. This should be a reasonable approximation as value added comprises wages and business cash flow (i.e. above-normal returns that may be disregarded in the case of services rendered by public bodies).

Columns 3 and 4 show goods and services that are taxed as they should be, that is, subject to VAT on turnover (output) with credit (deduction) for the VAT on purchases (inputs). Interestingly, only 22% of the potential base is subject to the standard rate and 16% to the lower rate. Columns 5–7 show the goods and services that are exempt or rather taxed on inputs. The amount of exempt goods and services that are input-taxed is 60% of a modern VAT base. This is indicative of the shortcomings of the VAT. After all, the VAT on the inputs for these goods and services, which cannot be invoiced to customers, constitutes an indeterminate and

Table 20.1 The Netherlands: composition and yield of the VAT base (2015, in million euros)

Consumption expenditures (including social benefits in kind)	Base modern VAT	Base actual VAT					Yield and rate		Notes
		Output taxed		Input taxed			Tax	Effective tax rate (%)	
		Standard rate (21%)	Reduced rate (6%)	Exempt	Fixed assets	Intermediate use			
(1)	(2)	(3)	(4)	(5)	(6)	(7)	(8)	(9)	
A. Households	**434,835**	**99,510**	**72,495**	**242,559**	**30,723**	**100,922**	**38,323**	**8.8**	
1. Predominantly taxable	***173,173***	***94,701***	***68,544***	***9,928***	***1,524***	***5,469***	***24,105***	***13.9***	
Foodstuffs	32,496	1,156	31,340				2,123	6.5	21% animal feed
Restaurants and hotels	19,871	4,034	15,837				1,797	9.0	21% alcoholic beverages
Water	1,080		1,080				65	6.0	
Non-alcoholic beverages	1,820		1,820				109	6.0	
Personal care products	9,342	3,463	5,879				1,080	11.6	6% dressings, prescription-free medicines, sun cream, toothpaste
Alcoholic beverages	2,891	2,891					607	21.0	See also restaurants and hotels
Tobacco	3,956	3,956					831	21.0	
Energy	5,821	5,821					1,222	21.0	
Motor fuel	8,380	8,380					1,760	21.0	
Durable consumer goods	47,193	45,138	2,055				9,602	20.3	6% art objects, walkers, books, medical instruments
Communication	6,538	6,113		425	70	596	1,413	21.6	Intermediate, 21% €539 m; 6% €21 m; exempt, €36 m
Transportation	6,894	621	3,801	2,472	1,366	1,374	438	6.4	Intermediate, 21% €936 m; 6% €2 m; exempt, €436 m
House and garden	5,683	2,916	1,343	1,424			693	12.2	6% maintenance services

Other goods and services	21,208	10,212	5,389	5,607	88	3,499	2,465	11.6	6% pets, preservatives, periodicals, horticultural products; intermediate, 21% €2,473 m; 6% €321 m; exempt, €705 m
2. Predominantly exempt	***261,662***	***4,809***	***3,951***	***232,631***	***29,199***	***95,453***	***14,217***	***5.4***	
Medical and social care	115,794	800		114,994	4,389	21,828	3,039	2.6	Government salaries, €45,190 m; intermediate, 21% €8,165 m; 6% €6,697 m; exempt, €6,966 m
Education	23,344			23,344	2,371	6,655	1,110	4.8	Government salaries, €23,344 m; intermediate, 21% €5,131 m; 6% €530 m; exempt, €994 m
Recreation and culture	14,729	1,098	3,874	9,757	158	1,769	757	5.1	21% commercial radio/TV; government salaries, €3,813 m; intermediate, 21% €1,141 m; 6% €344 m; exempt, €284 m
Rents and rental values	63,868	332	77	63,459	19,230	35,657	6,304	9.9	Intermediate, 21% €9,861 m; 6% €1,997 m; exempt, €23,799 m
Financial and business services	23,656	2,579		21,077	3,051	29,444	3,007	12.7	Intermediate, 21% €8,426 m; 6% €920 m; exempt, €20,098 m
B. Non-profit institutions	**5,444**			5,444					
C. Governments	**29,556**			29,556	11,954	26,031	6,126	20.7	Government salaries, €29,556 m; intermediate, 21% €16,836 m; 6% €1,330 m; exempt, €7,865 m
Grand totals	**449,564**	**99,510**	**72,495**	**272,115**	**42,677**	**125,953**	**44,548**	**9.9**	

Source: Statistics Netherlands, expenditure categories (excluding VAT) by VAT rates 2015. The base of the modern VAT for the exempt sectors (i.e. education, medical and social care, recreation, and culture) is assumed to consist of the remuneration of (government) employees found in the national accounts (Nationale Rekeningen 2017, available online at https://www.cbs.nl/nl-nl/publicatie/2018/30/nationale-rekeningen-2017) in addition to private consumption expenditures on these categories. The taxable inputs (intermediate goods and fixed assets) of exempt transactions and sectors are used to calculate the VAT on inputs. The effective tax rate is the yield as a percentage of the modern VAT base.

capricious element in sales prices, which distorts producer and consumer decisions and complicates the application of the VAT.

The capricious taxation of most goods and services is also apparent from the effective tax rates (column 8), that is, actual VAT receipts as a percentage of the modern VAT base. The standard rate of 21% is only applicable to alcoholic beverages, tobacco, energy, motor fuel, durable consumer goods, and communication services. Further, the table shows that the effective tax rate on foodstuffs, restaurants, and hotels equals the nominal rate of 6%. As expected, exempt services are taxed at lower effective rates, ranging from 2.6% on medical and social care to 12.7% on financial and business services. The total effective tax rate is close to 10% compared to the standard rate of 21% and a lower rate of 6% (currently 9%).[4] The most important message of the table is that the exemptions and lower rate result in a muddle of effective tax rates, a situation that is difficult to justify in a country capable of levying a modern VAT and having an advanced social benefit system to compensate lower-income groups for the regressive impact of the VAT.

20.4 Collection-Efficiency and Welfare Costs

The conclusion is inescapable: the EU VAT is not the efficient revenue-raising instrument that it can be. The defect is encapsulated by the VAT's C-efficiency, which is 1 (one) for a uniform rate VAT on all consumption expenditures. The difference between unity and the actual C-efficiency comprises the VAT that is not levied on account of the exemptions, lower rates and the threshold (called the policy gap), and shortcomings due to laps in the compliance and implementation of the VAT (called the compliance gap).

The Organization for Economic Co-operation and Development (OECD, 2018, p. 90) computed the C-efficiency of the Dutch VAT (excluding governments) at 0.51 in 2016. This was slightly higher than the OECD's unweighted average of 0.50, but somewhat lower than the average of the other EU member states (i.e. 0.52). In sharp contrast, the C-efficiency of the modern New Zealand VAT, which taxes nearly all goods and services at a uniform rate of 12.5% was 0.95 in the same year. The policy gap dominates the compliance gap in the EU. Bettendorf and Cnossen (2015), for example, calculated the policy gap of the Dutch VAT at 44% of potential receipts and the compliance gap at 2%. Obviously, closing the policy gap is not meant to increase VAT revenues per se. Rather, under an equal yield assumption, the 'extra' revenue from a broader base and a single rate can be used

[4] On the basis of Table 20.1, the VAT's yield can be calculated at 44,548 million euros, which is close to the actual yield of 44,589 million euros (see Table 2.3.1 of Miljoenennota, 2016).

to lower the standard rate or other taxes that are more distortionary than the VAT.

Copenhagen Economics (2013) calculated the efficiency gain that could be reaped if various exempt supplies were taxed (with credit for the VAT on intermediate goods and fixed assets). It analysed the effects of six core services (i.e. cultural activities, education, healthcare, garbage collection, postal services, and radio and television broadcasts), which, jointly, contributed 14.2% of GDP in the EU-27 (excluding Croatia) in 2010. The efficiency gain of fully taxing these services, which is what New Zealand does, would be 0.34% of GDP. If governments were to be included, the gain might well approach 0.5% of GDP. Copenhagen Economics notes further that in the absence of the self-supply bias, full taxation should have a significant positive effect, particularly on medium-sized and small businesses, which account for 60% of business services in the affected sectors.

While the efficiency gain may not seem exceptionally large, it is the sort of gain that highly developed countries should be looking for if they want to increase their welfare. Not surprisingly, Copenhagen Economics (2013, p. 12) concludes: 'we recommend to look towards a full taxation solution'. With this in mind, in the following sections, I examine the EU exemptions in greater detail.

20.5 Governments

Governments—central, regional, and local—and other public bodies are considered out-of-scope of the EU VAT, subject to some highly contentious conditions (as evidenced by a vast body of jurisprudence reviewed by Henkow, 2013): that they should be governed by public law, that they should be operated under public authority, and that their activities should not involve significant distortions of competition. 'Out-of-scope' means that governments do not enter the VAT's ambit. This expresses the view that governments should be viewed as final consumers (i.e. not be subject to tax and therefore not entitled to credit for the tax on inputs). Incidence theory, however, holds that only people, not institutions, bear taxes; their disposable income is reduced. Accordingly, services provided by governments to their citizens/consumers should be taxed in full, if feasible, just like goods and services produced by the private sector. Exceptions should only be made for pure public goods (defence, public administration, law and order) for which it is not possible to set a 'price', and for the redistribution of income and wealth, which does not constitute consumption (see the influential paper by Aujean, Jenkins, and Poddar, 1999).

Although, in terms of revenue, the taxation of many goods and services provided by public bodies would largely be in the nature of a pay-out and claw-back arrangement, the VAT on the inputs of exempt bodies causes the same non-neutralities and complexities as other exemptions: distortion of input choice, self-supply bias, unfair competition, and tax avoidance. Summing up the situation, Aujean (2010, p. 514), an astute observer and long-time participant in the debate on EU VAT, has labelled the VAT treatment of public bodies 'complex, inefficient, costly, and legally uncertain'. In the same vein, de la Feria (2009), another able tax lawyer, has documented the highly complex web of conditions, derogations, movements into and out of scope of VAT, and transitions between 'exempt' situations, 'taxable' situations, and 'non-taxable because out-of-scope situations'. She has attempted to lay this down in a flow chart, which shows that it is almost impossible to establish and apply a single consistent VAT treatment to all public-sector bodies. De la Feria opines that the EU VAT Directive is becoming more out of step with economic realities as time passes. The EU treatment, moreover, entails very significant compliance and administrative costs, as well as frequent and costly litigation.

The taxation of as many supplies by public bodies as possible would promote simplicity, accountability, transparency, and the workings of the VAT. Apart from eliminating most distortions, delineation issues regarding taxable versus non-taxable activities would become redundant. In short, the VAT chain would remain intact through to the consumer level. Although public bodies do not pursue profit maximization per se, cost minimization should be their aim, and this goal is promoted by applying the VAT as widely as possible.

The main issue that arises in taxing public goods and services is that many tend to be made for nil, nominal, or break-even consideration, and that they are usually financed through a variety of means that include charges, user fees, taxes, subsidies, grants, budgetary allocations, and funds from borrowing, often without a direct link to the supplies. Under modern VATs, all of these means of financing, regardless of their form, are included in the VAT base. Full inclusion prevents tax avoidance. As an example, Copenhagen Economics (2013) notes that, if taxed, public bodies can avoid the VAT under present arrangements by transforming product subsidies (taxable under the EU VAT Directive) into budget subsidies (not taxable). Budget subsidies, therefore, should also be included in the taxable base, which is what modern VATs do. The full taxation of public bodies, as is done in New Zealand and Australia, would, of course, require adjustments on the expenditure side of the budget.

An alternative, found in Canada, would be to refund the input tax of municipalities, to exempt provincial governments and to zero rate the supplies for the central government without further ado (Gendron, 2013). This would also eliminate most distortions and complexities, except for the competitive advantage governments would have if goods and services can also be provided by the private sector, which would be subject to the full VAT. Input VAT refunds are also provided under the VAT compensation schemes in various EU member states, but Wassenaar and Gradus (2004) conclude that their haphazard application hardly solves the self-supply bias and the investment disincentive. Copenhagen Economics (2013) estimates that the zero-rating of the services included in its study, as opposed to full taxation, would only increase welfare by 0.02% of GDP. Clearly, the situation calls for deeper reforms, preferably full taxation or close to comprehensive refund schemes, as in Canada.

20.6 Healthcare, Education, Social, and Cultural Services

Healthcare, education, and various social services—called activities in the public interest—are often considered 'merit goods' whose consumption should not be constrained by the imposition of VAT. However, even if the merit-good argument is acknowledged, full taxation of the output (including subsidies, if any) of hospitals, schools, universities, and various forms of social assistance in combination with increased subsidies could leave the total net amount of the (VAT-inclusive) charge for the services unaffected without distorting the exempt entities' input choices and outsourcing activities and without discriminating against similar taxable services provided by the private sector (which should then also be subsidized).

Accordingly, under New Zealand's Goods and Services Tax (GST), supplies by health organizations, educational institutions (except elementary schools), cultural organizations, social assistance agencies, child welfare groups, postal services, and public broadcasting companies, all exempt in the EU (see Box 20.1), are taxable.[5] According to Aujean et al. (1999), this has 'permitted there [i.e. in New Zealand] a dramatic simplification of VAT rules as they apply to public bodies'. The effect on revenue, moreover, would be nil, to the extent that the charge for the activities as well as their financing are determined by public bodies. Much the same effect is attained in Canada, which refunds the GST on the inputs of the MUSH sector—Municipalities (up to 100%), Universities (67%), Schools (68%), and Hospitals (83%)—percentages that have increased over time and that are moving towards full refunds (Gendron, 2013). Note, however, that the refunds may be aggravating the competitive distortion with regards to the private sector.

20.7 Property and Casualty Insurance

Insurance services are exempted from VAT in the EU, because at the level of the policyholder the taxable intermediation charge cannot be separated from the

[5] Of course, social services in the form of benefit pay-outs should not be taxed as they are not consumption, but their administrative cost does add value to the economy and should be included in the VAT base.

non-taxable capital transfer to the common pool from which indemnity and contingency payments are made. Instead, most member states subject insurance premiums to anachronistic, cascading insurance taxes or stamp duties, which should have no place in a modern tax system based on notions of equal treatment and neutrality. Further, no sensible argument can be made for why the VAT on insurance services should depend on the ratio between taxable inputs and exempt sales.

By contrast, modern VATs avoid the problem of determining taxable value added on the basis of individual policies by shifting it to the level of the insurance company, where value added is the difference between premium receipts, on the one hand, and indemnity pay-outs and taxable purchases, on the other. This difference is taxed by collecting VAT on insurance premiums (and permitting a credit for the VAT on the taxed inputs of insurance companies), and imputing a tax credit to indemnity payments (to be offset against the VAT on premiums).[6] The VAT on insurance premiums would be creditable by clients liable for VAT, who should be obliged to include the imputed tax credit received along with indemnity payments in their VAT return. However, a non-taxable recipient of the amount of the tax credit included in the indemnity payment would not have to file a return for it (not being taxable, the recipient would not have been able to offset the VAT on the insurance premium either). Instead, they would pay VAT on the replacing asset or keep their capital intact. VAT would continue to be imposed on warranties embedded in product prices.

While property and casualty insurance can thus be taxed, health and life insurance should probably remain exempt. Both forms of insurance are mostly taken out by individuals; hence, cascading effects are unlikely to occur (and thus taxation on the basis of the sum of payroll and business cash flow could be considered an alternative). For VAT purposes, health insurance would then be treated in the same way as other health services if these were to remain exempt, while life insurance—a long-term savings vehicle akin to pensions—would be exempted along with other financial business-to-consumer (B2C) margin-based services. A complication, too, is that the intermediation charge is not a constant portion of the gross premium, but increases with the duration of the insurance. Furthermore, health insurance premiums are often universal, compulsory, and sometimes progressive against income.

[6] Correct treatment would also imply that insurers' investment returns, which are eligible for a reverse credit, if paid out, should be taxed, although this is not done anywhere. For a review and evaluation of the EU situation and a detailed reform proposal along the lines sketched here, see Cnossen (2013).

20.8 Financial Services

The EU VAT Directive exempts financial services entirely, whether fee- or margin-based. This implies that B2C services tend to be undertaxed and business-to-business (B2B) services overtaxed. Margin-based services are difficult to tax under the tax-credit-method VAT, because the value of the intermediation charge (which should be taxed) is embedded in interest rates, returns or rewards which (along with the principal) should not be taxed, because they are not consumption but income. Because the value of the intermediation charge is not known, VAT cannot be charged on it and passed on to clients on a transaction-by-transaction basis, necessary if VAT-liable customers are to credit the tax against their VAT on output (see the leading paper by Poddar, 2003).

By contrast, fee-based services can be taxed without further ado, as is done in countries with a modern VAT. Taxing fee-based services would raise the tax on B2C services and enable business users of financial services to credit the tax on fee-based services in full. It is surprising that EU member states do not yet tax explicit financial fees and commissions. Admittedly, some fee-based services might be substituted by margin-based services, but disintermediation has made this less likely (Poddar, 2003). Moreover, financial services performed against a fee can be listed, and hence taxed, as is done in South Africa, for instance. Because higher-income people tend to consume more financial services than lower-income people, the distribution of the tax increase associated with taxing fee-based services would tend to be progressive with respect to income.

This leaves the distortionary effect of the exemption of margin-based services rendered to taxable businesses, which are not entitled to a credit for the VAT included therein. To remedy this effect, consideration should be given to allowing partial formula-based recovery of the input VAT incurred in rendering B2B margin services by financial institutions. Australia, New Zealand, and Singapore have instituted rules to that effect. New Zealand, for instance, zero-rates supplies of financial services to non-financial businesses, whose turnover, measured over a twelve-month period, consists of at least three-quarters of taxable supplies (Pallot, 2011). The rebatable GST (in principle, identical to VAT) of the financial services provider is determined on the basis of common apportionment rules, notably the turnover method. A look-through provision ensures that the input GST of a financial services provider is also zero-rated if the services are rendered to another financial services provider, which, in turn, makes supplies to registered businesses that are eligible to purchase zero-rated financial services.

Alternatively, financial services could be taxed under an addition-method VAT on the sum of payroll and business cash flow.[7] Denmark and Israel do so, although

[7] For a discussion of how value added can be measured and taxed, see Cnossen (2019).

Denmark does not include business cash flow in the base and Israel taxes profits instead. Although these approaches result in a fuller taxation of B2C services, they do not permit the passing on of input-VAT on a transaction-by-transaction basis and, hence, they increase the distortion of the VAT with respect to B2B financial services.

20.9 Lotteries and Gambling

EU practice is to exempt games of chance from VAT. In contrast, countries with a modern VAT tax most games of chance. Lotteries can be taxed on ticket sales (output), while a reverse charge can be imputed to pay-outs (inputs), similar to the best-practice VAT treatment of property and casualty insurance. The value added of the lottery industry would thus be taxed after providing a credit for the VAT on inputs against the gross tax liability (net of the VAT imputed to pay-outs). Casinos can be included in the VAT base under the margin method, where the margin is the difference between the sales of tokens and chips, on the one hand, and pay-outs, on the other. Again, a credit for VAT on other inputs should be allowed against the tax liability (for a fuller treatment, see Schenk, 2010). Both approaches yield the same result. VAT should be applied to transactions involving games of chance, regardless of whether or not lotteries and gambling are subject to externality-correcting excises.

20.10 Immovable Property

Obviously, it would be very difficult, administratively and politically, to tax the rental value of owner-occupied dwellings and, by extension, rental payments, as should be done under a fully fledged VAT. For this reason, the EU VAT Directive exempts residential as well as non-residential immovable property, but taxes new buildings (and the land on which they stand). Because the purchase price of a new building may be taken to represent the present discounted value of its future rents or rental values, the VAT on the purchase price may be considered a good proxy for the discounted value of the VAT that should have been levied on the future flow of building services. Further, to avoid potential discrimination and cascading of tax, the EU's exemption approach provides for an option to include non-residential buildings in the VAT base, obviously with a credit for the tax on new buildings and other inputs. Note that the exemption method needs a definition of specified non-residential use, such as hotel accommodation, boarding houses, camping facilities, and parking space—these should be taxable on the rates charged to customers.

By contrast, modern VATs tax the sale and leasing of *all* non-residential buildings, which provides for a fuller inclusion of immovable property in the

VAT base, because future increases in value will also be taxed. Accordingly, this tax approach should be preferred.[8]

Ideally, the tax approach should be complemented by the taxation of the increase in the value of residential buildings realized at the time of their sale (while refunds should be made if the value has declined), similar to the VAT margin scheme for second-hand goods. If value increases were taxed, transfer or registration duties, which exhibit the same capricious effects as a cascading turnover tax, should be abolished. Also, an input tax credit should be provided for the VAT paid in respect of major renovations. Admittedly, the VAT on increases in value causes lock-in effects, which discourage residential mobility, but this effect also occurs under the transfer or registration duty. Taxing immovable property more comprehensively under the VAT would most likely mitigate the regressive impact of the VAT, as housing tends to be an income-elastic item of consumption.

20.11 Registration Threshold and Agriculture

The EU VAT Directive prescribes a registration threshold of 5,000 euros, but derogations show a wide range of thresholds across EU member states. Previously, the Dutch VAT, for instance, did not have a registration threshold, although VAT liabilities of small businesses of 1,345 euros or less did not have to be paid. From 2020, however, the government has simplified the small-business exemption by introducing a general threshold of 20,000 euros, still one of the lowest in the EU.

This begs the question of what the best-practice level of a threshold should be. Obviously, at least two competing considerations enter the equation: revenue and operational (administration and compliance) costs. The revenue loss (gain) of increasing (reducing) the threshold must be balanced against the lower (higher) administrative cost of applying the VAT to a smaller (larger) number of registrants. Further, it should be considered that compliance costs (as a percentage of sales) tend to be much higher for small businesses than for large businesses. In the UK, for instance, the compliance costs of small businesses, as a percentage of turnover, have been estimated to be on average twenty times the compliance costs of large businesses (see Sandford, Godwin, and Hardwick, 1989).

Because compliance costs tend to be fixed costs, their incidence is likely to be regressive with respect to income, though this is an aspect that should be balanced against the competitive advantage that small exempt businesses may enjoy with respect to their larger taxable competitors. In addition, the cost of the economic

[8] Incidentally, the EU's exemption approach is equivalent to the modern tax approach, if, under the former, all owners of non-residential buildings were to opt for registration and payment of VAT, but this is not likely to happen. For a full treatment of the exemption and tax approaches, reference is made to Cnossen (2011).

distortions that can be associated with behavioural changes of businesses just below or above the threshold should be taken into account. Presumably, these costs increase as the threshold increases. Liu and Lockwood (2015) show that there is bunching around the threshold, and the amount of bunching is negatively related to the intensity of input use and positively related to the share of B2C transactions, consistent with the conceptual framework that they develop.

Apart from the cost of the economic distortions, the trade-off between revenue and operational costs is optimized, loosely speaking, at the point where the additional revenue from lowering the threshold equals the additional operational costs incurred. Keen and Mintz (2004) have formalized this trade-off in the following simple rule:

$$z^* = \frac{\delta A + \Gamma}{(\delta - 1)\tau v(z)}.$$

Here, z^* is the threshold that maximizes revenue, A denotes the administrative costs (assumed to be fixed), Γ denotes the compliance costs (also fixed), δ denotes the (constant) marginal cost of public funds, τ is the VAT rate, and v is the ratio of value added to sales. Based on the estimate of operational costs for developed countries given by Cnossen (1994)—US$100 for administrative costs and US$500 for compliance costs—a VAT rate of 15%, a ratio of value added to sales of 35%, and a marginal cost of public funds of 1.3, Keen and Mintz compute an optimal threshold for developed countries of US$40,000 (36,000 euros), nearly twice the size of the proposed threshold in the Netherlands.

Obviously, the Keen–Mintz formula—in contrast to the Liu–Lockwood framework—does not take account of the economic distortions noted above. If it did, the recommended threshold might be lower. However, a much higher threshold than the current Dutch version would appear to save on administrative and compliance costs. A relatively generous threshold without further ado would also seem to be the most appropriate approach to exempt small farmers from VAT. Before 2018, farmers were not obliged to register for VAT (although they could opt to do so), while their VAT on inputs was presumptively washed out through a flat-rate compensation scheme providing purchasers of agricultural products a tax credit for the estimated input VAT incurred by farmers. As pointed out by Cnossen (2018), this is an arbitrary form of input relief, which is out of date and in conflict with a modern VAT. Currently, Dutch farmers have to register for VAT subject to the newly introduced threshold.

20.12 Differentiated Rates

In contrast to a modern VAT, the VATs in most member states have differentiated rate schedules (Denmark is a notable exception). The reduced rates are supposed to mitigate the VAT burden on lower-income households, although Bettendorf and Cnossen (2015), on which this section draws, show that in the Netherlands higher-income groups benefit nearly twice as much from the lower rate on foodstuffs (and cultural activities) than lower-income groups—an odd way of trying to help the poor. The income tax and the social benefit system, moreover, are much more effective alternatives for influencing the income distribution.

The economic argument in favour of a uniform rate is that it does not distort consumer and producer choices. Eliminating the reduced rate, therefore, involves a welfare gain, which has been quantified by the Institute for Fiscal Studies (2011) for the UK and Belgium (regrettably, no analysis has been done for the Netherlands). An increase in the reduced rates (including the zero rate on food and dwellings in the UK) to the level of the standard rate implies a welfare gain of 3.5% of total VAT receipts in the UK and 4.6% for Belgium. In an alternative scenario, the elimination of the reduced rate is combined with a reduction of the standard rate by five percentage points, so that VAT yields stay the same. This results in a welfare gain per household of 1.07 euros per week in the UK and 0.74 euros per week in Belgium. Plausibly, a similar welfare gain would be realized for the Netherlands, because the differentiated rate involves roughly the same revenue loss as in Belgium.

A further argument is that a uniform rate contributes to a simpler VAT system with lower administration and compliance costs. For 2007, the VAT compliance costs for the Dutch business community were estimated at 408 million euros (excluding costs of invoicing; van Weeghel et al., 2010). In 2008, the Ministry of Finance estimated that a uniform VAT rate would reduce these costs by some 100 million euros (Tweede Kamer der Staten-Generaal, 2009). Also, the direct administrative costs of the VAT, estimated at 138 million euros, would go down. Compared with a dual rate structure, a uniform rate is also less sensitive to lobbying activities, while misclassifications, intentional or not, should not occur. A disadvantage of abolishing the reduced rate is that Dutch inhabitants of border areas might buy their foodstuffs in Belgium and Germany. However, the lower Dutch standard rate would attract Belgian and German buyers for other products. In any event, cross-border purchases are more of a problem for excisable goods than for goods and services subject to VAT (see the overview in Cnossen, 2003).

20.13 Summary and Conclusion

In this chapter, I have argued for modernizing the Dutch (and EU) VAT by broadening the base and levying a uniform rate. Base broadening would eliminate the distortions and complexities associated with skewed input choices, self-supply bias, export taxation, contentious input tax allocation, and exemption creep. Following New Zealand's example:

- governments, particularly provinces and municipalities, should be made liable to VAT, as in New Zealand;
- education (except elementary schools), healthcare, and social and cultural establishments can be brought into the VAT base without increasing the cost for students, patients, or other users;
- property and casualty insurance should be subject to VAT, and the distortionary stamp duty on insurance abolished;
- fee-based financial services should be made taxable and a scheme should be developed that would permit the recovery of the input VAT by financial institutions in supplying B2B services;
- lotteries and gambling should be brought into the VAT base;
- all non-residential property should be subject to VAT and it is suggested to impose VAT on the gain realized on the transfer of residential property, while the distortionary transfer duty should be abolished;
- the threshold should be reviewed; and
- the lower rate should be increased (and the standard rate reduced) in a move towards one single rate.

But for the EU VAT Directive, most of these reforms can be implemented without much further ado. The taxation of governments, education, and healthcare may be somewhat problematic as it would involve important changes on the expenditure side of the budget. The greater neutrality that would be achieved by taxing these sectors fully can also be achieved by zero-rating the bodies involved in providing government, education, and healthcare services. While this would not remove the competitive distortion with respect to the private sector, it would eliminate the input choice distortion, the self-supply bias, and various administrative complications. Also, it would permit an optical reduction in the overall tax ratio.

The EU VAT Directive is the most important obstacle to these reforms. However, if the EU cannot reach a consensus on the adoption of improvements to the EU VAT Directive, perhaps member states themselves should be allowed to do so, subject to approval by the EU VAT Committee. Arguably, a modern VAT, which does not affect the workings of the single market, unlike the current EU VAT, cannot be considered to infringe on the principles of free trade and free competition (i.e. to violate the EU Treaty).

References

Acosta-Ormaechea, S. and Morozumi, A. (2019), 'The value added tax and growth: design matters', International Monetary Fund (IMF) Working Paper no. 19/96.

Aujean, M. (2010), 'Commentary', *Tax Law Review*, 63, 509–16.

Aujean, M., Jenkins, P., and Poddar, S. (1999), 'A new approach to public sector bodies', *International VAT Monitor*, 10, 144–9.

Bettendorf, L., and Cnossen, S. (2015), 'The long shadow of the European VAT, exemplified by the Dutch experience', *FinanzArchiv*, 71, 118–39.

Cnossen, S. (1994), 'Administrative and compliance costs of the VAT: a review of the evidence', *Tax Notes International*, 8, 1649–68.

Cnossen, S. (2003), 'Is the VAT's Sixth Directive becoming an anachronism?' *European Taxation*, 43, 434–42.

Cnossen, S. (2011), 'A proposal to improve the VAT treatment of housing in the European Union', *Fiscal Studies*, 32, 455–81; reprinted in R. de la Feria (ed.), *VAT Exemptions: Consequences and Design Alternatives*, Wolters Kluwer, Alphen aan de Rijn, 225–52.

Cnossen, S. (2013), 'A proposal to apply the Kiwi-VAT to insurance services in the European Union', *International Tax and Public Finance*, 20, 867–83.

Cnossen, S. (2018), 'VAT and Agriculture: Lessons from Europe', *International Tax and Public Finance*, 25, 519–51.

Cnossen, S. (2019), *Modernizing VATs in Africa*, Oxford University Press, Oxford.

Copenhagen Economics (2013), 'VAT in the public sector and exemptions in the public interest', Final Report for TAXUD/2011/DE/334, European Commission, Brussels.

Crawford, I., Keen, M., and Smith, S. (2010), 'Value added tax and excises', in J. Mirrlees et al. (eds), *Dimensions of Tax Design: The Mirrlees Review*, Volume 1, Oxford University Press for the Institute for Fiscal Studies, Oxford, 275–422.

de la Feria, R. (2009), 'The EU VAT treatment of public sector bodies: slowly moving in the wrong direction', *Intertax*, 37, 148–65.

Diamond, P. A. and Mirrlees, J. A. (1971), 'Optimal taxation and public production I: production efficiency', *American Economic Review*, 61(1), 8–27.

Ebrill, L., Keen, M., Bodin, J-P., and Summers, V. (2001), 'The Modern VAT', International Monetary Fund, Washington, DC.

Gendron, P.-P. (2013), 'VAT treatment of public sector bodies: the Canadian model', in R. de la Feria (ed.), *VAT Exemptions: Consequences and Design Alternatives*, Wolters Kluwer, Alphen aan de Rijn, 103–33.

Henkow, O. (2013), *The VAT/GST Treatment of Public Bodies*, Wolters Kluwer, Alphen aan den Rijn.

Institute for Fiscal Studies (2011), 'Quantitative analysis of VAT rate structures, in Institute for Fiscal Studies, CPB, CAPP, CASE, CEPII, ETLA, IFO, and IHS, *A Retrospective Evaluation of Elements of the EU VAT System*', report prepared for the European Commission, TAXUD/2010/DE/328.

Keen, M. (2013), 'The anatomy of the VAT', *National Tax Journal*, 66, 423–46.

Keen, M. and Mintz, J. (2004), 'The optimal threshold for a value-added tax', *Journal of Public Economics*, 88, 559–76.

Liu, L. and Lockwood, B. (2015), 'VAT notches', Oxford University Centre for Business Taxation Working Paper WP15/06.

Miljoenennota (2016), Ministry of Finance, The Hague (https://www.rijksoverheid.nl/documenten/begrotingen/2015/09/15/miljoenennota-2016).

OECD (2018), *Consumption Tax Trends: VAT/GST and Excise Rates, Trends and Policy Issues*, OECD Publishing, Paris.

Pallot, M. (2011), 'Financial services under New Zealand's GST', *International VAT Monitor*, 22, 310–15.

Poddar, S. (2003), 'Consumption taxes: the role of the value-added tax', in P. Honohan (ed.), *Taxation of Financial Intermediation: Theory and Practice for Emerging Economies*, Oxford University Press for the World Bank, New York, 345–80.

Sandford, C., Godwin, M., and Hardwick, P. (1989), *Administrative and Compliance Costs of Taxation*, Fiscal Publications, Bath.

Schenk, A. (2010), 'Gambling and lotteries', in R. Krever (ed.), *VAT in Africa*, Pretoria University Law Press, Pretoria, 47–70.

Tweede Kamer der Staten-Generaal (2009), 'Uniform BTW-tarief: Aspecten en Overwegingen in Kort Bestek' (https://www.tweedekamer.nl/ downloads/document?id=0e44b38d-5c91-4805-82ba-10b236a030b2&title=Uniform %20BTW-tarief%3A%20Aspecten%20en%20overwegingen%20in%20kort%20 bestek.doc).

van Weeghel, S. et al. (2010), *Continuïteit en vernieuwing: een visie op het belastingstelsel*, Ministry of Finance, The Hague.

Wassenaar, M. C. and Gradus, R. H. J. M. (2004), 'Contracting out: the importance of a solution to the VAT distortion', *CESifo Economic Studies*, 50, 377–96.

21

Options for Taxation of the Financial Sector

*Ben Lockwood**

21.1 Introduction

The financial services sector is a large and growing part of any modern economy, and the Netherlands is no exception. For example, the share of finance and insurance in value added for the Netherlands in 2018 was 6.8%, one of the highest in the European Union (EU), only exceeded by the United Kingdom at 6.9% and Luxembourg at 26.5%.[1] Because of the technical difficulties of imposing VAT on some financial services, it has long been believed that this sector of the economy is under-taxed. Again, this issue is of particular significance for the Netherlands, as its banking sector is relatively large: the ratio of bank assets to GDP in 2017 was about 370%, well above the EU average, and the largest five banks comprise 85% of that total.[2]

This concern about under-taxation has taken on new urgency since the financial crisis of 2008, and indeed new taxes, such as bank levies, financial activity taxes (FATs), and financial transactions taxes (FTTs), have been introduced in many countries. Finally, in several countries, reforms to the VAT have been recently introduced to bring financial services more within scope of VAT. For example, zero-rating, rather than exemption, of business-to-business (B2B) supplies of financial services was introduced in New Zealand in January 2005.

In this chapter, I provide an overview and evaluation of these recent developments. First, in Section 21.2, I survey a range of options for dealing with the underlying problem, which is that financial services are not fully within the scope of VAT. I then look more closely at the possible revenue consequences of bringing financial services within the scope of VAT.

I then turn to the two entirely new taxes that have been introduced following the financial crisis. Both of these obviously have the practical attraction that they raise revenue, and they also probably play a political role by demonstrating tough action against the banking sector. In Section 21.3, I argue that some of the FATs

* Ben Lockwood (b.lockwood@warwick.ac.uk) is Professor of Economics at the University of Warwick and a fellow of the CEPR and the Centre for Business Taxation, University of Oxford.
I would like to thank Bas Jacobs and Sijbren Cnossen for very helpful comments.

[1] These data are from OECD (2020).

[2] These figures are from the European Banking Federation (2019).

Ben Lockwood, *Options for Taxation of the Financial Sector* In: *Tax by Design for the Netherlands*.
Edited by: Sijbren Cnossen and Bas Jacobs, Oxford University Press.
DOI: 10.1093/oso/9780192855244.003.0021

currently in use are close to an addition-based VAT, and suffer from the same problems. As regards the bank levy, I argue in Section 21.4 that there seems to be a strong conceptual and empirical case that excessive bank leverage imposes negative externalities on the rest of the economy. I discuss whether the bank levy, as currently designed, is the right corrective tax, and whether it is preferable to regulation. I draw some conclusions in Section 21.5.

21.2 VAT and Under-Taxation of Financial Services

21.2.1 Financial Services and the Under-Taxation Problem

In the discussion that follows, I define financial services to include payment services (credit/debit cards, electronic payments), savings intermediation, asset management, trading of stocks, bonds and foreign exchange, derivatives, and the provision of insurance.

As is well known, the difficulty in imposing VAT on these services is that many of these services are not conventionally priced, but are only implicitly priced by the margin charged by the financial institution as an intermediary (Ebrill et al., 2001). The classic example is that of a financial intermediation between savers and borrowers. For example, consider a bank that, for example, pays 3% on deposits, and charges 5% on loans; so the total price of intermediation of (say) \$100 is $0.02 \times \$100 = \$2$. The fact that this price is not divided between the depositor and the borrower makes it hard—if not impossible—to charge VAT in the conventional way.

The value of margin-based services of this kind can be computed from national accounts data and it is referred to as the FISIM (i.e. financial intermediation services indirectly measured). Table 21.1 gives some idea of the size of the FISIM, relative to both the total output of the financial services sector and national GDP, for the Netherlands.

We see that, for the Netherlands, almost half the value of output of the financial services sector is not explicitly priced and therefore certainly not subject to VAT. Of course, the fact that margin-based financial services are not currently

Table 21.1 FISIM in the Netherlands

	2012	2013	2014	2015	2016	2017
FISIM as a percentage of GDP	2.82	2.89	2.82	2.72	2.55	2.27
FISIM as a percentage of output of the finance and insurance sector	41.61	43.60	42.28	41.95	41.94	38.76

Source: Netherlands National Accounts and author's calculations.

subject to VAT does not imply, from a theoretical point of view, that they should be taxed. However, the theoretical literature on this topic is, in fact, unanimous that it is desirable to tax these, although there is some debate over the correct rate (Auerbach and Gordon, 2002; Lockwood, 2014).

21.2.2 Options for the VAT Treatment of Financial Services

Assuming that it is desirable to apply VAT to all financial services, how can this be done? Table 21.2 gives some possible options for the VAT treatment of financial services, and I consider these options one by one. In each case, the table gives comments on any distortion of producer and consumer choices created by the tax option, administrative complexity, and the revenue cost, relative to the benchmark of fully imposing VAT on financial services at zero administrative cost – a *comprehensive* VAT on financial services.[3] It should be emphasized that this benchmark is purely conceptual, as there is currently no way of achieving it in practice.[4] The final column gives information on countries where the method in question is used to tax financial services.

The first option is full exemption of margin-based and fee-based services. This is quite close to the regime for many countries in the EU, where the Sixth Directive gives a list of a number of financial services that must be exempt from VAT, and another list of financial services where individual countries have an option to tax. The first list is quite extensive and includes core financial activities, such as the taking of deposits, granting of credit, and insurance.[5] So, all EU countries, except those that explicitly offer the option to tax, are close to full exemption.

The disadvantages of full exemption are well known and are discussed in the first row of Table 21.2. First, there is under-taxation of business-to-consumer (B2C) transactions, leading to financial services being under-priced relative to other goods and services that are subject to VAT. Second, there is the problem that financial services providers cannot reclaim VAT on inputs—so-called embedded VAT. This embedded VAT is sometimes referred to as input taxation. Third, there is an effect on revenue, relative to comprehensive taxation, which conceptually, may be positive or negative, as discussed further in Section 2.3 below.

Embedded VAT gives rise to a number of economic distortions. First, financial services providers have an incentive to provide inputs, such as IT services,

[3] For options 2,3 and 4, for clarity, the revenue effects are expressed in comparison to option 1.

[4] The cash-flow method, the fifth option in the table, eliminates all economic distortions but is administratively very costly.

[5] Article 235 of the Council Directive 2006/112/EC of 28 November 2006 on the Common System of Value Added Tax, Official Journal of the European Union (OJ) L347/1, recasting Sixth Council Directive 77/388/EEC of 12 May 1977 on the Harmonisation of the Laws of the Member States relating to Turnover Taxes—Common System of VAT: Uniform Basis of Assessment, (1977) OJ L145/01.

Table 21.2 Comparison of VAT methods for taxing financial services

Method	Distortion of choices of VAT-registered entities	Distortion of consumer choices	Administrative complexity	Revenue cost	Examples of countries where found
Transactions-based					
Full exemption of margin and fee-based services	Self-supply bias, cascading, loss of international competitiveness	Under-taxation of B2C services	Major definitional and apportionment issues	Can be positive or negative	EU member states except those using the option to tax; African countries not in the Southern African Customs Union
Option to tax B2B services and exemption of B2C services	Distortions reduced relative to full exemption	Under-taxation of B2C services	Definitional and apportionment issues mitigated depending on use of option	Greater than under full exemption	Austria, Belgium, Estonia, France, Germany, Lithuania
Taxation of fee-based services and exemption of margin-based services	Distortions reduced relative to full exemption, especially with partial input recovery	Under-taxation of B2C services, but less than under full exemption	Number of definitional and apportionment issues less than under full exemption	Less than under full exemption, but higher with partial input recovery	Australia, Botswana, Malaysia, Namibia, Singapore, South Africa, Tanzania
Zero-rating of B2B services and exemption of B2C services	Distortions minimized	Under-taxation of B2C services	Definitional and apportionment issues mitigated	Greater than under full exemption	New Zealand
Cash-flow approach with TCAs	No distortions if pure rate of interest correctly estimated	No distortions if pure rate of interest correctly estimated	Substantial	None	None

Accounts-based					
Addition method	Cascading because input VAT cannot be reclaimed by purchasers of financial services	Distortions due to cascading	Cannot handle rate differentiation and exemptions	Extra revenue because of cascading	Iceland, Israel
Subtraction method	Cascading because input VAT cannot be reclaimed by purchasers of financial services	Distortions due to cascading	Cannot handle rate differentiation and exemptions	Extra revenue because of cascading	Japan (to some extent)

Source: This table is based on Table 13.4 of Cnossen (2019, pp. 219–20).

catering, or cleaning, themselves rather than purchase these services from other firms, even though other firms could provide these services at lower cost or higher quality. This is called self-supply bias. Second, there is the problem that financial services providers pass on embedded VAT to their customers in the form of higher prices. This will in turn distort the choices of firms who purchase financial services as inputs—so-called tax cascading. Finally, the cost of embedded VAT puts these financial services providers at a competitive disadvantage relative to other providers that do not pay VAT or can claim back input VAT. This is a common complaint made by EU-based international banks.

Finally, even in the EU, some fee-based financial services are subject to VAT, the details varying by country.[6] So, banks and other providers will typically supply a mixture of exempt and non-exempt services. EU countries, and others, use apportionment rules to determine the share of the cost of inputs that can be allocated to non-exempt outputs and thus can be reclaimed. These rules are often complex and open to several interpretations, and thus can impose an administrative burden.[7]

A second possibility, shown in the second row of Table 21.2, is the option to tax. The Sixth Directive gives the EU member states the right to introduce legislation that grants financial institutions the option of letting themselves be taxed in return for the possibility of deducting their input VAT. The member states have considerable leeway in designing such legislation.[8] The advantages and disadvantages of this option are given in the second row of Table 21.2. In principle, relative to the first option of full exemption, pricing distortions will be lower, and apportionment issues will be less severe, but there will be a loss of revenue due to the higher level of input VAT recovery. However, in practice, despite the existence of the option to tax, most EU member states do not make use of it. Moreover, in the six countries where this option is used, financial institutions often do not opt in. As a result, the prevailing VAT regime for financial services in Europe is close to exemption.

A third option is taxation of all fee-based services and exemption of margin-based services. The economic effects of this are similar to the option to tax;

[6] For example, in the United Kingdom, the list of services currently subject to VAT includes book-keeping services, debt collection, depository and trustee services, equipment leasing, investment, finance and taxation advice, management consultancy, merger and takeover advice, and portfolio management.

[7] For example, in the case of the Netherlands, a survey in 2007 states the apportionment rule as follows: 'only that part of the input VAT is deductible which corresponds to the ratio of the entrepreneur's total consideration derived from the other transactions to that derived from all transactions ("pro rata"). However, Article 11(2) of the VAT Implementing Order provides that, where it is found that, taken as a whole, actual use of the goods and services used for mixed purposes deviates from the pro rata, input VAT in respect of those goods and services is deductible on the basis of their actual use' (IBFD, 2006).

[8] For example, Austria restricts the option to only two types of transactions: credit for the purpose of acquiring a taxable good or service, and certain credit card transactions. Germany allows financial institutions to apply the option on a transaction-by-transaction basis, but restricts it to taxable customers. Likewise, the rules in Belgium, Estonia, France, and Lithuania differ considerably.

distortions are reduced relative to full exemption, and under-taxation of financial services is less than under full exemption. One difference, however, is that the option to tax only involves B2B customers; so, relative to that, taxation of fee-based services will involve VAT being charged even on B2C transactions. This mitigates the under-pricing of financial services to final consumers.

One additional feature of taxation of the third option in Australia and Singapore is partial input VAT recovery. In Australia, firms that make a relatively small amount of financial supplies, compared with their taxable supplies or GST-free supplies, can claim full input tax credits for those inputs related to taxable supplies.[9] Also, once over that limit, firms can claim a tax credit equivalent to 75% of the GST paid on a defined list of inputs acquired to make exempt financial supplies. The purpose of the credit is to mitigate the self-supply bias, but this does not address the problem of cascading or international competitiveness. Further, Poddar and Kalita (2010) question the efficiency of the approach, noting that the definition of input services eligible for the 75% credit is not simple, somewhat arbitrary, and will likely require constant review as patterns of outsourcing evolve.

In Singapore, financial services are taxable if they are provided in return for a brokerage fee, commission or similar form of compensation, while most core financial services are exempt. However, financial institutions can claim input VAT credits using two methods. The 'special method' requires segregation of financial services eligible for the zero rate from total services provided to all customers, similar to the New Zealand approach. The 'fixed input tax recovery method' relies on input VAT recovery rates that depend on the type of financial institution and reflect the mix of their business and non-business customers. The purpose of the method is to prevent cascading (and to preserve the price competitiveness of the financial institutions). However, this method under-taxes financial services provided to consumers, even more than pure exemption would do.

A fourth option is zero-rating of B2B services and exemption of B2C services. This was introduced in New Zealand on 1 January 2005. Since then, supplies of financial services to GST-registered persons whose taxable supplies equal or exceed 75% of their total supplies may be zero-rated, when the financial services provider elects to do so. Clearly, a provider that takes this option will avoid all the biases associated with full exemption on their B2B sales. However, there will still be exemption on B2C sales, resulting in under-taxation of these. Finally, the revenue cost of this option will be relatively high as the government loses all the embedded VAT on inputs.

A fifth option is the cash-flow approach with tax calculation accounts (TCAs). Unlike all other options considered so far, this directly extends the invoice-credit method of levying VAT to margin-based transactions, essentially by dividing

[9] The GST is the Goods and Services Tax, which is New Zealand's version of the VAT.

FISIM between the parties to the financial transaction, to create an artificial price to each party. It is explained in detail in chapter 8 of the *Mirrlees Review*, where a strong case is made for it (Mirrlees et al., 2010). This option has the advantage that it is fully consistent conceptually with existing VATs, but it is administratively complex and has thus far not been implemented in practice.

One particular problem is that dividing FISIM between, for example, a depositor and a borrower requires a reference rate of interest, which is supposed to reflect the pure cost of funds to the bank. Modern national accounting standards do require sectoral allocation of FISIM (to households, government, firms, etc.), and so definitions of this reference rate have been developed for this purpose.[10] However, views on the reference rate continue to evolve and any changes in this rate would affect the VAT liabilities of VAT-registered depositors and borrowers under this method, creating considerable tax uncertainty.

A second problem is that currently, lending rates are not adjusted for default risk, and so generally overestimate the consumption of FISIM by borrowers. For example, in the United Kingdom, the Office of National Statistics (2017) calculated that in the aftermath of the financial crisis of 2008, FISIM output adjusted for default risk would be reduced between 15% and 33%.

The final two options take a different approach as they do not levy VAT on a transaction basis, but on an entity or taxpayer basis. The addition method exploits the fact that value added created by a firm (i.e. the value of outputs minus the value of inputs, including capital inputs) is by definition equal to its wages paid plus cash-flow profit. Indeed, cash-flow profit is usually defined as residually as value added minus wages (Ebrill et al., 2001). Then, a VAT on an addition basis taxes both cash-flow profits and wages at some rate of VAT. Currently, two countries have something close to this for taxation of the financial sector. In Israel, banks and other financial institutions currently pay taxes at the rate of 17% based on their total payroll and on profits. Iceland currently taxes the payroll of financial institutions at 5.5% and their profits at 6%, although these taxes are formally financial activity taxes rather than a VAT (KPMG, 2017).

Levying VAT on an addition basis gives rise to a number of new problems. First, as just noted, an addition-based VAT and a transaction-based VAT will have the same base for a given firm only if the profit base is cash-flow profit, which is not the case in either Israel or Iceland. Moreover, this kind of VAT, if used just for the financial sector, will lead to tax cascading. Specifically, if a financial services firm is subject to an addition-based VAT, there is no mechanism for the firms to which it sells to recover any addition-based VAT included in the price of its

[10] For example, in the United Kingdom, the internal reference rate in sterling is now calculated using accrued interest receivable in sterling on loans by monetary financial institutions divided by the corresponding average stock on loans. The internal reference rate is comparable and slightly above the London Interbank Offered Rate (LIBOR) sterling three-month rate (Office of National Statistics, 2017).

services. Finally, because this approach taxes at the level of the entity, not the transaction, this approach cannot easily cope with rate differentiation and exemptions.

The final method is the subtraction method, which works as follows. At the end of a reporting period, a business calculates the value of all taxable sales, then subtracts the sum of all taxable purchases, and the VAT rate is applied to the difference. In principle, a subtraction-based VAT used just in the financial sector, because it is entity-based rather than transaction-based, gives rise to exactly the same problems as an addition-based VAT. Japan uses a subtraction-method VAT, but for all entities, not just the financial sector, and it contains all the invoice requirements and rules of the credit-invoice method, so in practice it is not that different from the VATs used in other countries.

How does this discussion relate to the current situation in the EU, and in the Netherlands in particular? The Sixth Directive of the EU currently exempts a very wide range of financial services, so it seems desirable to move to a regime, as in Australia or New Zealand, where the list of exempt services is as small as possible. In addition, embedded VAT (VAT input taxation) creates a large number of distortions, which could be reduced by moving to the New Zealand approach of zero-rating B2B sales of financial services. This still leaves the problem that exempt B2C services are under-taxed. However, in principle, this can be partially resolved by the imposition of a FAT or bank levy. Both of these are discussed below.

21.2.3 Estimates of Revenue Gains

Table 21.2 gives a general qualitative description of how we might expect revenues to decrease or increase, relative to a comprehensive VAT on financial services. Here, I discuss these effects in more depth, and I briefly review some attempts that have been made to quantify them.

There are three possible effects of bringing financial services entirely in the scope of VAT. First, revenues increase because VAT is charged on final consumption of financial services. Second, revenues decrease because VAT on inputs to the financial services sector (embedded VAT) is now deductible. Third, revenues further decrease because the removal of embedded VAT will generally reduce the prices to final consumers of other goods and services that use VAT as an input. Note that, as observed by Ebrill et al. (2001), it is possible for the second and third effects to dominate the first (e.g. if most financial services are consumed by VAT-registered entities rather than final consumers). In this case, VAT revenues will actually *fall* if financial services are fully taxed. It should also be noted that the size of all effects will depend on behavioural responses. For example, households may demand fewer financial services when they become more expensive, dampening the first positive revenue effect described above.

Some early studies of the revenue gains from ending exemption on financial services ignore behavioural responses. A study by the European Commission (2011) finds that ending exemption would increase EU-27 tax revenues by 15 billion euros. Lockwood (2011) finds that ending exemption within the EU would increase EU-27 tax revenues by 1–2 billion euros, but it could reduce it under some assumptions. These two studies have a common conceptual framework and common data (Eurostat sectoral accounts and input–output tables); the differences are driven by detailed assumptions, especially calculations of embedded input VAT and how this is passed through to prices.[11] Overall, these effects are small: for comparison, according to Eurostat, total tax receipts for the EU-27 in 2011 were about 5,200 billion euros.

More recently, Buettner and Erbe (2014) computed the effects of repealing the VAT exemption in Germany. Their baseline estimate indicates that tax revenues would increase by 1.2 billion euros, or 0.9% of VAT revenues. Again, these estimates exclude behavioural effects but, as in Lockwood (2011), assume that the elimination of embedded VAT is fully passed though in the form of lower prices.

More recent studies use computable general-equilibrium models to take into account behavioural effects. For Australia, Murphy (2017) studies the effect of ending existing exemptions of the financial services sector in Australia. He finds that this has the favourable effect of raising additional revenue with only a slight excess burden for consumers. But again, the changes relative to overall tax revenue are quite small.[12] Chisari, Estache, and Nicodème (2013) study the application of a 15% VAT to the financial sector in Belgium. They do not look explicitly at revenue effects, but find that this reform has a small negative effect on GDP growth and welfare.

Two conclusions could be drawn here. The first is that these effects are relatively small, so there is no strong revenue argument for or against bringing

[11] First, the European Commission implicitly assumes full pass-through of output VAT into prices but no pass-through of reduction in cost due to recovery of input VAT. In contrast, Lockwood (2011) assumes full pass-through of both taxes, following Huizinga (2002). Second, the European Commission ignores tax on tax/tax-cascading effects, as a result of implicitly assuming no pass-through of the elimination of irrecoverable VAT in the form of a lower output price. Third, the European Commission has a lower estimate of the tax revenue lost from no longer collecting 'embedded' input VAT. Empirically, Chiorazzo and Milani (2011) find some evidence that input VAT is passed through to loan and deposit rates.

[12] According to Murphy (2017): 'In particular, switching from a GST input tax to a GST consumption tax on the exempt financial services would raise an additional $2.3 billion in annual revenue while reducing consumer welfare by only $0.3 billion.... By comparison, raising the same amount of additional revenue through an increase in the general rate of GST would leave consumers worse off by $0.6 billion on an annual basis (a marginal excess burden of 24% applied to an additional $2.3 billion in revenue).' For comparison, total tax revenue in Australia in 2016 was $487 billion.

financial services fully within the scope of VAT—assuming it could be done. In particular, this implies that the cost of the New Zealand option might not be that high. Second, there is considerable uncertainty surrounding the size of these effects, as there is with all revenue forecasting.

21.3 Financial Activity Taxes

In an influential 2010 paper, the IMF recommended that 'Any further contribution from the financial sector that is desired should be raised by a Financial Activities Tax (FAT) levied on the sum of the profits and remuneration of financial institutions, and paid to general revenue' (IMF, 2010). Subsequently, a number of countries have introduced FATs. For example, as of 2017, Denmark has imposed a tax of 14.1% on the total annual salary cost (pension, bonuses, labour market contributions, benefits, etc.) associated with VAT exempt activities. Iceland and Norway have similar taxes, with various provisions to ensure that only wages and profits arising from VAT-exempt activities are taxed (KPMG, 2017).

A first question to ask is: how does a FAT differ from VAT on addition basis, such as that used by Israel? As made clear in IMF (2010), this depends on how the base is defined. The base could include profits above a 'normal' level and 'high' remuneration—in this way targeting rents. If the FAT were applied to all remuneration, it would then be similar to an addition-based VAT. So, while FATs are an effective way of raising revenue from the financial services sector, they are subject to the same problems as an addition-based VAT. Moreover, there might be boundary issues in deciding which cash inflows and outflows reflect 'real' activities and which reflect 'financial' activities, if the FAT rate is different to the regular VAT rate. For example, in Denmark, the standard rate of VAT is 25%, but the FAT rate is only 14%; thus, there is an incentive for financial services firms to re-classify activities as VAT exempt if they use few taxed inputs and are mostly B2C. So, overall, from an economic point of view, a FAT is a rather inferior way of dealing with under-taxation of the financial sector.

21.4 Bank Levies

Since 2008, at least fourteen countries have introduced bank levies, which are taxes based on the liabilities of banks (Devereux, Johannesen, and Vella, 2015). In eleven of these countries (i.e. Austria, Belgium, Cyprus, Germany, Latvia, the Netherlands, Portugal, Romania, Slovakia, Sweden, and the United Kingdom), taxes are based on measures of bank liabilities such as non-insured deposits. Two main arguments have been offered in support of such levies. First, a bank levy raises revenue that would be available for any future bailouts. The IMF (2010) suggests that this revenue might be allocated to an earmarked bailout fund.

Second, it is now generally accepted that high bank leverage (the ratio of debt to assets) and investment in more risky assets, at a given level of leverage, have negative external effects on the economy as a whole, and that a bank levy can help lower leverage and/or investment in excessively risky assets. How big are these negative external effects? There are quantitative calculations of their size, which proceed by first calculating the effect of bank leverage on the probability of a financial crisis, and then multiplying that effect by the cost of a financial crisis, typically in percentage points of GDP.

For example, the OECD has recently estimated the median cost of the 2008 financial crisis across OECD countries at about 6% of GDP (Ollivaud and Turner, 2015). As for the effect of bank leverage on the probability of crisis, De Mooij, Keen, and Orihara (2013), from their own estimates and the earlier literature, have shown that the effect of the aggregate leverage ratio of banks in a country on the probability of a crisis is highly non-linear. At realistic levels of the initial leverage (94%, roughly the median in their sample), the marginal effect of a 1 percentage point increase in the leverage ratio on the probability of a financial crisis can be between 1.5 and 7.3 percentage points. So, the overall effect of a marginal increase in leverage can be large, up to half a percentage point of GDP.[13]

Given that these externalities exist, how should bank levies be designed to mitigate them? One of the first papers on this topic was by Keen (2011), who studied a simple model with one bank whose only choice variable is a capital to lending ratio. A low capital ratio raises the risk of the bank's collapse and/or bailout. In this setting, it is shown that a tax on deposits (bank liabilities) increases the capital ratio of the bank. So, the behaviour of the bank can be fully controlled by the bank levy. Further, in his model, a fall in the capital ratio imposes a negative externality on the rest of the economy, either through bank collapse or through a bailout. Given that the bank levy controls the capital ratio, these externalities can be internalized by a Pigouvian tax on bank deposits.

However, Keen's model, while an important first step, suffers from some limitations. In particular, subsequent work in the area has clarified how the appropriate base for the tax depends on modelling assumptions. For example, unlike Keen (2011), Acharya et al. (2017) allow for multiple banks and multiple risky investment opportunities for each bank. They show that each bank's contribution to systemic risk can be measured by its systemic expected shortfall (SES), which they describe as 'its propensity to be undercapitalized when the system as a

[13] De Mooij, Keen, and Orihara (2013) use an earlier, much higher estimate of the cumulative output cost of financial crises of 23%, taken from Laeven and Valencia (2010), who measured the output loss relative to the pre-crisis tend, rather than to a more sophisticated counterfactual in the OECD study. This, of course, makes the externality even bigger.

whole is undercapitalized'. The optimal Pigouvian tax is proportional to the SES, not borrowing. The SES depends positively on bank borrowing, but also on other factors, such as correlation in bank returns on assets.

The work of Acharya et al. (2017) also implies that the SES will generally vary across banks. An implication is that (as in the textbook 'polluter pays' principle), the Pigouvian tax will generally be bank-specific, as a bank's contribution to systemic risk depends on its leverage, its size and its degree of interconnectedness with the financial system. So, in practice, any tax that is not bank-specific does not correctly internalize the negative externalities of leverage.

Finally, before turning to practical experience with bank levies, I mention two further issues. The first is that, ultimately, one of the reasons for high bank leverage is that interest on debt is usually deductible from the corporate income tax (CIT) base. For example, De Mooij et al. (2013) find a strong positive association between the CIT rate and bank leverage. So, it could be argued that a better targeted tax reform would be to reduce or eliminate the debt bias of the CIT. While there are moves in this direction, they are slow, and so a bank levy has the attraction of a quick fix.[14] It is also the case that even if the debt bias of the CIT could be eliminated, the Pigouvian externalities discussed above still remain.

A second issue is the role of bank regulation. For example, minimum capital requirements for banks are governed by the Basel III agreement, and currently impose a minimum ratio of core capital to assets of 3%. One might then ask whether Pigouvian taxes are even necessary given this regulation instrument, when it is set optimally.[15] Keen (2011) shows theoretically that, in the presence of uncertainty, there are conditions under which taxation is preferred to regulation. However, in practice, the choice is not between one or the other instrument but how to use both. In particular, as already remarked above, banks in practice will choose both total leverage and the allocation of borrowing to different risk classes of assets. Both of these decision margins may have negative externalities, so, in principle, both taxation and regulation may be needed to control these decisions.

Cannas et al. (2014) provide some evidence here. Using a simulation model for the EU based on bank balance-sheet data, they calculate the correlation between individual bank contributions to systemic risk and the base of either a FAT or a bank levy. They approximate the current Basel III framework by assuming a capital to debt ratio of 8%. They allow for contagion effects in their modelling

[14] For example, Belgium, Cyprus, Italy, and Turkey have introduced an allowance for corporate equity (ACE). This retains the deduction for interest but adds a similar deduction for the normal return on equity (see Hebous and Klemm, 2018).

[15] Some have argued that the Basel III requirement is too low. For example, in a letter to the *Financial Times*, Admati et al. (2010) say 'Basel III is far from sufficient to protect the system from recurring crises. If a much larger fraction, at least 15%, of banks' total, non-risk-weighted, assets were funded by equity, the social benefits would be substantial.'

(i.e. that failure can be driven by the default of the other banks), using data on interbank exposures between banks. With contagion, bank levies outperform FATs (in the sense of a higher correlation), mainly because of their stronger correlation with the size of financial institutions, a prime determinant of risk. One interpretation of these results is that bank levies may be effective ways of controlling individual bank contributions to systemic risk, even when there is a minimum capital requirement.

However, Cannas et al. (2014) do not model the behavioural responses of banks to the imposition of a FAT or bank levy in the presence of a capital requirement. This is a question addressed by Devereux et al. (2015). They show theoretically that, in the presence of a penalty for under-capitalization (a simple representation of the Basel III regime), an increase in a bank levy has two effects: it increases not only capital held by banks, as in Keen (2011), but also the riskiness of lending. The second, unintended effect arises because while the levy reduces the total amount of lending by the bank, this mechanically moves the bank further away from the capital requirement constraint, allowing the bank to choose a more risky but higher return portfolio of lending. Devereux et al. (2015) find empirical evidence in support of this effect; in particular, bank levies have a significant positive effect on the capital to asset ratio, but at the same time increase measures of portfolio risk.

In practice, the base of the levy is usually some measure of bank liabilities, as in Keen (2011). This is the case for levies in eleven countries (i.e. Austria, Belgium, Cyprus, Germany, Latvia, the Netherlands, Portugal, Romania, Slovakia, Sweden, and the United Kingdom). While these levies are conceptually similar, they vary along several dimensions. First, most of the levies fall on total liabilities net of own funds and customer deposits that are guaranteed under a deposit insurance scheme, but two countries (Cyprus and Portugal) include insured deposits in the levy base. Second, most levies treat short-term and long-term liabilities symmetrically, but two countries (the Netherlands and the United Kingdom) apply a reduced rate to liabilities with a maturity exceeding one year. Third, most of the levies apply a flat rate, but four countries (Austria, Germany, the Netherlands, and the United Kingdom) have a progressive rate structure where small banks are taxed at lower rates than large banks, or not taxed at all. This is clearly an attempt to deal with the heterogeneity problem.

Finally, one concern for policymakers is that banks may pass though the cost of the levies to households and firms, thus reducing the interest rates on deposits, and increasing the rates on loans. If this is the case, then consumers and firms, rather than banks, will bear the burden of internalizing the externality, which may be undesirable from a distributional point of view. Using bank-level evidence for 23 EU countries in the period 2007–13, Kogler (2016) shows some pass-through of bank levies to lending and deposit rates, and net interest margins. Market characteristics and capital structure influence the magnitude: the lending rate strongly increases in concentrated markets, and the pass-through is weak for well-capitalized banks. Overall, though, the effects are modest, with pass-through to lending being no more than 5% of the tax, on average.

21.5 Conclusions

I have evaluated three different options for increasing taxation of the financial sector: (1) bringing financial services more within the scope of VAT; (2) the use of FATs; (3) the use of bank levies. The degree to which financial services are exempt from VAT varies considerably, and best practice is probably New Zealand's approach of zero-rating financial services sold to VAT-registered customers. FATs, used in some countries, are effective revenue-raisers but a poor substitute for a transactions-based VAT on financial services, as they do not integrate well with an invoice-credit VAT and they give rise to additional distortions. There are probably stronger arguments for using bank levies rather than FATs, as bank levies are better targeted to the reduction of excessive bank leverage. There are strong theoretical arguments for some form of bank levy but the interaction of the levy with banking regulation needs to be considered.

References

Acharya, V. V., Pedersen, L. H., Philippon, T., and Richardson, M. (2017), Measuring systemic risk, *Review of Financial Studies*, 30, 2–47.

Admati, A. R. et al. (2010), 'Healthy banking system is the goal, not profitable banks', *Financial Times*, 9 November (https://www.gsb.stanford.edu/faculty-research/excessive-leverage/healthy-banking-system-goal).

Auerbach, A. J. and Gordon, R. H. (2002), 'Taxation of financial services under a VAT', *American Economic Review*, 92(2), 411–16.

Buettner, T. and Erbe, K. (2014), 'Revenue and welfare effects of financial sector VAT exemption', *International Tax and Public Finance*, 21, 1028–50.

Cannas, G., Cariboni, J., Marchesi, M., Nicodème, G., Giudici, M. P., and Zedda, S. (2014), 'Financial activities taxes, bank levies, and systemic risk', European Commission, Taxation papers, Working Paper 43-2014.

Chiorazzo, V. and Milani, C. (2011), 'The impact of taxation on bank profits: evidence from EU banks', *Journal of Banking and Finance*, 35, 3202–12.

Chisari, O., Estache, A., and Nicodème, G. (2013), 'Efficiency and equity effects of taxing the financial sector: lessons from a CGE model for Belgium', CEPR Discussion Paper no. DP9320.

Cnossen, S. (2019), *Modernizing VATs in Africa*, Oxford University Press, Oxford.

De Mooij, R. A., Keen, M. M., and Orihara, M. M. (2013), 'Taxation, bank leverage, and financial crises', International Monetary Fund Working Paper no. 13/48.

Devereux, M. P., Johannesen, N., and Vella, J. (2015), 'Can taxes tame the banks? Evidence from the European bank levies', Saïd Business School Working Paper 2015–5.

Ebrill, L., Keen, M., Bodin, J.-P., and Summers, V. (eds) (2001), *The Modern VAT*, International Monetary Fund, Washington, DC.

European Banking Federation (2019), 'The Netherlands' banking sector: facts and figures' (https://www.ebf.eu/the-netherlands/).

European Commission (2011), 'Impact Assessment, accompanying the document, Proposal for a Council Directive on a common system of financial transaction tax and amending Directive 2008/7/EC', SEC(2011), Brussels.

Hebous, S. and Klemm, M. A. D. (2018), 'A destination-based allowance for corporate equity', CESIfo Working Paper no. 7363.

Huizinga, H. (2002), 'A European VAT on financial services?' *Economic Policy*, 17, 497–534.

IBFD (2006), *VAT Survey: Financial Services*, International Bureau of Fiscal Documentation, Amsterdam.

IMF (2010), *A Fair and Substantial Contribution by the Financial Sector: Final Report for the G-20*, International Monetary Fund, Washington, DC.

Keen, M. (2011), 'The taxation and regulation of banks', IMF Working Paper no. 1–38.

Kogler, M. (2016), 'On the incidence of bank levies: theory and evidence', University of St Gallen Discussion Paper no. 2016–06.

KPMG (2017), 'Special taxes in the financial sector: Nordic comparison' (https://home.kpmg/content/dam/kpmg/fi/pdf/2017/11/Bank%20levies_Nordic%20comparison.pdf).

Laeven, M. L. and Valencia, F. (2010), 'Resolution of banking crises: the good, the bad, and the ugly', International Monetary Fund Working Paper no. 10–146.

Lockwood, B. (2011), 'Estimates from National Accounts Data of the revenue effect of imposing VAT on currently exempt sales of financial services companies in the EU', appendix 2, in *How the EU VAT Exemptions Impact the Financial Sector*, PricewaterhouseCoopers (PwC), pp. 84–110.

Lockwood, B. (2014), 'How should financial intermediation services be taxed?', in R. De Mooij and G. Nicodème (eds), *Taxation and Regulation of the Financial Sector*, MIT Press, Cambridge, MA, pp. 133–56.

Mirrlees, J. et al. (eds) (2010), *Dimensions of Tax Design: The Mirrlees Review*, Oxford University Press for the Institute for Fiscal Studies, Oxford.

Murphy, C. W. (2017), 'GST and how to tax Australian banking', *Australian GST Journal*, 17, 84–105.

OECD (2020), 'Value added by activity (indicator)' (https://data.oecd.org/natincome/value-added-by-activity.htm).

Office of National Statistics (2017), 'Financial intermediation services indirectly measured (FISIM) in the UK revisited'.

Ollivaud, P. and Turner, D. (2015), 'The effect of the global financial crisis on OECD potential output', OECD Journal: Economic Studies, 2014(1), 41–60.

Poddar, S. and Kalita, J. (2010), 'Treatment of financial services under a UAE VAT', in E. Ahmad and A. Al Faris (eds), *Fiscal Reforms in the Middle East: VAT in the Gulf Cooperation Council*, Edward Elgar, Cheltenham, pp. 256–282.

22

Excise Duties to Correct Market and Individual Failure

*Sijbren Cnossen**

22.1 Introduction

Cherished politically because of their potentially high yield, economically, excise duties are seen primarily as proxies for charging (internalizing) the costs of damage—physical, financial, psychological—imposed on other people by those who smoke, drink, eat sugary foods, gamble, pollute, guzzle fossil fuels, and use roads. An individual who drives a car uses petrol and thus contributes to global warming from which the whole world suffers. The car also emits substances that harm the health of others and can cause traffic jams. It is fair and efficient for the 'offender' to have to pay for the social or 'external' costs borne by others, ideally in the form of an amount (called excise duty) that is equal to the marginal damage caused (Pigou, 1920). In this way, the individual can adjust the decision whether or not—and to what extent—to participate in traffic to the appropriate optimum level.

The economic approach to dealing with external costs is based on the principle of consumer sovereignty, which holds that the freedom of choice of a rational person should not be impeded as long as he or she is fully aware of the consequences of his or her choice and does not impose costs on other people (Becker and Murphy, 1988). But many people are not aware, or are not sufficiently aware, of the consequences of their behaviour, or they are simply myopic and tend to discount the short-term costs of their activities at a higher rate than the long-term costs.[1] 'I'll stop smoking next year', they say, 'but not yet', with the 'next year' continuing to be the next year. Self-control is a scarce commodity. Therefore, in addition to external costs (damage to third parties), there are 'internal' costs (damage to oneself) that the consumer does not take into account. An excise duty can then be a correction for the consumer's short-sightedness.

* Sijbren Cnossen (cnossen@ese.eur.nl) is Professor of Economics at the University of Pretoria and Academic Partner at CPB Netherlands Bureau for Economic Policy Analysis.

[1] There is no consensus in the literature as to whether policy makers should or should not respect the short-term and long-term preferences of consumers in order not to fall into paternalistic interventions (Bernheim and Taubinsky, 2018).

Sijbren Cnossen, *Excise Duties to Correct Market and Individual Failure* In: *Tax by Design for the Netherlands*.
Edited by: Sijbren Cnossen and Bas Jacobs, Oxford University Press.
DOI: 10.1093/oso/9780192855244.003.0022

Internal costs are considerably more difficult to measure than external costs. For external costs, an estimate must be made of the extra healthcare, property damage, loss of productivity (insofar as it does not result in lower wages and is therefore internalized), and other costs caused by the 'perpetrators' that they should take into account. In this respect, the excise functions as an insurance premium: a contribution to a common pool from which external costs are paid for.[2] Internal costs are about the damage consumers do to themselves in the form of, for instance, reduced health or a shorter life span, but only insofar as they have not rationally traded the costs of that damage for the value of the enjoyment of a cigar, drink, bet, or whatever else. There is then no issue of a lack of self-control but of rational acceptance of the risk associated with consumption. The internal effects will therefore be greatest for people with limited cognitive insight, which usually correlates with low earning capacity. Internal and external effects mirror each other, although the benefit of the reduction in external costs through an improved choice benefits third parties, while the benefit of a decrease in internal costs benefits the consumers themselves. In either case, the government collects the extra revenue, if any.

A problem with excisable products, especially if they are addictive, is that the demand for them is generally relatively inelastic. As a result, those on lower incomes with the same quantitative level of consumption will pay more tax as a percentage of income than those on higher incomes. In other words, the burden distribution is regressive. On these grounds, politicians often object to the introduction or increase of excise duties. In recent literature, however, it has been pointed out that people on lower incomes will benefit relatively more from an internal-cost internalizing excise duty (in the sense of better health, for example) if they consume relatively more than higher-income groups and the price elasticity of demand is higher for them.[3] This appears to be the case for many products subject to excise duty.

In summary, when studying the level and functioning of the excise duties, external and internal costs and preference heterogeneity between incomes are important factors to take into account. Obviously, supply and demand elasticities play a crucial role in estimating the optimum level of excise duty. In addition, duty-equivalent measures, such as regulations and information provision, should not be overlooked; they reduce the level of the optimal excise duty. Finally, external and internal costs will be related to the number, volume, weight, strength

[2] This should not be considered a form of earmarking, a subject that is often raised in discussions on excise taxation, but which should be analysed on its own merits.

[3] Note that the principle of optimal taxation (Atkinson and Stiglitz, 1976) prescribes that if differences in consumption can be attributed to causal income differences, goods should not be taxed or subsidized for redistribution purposes. We have the income tax for that. However, if differences in consumption can be attributed to differences in preference between different income levels, then those differences are a 'tag' that can be useful for redistribution purposes.

or other physical characteristics of products, subject to duty and not to their value. The correction for external and internal costs should therefore be expressed in a specific amount that is periodically indexed for inflation (Cnossen and Smart, 2005). Furthermore, VAT should be imposed on the excise-duty-inclusive price of products (and the import duty, if levied).

Against this background, in this chapter I discuss and assess Dutch excise duties on tobacco and alcohol and I investigate the possibility of excise duties on games of chance, soft drinks and sugar, fireworks and plastics. The excise duties on CO_2 emissions, a pure externality, and transport are discussed in other chapters.

22.2 Tobacco Products

The Dutch health authorities consider smoking a deadly disease, whose costs can be estimated at around 13% of the total disease burden (SEO, 2016). Although the number of smokers has fallen in recent years, one in five adults is still addicted to smoking (Table 22.1). The consequences do not lie. In addition to every person who dies as a result of a smoking-related illness, there are twenty people who become chronically ill due to smoking. Second-hand smoke is also dangerous (especially for children): 8.6% of people who die prematurely die because of the smoking behaviour of others. The Stichting Economisch Onderzoek (SEO, 2016) estimates the total public and private costs (middle scenario) of smoking, mainly caused by loss of life years and quality of life, at 33 billion euros per year (around 2,000 euros per capita; 4,000 euros per smoker) or 0.4% of GDP in 2013.

In Germany (Neubauer et al., 2006; 2003 data) and Sweden (Bolin et al., 2011; 2007 data), the total costs (healthcare, mortality, lower productivity) of smoking are estimated at 0.36% and 0.82% of GDP, respectively. If we project these figures on to the Dutch situation and correct for differences in smoking prevalence (Tobacco Collaborators, 2017) and years of observation, the costs would amount to approximately 0.5% for the country, which roughly corresponds to the conclusion of the SEO.

Smokers usually have shorter lives than non-smokers, which saves on pension and social benefits and healthcare costs for old-age ailments. Warner et al. (1995) point out that these savings must be deducted from the costs caused by smokers. From an economic perspective, it is therefore the net costs that are important. Based on this reasoning, Tiihonen et al. (2012) conclude that the life-cycle costs of Finnish smokers are lower than those of non-smokers. Smokers live 8.6 years fewer than non-smokers and they miss 7.3 years in retirement. However, if a value could be attributed to the loss of life years, then not smoking would yield a benefit of 70,000 euros per individual. Barendregt, Bonneux, and van der Maas (1997) came to a similar conclusion for the Netherlands.

Table 22.1 Basic statistics on tobacco consumption and taxation

Consumption, costs, and collections (2015)	
Smoking prevalence	
Adult males	21.3%
Adult females	18.6%
Male youths	8%
Female youths	7%
E-cigarettes	
Males	3.3%
Females	2.9%
WHO Framework Convention (ratified 27-01-2005)	protection, warnings, aids, advertisement bans
Annual deaths from smoking-related diseases	20,000
People with chronic health conditions	400,000
Total costs per annum	€33 billion (€2.000 per head)
Estimated gross external costs per annum	€4.5 billion
Excise collections (2018)	€2.5 billion
Duty rates (2019)	
Cigarettes (most smoked brand)	
Retail price including tax (pack of 25)	€7.74
Specific excise duty (€175.20/1000)	€4.38
Ad valorem excise duty (5% of TIRSP)	€0.39
Total excise duty	€4.77
VAT (17.36% of TIRSP)	€1.34
Total tax	€6.17
Retail price excluding tax	€1.57
Roll-your-own	€108.94 per kg
Cigars	7% of TIRSP + 17.36% VAT

Note: TIRSP is the tax-included retail selling price.

Source: SEO (2016); World Health Organization (2017); European Commission (2019).

The costs caused by smokers can be confronted with the taxes imposed on tobacco products. The lower panel of Table 22.1 shows the excise duties and VAT for various tobacco products, in particular cigarettes, levied in accordance with the European Union Directive 2011/64/EU regarding the structure of the excise on tobacco products on tobacco taxation (Council of the European Union, 2011). The total excise duty is 62% of the weighted average retail price and, if VAT is also taken into account, the total tax burden is almost 80% of the retail price (400% of the sales price excluding taxes). This is more than the burden of 75% that has been agreed to under the Tobacco Framework Convention. Roll-your-own is relatively undertaxed compared with cigarettes (assuming that one cigarette contains 0.75 g of tobacco) and cigars are a tax bargain.

The excise duty on cigarettes, the most important, is almost entirely specific (and is automatically adjusted for inflation). The specific excise, unlike an ad valorem excise, does not affect the quality of the product and does not discriminate against more expensive imported tobacco varieties. It is difficult to determine the optimum level of excise duty. High taxes will stimulate the smuggling of untaxed and often inferior products. According to the press bureau ANP (2017), the consumption of contraband cigarettes, mainly from Poland and Russia, amounts to 6% of total consumption. In addition to the excise duty, primary healthcare intervention and information dissemination are important non-tax measures to reduce the incidence of smoking. Fortunately, as Table 22.1 indicates, the prevalence of smoking among adolescents of 15 years or younger is much lower than among adults. Perhaps this is an indication that anti-smoking policies are having the desired results.

It is generally assumed that the tobacco excise duty places a disproportionate burden on smokers with a low income. For the United States, however, Gruber and Köszegi (2008) argue that if time-inconsistent behaviour (internal costs) is taken into account, lower-income groups will benefit more from an increase in the excise duty on cigarettes than higher-income groups. They calculate an optimal excise duty, based on an estimate of the health costs of an average smoker, of more than US$35 per pack. The tax burden even becomes progressive in their model because the higher price elasticity of lower-income people means that they will drastically reduce their smoking behaviour, more than the excise duty they pay or the pleasure they forego by giving up smoking. However, cigarette excise duties will remain (very) regressive for low-income smokers who do not know how to quit, no matter how the tax burden is measured (Remler, 2004).

The health risks of smoking can also be reduced by providing smokers with the nicotine to which they are addicted without the smoke that harms their health (Royal College of Physicians, 2016). This can be done by administering medical nicotine but also by taxing e-cigarettes, which prove to be a potentially effective substitute for the nicotine that smokers need, lower than ordinary cigarettes. Although traces of carcinogens, oxidants, and other harmful substances have also been found in e-cigarettes, their health risks do not appear to be greater than 5% of comparable risks of smoking ordinary cigarettes. E-cigarettes appear to be a successful bridge to the complete cessation of smoking, especially if they are used as an alternative rather than as a complement to cigarettes. Of course, the Dutch equivalent of the Food and Drugs Administration should monitor the quality of e-cigarettes with a focus on lung complications due to vaping.

22.3 Alcoholic Beverages

Alcohol permeates all parts of Dutch culture: it is used before, during, and after meals, when celebrating a birth and when mourning, to socialize or relax, or to just get drunk. As shown in Table 22.2, more than 70% of Dutch adults (15+) drink, on average, some 12 litres of pure alcohol per year. Conversely, this corresponds per

Table 22.2 Basic statistics on alcohol consumption and taxation

Total consumption, of which	12.0
Beer (351 bottles; pure lt)	5.8
Wine (91 bottles; pure lt)	4.3
Spirits (7 bottles; pure lt)	1.9
Male/female (pure lt, drinkers)	16.7/5.8
Drinking patterns	
Abstainers (% 15+), past 12 months	27.9%
Moderate drinkers (% of drinkers)	70.3%
Heavy drinkers (% of drinkers, 4–6 glasses)	14.2%
Addictive drinkers (% of drinkers, >6 glasses)	5.5%
Young drinkers (%, <18)	30.5%
Duty rates, collections and costs	
Excise duty by beverage	
Beer (5%, 0.33 lt, 11-15 Plato)	€0.09
Wine (12%, 0.75 lt)	€0.66
Spirits (35%, 0.70 lt)	€4.13
Excise duty by alcohol content	
Spirits	€100
Wine	€33
Beer	€32
Excise duty collections (billion)	€1.2
Cost of abusive alcohol consumption	
Public health costs (billion)	€2.3–2.9
Healthcare costs (1% of total; million)	€800
Alcohol-related deaths	900

Source: RIVM (2016); Statistics Netherlands (2017); WHO (2018); and Douane Belastingdienst (2019).

adult to 727 bottles of beer (0.33 lt/5%), 133 bottles of wine (0.75 lt/12%), or 49 bottles of spirits (0.70 lt/35%). Two drinks (10 mg ethanol per consumption) per day for a man and one drink for a woman are not considered medically harmful. However, 14% of the people who drink have four to six glasses daily; they are heavy drinkers. Another 5.5% are addicted to alcohol (more than six glasses per day), so one in five drinkers is drinking too much. Men drink twice as much as women on average. One in five youngsters attending school is a binge drinker (five glasses on a single occasion).

Just as in other European countries, alcohol is a problem in the Netherlands. Heavy drinking can lead to violent behaviour, can cause accidents, and can have harmful consequences for health (organ damage, birth defects). The costs for public health are estimated at 2.3–2.9 billion euros. Alcohol-related deaths amount to 900 per year (about the same as the number of people living longer due to moderate alcohol consumption). Based on Anderson and Baumberg (2006), Cnossen (2007) calculated the external costs of alcohol abuse at

0.5–0.7% of GDP, with a lower limit on direct costs (healthcare, crime, traffic accidents) and an upper limit that also includes the costs of productivity loss and premature death. He calculated the low and high costs per adult (158 and 241 euros, respectively) and per litre of pure alcohol (16 and 24 euros, respectively). The excise duties, however, were only 64 euros per adult and the effective tax per litre of pure alcohol was merely 6.60 euros.

The lower panel of Table 22.2 shows the rates of excise duty on different types of alcoholic beverages. Although the definitions are harmonized in accordance with the European Union Directives 92/83/EEC and 92/84/EEC (Council of the European Union, 1992a,b), the duties vary considerably between member states. In most member states, 'national' drinks are favoured in terms of alcohol content. For example, thirteen member states do not levy excise duties on wine; the beer duty is very low in Germany and the Czech Republic; and the distilled excise duty is relatively low in the United Kingdom. All alcoholic beverages are subject to the standard VAT rate that must be at least 16%. For the Netherlands, the standard VAT rate is 21% or 17.34% of the price including excise duty.

As indicated in Table 22.2, the excise duty collections do not cover the costs of alcohol abuse. A complicating factor is that the costs of alcohol abuse, unlike smoking, do not increase linearly with the increase in consumption, but exponentially. The top 10% of the drinking population, which consumes between one-third and one-half of all alcohol, is responsible for 90% of the costs. Moderate drinkers, however, hardly incur costs. Hence, an increase in excise duty to reduce the high costs of excessive drinkers greatly reduces the consumer surplus of moderate drinkers. Hummel, Jacobs, and Oosterveen (2016), who concluded that 'the social benefits of alcohol may be billions of euros higher than the RIVM report [2016] currently calculates', have shown that this reduction should not be ignored.

Table 22.2 indicates that the excise duties on spirits, wine, and beer differ according to alcohol content. Spirits are taxed relatively heavier than wine or beer. Griffith, O'Connell, and Smith (2019) show that this is optimal if there are heterogeneous consumption externalities in differentiated product markets. If heavy drinkers have a preference for spirits over wine or beer, then a relatively higher excise duty per unit of alcohol on spirits is an effective way to reduce the amount of ethanol purchased by heavy drinkers, without having to confront moderate drinkers of wine and beer with higher excise duty costs. Seen in this light, the excise duty differentiation according to alcohol content between spirits, wine, and beer appears to be justified.

The use of excise duty differentiation to reduce heavy (episodic) drinking should be supplemented with regulations aimed at specific problem groups, such as young and heavy drinkers. Cost-effective measures that have a noticeable effect on alcohol abuse (and thus reduce the need for an increase in excise duty) are limited physical availability (by no means optimal in the Netherlands) and a ban on drink-driving. In addition, legal liability in connection with the sale of alcohol to minors or alcoholics is important. The cost- effectiveness of limiting alcohol abuse through regulatory measures has been exhaustively investigated by Babor et al. (2003).

The large differences in alcohol excise duties in the European Union imply that high-excise duty policies of some member states are constrained by the opportunities of buying alcohol in neighbouring countries. Cross-border shopping occurs when there are large price differences over small distances, such as in the Öresund area and between Helsinki and Talinn (Karlsson and Tigerstedt, 2005). At least one in six tourists in the European Union returns annually from abroad with an average of 2 litres of pure alcohol (Leifman, 2001). Smuggling is also a serious problem in the European Union. For the EU-15, in 1998, a High Level Group on Fraud in the Tobacco and Alcohol Sectors calculated that in 1996 about 8% of total excise tax collections was foregone due to illegal practices (Council of Economic and Finance Ministers, 1998). It is likely that this percentage is now higher. Wells, Gerrard, and Hubbard (2005) believe that the majority of the illicit trade in alcoholic beverages consists of imports by high-excise duty states from low-excise duty states, so-called bootlegging.

Minimum rates for alcoholic beverages were agreed in the European Union in 1992. These rates have not been increased since then; in other words, they have fallen by 60% in real terms. This is not helpful in curbing economically wasteful, albeit legal, cross-border shopping. Wasteful because this activity, like other forms of tax avoidance, generates an excess burden, incurred in the pursuit of a transfer, namely a tax saving. It is necessary to increase the minimum rates, but it is difficult given the zero rate on wine in many member states and the 'per unit of alcohol' excise duty relationship to be observed between beer, wine, and spirits. The external and internal costs will also differ between member states. These costs appear to be lower in Southern European countries than in Northern European countries.

22.4 Lotteries and Casinos

Engaging in games of chance (mainly lotteries and casinos) has much in common with smoking and drinking; there even seems to be co-morbidity (Petry, Stinson, and Grant, 2005). Like smokers, gamblers mainly bear the negative consequences of their actions themselves, although their family members also suffer. As with alcohol, restrictions on participation in games of chance (due to excise duties or supply regulation) will be at the expense of the consumer surplus of recreational players. The demand elasticity of recreational players, as well as moderate drinkers, is high, but the opposite applies to addicted gamblers and drinkers. Note that lotteries are hardly addictive because the possibility of immediate repetition does not occur (Griffiths, 1999). Another difference is that lotteries and casinos are often public companies where supply restrictions increase the price, while dividend payments substitute for taxes with similar qualitative effects (Clotfelter, 2005). In the Netherlands, the Holland Casino state monopoly was privatized in 2016 and placed under the supervision of the Gaming Authority.

In the Netherlands, lotteries and casinos are subject to a gambling tax of 30.1% on pay-outs. Excise duties to internalize external and internal costs are not levied, although these costs undoubtedly occur. Examples of external costs are questionable ways of obtaining play money and the loss of income of financially dependent family members. Internal costs are the lack of self-control insofar as the risk of loss has not been rationally accepted, which appears to be rare (Forrest, 2008). An indication of high internal costs is also that the prevalence of suicide is greater among problem gamblers than among all other forms of addiction (Rosenthal and Fong, 2004). A not unimportant point to note is that lower-income groups spend a disproportionate share of their income on participating in lotteries (Smith, 2008). Taxes on gambling are therefore regressive (Clotfelter, 2005), just as regressive as tobacco duty is. This effect is enhanced if the proceeds from lotteries, as is often the case, are spent on, for example, the arts (Feehan and Forrest, 2007)—in other words, income-elastic items of consumption.

Gambling has become socially acceptable in the Netherlands. An estimated 8.4 million players regularly take a chance. Of this number, approximately 96,700 players are at risk, of which approximately 79,000 are problem gamblers, which is less than 1% of the total number of players (Netherlands Gaming Authority, 2017). Further, there are some 42,000 slot machines in the country, which are known as the crack cocaine of the gambling world. The possibility and temptation of continuing to gamble by displaying frequent near-win situations fosters addiction. Studies that estimate external and internal costs have, as far as I have been able to ascertain, not been made.

There seems to be little to be said for making games of chance subject to excise duty. The demand elasticity of problem gamblers is so low that an internal cost charge, such as with alcoholic beverages, will have little or no effect. In addition, it can be assumed that the consumer surplus of recreational players is considerable—greater than the sum of 472 million euros collected through gambling tax in 2017 (Statistics Netherlands, 2018b) and the annual dividend of Holland Casino, estimated at 10 million euros (Staatssecretaris van Financiën, 2016). The chance that an excise duty would be avoided has increased considerably due to the rise of internet gambling. It would be virtually impossible to monitor online gambling for tax purposes. However, games of chance should be included in the VAT base by taxing lottery tickets and imputing VAT to pay-outs. Casino visitors should be subject to VAT on the difference between the values of chips played and returned, the so-called margin (Schenk, 2010).

22.5 Soft Drinks and Sugar

The Netherlands levies an excise tax of 8.83 euros per hectolitre on fruit juices, vegetable juice, mineral water, mixtures of fruit and vegetable juice, and lemonades. Apart from the revenue, the excise duty, which is based solely on volume, lacks a clear justification. Mineral water contains no sweeteners, and fruit and vegetable juices contain vitamins and minerals that are healthy. Elsewhere, policies are better focused. In about forty countries in the world, soft drinks, especially sugar-sweetened beverages (SSBs), are subject to excise duty because their over-consumption is associated with tooth decay, being overweight, obesity (13% higher probability), and heart and vascular diseases (17% more likely); see International Diabetes Federation (2016) and Allcott, Lockwood, and Taubinsky (2019).

According to Statistics Netherlands (2018a), around 14% of the Dutch population is affected by obesity, two and a half times as many as in the early 1980s. Another 36% of the population is overweight (body mass index > 25). These percentages are lower than in most other OECD countries, but still cause for concern. The World Health Organization recommends limiting free sugar intake to 50 g per day. Compliance with this guideline in the Netherlands leaves something to be desired, especially among children (Sluik et al., 2016). With an average of 102.5 g per day, the Dutch consume twice as much as the recommended limit (Euromonitor International, 2019), making it the third largest sugar-consuming country in the world; the situation is worse only in the United States and Germany.[4]

In a recent highly detailed study for the United States, Allcott et al. (2019) estimate the optimal excise duty on SSBs at US$0.01–0.021 per ounce (= 28.35 g): US$0.08 for external costs, US$0.01 for internal costs (inflated by 20% due to the progressive effect of the correction), and a reduction of US$0.05 due to the regressive incidence of the financial costs of the excise duty. On balance, the authors come up with an excise duty of approximately US$0.015 per ounce, roughly 4 eurocents per 100 g of sugar. For policymakers who prefer to ignore internal costs, they say that a duty of US$0.04 per ounce internalizes external costs. The thorough study by Allcott et al. (2019) provides a good basis for a similar analysis for the Netherlands.

But the story does not end with SBBs. Although the volume of SSB consumption is large, SSBs only rank 1,726th in terms of sugar content per 100 g compared with other selected foodstuffs. As Table 22.3 shows, there are many foodstuffs with considerably more sugar per 100 g of weight than SSBs, such as candy, honey, pudding, junk food, etc. Therefore, if a reduction in sugar consumption is to be

[4] See Walvin (2018) for an entertaining, informative and extremely bleak global history of sugar that corrupted the world.

Table 22.3 Ranking of the sugar content of foodstuffs

Rank	Description	Sugar (g) per 100 g of foodstuff
1	Sugars, granulated	99.80
14	Candies, fondant, prepared-from-recipe	88.90
18	Honey	82.12
23	Puddings, coconut cream, dry mix, regular	80.54
25	Candies, butterscotch	80.46
38	Syrups, corn, high-fructose	75.65
57	Candies, jellybeans	70.00
146	Cereals, ready-to-eat, Post Golden Crisp	53.60
212	Cookies, sugar wafer, chocolate-covered	51.72
264	Cake, white, prepared from recipe, without frosting	35.49
1172	Beverages, fruit-flavoured drink, less than 3% fruit juice,not fortified with vitamin C (**first SSB in list**)	15.85
1275	Beverages, energy drink with carbonated water and high-fructose corn syrup	13.75
1378	Beverages, fruit juice drinks, greater than 3% fruit juice, high vitamin C and added thiamine	12.11
1413	Beverages, the Coca-Cola-company, Minute Maid, lemonade	11.67
1697	Beverages, coffee, ready-to-drink, iced, mocha, milk-based	9.23
1726	Beverages, carbonated cola, fast-food cola (**last SSB in list**)	8.77

Source: United States Department of Agriculture, Agriculture Research Service, Food Composition Database, 9 July 2018 (https://reedir.arsnet.usda.gov/codesearchwebapp/(S(ypb0cp4r2gjzibqf1pnzgyk4))/codesearch.aspx).

taken seriously, then the excise net must be cast further than SSBs. If substitutes (e.g. chocolate, candy, glazed sugar products) are not included in the base, the burden distribution of the excise duty might also be more regressive, because higher-income groups spend as much or more on these products than on cold drinks with carbon dioxide. For these reasons, several countries, including Denmark, Finland, and Norway, have included sugar and confectionery in the excise duty base, in addition to SBBs.

22.6 Fireworks

According to a national newspaper (NRC.nl, 2019), the material damage suffered by private individuals as a result of the irresponsible use of fireworks at the end of 2018 amounted to 15–20 million euros, 20–30% of the total sales of 70 million euros. The medical costs of torn fingers and burnt-out eye sockets, and the costs associated with deploying additional police, fire brigades, hospital staff, etc., are not included. The total damage (less the damage suffered in private) is paid by insurance companies and the government (i.e. by the population at large).

In order to recover the cost of the damage indirectly from perpetrators, Kalshoven (2019) argues in favour of introducing an excise duty on fireworks as a number of US states do (e.g. 12% of the retail value in Pennsylvania). Enforcing the excise duty (along with a prohibition on specified fireworks) would not be easy. Fireworks can be obtained tax-free in Belgium, although shooting there is prohibited—an example of good Dutch salesmanship! Supervision and fines are more obvious instruments than excise duty.

22.7 Stray Plastic and Packaging

The world, including the Netherlands, is drowning in plastic. As stated at the World Economic Forum (2019), the world produced 311 million tonnes of plastic in 2014, a volume that is expected to triple by 2050 if nothing is done to limit production. The environmental damage caused by plastic litter is enormous. Every square kilometre of ocean now contains 13,000 pieces of plastic waste that end up in the sea, and hence also in the animal and human food chain. Plastic has been found in the stomachs of sperm whales, in tap water, and in table salt. It has recently been observed that microplastic moves through the air and can therefore be inhaled. As another example, the production of four plastic bottles generates a quantity of greenhouse gas emissions that corresponds to a mile's drive in a medium-sized petrol car.

The most immediate problem concerns single-use plastic products—bags, cotton buds, cutlery, plates, straws, stirrers—that make up 70% of all plastics; these are also called maritime plastics because they litter European beaches. The Ellen MacArthur Foundation (https://www.ellenmacarthurfoundation.org/) estimates the cost of single-use plastics along with greenhouse gas emissions during production at US$40 billion (equivalent to 36 billion euros). Excise duties, along with regulations and covenants such as the New Plastics Economy Global Commitment (https://www.newplasticseconomy.org/projects/global-commitment) announced by UN Environment Programme and the Ellen MacArthur Foundation in October 2018, should be able to reduce the problem to a manageable size.

Several European countries link the imposition of an excise tax on plastics used as packaging material to the simultaneous prohibition of single-use plastics. The ban is aimed at prohibiting the thinnest and least durable single-use plastics, on the philosophy that thicker plastic bags will encourage reuse. The Irish PlasTax law of 2002 (Anastasia and Nix, 2016), which initially imposed a surcharge of 0.15 euros per bag (now 0.22 euros per bag), is one of the more successful examples of reducing the use of plastics in Europe. Within just six months, the use of single-use plastic bags decreased by 90%. In the first three months after the introduction of the ban, stores issued 277 million plastic bags fewer than the year before. Plastic bags used for food safety and hygienic purposes are exempt from the excise duty.

As part of a larger packaging tax introduced in 1994, Denmark taxes plastic bags to promote the use of reusable bags. However, the tax is paid by retailers when they buy the bags instead of by shop visitors, which produces less impressive results than the Irish PlasTax. This is in line with the finding by Hogg and Sherrington (2011) that levies on plastic bags are usually more successful when they are charged directly to consumers. Nevertheless, the consumption of plastic bags in Denmark has fallen by 66%. From 2022, the United Kingdom intends to levy a tax on packaging plastics that contain less than 30% recycled plastic, making recycled plastic cheaper than new plastic that costs less without the new tax (HM Treasury, 2019). Belgium levies an eco-tax on disposable plastic bags, disposable kitchen utensils, food foil, and aluminium foil.

The European Commission (2015, 2018) has developed a comprehensive action plan for a circular economy, including a *Strategy for Plastics*, with specific recycling targets. The directives based on this plan have to be implemented by the member states by mid-2020. The Netherlands is among the leaders in recycling plastics in the European Union. It tries to discourage environmental degradation by reducing the use of single-use plastics by charging a nominal amount of 0.20 euros for each plastic bag supplied for store purchases. The results of the anti-plastic policy through excise duties are not yet in.

22.8 Policy Recommendations

In this chapter, I have shown that excise duties can play an important role in internalizing external and internal costs associated with the abuse of potentially harmful products. In this way, people are confronted with the full costs of their choice, so that they will make better decisions, in particular if the excise duties are supplemented with appropriate regulations and information dissemination.

Based on the findings in this chapter, and in analogy with Allcott et al. (2019), I derive the following principles for an optimal excise duty policy.

- With excise policy, focus on combatting externalities and internalities, not on reducing consumption. The costs and benefits of potentially harmful behaviour should be balanced against each other. The pleasure of a cigar, drink (sugar-sweetened or with alcohol), or gamble should be taken into account.
- Focus policy to combat the abuse by people who (potentially) cause the greatest external and internal costs, such as young and heavy smokers, drinkers, gamblers, and people who consume too much sugar. Policies that focus on young 'perpetrators' who are not yet addicted are preferable.
- Replace the ill-targeted soft drinks duty with a specific duty on sugar.
- Prohibit plastic packaging materials and single-use items.

- Include positive internal effects in evaluating the (regressive) burden distribution of excise duties—not just who pays the tax.
- Tax substitutes for potentially harmful products, such as e-cigarettes, lotteries, and pure-fruit drinks, only if they cause demonstrable health risks.
- Tax physical quantities, not prices, of products that cause external and internal costs, because they are directly related to social and individual damage.
- Make regulations on availability, information provision, packaging, etc., an essential complementary part of a focused excise duty policy; they reduce the level of the optimal excise duty.
- Strive for an increase in the minimum excise duties on alcoholic beverages in the European Union in order to avoid loss of welfare and revenue. Align the excise duty policy with that of neighbouring states with which much border traffic takes place.

The purpose of these recommendations is not to generate more government revenue or to reform society through excise duties, but to confront people more fully with the full impact of their activities. Extra revenue can be used to reduce other taxes.

References

Allcott, H., Lockwood, B. B., and Taubinsky, D. (2019), 'Should we tax sugar-sweetened beverages? An overview of theory and evidence', *Journal of Economic Perspectives*, 33(3), 202–27.

Anastasia, M. and Nix, J. (2016), 'Plastic bag levy in Ireland, Institute for European Environmental Policy' (https://ieep.eu/uploads/articles/attachments/7f91cb97-8cb7-49c3-9cf0-d34062a9192e/IE%20Plastic%20Bag%20Levy%20conference%20draft.pdf?v=63673818840).

Anderson, P. and Baumberg, B. (2006), 'Alcohol in Europe', Institute of Alcohol Studies, London.

ANP (2017), 'Rokers steken vaker illegale peuk op' (https://www.dvhn.nl/binnenland/Rokers-steken-vaker-illegale-peuk-op-22334638.html).

Atkinson, A. B. and Stiglitz, J. B. (1976), 'The Design of Tax Structure: Direct versus Indirect Taxation', *Journal of Public Economics*, 6, 55–75.

Babor, T. F. et al. (2003), *Alcohol: No Ordinary Commodity: Research and Public Policy*, Oxford University Press, Oxford.

Barendregt, J. J., Bonneux, L., and van der Maas, P. J. (1997), 'The healthcare costs of smoking', *New England Journal of Medicine*, 337, 1052–7.

Becker, G. S. and Murphy, K. M. (1988), 'A theory of rational addiction', *Journal of Political Economy*, 96, 675–700.

Bernheim, B. D. and Taubinsky, D. (2018), 'Behavioral public economics', in B. D. Bernheim, S. DelleVigna, and D. Laibson (eds), *Handbook of Behavioral Economics: Applications and Foundations I*, Elsevier, Amsterdam, 381–516.

Bolin, K., Borgman, B., Gip, C., and Wilson, K. (2011), 'Current and future avoidable costs of smoking—estimates for Sweden 2007', *Health Policy*, 103, 83–91.

Clotfelter, C. T. (2005), 'Gambling taxes', in S. Cnossen (ed.), *Theory and Practice of Excise Taxation: Smoking, Drinking, Gambling, Polluting, and Driving*, Oxford University Press, Oxford, 84–119.

Cnossen, S. (2007), 'Alcohol taxation and regulation in the European Union', *International Tax and Public Finance*, 14, 699–732.

Cnossen, S. and Smart, M. (2005), 'Taxation of tobacco', in S. Cnossen (ed.), *Theory and Practice of Excise Taxation: Smoking, Drinking, Gambling, Polluting, and Driving*, Oxford University Press, Oxford, 20–55.

Council of Economic and Finance Ministers (1998), 'Report of the High Level Group on fraud in the tobacco and alcohol sectors' (https://www.verginet.net/ UserFiles/File/Avrupa_Birligi/4/report_High_Level_sectors.pdf).

Council of the European Union (1992a), 'European Union Directive 92/83/EEC, on the harmonization of the structures of excise duties on alcohol and alcoholic beverages' (https://www.legislation.gov.uk/eudr/1992/83).

Council of the European Union (1992b), 'European Union Directive 92/84/EEC of the Council of 19 October 1992 on the approximation of the rates of excise duty on alcohol and alcoholic beverages' (https://op.europa.eu/s/n3xD).

Council of the European Union (2011), 'Council Directive 2011/64/EU of 21 June 2011 on the structure and rates of excise duty applied to manufactured tobacco, Official Journal of the European Union (OJ) L176/24' (https://eur-lex.europa.eu/LexUriServ/LexUriServ.do?uri=OJ:L:2011:176:0024:0036:EN:PDF).

Douane Belastingdienst (2019), *Tarievenlijst Accijns en verbruiksbelastingen*.

Euromonitor International (2019), 'Country Report—Sugar Confectionary in the Netherlands', Euromonitor International, London.

European Commission (2015), 'A European Strategy for Plastics in a Circular Economy', European Commission, Brussels.

European Commission (2018), 'Single-Use Plastics: New EU Rules to Reduce Marine Litter', European Commission, Brussels.

European Commission (2019), 'Excise Duty Tables, Part III—Manufactured Tobacco', (01/03/2019) (https://ec.europa.eu/taxation_customs/sites/taxation/files/resources/documents/ taxation/excise_duties/tobacco_products/rates/excise_duties-part_iii_tobacco_en.pdf).

Feehan, P. and Forrest, D. (2007), 'The distribution of UK lottery grants across local authority areas', *Applied Economic Letters*, 14, 361–5.

Forrest. D. (2008), 'Gambling policy in the European Union: too many losers', *FinanzArchiv*, 64, 540–69.

Griffith, R., O'Connell, M., and Smith, K. (2019), 'Tax design and the alcohol market', *Journal of Public Economics*, 172, 20–35.

Griffiths, M. (1999), 'Some comments on "Health-related correlates of gambling on the British National Lottery" by Reid et al.', *Psychological Reports*, 85, 143–4.

Gruber, J. and Köszegi, B. (2008), 'A Modern Economic View of Tobacco Taxation', International Union against Tuberculosis and Lung Disease, Paris.

HM Treasury (2019), 'Consultation outcome, Plastic packaging tax' (https://www.gov.uk/government/consultations/plastic-packaging-tax).

Hogg, D. and Sherrington, C. (2011), 'A comparative study on economic instruments promoting waste prevention', Final Report to Bruxelles Environnement, eunomia, Bristol.

Hummel, A. J., Jacobs, B., and Oosterveen, M. (2016), 'Een nuchtere blik op de kosten en baten van alcohol', *ESB Economie en Samenleving*, 101, 766–9.

International Diabetes Federation (2016), 'IDF Europe Position on Added Sugar', Brussels, Belgium.

Kalshoven, F. (2019), 'Waarom een vuurwerkbelasting hard nodig is', *de Volkskrant*, 4 January 2019.

Karlsson, T. and Tigerstedt, C. (2005), 'Alcohol policy: changing climate and changing structures in the Nordic Countries', presentation at *Alcohol—Use, Harm and Policy*, a research-based Nordic-Baltic Seminar, Riga, 3 October.

Leifman, H. (2001), 'Estimations of unrecorded alcohol consumption levels and trends in 14 European countries', *Nordisk Alkohol- & Narkotikatidskrift* 18 (1 suppl), 54–70.

Netherlands Gaming Authority (2017), *Gokken in Kaart*, Intraval, Groningen-Rotterdam.

Neubauer, S., Welte, R., Beiche, A., Koenig, H. H., Buesch, K., and Leidi, R. (2006), 'Mortality, morbidity and costs attributable to smoking in Germany: update and a 10-year comparison', *Tobacco Control*, 15, 464–71.

NRC.nl (2019), https://www.nrc.nl/handelsblad/2019/01/02/#101.

Petry, N., Stinson, F., and Grant, B. (2005), 'Comorbidity of DSM-IV pathological gambling and other psychiatric disorders: results from the National Epidemiologic Survey on alcohol and related conditions', *Journal of Clinical Psychiatry*, 66, 564–74.

Pigou, A. C. (1920), *The Economics of Welfare*, Macmillan, New York.

Remler, D. K. (2004), 'Poor smokers, poor quitters, and cigarette tax regressivity', *American Journal of Public Health*, 94, 225–9.

RIVM (2016), 'Maatschappelijke kosten-baten analyse van beleidsmaatregelen om alcoholgebruik te verminderen, Rijksinstituut voor Volksgezondheid en Milieu', RIVM Rapport 2016-0146.

Rosenthal, R. and Fong, T. (2004), 'The Etiology of Pathological Gambling', report to the California Office of Problem Gambling, Sacramento.

Royal College of Physicians (2016), 'Nicotine without smoke—tobacco harm reduction', a report by the Tobacco Advisory Group, Lavenham Press, Suffolk.

Schenk, A. (2010), 'Gambling and lotteries', in R. Krever (ed.), *VAT in Africa*, Pretoria University Law Press (PULP), Pretoria, South Africa, 47–70.

SEO (2016), 'Kosten van roken', Stichting Economisch Onderzoek (SEO) Report no. 2015–53.

Sluik, D., van Lee, L., Engelen, A. I., and Feskens, E. J. M. (2016), 'Total, free, and added sugar consumption and adherence to guidelines: the Dutch National Food Consumption Survey 2007–2010', *Nutrients*, 8, 70.

Smith, S. (2008), 'Lotteries as a source of revenue', in M. Viren (ed.), *Lotteries in a Changing Market Environment*, Palgrave Macmillan, Basingstoke, 99–125.

Staatssecretaris van Financiën (2016), 'Toekomstplannen met Holland Casino', Brief aan de Tweede Kamer der Staten-Generaal, no. 139, 11 May 2016.

Statistics Netherlands (2017), https://www.volksgezondheidenzorg.info/onderwerp/alcoholgebruik/cijfers-context/huidige-situatie.

Statistics Netherlands (2018a), '100 duizend volwassenen hebben morbide obesitas' (https://www.cbs.nl/nl-nl/nieuws/2018/27/100-duizend-volwassenen-hebben-morbide-obesitas).

Statistics Netherlands (2018b), 'Overheid; ontvangen belastingen 1995–2017' (https://opendata.cbs.nl/statline/#/CBS/nl/dataset/82569ned/table?fromstatweb).

Tiihonen, J., Ronkainen, K., Kangasharju, A., and Kauhanen, J. (2012), 'The net effect of smoking on healthcare and welfare costs: a cohort study', *BMJ Open*, 2(6), e001678.

Tobacco Collaborators (2017), 'Smoking prevalence and attributable disease burden in 195 countries and territories, 1990–2015: a systematic analysis from the Global Burden of Disease Study 2015', *The Lancet*, 389, 1885–1906.

Walvin, J. (2018), *Sugar: The World Corrupted: From Slavery to Obesity*, Pegasus Books, New York.

Warner, J. K. E., Chaloupka, F. J., Cook, P. J., Manning, W. C., Newhouse, J. P., Novotny, J. P., Schelling, T. C., and Townsend, J. (1995), 'Criteria for determining an optimal cigarette tax: the economist's perspective', *Tobacco Control*, 4, 380–6.

Wells, M., Gerrard, P., and Hubbard, D. (2005), 'Oral evidence to the Treasury (Sub-) committee on Excise Duty Fraud, 17 November 2004, in House of Commons Treasury Committee, *Excise Duty Fraud: Fourth Report of Session 2004–05*', HM Stationery Office, London.

World Economic Forum (2019), 'Plastic is a global problem. It's also a global opportunity' (https://www.weforum.org/agenda/2019/01/plastic-might-just-be-the-solution-to-its-own-problem/).

World Health Organization (2017), 'WHO report on the global tobacco epidemic, country profile Netherlands' (https://www.who.int/tobacco/global_report/2017/en/).

World Health Organization (2018), 'Netherlands, alcohol consumption: levels and patterns', in Global Status Report on Alcohol and Health 2018, WHO, Geneva (https://www.who.int/substance_abuse/publications/global_alcohol_report/profiles/nld.pdf?ua=1).

Index